FROM ST. FRANCIS TO DANTE.

FROM
ST. FRANCIS TO DANTE

TRANSLATIONS FROM THE CHRONICLE OF THE
FRANCISCAN SALIMBENE ;
(1221-1288)

WITH NOTES AND ILLUSTRATIONS FROM OTHER
MEDIEVAL SOURCES.

BY
G. G. COULTON, M.A.

SECOND EDITION, revised and enlarged

Introduction by Edward Peters

UNIVERSITY OF PENNSYLVANIA PRESS

Philadelphia

First published 1907

First *Pennsylvania Paperback* edition 1972
Introduction © 1972 by the University of Pennsylvania Press, Inc.

Library of Congress Catalog Card No. 68–10910

ISBN (cloth) 0–8122–7672–8
ISBN (paper) 0–8122–1053–0

Printed in the United States of America

CONTENTS.

"Un livre de bonne foy": The Chronicle of Salimbene and Its Translator

CHRONICLES and other narrative literary documents constituted for centuries the principal sources for the social and political history of the Middle Ages. From the late nineteenth century on, however, social historians have turned with increasing frequency and satisfaction to other kinds of sources. Parish and episcopal records, wills, tax rolls, accounts of family wealth, and the documentation of investments in companies, long-range commercial projects, and public charitable funds have provided more information about the social and economic profile of medieval society in the aggregate than even the most detailed and impersonal narrative literary accounts. Indeed, to know about some parts of medieval society—the life of rural communities, the social structure of towns and single families, and the vicissitudes of social and economic mobility—the most recently exploited kinds of source material are indispensable. They respond readily and regularly to questions of accuracy, reliability, impartiality, and consistency, the very questions whose solution has caused a revolution in the disciplines of social history and sociology from Max Weber's day to our own. Without the information they provide no satisfactory picture of medieval—or any other— society could responsibly be drawn.

The narrative literary materials of medieval social history have recently fallen on hard times, and, in the light of recent techniques of social analysis and description, they have prodigious faults. More dependent upon chance, whim, and the accidental or arbitrary possession of information on the author's part, they seem to bring few acceptable answers to the questions now most frequently asked about the structure and character of medieval society. Their authors, ill-informed, often prone to enormities

of baseless generalization, incapable of distinguishing in importance between the birth of a two-headed calf and an urban up-
rising, obviously indebted to strict rhetorical or epistemological
convention, appear to offer far fewer rewards and far more
pitfalls than the safer and—one hopes—less imaginative notaries
and clerks who kept their impersonal records so conscientiously.

Yet for some purposes and for many questions, chronicles and
other narrative sources remain indispensable. They appeal
inveterately to an appetite for serial narration and a single-
minded point of view which scholars and general readers alike
still possess. They offer, however disconcertingly, a picture of
life that few sets of statistics and few profiles compiled from
them can match. To the degree that the dimension of historical
experience constituted by men's accounts of their own times is a
valid one, chroniclers' accounts illuminate not only certain historical periods, but historical mental structures as well. To the
reader who wants to know how some individuals in the Middle
Ages perceived the events and personalities of their own times,
they are almost the only sources worth reading. When the men
who wrote them happened to be gifted writers, their reading can
be not only informative, but exciting and satisfying in a way no
tax register, will, or corporation record can hope to be.[1]

Sometimes—more often than one might think—gifted men did
write them. Although the character of narrative literary sources
varies widely from century to century and from place to place,
perceptive and intelligent men did sometimes set out to describe
what they thought was particularly important about their own
worlds in the genres of chronicle and annal, memoirs and saints'
lives, family or institutional history, and the deeds of famous
men. Sometimes their work indicates a major change in men's
perceptions of broad social bonds and historical causation: this
is often the case in the earliest of these materials, the histories
of the barbarian Christian peoples who came to inhabit Roman
and non-Roman Europe between the fifth and the tenth centuries.
The histories of the Goths, Franks, Lombards, and English,
written by men of such varying reliability and skill as Isidore of

Seville, Gregory of Tours, Paul the Deacon, and Bede, would be of immense importance even if other, less literary sources had managed to survive.[2] Even in the troubled ninth and tenth centuries the late Carolingian annals and the early Anglo-Saxon chronicles sometimes offer eloquent and touching accounts of a society assaulted by new enemies in a course of events whose complex details were often only dimly perceived by those recording them. In the later middle ages the long—sometimes interminable—chivalric and dynastic histories, so vexing to their later humanist revisers, were occasionally illuminated by the verbal opulence of a Froissart or the incisiveness of a Commines. During the period from 1100 to 1300 one finds an analogous degree of insight and skill in a different kind of narrative, the chronicle-memoirs compiled by observant, intelligent writers from their own experience and from the more frequent use of documents. As some twelfth-century men became interested in themselves and their fellows as distinct personalities, developed a literary language and a technique for sharp and detailed characterization, and began to envision the continuity of problems and personalities over prolonged periods of time, they created truly memorable and highly readable records of some of the most important individuals and events in European history. The language they helped to shape—a flexible, responsive, living Latin—reflects a technical virtuosity which was only later to influence prose vernaculars.[3]

In their different ways, the *Memoirs* of Guibert de Nogent, the *Jerusalem History* of Fulcher of Chartres, *The Murder of Charles the Good* by Galbert of Bruges, and the *Chronicle* of Jocelyn of Brakelond all reflect this new realism, sharpness, and acute sense of personality and event.[4] But the thirteenth century witnessed the greatest works in this genre. Matthew Paris and even more so Salimbene are two of Europe's best historians.[5] They represent the flowering of a literary tradition that lay behind the vernacular narratives of Villehardouin and Joinville and influenced the literary character of moral tales and miracle stories in the work of Caesarius of Heisterbach and Jacobus de Voragine.

One of the greatest products of the movement they represent and culminate is the unique body of Franciscan literature that so helped to shape the sensibility of the late thirteenth and fourteenth centuries. This thrust toward realism, the sharp depiction of personalities and events, the stamp of the writer's own personality and his handling of the passage of time was certainly one of the bases for the later literary triumphs of Dante, Boccaccio, and Chaucer.

No work in this remarkable genre surpasses in richness of detail, vivacity, and color the *Chronicle* which the Franciscan friar Salimbene di Guido di Adam of Parma wrote between 1283 and 1288 for the edification of his favorite niece Agnes, a nun who wished to know something about her ancestors and relatives and to possess an account of those "for whom she ought to pray." Sister Agnes, if she ever received the manuscript, got far more than she had asked for. Although many pages of the unique autograph manuscript that now survives appear to have been missing long before the first printed edition of 1857, it is clear that Salimbene wrote a kind of world history in which, as a recent French translator remarks, "he mixes up his own history with the history of the world and the history of his own Order."[6] Salimbene's *Chronicle* is in fact a vast mélange of autobiography, memoirs of political and religious life in thirteenth-century Italy and France, and a collection of individual portraits of innumerable well-known and obscure individuals. Luigi Salvatorelli has said of it:

> The greatest work of Italian historiography of the thirteenth century is the *Chronicle* (1168-1287) of the minorite Salimbene of Parma, incomparable particularly for the period of his own life in its lively and varied depiction of political and religious society. The figures of great men, the vivacious narrative description of individual episodes, representations of ideological currents and popular movements, anecdotes, proverbs, *bons mots,* and snatches of popular poetry extraordinarily animate his work and constitute the most precious witness we possess to the Italian spirit of his time.[7]

The *Chronicle* of Salimbene is so distinctive a work that its author has been compared most frequently, not to other medieval writers at all, but to the greatest memoir-writers of early modern Europe: Montaigne, Pepys, Boswell, Goldoni, and Saint-Simon. The range of the work, Salimbene's personal acquaintance with the most powerful individuals of his time, his own distinctive likes and dislikes, and his often touching and naive frankness make his work indispensable for the study of life and thought in the thirteenth century and one of the greatest—if most idiosyncratic—literary monuments of the middle ages.

The first printed edition of Salimbene's work appeared in 1857, but it was neither very accurate nor very widely read, and Salimbene first became available to scholars in the edition of O. Holder-Egger in the *Monumenta Germaniae Historica* between 1905 and 1913.[8] In 1906, however, the English medievalist George Gordon Coulton, convinced that first-person narratives by contemporary observers and participants in events were the most personally and professionally useful of documents, published the present abridgement and translation of the *Chronicle*. Coulton had been working on Salimbene and other thirteenth-century authors since 1897, and he had found that the friar's observations on the religious life of his age offered the best kind of understanding, not only of the theories, laws, and ideals behind institutions and practices, but—far more important to him—of the varied and often disappointing life they necessarily lead in the flesh. Coulton's preference for narrative history, particularly the genres of biography and autobiography, led to a number of English translations of important and hitherto neglected medieval texts. This preference, carried to very learned but extraordinarily anecdotal extremes in his own later work, led Coulton to apply to Salimbene's *Chronicle* Montaigne's famous description of his own *Essais: un livre de bonne foy,* "an honest book." Forty-one years later, Coulton applied the same phrase to his own masterpiece, *Five Centuries of Religion.* For a more effective understanding of Salimbene's *Chronicle* in this, still its only English translation, something must be said, not only of

Salimbene's life and thought, but of the enormous erudition and personal concerns which led Coulton to translate this "honest book" as he did.

The thirteenth century opened with the pontificate of the youngest and most effective of the great medieval lawyer-popes, Innocent III (1198–1216) and closed with that of one of the oldest and ultimately least effective, Boniface VIII (1294–1303). Between these men there occurred perhaps the greatest range of papal styles of any century: great and sympathetic administrators, hermits, crusaders, and devotional geniuses, as well as the first important papal products of that political factionalism which was to plague the fourteenth and fifteenth centuries.[9] The other nominal authority in universal Christendom, the Holy Roman Empire, was transformed from the confusion following the death of Henry VI in 1197 to the most compact and complex secular state ever conceived, under Frederick II (1220–1250), plunged as abruptly into the great Interregnum of 1250 to 1273, and ended the century with the establishment of the power of princely electors on the one hand, and the beginnings of the dynastic struggle between the Habsburg and Luxemburg houses on the other.[10]   The "other" Christian empire, the old Roman Empire with its capital at Constantinople, had been captured by western Christians during the Fourth Crusade (1204–1207) and was lost finally to its Latin emperors in 1261, when another native line of Byzantine aristocrats attempted to reestablish imperial authority over a diminished world.[11]   Jerusalem, lost to the Christians since 1187, had been restored briefly by a treaty arranged between Frederick II and the sultan of Egypt, only to be closed again a few years later.   In 1291, with the fall of Acre, the last Christian stronghold in the Holy Land fell to Islam.

During the thirteenth century the monarchy of France witnessed the triumph of the last Capetians, from Philip II Augustus (1180–1223) to Louis IX (1226–1270) and Philip IV (1285–1314), and a vast increase both in the territory ruled by the crown and in the place held by the royal dynasty in the minds of all the king's subjects.[12] At the same time, in spite of assiduous and intelligent governmental institutions, the monarchy of England under John (1199–1216), Henry III (1216–1272), and Edward I (1272–1307) witnessed the growing concept of a *communitas regni*, a community of the realm, which developed to a certain degree independent of the king until Edward's reign and is the basis of the struggles for control over the government and crown which plagued the last years of both John and Henry III.[13] In the Iberian peninsula, the southern drive of the Castilian, Aragonese, and Portuguese *reconquista* culminated in the triumph of Las Navas de Tolosa in 1212 and in the subsequent cultural eminence and political disorders under Alfonso X in Castile. Aragon, sharing the goals of the reconquista but possessing stronger connections with southern France and the Mediterranean, became involved first with the crusades in southern France against heretics and, later, with the wider world of political affairs in the central and eastern Mediterranean, particularly the conquest of Sicily in 1282–1302 and the subsequent inroads into the Byzantine maritime world.[14] The century also witnessed powerful German and Slavic expansion into the lands between the Elbe and the Vistula, and the establishment of a new central Europe whose character has only recently begun to be investigated dispassionately.[15]

In terms of Europe's relations with the wider world, the Crusade idea, long a symbol of united Christian opposition to Islam, was rapidly in decline by the end of the century, and new, occasionally more curious and tolerant, attitudes toward non-Christians had begun to develop.[16] The expansion and consolidation of Mongol power in Asia had opened new lands in new security to European travellers, merchants and missionaries alike. The middle of the thirteenth century witnessed the first reports of the papal emissaries to the Mongol khans, and their memoirs of these encounters, the narratives of John of Plano Carpini and Simon of Saint-Quentin, were quickly taken up and included in the most extensive universal history written during the century, the *Speculum historiale* of Vincent of Beauvais. The very end of the century witnessed both the instructions to Italian merchants trading in China in the handbook of Francesco Pegolotti and the account of his eighteen years spent in China by Marco Polo, a Venetian captive, dictated to a down-at-heel writer of knightly romances in a Genoese jail.[17]

Changes in politics, theories of power, and the character of rulership paralleled other changes in deeper strata of society and in the bonds which held society together. Trade increased in both volume and complexity, towns attempted to shake themselves free of old rulers and either managed to thrive at the end of the century as flourishing city-republics, such as Florence, or gave themselves to the arbitrary rule of individuals and families or the more considered rule of boards of aristocratic directors, as did Milan and Padua on the one hand, or Venice, on the other. Associations of teachers and students—the universities—which had begun the century by frantically collecting for themselves defensive privileges against frequently hostile local town populations and authorities, ended it by exercising a local and universal authority and possessing an economic status never attained before and rarely since. It was the century of Aquinas, Bonaventure, and Duns Scotus, of double-entry bookkeeping, marine insurance, and corporation law, of Leonardo of Pisa, Michael Scot, and Roger Bacon. Most conspicuously, it was the century of St. Francis and Dante.

For all of its great and small degrees of temporal change and new enthusiasms, the thirteenth century was concerned with the condition of its soul, and few other periods in European history witnessed comparably energetic and ingenious attempts to find a satisfactory spiritual life. The century opened with the Fourth Lateran Council in 1215, which drew into a coherent and consistent dogmatic structure many of the results of the theological thought and the conciliar pronouncements of the twelfth century. At the same time, the Council vigorously launched an attack, not only on the infidels outside Christendom, but on the enemies inside—particularly the heretics, but, on a broader scale, the Jews too, who were expelled from kingdom after kingdom throughout the century. The century witnessed the vast summaries of dogma and apologetics from the scholastic philosophers and theologians, and it closed with the remarkably introspective analyses of Christian society and its ills which Pope Gregory X solicited for the Second Council of Lyons in 1274 and with the furious conflict between Boniface VIII and Philip the Fair of France. The most striking characteristic of institutional Christianity in the thirteenth century, however, is its flexibility in responding to religious crises and its ultimate willingness to create new institutions to respond to new problems. In their own very different ways, the Inquisition and the new religious orders all reflect this persistent responsiveness. For the thirteenth century is, *par excellence,* the century of the Orders—the Dominicans and the Franciscans, or, more properly, the Order of Preachers and the Order of Friars Minor. Created as individual responses to the growth of heresy and the spiritual alienation of townspeople, the Dominicans and Franciscans, moved and directed by the great personalities of their founders and their remarkable successors, quickly touched all aspects of thirteenth-century life with their distinctive and compelling energies, resources, and influences. Town and university life, the papacy and the curia, the political powers of the temporal world, even the Mongol rulers of Asia, all found the Orders at work in their very backyards.[18]

It is not by accident that so many men and women of the century belonged to the orders, joined them or one of their branches before the end of their lives, shared in their spiritual benefits, patronized them while prosperous, and turned to their ministering institutions when destitute. Saint Dominic was the "athlete of God," and Saint Francis "Christ's minstrel." Little wonder, then, that the spread of Franciscan and Dominican culture and spirit was so extensive, little wonder that the greatest minds of the century spent their lives in the orders and that the greatest powers of the world patronized them, little wonder that the greatest chronicler of thirteenth-century life should be a Franciscan.

If two aspects of his life may be singled out as shaping
Salimbene's mind and spirit, they are unquestionably his roots in
two of the most characteristic thirteenth-century institutions, the
city and the Order. His urban upbringing and his Franciscan life
created in him a distinctive character—proud, gregarious, cosmo-
politan—and his own talents responded to these influences in a
distinctive way. In an age when students and merchants, church
officials and pilgrims, beggars, soldiers, and lepers were the most
numerous and most conspicuous travellers on the roads and
waterways of Europe, the new Orders constituted a notably new
body of travellers, and the Orders' spread of houses and patrons
throughout Europe brought Franciscans and Dominicans not
only to the most far-flung corners of Europe, but to Damietta,
Karakorum, and Peking. If Salimbene's childhood in Parma and
his family background imparted to him a degree of cosmopolitan-
ism and a hunger for new experiences, his life as a Franciscan
gave him the opportunity to travel widely, to know personally
great and lesser men and to observe their activities, and a set of
unique criteria for explanation and judgment.

Salimbene was born on 9 October, 1221, in Parma, the son of
wealthy parents from established families. His godfather was
Balian of Sidon, a warrior who had distinguished himself at
the siege of Damietta during the Fifth Crusade in 1218–19.
Salimbene attended the studies in liberal arts available to most
boys of his status in the Italian city-republics, and in Parma he
had an opportunity to hear about, and sometimes observe directly,
some of the most important events of the early thirteenth century. In 1233, for example, when Salimbene was 12, there
occurred one of those periodic collective manifestations of spiritual enthusiasm in which a vigorous religious spirit appears to
have taken over many of the city-republics of Italy. During the
Great Alleluia, as the events of 1233 were called, holy men,
hermits, and popular religious leaders exerted a particularly
intense influence over the spiritual and civic lives of men and
women, and many of the conditions of life which men thought
led to civic violence and disorders were briefly ameliorated.

Briefly, because the spirit which informed the Great Alleluia did not stay long, although its experience appears to have marked the religious and civic sensibilities of many of those who lived through it. Two years later, in 1235, the great war-elephants of the Emperor Frederick II came through Parma, and the looming figure of the emperor must have dominated Salimbene's political and religious consciousness at least as much as it did that of everyone else.[19]

In 1238 Salimbene, then seventeen and expected confidently to follow in his father's secular footsteps, suddenly joined the Franciscan Order. In spite of his father's energetic protests, which included letters from the emperor, personal contact with the minister-general of the Order, and a prolonged, terribly painful (for Guido di Adam) but unsuccessful personal confrontation between father and son at Fano, Salimbene never wavered from his decision. Given the privilege of his choice of residence, possibly as a reward for his steadfastness, Salimbene chose the city of Lucca, where he remained until 1241. From 1241 to 1243 Salimbene was in Siena, where he met the first of St. Francis' companions, Bernard of Quintavalle, and several of the Franciscan musicians whose company and acquaintance so seems to have pleased him throughout his life. From 1243 to 1247 Salimbene was at Pisa, where he met Hugh de Digne, the great exponent of the spiritualism of Joachim of Flora, and was ordained deacon.[20] In 1247 Salimbene travelled from Pisa to Cremona, then to Parma, then into France, where he was sent for further study in theology.

The years 1247 to 1249 were the most crowded and exciting of the friar's life. He met Pope Innocent IV at Lyons "and talked with him familiarly," and then he travelled to Villefranche, where he met and also spoke at great length with John of Plano Carpini, the first papal emissary to the Mongol khans, who had just returned from Karakorum. In 1248 Salimbene went from Villefranche to Troyes, Provins, Paris, where he remained only for a week, to Auxerre, Sens, then to Marseilles, Hyères, Aix, Arles, back to Hyères, and then on to Genoa, where he was ordained priest. In 1249 he returned to Hyères from Genoa, and then went on to Avignon, Lyons, Genoa, Parma, Bologna, and finally to Ferrara, where he was to remain for seven years, until 1256. The range of Salimbene's travels during these years, the extraordinary number of great men he not only met, but appears to have taken somewhat excessive pride in having become friendly with, is a census of places and personalities uniquely characteristic of the mid-thirteenth century: Pope Innocent IV, Frederick II, John of Plano Carpine, Hugh de Digne, Gerardo da Borgo San Donnino, Bernard of Quintavalle, King Louis IX of France.

After 1249, as Scivoletto points out, Salimbene provides fewer details about himself and his own life, and, in a sense, he disappears as a character in his own chronicle.[21] His seven years in Ferrara were followed by fourteen years in various houses in the Emilia, principally Reggio and Modena, and in Bologna. He seems to have spent the 1270s in the Romagna, and by 1283–1285 was back in Reggio again, where he began to write his *Chronicle*. In 1287 he moved to Montefalcone, where he died, about the age of sixty-seven, in 1289, his life, as Coulton reminds us, overlapping that of St. Francis by five years and that of Dante by twenty-five. His mind must have remained sharp to the last, because the vivid portraits and minute detail which fill his *Chronicle* are clearly drawn from life, and the influences of his youthful opinions still seem to color his judgement of men and events. As Scivoletto sums him up:

> With one foot in the convent and the other in the world, always ready to put aside his breviary in order to get out into the midst of a crowd and witness the events of the day for himself, always desirous of getting close to the most notable individuals of his age, Salimbene succeeded in this manner in garnering the echo of all those events of nearly an entire century, one of the most exciting in Italian history.[22]

His character, his long years, and his great travels had given Salimbene both curiosity and the most abundant means for its satisfaction, the ability to perceive the importance of men and events and the criteria for organizing them into a narrative. His predictable preferences for ecclesiastical authority, his political guelfism, his criticism of laymen (particularly Frederick II) who afflicted the clergy, these were only a few of the constants which influenced his judgement. His pride in his city of Parma and its defiance of Frederick II surely reflects the consciousness of the citizen beneath the Franciscan habit, and Salimbene's early flirtations with the joachite spirituals persisted to color his descriptions of the major political and ecclesiastical movements of his day. Yet his endorsement of ecclesiastical authority did not prevent him from expressing the most pointed—not to say impolite or even scatological—criticism of deficient prelates and religious, nor did his Franciscan sympathies make him more than a *pro forma* follower of St. Francis. Even today, Salimbene's off-color stories and descriptions of his own appetites sometimes render him a dubious asset to Franciscan historians, a kind of black sheep who makes up in information and detail what he all too obviously lacks in the spirit. Never reluctant to include himself and his own opinions in the details of his vast canvas, Salimbene did not do so undeservedly. He himself is as interesting as anyone he writes about.

There are parts of Salimbene's *Chronicle,* of course, which are important for other reasons than the friar's uniquely personal view of thirteenth-century affairs and his discursive style. The *Chronicle* is the only adequate source for the history of the early Franciscan expansion into France and the most detailed exposition of what Coulton terms "Cloister Life" within Franciscan communities.[23] The *Liber de prelato,* a treatise incorporated into the *Chronicle* and dealing, usually in an extraordinarily hostile manner, with Brother Elias, the minister-general of the order and a renegade supporter of Frederick II, is part of an important Franciscan controversy, one which would not be settled until the fourteenth century. Salimbene's early acquaintance with joachite spiritualism, and particularly his friendships with such supporters of that movement in the Franciscan Order as Gerardo da Borgo San Donnino and Hugh de Digne offers an illuminating contribution to the history of the "Spiritual Franciscan" that later shook the religious world of the late thirteenth and early fourteenth centuries.[24] Finally, although not exclusively, Salimbene's personal portraits of such figures as Pope Innocent IV, Frederick II, and Louis IX of France offer invaluable dimensions to our knowledge of these powerful men. On a level apart from politics and major spiritual movements, Salimbene provides us with information concerning popular religious and lay poetry and music which is hard to find at all outside his *Chronicle*. His moving portrait of Brother Rinaldo of Arezzo, who struggled so mightily with his conscience upon becoming bishop of that city that he quickly resigned his dignity before the Pope and Cardinals in Consistory at Perugia and became again a begging friar, illuminates a corner of the history of the medieval episcopate as do few other documents or passages. Further, on a level not yet satisfactorily explored by even the most innovative social historians, that of scatology, Salimbene provides a wealth of anecdotal material which Coulton felt obliged by decency to leave in Latin in an appendix to his translation. The jests of the immortal Brother Diotisalve at the expense of would-be-saints and Florentines reveal medieval humor at its most scurrilous and witty, and yet are not any more inconsistent with the tone of the rest of the *Chronicle* than are the interminable sequences of Biblical proverbs and saws in which Salimbene so delights or his indiscriminate hopping from topic to topic as the spirit moves him.

Salimbene's English translator was a man in many ways as interesting as the friar himself. Born in 1858 to a prosperous family in Lynn, Coulton spent the years 1877–1881 at Cambridge, and then accepted a series of teaching appointments at various boys' schools, planning eventually to enter the Anglican priesthood. In 1883 he was ordained Deacon and began at the same time his intensive reading of medieval Latin literature, a project inspired by personal inclination rather than any academic influences. During this period he read particularly Thomas à Kempis'

Imitation of Christ, the letters of Sts. Jerome and Bernard, and the *Confessions* of St. Augustine. In many ways, these readings directed much of his later approaches to religious and social history. He once wrote of them:

> In the attempt to disentangle what a man was from what
> he would have liked to be and shows to the world, there is,
> to my mind, more interest and profit than in meditating
> over the characters and the problems of even so fine a
> novel as Mr. E. M. Forster's *Passage to India.* Not only in
> the ponderables, but in imponderables also, I cannot help
> preferring the autobiography or intimate biography.[25]

By 1885, however, Coulton had rejected the possibility of Holy Orders, partly because of his criticism of what he considered the excessively conservative and unscholarly character of late nineteenth-century Anglican theology. His reading of Renan and Origen had shaped in him a kind of social-liberal Protestantism which he was never to lose, and whose influence echoes through the pages, not only of *From St. Francis to Dante,* but through the rest of his monumental life's work as well, leading one American reviewer of his later works to refer to him as "a *feste burg* of Protestant theology today." Closely tied to his religious ideas were concerns for social and educational reform so articulate and intense that they might have turned Coulton, as F. M. Powicke remarked, into a permanently frustrated social critic:

> As one reads his autobiography one cannot but feel that
> his interest in history may have saved him from a life of
> frustration. The cultivated, courteous, well-informed but
> ineffective agitator is a well-known, if uncommon type.
> Nearly always right, wiser than those whom he tends to
> weary, he fails for one reason or another to carry conviction.
> Coulton managed to escape this danger.[26]

After 1885 Coulton taught in Germany, near Heidelberg, and he then resumed his teaching in English secondary schools until a prolonged illness and recovery in 1896 gave him the opportunity to travel for a year on the Continent, reading and looking according to his own whim. It was in Italy in 1897 that Coulton

purchased his copy of Salimbene's *Chronicle.* From 1897 to
1911 Coulton taught at the Eastbourne school, presided over by
his old college friend H. von E. Scott, later one of the translators,
at Coulton's suggestion, of *The Dialogue on Miracles* by the
thirteenth-century moralist Caesarius of Heisterbach.[27] In 1900
Coulton was given an appointment as a University Extension
lecturer, and in 1903 he married. By then, he remarks in his
autobiography, he had begun to face the problems caused by the
accumulation of notes on his two decades of reading medieval
documents. He was by then forty-five years old, with an uncertain future, a very small income, and no financial resources.

In 1906 the first product of his research appeared:

> Now, therefore, I decided to take an autobiography as my
> main theme, and fill it out into a volume which might have
> been called *Salimbene and his Circle.* But, as Salimbene
> was then almost unprocurable and unknown, I called the
> book *From St. Francis to Dante.* For in fact this frank
> and well-informed friar, born in 1221 and writing his last
> words about 1288, goes very far to fill one of the most re-
> markable centuries in Italian and European history. It is
> not altogether creditable to our Universities that, amid
> their countless pupils' monographs, they still have produced
> no exhaustive study either of Salimbene's *Chronicle* or of
> the contemporary *Diary* of Odo Rigaldi, Archbishop of
> Rouen (1248–1269), or of Johann Busch in the fifteenth
> century.[28]

Between 1906 and 1950 the fruits of Coulton's vast erudition
and enormous labors began to appear with regularity. In 1906
and 1908 he published first *Chaucer and His England* and then
A Medieval Garner, the latter reprinted by the Cambridge University Press in 1932 under the title *Life in the Middle Ages,* a
work still useful to students—and still used by them, since its
current incarnation is four paperback volumes of that title.
The format of Coulton's research, his collection of notes on his
reading, was designed as much by financial necessity as scholarly
method. Never able to afford to buy the books he needed in any
quantity, Coulton three times sold his personal library to support

himself and his family, and his only research materials at any given time were his own painfully compiled collections of notes. These in turn shaped his books and imparted to them the anecdotal character which his critics have, sometimes unjustly, attacked. Thus, if his work often reveals the faults of his method, lacking most conspicuously the compactness and spare argument that readers now demand of social history, it inevitably profits from the detailed familiarity with the largest and most diverse body of research materials that any historian ever made his own. The beginnings of that method are revealed in Coulton's first book. In addition to translating and annotating "all that is of primary interest" in the *Chronicle* of Salimbene, Coulton included illustrative and little-known texts from other contemporary sources to illuminate further several points raised by the friar. In time, these additional materials range from the late twelfth and early thirteenth centuries in citations from the sermons of Jacques de Vitry and the stories of Caesarius of Heisterbach, to the mid-fourteenth century in the selections from Benvenuto da Imola, the commentator on Dante's *Divine Comedy*, and the storyteller Sachetti. In between there is material from the sermons of Berthold of Regensburg, the saints' tales of Jacobus de Voragine, the moral treatises of Roger Bacon and St. Bonaventure, selections from the Dominican *Vitae Patrum*, the *Chronicle of Parma*, and Joinville's *Life of Louis IX*. Not one selection is ill-chosen, and in the aggregate they cross-illuminate Salimbene's text very effectively.

In 1911 Coulton decided to leave Eastbourne for the town of Cambridge, and moved his family there, supporting them by putting up students, tutoring them, and continuing his Extension lectures, still without any formal academic appointment or prospect of one. In 1911 he was invited to deliver the Birkbeck lectures in ecclesiastical history, an opportunity which he later claimed allowed him to lay out the foundation for his later great work *Five Centuries of Religion*, the four volumes of which appeared intermittently in 1923, 1927, 1936, and 1950. In 1912 Coulton and Z. N. Brooke were invited to complete a course of lectures in medieval history at Cambridge University, and in 1919 Coulton was invited to succeed G. C. Macaulay in the University Lectureship in English. At the same time he was offered the Research Fellowship at St. John's College, Cambridge. At the age of sixty-one, then, Coulton finally received the formal academic affiliation without which few, if any, modern scholars would today consider even beginning their work. At about this time a Parisian journalist satirically described Coulton's appearance after a lecture:

> Imagine the queerest and most absurd figure! A scarlet face, a disproportionately lanky body, clothes too short and too tight, awkward gestures, and a collar and necktie to make you split with laughter—and there you have the honorable Mr. Coulton.[29]

Coulton was to remain a figure of scholarly controversy throughout his life, and his methods and features were to be described and drawn more than once, perhaps most affectionately by G. R. Owst in his drawing reproduced in Coulton's autobiography, and perhaps most objectively by Dom David Knowles:

> Coulton had, very deeply ingrained, two atavistic prejudices which ever since the age of Wyclif have possessed a large section of his countrymen, the one a fear and mistrust of ecclesiastical potentates in general and of Romans in particular, the other a conviction that monasticism is an unnatural institution which of itself always leads inevitably to disaster. To these he added an almost emotional attachment to a particular point of historical accuracy, viz. the ability to support one's assertions by exact references to authorities, accompanied by a readiness to alter or withdraw publicly from any error once it had been indicated. . . . To this it should be added that Coulton had in full measure the distinctive qualities of the controversialist: persistence, love of the reiterated question, the ability to focus attention on a single tree in the forest, a desire for printed acknowledgement, and great self-assurance.[30]

The controversies in which Coulton became involved, however, did not invariably spring from his attitudes to ecclesiastical authority and monasticism on the one hand, or from his insistence upon meticulous scholarship on the other. His own faith in the idea of progress and his concept of enlightened Protestantism may well have caused him to appear to no less distinguished a scholar than Gaines Post, "beneath the cloak of *Historismus* . . . really a Bossuet with a liberal-protestant philosophy of history."[31]   But Coulton also had real objects of criticism before him. The late-Romantic nostalgia for an imaginary medieval period, carried to obsessive extremes by the pre-Raphaelites and soon to influence even the work of Ezra Pound and T. S. Eliot; an effective and scholarly Roman Catholic view of the middle ages as a period of constructive ecclesiastical guidance of society distracted in its great mission only by willfully malicious heretics and unbelievers and revealed in a false light by opinionated historians like Coulton himself; and the inclination of administrative historians to neglect the purely human qualities of the men who shaped and ruled medieval society, these became, too, the objects of Coulton's vast revision of medieval ecclesiastical history.   Like those of his older American contemporary Henry Charles Lea, Coulton's studies were informed by a personal and confessional point of view, tenaciously held, but always courteously defended.   Like Lea, Coulton was too great an historian to allow those values to distort the scholarly accuracy of his own work, although, to be sure, Coulton was sometimes too ready to reject, not only an error and the refusal to withdraw it, but the personal character and the entire scholarly value of the work of his opponents.   It is no accident that Coulton admired the work of Lea and included in his sharpest criticism such scholars as Henry Adams and Henry Osborn Taylor for what he considered their unscholarly nostalgic hypotheses and their unsatisfactory treatment of source materials.[32]

Within his own fields of expertise, Coulton thus drew a portrait of the religious life of the eleventh through the sixteenth centuries which has remained to this day a vigorous and argumentative, but provoking and enlightening description of institutions and the men who had to make them work.   Once this has been said, however, it must also be said that his unrivalled familiarity with particular kinds of source materials—chronicles, cartularies, devotional literature of all kinds, official correspondence, and works of literature proper—did not extend to other kinds of sources and other social groups and movements that have been more thoroughly studied in recent years. Lawyers, civil servants both high and low, those men involved more in the business than in the theory of rulership, escape much of his scrutiny. Canon law, medieval science and technology, and the wider world of ecclesiastical affairs outside of monasticism and the religious orders receive less of his attention. Moreover, just when these men and materials were beginning to attract the attentions of social historians, Coulton was working from notes and editions which he had begun to compile in the 1880s. Coulton himself remarked that the Birkbeck lectures of 1911 foreshadowed the major themes of *Five Centuries of Religion,* but it will strike the reader of the later work to what extent some of those themes are already outlined in Coulton's translation of Salimbene in 1906. Coulton's extraordinarily long life and the circumstances of his early research have often been ignored by his critics, and much of the criticism directed against him has been as much confessional as professional in character and inspiration.

Coulton remained a vigorous, productive scholar—and polemicist—until the end of his life. In 1944 A. C. Krey published a memoir of a lecturing tour by Coulton in the United States:

> For several years now he has been teaching at Toronto University, and, in his spare moments, delivering lectures at universities scattered over the continent. He was eighty-three years old when he came to the University of Minnesota (in 1941). It was not difficult to identify the tall, spare figure whose total luggage consisted of a walking stock and a rucksack strapped to his back. The rucksack was so choked with contents that it could not be closed. . . . His lecture that afternoon at Minnesota was delivered in a sprightly manner, and when after tea I took him back to his room, I learned that he had spent his "rest" reading

proof of the last volume of his *Five Centuries of Religion*.
It was the galley proof that had so bulged his rucksack.[33]

George Gordon Coulton's life was one of continuous scholarship,
accomplished method, shaped by a distinctive, even idiosyncratic,
personal view of his own time and the middle ages. Interested
primarily in life—daily life, the lives of individual men who, forced
to live with what to Coulton was an impossible and even unnatural
ideal, fell too frequently into the negation of that ideal—Coulton
turned to autobiography and biography, personal memoirs, and
other first-person accounts and constructed upon them his vision
of medieval monastic and religious history. "As early as Heidelberg days," he wrote,

> I had formed a plan for competing with fiction by writing
> a series of biographies founded upon those memoirs which
> are now forgotten because their very bulk and multitude
> discourage the reader, but which are full of striking literary
> possibilities. I began with the autobiography of Johann
> Gottfried Seume, whose *Tramp to Syracuse* had much
> attracted me; and these beginnings are somewhere among
> my papers. Mr. Lytton Strachey's brilliant volumes, and
> even those of his imitators, have shown now what possi-
> bilities lie in that direction; and it would not be surprising
> if, fifty years hence, a body of brief biographies should have
> been created which could compete on equal terms with the
> novels of that future day.[34]

From St. Francis to Dante was Coulton's first venture into
biographies built out of memoirs, but it was not his last, and the
recent revival of scholarly interest in historical biography has
indicated that once again, for all of his obsessive interests,
Coulton was right. Coulton's indictment of scholarship for failing to deal with the subject of biography had and has a great
deal of validity to it. The *Memoirs* of Guibert of Nogent, the
first English translation of which Coulton himself sponsored, had
to wait until 1907 for a scholarly edition of the Latin text and
until 1970 for a scholarly English translation and introduction.
The "Diary" of Odo Rigaud was not translated until 1964, and,

aside from one study in Dutch, the great Netherlands monastic reformer of the fifteenth century, Johann Busch, is still best known to English readers from forty detailed pages in Volume Four of Coulton's own *Five Centuries of Religion*.[35] Salimbene, of course, has done worst of all. There has been little work done on his *Chronicle* in English, less in other modern scholarship except for Italian and German, between Coulton's translation and today. The English reader owes his Salimbene, the most important chronicler of thirteenth-century life, still to Coulton, with his inveterate respect for *livres de bonne foy* and his insight into their value as essential tools for living social history.

In one other respect, and that not least important, Coulton deserves our admiration. Continually attacked for the darkness of his portrait of late medieval religion, Coulton responded that, if he had chosen, the picture would have been much darker, and that he had the sources to prove it. Attacking what he considered the failure of medieval religion, he did so out of a profound and enduring concern for the welfare of society and religion in his own time. He championed not only the enlightened Catholicism and Protestantism of the late nineteenth and twentieth centuries, but their dependence upon accurate historical information in order to remain enlightened. He thus laid great emphasis upon the rights and needs of an informed literate public to information concerning even the most remote of historical questions and demanded that this information be made available in inexpensive, accurate translations. Coulton's concept of the necessity of an informed, non-specialist public is still of compelling concern to even more specialized historians. It was, finally, this aspect of his convictions which inspired his somewhat off-hand definition of a "philosophy" of history. Once, when he was criticized for providing the materials for history rather than "history" itself, Coulton answered that it did not matter to him if scholars said "that what I write is not, strictly speaking, history, so long as the stuff is reasonably true, and conveys to the public a reasonably clear impression of what men did and thought in the past." "What men did and thought in the past" is, of course, also the definition of history of no less an authority than Frederick William Maitland. On another occasion, Coulton defended the translation of medieval source materials for non-specialists on the grounds that the "public were getting, in the matter of accessible and very important information, good value for their money." Important information and good value for money are not the terms that would occur first to modern historians in response to questions concerning the social value of their work, but they were Coulton's criteria for value, and they were—and are—not bad ones.[36] Stubbornly Aristotelian in his insistence on testing general theories and ideals in terms of detailed individual cases, a proponent of historicism in his conviction that men's perception of their own times was at least as important as historians' perception, Coulton created an impressive and useful body of historical scholarship, still indispensable to specialist and general reader alike, humane, literate, and alive. He applied the same touchstone to the work of Salimbene and others as he did to his own work and to that of his contemporaries—that it produce "honest books" which gave the public "good value for its money."

EDWARD PETERS
Philadelphia, 1972

NOTES

1. Among recent studies of the chronicle-genre are those of William J. Brandt, *The Shape of Medieval History: Studies in Modes of Perception* (New Haven, 1966), and Robert W. Hanning, *The Vision of History in Early Britain* (New York, 1966). A systematic introduction to the different genres of historical sources for the middle ages is R. C. Van Caenegem and F. L. Ganshof, *Kurze Quellenkunde des westeuropäischen Mittelalters* (Göttingen, 1962).

2. These accounts are discussed and briefly described in M. L. W. Laistner, *Thought and Letters in Western Europe, A.D. 500–900* (London, 1957) and in considerably greater detail in Wattenbach-Levison, *Deutschlands Geschichtsquellen im Mittelalter*, ed. H.

Löwe and R. Buchner, 4 vols. with Beiheft (Weimar, 1952–1963). The most recent study of Bede is Peter Hunter Blair, *The World of Bede* (London, 1970).

3. There is a stimulating discussion of this point for the twelfth century in Christopher Brooke, *The Twelfth Century Renaissance* (New York, 1969). See also Erich Auerbach, *Mimesis: The Representation of Reality in Western Literature* (Princeton, 1953), 203–31.

4. For Guibert's *Memoirs*, see John F. Benton, ed. and trans., *Self and Society in Medieval France: The Memoirs of Abbot Guibert of Nogent* (New York, 1970). For Fulcher, see E. Peters, ed., *The First Crusade: The Chronicle of Fulcher of Chartres and Other Source Materials* (Philadelphia, 1971); for Jocelyn, see H. E. Butler, ed. and trans., *The Chronicle of Jocelin of Brakelond* (London and Edinburgh, 1949). Galbert's work has been translated by J. B. Ross (rep. New York, 1967).

5. Matthew Paris' Chronicle has been translated by J. A. Giles (London, 1852–54), in three vols. See V. H. Galbraith, *Roger Wendover and Matthew Paris* (Glasgow, 1944).

6. M.-T. Laureilhe, in her introduction to Placid Hermann, O.F.M., trans., *XIIIth Century Chronicles: Jordan of Giano, Thomas of Eccleston, Salimbene degli Adami* (Chicago, 1961), 195.

7. Luigi Salvatorelli, *L'Italia Comunale* (Milan, 1962), 599. See Bibliographical Note below, p. xxxiv.

8. A full discussion of the manuscript and printed editions of Salimbene's work will be found in *Salimbene di Adam, Cronica*, ed., G. Scalia, 2 vols. (Bari, 1966).

9. Most recently, see Geoffrey Barraclough, *The Medieval Papacy* (New York, 1968); R. W. Southern, *Western Society and the Church in the Middle Ages* (Baltimore, 1970); Walter Ullmann, *The Growth of Papal Government in the Middle Ages* (London, 3rd ed., 1970); David Knowles and Dimitri Obolensky, *The Middle Ages*, Volume II of *The Christian Centuries* (London, 1969).

10. See Friedrich Heer, *The Holy Roman Empire* (London, 1969), and C. C. Bayley, *The Formation of the German College of Electors in the Mid-Thirteenth Century* (Toronto, 1949).

11. For thirteenth-century Byzantium, see J. Hussey, ed., *The Cambridge Medieval History*, Volume IV (Cambridge, 2nd ed., 1966–67) and D. Geanakoplos, *The Emperor Michael Palaeologus and the West* (Cambridge, Mass., 1959). The study by Steven Runciman, *The Sicilan Vespers* (Cambridge, 1958) is very useful for the Mediterranean world as a whole during this period.

12. See Robert Fawtier, *The Capetian Kings of France: Monarchy and Nation (987–1328)*, trans. L. Butler and R. J. Adam (London, 1962) and the various studies by Joseph R. Strayer, now partially collected in his *Medieval Statecraft and the Perspectives of History* (Princeton, 1971).

13. See F. M. Powicke, *The Thirteenth Century* (Oxford, 2nd ed., 1962), with bibliography. See also R. W. Southern, "England's First Entry into Europe," in his *Medieval Humanism and Other Studies* (New York, 1971), 135–57; F. M. Powicke, "England and Europe in the Thirteenth Century," in his *Ways of Medieval Life and Thought* (rep. New York, 1964), 115–29; Roger Wickson, *The Community of the Realm in Thirteenth Century England* (London, 1970).

14. Most recently, Gabriel Jackson, *Medieval Spain* (New York, 1972); J. Lee Shneidman, *The Rise of the Aragonese-Catalan Empire, 1200–1350*, 2 vols. (New York, 1970); R. I. Burns, "Christian-Islamic Confrontation in The West: The Thirteenth Century Dream of Conversion," *American Historical Review* 76 (1971), 1386–1434.

15. Geoffrey Barraclough, ed., *Eastern and Western Europe in the Middle Ages* (New York, 1970), with extensive bibliography.

16. See Palmer Throop, *Criticism of the Crusade* (Amsterdam, 1940), and the study of R. I. Burns cited above, n. 14. See also the sources and bibliography in E. Peters, ed., *Christian Society and Crusades, 1198–1229* (Philadelphia, 1971).

17. See Christopher Dawson, ed., *Mission to Asia* (New York, 1955); Gregory D. Guzman, "Simon of Saint-Quentin and the Dominican Mission to the Mongol Baiju: A Reappraisal," *Speculum* 46 (1971), 232–49; Leonardo Olschki, *Marco Polo's Asia* (Berkeley and Los Angeles, 1960); P. Chaunu, *L'expansion européene du XIIIe au XVe siècle* (Paris, 1969), with extensive bibliography.

18. For the Dominican Order, see M. H. Vicaire, *St. Dominic and his Times* (London, 1964) and R. F. Bennett, *The Early Dominicans*

(Cambridge, 1937). The best introduction to Franciscan history and literature is now John Moorman, *A History of the Franciscan Order* (Oxford, 1968). Convenient translations of some early Franciscan literature are B. Fahy, O.F.M. and P. Hermann, O.F.M., *The Writings of St. Francis of Assisi* (Chicago, 1964); P. Hermann, O.F.M., *St. Francis of Assisi: First and Second Life of St. Francis* (Chicago, 1963); L. Sherley-Price, *The Little Flowers of Saint Francis* (Baltimore, 1959).

19. See Ernst Kantorowicz, *Frederick the Second*, trans. E. O. Lorimer (rep. New York, 1957); James Powell, *The Liber Augustalis* (Syracuse, 1971).

20. On the spiritualism of Joachim of Flora and its influence from the thirteenth to the eighteenth centuries, see Marjorie Reeves, *Prophecy in The Later Middle Ages* (Oxford, 1969), with bibliography. See also Decima L. Douie, *The Nature and Effect of the Heresy of the Fraticelli* (Manchester, 1932).

21. Nino Scivoletto, *Fra Salimbene da Parma e la storia politica e religiosa del secolo decimoterzo* (Bari, 1950), the best recent fulllength study.

22. *Ibid.*, 45

23. See the remarks of M.-T. Laureilhe, cited above, n. 6, and below, 57–71, 85–111.

24. A fuller discussion of the *Liber de prelato* may be found in Rosalind B. Brooke, *Early Franciscan Government* (Cambridge, 1959), 45–55.

25. G. G. Coulton, *Fourscore Years: An Autobiography* (Cambridge, 1944), 306.

26. F. M. Powicke, "Three Cambridge Scholars," in his *Modern Historians and the Study of History* (London, 1955), 136. The section of this essay devoted to Coulton is perceptive, sensitive, and generous.

27. H. von E. Scott and C. C. Swinton Bland, tr., Caesarius of Heisterbach, *The Dialogue on Miracles* (London, 1929), 2 vols. This translation, as well as Swinton Bland's translation of Guibert of Nogent's *Memoirs*, were both inspired by Coulton. On the latter, see the exchange between Coulton and F. M. Powicke in *History*, n.s. 8 (1923–24) and 9 (1924–25).

28. Coulton, *Fourscore Years*, 306–7. Odo Rigaldi, or Eudes Rigaud, entered the Franciscan order in 1236, was made Archbishop of Rouen in 1247, and kept a register of his episcopal visitations throughout his archdiocese between the years 1248 and 1269. This is the "Diary" of which Coulton speaks. Rigaud went on the Crusade to Tunis with Louis IX in 1270 and attended the Second Council of Lyons in 1274. He died in July, 1275. His *register* has only recently been translated into English: Sidney M. Brown, *The Register of Eudes of Rouen*, ed. J. F. O'Sullivan (Records of Civilization: Sources and Studies No. LXXII) (New York, 1964). The only extensive English work on Johann Busch, the Netherlands monastic reformer of the fifteenth century, is still G. G. Coulton, *Five Centuries of Religion*, Vol. IV, *The Last Days of Medieval Monachism* (Cambridge, 1950), 81–120. The standard work on the autobiographical genre in the middle ages is Georg Misch, *Geschichte der Autobiographie*, Vols. II and III (Frankfurt, 1955–62). An English translation only of Volume I of this work has appeared as *A History of Autobiography in Antiquity*, 2 vols. (London, 1950). See also Paul Lehmann, "Autobiographies of the Middle Ages," *Transactions of the Royal Historical Society*, 5th series, Vol. III (1953), 41–52. On the genre of biography there is incomparably less. See R. Boszard, *Über die Entwicklung der Personendarstellung in der mittelalterlichen Geschichtsschreibung* (Zürich, 1944) and Walter Ullmann, *Principles of Government and Politics in the Middle Ages* (New York, 1966), 299–305, with some further bibliography. Some medieval material is discussed in T. A. Dorey, ed., *Latin Biography* (London, 1967). The most suggestive recent study is John F. Benton's introduction to the *Memoirs* of Guibert de Nogent, cited above, n. 4.

29. Coulton, *Fourscore Years*, 315n.

30. David Knowles, "Cardinal Gasquet as an Historian," in his *The Historian and Character* (Cambridge, 1963), 240–63 at 258–59. See also Gerald Christianson, "G. G. Coulton: The Medieval Historian as Controversialist," *Catholic Historical Review* 57 (1971), 421–41. I am grateful to Professor W. R. Jones of The University of New Hampshire for this reference.

31. *Speculum* 14 (1939), 241.

32. See, e.g., Coulton's Appendix, "American Medievalists," in *Five Centuries of Religion*, Vol. I, *Saint Bernard and His Predeces-*

sors and Successors, 1000-1200 (Cambridge, 1923), 521–22. On the varieties of medievalism in the nineteenth and twentieth centuries, see Philip Gleason, "Mass and Maypole Revisited: American Catholics and The Middle Ages," *Catholic Historical Review* 57 (1971), 249–74, with extensive bibliographical notes.

33. *American Historical Review* 50 (1944–45), 300–301.

34. Coulton, *Fourscore Years*, 306.

35. See above, n. 28.

36. Some of Coulton's conclusions on the nature of medieval history have recently been supported by Geoffrey Barraclough, *History in a Changing World* (Oxford, 1955) and in *The Medieval Papacy*, 205.

Bibliographical Note

On the thirteenth century in general, the best recent study is Léopold Genicot, *Le XIIIe siècle européen* (Paris, 1968), with extensive bibliography and surveys of recent historical concerns. On the city-states of Salimbene's Italy, see the short history by Daniel Waley, *The Italian City-Republics* (New York, 1968). A much more detailed study is Luigi Salvatorelli, *L'Italia Comunale* (Milan, 1940), and a profusely illustrated volume on social life is A. Viscardi and L. Barni, *L'Italia nell'Età Comunale* (Turin, 1966), an important volume in the general series *Società e costume, panorama di storia sociale e tecnologica*. An older work in English is W. F. Butler, *The Lombard Communes* (New York, 1906). A good history of much of later thirteenth-century Europe is Steven Runciman, *The Sicilian Vespers* (Cambridge, 1958), and the most recent, but not entirely satisfactory survey of thirteenth-century Italian culture in English is Helène Nolthenius, *Duecento: The Late Middle Ages in Italy* (New York, 1968). John Larner, *Culture and Society in Italy, 1290–1415* (New York, 1971), although it deals mostly with a later period, is a model of the best methods of recent cultural history and extremely informative for Dante's lifetime and the later period treated by Salimbene. One of the most provocative of recent comprehensive studies of the thirteenth century is Archibald R. Lewis, "The Closing of the Medieval Frontier," *Speculum* 33 (1958), 475–83. An excellent brief introduction to medieval culture is John W. Baldwin, *The Scholastic Culture of the Middle Ages, 1000–1300* (Lexington, Mass., 1971).

PREFACE TO FIRST EDITION.

THERE are many nowadays, and of the best among us, who still halt between the medieval and the modern ideals. In their just dislike of much that is blameworthy in the present, they are often tempted to imagine Religion as a lamp glimmering in the far depths of the past, dimmer and dimmer to human eyes as the world moves onward down the ages. At other times, with the healthy instinct of life, they cling to the more hopeful conception of Faith as a sacred flame kindled from torch to torch in the hands of advancing humanity—varying and dividing as it passes on, yet always essentially the same—broadening over the earth to satisfy man's wider needs, instead of fading away in proportion as God multiplies the souls that need it.

These two ideals are mutually exclusive, and the choice is plain if historians would write plainly. Medieval history has been too exclusively given over to the poet, the romancer, and the ecclesiastic, who by their very profession are more or less conscious apologists. Yet we cannot understand the present until we face the past without fear or prejudice. The thirteenth century—the golden age of the old ideal—is on the one hand near enough for close and accurate observation, while it is sufficiently distant to afford the wide angle needed for our survey.

This present study lays no claim to impartiality in one sense, for I cannot affect to doubt which is the higher of the two ideals. At the same time, when I first fell in love with the Middle Ages, thirty years ago, it was as most people begin to love them, through Chaucer and the splendid relics of Gothic art. An inclination, at first merely æsthetic, has widened and deepened with the growing conviction that the key to most modern problems is to be found in the so-called Ages of Faith. Even here, where the very conception of my work compels me to run counter to many cherished convictions, I have honestly tried to avoid doubtful statements or exaggerations, and am ready to guarantee this by the only pledge in my power—by an offer which I have already made (in substance) several times in vain. Many writers disparage modern civilization in comparison with what seems to me a purely imaginary past. If any one of these will now take me at my word, I will willingly accept his severest criticisms to the extent of thirty-two octavo pages, restrict my reply within the same limit, and publish the whole at my own expense without further comment. If my contentions are false, I am thus undertaking to offer every facility for my own exposure.

I must here record my special thanks to Prof. L. Clédat of Lyons, and Geheimrath-Prof. O. Holder-Egger of Berlin. The former, who had once projected a complete edition of Salimbene, generously put his very extensive collations at my service : and the latter, who has at last published the Chronicle with a perfection of scholarly apparatus which leaves nothing to be desired, has not only met my enquiries with the most ungrudging courtesy, but has kindly supplied me with advance sheets of his great work.

G. G. COULTON.

EASTBOURNE, *July, 1906.*

PREFACE TO SECOND EDITION.

THE present edition contains a considerable amount of fresh matter from Salimbene's chronicle, omitted from the first mainly for the insufficient reason that I had already published it elsewhere. The notes and appendices have been even more extended, especially on points where different critics seemed to think the evidence inadequate.

Apart from the more obvious advantages of a second edition, an author must always welcome the further opportunity of explaining himself; especially when he has struck for a definite cause and provoked hard knocks in return. To most of my reviewers I owe hearty thanks, and certainly not least to a *Guardian* critic, whose evident disagreement with me on important points did not prevent him from giving me credit for an honest attempt to describe the facts as they appeared to one pair of eyes. In that recognition an author finds his real reward : after all, even Goethe was content to say, " I can promise to be sincere, but not to be impartial."* Genuine impartiality is one of the rarest of virtues, though there have always been plenty of authors who shirk thorny questions, or who concede points to the weaker side with the cheap generosity which impels a jury to find for a needy plaintiff against a rich man. Never, perhaps, was this kind of impartiality so common as at present, when (to quote a recent witty writer) "the fashion is a Roman Catholic frame of mind with an agnostic conscience : you get the medieval picturesqueness of the one with the modern conveniences of the other." Even the Editors of the Cambridge Modern History, fearing more the

---

* Goethe's Maxims and Reflections, translated by T. Bailey Saunders, p. 91.

suspicion of partiality than the certainty of an error, have allowed two contributors to contradict each other almost categorically, within a few pages, on one of the most important points in the first volume * Direct references to authorities are forbidden by the plan of the History : there is, of course, nothing to warn the ordinary reader how far one of the two contributors surpasses the other in originality and depth of research ; and it is practically left to him to accept whichever of the two statements fits in best with his preconceived opinions. We cannot imagine a great co-operative work on Natural Science written nowadays on these principles ; and this alone would go far to account for the present unjust neglect of history by readers of an exact turn of mind. Yet there is a further reason also ; for to shirk disputed questions is to neglect matters of the deepest interest : and the elaborate dulness of many official histories is a libel on the many-coloured web of human life.

Eleven years ago, finding it impossible to get from the accredited text-books satisfactory information on points which I had long studied in a desultory way, I began systematic work for myself within a narrow area, and soon found how little the original documents are really studied, and how much one historian is content to take at second-hand from another. In cases like this, anything that can be done to sweep away ancient cobwebs is a real gain. I knew that I should make mistakes, as even officialism is far from infallible, and we have recently seen a reviewer fill three and a half quarto columns with the slips made by one of our most dignified professors in a single octavo volume. I knew also that, however correct my facts, the very effort to expose widely-accredited fallacies would give a certain want of perspective to my work. But, without for a moment supposing that this book would by itself give anything like a complete picture of medieval life, I yet believed that our forefathers' " common

* Cambridge Modern History, vol. i, p. 632: cf. 660, 672, 674-6.

thoughts about common things " would never really become intelligible without informal and frankly personal studies of this kind; and the public reception has now strengthened this belief.

I have, however, departed even more from official usage in another matter—the direct criticism of many misstatements which have gained currency by reaction from the equally one-sided Protestantism of a century ago, more especially through the writings of Abbot Gasquet. While it is to the direct interest of all Roman Catholic clergy, and of many High Churchmen, to misread certain facts of history, there are comparatively few who have the same official excuse for equal vigilance and persistence on the other side. The extreme dread of partiality, into which modern literature has swung from the still worse extreme of blind partisanship, restrains first-rate historians from speaking with sufficient plainness, even in the few cases where they have found time to convince themselves, by carefully verifying his references, of an author's inaccuracy. So long, therefore, as the most authoritative writers salve their consciences by merely describing certain books as able pleas from the Roman Catholic point of view, the public will never grasp what this indulgent phrase really means. Moreover, the euphemism itself would seem to imply a very low view both of history and of religion. No man of science would content himself with such equivocal language in the face of systematic distortions and suppressions of evidence, however personally respectable the literary offender might be. For it is absolutely necessary here to separate the personal and the literary questions as much as possible. The fact that an author is sincerely attached to a particular church, in which he also holds a high official position, is thoroughly honourable to him personally ; but it aggravates the ill effect of his interested misstatements. Not charity, but cynicism underlies the plea which is constantly implied, if not expressed, that certain religious beliefs should be allowed wide licence in the treatment of historical facts—that a writer's public falsehoods may be considered an almost inseparable accident of his private creed, a superfetation of his excessive piety.   No bitterer condemnation could be imagined than this contemptuous leniency which most men extend to a priest's misstatement in the name of Christian Truth. Moreover, we all know Roman Catholics whose theory and practice alike contradict this plea.   It was Lord Acton who said, after years of struggle against official distortions of history, " the weight of opinion is against me when I exhort you never to debase the moral currency or to lower the standard of rectitude, but to try others by the final maxim that governs your own lives, and to suffer no man and no cause to escape the undying penalty which history has the power to inflict on wrong."   Nor did Lord Acton stand alone here : for cultivated laymen show an increasing repugnance to the crooked historical methods which are still only too popular in ecclesiastical circles ; and certain apologists pay already to truth at least the unwilling homage of anonymity.   Legends, which once stalked boldly abroad, are fain to lurk now in unsigned articles for the *Church Times,* or to creep into corners of the *Athenæum* while the editor nods, or to herd with other ancient prejudices in the *Saturday Review.* Yet, to clear the ground thoroughly, it is necessary sometimes to pursue them even into this last ditch, and to show the public how, in spite of the high general tone of our periodical literature, the editorial *we* must inevitably cover some creatures which do well become so old a coat.   When the *Saturday* proclaims, with its traditional wealth of epithet, that our writings lack the odour of sanctity, we may profitably point out that there have always been two separate voices on that journal.   As in the days of the Stephens and J. R. Green, it still doubtless owes its real flavour to witty latitudinarians, and only keeps a few *vrais croyants* on the premises to do the necessary backbiting.

I realise as clearly, perhaps, as some of my critics, how inadequate and unsatisfactory mere negative work must necessarily be. But, having once liberated my soul by plainly exposing the dislike felt by a certain school of historians and critics for the open discussion of actual medieval documents, I hope presently to pass on to a more constructive picture of social life in the past. Yet it may still be doubted whether any history of the Middle Ages can at present avoid controversy without falling into superficiality : and the blame of these conditions lies partly with the want of proper organization at our universities, though there are recent signs of a real awakening. All history is a chain which may break at any point unless each link has been forged with separate care. We cannot understand our place in the modern world without comprehending the French Revolution and the Reformation : nor can we understand these without an accurate conception of the *ancien régime* which each replaced. For instance (to state the problem which the Cambridge History sometimes obscures), were the clergy, from whom the laity revolted four hundred years ago, such as would be tolerated by any civilized country of to-day ? The question is far from insoluble ; it may almost be said that judgment has already gone by default, since Dr. Lea's *Sacerdotal Celibacy* has held the field for forty years. Certainly, if it were made worth their while, one or two able men could in a few years work through the evidence, and bring the public to the same rough agreement as has long been reached on many subjects once as contentious as this. Dozens of important questions similarly await a solution before any real history of medieval life can be written ; and, in default of such organized study as we have long seen in physical science, most of this necessary foundation-work will continue to be done slowly and fitfully by volunteers, amateurs, and controversialists, while the universities are raising enormous monuments on the quicksands of our present uncertainties. The forthcoming Cambridge Medieval History cannot possibly come

near to finality, even in the limited sense in which that word can
ever be rightly used. Large numbers of vital documents are
still unprinted : many even of the printed volumes are not yet
digested, and generations of acute controversy are likely to elapse
before a real historian of the Middle Ages could find such
materials as Gibbon found ready to his hand. It is pathetic to
see how much of professional historiography is still a mere pour-
ing of old wine into new bottles, and to think that Carlyle wrote
half a century ago " After interpreting the Greeks and Romans
for a thousand years, let us now try our own a little. . . . How clear
this has been to myself a long while ! Not one soul, I believe,
has yet taken it into him. Universities founded by "monk ages"
are not fit at all for this age. . . . What all want to know is
the condition of our fellow men ; and, strange to say, it is the
thing of all least understood, or to be understood as matters go."*
The condemnation of the universities is, of course, couched in
terms of Carlylean exaggeration : but it can scarcely be denied
that the official schools are still tempted—through official
timidity, or natural laziness, or mere muddle—to neglect those
questions of past history which are indeed most contentious, but
which go nearest to the roots of human life.

---

* Froude's "Early Life of Thomas Carlyle" (1891), vol. ii, pp. 16, 85.

CHAPTER I

The Autobiography of Brother Salimbene.

THIS—the most remarkable autobiography of the Middle Ages—is only now beginning to take its proper place in history. Inaccessible until lately even to most medieval scholars, it is now at last being published in its entirety under the admirable editorship of Prof. Holder-Egger, in the *Monumenta Germaniæ* (Vol. xxxii, Scriptores). An edition was indeed published in 1857 at Parma : but this was printed from an imperfect transcript, mutilated in deference to ecclesiastical susceptibilities. The original MS., after many vicissitudes, had been bought into the Vatican library in order to render a complete publication impossible ; and it was only thrown open to students, with the rest of the Vatican treasures, by the liberality of the late Pope Leo XIII. Even now, the complete Salimbene will never be read ; for many sheets have been cut out of the MS., and parts of others erased, by certain scandalized readers of long ago :[1] but, in the shape in which we have him at last, he is the most precious existing authority for the ordinary life of Catholic folk at the period which by common consent marks the high-water line of the Middle Ages.

There have been few more brilliant victories in history than those of St. Francis, and few more pathetic failures. The very qualities which put him in a class by himself, and command admiration even from his least sympathetic critics, foredoomed his ideal to a fall as startling as its rise. The generation which followed him was at least as far from fulfilling his hopes as the First Empire was from realizing the ideal of 1789. In each case, an impulse was given which shook Europe to its foundations, and still vibrates down the ages. But in each case there was something of necessary blindness in the passionate concentration of the original idea ; so that the movement soon took quite a different direction, and liberated quite different forces, from those which had been comtemplated by the men who threw their whole soul into the first blow. In Dante's lifetime, not a century after St. Francis's death, friars were burned alive by their brother friars for no worse fault than obstinate devotion to the strict Rule of St. Francis. The Saint was the especial Apostle of Poverty : yet that century of steadily-growing wealth and luxury which stirred Cacciaguida's gall so deeply (Par. xv. 97 foll.) coincided precisely with the century of first and purest Franciscan activity : especially if we read the poet in the light of contemporary chroniclers, who date the change from "the days of Frederick II." St. Francis was born in that age of Bellincion Berti to which Dante looked back as so simple, so sober, and so chaste ; and if he had come back to earth on the centenary of his death, he would have found himself "in the days of Sardanapalus." Making all allowance for Dante's bitterness, and for his characteristically medieval praise of past times at the expense of the present, still we cannot doubt that the change was real and far-reaching. It was in Dante's life-time, for instance, that the custom of buying Oriental slaves grew up, with other similar luxuries which the friars were quite powerless to banish, even when they did not themselves set the example.[2]

Again, Innocent III had seen in a vision St. Francis propping the falling Church : yet this hope, too, was partly belied by the facts of later history. The friars, it is true, seemed for a time to have entirely checked the growing spirit of antisacerdotalism ; but they brought among the clergy themselves a ferment of free thought which only found its proper outlet at the Reformation ; just as the Oxford movement, though initiated as a protest not against the Low Church but against Liberalism, has worked in the long run for Liberalism within our own communion. The Church, in the narrower sense in which Innocent and Francis understood the word, was partly propped, but also seriously shaken, by the thrust of the Franciscan buttress.

Yet the true kernel of St. Francis's teaching has lived and grown : he has given an undying impulse to the world's spiritual life. He showed that a man need not leave the world to live the highest life—that indeed he can scarcely live the highest life except in the world—and, in spite of occasional hesitation on the Saint's own part, in spite of the blindness of many of his most devoted successors, this is a lesson which men have never since forgotten. In this at least, the twentieth century is more Franciscan than the thirteenth ; that you may find a true saint in cricketing flannels or at a theatre, or selling you a pennyworth of biscuits without any airs whatever behind the counter of a village shop. Society in general has grown sufficiently decent to render the retirement into monastic life almost or quite unnecessary : and therefore, though there has been no age in which monks might so easily live in undisturbed retirement as in our own (if indeed they would seek such retirement, and avoid worldly politics), yet monastic vocations among grown-up men and women are extremely rare even in Roman Catholic countries. The good man seldom dreams of cutting himself off from society : and both he and society find themselves the better for it.

The persistence with which most English writers on St. Francis ring the changes on M. Sabatier's admirable biography without refreshing themselves at original sources is apt to create a very artificial atmosphere. Indeed, M. Sabatier himself seems at times to forget the essential impracticability of the strict Franciscan ideal. When he writes that there was something " which all but made of the Franciscans the leaven of a quite new civilization " in " the thought . . that the return of the Spirit of Poverty to dwell on the earth should be the signal for a complete restoration of the human race " (*Sacrum Commercium*, p. 8) he himself would probably frankly confess, on second thoughts, that his enthusiasm has carried him too far. The idea of a formal and absolute renunciation of property was from the first as essentially incapable of regenerating the world as the idea of formal celibacy was of settling " the social problem." It was simply a religious charge of the Light Brigade—magnificent in its moral effect, eternally inspiring within its own limits, but vitiated by a terrible miscalculation of the opposing forces. It had no more effect on the growing luxury of the 13th century than had the Six Hundred on the solid Russian army. Military suicide is in the long run as fatal to victory in the Holy War as in any other : and many of the worst treasons to the Franciscan spirit may be traced directly to the Saint's own exaggerations. The Franciscan legend in England seems in danger of becoming almost as artificial as the Napoleonic legend in France : the strain of praise is pitched higher and higher by each successive writer, till it comes very near to the falsetto of cant. The time seems almost at hand when those who cared for the Saint before M. Sabatier's *Life* was published will feel like those who cared for art before the coming of Æstheticism. The cycle of early Franciscan legends is studied almost as the Bible was two hundred years ago—as a Scripture rather desecrated than honoured by illustration from outside sources. Miss Macdonell's *Sons of Francis*, in spite of the lacunæ in her scholarship, is, however, a real attempt to illustrate the Saint's life by those of some of his nearest companions and most distinguished followers. But even

she moves almost altogether in the plane of exceptional manifestations, and lacks the deeper knowledge of contemporary
manners which is necessary for a comprehension of the average
friar. Yet it is in fact almost as important to understand the
average friar as to understand St. Francis himself, if we would
realize the 13th century. And though Salimbene himself cannot
be called an average friar—he was in many ways far above the
ordinary—yet there is no other single book in which the ordinary
friar, and the world on which he looked out, may so well be
studied.

The author's time and circumstances were among the most
favourable that could possibly be conceived for an autobiographer.
He was a citizen of one of the busiest cities of Italy during incomparably the most stirring period of its history. A Franciscan
of the second generation, overlapping St. Francis by five years
and Dante by twenty-five, he knew personally many of the foremost figures in Franciscan and Dantesque history : and the course
of his long and wandering life brought him into contact with
many real saints, and still more picturesque sinners, whom he
describes with the most impartial interest. His naturally observant and sympathetic mind had been ripened, when he wrote, by
forty years' work in the busiest, most popular, most enterprising
religious order that ever existed :

> " Lo, goode men, a flye, and eek a frere
> Wol falle in every dyshe and mateere."

And, rarest and most precious circumstance of all, he is among
the frankest of autobiographers, not so much composing as
thinking aloud. Like Pepys, whom he resembles so closely in
other ways, he wrote with small thought for posterity : the Chronicle was apparently designed at first for the edification of his dear
niece, a nun of his own order. As he tells us (p. 187), " Moreover,
in writing divers chronicles I have used a simple and intelligible
style, that my niece for whom I wrote might understand as she
read ; nor have I been anxious and troubled about ornaments of
words, but only about the truth of my story. For my niece
Agnes is my brother's daughter, who, having come to her fifteenth
year, entered the order of St. Clare, and continues in the service
of Jesus Christ even to this present day, A.D. 1284, wherein I
write these words. Now this Sister Agnes, my niece, had an
excellent understanding in Scripture, and a good understanding
and memory, together with a delightful tongue and ready of
speech, so that it might be said of her, not without reason, ' Grace

is poured abroad in thy lips, therefore hath God blessed thee for ever.' "[3] We have here, therefore in Montaigne's words, " *un livre de bonne foy*." If some of the stories which the grey-headed friar chronicles for the edification of his aristocratic and cultured niece seem to us a trifle full-flavoured, we must remember that this was thoroughly characteristic of the Ages of Faith. After all, Madame Eglantine and her two fellow-nuns heard worse still on their pious journey to Canterbury : and the most classical educational writer of the Middle Ages, the Knight of La Tour Landry, records even stranger tales than Chaucer's for the instruction of his two motherless daughters. If, again, the friar's very plain-spoken criticisms of matters ecclesiastical may startle those who have indeed read their Dante, but who have been taught, perhaps, that Dante writes with peculiar bitterness as a disappointed man, this is only because many of the most important facts of thirteenth century history have never in modern times been fairly laid before the public. Nobody could gather from even the most candid of modern ecclesiastical historians that the crowning period of the Middle Ages seemed, to those who lived in it, almost hopelessly out of joint. The most pious, the most orthodox, the bravest men of the thirteenth century write as unwilling dwellers in the tents of Kedar. To them, their own world, whether before or after the coming of the Friars, was the mere dregs of the good old world of the past : and they expected God's final vengeance in the near future. Herein lies one of the principal, though hitherto imperfectly recognized, causes of the strange unprogressiveness of the Middle Ages : the strongest minds were hopelessly oppressed by the sight of the crying evils around them, and by the want of histories to teach them how, barbarous as the present was in so many ways, it yet marked a real improvement on the past.

The modern historian, therefore, cannot be too thankful for these memoirs, written without pose or effort, to interest his favourite niece, by a man who had looked sympathetically on many sides of the world in which St. Francis and Dante lived and worked. The learned Jesuit Michael, sadly as he is shocked by our author in many ways, cannot deny that this book presents a mirror of the times, and quotes with approval the verdict of Dove : " His character stands out in striking completeness of modelling by the side of the bas-reliefs of other medieval authors."[4] The dryness of the ordinary medieval chronicler, his apparent unconsciousness of any human interest beyond the baldest facts, is often exasperating : or again, when he betrays real interest, it is too often at the expense of fact. Not only lives of saints, but whole histories, were written avowedly by direct angelic revelation, pure from all taint of earthly documents.[5] But, fortunately for us, Salimbene had more modern notions of the historian's duty. With him, fact comes first, and even edification takes a subordinate place. " Whereas I may seem sometimes to digress from the matter in hand," he says, " it must be forgiven me. I cannot tell my stories otherwise than as they came about in very deed, and as I saw with mine own eyes in the days of the Emperor Frederick II ; yea, and many years after his death, even unto our own days wherein I write these words, in the year of our Lord 1284 " (185). Later on (217) he gives us further evidence of his anxiety to learn the exact truth of the stories current in his own day : and the passage is interesting also as exemplifying the difficulties which ordinary medieval writers experienced in producing even a single copy of their work. He is speaking of a book of his, which unfortunately has not survived : " The chronicle beginning ' *Octavianus Cæsar Augustus, etc.*,' which I wrote in the convent of Ferrara in the year 1250 ; the style of which chronicle I gathered from divers writings, and continued it as far as to the story of the Lombards. Afterwards I slackened my quill, and ceased to write upon that chronicle, being, indeed, so poor that I could procure neither paper nor parchment. And now we are in the year 1284 : yet I ceased not to write divers other chronicles which, in mine own judgment, I have excellently composed, and which I have purged of their superfluities, follies, falsehoods, and contradictions. Nevertheless, I could not purge them of all such ; for some things which have been written are now so commonly noised abroad that the whole world could not remove them from the hearts of men who have thus learnt them from the first. Whereof I could show many examples ; but to rude and unlearned people all examples are useless; as it is written in Ecclesiasticus, ' He that teacheth a fool, is like one that glueth a potsherd together.' " Nor are these mere idle boasts. With all his partiality here and there—a partiality the more harmless because it is so naïvely shown—Salimbene stands the test of comparison with independent documents quite as well as Villani. Among modern writers, those who have least reason to love him are glad to avail themselves of his authority. The footnotes to the three volumes of *Analecta Franciscana*, by which the friars of Quaracchi have laid modern students under such heavy obligations, swarm with references to Salimbene, whose data are constantly used to correct even so painstaking a compiler as Wadding.

Amid all that has been written of the thirteenth century, there is extraordinarily little to guide the general reader in a comparison between those men's real lives and ours. It is true that the main ebb and flow of their conflicts in Church and State has often been related ; the theory of their institutions has been described and analysed ; we have excellent studies of the lives and ideals of some of their greatest men. All this is most important, yet it says comparatively little to the ordinary reader, who, without leisure for special study, often craves nevertheless to compare other states of life with his own. Even the student of greater leisure and opportunities can find but little answer to the all-important question, " Which would be the better to live and die in, a world with those institutions and ideals, or a world with ours ? " Those who have set themselves most definitely to answer this question have too often placed themselves from the outset at a necessarily distorting point of view. They have painted the medieval life mainly after medieval theories of Church and State, or after the lives of a few great men. Yet there never was an age in which theory was more hopelessly divorced from practice than in the thirteenth century ; or in which great men owed more of their greatness to a passionate and lifelong protest against the sordid realities of common life around them. The Franciscan gospel of poverty and humility was preached to a world in which money and rank had far more power than in modern England ; and there is scarcely a page of the *Divina Commedia* that does not breathe a sense of the terrible contrast between Catholic theory and Catholic life. Dean Church, in one of his essays, shows himself fully alive to the danger of judging an age simply after the pattern of its great men.[6] Yet perhaps no writer on the Middle Ages followed this dangerous path more closely than Church's great Oxford master, with all his genius and his natural love of truth. Newman's pictures of the Middle Ages have all the charm and the earnest personal conviction of his best writings, but they have often scarcely more correspondence with the historical facts of any state of society than has Plato's *Republic*. A momentary survey of periods with which we are more familiar will at once show us how fatally history of this kind must take the colour of the writer's personal ideals and prepossessions, in the absence of unquestionable landmarks to correct the play of his imagination. What conception could we form of the real differences between our life and that of our seventeenth-century ancestors from even the most brilliant and penetrating comparisons between Jeremy Taylor and Liddon, Hobbes and Herbert Spencer, Clarendon and Carlyle ?   At the best, such studies could only illustrate and complete a real history written from very different sources.

Such sources are abundant enough for the actual ways and thoughts of the people in the Middle Ages : yet a vast amount of work remains to be done before the historian of the future can give us a full and intimate picture of thirteenth century life. The foundation needs first to be laid in a series of exhaustive monographs with full references, such as Dr. Rashdall' *Universities of Europe in the Middle Ages,* Dr. Dresdner's *Kultur-und Sittengeschichte der Italienischen Geistlichkeit,* and Dr. Lea's admirable books on the Inquisition, Confession, Indulgences, and Celibacy.   Yet such monographs are still far too few : many of the most important documents are still unprinted : many of those in print have been most imperfectly read and discussed ; and a period of acute controversy must necessarily come before we can arrive at even a rough agreement as to the main facts.   Though the history of medieval civilization needs most care of all— for here at every step we move among the flames, or at least over the smouldering ashes, of passionate convictions and pre-judices—it is still the one domain of history into which, in England at least, the scientific spirit has least penetrated.   Even the new series of English Church histories published by Messrs. Macmillan—nay, the Cambridge Modern History itself—are shorn of half their use to the serious student by the entire absence of references or similar guarantees of literary good faith.   No bank can exist in these days without publishing its balance-sheets : yet we are still expected to accept teaching which may be more vital than money, upon the *ipse dixit* of this or that writer.   Half our religious quarrels are due to this habit of writing without references, and therefore too often in reliance upon evidence which will not bear serious criticism.   The temptation is too strong for human nature.   Whether a writer's prepossessions be pro-medieval or anti-medieval, he can count upon a sympathetic public of his own, and upon comparative immunity from criticism ; since his separate blunders, unsupported by references, can be traced and exposed only with the greatest difficulty ; and, in the present state of public opinion, nobody thinks the worse of him for making the most sweeping statements without adequate documentary vouchers.   The inevitable result is that well-meaning men, whom a careful study of their opponents' sources would soon bring to some sort of rough agreement, spend their lives beating the air in wild attempts to strike an adversary who is heating himself with equally vain and violent demonstrations after his own fashion.   Moving in wholly different planes, with scarcely a single point of possible contact, they are necessarily carried farther apart at every step ; and the consciousness of their own good faith in the main compels them to look upon their mysteriously perverse adversaries as Jesuits or Atheists (as the case may be) in disguise. At the same time, the general reader is rather annoyed than interested by interruptions. I have, therefore, omitted footnotes as far as possible, not even marking the necessarily frequent omissions of repetitions and irrelevancies in direct quotations from Salimbene—omissions which sometimes run to a page or more— but simply giving page-references by means of which students can always verify my translations. To the general reader I offer the guarantee of good faith already explained in my preface, viz., an undertaking to print at my own expense the first criticism of my methods which any scholar may care to send me, to the extent of 36 octavo pages. Those who may wish to verify my illustrations from other sources will find full quotations in the notes (Appendix A), whither I have also relegated a good deal of detailed evidence interesting in its bearing upon my subject, but too lengthy to find a place in the text. I have found it hopeless, however, to give in a book of this compass more than a very small fraction of the evidence which I have collected during the past nine years to show that what Salimbene describes is nothing exceptional, but simply the normal state of thirteenth-century society. For he is indeed the natural and artless chronicler of ordinary life in the age of St. Francis and Dante. As with Pepys or Boswell, his very failings as a man are to his advantage as a historian ; and, for us, his lively interest in all sorts of men more than counter-balances his occasional lukewarmness of family affection. The figures which too often stalk like dim ghosts through the pages of far more famous authors, startle us here with their almost modern reality. They move indeed in a world differing from ours to an extent almost past belief, except to those who have carefully measured the strides of civilization even during the past century : yet the most startling of his anecdotes are cor-roborated by unimpeachable independent testimony. All the documents of the thirteenth century, from poems and romances to saints' lives and bishops' registers, yield to the patient student scattered bones from which a complete skeleton of the society of that time might be built up. Beyond this, there are a few authors who in themselves show us something more than mere bones— Joinville, for instance, and Cæsarius of Heisterbach, and Thomas of Chantimpré. But Salimbene alone shows us every side of his age, clothed all round in living flesh, and answering in every part to the dry bones we find scattered elsewhere.

The history of his MS. is sufficient to explain why he is as yet so little known : for it is difficult to do much with a notoriously imperfect text. The reader will, however, find a good deal about Salimbene in Gebhart's fascinating *L'Italie Mystique*, and *La Renaissance Italienne*. He has been the subject of learned monographs by Professors Clédat of Lyons and Michael of Innsbruck, the latter of whom analyses the book very fully and without too obvious partiality. A very short abstract of the Chronicle has been printed in English by Mr. Kington Oliphant; and, quite recently, Miss Macdonell has dealt with Salimbene at some length on pp. 252 foll. of her *Sons of Francis*. Lively and interesting as this chapter is, it fails, however, to give an adequate idea either of the contents of Salimbene's book, or of his value as a historian. The author, though she quotes from the Latin text, has evidently worked almost entirely from Cantarelli's faulty Italian translation, of which she herself speaks, somewhat ungratefully, with exaggerated scorn. Not only has she followed Cantarelli blindly in all his worst blunders—quoting, for instance, as specially characteristic of Salimbene's attitude towards Frederick II a paragraph, which, in fact, describes a different man altogether (p. 300)—but she adds several of her own. The greatest weakness of her study, however, is that her comparative unfamiliarity with other first-hand contemporary sources tempts her to depreciate Salimbene's value as a faithful mirror of his times. She evidently looks upon certain perfectly normal facts as strange and exceptional; and her essay, though well worth reading, fails in this respect to do justice to its subject.[7]

In the following pages I have made no attempt to translate the Chronicle in the exact state in which Salimbene left it. The good friar jotted things down just as they came into his head, with ultra-medieval incoherence : "For the spirit bloweth whither it listeth, neither is it in man's power to hinder the spirit," as he says after one of his wildest digressions. Whole pages are filled with mere lists of Scripture texts, often apparently strung together from a concordance, though he undoubtedly knew his Bible thoroughly well. Pages more are occupied with records of historical events compiled from other chronicles : the parentheses and repetitions are multitudinous and bewildering. The book as it stands is less a history than materials for a history, like the miscellaneous paper bags from which Hofrath Heuschrecke compiled the biography of Teufelsdröckh. The only possible way of introducing the real Salimbene to the modern public is to translate or summarize all the really characteristic portions of the Chronicle, reducing them by the way to some sort of order. But I have been compelled to omit a good deal both from my author's text and from the scope of my illustrations : for there is one side of medieval life which cannot be discussed in a book of this kind. To the darkest chapter in Celano's life of St. Francis I have barely alluded ; and I have turned aside altogether from the most terrible canto in the *Inferno.* The student will, however, find in Appendix C the original Latin of certain passages and allusions omitted from the text.

CHAPTER II

Parentage and Boyhood.

BROTHER Salimbene di Adamo was born of a noble family at
Parma, in 1221, the year of St. Dominic's death. One of
his sponsors was the Lord Balian of Sidon, a great baron of
France who had been viceroy for Frederick II in the Holy Land.
" My father was Guido di Adamo, a comely man and a valiant
in war, who once crossed the seas for the succour of the Holy
Land, in the days of Baldwin, Count of Flanders, before my
birth. And I have heard from him that, whereas other Lombards
in the Holy Land enquired of diviners concerning the state of
their houses at home, my father would never enquire of them ;
and, on his return, he found all in comfort and peace at home ;
but the others found evil, as the diviners had spoken. Furthermore, I have heard from my father that his charger, which he had
brought with him to the Holy Land, was commended for its
beauty and worth above those of all the rest who were of his
company. Again, I have heard from him that, when the
Baptistery of Parma was founded, he laid stones in the foundations
for a sign and a memorial thereof, and that on the spot whereon
the Baptistery is built had been formerly the houses of my
kinsfolk, who after the destruction of their houses, went to
Bologna " (37). In 1222 occurred the Great Earthquake in
Lombardy, attributed by the orthodox to God's anger against
the heretics, who swarmed in France, Germany and Italy, and
who in Berthold of Ratisbon's excited imagination numbered
a round hundred-and-fifty sects.[1] The common folk, however,
when their first panic was over, treated it rather as a joke :
" They became so hardened by the earthquake that, when a
pinnacle of a tower or a house fell, they would gaze thereon
with shouts and laughter. My mother hath told me how at the
time of that earthquake I lay in my cradle, and how she caught
up my two sisters, one under each arm, for they were but babes
as yet. So, leaving me in my cradle, she ran to the house of
her father and mother and brethren, for she feared (as she said),

lest the Baptistery should fall on her, since our house was hard by. Wherefore I never since loved her so dearly, seeing that she should have cared more for me, her son, than for her daughters. But she herself used to say that they were easier for her to carry, being better grown than I" (34). Yet he describes her as a most loveable woman, in spite of her perverse choice on that eventful day. "She was named the Lady Imelda, a humble lady and devout, fasting much and gladly dispensing alms to the poor. Never was she seen to be wroth; never did she smite any of her maidservants with her hand. In winter, she would ever have with her, for the love of God, some poor woman from the mountains, who found in the house both lodging and food and raiment all winter long; and yet my mother had other maids who did the service of the house. Wherefore Pope Innocent [the IVth, who knew her personally] gave me letters at Lyons that she might be of the order of St. Clare, and the same he gave another time to Brother Guido, my blood-brother, when he was sent on a mission from Parma to the Pope. She lieth buried in the convent of the ladies of St. Clare; may her soul rest in peace! Her mother, that is, my grandmother, was called the Lady Maria, a fair lady and a full-fleshed, sister to the Lord Aicardo, son to Ugo Amerigi, who were judges in Parma, rich men and powerful, and dwelt hard by the church of St. George " (55). The implication in this remark about the maid-servants is only too fully justified by all contemporary evidence. The *Confessionale*, a manual for parish priests, variously attributed to St. Bonaventura, St. Thomas Aquinas, and Albertus Magnus, specifies the canonical penances to be imposed for some sixty probable transgressions. One of them runs, "If any woman, inflamed by zealous fury, have so beaten her maid-servant that she die in torments within the third day, ... if the slaying have been wilful, let her not be admitted to the communion for seven years; but if it have been by chance, let her be admitted after five years of legitimate penance." A stock case in Canon Law is that of the priest who, wishing to beat his servant with his belt, had the misfortune to wound him with the dagger thereto attached. A Northumbrian worthy in 1279, striking at a girl with a cudgel, struck and killed by mistake the little boy whom she held in her arms; the jury treated it as a most pardonable misadventure, though he showed his sense of having sailed very close to the wind by absconding until the trial was over. It is necessary, indeed, on the threshold of any out-spoken study of medieval life, to recognise the essential difference between past and present manners in this matter of personal

violence. On this subject, as on so many others, a false glamour
has been thrown over the past by writers who have studied only
the theory of knightly courtesy, without making any attempt to
gauge the actual practice. The instances of brutality to women
in high life quoted by Léon Gautier and Alwin Schulz from the
Chansons de Geste might be multiplied almost indefinitely. The
right of wifebeating was formally recognised by more than one
code of laws : and it was already a forward step when, in the
thirteenth century, the *Coutumes du Beauvoisis* provided " que le
mari ne doit battre sa femme que *raisonnablement*." But what
were the limits of reason in this matter, to the medieval mind ?
We may infer them fairly well from the tales told by the Knight
of La Tour-Landry (1372) for the instruction of his daughters.
He tells, for instance, how a lady so irritated her husband by
scolding him in company, that he struck her to the earth with his
fist and kicked her in the face, breaking her nose. Upon this
the good Knight moralises, " And this she had for her euelle
and gret langage, that she was wont to saie to her husbonde.
And therefor the wiff aught to suffre and lete the husbonde
haue the wordes, and to be maister, for that is her worshippe."
This was also the opinion of St. Bernardino, who said in a
public sermon : " And I say to you men, never beat your wives
while they are great with child, for therein would lie great peril.
I say not that you should never beat them, but choose your time.
. . . . I know men who have more regard for a hen that
lays a fresh egg daily, than for their own wives : sometimes the
hen will break a pot or a cup, and the man will not beat her, for
the mere fear of losing the egg that is her fruit. How stark
mad are many that cannot suffer a word from their own lady
who bears such fair fruit : for if she speak a word more than
he thinks fit, forthwith he seizes a staff and begins to chastise
her : and the hen, which cackles all day without ceasing, you
suffer patiently for her egg's sake. . . . . Many a man, when
he sees his wife less clean and delicate than he would fain see
her, strikes her forthwith ; and the hen may befoul your table,
and yet you have patience with her : why not, then, with her to
whom you owe patience ? Seest thou not the hog, too, always
grunting and squealing and defiling thy house ! yet thou sufferest
him until slaughter-time. Thy patience is but for the fruit's
sake of the beast's flesh, that thou mayst eat it. Bethink thee,
wretch, bethink thee of the noble fruit of thy lady, and have
patience ; it is not meet to beat her for every trifle, no ! "
Moreover, it is the same story if we pass upwards from such a
citizen's house, where the pigs and the fowls were as familiar as

in an Irish cabin, and peep into the palace of Frederick II, the
wonder of the world. Weary of his wife, the Emperor had
seduced her cousin: and Jean de Brienne, exasperated by this
double wrong to his daughter and his niece, talked loudly of
washing it out in blood. Therefore the Emperor "so threatened
and beat the Empress as almost to slay the babe in her womb."
We get a similar glimpse of the relations between Frederick's
father and mother—the Costanza of Par. iii, 118. "I have
heard," writes Etienne de Bourbon, "that when the father of the
Ex-Emperor Frederick had gone to bed, and the Empress his
spouse would fain come to him, and had taken off in his presence
her head-attire with a great mass of false hair, then he began to
call his knights and squires, and in their presence, loathing that
hair as a piece of carrion, he cried aloud as one raving: ' Quick,
quick ! bear away this carrion from my room and burn it in the
fire, that ye may smell its evil savour : for I will have no dead
wife, but a living one.' " When these things were done in the
green tree of their honeymoon, we need scarcely wonder that
Salimbene should give a sad account of their married life in the
dry, after deep political differences had multiplied the causes of
quarrel. "There was grievous discord and war between these
two, so that wise and learned men were wont to say these are
not as Ecclesiasticus teacheth, ' man and wife that agree well
together : ' while, again, buffoons would say ' if one should now
cry Mate ! to the King, the Queen would not defend him ' " (359).
Nor was it the rougher sex alone which permitted itself such
violence, as Salimbene has already hinted. We may find the
exact antithesis of the good Imelda in Benvenuto da Imola's
description of another lady of high rank in Dante's Florence—
the Cianghella of Par. xv, 128. "She was most arrogant and
intolerable ; she was wont to go through the house with a
bonnet on her head after the fashion of the Florentine ladies,
and with a staff in her hand ; now she would beat the serving-
man, now the cook. So it befell once that she went to mass
at the convent of Friars Preachers in Imola, not far from
her own house ; and there a friar was preaching. Seeing,
therefore, that none of the ladies present rose to make room for
her, Cianghella was inflamed with wrath and indignation, and
began to lay violent hands on one lady after another, tearing hair
and false tresses on the one hand, wimple and veil on the other.
Some suffered this not, but began to return her blow for blow,
whereat there arose so great noise and clamour in the church
that the men standing round to hear the sermon began to laugh
with all their might, and the preacher laughed with them, so

that the sermon ended thus in merriment." One wonders how Cianghella's children were brought up; and we might almost be tempted to look for one of them in the contemporary boy who was sent by his mother " to the common prison of Florence, to be there retained until he return to his good senses."[2]

Salimbene, however, grew up under very different home influences. " My father's mother was the Lady Ermengarda. She was a wise lady, and was a hundred years old when she went the way of all flesh. With her I dwelt fifteen years in my father's house; how often she taught me to shun evil company and follow the right, and to be wise, and virtuous, and good, so often may God's blessing light upon her! For oft-times she taught me thus. She lieth buried in the aforesaid sepulchre, which was common to us and to the rest of our house " (54).

An equally definite religious influence was that of an old neighbour on the Piazza Vecchia: " The Lord Guidolino da Enzola, a man of middle stature, rich and most renowned and devoted beyond measure to the Church, whom I have seen a thousand times. Separating himself from the rest of the family, who dwelt in the Borgo di Santa Cristina, he came and dwelt hard by the Cathedral Church, which is dedicated to the glorious Virgin, wherein he daily heard mass and the whole daily and nightly offices of the Church, each at the fit season; and whensoever he was not busied with the offices of the Church, he would sit with his neighbours under the public portico by the Bishop's Palace, and speak of God, or listen gladly to any who spake of Him. Nor would he ever suffer children to cast stones against the Baptistery or the Cathedral to destroy the carvings or paintings[3]; for when he saw any such he waxed wroth and ran swiftly against them and beat them with a leather thong as though he had been specially deputed to this office; yet he did it for pure godly zeal and divine love, as though he said in the Prophet's words, ' The zeal of thy house hath eaten me up.' Moreover, this said lord, besides the orchard and town and palace wherein he lived, had many other houses, and an oven and a wine cellar; and once every week, in the road hard by his house, he gave to all the poor of the whole city who would come thither a general dole of bread and sodden beans and wine, as I have seen, not once or twice only, with mine own eyes. He was a close friend of the Friars Minor, and one of their chief benefactors " (609). For a man of such exceptional piety, Guidolino was unfortunate in his descendants. His son Jacobino, who bought Salimbene's father's house, was an usurer, and failed miserably as Podesta of Reggio, leaving a son who was the hero of a somewhat disreputable quarrel. His only daughter, the Lady Rikeldina, "was a worldly and wanton woman," and married a rich lord who "consumed all his substance with his banquetings and buffoons "and courtly fashions ; so that his sons must needs starve unless they would beg, as one of them told me even weeping."

The Chronicler has warm words of praise for most of his elder relations : "fair ladies and wise " ; " a very fair lady " ; " an honourable lady and devout " ; " a fair lady, wise and honourable, who ended her days in a convent " ; " the most fair lady Caracosa, excellent in prudence and sagacity, who ruled her house most wisely after her husband's death." There was evidently a definitely religious note in the family, though this, in good medieval society, was perfectly consistent with the fact that our chronicler's father had a son by a concubine named Rechelda (54). He had also three legitimate sons. First came Guido, by a first wife, "the lady Ghisla of the family de' Marsioli, who were of old noble and powerful men in the city of Parma. They dwelt in the lower part of the Piazza Vecchia, hard by the Bishop's Palace ; whereof I have seen a great multitude, and certain of them were clad in robes of scarlet, more especially such as were judges. They were also kinsfolk of mine own through my mother, who was daughter to the Lord Gerardo di Cassio, a comely old man, who died (as I think) at the age of one hundred years. He had three sons ; the lord Gerardo, who wrote the *Book of Composition*, for he was an excellent writer of the more noble style ; the Lord Bernardo, who was a man of no learning, but simple and pure ; and the Lord Ugo, who was a man of learning, judge and assessor. He was a man of great mirth, and went ever with the Podestas to act as their advocate " (55). This eldest brother Guido married into a greater family still. " My brother Guido was a married man in his worldly life, and a father, and a judge ; and afterwards he became a priest and a preacher in the Order of the Friars Minor. His wife was of the Baratti, who boast that they are of the lineage of the Countess Matilda, and that in the service of the Commune of Parma forty knights of their house go forth to war " (38). It was natural, therefore, that our chronicler, as he tells us on another page, should have owed special reverence to the great protectress of the Church whom Dante also set on so high a pinnacle, if we are to accept the almost unanimous opinion of the early commentators. When Guido became a friar, his wife entered a convent, and their only daughter was that Agnes for whom, in her Franciscan convent of Parma, Salimbene wrote part at least, of his Chronicle. It is noteworthy that of the sixty-two persons who are named in this genealogy, no less than fourteen became monks, friars, or nuns, while five were knights and three were judges.

After Guido came Nicholas, who " died while he was yet a child, as it is written, ' while I was yet growing he cut me off' " (38). " The third am I, Brother Salimbene, who entered the Order of the Friars Minor, wherein I have lived many years, as priest and preacher, and have seen many things, and dwelt in many provinces, and learnt much. And in my worldly life I was called by some *Balian of Sidon*, by reason of the above-mentioned lord who held me at the sacred font. But by my comrades and my family I was called *Ognibene* (*All-good*), by which name I lived as a novice in our Order for a whole year long " (38).

The name seems to indicate a docile, impressionable disposition, and all Salimbene's home memories point the same way. " From my very cradle I was taught and exercised in [Latin] grammar " (277). In other respects, his upbringing must necessarily have been rough, however favourable it may have been for those times. Home life even among the highest classes in the 13th century was such, in many of its moral and sanitary conditions, as can now be found only among the poor. The children had ordinarily no separate bedroom, but slept either with their parents or with servants and strangers on the floor of the hall. Thomas of Celano, describing the home education of St. Francis's day, and showing by his present tenses that things were still the same in the generation in which he wrote, gives a picture which we might well dismiss as an unhealthy dream if it were not so accurately borne out by the repeated assertions of Gerson 150 years later. " Boys are taught evil as soon as they can babble," says Celano, " and as they grow up they become steadily worse, until they are Christians only in name." As half-fledged youths they ran wild in the streets : and we cannot understand the Friars until we have realized how many of them had plunged into Religion, like Salimbene, just at the age when a boy begins to realize dimly the responsibilities of a man, and to look back upon what already seem long years spent—as his awakened imagination may now warn him with even hysterical emphasis— in the service of the Devil.

Our author had three sisters also, " fair ladies and nobly wedded," of whom the first was the Lady Maria, married to the Lord Azzo, cousin-german to the Lord Guarino, who was of kin to the Pope [Innocent IV]. He had many other relations and connections of noble rank and distinction in other ways. His musical tastes came partly by birth and partly by education.

(54). "My father's sister was the mother of two daughters, Grisopola and Vilana, excellent singers both. Their father, the Lord Martino de' Stefani, was a merry man, pleasant and jocund, who loved to drink wine; he was an excellent musician, yet no buffoon. One day in Cremona he beguiled and out-witted Master Gerardo Patechio, who wrote the *Book of Pests*[4]. But he was well worthy to be so out-witted, and deserved all that befell him."

Having come to the end of this genealogy—or nearly to the end, for he throws in occasional postscripts afterwards—he explains why he has entered into such full details. (56) "Lo here I have written the genealogy of my kinsfolk beyond all that I had purposed; yet, for brevity's sake, I have omitted to describe many men and women, both present and past. But since I had begun, it seemed good to me to finish the same, for five reasons. First, for that my niece, Sister Agnes, who is in the convent of the nuns at St. Clare in Parma, wherein she enclosed herself for Christ's sake while she was yet a child, hath begged me to write it by reason of her father's grandmother, of whom she could obtain no knowledge. Now therefore she may learn from this genealogy who are her ancestors both on the father's and on the mother's side. Moreover, my second reason for writing this genealogy was, that Sister Agnes might know for whom she ought to pray to God. The third reason was the custom of men of old time, who wrote their genealogies; whence it is written of certain folk in the book of Nehemiah that they were cast forth from the priesthood, for that they could not find the writings of their genealogies. The fourth reason was, that by reason of this genealogy I have said certain good and profitable words which otherwise I should not have said. The fifth and last was, that the truth of those words of the Apostle James might be shown, wherein he saith, 'For what is your life? It is a vapour which appeareth for a little while and afterwards shall vanish away.' The truth of which saying may be shown in the case of many whom death hath carried off in our days; for within the space of sixty years mine own eyes have seen all but a few of those whom I have written in the table of my kindred, and now they have departed from us and are no longer in the world. I have seen in my days many noble houses destroyed, in different parts of the world. To take example from near at hand, in the city of Parma my mother's house of the Cassi is wholly extinct in the male branch; the house of the Pagani, whom I have seen noble, rich, and powerful, is utterly extinct; likewise the house of the Stefani, whom I have seen in great multitude, rich men and powerful. Consider now that we shall go to the dead rather than they shall return to us, as David saith, speaking of his dead son. Let us therefore be busy about our own salvation while we have time, lest it be said of us as shall be said of those of whom Jeremiah speaketh, 'The harvest is past, the summer is ended, and we are not saved.' Of which matter 1 have written above at sufficient length." Dante students will no doubt notice the strong similarity between this last passage and Purg. XIV. 9, foll., where the Pagani are among the families whose decay the poet bewails. The same cry is constant through the Middle Ages, no doubt partly because the noble families, forming a specially fighting caste, were specially liable to sudden extinction; partly also because they led such irregular lives. Berthold of Ratisbon complains that "so few great lords reach their right age or die a right death," and ascribes this to their careless upbringing and to the oppressions which, when grown to man's estate, they exercise upon the poor[5].

CHAPTER III.

The Great Alleluia.

WHEN Salimbene was in his twelfth year, an event occurred which undoubtedly impressed him deeply, and probably determined his choice of a career. This was the great North Italian religious revival of 1233, which was called *The Alleluia*. There is an excellent article on this and similar medieval revivals in Italy by J. A. Symonds, in the *Cornhill* for January, 1875. But no chronicler tells the great Alleluia of 1233 with anything like the same picturesque detail as Salimbene. (70) " This Alleluia, which endured for a certain season, was a time of peace and quiet, wherein all weapons of war were laid aside ; a time of merriment and gladness, of joy and exultation, of praise and rejoicing. And men sang songs of praise to God ; gentle and simple, burghers and country folk, young men and maidens, old and young with one accord. This devotion was held in all the cities of Italy ; and they came from the villages to the town with banners, a great multitude of people ; men and women, boys and girls together, to hear the preaching and to praise God. And they sang God's songs, not man's ; and all walked in the way of salvation. And they bare branches of trees and lighted tapers ; and sermons were made at evening and in the morning and at midday, according to the word of the Prophet, ' Evening, and morning, and at noon will I pray and cry aloud, and He shall hear my voice.' And men held stations in the churches and the open places, and lifted up their hands to God, to praise and bless Him for ever and ever ; and they might not cease from the praises of God, so drunken were they with His love ; and blessed was he who could do most to praise God. No wrath was among them, no trouble nor hatred, but all was done in peace and kindliness ; for they had drunken of the wine of the sweetness of God's spirit, whereof if a man drink, flesh hath no more savour to him. Wherefore it is commanded to preachers, ' Give strong drink to them that are sad, and wine to them that are grieved in mind. Let them drink and forget their want, and remember their sorrow no more.'

And forasmuch as the Wise Man saith, 'Where there is no governor, the people shall fall,' lest it be thought that these had no leader, let me tell now of the leaders of those congregations. First came Brother Benedict to Parma, who was called the Brother of the Horn, a simple man and unlearned, and of holy innocence and honest life, whom also I saw and knew familiarly, both at Parma and afterwards at Pisa. This man had joined himself unto no religious congregation, but lived after his own conscience, and busied himself to please God ; and he was a close friend of the Friars Minor. He was like another John the Baptist to behold, as one who should go before the Lord and make ready for him a perfect people. He had on his head an Armenian cap, his beard was long and black, and he had a little horn of brass, wherewith he trumpeted ; terribly did his horn bray at times, and at other times it would make dulcet melody. He was girt with a girdle of skin, his robe was black as sackcloth of hair, and falling even to his feet. His rough mantle was made like a soldier's cloak, adorned both before and behind with a red cross, broad and long, from the collar to the foot, even as the cross of a priest's chasuble. Thus clad he went about with his horn, preaching and praising God in the churches and the open places ; and a great multitude of children followed him, oft-times with branches of trees and lighted tapers. Moreover I myself have oft-times seen him preaching and praising God, standing upon the wall of the Bishop's Palace, which at that time was a-building. And thus he began his praises, saying in the vulgar tongue, ' Praised and blessed and glorified be the Father.' Then would the children repeat in a loud voice that which he had said. And again he would repeat the same words, adding ' be the Son ; ' and the children would repeat the same, and sing the same words. Then for the third time he would repeat the same words, adding ' be the Holy Ghost ' ; and then ' Alleluia, alleluia, alleluia ! ' Then would he sound with his trumpet ; and afterwards he preached, adding a few good words in praise of God. And lastly, at the end of his preaching, he would salute the blessed Virgin after this fashion :—

'Ave Maria, clemens et pia, etc., etc.' "

But Brother Benedict was far outdone in popularity by the great Franciscan and Dominican preachers. There was Brother Giacomino of Reggio, a learned man, and in later life a friend of our chronicler's, who so wrought upon his hearers that great and small, gentle and simple, boors and burghers, worked for the building of the Dominican Church at Reggio. Blessed was he who could bring most stones and sand and lime on his back, without regard for his rich furs and silks, for Brother Giacomino would stand by to see that the work was well done. This Brother held a great preaching between Calerno and Sant' Ilario, whereat was a mighty multitude of men and women, boys and girls, from Parma and Reggio, from the mountains and valleys, from the field and from divers villages. And it came to pass that a poor woman of low degree brought forth among the multitude a man child. Then, at the prayer and bidding of Brother Giacomino, many of those present gave many gifts to that poor woman. For one gave her shoes, another a shirt, another a vest, another a bandage ; and thus she had a whole ass's load. Moreover, the men gave one hundred imperial *solidi*. One who was there present, and saw all these things, related them to me a long while afterwards, as I was passing with him through this same place ; and I have also heard the same from others." (73) There was another Franciscan of Padua, " who was preaching at Cumæ on a certain feast day, and a usurer was having his tower built : and the friar, impeded by the tumult of the workmen, said to his hearers ' I forewarn you that within such and such a time this tower will fall and be ruined to the very foundations ' : and so it came to pass, and men held it a great miracle. Note Ecclesiasticus xxxvii, 18 and Proverbs xvii, 16, and the example of the man who foretold the fall of the tower, and Grilla's son, and the three pumpkins, in one of which was a mouse : he happened to tell all things by chance as they were, and therefore he was hailed as a prophet" (74). Then there was " Brother Leo of Milan, who was a famous and mighty preacher, and a great persecutor and confuter and conqueror of heretics "—a panegyric which shows how soon the Order had lost the sweet reasonableness which was one of the most striking characteristics of St. Francis. " He was so bold and stout-hearted that once he went forward alone, standard in hand, before the army of Milan which was marching against the Emperor ; and, crossing the stream by a bridge, he stood long thus with the standard in his hands, while the Milanese shrank from crossing after him, for fear of the Emperor's battle-array. This Brother Leo once confessed the lord of a certain hospital at Milan, who was a man of great name and much reputed for his sanctity. While he was at his last gasp, Brother Leo made him promise to return and tell him of his state after his death, which he willingly promised. His death was made known through the city about the hour of vespers.

Brother Leo therefore prayed two Brethren, who had been his special companions while yet he was Minister Provincial, to watch with him that night in the gardener's cell at the corner of the garden. While, therefore, they all three watched, a light sleep fell upon Brother Leo ; and, wishing to slumber, he prayed his comrades to awake him if they heard anything. And lo ! they suddenly heard one who came wailing with bitter grief ; and they saw him fall swiftly from heaven like a globe of fire, and swoop upon the roof of the cell as when a hawk stoops to take a duck. At this sound, and at the touch of the brethren, Brother Leo awoke from his sleep and enquired how it stood with him, for ever he wailed with the same woful cries. He therefore answered and said that he was damned, because in his wrath he had suffered baseborn children to die unbaptized when they had been laid at the hospital door, seeing to what travail and cost the spital was exposed by such desertion of children. When, therefore, Brother Leo enquired of him why he had not confessed that sin, he answered either that he had forgotten it, or that he thought it unworthy of confession. To whom the Brother replied, ' Seeing that thou hast no part or lot with us, depart from us and go thine own way ! ' so the soul departed, crying and wailing as it went " (74). Brother Leo's subsequent history is interesting. The Chapter of Milan, disagreeing hopelessly about the election of an Archbishop, agreed to leave the choice in his hands. After due reflection, he announced, " Since you have so good an opinion of me, I name myself Archbishop." The people, surprised at first by this decision, presently applauded it, and the Pope approved. After sixteen years' rule, however, Leo left the city a prey to civil strife, and for fourteen years the Milanese refused to accept his successor, in spite of the army and the Papal anathemas with which he supported his claim.[1]

After Leo came Brother Gerard of Modena, " one of the first Brethren of our Order, yet not one of the Twelve. He was an intimate friend of St. Francis, and at times his travelling-companion " (75). He was of noble birth, strict morals, and great eloquence, though his learning was small. " He it was who, in the year 1238, prayed Brother Elias to receive me into the Order, and I was once his travelling-companion. When I call him to mind, I always think of that text, ' He that hath small understanding and feareth God is better than one that hath much wisdom, and transgresseth the law of the Most High.' With him I also lay sick at Ferrara of that sickness whereof he died ; and he went about New Year's tide to Modena, where he gave up the ghost. He was buried in the church of the Brethren Minor, in a tomb of stone ; and through him God hath deigned to work many miracles, which, for that they be written elsewhere, I here omit for brevity's sake." Several of these are recorded by Angelo Clareno (*Archiv.* Bd. ii. p. 268) ; they are mostly of the common type, but one bears a very suspicious resemblance to this bogus miracle which Salimbene relates immediately below. (76) " One thing I must not omit, namely that, at the time of the aforesaid devotion, these solemn preachers were sometimes gathered together in one place, where they would order the matter of their preachings ; that is, the place, the day, the hour, and the theme thereof. And one would say to the other, ' Hold fast to that which we have ordered ' ; and this they did without fail, as they had agreed among themselves. Brother Gerard therefore would stand, as I have seen with mine own eyes, in the Piazza Communale of Parma, or wheresoever else it pleased him, on a wooden stage which he had made for his preaching ; and, while the people waited, he would cease from his preaching, and draw his hood deep over his face, as though he were meditating some matter of God. Then, after a long delay, as the people marvelled, he would draw back his hood and open his mouth in such words as these : ' I was in the spirit on the Lord's day, and I heard our beloved brother, John of Vicenza, who was preaching at Bologna on the shingles of the river Reno, and he had before him a great concourse of people ; and this was the beginning of his sermon : Blessed are the people whose God is the Lord Jehovah, and blessed are the folk that he hath chosen to him to be his inheritance.' So also would he speak of Brother Giacomino ; so spake they also of him. The bystanders marvelled and, moved with curiosity, some sent messengers to learn the truth of these things that were reported. And having found that they were true, they marvelled above measure, and many, leaving their worldly business, entered the Orders of St. Francis or St. Dominic. And much good was done in divers ways and divers places at the time of that devotion, as I have seen with mine own eyes.[2] Yet there were also at the time many deceivers and buffoons who would gladly have sought to bring a blot upon the Elect. Among whom was Buoncompagno of Florence, who was a great master of grammar in the city of Bologna. This man, being a great buffoon, as is the manner of the Florentines, wrote a certain rhyme in derision of Brother John of Vicenza, whereof I remember neither the beginning nor the end, for that it is long since I read it, nor did I even then fully commit it to memory, seeing that I cared not greatly for it. But therein were these words following, as they come to my memory :—

John, in his Johannine way
Dances all and every day.
Caper freely, skip for joy,
Ye who hope to reach the sky !
—Dancers left and dancers right,
Thousands, legions infinite—
Noble ladies dance in rhythm,
Doge of Venice dances with 'em, etc., etc.[3]

Furthermore, this master Buoncompagno, seeing that Brother John took upon himself to work miracles, would take the same upon himself ; wherefore he promised to the men of Bologna that, in the sight of all, he would presently fly. In brief, the report was noised abroad through Bologna, and on the appointed day the whole city, men and women, boys and old men, were gathered together at the foot of the hill which is called Santa Maria in Monte. He had made for himself two wings, and stood now looking down upon them from the summit of the mountain. And when they had stood thus a long while gazing one at the other, he opened his mouth and spake, ' Go ye hence with God's blessing, and let it suffice you that ye have gazed on the face of Buoncompagno ! ' Wherefore they withdrew, knowing that they were mocked of him " (78).

John's strange career is described at length in Symonds's article, and still more fully in an exhaustive monograph by C. Sutter (*Johann v. Vicenza.* Freib. i/B. 1891). Matthew Paris (an. 1238) tells how he crossed rivers dryshod, and by his mere word compelled eagles to stoop in their flight. On the other hand, a contemporary satire on his reported miracles was attributed to Piero delle Vigne, and Guido Bonatti complained that he had sought for years in vain to meet any one of the eighteen men whom John was said to have raised from the dead.[4] At the back of all these legends, however, lies the certain fact that many cities of Italy entrusted him and other friars (e.g. Gerard of Modena) with dictatorial powers during this Alleluia year, permitting them to make or remodel laws as they pleased. John was made Lord of Vicenza, with the titles of Duke and Count ; and it was apparently these honours which finally turned his head. He used his power so recklessly that he was cast into prison, from which he emerged a discredited and neglected man. But, already in the Alleluia year, Salimbene tells us how he " had come to such a pitch of madness by reason of the honours which were paid him, and the grace of preaching which he had, that he believed himself able in truth to work miracles, even without God's help. And when he was rebuked by the Brethren for the many follies which he did, then he answered and spake unto them :

' I it was who exalted your Dominic, whom ye kept twelve years hidden in the earth, and, unless ye hold your peace, I will make your saint to stink in men's nostrils and will publish your doings abroad' (78). For [at the time of the Alleluia] the blessed Dominic was not yet canonized, but lay hidden in the earth, nor was there any whisper of his canonization ; but, by the travail of this aforesaid Brother John, who had the grace of preaching in Bologna at the time of that devotion, his canonization was brought about. To this canonization the Bishop of Modena gave his help ; for he, being a friend of the Friars Preachers, importuned them, saying, ' Since the Brethren Minor have a saint of their own, ye too must so work as to get yourselves another, even though ye should be compelled to make him of straw ' (72). So, hearing these words of Brother John, they bore with him until his death, for they knew not how they might rise up against him.[5] This man, coming one day to the house of the Brethren Minor, and letting shave his beard by our barber, took it exceeding ill that the brethren gathered not the hairs of his beard, to preserve them as relics. But Brother Diotisalve, a Friar Minor of Florence, who was an excellent buffoon after the manner of the Florentines, did most excellently answer the fool according to his folly, lest he should be wise in his own conceit. For, going one day to the convent of the Friars Preachers, when they had invited him to dinner, he said that he would in no wise abide with them, except they should first give him a piece of the tunic of Brother John, who at that time was there in the house, that he might keep it for a relic. So they promised, and gave him indeed a great piece of his tunic, which, after his dinner, he put to the vilest uses, and cast it at last into a cesspool. Then cried he aloud saying, ' Alas, alas ! help me, brethren, for I seek the relic of your saint, which I have lost among the filth.' And when they had come at his call and understood more of this matter, they were put to confusion ; and, seeing themselves mocked of this buffoon, they blushed for shame. This same Brother Diotisalve once received an Obedience (i.e., command) to go and dwell in the province of Penna, which is in Apulia. Whereupon he went to the infirmary and stripped himself naked, and, having ripped open a feather bed, he lay hid therein all day long among the feathers (Lat. in pennis), so that, when he was sought of the brethren, they found him there, saying that he had already fulfilled his Obedience ; wherefore for the jest's sake he was absolved from his Obedience and went not thither. Again, as he went one day through the city of Florence in winter time, it came to pass that he slipped upon the ice and fell at full length.

At which the Florentines began to laugh, for they are much given to buffoonery ; and one of them asked of the friar as he lay . . . . ." (79). The dialogue which our good Franciscan here records is unfortunately quite impossible in modern print. He himself had evidently some qualms about reporting it, for he goes on : " The Florentines took no offence at this saying, but rather commended the friar, saying 'God bless him, for he is indeed one of us !' Yet some say that this answer was made by another Florentine, Brother Paolo Millemosche (Thousand-flies) by name. Now we should ask ourselves whether this brother answered well or not ; and I reply that he answered ill, for many reasons. First, because he acted contrary to the Scripture which saith, ' Answer not a fool according to his folly, lest thou also be like unto him.' Secondly, for that the answer was unhonest, since a religious man ought to answer as becometh a religious. Whence James saith, 'If any man among you seem to be religious, and bridleth not his tongue, but deceiveth his own heart, this man's religion is vain.' Again, ' If any man speak, let him speak as the speech of God.' And Jerome saith, ' Blessed is the tongue which knoweth not to speak, save of God only.' (Also Eph. iv, 29 and Coloss. iv, 6). Thirdly, in that he spake an idle word, whereof our Lord saith (Matt. xii, 36). Now that word is idle which profiteth neither to speaker nor to hearer, wherefore our Lord addeth (Matt. xii, 37) ; Ecclesiasticus saith (xxii, 27). Fourthly, in that he who speaketh unhonest words showeth that he hath a vain heart, and moreover giveth to others an ensample of sin (1 Cor. xv. 33). But hear the remedy or vengeance (Isa. xxix. 20). Of the vain heart we may say that which is spoken of the eye. For even as the immodest eye is the messenger of an immodest heart, so the vain word showeth a vain heart. Therefore saith the Wise Man (Prov. iv. 23 and xxx. 8). Fifthly, because silence is commanded us (Lam. iii. 28 ; Isa. xxx. 15 ; Exod. xiv. 14 ; Ps. cvii. 30). It is written that the Abbot Agatho kept a pebble three whole years in his mouth that he might learn to be silent. Sixthly, because much speaking is condemned (Prov. x, 19, and 7 similar texts). Note the example of the philosopher Secundus, by whose speech his mother met her death ; and he, by reason of penitence, kept silence even to the day of his death ; to whom we might indeed say, ' If thou hadst kept silence, thou wouldst have been a philosopher.'[6] Again, the Apostle bade that ' women should keep silence in churches, for it is not permitted unto them to speak, but they are commanded to be under obedience, as also saith the law ; and if they will learn anything, let them ask their husbands at home, for it is a shame for women to speak in the church.' For women do indeed speak much in church ; wherefore some say that the Apostle forbade not to women useful and laudable speech, as when they praise God, or when they confess their sins to the priest ; but he forbade their presuming to preach, an office which is known to belong properly to men. Which, indeed, is evident from this, that the Apostle was speaking only of the office of preaching. But Augustine saith that speech is therefore forbidden to woman, because she once confounded the whole world by speaking with the serpent. . . . The eighth and last reason is, that he who speaketh base and unprofitable and vain and unhonest words in the Order of the Friars Minor should be accused and punished for his deeds if they are seen, or his words if they are heard. And this is right, since the Lord's words are clean words ; and in the Rule of the Friars Minor it is said that their speech should be well-considered and clean for the profit and edification of the people, etc.[7] . . . . Yet Brother Diotisalve, by reason of whom I have written this, may be excused for manifold reasons. However, his words should not be taken for an example, to be repeated by another, for the Wise Man saith, 'As a dog that returneth to his vomit, so is a fool that repeateth his folly.' Now the first reason for his excuse is that he answered the fool according to his folly, lest he should seem wise in his own eyes. The second is, that he meant not altogether as his words sounded ; for he was a merry man, as Ecclesiasticus saith, 'There is one that slippeth with the tongue, but not from his heart.' . . . . The third reason is that he spake to his fellow-citizens, who took no ill example from his words, for they are merry men and most given to buffoonery. Yet in another place that brother's words would have sounded ill. . . . Moreover I know many deeds of this Brother Diotisalve, as also of the Count Guido [da Montefeltro], of whom many men are wont to tell many tales, yet as these are rather merry than edifying, I will not write them.[8] . . . . Yet one thing I must not omit, namely, that the Florentines take no ill example if one go forth from the Order of Friars Minor, nay, they rather excuse him, saying, 'We wonder that he dwelt among them so long, for the Friars Minor are desperate folk, who afflict themselves in divers ways.' Once, when the Florentines heard that Brother John of Vicenza would come to their city, they said, 'For God's sake let him not come hither, for we have heard how he raiseth the dead, and we are already so many that there is no room for us in the city.' And the words of the Florentines sound excellently well in their own idiom. Blessed be God, Who hath brought me safe to the end of this matter."

I have given these anecdotes and quotations with some approach to fullness in spite of their apparent irrelevance to the Alleluia, because they are well calculated to give the reader an idea of Salimbene's discursive style, and to prepare him for many strange things which will come later in this autobiography. It may indeed seem startling that a friar should feel it necessary to point out to a nun (for here the reference to his niece seems obvious) that St. Paul does not mean to forbid women from joining in the service as members of the congregation; or again, that he should relate with such complacent triumph the success of bogus miracles concocted by two of the greatest revivalists in the century of St. Francis. For not only had Gerard been a close companion of St. Francis, but he was also one of the six "solemn ambassadors" sent to the Pope in 1236 to protest against Brother Elias. It was evidently he who had the main share in Salimbene's conversion, and after his death he was honoured as a saint. That such a person deliberately reinforced his preaching by false miracles seems strange enough; but that a clever man like Salimbene should tell it in this matter-of-fact way, in the same breath in which he alludes to real miracles wrought by his sainted friend, seems to the modern mind absolutely inexplicable, and the Jesuit professor Michael discreetly slurs over the whole story. But the curious reader may find abundant evidence of the same kind in the *Treatise on Relics* of St. Anselm's pupil, the Abbot Guibert of Nogent, and in the Papal letter of 1238 to the Canons of the Holy Sepulchre at Jerusalem, who forged annually on Easter Eve miraculous flames of fire which even Guibert, a century earlier, had believed to be genuine. One of the greatest men of Salimbene's century, Cardinal Jacques de Vitry, relates with approval an equally false miracle of a priest who slipped a bad penny instead of the Host into the mouth of a miserly parishioner at Easter communion, and then persuaded the man that the Lord's body had been thus transmuted, for his punishment, into the same false coin which he had been wont to offer yearly at that solemnity. Cæsarius of Heisterbach sees nothing but a triumph for the Christian religion and for the "God of Justice" in the fact that a cleric of Worms, who had seduced a Jewess, tricked the parents into believing that the child to be born would be Messiah, a hope which was miserably frustrated when the infant proved to be a girl. The good Bishop Thomas of Chantimpré does indeed blame the readiness of certain prelates in religion to tell lies for the profit of their house; yet even he approves a wife's pious deceit. The early Franciscan records simply swarm with pious thefts and pious lies. St. Rose of Viterbo, St. Elizabeth of Hungary, St. Elizabeth of Portugal, the blessed Viridiana, all boast an incident of this sort as one of their chief titles to fame ; " a pious theft," says the approving Wadding of the last case, in so many words.[9] St. Francis himself began his public career with such a pious theft ; and it is very difficult to understand how, in the face of the early biographers, so admirable a writer as M. Sabatier can speak of the Foligno incident as though the horse and cloth had really been the Saint's own. At the same time, he is a great deal too careful to allow himself anything like Canon Knox-Little's astounding assertion that St. Francis's theft is a figment of "modern biographers," and an example of "modern prejudice or stupidity in dealing with the facts of the Middle Ages." If the Canon had consulted so obvious an authority as Wadding, he would have found that, even in the face of Protestant attacks, the learned and orthodox Romanist Sedulius felt obliged to admit the evidence against St. Francis. Moreover, Wadding himself, in the middle of the 17th century, deeply as he resents criticism on this point, ventures only upon a half-hearted defence. His main argument, involved in a cloud of words which betrays his embarrassment, amounts merely to a plea that the goods *might* have been the saint's own, or that he *might* have thought them such ; and, admitting the possibility that neither of these alternatives were true, he falls back on a timid defence which really embodies, in more cautious language, the 13th century theory. " He [Francis] received from Christ, speaking plainly to his bodily ears, the command to restore this church, and although the Lord's words intended otherwise, yet he understood them to lay on him the task of repairing that building [of St. Damian]. Now he knew full well that Christ bade no impossibilities, whence he inferred not without probability that, if he was to obey the divine command, it was lawful to him to take of his father's goods where his own sufficed not." His action, concludes Wadding, was therefore worthy not of blame but of praise (Vol. i. p. 32). To Salimbene and his readers in the 13th century, the line of thought thus laboriously worked out by the 17th century apologist was natural and instinctive. The miracles had impressed men who would otherwise have paid no attention to the Revival ; they were a most successful stratagem in the Holy War : they would have been discreditable only if they had failed. Yet, even then, there were a few who realized that " nothing can need a lie," and who were almost as much embarrassed as edified by the frequency of miraculous claims around them or in their midst. David of Augsburg, whose fundamental good sense remained unshaken by his religious fervour, wrote very strongly on this point. " Visions of this sort have thus much in common, that they are vouchsafed not only to the good, but often to the evil also. Moreover, that they are sometimes true and teach the truth, sometimes deceptive and delusive as Ezekiel saith (xiii. 7.) Moreover, that they neither make nor prove their seer holy : otherwise Baalam would be holy, and his ass who saw the Angel, and Pharaoh who saw prophetic dreams. Moreover, even if they are true, yet in themselves they are not meritorious ; and he who sees many visions is not therefore the better man than he who sees none, as also in the case of other miracles. Moreover, many men have often been more harmed than profited by such things, for they have been puffed up thereby to vain-glory : many also, thinking themselves to have seen visions, when in fact they had seen none, seduced themselves and others, or turned them aside to greed of gain : many again have falsely feigned to see visions, lest they should be held inferior to others, or that they might be honoured above others, as holier men to whom God's secrets were revealed. Moreover, in some folk such visions are wont to be forerunners of insanity ; for when their brain is addled, and clouded with its own fumes, the sight of their eyes is confounded also, until a man takes for a true vision that which is merely fantastic and false, as Ecclesiasticus saith (xxxiv. 6.)"[10]

These words of David's are all the more weighty, because he was the master of the greatest of 13th century mission-preachers, whose fame spread through Europe only a few years after the Great Alleluia. About the year 1250, chroniclers of cities far distant from each other mention the startling appearance among them of this Berthold of Ratisbon, whom Salimbene describes at some length on a later page, in connexion with John of Parma's friends (559). " Now let us come to Brother Berthold of Allemannia* of the order of Friars Minor ; a priest and preacher and a man of honest and holy life as becometh a Religious. He expounded the Apocalypse,[11] and I copied out his exposition of the seven bishops of Asia only, who are brought forward under the title of Angels in the beginning of the Apocalypse : this I did, to know who those angels were, and because I had Abbot Joachim's exposition of the Apocalypse, which I esteemed above all others. Moreover, this Berthold made a great volume of sermons for the whole course of the year, both for feast days and *de tempore*, *i.e.*, for the Sundays of the

---

* Ratisbon is in the district of Germany once inhabited by the Allemanni.

whole year. Of which sermons I copied two only, for that they treated excellently of Antichrist : whereof the first was on Luke ii. 34, and the other on Matt. viii, 23 : for both teach most fully both of Antichrist and of the awful judgment.[12] And note that Brother Berthold had of God a special grace of preaching, and all who have heard him say that from the apostles even to our own day there hath not been his like in the German tongue. He was followed by a great multitude of men and women, sometimes sixty or a hundred thousand, sometimes a mighty multitude from many cities together, that they might hear the honeyed words of salvation which proceeded from his mouth, by His power who 'giveth His voice a voice of might' and 'giveth word to them that preach with much virtue.' He was wont to ascend a belfry or wooden tower made almost after the fashion of a campanile, which he used for a pulpit in country places when he wished to preach : on the summit whereof a pennon also was set up by those who put the work together, so that the people might see whither the wind blew, and know where they ought to sit to hear best. And, marvellous to relate ! he was as clearly heard and understood by those far from him as by those who sat hard by ; nor was there one who rose and withdrew from his preaching until the sermon was ended. And when he preached of the dreadful day of doom, all trembled as a rush quakes in the water : and they would beg him for God's sake to speak no more of that matter, for they were terribly and horribly troubled to hear him.[13] One day when he was to preach at a certain place, it befel that a peasant prayed his lord to let him go, for God's sake, to hear Brother Berthold's sermon. But the lord answered ' I shall go to the sermon, but thou shalt go into the field to plough with the oxen,' as it is written in Ecclesiasticus ' Send him to work, lest he be idle.' So when the peasant one day at high dawn had begun to plough in the field, wondrous to relate ! he heard the very first syllable of Brother Berthold's sermon, though he was thirty miles away at that time. So he loosed the oxen forthwith from the plough, that they might eat, and he himself sat down to hear the sermon. And here came to pass three most memorable miracles. First, that he heard and understood him, though he was so far away as thirty miles. Secondly, that he learnt the whole sermon and kept it by heart. Thirdly, that after the sermon was ended he ploughed as much as he was wont to plough on other days of un- interrupted work. So when this peasant afterwards asked of his lord concerning Brother Berthold's sermon, and he could not repeat it, the peasant did so word for word, adding how he had heard and learnt it in the field. So his lord, knowing that this

was a miracle, gave the peasant full liberty to go and hear freely
Brother Berthold's preaching, whatever task-work he might have
to do.

Now it was Brother Berthold's custom to order his sermons
which he intended to preach now in one city, now in another, at
divers times and in divers places, that the people who flocked to
hear him might not lack food. It befel upon a time that a certain
noble lady, inflamed with great and fervent desire to hear him
preaching, had followed him for six whole years from city to city
and town to town, with a few companions and carrying her wealth
with her ; yet never could she come to private and familiar talk
with him. But when the six years were past, all her goods
were wasted and spent, and on the Feast of the Assumption of
the Blessed Virgin, neither she nor her women had food to eat ;
so she went to Brother Berthold and told him all her tale from
beginning to end. Brother Berthold, therefore, hearing this, sent
her to a certain banker, who was held the richest of all in that
city, bidding her tell him in his name, to give her for her food
and charges as many moneys as the worth of one single day of
that Indulgence for which she had followed the Brother these
six years.[14] The banker hearing this, smiled and said, ' And how
can I know the worth of the Indulgence for one day whereon
you have followed Brother Berthold ? ' And she, ' The man of
God bade me tell you to lay your moneys in one scale of the
balance, and I will breathe into the other scale, and by this sign
ye may know the worth of my Indulgence.' Then he poured in
his moneys abundantly and filled the scale of the balance ; but
she breathed into the other scale, and forthwith it was weighed
down, and the moneys kicked the beam as suddenly as if they
had been changed to the lightness of feathers. And the banker
seeing this was astonished above measure ; and again and again
he heaped moneys upon his side of the balance ; yet not even so
could he outweigh the lady's breath ; for the Holy Ghost lent
such weight thereto that the scale whereon she breathed could be
counterbalanced by no weight of moneys. Wherefore the
banker, seeing this, came forthwith to Brother Berthold with the
lady and her whole company of women ; and they told him in
order all those things which had come to pass. And the banker
added, ' I am ready to restore all my ill-gotten gains and to dis-
tribute my own goods for God's sake amongst the poor, and I
desire to become a good man ; for in truth I have to-day seen
marvellous things.' So Brother Berthold bade him minister the
necessities of life abundantly to that lady by reason of whom he
had seen this marvel, and to them that were with her. This he

fulfilled readily and gladly to the praise of our Lord Jesus Christ, to whom is glory and honour for ever and ever. Amen.

Another time, as Brother Berthold was passing at eventide by a certain road with a lay-brother his comrade, he was taken by the hired ruffians (*assassinis*) of a certain Castellan and brought to his castle ; where all that night he was kept chained and in evil plight. (Now this Castellan had so provoked his fellow-citizens that they had caused a picture to be painted in the Palazzo Communale shewing forth his punishment if ever he were taken —that is, the doom of hanging.) And on the morrow at dawn the chief executioner came to the Castellan his lord, and said, ' What are your lordship's commands with respect to those Brethren who were brought to us yesterday ? ' He answered, ' Away with them,' which was as much as to say, ' Slay them : ' for that was the custom of this Castellan and his ruffians, that some they robbed and others they slew; and others again they cast into the castle dungeons until they should redeem themselves with money : otherwise they must needs be slain. Now Brother Berthold slept : but the lay brother his comrade was awake and said his Mattins ; and, hearing the sentence of death pronounced upon them by the Castellan (for there was but a party-wall between them) he began to call again and again on Brother Berthold. The Castellan therefore, hearing the name of Brother Berthold, began to think within himself that this might well be that famous preacher of whom such marvels were told ; and forthwith he recalled his executioner and bade him do the Brethren no harm, but bring them before his face. When therefore they came before him he enquired what might be their names : whereto the lay-brother answered, ' My name is such-and-such : but my comrade here is Brother Berthold, that renowned and gracious preacher, through whom God worketh so great marvels.' The Castellan hearing this forthwith cast himself down at Brother Berthold's feet ; and having embraced and kissed him he besought for God's sake that he might hear him preach, for he had long time desired to hear the word of salvation from his lips. To this Brother Berthold consented on condition that he should call together before him all the ruffians whom he had in his castle, that they also might hear his sermon : which he gladly promised. When therefore the lord had called his ruffians together and Brother Berthold had gone aside for a while to pray to God, then came his comrade and said to him, ' Know now, Brother, that this man condemned us even now to death : therefore if ever you have preached well of the pains of hell and the joys of Paradise, you need now all your skill.' At which words

Brother Berthold betook himself wholly to prayer; and then, returning to that assembly, he spake the word of salvation with such exceeding glory that all were moved to tears. And before his departure thence he confessed them all of their sins, and bade them depart from that castle and restore their ill-gotten gains and continue in penance all the days of their life : 'and so,' said he, 'shall ye come to everlasting life.' But the Castellan fell down at his feet, and besought him with many tears that, for the love of God, he would deign to receive him into the order of St. Francis : so he received him, hoping that the Minister General would grant him this grace.[15] Then he would fain have followed Brother Berthold on his journey, but he suffered him not, for the fury of the people whom he had provoked and who had not yet heard of his conversion. So Berthold went on his way into the city, and the people were gathered together to hear his sermon on the shingles of a river bed ; the pulpit was set up over against the gibbet whereon hung the bodies of thieves. (Thou, when thou hearest this, picture it to thyself as though it were upon the shingles of the River Reno at Bologna.[16]) So the aforesaid Castellan, after Brother Berthold's departure, was so inflamed with divine love, and so drawn with desire of hearing the preacher that he thought no more of all the evils which he had wrought to that city, but came alone to the place of preaching, where he was forthwith known, and taken, and led straight to the gallows : so that all ran after him crying 'Let him be hanged, and die a felon's death, for he is our most mortal foe.' Brother Berthold therefore, seeing how the multitude ran together and departed from his sermon, marvelled greatly, and said : 'Never before have I known the people depart from me until my sermon was ended and the blessing given.' And one of those who remained answered, 'Father, marvel not, for that Castellan who was our mortal foe, is taken, and men lead him to the gallows.' Whereat Brother Berthold trembled greatly and said with sorrow, 'Know ye that I have confessed him and all them that are with him ; and the others I have sent away to do penance, and him I had received into the order of St. Francis : he was come now to hear my sermon : let us all hasten therefore to loose him.' Yet though they made all haste to the gallows, they found that he had even then been drawn up, and had given up the ghost. Nevertheless, at Berthold's bidding, men took him down, and round his neck they found a paper written in letters of gold with these words following : 'Being made perfect in a short space, he fulfilled a long time : for his soul pleased God : therefore he hastened to bring him out of the midst of iniquities.' (Wisdom iv, 13, 14). Then Brother Berthold sent to the convent of Friars Minor in that city, that the Brethren might bring a cross and a bier and a friar's habit, and see and hear what marvels God had wrought. And when they came he expounded to them all the aforesaid story, and they brought his body and buried it honourably in their convent, praising the Lord who worketh such wonders."

A comparison of these stories in Salimbene with Wadding (vol. iv, p. 345 foll.) or the parallel passages in *xxiv Gen.*, *pp.* 238-9, clearly brings out the good friar's superiority to the general run of medieval chroniclers. Upon one of these stories we have, by rare good fortune, the criticism of the hero himself. A precious fragment printed in the *Analecta Franciscana* (vol. 1, p. 417) describes how, when Berthold came to France, St. Louis wished to see and speak with him. "And addressing him in Latin, he added : ' Good Brother, I know but little of the Latin tongue.' ' Speak boldly, my Lord King,' answered Brother Berthold, ' for it is no shame or wrong for a king to speak false Latin.'" The writer then relates how the King of Navarre, who was present at this interview, recounted to St. Louis, in the preacher's own presence, the story here told by Salimbene about the peasant who heard the sermon thirty miles off—or, as the king more modestly put it, at three miles' distance. Berthold's reply was " ' My Lord, believe it not and put no faith in tales of this sort which men tell of me as though they were miracles. For this I believe to be false, nor have I ever heard that it was true. But there are a sort of men who, for greed of filthy lucre or for some other vain cause, follow with the rest of the multitude after me, and invent sometimes such stories, which they tell to the rest.' Whereat both kings were much edified, perceiving clearly that this Brother . . . . . . loved the truth better than popular favour or the sound of empty praise."

CHAPTER IV.

Conversion.

"BLESSED be God," wrote Salimbene at the end of the long digression into which he had been tempted on the subject of Diotisalve's witticisms : "blessed be God who hath brought me safe to the end of this matter!" He is therefore conscious of his failing, and will no doubt hasten back to his main subject : to that great Alleluia which probably determined his own choice of a career. . . . .

Nothing lies farther from his thoughts : he goes on in the same breath with a fresh digression, smacking still less of revivalism than the first (83). "There lived in these days a canon of Cologne named Primas, a great rogue and a great buffoon, and a most excellent and ready versifier ; who, if he had given his heart to love God, would have been mighty in divine learning, and most profitable to the Church of God." Here follow a few specimens of his epigrams, interesting only to the student. "Moreover he was once accused to his archbishop of three sins, namely of incontinence or lechery, of dicing, and of tavern-haunting. And he excused himself thus in verse." Here Salimbene quotes at length the witty and profligate verses so well known in their attribution to Walter Map, of which Green gives a spirited extract in his *Short History* (p. 116) :—

> "Die I must, but let me die drinking in an inn !
> Hold the wine-cup to my lips sparkling from the bin !
> So, when angels flutter down to take me from my sin,
> 'Ah, God have mercy on this sot,' the cherubs will begin !"

Professor Michael is much scandalized by the impenitent jovial-ity with which the friar quotes *in extenso*, on so slight a pretext, a poem which could scarcely be rendered into naked English. But Salimbene only followed the custom of his time ; the same poem, with a collection of others beyond comparison worse, was kept religiously until modern times in the great monastery of Benediktbeuern, and in fact nearly all the ultra-Zolaesque literature of the middle ages (except that of the Fabliaux) has come down to us through Church libraries. Nor is there the least *a priori* reason against Salimbene writing such things to Sister Agnes : for nuns were often accustomed to hear songs of unbecoming purport sung in the churches during the Feast of Fools, and not infrequently joined themselves in the songs and the dancing.[1]

As Diotisalve and Primas drove the Alleluia out of Salimbene's head, so did like worldly vanities banish it from men's hearts in Northern Italy after those few months of 1233 were past. All such religious revivals have been short-lived in direct proportion to the suddenness of their origin. No doubt they left behind in many minds some real leaven, however small, of true religion : but the mass swung back all the more violently into their old groove : and those populations which had suddenly thrown away their swords and sworn with tears an eternal peace, were again in a month or two as busy as ever with the ancient feuds. During the Alleluia itself, many earnest men must have felt the fear expressed on a similar occasion by a pious chronicler of the fifteenth century : " Now may God grant that this be peace indeed, and tranquillity for all citizens ; whereof I doubt." Jacopo da Varagine, author of the Golden Legend, describes a similar religious revival and pacification at which he himself played a prominent part in 1295 ; yet, since nothing is pure in this world, the year was not yet out before the Devil inspired the citizens again with such a spirit of discord that there were several days of street fighting, in which a church was burned to the ground. In the year after the great Alleluia, Salimbene records, without comment, how there was a great battle in the plain of Cremona between the seven principal towns of Lombardy, in spite of natural calamities in which they might well have seen the finger of Providence. For (88) " There was so great snow and frost throughout the month of January that the vines and all fruit-trees were frost-bitten. And beasts of the forest were frozen to death, and wolves came into the cities by night : and by day many were taken and hanged in the public streets. And trees were split from top to bottom by the force of the frost, and many lost their sap altogether and were dried up." The next year came another bitter winter and greater destruction of vines : but the warm weather was again marked by the usual civil wars. In this year 1235 . . . the men of Parma and Cremona, Piacenza and Pontremoli, went with those of Modena to dig the Scotenna above Bologna ; for they would fain have thrown the stream against Castelfranco to destroy it. And no

man was excused from the labour ; for some digged, others
carried earth, both nobles and common folk " (92).   Salimbene
more than once speaks of the month of May, in Old Testament
phrase, as "the time when kings go forth to war." " Every
spring," as Ruskin put it, " kindled them into battle, and every
autumn was red with their blood."   The worst horrors of civil
war recorded by Salimbene come *after* the great Alleluia of
1233.

It must be noted also to what an extent this, like most other
religious movements in the Middle Ages, came from the people
rather than from the hierarchy.   Brother Benedict of the Horn
had no more claim to Apostolical Succession than General
Booth,—or, for the matter of that, than St. Francis when he first
began to preach.   There is no hint that either of them had at
first any episcopal licence even of the most informal kind, any
more than the Blessed Joachim of Fiore and St. Catherine of
Siena, and Richard Rolle of Hampole, who all set an example of
lay preaching.   No doubt the practice was contrary to canon law :
but the thing was constantly done ; and, so long as the preacher
did not become a revolutionary, it seems to have caused neither
scandal nor surprise.   Matthew Paris (ann. 1225) describes a
wild woman-preacher of this sort, not with contempt, but with
warm admiration.   The canonization of saints, in the same way,
almost always came from the people and the lower classes.
Nothing is more false than to suppose that the medieval Church
was disciplined like the present Church of Rome.   It was as
various in its elements, with as many cross-currents and as many
conflicts of theory with practice, as modern Anglicanism ; and
much which seems smooth and harmonious to us, at six hundred
years' distance, was as confusing to contemporaries as a Fulham
Round-Table Conference.   Again, the oft-quoted saying of
Macaulay, that Rome has always been far more adroit than Protestantism in directing enthusiasm, is true (so far as it is true at
all) only of Rome since the Reformation.   What Darwin took at
first for smooth unbroken grass-land proved, on nearer examination, to be thick-set with tiny self-sown firs, which the cattle
regularly cropped as they grew.   Similarly, that which some love
to picture as the harmonious growth of one great body through
the Middle Ages is really a history of many divergent opinions
violently strangled at birth ; while hundreds more, too vigorous
to be killed by the adverse surroundings, and elastic enough to
take something of the outward colour of their environment,
grew in spite of the hierarchy into organisms which, in their
turn, profoundly modified the whole constitution of the Church.

If the medieval theory and practice of persecution had still been in full force in the eighteenth century in England, nearly all the best Wesleyans would have chosen to remain within the Church rather than to shed blood in revolt; and the rest would have keen killed off like wild beasts. The present unity of Romanism, so far as it exists, is due less to tact than to naked force ; so that in the Middle Ages, when communication was difficult and discipline of any kind irregularly enforced, the religious world naturally heaved with strange and widespread fermentations. It is true that the modern Church historian generally slurs them over : yet they were very pressing realities at the time.

Amid these wars, Salimbene records one very dramatic scene (88). The Bishop of Mantua, whose sister was afterwards " *mea devota* "—i.e., one of Salimbene's many spiritual daughters—was murdered in a political quarrel. " And note that the College of Canons and Clergy at Mantua sent news of the murder to the Pope's court by a special envoy of exceeding eloquence : who, young though he was, spake so that Pope and Cardinals marvelled to hear him. And, having made an end of speaking, he brought forth the Bishop's blood-stained dalmatic, wherein he had been slain in the Church of St. Andrew at Mantua, and spread it before the Pope, saying : ' Behold, Father, and see whether it be thy son's coat or not.' And Pope Gregory IX, with all his cardinals, wept at the sight as men who could not be comforted ; for he was a man of great compassion and bowels of mercy. And the Avvocati of Mantua, who slew this their Bishop, were driven forth from their city without recall, and they wander in exile even to this present day : in order that perverse and incorrigible men (of whom and of fools the number is infinite)[2] and pestilent men who ruin cities, may all know that it is not easy to fight against God. Note that folk say commonly in Tuscany—' *D'ohmo alevandhizo, et de pioclo apicadhizo no po l'ohm gaudére:* ' which is, being interpreted, ' A man hath no joy of a man who is a foreigner, nor of a louse which clingeth : ' that is, thou hast no solace of another man's louse which clingeth to thee, nor of a stranger man whom thou cherishest. Which may be seen in Frederick II, whom the Church cherished as her ward, and who afterwards raised his heel against her and afflicted her in many ways. So also it may be seen in the Marquis of Este who now is,[3] and in many others." After which Salimbene loses himself in a long sermon on martyrs, from Abel and Zacharias to Becket ; from whose legend he quotes a series of absolutely apocryphal stories relating the miraculous torments amid which his murderers severally expired. Then the good friar goes on with his common story of wars and bloodshed : for of the 76 years covered by the Chronicle proper, only 21 are free from express record of war in the writer's own neighbourhood, while several of the others were years of famine or pestilence. Salimbene, as he played about the streets of Parma, saw the heralds of the mighty host that Frederick was bringing to crush the rebellious cities of Lombardy, " an elephant, with many dromedaries, camels, and leopards," and all the strange beasts and birds that the great Emperor loved to have about him (92). Two years later, another imperial elephant came through Parma armed for war, with a great tower and pennons on its back, " as described in the first book of Maccabees and in the book of Brother Bartholomew the Englishman " (94). From his earliest childhood he had been familiar with the trophies of the bloody fight at San Cesario—a number of mangonels taken from the vanquished Bolognese, and ranged along the Baptistery and the west front of the Cathedral, almost under the windows of his father's house (60). And now in his seventeenth year the sad side of war was for the first time brought vividly before his bodily eyes. The Bolognese in their turn had destroyed Castiglione, a fortress of friendly Modena ; and Parma itself was threatened (95). " Then the Advocate of the Commune of Parma (who was a man of Modena) rode on horseback, followed by a squire, through the Borgo di Sta. Cristina, crying again and again with tears in his voice, ' Ye lords of Parma, go and help the men of Modena, your friends and brothers !' And hearing his words my bowels yearned for him with a compassion that moved me even to tears. For I considered how Parma was stripped of men, nor were any left in the city but boys and girls, youths and maidens, old men and women ; since the men of Parma, with the hosts of many other cities, had gone in the Emperor's service against Milan."

In the next year, 1238, came the turning point of Salimbene's life. The Alleluia had impressed him deeply : Gerard of Modena, one of the most distinguished men of the Order, took a personal interest in his conversion : and on February 4th, at the age of sixteen years and a few months, he slipped away from his father's home and was admitted that same evening as a novice among the Franciscans of Parma. Within the brief space of three hundred yards he had passed from one world to another. A friend of his, Alberto Cremonella, was admitted at the same time, but went out during his noviciate, became a physician, and later on entered the Cistercian Order.

Sixteen years may seem a strangely immature age at which

to renounce the world for life ; yet very many joined the Friars
at an earlier age than this. Conrad of Offida and John of La
Vernia, two of the most distinguished Franciscans of the first
generation, were only fourteen and thirteen respectively when
they joined the Order. Salimbene's contemporary, Roger Bacon,
asserts that most Friars had joined before they were of age, and
that in all countries they were habitually received at any age
between ten and twenty years. Thousands become friars, he
says, who can read neither their grammar nor their psalter.
Richard de Bury, Bishop of Durham, accused the friars of
attracting boys by presents of apples and wine ; and in 1313 the
University of Oxford passed a statute forbidding them to receive
novices below eighteen years of age. The crude spirit of adventure which prompts a modern schoolboy to go to sea, sometimes
found a vent six hundreds years ago in an equally ill-regulated
religious enthusiasm. Only nine years before Salimbene's birth,
Northern Italy had witnessed the Boys' Crusade, which originated on the Rhine and swelled to a troop of seven thousand youths
and children, many of whom were of noble families, and who
expected to cross the sea dry-shod from Genoa to the Holy Land.
The Genoese, scandalized by the moral disorders which reigned
among them, and judging them " to be led by levity rather than
by necessity," closed their gates upon the juvenile pilgrims, who
were dispersed and perished miserably. Salimbene tells the story
on p. 30, and the author of the Golden Legend makes the
startling assertion that the fathers of the well-born boys had sent
harlots with their children.[4]

Albert and Salimbene had chosen their time well ; for Brother
Elias, the powerful Minister-General of the Order, was at that
moment passing through Parma ; and, once received by him in
person, they would be pretty safe from all outside interference.
They found the great man on a bed of down in the guesten-hall :
for the easy-chair was not a medieval institution, and even kings
or queens would receive visitors seated on their beds. Brother
Elias " had a goodly fire before him, and an Armenian cap on his
head : nor did he rise or move from his place when the Podesta
entered and saluted him, as I saw with mine own eyes : and this
was held to be great churlishness on his part, since God Himself
saith in Holy Scripture, ' Rise up before the hoary head, and
honour the person of the aged man.' " After all, however, such
boorishness was natural to Brother Elias, who in his youth had
been glad to earn a scanty living by sewing mattresses and teaching little boys to read their psalter. Brother Gerard of Modena
was also present : and at his prayer the young Salimbene was re-

ceived into the Order. The Abbot of St. John's at Parma had
sent for the Brethren's supper a peasant loaded with capons
hanging before and behind from a pole over his shoulders ; the
friars took the boy to sup in the infirmary, where more delicate
fare could be had than the ordinary Rule permitted. Here,
" though I had supped magnificently in my father's house, they
set an excellent meal before me again.[5] But in course of time
they gave me cabbages, which I must needs eat all the days of
my life : yet in the world I had never eaten cabbages—nay,
I abhorred them so sore that I had never even eaten the flesh
stewed with them. So afterward I remembered that proverb
which was often in men's mouths : ' The kite said to the chicken
as he carried him off—' You may squeak now, but this isn't the
worst.'[6] And again I thought of Job's words, ' The things
which before my soul would not touch, now through anguish
are my meats ' " (99).   Salimbene kept his eyes and ears open
that evening : for he was in the presence of one of the greatest
men in Italy. As a grown man he was far from approving
Brother Elias's policy, of which he has left the most detailed
criticism now extant. (96 foll.) This most thorny question,
however, is exhaustively discussed in Lempp's *Frère Elie de
Cortone,* and well summarized by Miss Macdonell ; so I shall
quote elsewhere only such of our chronicler's remarks as throw
definite light upon the general conditions of the Order.
    Once admitted, he was sent forthwith to Fano, in the Mark of
Ancona, some hundred and fifty miles from Parma. Guido
di Adamo was a man of influence, and only too likely to resent
the loss of his son and heir : for the proselytizing methods of
the friars constantly caused bitter family quarrels. " Greedy
and injurious men ! " complains an Italian dramatist of the next
century, " who think they have earned heaven when they have
separated a son from his father ! " The friars in their turn,
enforced the strictest separation from all friends during the year
of the noviciate. As St. Bonaventura's secretary writes—" To
speak with outsiders, whether lay folk (even such as serve the
Brethren) or Religious of any Order, is absolutely forbidden to
the novices except in the presence of a professed friar, who shall
hear and follow all the words spoken on either side ; nor may
the novices without special licence be allowed to go to the gate or
to outsiders."[7] How necessary was this rule in the friars' interest,
Salimbene's own words will show. (39.) " My father was sore
grieved all the days of his life at my entrance into the Order of
the Friars Minor, nor would he be comforted, since he had now
no son to succeed him. Wherefore, he made complaint to the

Emperor, who had come in those days to Parma, that the Brethren Minor had robbed him of his son. Then the Emperor wrote to Brother Elias, Minister-General of the Order, saying that, as he loved his favour, he should hearken to him and give me back to my father. Then my father journeyed to Assisi, where Brother Elias was, and laid the Emperor's letter in the General's hand, whereof the first words were as follows : *To comfort the sighing of our trusty and well-beloved Guido di Adamo, etc.* Brother Illuminato,[8] who in those days was scribe and secretary to Brother Elias, and who was wont to write in a book, apart by themselves, all the fair letters which were sent by princes of the world to the Minister-General, showed me that letter, when in process of time I dwelt with him in the convent of Siena. Wherefore Brother Elias, having read the Emperor's letter, wrote forthwith to the Brethren of the convent of Fano, where I then dwelt, bidding them, if I were willing, to give me back to my father without delay, in virtue of holy obedience ; but if they found me unwilling to return, then should they keep me as the apple of their eye. Whereupon many knights came with my father to the house of the Brethren in the city of Fano, to see the issue of this matter. To them I was made a gazing-stock ; and to myself a cause of salvation. For when the Brethren and the laymen had assembled in the chapter-house, and many words had been bandied to and fro, my father brought forth the letter of the Minister-General, and showed it to the Brethren. Whereupon Brother Jeremiah the Custode, having read it, replied to my father, ' My Lord Guido, we have compassion for your grief, and are ready to obey the letters of our father. But here is your son : he is of age, let him speak for himself. Enquire ye of him : if he is willing to go with you, let him go in God's name. But if not, we cannot do him violence, that he should go with you.' My father asked therefore whether I would go with him, or not. To whom I answered, ' No ; for the Lord saith, " No man, putting his hand to the plough, and looking back, is fit for the kingdom of God." ' And my father said to me : ' Thou hast no care then for thine own father and mother, who are afflicted with divers pains for thy sake ? ' To whom I made answer, ' No care have I in truth, for the Lord saith, " He that loveth father or mother more than Me, is not worthy of Me." Thou, therefore, father, shouldst have a care for Him, Who for our sake hung on a tree, that He might give us eternal life. For he it is Who saith, ' For I came to set a man at variance against his father,' etc., etc. (Matt. x. 35, 36, 32, 33). And the Brethren marvelled and

rejoiced that I spake thus to my father. Then said he to
the Brethren, 'Ye have bewitched and deceived my son, lest
he should obey me. I will complain to the Emperor again
concerning you, and to the Minister-General. Yet suffer me
to speak with my son secretly and apart ; and ye shall see
that he will follow me without delay.' So the Brethren suffered
me to speak alone with my father, since they had some small
confidence in me because of my words that I had even now
spoken. Yet they listened behind the partition to hear what
manner of talk we had : for they quaked as a rush quakes in the
water, lest my father by his blandishments should change my
purpose. And they feared not only for the salvation of my
soul, but also lest my departure should give occasion to others
not to enter the Order. My father, therefore, said to me :
'Beloved son, put no faith in these filthy drivellers[9] who have
deceived thee, but come with me, and all that I have will I give
unto thee.' And I answered and spake to my father : 'Hence,
hence, father : the Wise Man saith in his Proverbs, in the third
chapter, "Hinder not from well-doing him who hath the power :
if thou art able, do good thyself also."' And my father answered
even weeping, and said to me, 'What then, my son, can I say
to thy mother, who mourneth for thee night and day ?' And
I spake unto him : 'Say unto her for my part, Thus saith thy
son : "When my father and mother forsake me, then the Lord
will take me up."' My father, hearing all this, and despairing
of my return, threw himself upon the earth in the sight of the
Brethren and the layfolk who had come with him, and cried, 'I
commit thee to a thousand devils, accursed son, together with
thy brother who is here with thee, and who also hath helped
to deceive thee. My curse cleave to thee through all eternity, and
send thee to the devils of hell !' And so he departed, troubled
beyond measure ; but we remained in great consolation, giving
thanks unto God, and saying to Him, 'Though they curse, yet
bless Thou. For he who is blessed above the earth, let him be
blessed in God. Amen.' So the layfolk departed, much edified
at my constancy : and the Brethren also rejoiced greatly that
the Lord had wrought manfully through me His little child ;
and they knew that the words of the Lord are true, Who saith,
'Lay it up therefore in your hearts, not to meditate before how
you shall answer. For I will give you a mouth and wisdom, which
all your adversaries shall not be able to resist and gainsay.' In
the following night the Blessed Virgin rewarded me. For
methought I lay prostrate in prayer before the altar, as is the
wont of the Brethren, when they arise to matins : and I heard

the voice of the Blessed Virgin calling unto me. And, raising my face, I saw her sitting upon the altar, in that place where the Host and the chalice are set. And she had her little Child in her lap, Whom she held out to me, saying, 'Draw thou nigh without fear, and kiss my Son Whom thou hast confessed yesterday before men.' And when I feared, I saw that the Child opened His arms gladly, awaiting my coming. Trusting, therefore, in the cheerfulness and innocence of the Child, no less than in this so liberal favour of His mother, I came forward and embraced and kissed Him; and His gracious mother left Him to me for a long space. And since I could not take my fill of Him, at length the Holy Virgin blessed me, saying: 'Depart, beloved son, and take thy rest, lest the Brethren should rise to matins, and find thee here with us.' I obeyed, and the vision disappeared: but in my heart remained so great sweetness as tongue could never tell. In very truth I avow, that never in this world had I such sweetness as that. And then I knew the truth of that scripture which saith, 'To him who hath tasted of the spirit, there is no taste in any flesh.'

"At that time, while I was still in the city of Fano, I saw in a dream that the son of Thomas degli Armari, of the city of Parma, slew a monk; and I told the dream to my brother. And after a few days there came through the city of Fano Amizo degli Amici, going into Apulia to fetch gold from thence; and he came unto the house of the Brethren, where he saw us: for he was our acquaintance and friend and neighbour. And then, beginning from another matter, we enquired how it might be with Such-an-one (now his name was Gerard de' Senzanesi), and he said to us: 'It is ill with him, for the other day he slew a monk.' Then we knew that at times dreams are true. Furthermore, at that time also, when first my father passed through the city of Fano, journeying towards Assisi, the Brethren hid me many days, together with my brother, in the house of the Lord Martin of Fano, who was a Master of Laws, and his palace was hard by the seaside. And at times he would come to us and speak to us of God and of the Holy Scriptures, and his mother ministered unto us. Afterwards he entered the Order of the Friars Preachers, wherein he ended his life with all praise. While then he was yet in that Order, he was chosen Bishop of his own city: but the Preachers would not suffer him to accept it, for they were not willing to lose him. He would have entered our Order, but he was dissuaded therefrom by Brother Taddeo Buonconte, who was himself thereof. For our Brethren lay sore upon Taddeo that he should return all ill-gotten gains, if he

would be received among us : and he said to the Lord Martin,
' So will they do with thee also, if thou enter the Order.'   So
he feared, and entered the Order of Preachers, which perchance
was better for him and for us." This restitution of ill-gotten
gains was a very sore point with both Orders.

As Salimbene had learnt Latin " from his very cradle," so
now, from the very first days of his conversion, he set himself to
study theology.   Forty-six years afterwards, on the anniversary
of his entrance, he looks back with pardonable complacency
over this long term of study.   (277) " From my very earliest
noviciate at Fano in the March of Ancona, I learned theology
from Brother Umile of Milan, who had studied at Bologna under
Brother Aymo, the Englishman; which same Aymo, in his old
age, was chosen Minister-General of our Order, and held that
office three years, even to his death.   And in the first year of my
entrance into the Order I studied Isaiah and Matthew as Brother
Umile read them in the schools : and I have not ceased since then
to study and learn in the schools.   And as the Jews said to Christ,
' Six and forty years was this temple in building,' so may I also
say : for it is 46 years to-day, Saturday the Feast of St. Gilbert,
in the year 1284, whereon I write these words, since I entered
the Order of Friars Minor.   And I have not ceased to study
since then : yet not even so have I come to the wisdom of my
ancestors."

Chapter V.

A Wicked World.

BUT Salimbene's stay at Fano was brief. The friary lay outside the walls, by the sea-shore, and he was haunted by the idea that his father had hired pirates to seize and kidnap him. He therefore gladly welcomed a message from Brother Elias, who, delighted at the boy's constancy in cleaving to the Order, sent him word that he might choose his own province. He chose Tuscany, and went thither after a brief stay at Jesi. On his way, he changed his home name for that which he was to bear during the rest of his life. (38) " Now as I went to dwell in Tuscany, and passed through the city of Castello, there I found in an hermitage a certain Brother of noble birth, ancient and fulfilled of days and of good works, who had four sons, knights, in the world. This was the last Brother whom the blessed Francis robed and received into the Order, as he himself related to me. He, hearing that I was called All-good, was amazed, and said to me, ' Son, there is none good but One, that is, God.[1] From henceforth be thou called no more *Ognibene* but Brother *Salimbene* (Leap-into-good), for thou hast well leapt, in that thou hast entered into a good Order.' And I rejoiced, knowing that he was moved with a right spirit, and seeing that a name was laid upon me by so holy a man. Yet had I not the name which I coveted : for I would fain have been called Dionysius, not only on account of my reverence for that most excellent doctor, who was the disciple of the Apostle Paul, but also because on the Feast of St. Dionysius I was born into this world. And thus it was that I saw the last Brother whom the blessed Francis received in the Order, after whom he received and robed no other. I have seen also the first, to wit, Brother Bernard of Quintavalle, with whom I dwelt for a whole winter in the Convent of Siena. And he was my familiar friend ; and to me and other young men he would recount many marvels concerning the blessed Francis ; and much good have I heard and learnt from him."

In Tuscany, Salimbene dwelt in turn in the convents of Lucca, Siena, and Pisa.   It is possible that he was twice at Pisa, since he had there an adventure which seems to imply that he was scarcely yet settled in the Order.   At any rate it belongs logically, if not chronologically, to this place.   (44) " Now at Pisa I was yet a youth, and one day I was led to beg for bread by a certain lay-brother, filthy and vain of heart (whom in process of time the Brethren drew out of a well into which he had thrown himself, in a fit of I know not what folly or despair.   And a few days later, he disappeared so utterly that no man in the world could find him : wherefore the Brethren suspected that the devil had carried him off : let him look to it !).   So when I was begging bread with him in the city of Pisa, we came upon a certain court-yard, and entered it together.   Therein was a living vine, overspreading the whole space above, delightful to the eye with its fresh green, and inviting us to rest under its shade.   There also were many leopards and other beasts from beyond the seas, whereon we gazed long and gladly, as men love to see strange and fair sights.   For youths and maidens were there in the flower of their age, whose rich array and comely features caught our eyes with manifold delights, and drew our hearts to them. And all held in their hands viols and lutes and other instruments of music, on which they played with all sweetness of harmony and grace of motion.   There was no tumult among them, nor did any speak, but all listened in silence.   And their song was strange and fair both in its words and in the variety and melody of its air, so that our hearts were rejoiced above measure.   They spake no word to us, nor we to them, and they ceased not to sing and to play while we stayed there : for we lingered long in that spot, scarce knowing how to tear ourselves away.   I know not (I speak the truth in God), how we met with so fair and glad a pageant, for we had never seen it before, nor could we see any such hereafter.[2]   So when we had gone forth from that place, a certain man met me whom I knew not, saying that he was of the city of Parma : and he began to upbraid and rebuke me bitterly with harsh words of scorn, saying ; ' Hence, wretch, hence !   Many hired servants in thy father's house have bread and flesh enough and to spare, and thou goest from door to door begging from those who lack bread of their own, whereas thou mightest thyself give abundantly to many poor folk.   Thou shouldst even now be caracoling through the streets of Parma on thy charger, and making sad folk merry with tournaments, a fair sight for the ladies, and a solace to the minstrels.   For thy father wasteth away with grief, and thy mother well-nigh

despaireth of God for love of thee, whom she may no longer see.'
To whom I answered : 'Hence, wretch, hence thyself ! For
thou savourest not the things which are of God, but the things
which are of fleshly men : for what thou sayest, flesh and blood
hath revealed it to thee, not our Father which is in heaven.'*
Hearing this, he withdrew in confusion, for he wist not what to
say. So, when we had finished our round [of begging], that
evening I began to turn and ponder in my mind all that I had
seen and heard, considering within myself that if I were to live
fifty years in the Order, begging my bread in this fashion, not
only would the journey be too great for me (I Kings xix, 7), but
also shameful toil would be my portion, and more than my
strength could bear. When, therefore, I had spent almost the
whole night without sleep, pondering these things, it pleased
God that a brief slumber should fall upon me, wherein He
showed me a vision wondrous fair, which brought comfort to
my soul, and mirth and sweetness beyond all that ear hath
heard. And then I knew the truth of that saying of Eusebius,
'Needs must God's help come when man's help ceases : ' for I
seemed in my dream to go begging bread from door to door,
after the wont of the Brethren ; and I went through the quarter
of St. Michael of Pisa, in the direction of the Visconti ; because in
the other direction the merchants of Parma had their lodging,
which the Pisans call *Fondaco* ; and that part I avoided both
for shame's sake, since I was not yet fully strengthened in Christ,
and also fearing lest I might chance to hear words from my
father which might shake my heart. For ever my father pursued
me to the day of his death, and still he lay in wait to withdraw
me from the Order of St. Francis ; nor was he ever reconciled
to me, but persisted still in his hardness of heart. So as I went
down the Borgo San Michele towards the Arno, suddenly I lifted
my eyes and saw how the Son of God came from one of the
houses, bearing bread and putting it into my basket. Likewise
also did the Blessed Virgin, and Joseph the child's foster-father,
to whom the Blessed Virgin had been espoused. And so they
did until my round was ended and my basket filled. For it is
the custom in those parts to cover the basket over with a cloth
and leave it below ; and the friar goes up into the house to beg
bread and bring it down to his basket. So when my round was
ended and my basket filled, the Son of God said unto me : 'I

* Salimbene here, as usual, reinforces his speech with several other texts—
Rev. iii, 17 ; Jer. ii, 5 ; Ecc. i, 2 ; Ps. lxxvii, 33 ; and lxxii, 19 ; Job xxi, 12, 13 ;
and 1 Cor. ii, 14.

am thy Saviour, and this is My Mother, and the third is Joseph who was called My father. I am He Who for the salvation of mankind left My home and abandoned Mine inheritance and gave My beloved soul into the hands of its enemies . . .'" Under the thin veil of our Lord's speech to him, the good friar here launches out into a long and rambling disquisition on the merits of voluntary poverty and mendicancy: a theme so absorbing that he more than once loses sight of all dramatic propriety. Not only does he make our Lord mangle the Bible text, quote freely from apocryphal medieval legends, and cite the tradition recorded by " Pietro Mangiadore " that the widow of 2 Kings IV had been the wife of the prophet Obadiah, but more than once we find Him inadvertently speaking of God in the third person.[3]   There are, however, one or two points of interest in this wilderness of incoherent texts and old wives' tales. Salimbene, who (as he tells us elsewhere) had at least one Jewish friend, gives us an interesting glimpse of thirteenth century apologetics. " Moreover in my vision I spake again to the Lord Christ, saying : ' Lord, the Jews who live among us Christians learn our grammar and Latin letters, not that they may love Thee and believe in Thee, but that they may carp at Thee and insult us Christians who adore the crucifix ; and they cite that scripture of Esaias, "They have no knowledge that set up the wood of their graven work, and pray unto a god that cannot save." ' "   He represents the Jews, in fact, as objecting the texts which a modern Jew might quote ; while he himself meets their objections with arguments which no modern apologist would dare to use.   Indeed, his wordy and futile apologia illustrates admirably a well-known ancedote of St. Louis.   " The holy king related to me " (writes Joinville, x. 51) " that there was a great disputation between clergy and Jews at the Abbey of Cluny. Now a knight was present to whom the Abbot had given bread for God's sake ; and he prayed the Abbot to let him say the first word, which with some pain he granted.   Then the knight raised himself on his crutch, and bade them go fetch the greatest clerk and chief rabbi of the Jews : which was done. Whereupon the knight questioned him : ' Master,' said he, ' I ask you if you believe that the Virgin Mary, who bare God in her womb and in her arms, was a virgin mother, and the Mother of God?'   And the Jew answered that of all this he believed naught.   Then answered the knight that he had wrought great folly, in that he believed not and loved her not, and yet was come into her minster and her house. ' And of a truth,' said the knight, ' you shall pay it dear.'   With that he lifted his crutch and smote the Jew under the ear and felled him to earth. And the Jews turned to flight and bare off their wounded rabbi ; and thus was the disputation ended. Then came the Abbot to the knight and said that he had wrought great folly. But he said that the Abbot had wrought more folly to ordain such a disputation : 'For here,' he said, 'are many good Christians present who, or ever the dispute had been ended, would have departed in unbelief, for they would never have understood the Jews.' 'So say I,' added the king, 'that none should dispute with them, but if he be a very learned clerk. The layman, when he hears any speak ill of the Christian faith, should defend it, not with words but with the sword, which he should thrust into the other's belly as far as it will go.'" The story is all the more instructive because St. Louis was, in practice, extremely kind to the Jews in comparison with most medieval princes. Another medieval practice admirably illustrated by these pages of Salimbene's is the wresting of Scripture to prove a preconceived theory, by distortion of its plain meaning, interpolation of words or phrases, and quotations from the Gloss,* as of equal authority with the Bible text. These time-hallowed liberties in the interpretation of Scripture go far to explain why medieval religious controversy, even among Christians, nearly alway ended in an appeal to physical force. So long as a word and a blow was looked upon as the most cogent religious argument, men seldom attempted either to understand their opponents' position or to weigh seriously their own arguments. And so in this passage our good friar loses himself in his own labyrinth of texts, and at last confesses that most of this elaborate dialogue has been a mere afterthought,—a "story with a purpose." It was written, he tells us, to confute Guillaume de St. Amour and other wicked people who, seeing how far the friars had already drifted from the Rule of St. Francis, accused them of being the "ungodly men" of 1 Tim. iii. 5–7 and iv. 3, come as heralds of the last and worst age of the world. There was, however, enough truth in the first portion of the vision to support Salimbene himself (53). "Wherefore, after this vision aforesaid, I had such comfort in Christ, that when jongleurs or minstrels came at my father's bidding to steal my heart from God, then I cared as little for their words as for the fifth wheel of a waggon. For upon a day one came to me and said, 'Your father salutes you and says thus : "Your mother would fain see you one day ; after which she would willingly die on the morrow."' Wherein he thought to have spoken words that would grieve me sore,

* i.e., the traditional notes.

to turn my heart away ; but I answered him in wrath : 'Depart from me, wretch that thou art; for I will hear thee no more. My father is an Amorite unto me, and my mother a daughter of Heth.' And he withdrew in confusion, and came no more."

Yet, manfully as Salimbene might resist during his novicate all temptations to apostasy (for so the Brethren called it, however unjustly), he felt a natural human complacency in looking back as an old man on what he had given up. Speaking of Cardinal Gerardo Albo, he tells us, "He was born in the village of Gainago, wherein I, Brother Salimbene, had once great possessions " : and he repeats the same phrase a second time, when he comes again to speak of the great Cardinal. Similarly, he cannot think without indignation of the miserable price at which his father's house was sold when poor Guido was gone, leaving his wife and children dead to the world in their respective convents. "The Lord Jacopo da Enzola bought my house in Parma hard by the Baptistery ; and he had it almost for a gift, that is, for a sum of small worth in comparison with that whereat my father justly esteemed it." Finally, he dwells with pardonable pride on the honours to which he might have attained, under certain very possible contingencies, even as a friar. In those, as in later, days, there was no such friend for a cleric as a Pope's nephew : and Salimbene, speaking of a nephew of Pope Innocent IV, continues : (61) "I knew him well, and he told me that my father hoped to procure from Pope Innocent my egress from the Order ; but he was prevented by death. For my father, dwelling hard by the Cathedral Church, was well known to Pope Innocent, who had been a canon of Parma and was a man of great memory. Furthermore, my father had married his daughter Maria to the Lord Azzo, who was akin to the Lord Guarino, the Pope's brother-in-law ; wherefore he hoped, what with the Pope's nephews and what with his own familiar knowledge of him, that the Pope would restore me to my home, especially since my father had no other sons. Which, as I believe, the Pope would never have done ; but perchance to solace my father he might have given me a Bishopric or some other dignity : for he was a man of great liberality."

However, for good or for evil, our chronicler is now irrevocably rooted in his cloister, and his father has no sons left to him in the world. The two last males of his house have definitely exchanged all their earthly possessions for a heavenly. (56) "I, Brother Salimbene, and my Brother Guido di Adamo destroyed our house in all hope of male or female issue by entering into Religion, that we might build it in Heaven. Which may He grant us Who liveth and reigneth with the Father and the Holy Ghost for ever and ever. Amen." One needs, of course, at least a homœopathic dose of Carlyle's "stupidity and sound digestion" to live at peace anywhere ; but to nine friars out of ten the gain of the celestial inheritance would seem as certain henceforth as the loss of the terrestrial : for it is an ever-recurring commonplace in Franciscan chronicles that the Founder had begged and obtained a sure promise of salvation for all his sons who should remain true to the Order. But, if we would fully understand the rest of Salimbene's earthly life, we must pause a moment here to take stock of the old world he had left, and of the new world into which he had so intrepidly leapt at the age of sixteen years.

One would be tempted to say that "the world," in the thirteenth century, deserved almost all the evil which religious men were never weary of speaking about it. It is scarcely possible to exaggerate the blank and universal pessimism, so far as this life is concerned, which breathes from literature of the time. It is always rash to assert a negative ; yet after long search in likely places, I have found only one contemporary author who speaks of his own brilliant century as marking a real advance, in morals and religion, on the past. This is Cardinal Jacques de Vitry, who died in 1244, before the decline of the friars was too obvious to be blinked, and who wrote earlier still, while St. Francis was alive. Moreover, even his testimonial to the improvement during his own days must be taken in connection with his astounding descriptions of the moral and religious squalor which reigned before the advent of Francis and Dominic. What is more, he plainly tells us that he looks upon even this new Revival as the last flicker of an expiring world. The Franciscan Order, he says, "has revived religion, which had almost died out in the eventide of a world whose sun is setting, and which is threatened by the coming of the Son of Perdition : in order that it might have new champions against the perilous days of Antichrist, fortifying and propping up the Church."[4]

Slender as were Vitry's hopes, his compeers were more hopeless still. Most of them, however pious and learned and brave, simply ring variations on the theme which to us seems so incongruous on the lips of our remote ancestors : "The world is very evil, the times are waxing late !" Read the great poem of Bernard of Morlaix from which this hymn is translated, and you will find page after page of bitter and desperate lamentations on the incorrigible iniquity of the whole world. The greatest of all medieval historians, Matthew Paris, had no doubt that the

thirteenth century marked the last stage of senile decay. Adam
Marsh, one of the greatest and most strenuous of the early
Franciscans in England, is never weary of alluding to "these
most damnable times," "these days of uttermost perdition,"
in which "no man can fail to see plainly that Satan is either
already loosed or soon to be loosed, except those whom (according
to the Scripture) the Lord hath struck with madness and blindness." Grosseteste, unsurpassed in learning and energy among
our Bishops, complained in a sermon before the Pope at Lyons
that (leaving heretics aside) even the Catholic population was,
as a body, incorporate with the Devil. Innocent III writes in
a Bull of "the corruption of this world, which is hasting to old
age." St. Francis, at the end of his life, sighed over "these times
of superabundant malice and iniquity." St. Bonaventura,
Vincent of Beauvais, Humbert de Romans, Gerard de Frachet,
Thomas of Chantimpré, Raimondo da Vigna (to name only
distinguished friars who were not tempted to minimize the work
of their Orders towards the betterment of the world), echo the
same despairing cry.[5] Dante shares their belief that the end of
the world is at hand, and leaves but few seats still vacant in
his Paradise (xxx. 131 ; cf. Convivio ii. 18.) His Ubertino da
Casale gives a curious reason for thinking that the world will just
last his own time : viz, Petrus Comestor,* in his commentary on
Gen. ix. 13, had written "that the rainbow will not appear for
30 or 40 years before the Day of Doom ; but the rainbow hath
appeared this year [1318] . . . wherefore we have now at least
30 or 40 years before Doomsday."[6]
If Dante or St. Francis could come back to life for a single
day, their first and greatest surprise would probably be that the
world still exists after six hundred years, far younger and more
hopeful than in their days ; a world in which even visionaries
and ascetics look rather for gradual progress than for any sudden
and dramatic appearance of Antichrist. But more significant
even than the chorus of misery and despair from thirteenth-
century theologians and poets is the deliberate pessimism of a
cool and far-sighted genius like Roger Bacon. He anticipated
the verdict of modern criticism on the boasted philosophy of his
contemporaries : that, with all its external perfection, it rested
upon a Bible and an Aristotle frequently misunderstood, and
showed a fatal neglect of the mathematical and physical sciences.
But in the domain of history he shared the ignorance of his
time, and was deprived of that assurance of progress in the past,

* The Mangiadore of Par. xii. 134.

which is one of the mainsprings of future progress for the world.
The passage is so significant both of the barbarous atmosphere
which stifled the greatest minds of the thirteenth century, and
of the limited outlook which paralyzed their best energies, that
I must give a full summary of it here. It was written in 1271,
two whole generations after St. Francis began to preach; and
the writer, it must be remembered, was himself a Franciscan.

Wisdom, he says, is intimately connected with morality; and
although there has been a vast *extension* of learning of late—
especially through the Friars during the last forty years—and,
by the Devil's wiles, much *appearance* of learning—yet "never
was so much ignorance, so much error as now . . . For more
sins reign in these days of ours than in any past age, and sin is
incompatible with wisdom. Let us see all conditions in the
world, and consider them diligently everywhere: we shall find
boundless corruption, and first of all in the Head." The court
of Rome is given up to pride, avarice, and envy; "lechery
dishonours the whole Court, and gluttony is lord of all." Worse
still when, as lately happened, the Cardinals' quarrels leave the
Holy See vacant for years. "If then this is done in the Head,
how is it in the members? See the prelates: how they hunt
after money and neglect the cure of souls. . . . Let us consider
the Religious Orders: I exclude none from what I say. See
how far they are fallen, one and all, from their right state; and
the new Orders [of Friars] are already horribly decayed from
their first dignity. The whole clergy is intent upon pride,
lechery, and avarice: and wheresoever clerks are gathered
together, as at Paris and Oxford, they scandalize the whole
laity with their wars and quarrels and other vices." Princes
and Barons live for war: "none care what is done, or how, by
hook or by crook, provided only that each can fulfil his lust:"
for they are slaves to sensuality. The people, exasperated by
their princes, hate them and break faith with them whenever
they can. But they too, corrupted by the example of their
betters, are daily busy with oppression or fraud or gluttony or
lechery. Yet we have Baptism, and the Revelation of Christ,
and the Sacrament of the Altar, which men cannot really believe
in or revere, or they would not allow themselves to be corrupted
by so many errors. With all these advantages, how do we stand
in comparison with the ancient philosophers? "Their lives
were beyond all comparison better than ours, both in all decency
and in contempt of the world, with all its delights and riches and
honours; as all men may read in the works of Aristotle, Seneca,
Tully, Avicenna, Alfarabius, Plato, Socrates, and others; and

so it was that they attained to the secrets of wisdom and found out all knowledge. But we Christians have discovered nothing worthy of these philosophers, nor can we even understand their wisdom; which ignorance springs from this cause, that our morals are worse than theirs." Therefore many wise men believe that Antichrist is at hand, and the end of the world. We know, however, from the Bible, that the fulness of the Gentiles must first enter in, and the remnant of Israel be turned to the Faith: which still seems far from accomplishment: for along the Baltic we have vast populations of pure heathens, to whom the word of God has never been preached, though they are nearer to Paris than Rome is. It may be that still, as of old, the long-suffering God will withhold his Hand awhile: "yet since the wickedness of men is now fulfilled, it must needs be that some most virtuous Pope and most virtuous Emperor should rise to purge the Church with the double sword of the spirit and the flesh: or else that such purgation take place through Antichrist, or thirdly through some other tribulation, as the discord of Christian princes, or the Tartars and Saracens and other kings of the East, as divers scriptures and manifold prophecies tell us. For there is no doubt whatever among wise men, but that the Church *must* be purged: yet whether in the first fashion, or the second, or the third, they are not agreed, nor is there any certain definition on this head."[7]

That Bacon, on his lonely pinnacle of contemplation, found the world of the thirteenth century almost intolerable, will seem natural enough to those who follow the revelations which flow so freely even from Salimbene's jovial pen. It is less natural, at first sight, that he should have done his own age the injustice of placing it on a far lower moral level than the Rome of Seneca or the Greece of Aristotle. But the cause is very simple; he knew nothing whatever of the inner life of ordinary Greece and Rome: he had only spent long years in studying the religious and philosophical writings of their greatest men. In a word, he had studied Antiquity as Newman studied the Middle Ages: and this false ideal of the past disabled him from making the best of the realities among which God had placed him.[8]

This false perspective, however, was inevitable in the thirteenth century. Men could not know the real past; and the present seemed only a chaos of conflicts and uncertainties. A broader view of history might have taught them how the very ferment of their own age was big with a glorious future; but such a wider view was impossible in those days of few and untrustworthy books. So they saw no hope in this world; no hope but in a *Deus ex machina.* Some Good Emperor and Good Pope shortly to come, or else Christ's second Advent and the end of all things—that was the heart's cry of the crowning period of the Middle Ages ! Dante shared this longing for a Good Emperor and a Good Pope ; but he lived to see Henry of Luxemburg poisoned, Boniface VIII triumphant, and the Babylonian Captivity of Avignon. This expectation of a *Deus ex machina* seems to die out towards the end of the fourteenth century ; undoubtedly the Black Death made men take more serious stock of the real grounds of their faith. Gerson spoke of the world in which he lived with all Dante's loathing and contempt, but his hopes rested on a General Council to reform the otherwise hopeless Church.[9] Meanwhile the lay element increased steadily in power : its influence may be traced in the growing magnificence of church buildings, furniture, and ritual. Presently powerful laymen set their hands, one by one, to assist that regeneration which the Church by herself had tried in vain to bring about : and then came the Reformation, with its slow evolution of a better world—a world which, with all its faults, enjoys such a combination of individual liberty and public order as would have seemed Utopian to the most hopeful minds of the thirteenth century.

If there had been nothing else in those days to render modern liberty and order impossible, there was the ingrained habit of civil and religious war. The fanatical craving of the Middle Ages for an outward unity fatally frustrated all real inward peace, as the greedy drinker chokes and spills in his own despite. The civil wars of Salimbene's Italy were not worse than those of Stephen's England, or the France of Charles VI, to leave less civilised countries out of the question : and Guibert of Nogent's autobiography indicates a state of things quite as bad in the North of France during St. Bernard's generation. Again, our good friar takes no cognizance of the still more horrible religious wars against the Albigenses and Stedingers, and the half-converted heathen of Prussia. Yet, omitting all those touches which would add so much deeper a gloom to any comprehensive picture of the Middle Ages, here is Salimbene's description of what went on as the necessary consequence of quarrels between Pope and Emperor, in that outer world upon which he now looked out in comparative safety from under his friar's cowl. (190) " But here, that you may know the labyrinth of affairs, I must not omit to tell how the Church party in Modena was driven forth from the city, while the Imperial party held it. So it was also in Reggio ; and so also, in process of time, in Cremona. Therefore in those days was most cruel war, which endured many years. Men could neither plough, nor sow, nor reap, nor till vineyards, nor gather the vintage, nor dwell in the villages : more especially in the districts of Parma and Reggio and Modena and Cremona. Nevertheless, hard by the town walls, men tilled the fields under guard of the city militia, who were mustered quarter by quarter according to the number of the gates. Armed soldiers thus guarded the peasants at their work all day long : for so it must needs be, by reason of the ruffians and bandits and robbers who were multiplied beyond measure. For they would take men and lead them to their dungeons, to be ransomed for money ; and the oxen they drove off to devour or to sell. Such as would pay no ransom they hanged up by the feet or the hands, and tore out their teeth, and extorted payment by laying toads in their mouths, which was more bitter and loathsome than any death. For these men were more cruel than devils, and one wayfarer dreaded to meet another by the way as he would have dreaded to meet the foul fiend. For each ever suspected that the other would take and lead him off to prison, that 'the ransom of a man's life might be his riches.' And the land was made desert, so that there was neither husbandman nor wayfarer. For in the days of Frederick, and specially from the time when he was deposed from the Empire [by the Pope], and when Parma rebelled and lifted her head against him, ' the paths rested, and they that went by them walked through bye-ways.' And evils were multiplied on the earth ; and the wild beasts and fowls multiplied and increased beyond all measure,—pheasants and partridges and quails, hares and roebucks, fallow deer and buffaloes and wild swine and ravening wolves. For they found no beasts in the villages to devour according to their wont : neither sheep nor lambs, for the villages were burned with fire. Wherefore the wolves gathered together in mighty multitudes round the city moats, howling dismally for exceeding anguish of hunger ; and they crept into the cities by night and devoured men and women and children who slept under the porticoes or in waggons. Nay, at times they would even break through the house-walls and strangle the children in their cradles.[10] No man could believe, but if he had seen it as I have, the horrible deeds that were done in those days, both by men and by divers beasts. For the foxes multiplied so exceedingly that two of them even climbed one Lenten-tide to the roof of our infirmary at Faenza, to take two hens which were perched under the roof-tree : and one of them we took in that same convent, as I saw with mine own eyes. For this curse of wars invaded and preyed upon and destroyed the whole of Romagna in the days when I dwelt there. Moreover, while I dwelt at Imola, a certain layman told me how he had taken 27 great and fair cats with a snare in certain villages that had been burnt, and had sold their hides to the furriers : which had doubtless been house-cats in those villages in times of peace." When we consider that the moral disorders of the time were almost as great as the political disorders ; and that the lives of the Saints constantly describe their heroes as meeting with worse religious hindrances in their own homes than they would be likely to find in a modern Protestant country—then we shall no longer wonder that so many escaped from a troubled world into what seemed by comparison the peace of the cloister.

CHAPTER VI.

Cloister Life.

BUT the cloister itself was only half a refuge. In vain did each generation try afresh to fence "Religion" with an impenetrable wall, for within a few years "the World" had always crept in again. Most men brought with them into the cloister a great deal of the barbarous world without; the few who cast off the old man did so only after such a struggle as nearly always left its life-long shadow on the mind. I have pointed out elsewhere how false is the common impression that "Puritanism" and "Calvinism" were born with the Reformation.[1] The self-imposed gloom of religion—the waste and neglect of God's visible gifts in a struggle after impossible otherworldliness—the sourness and formalism and hypocrisy which are the constant nemesis of so distorted an ideal, meet us everywhere in the 13th century, and nowhere more inevitably than among the friars of St. Bonaventura's school. There is, I believe, no feature of Puritanism (as distinct from Protestanism in general) which had not a definite place in the ideals of the Medieval Saints. The "personal assurance of salvation" which Newman mentions as specially characteristic of "Calvinism or Methodism," was in fact specially common among the early Friars.[2] So was the dislike of church ornaments and church music ; high officials in the Order were disgraced for permitting a painted window or a painted pulpit in their churches ; and even in the 17th century there were many who believed that St. Francis had forbidden music altogether. St. Bernard speaks of the profusion of paintings and carvings in monastic churches as little short of heathenism ; and he argues most emphatically that the highest religion is least dependent on such extraneous aids to devotion.[3] Multitudes of beautiful works of art were mutilated, and noble buildings destroyed, by the vandalism of the very ages which gave them birth ; and the iconoclasm of the reformers was simply the medieval spirit of destructiveness working under particularly favourable conditions. Moreover, the selfish view of salvation which is often spoken of as distinctively Puritan—the idea of the Christian race as a sort of jostle for heaven—was particularly medieval, and particularly monastic. It is true, St. Francis did much to shake the idea ; but it was soon flourishing again in his own Order ; and the ideal friar of St. Bonaventura's school is almost as deeply imbued with what St. Jerome calls " holy selfishness " as the older monks themselves. The tenet of the certain damnation of unbaptized infants, so often charged against Calvinism, is maintained universally, I believe, by orthodox medieval theologians. St. Bonaventura (following St. Gregory, and in company with Aquinas, Gerson, and numbers of others almost as eminent) reckons among the delights of the blest that they will see the damned souls writhing below them in hell. One anecdote will show how little the early Franciscans realized the lesson which the modern world has learnt from St. Francis and from others who have followed in his steps—that to save our own souls we not only *need* not, but almost *must* not, avoid our fellow-men, or break off the ordinary relations of life. The Blessed Angela of Foligno was the spiritual instructress of Dante's Ubertino da Casale ; she is singled out by Canon Knox-Little for special praise among the Franciscan saints. On her conversion to God she " mourned to be bound by obedience to a husband, by reverence to a mother, and by the care of her children," and prayed earnestly to be released from these impediments. Her prayer was heard, and " soon her mother, then her husband, and presently all her children departed this life." The story is told with admiration by one Franciscan chronicler after another, even down to the sober Wadding in the middle of the 17th century. St. Francis's admirable combination of cheerfulness and religion passed to but few of his disciples, as we realise at once when we wander afield beyond the charmed circle of the *Fioretti* legends. In the generations between St. Francis and Dante there were merry and sociable friars, and there were deeply religious friars ; but from a very early period the merry and the serious were divided into almost irreconcilable parties within the Order.

I had hoped to give at this point as full a picture as possible of inner Franciscan life in the later 13th century, by way of introducing my reader to Salimbene's experiences, but this would take me so far from my main purpose that I must reserve it for another time. At the same time it is necessary to give a few details, if only to disabuse the reader who may have formed his notions of ordinary Franciscan life from the *Fioretti* alone. That immortal book, true as it is within its own limits, no more gives us the life of the average friar than the *Vicar of Wakefield* shows us the average country parson of the 18th century. Many important inferences which might be drawn from it are most directly contradicted by St. Bonaventura (d. 1274), by other writers of his school, by the earliest chronicles of the Order, and —most incontrovertible evidence of all—by dry official documents. The *Fioretti* will always remain an inspiring example of what *some* men have done, but for the purposes of historical comparison the main question is, "How do *most* men live?"; and from this the *Fioretti*, by themselves, would often lead us far astray. Nowhere within so small a compass can we so clearly realize average Franciscan life as from the directions to novices and older brethren compiled by St. Bonaventura, by his secretary Bernard of Besse, and by his contemporary David of Augsburg. These little books have been republished in a cheap form by the Franciscans of Quaracchi, and should be studied by all who wish to understand the 13th century friar.* But the reader must be prepared for things undreamt of in M. Sabatier's *St. Francis*, admirable as that book is on the whole as a picture of the Order during the saint's lifetime. Nothing is more remarkable in religious history than the rapid changes in Franciscan ideals and practice within a very few years.

The manuals of St. Bonaventura's school—and their evidence is entirely borne out by such early documents as were composed without the poetic preoccupations which moulded the *Fioretti*— show a conventual ideal almost as gloomy as that of earlier monasticism. Of the Puritanism I have already spoken; the ideas of discipline were equally formal and lifeless. Novices are bidden not to *thee* or *thou* their seniors in the Order. To carry flowers or a staff, to twirl the end of one's girdle-cord, to sit with crossed legs, to laugh, to sing aloud, are all unworthy of Franciscan decorum. So far from ever talking familiarly with a woman, or touching her hand, the friar must not even look at one when he can help it. Warning is heaped upon warning to show that spiritual friendship in these matters is even more dangerous than ordinary friendship; many pillars of the Order have fallen through this. The friar is thus cut off for life not only from the help of women, but from any free and personal influence over them.[4] Again, to carry news is unfranciscan, or to speak of contingent matters without some such qualification as D.V.; or

* The Italian translation of Bernard of Besse's book, published by the same community, must, however, be used with caution, as the text is softened down by omissions and other similar changes, to avoid shocking the modern reader.

to say *How d'ye do* ? to people in whose health you have no special interest. As David of Augsburg sums it up, wherever the friar has no special prospect of spiritual profit, he is to look upon worldly folk with no more interest " than if they were so many sheep."

Of course the average friar did not conform to all these rules. We cannot even begin to understand medieval life until we realize that the laws and regulations of those days represented only pious aspirations, all the more soaring because they were so little expected to bear fruit in fact. No doubt the average friar, in his easy sociability, resembled the friar of Chaucer and of Shakespeare, but the fact remains that the Constitutions of his Order, and the byelaws of his convent, required him to be quite a different person. Moreover (literary enjoyment and dilettante sentiment apart), we may well be glad that these most picturesque figures of the past are no longer living among us in their primitive shape. Brother Juniper running naked in our streets—or St. Francis himself ; for on at least one occasion the earliest authorities expressly deny him even the scanty garments in which later prudery clokes him—we may well be glad to keep such children of nature within the covers of old books. We revel in Jacopone da Todi's eccentricities, but we are happy to live 600 years to windward of him. And, in this respect, the sober prose documents are in complete agreement with the *Fioretti* : they show us many traces not only of the old unregenerate Adam, but, what is more, of the 13th century Adam, only dimly realizable at the best by politer readers of to-day. The directions for behaviour in refectory and in church are startling indeed, for they exemplify something more than that " morbid craving for an indulgence of food and drink, making mockery of their long fasts and abstinence," which Mr. McCabe describes as general among modern friars. St. Francis himself had noted and legislated against this gluttony, and the complaints continue through St. Bonaventura and others down to Ubertino da Casale. " Fall not upon thy meat with tooth and claw like a famished dog," pleads David of Augsburg ; and St. Bonaventura's secretary enters into minuter details. " Cleanliness should be observed not only as to thine own and thy fellows' food, but as to the table also whereat thou eatest. Beware, in the name of cleanliness and decency alike, of plunging into dish, cup, or bowl that which thou hast already bitten and art about to bite again. It is a foul thing to mingle the leavings of thine own teeth with others' meat. Never grasp the cup with fingers steeped in pottage or other food, nor plunge thy thumb into the goblet, nor blow upon the drink in the cup or upon any meat whatsoever. It is indecent for a man to plunge his fingers into the pottage and fish for gobbets of meat or potherbs with bare hands in lieu of spoon, thus (as Hugh of St. Victor writes) washing his hands and refreshing his belly with one and the same broth." The friar is further warned not " to cast forth upon the table the superfluity of his fish or other meat, to crack nuts with his teeth for another guest, to cough or sneeze without turning away from the table, to . . ." but the rest of this warning must be left to the decent obscurity of the original. It is sufficient to remind the reader that even sybaritic worldlings in the thirteenth century possessed neither handkerchief nor fork, and that their most elaborate refinements of manners under these difficulties will scarcely bear description in a less downright age. . . . Again, " the cleanliness of the table demands that the cloth should by no means be fouled through frequent or superfluous wipings of thy knife or thy hands ; least of all should it be submitted to purging of teeth. For it is a base and vile thing to befoul the Brethren's common cloths and towels with rubbing of thy gums. He who dishonoureth the common goods offendeth against the community." It is only fair to add that many of these rules for behaviour are adapted from those drawn up by Dante's Hugh of St. Victor for his fellow-monks ; and that, on the whole, the friars were apparently just one shade more civilized at table than the members of a great Augustinian convent a century earlier, of whom Hugh complains that many rushed upon their meat like a forlorn hope at the breaches of a besieged city. The great Dominican General Humbert de Romans makes similar complaints of his brother-friars' behaviour at table.[5]

But even more significant than these hints on table manners are the indications which may be gathered as to the conduct of divine service. St. Bonaventura twice alludes to the extreme length of the services, assuming that the novice in confession will have to accuse himself " of much negligence and irreverence in the matter of thine Hours, for thou sayest them sleepily and indevoutly and with a wandering heart and imperfectly, omitting at times whole verses and syllables." David of Augsburg speaks of the common temptation to melancholy or levity in the friar's mind, " whence we are forced to attend divine service with a mind that struggles against it, like puppies chained to a post; and this is the vice of *accedia*, the loathing of good.[*] Many, even among Religious, are sick of this disease, and few overcome

---

* Cf. Inf. vii, 123.

it." Salimbene bears the same testimony in his own racy style *à propos* of the changes made by the great Innocent III, who (31) " corrected and reformed the church services, adding matter of his own and taking away some that others had composed ; yet even now it is not well ordered, as many would have it and as real truth requires. For there are many superfluities which beget rather weariness than devotion, both to hearers and to officiants ; as, for instance, at Prime on Sundays, when priests have to say their masses and the people await them, yet there is none to celebrate, for they are yet busied with Prime. So also with the recitation of the eighteen psalms at Nocturns on Sunday before the *Te Deum*. For these things beget sheer weariness, not only in summer, when we are harassed by fleas and the nights are short and the heat is intense, but in winter also. There are yet many things left in divine service which might be changed for the better. And it would be well if they were changed, for they are full of uncouth stuff, though not every man can see this." Cæsarius of Heisterbach, again, has many tales of Brethren who slumber in church. Within the walls of the sanctuary his saints are as drowsy as his sinners, and, while the idle Cistercian is dreaming of Hell, the industrious Cistercian, no less oblivious of earthly psalmody, is rapt into the Seventh Heaven. In spite of the theoretical gravity of the sin, the stern moralist unbends to humour in writing of a lapse so natural and so inevitable in practice. " A certain knight of Bonn once made his Lenten retreat in our abbey. After that he had returned to his home, he met our Abbot one day and said to him, ' My Lord Abbot, sell me that stone which lieth by such and such a column in your choir, and I will pay whatsoever price thou wilt.' Our Abbot asked, ' What need hast thou thereof ? ' ' I will lay it,' he replied, ' at my bed's head, for it hath such virtue that the wakeful need but lay his head thereon and forthwith he falleth asleep.' . . . Another noble, who had been at our abbey for a similar penitence, is reported to have said in like words, ' the stones of the Abbey choir are softer than all the beds of my castle.' " There is an almost equally amusing story in the Dominican *Vitæ Fratrum* about a friar who was haunted all through service by a devil offering to his lips a contraband cheese-cake, " such as the Lombards and French call a *tart*." It was precisely during those long, monotonous hours that a man's besetting sin haunted him most inexorably, as Nicholas of Clairvaux reminded his Brethren. " The great patriarch Abraham," he adds, " could scarce drive away these unclean fowls from his sacrifice, and who are we to presume that we shall put them to flight ?

Who of us can deny that he hath been plunged, if not altogether submerged, in this river?" It is the more necessary to insist upon this point, because of the false sentiment lavished on the monastic ideal by modern writers who would not touch with one of their fingers the burden of the strict monastic Rule. It is the merest cant to expatiate on that Rule without facing the fact that few ever came even within a measurable distance of strict conformity to it; while far more, having taken the vows without full understanding, bore afterwards not only the natural weariness of human flesh and blood, but the added burden of a system which less and less commended itself to their reason.[6] Monks and friars were men like ourselves, who, finding themselves pledged by profession to an impossible theory of life, struck each an average depending on his own personal equation, varying in separate cases from the extreme of self-denial to the extreme of self-indulgence, but in the main following the ordinary lines of human conduct. Not one human being in a million can pray in heart for seven hours a day ; few can even dream of doing so, and drowsiness in church is a commonplace of medieval monastic writers. Of the saintly and ascetic Joachim of Flora, for instance, his enthusiastic biographer assures us that he slept but little at any time, and least of all in church. It is the same contrast which meets us everywhere in the Middle Ages. Over-strained theories bore their fruit in extreme laxity of practice ; and good men, distressed at this divergence, could imagine no better remedy than to screw the theory one peg higher.[7]

If outraged nature demanded a modicum of slumber during service, much of the same excuse can be pleaded, and was in fact allowed by the moralist, for irreverence. The extraordinary licence of behaviour in medieval churches was the necessary outcome of the elaborate medieval ritual, and of the small extent to which the words were understood even by the average officiant. Friars are warned not to laugh during service, or make others laugh, or pursue their studies, or walk about, or cleanse lamps, or come in late, or go out before the end. They must doff their hoods now and then at the more solemn parts, not toss their heads or stare around in their stalls ; "It is blameworthy . . . . to busy thyself with talk while the office of the Mass is being celebrated, for Canon Law forbiddeth this at such times even to the secular clergy."[8] The same warning was needed by the layfolk in the nave, who (as Ubertino complains) were always loafing about in the friars' churches "rather for the sake of curiosity and gossip than for spiritual profit." Care must be taken to guard these layfolk, ignorant of the different steps of the Mass, from the idolatry of adoring prematurely an unconsecrated wafer. Moreover, an officiating friar himself would frequently trip in his reading, to the irreverent glee of self-righteous Brethren, who scandalized others by their laughter or comments.[9]

There remains one more point to be noticed, if we are to realize the difference between Salimbene's surroundings and our own. Many of his stories and allusions, far too natural then to need any special explanation from him, will seem scarcely credible in our age to those who have not yet realized facts which the 13th century took as matters of course. In studying medieval religious manners, we come to a point at which it is difficult to distinguish irreverence from the prevailing coarseness and uncleanliness of the times. The familiarity with which the people treated their churches had something pleasant and homely then, as it has in modern Italy. The absence of a hard-and-fast line between behaviour within and without the sacred building is in many ways very touching ; yet, in a rude society, this familiarity had great inconveniences. The clergy often brought their hawks and hounds to church ; and similar instances are recorded by Salimbene. For instance, when the Bishop of Reggio was buried in his own cathedral, it was quite natural for a dog to be present, and to show no better manners than a modern Protestant beast ; nor were the citizens in the least deterred by reverence for the holy place when they wished to desecrate an unpopular governor's tomb by filthy defilements. It is natural, therefore, that the Franciscan precepts for behaviour in church should resemble the counsels for table-manners. "While a single voice is reading in choir, as in the collects, chapters, or lessons, thou must take good heed to make no notable sound of spitting or hawking, until the end of a period, and the same care must be taken during a sermon or a reading." A far more detailed warning lower down proves incontestably that, in personal cleanliness and respect for the church floor, the Italian of the thirteenth century was far behind even the Italian of to-day. It was the same elsewhere ; in Provence, for instance, the dainty and aristocratic Flamenca is described as gratifying her lover with a momentary sight of her mouth as she lowered her wimple to spit in the church porch. And, as usual, we find that the neglect of cleanliness is accompanied by an almost corresponding bluntness of moral feeling ; the warnings on this score point to a state of things which may indeed stagger a modern reader. The friar is bidden to observe the most scrupulous cleanliness at Mass ; the server must " never blow his nose on the priestly garments, especially upon the chasuble," a warning which is repeated in even more grisly detail lower down : "moreover, he who ministers at mass must so keep his surplice (if he have one), as never in any degree to blow his nose on it, nor use it to wipe away the sweat from his face or any other part : neither let him expose its sleeves to drag, especially in the dust, over wood, stones, or earth." What was worse, the offenders sometimes made a merit of their offence. "Certain careless [friars] . . . . can scarce keep [the long sleeves of their frocks], which have frequently been exposed to the utmost dirt, away from their fellows' food, from the altar, or from the very maniple of the chalice. Such, who would fain please [God] by their very filth, brand their more careful brethren with the reproach of fastidiousness, and strive to colour their own vicious negligence with the show of virtue."[10]   We may here read between the lines a further, and just, cause for the unpopularity of the Spirituals, with their stern insistence upon the Saint's sordid example in dress, and their pride in wearing garments not only as coarse but also as old as possible.   Many uncompromising old Spirituals wore, as others complained, frocks that had shrunk to the dimensions of an Eton jacket,[11] and one such garment attained to a certain historical notoriety in the Order.   Brother Carlino de' Grimaldi, probably a scion of one of the greatest families in Genoa, had washed his frock (we are not told after how long an interval) and had spread it to dry in the sun.   Here at last it lay at the mercy of the Brethren, who, having probably more than mere doctrinal differences to avenge, cut it into small pieces which they desecrated with medieval ingenuity.[12]   It is necessary to face this subject, since there is no other, except that of compulsory celibacy, which illustrates more clearly the practical weakness of the strict Franciscan Rule.   The ideal of absolute and uncompromising poverty was in fact hopelessly retrograde.   Even without such ascetic exaggerations, the very Rules of the religious Orders forbade cleanliness in the modern sense.   Father Taunton (*Black Monks of St. Benedict*, i. 83) does indeed take some pains to combat this impression ; but the documents to which he refers flatly contradict his assertions, nor have I been successful in eliciting further references from him.   Among the real hardships of a strict monk's life, this would have been the most intolerable, during his noviciate at least, to a modern Englishman.   It sometimes shocked even the medieval layman, accustomed as he was, in the highest society, to many of the conditions of slum life. Cæsarius describes the conversion of a knight who had long wished to enter the cloister, but who always hung back, " on the

cowardly plea that he feared the vermin of the garments (for
our woollen clothing harbours much vermin.)" The Abbot
laughed away the scruples of the valiant soldier who would suffer
such tiny creatures to scare him away from the Kingdom of
God ; and indeed, once admitted, the knight was soon sufficiently
hardened to boast that " even though all the vermin of the monks
should fall upon my single body, yet should they not bite me
away from the Order."[13] Salimbene speaks jestingly on the same
topic, quoting (1285-336) "those verses which men are wont to
repeat :—

> ' Three are the torments that rhyme—ex,
> *Pulex* and *culex* and *cimex.*
> Mighty to leap is the *pulex*,
> Swift on the wing is the *culex* ;
> But the *cimex*, whom no fumigation can slay,
> Is a monster more terrible even than they.' "*

Bernard of Besse (p. 327) bears far more significant witness
in solemn prose. The strict rule of poverty would have
condemned the uncompromising Franciscan to something less
than ordinary monastic cleanliness, as it would have condemned
him also to ignorance.[14] In short, all the early writings on the
discipline of the Order, as well as the early collections of legends,
point to the impossibility of carrying out the Franciscan ideal
on a large scale, and under the conditions which the age demanded.
As the strict rule of poverty would have condemned the Order
to barbarism, so the vow of chastity could not in those days be
kept with anything like the strictness which modern society
demands from a religious body, by any but an order of virtual
hermits. The ascetic writers of the time assure us, over and
over again, that this virtue needed a perpetual consciousness of
living in a state of siege, a deliberate aloofness from one half of
mankind, which was patently impossible for any missionary body
on the enormous scale of the Franciscan Order. What the early
disciplinarians prophesy as imminent, later writers complain of
as an accomplished fact. Gower and the author of *Piers Plowman*,
though they both hated heretics as heartily as Dante did, asserted
roundly that the friar was a real danger to family life. Benvenuto,
in his comment on Par. xii. 144, specifies lubricity as one of
the vices of the friar of his day, and Sacchetti speaks even more
strongly. Again, Busch in the 15th century names " the

---

* In *x* finita tria sunt animalia dira :
Sunt pulices fortes, cimices culicumque cohortes ;
Sed pulices saltu fugiunt, culicesque volatu,
Et cimices pravi nequeunt fœtore necari.

unreformed friars " as those who most infected other religious Orders with the seeds of decay.[15] Like the monks, they had often pledged themselves as boys to that which no boy can understand, while their manner of life exposed them to far more temptations than the average monk. It is impossible to do more than allude to this subject here, in the text; but I take the opportunity of pointing out that I have more than once requested, both privately and publicly, references for the most important statements of monastic apologists, such as Abbot Gasquet, and that these references have been steadily refused. On the other hand, I have given very definite evidence for my own contentions in the *Contemporary Review*, and in a separate pamphlet.[16] Apologists of the Middle Ages have played upon the unwillingness of modern Englishmen to believe facts which can be proved to the hilt from contemporary records, though for obvious reasons those who know these facts find it difficult to publish them. There can be no better testimony to the civilizing work of the Reformation than that the average educated Anglican cannot now bring himself even to imagine a state of things which is treated as notorious by medieval satirists and moralists, and is recorded in irrefragable documents. Charges which would be readily enough believed in modern Italy or Spain find little acceptance in a country like ours, where monks and nuns, living in a small minority under a glare of publicity and criticism, keep their vows with a strictness far beyond the average of the Middle Ages.

The third vow, that of obedience, was as radically modified as the two others by the growth of St. Francis's originally small family into an enormous Order. The most significant anecdote on this point is quoted by Wadding under the year 1258. In this year died one Brother Stephen, who deposed as follows to Thomas of Pavia, Provincial Minister of Tuscany—a great friend of Salimbene's, it may be noted—"I, Brother Stephen, dwelt for a few months in a certain hermitage with St. Francis and other brethren, to care for their beds and their kitchen; and this was our manner of life by command of the Founder. We spent the forenoon hours in prayer and silence, until the sound of a board [struck with a mallet, like a gong] called us to dinner. Now the Holy Master was wont to leave his cell about the third hour [9]; and if he saw no fire in the kitchen he would go down into the garden and pluck a handful of herbs which he brought home, saying, 'Cook these, and it will be well with the Brethren.' And whereas at times I was wont to set before him eggs and milk food which the faithful had sent us, with some sort of gravy stew [*cum aliquo jusculento*], then he would eat cheerfully with the rest and say, 'Thou hast done too much, Brother; I will that thou prepare naught for the morrow, nor do aught in my kitchen.' So I, following his precepts absolutely, in all points, cared for nothing so much as to obey that most holy man ; when therefore he came, and saw the table laid with divers crusts of bread, he would begin to eat gaily thereof, but presently he would chide me that I brought no more, asking me why I had cooked naught. Whereto I answered, 'For that thou, Father, badest me cook none.' But he would say, 'Dear son, discretion is a noble virtue, nor shouldest thou always fulfil all that thy Superior biddeth thee, especially when he is troubled by any passion.'" This anecdote, which is quite worthy of the *Fioretti*, gives us a most instructive glimpse into the strength and weakness of the Saint's society. All his ways were intensely human and personal, but everything depended on his own spirit and his own presence. Nobody could have been angry with a saint who confessed so naïvely that he did not wish to be taken at his word: yet one sees at a glance how necessarily the increase of the Order thrust his direct authority into the background, and how naturally, while the veneration for his sanctity steadily increased, he himself fell from the position of a working Head into that of a Dalai Lama, a sort of living relic, mighty to conjure with, but comparatively passive in the hands of others, and only liberating his soul by the deathbed protest of his "Testament" against those hateful courses upon which the Order had already embarked almost beyond recall.

In considering this revolt against St. Francis's rule, we must bear in mind that it was the very intensity of the Saint's ideal which caused that recoil, by a natural law as inevitable as gravitation. Thomas of Eccleston's history, which is constantly quoted as the most vivid picture of the Order's inner life, avowedly refers to a state of things already dead and gone within thirty years of the Saint's death ; already the writer speaks of the persecutions endured by those who strove for the original purity.[17] It is idle to charge this decay to Brother Elias, or to any man or group of men ; it was fatally involved in the very ideal of the Saint. As he hastened his own death by sinning grievously against Brother Body, just so he hastened the decay of his Order. Admirably as he protested against some of the crazy asceticisms of his age, he was still too much a child of his time. It is difficult to wish anything away from St. Francis's own life, as it is difficult for an Englishman to regret the Charge of the Light Brigade. But, when our present age is taunted for its alleged soullessness by reactionaries whose eyes are too weak

to face the growing light of the times in which they live, it may
be profitable to point out that in the Holy War, as in all other
wars, we need not only courage and sudden self-sacrifice, but also
calm judgment and even a certain amount of routine work.

The self-imposed hardships of an average friar's life were very
real, until at least the middle of the 13th century. Men were
not wanting, even then, who managed to live more luxuriously in
the Cloister than they could ever have done in the World, as
their Superiors frequently complained : but quite a considerable
portion of the early friars had been boys of good family and
position, to whom, after the first plunge, the trial was severe,
for some years at least. We see something of this in the case
of Salimbene, richly as his opportunities of travel and study in-
demnified him for those cabbages which his soul abhorred. We
may gather it also from the very frequent mention of apostasies,
either contemplated or carried out, in collections of Mendicant
legends ; and Berthold of Ratisbon, preaching to his Brethren
about the middle of the century, implies the same. " Almost
all Religious who have failed or still fail, in all religious Orders,
have perished or still perish by reason of the evil example which
they have seen and still see among the rest to whom they come.
For almost all enter Religion with a mind most readily disposed
to all good. But when on their entry they find one impatient,
another wrathful, another carnal, another dissolute, another
agape for news, another a mere trifler, another backbiting,
another slothful, another breaking St. Francis's prohibition
against receiving money, then they follow in their ways and
become like unto them." He goes on to speak in the same breath
of " so many in Religion " who thus " are corrupted and perish " ;
and the whole tenour of his sermons to his fellow-friars implies
that, among the crowds who pressed with more or less precipita-
tion into the Order (for the year of novitiate was not always
strictly enforced) there were comparatively few who even
approached its strict ideal. We get glimpses of this even in the
records of the heroic age, and in those of a generation later the
fact is gross and palpable. As St. Bonaventura shows us, the
development from the friar of the *Fioretti* to something very like
the friar of Chaucer was rapid and inevitable. Among even the
best-intentioned of the first generation, few were able to keep
their ascetic enthusiasm to the end.[18] " When those who first
kept the Order in its vigour are taken away or become enfeebled
in body," writes the Saint, "then they can no longer give
to their juniors the same strict examples of severity as of old ;
and the new Brethren, who never saw their real labours, imitate

them only in that which they now behold in them, so that they become remiss, and spare their bodies under a cloke of discretion, saying that they will not destroy their bodies as did the Brethren of old. And, for that they see not the inner virtues which their elders had, they are negligent on both sides, neither exercising themselves in outward things nor grasping the inward virtues." Berthold makes the same complaint in his own style. " Many take good care to avoid serious penance, clapping on bandages before they are wounded, . . . sparing themselves as tenderly as though they were silkworms, or silken stuff, or as though their flesh were as brittle as an eggshell." Again, "they spare their bodies almost as tenderly as the relics of saints" ; if one of them has but a little grace " he is like a hen, cackling so loudly over a single egg, that all grow weary of her, wherefore she is driven forth from the house and loses her egg." " Some [friars'] hearts are as the flesh of an old brood-hen, nay, as that of an old wild duck, which can scare be sodden ; for indeed a wild duck was taken for our convent which we boiled three days long and yet it lacked all natural tenderness, being still so tough that no man could cut it with a knife, nor would any beast eat thereof. Ye marvel at this in nature, far more should ye marvel that some— and thou thyself perchance among them—are stewed in the kitchen of Religion for nine or ten years, nay, for twelve, thirteen, or thirty years, and yet are ye altogether hard-hearted, and, what is more, impatient."[19]

It will be necessary to glance again at the Friars as a whole towards the end of the book ; meanwhile the present chapter may prepare the reader for Salimbene's experiences in the Order. Miss Macdonell seems to think that the average friar was a more serious person than our chronicler ; I cannot understand anyone thinking so who has read carefully the disciplinary works of St. Bonaventura's school, the Constitutions of the Order, Angelo Clareno's *Seven Tribulations* as edited by Father Ehrle, and Berthold of Ratisbon's Sermons to his Brethren. A study of those works is calculated to make us accept Salimbene at something nearer to his own estimate—as standing above the common average of his fellows in nearly all respects, while he is far above that average in natural gifts, learning, and experience of the world.

CHAPTER VII.

Frate Elia.

SALIMBENE had scarcely completed his novitiate, when a storm burst which had long been brewing within the Order. The Minister-General Elias, leader of the party which frankly abandoned the first strict ideal, and builder of the splendid basilica which now covers the Saint's bones, was deposed from his office after a bitter struggle. Instead of bearing his defeat patiently, Elias " gave scandal to the Pope, to the Church, and to his Order," by joining the Emperor Frederick, then excommunicate and at war with the Pope. Franciscan frocks were thus seen flitting about in the rebel camp, for Elias had taken others over with him : and he rode abroad publicly with the Emperor, whose trusted counsellor he at once became. " Which was an evil example to the country folk and the rest of the laity, for whensoever the peasants and boys and girls met the Brethren Minor on the roads of Tuscany, they would sing (as I myself have heard a hundred times)

> ' Frat' Elia is gone astray,
> And hath ta'en the evil way.'

At the sound of which song the good Brethren were cut to the heart, and consumed with deadly indignation " (160).

Nor does Salimbene's story of these first years leave by any means an impression of perfect harmony among those who remained within the Order, though, as will presently be seen, he himself made many friends there. To begin with, his gall was stirred by the way in which lady-superiors of Clarisses often lorded it over their fellow-nuns : for our friar was no believer in " the monstrous regiment of women." He describes (63) the " churlishness and avarice " of the Lady Cecilia, niece to Pope Innocent IV, and Abbess of a rich convent of Clarisses at Lavagna. The Clarisses of Turin had been driven from their convent by the ravage of war—a common story, as the pages of Wadding show—

and the Visitor of the Lombard province was doing his best to find other homes for the poor nuns. One only, the last of all, was brought to this rich convent; yet the Abbess, in her "hardness of heart and avarice and folly," refused to receive a fresh inmate, and drove the poor refugee ignominiously from her door, in spite of the Visitor's anathema. "Hereupon an ancient and devout Sister of the convent cast herself down before the altar and appealed against the Abbess to God, Who presently answered, 'I have heard thy prayer, and she shall be no more Abbess.' So the Visitor sent a swift messenger forthwith to Chiavari to learn what had befallen that Abbess, and he found her dead and cursed and excommunicate and unabsolved; for even while the messenger was yet on his way, she began to be grievously sick and to fail for very faintness, and after divers torments she sank down on her bed and was at the point of death, crying, ' Sisters, I die! Hasten! Help! Bring me some remedy!' The Sisters came forthwith, pitying their Abbess, as was right. No mention was made of the salvation of her soul, not a word was spoken of confession. Her throat so closed that she could scarce breathe; and now, seeing death at hand, she said to the Sisters who were gathered round her, ' Go and take in that lady! Go and take in that lady! Go and take in that lady! For her sake hath God smitten me! For her sake hath God smitten me! For her sake hath God smitten me!' And with these words she yielded up her spirit, but it returned not to God Who gave it."

Salimbene thinks the lady might perhaps have behaved better if she had been sent to rule over a strange convent far away from her powerful kinsfolk; but, to his eyes, the root of the matter lay in the constitutional unfitness of women to bear rule, and he dilates on this subject in truly medieval fashion, with a wealth of Biblical and profane quotations: "for woman, whensoever she may, doth take gladly dominion to herself, as may be seen in Semiramis who invented the wearing of breeches. . . . . Blessed be God Who hath brought me to the end of this matter!'

Yet, in spite of this sigh of relief, we find our good friar recurring almost immediately to the same ungallant complaints, and again, à propos of an Abbess of Clarisses (67). This was again in the first days of his new vocation, at Lucca, where he formed an intimacy with an aristocratic pair of doubtful morals, of whom he writes with his usual naïveté: "In the year 1229 the Lord Nazzaro Gherardini of Lucca was Podesta of Reggio, when he built the bridge and the Porta Bernone. His statue was set up in marble on the Porta Bernone which he made, and there he sits on his marble horse in the city of Reggio. He was a comely knight and exceeding rich, my acquaintance and friend when I dwelt in the convent at Lucca. The Lady Fior d'Oliva, his wife, was a fair lady, plump and full-fleshed,* and my familiar friend and spiritual daughter (*devota*). She was of Trent, the wife of a certain notary, by whom she had two daughters, most fair ladies. But the Lord Nazzaro, when he was Podesta of Trent, took her from her husband and brought her, not unwilling, to the city of Lucca ; and his own wife, who was still alive, he sent to a castle of his, where she dwelt till her death.[1] The Lord Nazzaro died childless, and gave great riches to this lady, who, in course of time was beguiled (as she herself hath told me) into another marriage in the city of Reggio. He who took her to wife was Henry, son of Antonio da Musso, and she liveth yet in this year 1283 wherein I write. Both the Lord Nazzaro and the Lady Fior d'Oliva did much to comfort the Friars Minor of Lucca when the Abbess of the Clarisses at Gatharola stirred up the whole city of Lucca against the brethren, laying a blot on the elect, for that Brother Jacopo da Iseo would fain have deposed her because she bare herself ill in her office. For she was the daughter of a baker-woman of Genoa, and her rule was most shameful and cruel, and unhonest to boot, and she would fain have kept her rule by force, that she might still be Abbess. Wherefore, the better to hold her office, she lavished gifts on youths and men and worldly ladies, but especially on those who had any of near kin in her convent. And to such she would say, ' This is why the Friars Minor would fain depose me, for that I will not suffer them to sin with our daughters and sisters ; ' and so, as hath been said, she would have laid a blot on the elect, for she lied in her teeth. Yet for all that she was deposed, and the Friars recovered their honour and good report, and the city had rest from her troubling. I have therefore shown plainly how shameful is the dominion of women."

Salimbene records only one other noteworthy incident of these first days at Lucca. (164) " In the year of our Lord 1239 there was an eclipse of the sun, wherein the light of day was horribly and terribly darkened, and the stars appeared. And it seemed as though night had come, and all men and women had sore fear, and went about as if bereft of their wits, with great sorrow and trembling. And many, smitten with terror, came to confession, and made penitence for their sins, and those who were at discord made peace with each other. And the Lord Manfred da Cornazano, who was at that time Podesta, took the Cross in his hands and went in procession through the streets of Lucca, with

---

* *Pinguis et carnosa.* This is always high praise from Salimbene.

the Friars Minor and other men of religion and clerks. And the Podesta himself preached of the Passion of Christ, and made peace between those who were at enmity. This I saw with mine own eyes, for I was there, and my brother Guido di Adamo with me."

It was apparently from Lucca that he went to Siena, where he enjoyed the privilege already recorded of a whole winter's familiar intercourse with St. Francis's first disciple, Bernard of Quintavalle. (39) Here also he received his first tinge of Joachitic Millenarianism from Hugues de Digne and other enthusiasts, as will be seen later on. Already, like most of his brethren, Salimbene took an active part in politics, working for the Pope against the Emperor. (174) "The See of Rome was vacant from the year 1241 to 1243, for the cardinals were dispersed and at discord, and Frederick had so straitly guarded all the roads that many men were taken, for he feared lest any should pass through to be made Pope. Yea, and I myself also was often taken in those days; and then I learned and invented the writing of letters after divers fashions in cypher."

In spite of the preponderance of the lay element at Pisa, his next place of abode, he made very good friends there and loved the place. Although a powerful patron, Brother Anselm, Minister Provincial of Terra di Lavoro (552) "sent me letters that I should go with my brother Guido to dwell with him in his province, yet the Brethren of the convent of Pisa dissuaded us from the journey, for that they loved us." Long afterwards, writing of the disastrous defeat of the Pisans at Meloria, he cannot help showing his pity for the sufferings even of his political opponents : "God knows I sorrow for them and pity them in my heart, for I lived four years in the convent of Pisa a good forty years since." (535). Here also he was strengthened in his Joachism by "a certain abbot of the Order of Fiore, an aged and saintly man, who had placed in safety at Pisa all the books that he had of Abbot Joachim's, fearing lest the Emperor Frederick should destroy his abbey, which lay on the road from Pisa to Lucca. For he believed that in the Emperor Frederick all the mysteries of iniquity should be fulfilled. And Brother Rudolf of Saxony, our lector at Pisa, a great logician and theologian and disputer, left the study of theology by reason of those books of Joachim's, which were laid up in our convent, and became a most eager Joachite" (236).

As his stay at Lucca had been marked by an eclipse, so at Pisa he was startled by an earthquake. Two similar phenomena which occurred much later, in 1284, carry him back to these years

of his first vocation, and give occasion for an amusing anecdote
and a very characteristic dissertation. (547-9). " Brother
Roglerio of our Order, a native of Lodi, who had been a comrade of the Visitor of the Province of Bologna, was on his way
back from the Roman Court wherein he had been with a certain
Cardinal, and when he passed by Corenno, where he was to lodge,
the inhabitants of that place said unto him ' Holy father, we often
feel earthquakes in this place.' And immediately when they had
said this an earthquake was felt. So the Brother said ' He
looketh on the earth, and it trembleth ; He toucheth the hills, and
they smoke' : and again ' The earth trembled, and was still ' ;
and again ' Thou hast made the earth to tremble, Thou hast broken
it ; heal the breaches thereof, for it shaketh.' But when the
Brother had finished speaking thus, he looked round and saw a
certain building thatched with straw, and said that he would sleep
therein that night, ' For if I sleep in some other house, it may be
that the gutter-stones or tiles fall upon me, if the house be
brought low ; and there I shall die.' So the women of that
village, seeing and hearing these things, carried their beds into
that thatched building, that they might sleep in safety by the
side of the Friars. But a certain old man, seeing this, said to
Brother Roglerio ' Ye have done that which ye should not have
done. For ye should always be ready to accept death, that the
dust may return to the earth as it was, and the spirit unto God
who gave it.' To whom the Friar answered ' The blessed Jerome
saith that " It is prudent to fear all that may happen " ; and
Ecclesiasticus " The wise man feareth in all things " [also Prov.
xxviii. 14 and xi. 15 ; and Eccles xviii. 27].' All this I heard
from the mouth of Brother Roglerio." With regard to the
following eclipse, Salimbene quotes a whole string of Bible texts
connecting such natural catastrophes with the signs of the Last
Judgment, after which he continues (549), " I have multiplied these texts because at one time the sun is darkened, and at
another time the moon, and at times the earth will quake ; and
then some preachers, having no texts ready prepared for this
matter, fall into confusion. I remember that I dwelt in the convent of Pisa forty years since and more, and the earth quaked at
night on St. Stephen's day ; and Brother Chiaro of Florence of
our Order, one of the greatest clerks in the world, preached twice
to the people in the cathedral church there, and his first sermon
pleased them, but the second displeased. And this only because
he founded both sermons on one and the same text, which was a
token of his mastery, since he drew therefrom two discourses ;
but the accursed and simple multitude that knew not the law,

thought that he had preached again the same sermon, by reason
of that same text which had been repeated ; wherefore he reaped
confusion where he should have had honour. Now his text was
that word of Haggai, ' Yet a little while, and I will move the
heaven and the earth and the sea and the dry land.' Note that
earthquakes are wont to take place in cavernous mountains,
wherein the wind is enclosed and would fain come forth ; but
since it hath no vent for escape, the earth is shaken and trembles,
and thence we feel an earthquake. Whereof we have a plain
example in the uncut chestnut, which leaps in the fire and bursts
forth with might and main to the dismay of all who sit by."
Pisa, of course, is a city of the plain, but it is interesting to
know what ideas were raised in Salimbene's mind by the mountains
which stand round it on the horizon.

At Siena he had received the subdiaconate (329) ; at Pisa he
was ordained deacon (182) ; some time during the year 1247 he
left the province of Tuscany and went to Cremona, where he soon
found himself a close spectator of the bloody struggle between
Pope and Emperor. But before following him into that world of
treasons, stratagems, and spoils, let us glance at those memories
of Tuscan convents which most haunted his mind as an old man.

The Order in its early days, under St. Francis, had been
specially distinguished by its unsacerdotal character.[2] The saint
himself was never more than deacon ; and in a letter to the Order
he evidently contemplated the presence of two priests in a single
settlement of the Brethren as quite an exceptional case. Of the
twenty-five friars whom he sent to evangelize Germany in 1221,
thirteen were laymen, as were also five of the nine who began the
English mission in 1224 ; it was not until 1239 that a priest,
Agnello of Pisa, was elected Minister-General and could exclaim
in triumph to the assembled brethren, " Ye have now heard the
first mass ever celebrated in this Order by a Minister-General."
St. Francis had been content to impose on his brethren a plain
and brief Rule, without " constitutions " or byelaws ; St. Francis
and his early friars had lived not in convents but in hermitages.[3]
But in fourteen years the ideal of the Order was already so
changed that a young and ambitious student like Salimbene, in
spite of his close personal intercourse with several of the earliest
Brethren, could count it among the worst crimes of Brother
Elias to have followed here in the Founder's steps, though indeed he accuses him of having done so with a far different
intention.[4] He speaks of it as scandalous that he should have
had to associate with fifty lay brethren during his six years at
the two convents at Siena and Pisa, and that he, a clerk, should

have been subject at different times to a lay Custos and several lay Guardians. As to the lack of general Constitutions, though Salimbene is perfectly aware that neither St. Francis nor his immediate successor Giovanni Parenti had made any, yet he complains that the absence of such hard-and-fast rules under Elias resulted in a sort of anarchy; "in those days there was no king in Israel," he quotes (102); "but every one did that which seemed right to himself. For under [Brother Elias] many lay brethren wore the clerical tonsure, as I have seen with mine own eyes when I dwelt in Tuscany, and yet they could not read a single letter; some dwelt in cities, hard by the churches of the Brethren, wholly enclosed in hermits' cells, and they had a window through which they talked with women; and the lay-brethren were useless to hear confessions or to give counsel; this have I seen at Pistoia and elsewhere also. Moreover, some would dwell alone, without any companion,[5] in hospitals; this have I seen at Siena, where a certain Brother Martin of Spain, a little shrivelled old lay-brother, used to serve the sick in the hospital, and went alone all day through the city wheresoever he would, without any Brother to bear him company; so also have I seen others wandering about the world. Some also have I seen who ever wore a long beard, as do the Armenians and Greeks, who foster and keep their beard; moreover they had no girdle; some wore not the common cord, but one fantastically woven of threads and curiously twisted, and happy was he who could get himself the gayest girdle. Many other things I saw likewise, more than I can relate here, which were most unbecoming to the decency of the Franciscan habit. Moreover laymen were sent as deputies to the Chapter, and thither also a mighty multitude of other laymen would come, who had no proper place there whatsoever. I myself saw in a general chapter held at Sens a full 300 brethren, among whom the laymen were in the greater number, yet they did nought but eat and sleep. And when I dwelt in the province of Tuscany, which had been joined together out of three provinces, the lay-brethren were not only equal in numbers to the clerics, but even exceeded them by four. Ah God! Elias, 'thou hast multiplied the nation, and not increased the joy.' It would be a long and weary labour to relate the rude customs and abuses which I have seen; perchance time and parchment would fail me, and it would be rather a weariness to my hearers than a matter of edification. If a lay-brother heard any youth speaking in the Latin tongue, he would forthwith rebuke him, saying, 'Ha! wretch! wilt thou abandon holy simplicity for thy book-learning ? "* But I for my part would answer them thus from St. Jerome, ' Holy selfishness profiteth itself alone ; and howsoever it may edify Christ's Church with the excellence of its life, by so much it worketh harm if it resist not them who would destroy her.' In truth, as saith the proverb, an ass would fain make asses of all that he seeth. For in those days not only were laymen set above priests, but in one hermitage, where all were laymen save one scholar and one priest, they made the priest work his day in the kitchen in turn with the rest. So it chanced on a season that the Lord's day came to the priest's turn ; wherefore, entering the kitchen and diligently closing the door after him, he set himself to cook the potherbs as best he could. Then certain secular folk, Frenchmen, passed that way and earnestly desired to hear Mass, but there was none to celebrate. The lay-brethren therefore came in haste and knocked at the kitchen door that the priest might come out and celebrate. But he answered and spake unto them, ' Go ye and sing Mass, for I am busied in the work of the kitchen, which ye have refused.' Then were they sore ashamed, perceiving their own boorishness. For it was boorish folly to pay no reverence to the priest who confessed them ; wherefore in process of time the lay-brethren were brought to nought, as they deserved, for their reception was almost utterly forbidden,[6] since they comprehended not the honour paid them, and since the Order of Friars Minor hath no need of so great a multitude of laymen, for they were ever lying in wait for us [clerics]. For I remember how, when I was in the convent of Pisa, they would have sent to the Chapter to demand that, whensoever one cleric was admitted to the Order, one lay-brother should be admitted at the same time, but they were not listened to—nay, they were not even heard to the end—for their demand was most unseemly. Yet in the days when I entered the Order, I found there men of great sanctity, mighty in prayer and devotion and contemplation and learning ; for there was this one good in Brother Elias, that he fostered the study of theology in the Order."

If the clerics of the Order smarted under Brother Elias' encouragement of the lay-brethren, all alike groaned under his masterful government. Even in St. Francis's lifetime we can see a natural tendency to more mechanical methods of discipline as the Order grew in size ; in the Saint's " Epistle to a Minister " of 1223 the conception of discipline is still paternal, and the Minister's authority mainly moral ; but in the " Testament " of only three years later we find already a stern insistence on the

---

* *Pro tua sapientia scripturarum.*

necessity of imprisonment for heresy or certain forms of disobedience among the Brethren.   Again, among the Constitutions
passed at Padua in 1277 we find : "item, the General Chapter
commands that there be strong prisons in great numbers (*multi-
plices*), and at the same time humane." Salimbene's Tuscan re-
collections of the years 1239-1247 fill in these bare notices
admirably, and show the friction caused within the Order by the
strong-willed, unscrupulous man who did more than any other to
discipline these spiritual volunteers into a rigidly organized papal
militia.

(104) " The sixth defect of Brother Elias was that he afflicted
and reviled the Ministers Provincial, unless they would redeem
their vexation by paying tribute and giving him gifts.   For he
was covetous and received gifts, doing contrary to the Scripture
(Deut. xvi. 19) ; whereof we have an example in Alberto Balzo-
lano, the judge of Faenza, who changed his judgment on hearing
that a countryman had given him a pig.   Moreover the aforesaid
Brother Elias kept the Ministers Provincial so utterly under his
rod that they trembled at him as a rush trembles when it is shaken
under the water, or as a lark fears when a hawk pursues and
strives to take him.   And this is no wonder, for he himself was
a son of Belial, so that no man could speak with him.   In very
deed none dared to tell him the truth nor to rebuke his evil deeds
and words, save only Brothers Agostino da Recanati and Bonaventura da Iseo.*   For he would lightly revile such Ministers as
were falsely accused to him by certain malicious, pestilent, and
hot-headed lay-brethren his accomplices, whom he had scattered
abroad throughout the Provinces of the Order.   He would depose
them from their office of Minister even without fault of theirs,
and would deprive them of their books, and of their licence to
preach and hear confessions, and of all the lawful acts of their
office.   Moreover, he would give to some a long hood† and send
them from east to west, that is from Sicily or Apulia to Spain or
England, or contrariwise.   Moreover, he deposed from his
Ministership Brother Albert of Parma, Minister of the Province
of Bologna, a man of most holy life ; and he bade Brother Gerard
of Modena, whom he appointed by letter into the place of the
deposed Minister, to bring him to himself at Assisi clad in the hood
of probation.   But Brother Gerard, who was a most courteous man,
said nought of this matter to the Minister, only praying him that
he would be his companion on a pilgrimage to the shrine of the

---

* Not to be identified with Dante's Agostino or Bonaventura.
† i.e., degrade them to wear the novice's hood.

blessed father Francis. When therefore Brother Gerard was come
with Brother Albert near to Brother Elias' chamber, he brought
forth from his bosom two hoods of probation, whereof he placed one
on his own shoulders, and gave the other to the Minister of
Bologna, saying ' Place this on thine, father, and await my return
to thee.' So Brother Gerard went in to Elias and fell at his
feet saying, ' I have fulfilled thine obedience, in bringing to thee
the Minister of Bologna with a hood of probation, and behold
he watcheth without and is willing to do whatsoever ye command.'
When Elias heard this, all his indignation left him, and the spirit
sank wherewith he had swelled against him. So Brother Albert
was brought in and restored to his former rank ; moreover, he
obtained many favours also for his Province by the mediation of
Brother Gerard. Wherefore on account of this and other deeds
of that wicked man Elias, thoughts of revenge were bred in
the hearts of the Ministers, but they waited for the time when
they might answer a fool according to his folly. For Brother
Elias was a most evil man, to whom we may fitly apply those
words which Daniel saith of Nebuchadnezzar, ' And for the
greatness that he gave to him, all people, tribes, and languages
trembled, and were afraid of him ; whom he would, he slew ;
and whom he would, he destroyed ; and whom he would, he set
up ; and whom he would, he brought down.' Moreover, he sent
Visitors who were rather exactors than correctors, and who
solicited the Provinces and Ministers to pay tributes and grant
gifts ; and if a man gave not something into their mouth, they
prepared war against him. Hence it came about that the
Ministers Provincial in his time caused to be made at Assisi, at
their own expense, for the church of the blessed Francis, a
great and fair and sonorous bell, which I myself have seen,
together with five others like unto it, whereby that whole valley
was filled with delightful harmony. So likewise, while I dwelt
as a novice in the convent of Fano, I saw two brethren coming
from Hungary and bearing on sumpter-mules a great and
precious salt fish, bound up in canvas, which the Minister of
Hungary was sending to Brother Elias. Moreover, at the same
time, by the Minister's mediation, the King of Hungary sent
to Assisi a great goblet of gold wherein the head of the blessed
Francis might be honourably preserved. On the way, in Siena,
where it was laid one night in the sacristy for safety, certain
Brethren, led by curiosity and levity, drank therefrom a most
excellent wine, that they might boast thenceforward of having
drunk with their own lips from the King of Hungary's goblet.
But the Guardian of the convent, Giovannetto by name, a man

zealous for justice, a lover of honesty, and a native of Assisi, hearing this, bade the refectorer, a man of Belfort, who likewise was named Giovannetto—he bade him, I say, at the morrow's dinner, to place before each of those who had drunk from the goblet one of those little kitchen-pots called *pignatta*, black and stained, wherefrom each must drink will he nill he, in order that, if he would boast henceforward of having once drunk from the King's goblet, he might remember also how for that fault he had drunk from a foul pipkin."

Not content with these liberal contributions from all quarters, the General sought also for the Philosopher's Stone. (160) " He was publicly reported of dealing in alchemy, and it is certain that, whenever he heard of Brethren in the Order who, while yet in the world, had known aught of that matter or craft, he would send for them and keep them by him in the Gregorian Palace— for Pope Gregory IX had built himself a great palace in the convent of Friars Minor at Assisi, both in honour of St. Francis and that he himself might dwell there when he came to Assisi. In this palace, therefore, were divers chambers and many lodgings, wherein Elias would keep the aforesaid craftsmen, and many others also, which was as much as to consult a pythonic spirit (Deut. xviii, 11). Let it be imputed to him ; let him see to it " ! It may be that Elias' dealings in the black art were merely a popular fiction, but there was no doubt that the liberal contributions of the faithful were very often diverted from their proper object—a malpractice common everywhere in the 13th century, when pope after pope set the example of collecting money for the Crusades and spending it in private wars or in worldly pomp (157). " The seventh defect of Elias was that he would live in too great splendour and luxury and pomp. For he seldom went anywhither save to Pope Gregory IX and the Emperor Frederick II, whose intimate friend he was, and to Santa Maria della Porziuncula (where the Blessed Francis instituted his Order and where also he died), and to the convent of Assisi, where the body of the Blessed Francis is held in veneration, and to the House of Celle by Cortona, which is a most fair and delightful convent, and which he caused to be specially built for himself in the Bishopric of Arezzo, for he was to be found either there or in the convent of Assisi. And he had fat and big-boned palfreys, and rode ever on horseback, even if he did but pass a half-mile from one church to another, thus breaking the rule which saith that Friars Minor must not ride save of manifest necessity, or under stress of infirmity. Moreover, he had secular youths to wait on him as pages, even as the Bishops have, and these were

clad in raiment of many colours to wait on him and minister to
him in all things. Moreover, he seldom ate in the convent with
the other brethren, but ever alone in his own privy chamber,
which in my judgment was great boorishness, for

> The sweetest joys are vain as air
> Unless our friend may claim his share.

Moreover, he had his special cook in the convent of Assisi, Brother
Bartholomew of Padua, whom I have seen and known, and who
made most delicate dishes." An anecdote in the *Chronicle of
the xxiv Generals* (p. 229) at once corroborates Salimbene here,
and suggests that much of his information about Elias may have
come from his old comrade at Siena, the earliest disciple of St.
Francis. "Brother Bernard of Quintavalle, when he saw Brother
Elias on his horse, would pant hard after him and cry 'This is
too tall and big ; this is not as the Rule saith !' and would
smite the horse's crupper with his hand, repeating the same again.
And when Elias fared sumptuously in his own chamber, Brother
Bernard aforesaid would at times rise up in great zeal from the
table of the refectory, bearing in his hand a loaf of bread, a flesh-
hook and a bowl, and would knock at the door of Brother Elias's
chamber. When therefore the door was opened he would sit
down beside the Minister at his table, saying, 'I will eat with thee
of these good gifts of God :' whereat the General was inwardly
tormented, yet for that Bernard was held in the utmost reverence
throughout the Order, he dissembled altogether."

Elias, whose despotic rule and contempt of early traditions
made him so widely unpopular, had yet the magnetic attraction
of a born ruler of men. He enjoyed the love of St. Francis, the
close confidence of Emperor and Pope, even while they were at
war with each other, and the loyal attachment of his humble
intimates. As Salimbene continues, speaking of his special cook,
(157) "this man clung inseparably to Elias until the last day of
his life, and so also did all they of his household. For he had a
special household of twelve or fourteen brethren, whom he kept
by him in the convent of Celle, and they never changed the habit
of the Order "—i.e. they never acknowledged themselves truly
excommunicate for their adherence to an excommunicated man.
"And after the death of their evil pastor, or rather their seducer,
having understood that they were deceived, they returned to the
Order. Moreover, Elias had in his company one John, whose
surname was *de Laudibus* [of Lodi ?], a lay-brother, hard and keen,
and a torturer and most evil butcher, for at Elias's bidding he

would scourge the brethren without mercy. And [just before the Chapter of 1239] Elias, knowing that the Provincial Ministers were gathered together against him, sent commands to all robust lay-brethren throughout Italy whom he counted as his friends, that they should not fail to come to the General Chapter ; for he hoped that they might defend him with their cudgels." This plan was frustrated, however ; and after a stormy meeting, in which the Pope had to remind the friars that " it was not the fashion of Religious " to shout each other down with *Thou liest* and other abusive cries, Elias was deposed. His Man Friday, John of Lodi, whose great bodily strength is spoken of by another chronicler, died in the odour of sanctity, and miracles were wrought at his tomb : he had enjoyed the supreme privilege of touching the wound in the side of St. Francis. This is not in the least inconsistent with Salimbene's account; miracles were commonly worked at the tombs of men who in any way struck the medieval imagination, even as champions of a popular cause in purely secular politics, like Simon de Montfort or Thomas of Lancaster. St. Thomas à Becket would have done all that Salimbene here describes for the cause of discipline in a matter where his convictions were fixed.

Chapter VIII.

The Bitter Cry of a Subject Friar.

SO Elias was deposed ; yet still he troubled Israel. Not only was his life in his first retirement at Celle a scandal to the Rule, but presently he joined the Emperor's camp openly, as we have already seen. Salimbene has much to say of this :—and, when he describes the difficulties created by this single man, we must remember also how many more of the same sort would be created by the numerous supporters who had once raised him to the Generalship and had nearly succeeded in procuring his re-election in 1239. Indeed, the deposition of Elias marks only the beginning of the most serious Francisan dissensions. Salimbene tells how he went about justifying his apostasy, and how one friar withstood him to his face, finally dismissing him with St. Francis's contemptuous farewell, " Go thy way, Brother Fly." (161). Salimbene's dear friend, Gerard of Modena, who had known Elias well, went once to Celle, and laboured all day long to bring him back to the Order : but in vain. Moreover, as Gerard tossed on his sleepless pallet that night, " it seemed to him that devils like bats fluttered all night long through the convent buildings : for he heard the sound of their voices, and fear and trembling seized him, and all his bones were affrighted, and the hair of his flesh stood up. Wherefore, when morning was come, he took his leave and departed in all haste with his companion. So in process of time Brother Elias died : he had been excommunicated aforetime by Pope Gregory IX : whether he was absolved and whether he ordered things well with his soul, he himself knoweth now : let him look to it ! But in course of time (since, as the Wise Man saith, there is a time and opportunity for every business), a certain Custode dug up his bones and cast them upon a dunghill. Now if any would fain know whereunto this Brother Elias was like in bodily aspect, I say that he may be exactly compared to Brother Ugo of Reggio, surnamed Pocapaglia, who in the world had been a master of grammar, and a great jester and a ready speaker : and in the Order of the

Friars Minor he was an excellent and mighty preacher, who by his sermons and his parables confuted and confounded those who attacked our Order. For a certain Master Guido Bonatti of Forlì[1] who called himself a philosopher and astrologer, and who reviled the preaching of the Friars Minor and Friars Preachers, was so confounded by Brother Ugo before the whole people of Forlì that he not only feared to speak, but durst not even show himself during all the time that the Brother was in those parts. For he was brimful of proverbs, stories, and instances ; and they sounded excellently in his mouth, for he ever suited them to men's manners ; and he had a ready and gracious tongue, that the people were glad to hear him. Yet the ministers and prelates of the Order loved him not, for that he spake in parables, and would confound them with his instances and proverbs : but he cared little for them, since he was a man of excellent life. Let it suffice me to have said thus much of Brother Elias." (163).

The fall of Elias leads Salimbene to moralize on the advantages of constitutional as compared with absolute government in a religious Order. The Friars differed from the older Orders in their frequent change and re-election of officials, a system in which we find one of the many strong points of similarity between the Revival of the XIIIth century and the Wesleyan movement.[2] This frequent change had Salimbene's hearty approval. For one thing, familiarity was apt to breed contempt. (146) " I have seen in mine own Order certain Lectors of excellent learning and great sanctity who had yet some foul blemish (merditatem), which caused others to judge lightly of them. For they love to play with a cat or a whelp or with some small fowl, but not as the Blessed Francis was wont to play with a pheasant and a cicada, rejoicing the while in the Lord."[3]

Again, the official might have some strange defect which forbade his inspiring proper veneration ; for instance (137) " I was once under a minister named Brother Aldebrando, of whom Brother Albertino of Verona (whose sayings are much remembered) was wont to say in jest that there must have been a hideous idea of him in God's mind.[*] For his head was misshapen after the fashion of an ancient helmet, with thick hair on his forehead : so that whenever it fell to him, in the service for the octave of the Epiphany, to begin that antiphon, ' caput draconis ' (the dragon's head), then the brethren would laugh,

---

[*] Quod turpem ideam in Deo habuerat, an allusion to Plato's doctrine of ideas, according to which everything in the visible universe had its eternal exemplar in the Divine mind : so at least Plato was understood in the Middle Ages.

and he himself would be troubled and ashamed. But I used to recall that saying of Seneca, ' Of what sort, thinkest thou, is the soul within, where the outward semblance is so hideous ? ' . . . . Therefore we advise the Prelate, who is set for an example to others, to abstain from levities so far as in him lies ; and, if he indulged in such when he was a private person, let him quit them altogether when promoted to a prelacy : as a man did, whom the monks of a certain monastery chose for abbot as being the most disorderly (*dissolutum*) of all, hoping to live more laxly under his rule. But when he was made abbot, he caused the rule and statutes of his predecessors to be nobly kept. So the monks, being grieved beyond measure, said to their abbot ' we chose thee in the hope of fulfilling the desire of our hearts under thy rule : but thou seemest changed into another man.' To whom he answered ' My sons, this is the change of the right hand of the Most High.' . . . . But there are some who, as prelates, practise levities even as they did aforetime when they were private persons " (149).

Furthermore, a once vigorous prelate may fall into his second childhood, as (150) " I have ofttimes read in the *Liber Pontificalis* of Ravenna that a certain Archbishop of that see became so old as to speak childishly, for he was grown a babe among babes. So when the Emperor Charlemagne should come to Ravenna and dine with him, his clergy besought him to abstain from levity for his honour's sake, and for a good example in the great Emperor's presence : to whom he made answer, ' Well said, my sons, well said ; and I will do as ye say.' So when they were seated side by side at table, he patted the Emperor's shoulders familiarly with his hand saying, ' Pappa,† pappa, Lord Emperor ! ' The Emperor, therefore asked of those who stood by what this might mean : and they answered him, ' He would invite you in childish fashion to eat with him ; for he is in his dotage.' Then with a cheerful face the Emperor embraced him, saying, ' Behold an Israelite indeed, in whom there is no guile.' "

Therefore the Prelates (i.e., officials) of Religious Orders should be regularly and frequently changed, as the Captains and Podestas of the cities, in whose case the plan works admirably. It works admirably also amongst the Friars ; for (112) " Let it be noted that the conservation of religious Orders lieth in the frequent change of Prelates, and this for three reasons. First, lest they wax too insolent with their long prelacy, as we see in

† Cf. Dante, *Purg.*, xi. 105.

the abbots of the Order of St. Benedict, who, since they hold office for life and are not deposed, treat their subject monks as a mere rabble (*vilificant subditos suos*), and esteem them no more than the fifth wheel of a waggon, which is a thing of nought; and the abbots eat flesh with lay folk while the monks eat pulse in their refectory; and many other burdensome and unseemly things they do to their subjects, which they should not do, since they themselves choose to live in splendour and in the greatest liberty.[4] Moreover, not only do nature and human courtesy bid them not afflict their subjects nor do them evil, but Holy Scripture also, and the example of the Father, the Son, and the Holy Ghost. Of courtesy we have an example in a certain King of England, to whom, as he was at supper with his knights by a spring in a wood, a vessel of wine was brought such as the Tuscans call *fiascone*, and the Lombards *bottaccio*. Having asked, and received an answer that there was no more wine than this, he said; 'Here then is enough for all,' and poured the whole vessel into the spring, saying, 'Let all drink in common'; which was held to be a great courtesy in him.* Not so doth the miser who saith, 'I have found me rest, and now I will eat of my goods alone': not so do those Prelates who eat the finest white bread and drink the best and choicest wine in the presence of their subjects and of those who eat with them in the same house, and who give nought thereof to their subjects (which is held to be utter boorishness); and so also they do with other meats. Moreover some Prelates drink choice wine, yet give nought thereof to their subjects who are present, though these would as gladly drink as they; for all throats are sisters one to another.[5] But the Prelates of our time, who are Lombards, gladly take to themselves all that their throats and appetites crave, and will not give thereof to others. Indeed, that curse seems in our days to be fulfilled which Moses imprecated upon evil-doers, saying 'Thine ox shall be slain before thine eyes, and thou shalt not eat thereof.' The prelates of our days, for the most part, 'come for to kill and to steal and to destroy,' as is written in St. John; and as Micah saith 'the best of them is a briar, the most upright is as a thorn hedge.' And if some man would now write a dialogue concerning prelates, as St. Gregory did, he might rather find offscourings than holy prelates; for as Micah again saith, 'the good man is perished out of the earth, and there is none upright among men.' Yet after Christ's example the Prelates should

---

* This was probably the *Re Giovane* of *Inf.* xxviii. 135, who was a byeword for courtesy and liberality: cf. *Novellino*, 15, 16, 87.

minister to their subjects: as is indeed done in the Order of
Pietro Peccatore; for on fast days at Collation the priors pour
out drink to their subjects in memory of the Lord's example.
Now the head of the Order of Pietro Peccatore is in the church
of Santa Maria in Porto at Ravenna; and of the same Order is
the convent of Santa Felicula near Montilio in the Bishopric of
Parma, and several other houses in divers parts of the world."[6]
Not only does the Rule of St. Francis bid that the superiors
should be real servants of the Brethren, but they might learn
from the example even of a heathen like Julius Cæsar, who never
said to his soldiers " Go and do that," but " Let us come and do
this."

Salimbene goes on to complain that, whereas the Apostles and the
first Christians had all things in common, "it is not so nowadays"
even in Franciscan convents.   St. Francis's Rule prescribes that
the Minister should be a servant to all his brethren, and Christ
rebukes the Pharisees for taking the foremost places in the
synagogues, etc.: " Yet the prelates of our time do this, to the
very letter."   Our Lord, again, likened His care for mankind to
that of a hen for her chickens: but the evil prelate of to-day
rather resembles that ostrich of which Job writes, " she is
hardened against her young ones, as though they were not hers."
The hen defends her chickens against the fox, " which is a
stinking and fraudulent beast ": so should the prelate defend his
fellow-friars against the Devil or worldly tyrants.   The hen,
" finding a grain of corn, hideth it not, but rather crieth aloud
that her brood may flock to her: and when they are come she
casteth the grain before them without distinction of white or
black or brown, but giving to each alike: yet the prelates of
our days love not their subjects equally, but with a private love:
some they count as sons, others as stepsons or spurious: and the
same whom they invite to share their good cheer to-day, to the
same they give just as freely on the morrow.   But the rest who
sing the *invitatorium* and whose place is in the refectory (*i.e.* who
do not eat apart with the prelate,) stand all the while idle and
grumble and murmur, saying with the poet, ' The wild boar is
feared for his tusks, the stag is defended by his horns; while we
the peaceful antelopes are a helpless prey ': which is as much as
to say, ' the flies flock to the lean horse' " (118).   This favouritism
of our modern prelates in their invitations to good cheer is
contrary both to our Lord's words (Luke xiv. 12) and to the
example of St. Lawrence, which Salimbene quotes at length.
" But [modern prelates] have loved the glory of men more than
the glory of God, and therefore shall they be confounded.   For

they say, 'To-day I will give you a good dinner in the hope that
ye will give me the same to-morrow ' : of whom the Lord saith,
' Amen I say unto you, they have received their reward ' " (119).
   To these faults of unfairness and self-seeking the Prelates too
often add that of discourtesy : which Salimbene rebukes by
three Scriptural examples. Our Lord *desired* (not *commanded*)
Simon to draw back a little from the land : Simon himself said
to Cornelius, ' Arise, I myself also am a man ' : and the Angel
of the Apocalypse said the same to St. John. " Lo therefore
how our Lord and the Apostle Peter and the Angel honour God's
servants ; and how these boorish Prelates raise themselves above
them in their pride ! Note that in some religious Orders there
will at times be men who were noble in the world, rich and
powerful, and who are ancient in the Order both as to their own
days and as to the time of their entrance into Religion ; moreover, better still, they are spiritual and contemplative and devout
and amiable to the Brethren ; they are endowed also with wisdom
and learning, having a knowledge of books and a ready tongue
and mother-wit and honest morals. Yet over such men a Prelate
may be set who is of obscure birth, insufficient and unprofitable
in all the aforesaid qualities, and yet he will come to such pride
and folly that his heart will be lifted to pride against his
brethren, paying reverence to no man, but addressing all in the
singular number with ' *tu* ' ; which, as I may say, is not permitted
except for five reasons." Here he launches into a dissertation
from which we learn incidentally how little the use of the pro-
nouns was as yet fixed in Italian : for " the Apulians and Sicilians
and Romans say *thou* to the Emperor or the Pope himself, while
the Lombards say *you* not only to a child but even to a hen or a
cat or a piece of wood " (120). He admits, indeed, that " even
good Prelates have their persecutors and evil-speakers and
scorners," (120) for there are always sons of Belial, unbridled
and uncontrolled, like those who despised Saul. But he harks
back to the same complaints. " Doctors prescribe to their patients
many things which they themselves will not do when they are
sick : so Prelates know how to teach their subjects many things
which they will not do themselves : as the Lord said, ' For they
say and do not ' (122). As to what we said above, that he
who is chosen to a Prelacy should know his own insufficiency, if
he be insufficient, we say here that this can seldom be, for whosoever has dominion and authority believes himself forthwith
altogether sufficient, both in wisdom and in eloquence and in all
things necessary to a Prelate " (123). He is apparently thinking
mainly of the older Orders when he complains, *à propos* of

Ecclesiasticus xiv. 3, 4 (153) " we often see this fulfilled to the letter; for one Prelate will have much wealth heaped together, yet God doth not grant him power to eat thereof, but another coming after him will scatter them abroad." Against similar faults he has already quoted (136) " the example of that rich man who gave nought to the poor, and was utterly given up to gluttony and lechery, nor would he hear Mass or Gospel. So when the priests and clergy sang a Requiem over his corpse, the Crucifix thrust its fingers into its ears, saying that it would in no wise hear the man who had scorned to hear its voice." Prelates are apt to be hasty-tempered, and to excuse themselves by pleading a choleric complexion : such have no business in office, for (as we may see from Ecc. x. 5-7), " we cannot reduce a fool to silence by promoting him to the dignity of a Prelacy. This we see done daily ; for a man is promoted who is not worth three pence, (unless he chance to have them in his mouth) ; and this is done of private affection, while another man, though fit and sufficient, will find no grace." Nowadays, indeed, as often in the past, a man risks his immortal soul by accepting promotion in the Church (142) : a saint of old once cut off his own ears to avoid being made Bishop, and, when this proved an insufficient protection, swore that he would cut out his tongue also unless they left him in peace. This holy man, continues our chronicler, resembled the beaver, who will mutilate himself to escape from his pursuers. He cites the well-known example of Geoffroi de Péronne, prior of Clairvaux, who "was chosen Bishop of Tournay and whom Pope Eugenius and his abbot St. Bernard would have compelled to submit to the burden : but he fell on his face in the form of a cross at the feet of the abbot and the clergy who had elected him, saying : ' I may indeed, if ye elect me, be a runaway monk, but I shall never be a bishop.' When he was in his death-agony a monk, his dear friend, who sat by his bedside, said : ' Dear friend, now that we are being separated in the body, I pray thee (if by God's will thou art able) to reveal me thy state after death.' So, as he prayed after his friend's death in front of the altar, Geoffrey appeared to him in a vision saying : ' Lo here am I, Geoffrey thy brother ! ' To whom the other said ' Dear friend, how is it with thee ? ' Whereunto he replied, ' I am well ; but it has been revealed to me by the Holy Trinity that, if I had been promoted to a bishopric, I should have been among the number of the damned.' "

It will be as well to close this chapter with the summary of another most characteristic digression of Salimbene's. He has been quoting many shining examples of the past who might well

shame the authorities of his day into something better (132).
For post-Biblical times he chooses as typical heroes Saints
Silvester, Nicholas, and Thomas of Canterbury. The mention
of St. Nicholas leads him into a tirade which reads like a
fragment of the Wife of Bath's Prologue. It may well be
commended to the notice of those who have hastily inferred
that, because the Franciscans exaggerated the already exaggerated devotion to the Virgin Mary, they were therefore
possessed with a " chivalric respect for women " and " restored
woman to her rightful position in Christian society."[7] Salimbene,
it must be remembered, was no *farouche* ascetic : he tells us
more than once of the charming ladies whose director he has
been ; he was far from holding, with St. Bonaventura's cherished
secretary, that women are not fit objects for a friar even to gaze
upon. The quotations which he here heaps together are simply
commonplaces of the Middle Ages, and represent the ordinary
clerical attitude towards the fair sex. " Note," he writes, " that
it is said of St. Nicholas, 'he avoided the company of women' :
and herein he was wise ; for it was women who deceived the
children of Israel (Num. xxxi.). Wherefore it is written in
Ecclesiasticus, ' Behold not every body's beauty ; and tarry
not among women. For from garments cometh a moth, and
from a woman the iniquity of a man.' Again, in Ecclesiastes,
' I have found a woman more bitter than death, who is the
hunter's snare, and her heart is a net, and her hands are bands.
He that pleaseth God shall escape from her : but he that is a
sinner, shall be caught by her.' In Proverbs again, ' Why art
thou seduced, my son, by a strange woman, and art cherished
in the bosom of another ? ' Again in the sixth chapter, ' Let not
thy heart covet her beauty, be not caught with her winks : For
the price of a harlot is scarce one loaf : but the woman catcheth
the precious soul of a man.' And again in the twenty-third, ' For
a harlot is a deep ditch : and a strange woman is a narrow pit.
She lieth in wait in the way as a robber, and him whom she
shall see unwary, she shall kill.' Moreover, Jerome saith, ' It is
perilous to be ministered to by one whose face thou dost frequently
study ' :* and again, ' Believe me, he cannot be whole-hearted
with God to whom women have close access ' ; and again, ' With
flames of fire doth a woman sear the conscience of him who
dwelleth by her ' ; and again, ' Where women are with men,

---

* Lady readers may be glad to learn that, among all the *soi-disant* patristic
quotations in this passage, only this first from St. Jerome is genuine. Prof.
Holder-Egger has tracked six of the rest to spurious works of the Fathers here
named ; but even his industry has not been able to indentify the remaining two.

there shall be no lack of the devil's birdlime.' Again the poet saith, 'Wouldst thou define or know what woman is? She is glittering mud, a stinking rose, sweet poison, ever leaning towards that which is forbidden her.' And another poet, ' Woman is adamant, pitch, buckthorn, † a rough thistle, a clinging burr, a stinging wasp, a burning nettle.' And yet another, 'Man hath three joys—praise, wisdom, and glory : which three things are overthrown and ruined by woman's art ' : and Augustine saith, ' As oil feedeth the flame of a lamp, so doth a woman's conversation feed the fire of lust.' And Isidore, ' As the green grass groweth by the waterside, so also groweth concupiscence by looking upon women.' And John Chrysostom : ' What else is woman but a foe to friendship, an inevitable penance, a necessary evil, a natural temptation, a coveted calamity, a domestic peril, a pleasant harm, the nature of evil painted over with the colours of good : wherefore it is a sin to desert her, but a torment to keep her.' And Augustine : ' Woman was evil from the beginning, a gate of death, a disciple of the serpent, the devil's accomplice, a fount of deception, a dogstar to godly labours, rust corrupting the saints ; whose perilous face hath overthrown such as had already become almost angels.' Likewise Origen : ' Lo, woman is the head of sin, a weapon of the devil, expulsion from Paradise, mother of guilt, corruption of the ancient law.' " To this whole page Salimbene has affixed the heading " Here the author shows that women are to be avoided : see below folio 323." And on that folio (p. 270) he subjoins another string of the same or similar quotations, with the addition of one (genuine, alas ! this time) from St. Augustine. " Among all the Christian's battles the sorest are the struggles of chastity, wherein is continual conflict and seldom victory " : a warning which is enforced by the tale of St. Chrysanthus and his temptations.

We see then that, in spite of all Salimbene's varied interests and thoroughly human point of view, even in spite of his little religious idylls, there was one hiatus in his sympathies. He might have thousands of women under his spiritual guidance ; he might strike up piquant and dangerous Platonic friendships with one or two ; but his very profession shut him off from that free and natural social intercourse without which neither sex can really understand the other.

> " For, trusteth wel, it is impossible
> That any clerk wol speke good of wyves,
> (But if it be of hooly Seintes lyves),
> Ne of noon other womman never the mo."
>   CHAUCER, *Cant. Tales*, D. 688.

† From which a sort of Black Draught was concocted in the Middle Ages.

CHAPTER IX.

Convent Friendships.

SALIMBENE was eminently a sociable man, and he has much to tell us of his friends. Many such descriptions will come later on in other contexts, but it will be well to collect in this chapter such scattered notices as may give an idea of the cheerful side of Franciscan life, in contrast to the troubles and discontents to which he so frequently alludes.

The Friars were still, until some time after his death, the most real intellectual and moral force in Christendom. All the great Schoolmen of this period were Friars; all or nearly all the great preachers; and the movement gave a great stimulus to poetry and to art. Salimbene found in his Order full scope for his love of travel, his eager (if somewhat random) curiosity, and his passion for music. All his closest friends seem to have been musicians; and he has left us delightful portraits of these minstrels of God. (181) "Brother Henry of Pisa was a comely man, yet of middle stature, free-handed, courteous, liberal, and ready. He knew well how to converse with all, condescending and conforming himself to each man's manners, gaining the favour both of his own brethren and of secular persons, which is given but to few. Moreover, he was a preacher of great weight and favour with both clergy and people. Again, he was skilled to write, to miniate (which some call *illuminate*), for that the book is illuminated with the scarlet *minium*),[1] to write music, to compose most sweet and delightful songs, both in harmony and in plain-song. He was a marvellous singer; he had a great and sonorous voice, so that he filled the whole choir; but he had also a flute-like treble, very high and sharp; sweet, soft, and delightful beyond measure. He was my Custos in the Custody of Siena, and my master of song in the days of Pope Gregory IX. Moreover he was a man of good manners and devoted to God and the Blessed Virgin and Blessed Mary Magdalene; and no wonder, for the church of his *contrada* at Pisa was dedicated to this saint. Having heard a certain maidservant tripping through the cathedral church of Pisa and singing in the vulgar tongue,

> " If thou carest not for me,
> I will care no more for thee,"

he made then, after the pattern of that song, words and music of this hymn following :—

> "Christ Divine, Christ of mine,
> Christ the King and Lord of all." [2]

Moreover, because when he was Guardian and lay sick on his bed in the infirmary of the convent of Siena, he could write no music, therefore he called me, and I was the first to note one of his airs as he sang it." Salimbene goes on to enumerate other compositions of Brother Henry's, the last of which reminds him of another musical friend. " Now the second air of these words, that is, the harmony, was composed by Brother Vita of the city of Lucca, and of the Order of Friars Minor, the best singer in the world of his own time in both kinds, namely, in harmony and in plain-song. He had a thin or subtle voice, and one delightful to hear. There was none so severe but that he heard him gladly. He would sing before Bishops, Archbishops, and the Pope himself ; and gladly they would hear him. If any spoke when Brother Vita sang, immediately men would cry out with Ecclesiasticus, 'Hinder not music.' Moreover, whenever a nightingale sang in hedge or thicket, it would cease at the voice of his song, listening most earnestly to him, as if rooted to the spot, and resuming its strain when he had ceased ; so that bird and friar would sing in turn, each warbling his own sweet strains. So courteous was he in this that he never excused himself when he was asked to sing, pleading that he had strained his voice, or was hoarse from cold, or for any other reason ; wherefore none could apply to him those oft-quoted verses [of Horace], 'All singers have this fault, that they can never be brought to sing when they are begged to perform among friends.' He had a mother and sister who were delightful singers. He composed this sequence, ' *Ave mundi*,' both words and air. He composed many hymns in harmony, wherein the Secular clergy specially delight. He was my master of song in his own city of Lucca. Again, the Lord Thomas of Capua having written that sequence, 'Let the Virgin Mother rejoice,' and having begged Brother Henry of Pisa to compose an air to it, he composed one delightful and fair and sweet to hear, whereto Brother Vita composed the secondary air, or harmony ; for whenever he found any plain-

chant of Brother Henry he would gladly compose a harmony
thereto. Moreover, the Lord Philip, Archbishop of Ravenna,
took this Brother Vita to be of his household, both because he
was of his own country, and because he was a Friar Minor,
and because he knew so well to sing and write. He died at
Milan, and was buried in the Convent of the Friars Minor. He
was slender and lean of body, and taller of stature than Brother
Henry. His voice was fitter for the chamber than for the choir.
Oft-times he left the Order, and oft-times returned : yet he never
left us but to enter the Order of St. Benedict ; and when he
wished to return, Pope Gregory IX was ever indulgent to him,
both for St. Francis's sake, and for the sweetness of his song.
For once he sang so enchantingly that a certain nun, hearing his
song, threw herself down from a window to follow him ; but this
might not be, for she broke her leg with the fall.   This was no
such hearkening as is written in the last chapter of the Song of
Songs, ' Thou that dwellest in the gardens, the friends hearken :
make me hear thy voice.'   Truly, therefore, spake Brother Giles
of Perugia (not that he was of Perugia, but that there he lived
and ended his days—a man given to ecstasies and rapt in divine
contemplation, the fourth Brother admitted to our Order, after
St. Francis—), truly he spake, ' It is a great grace of God to have
no graces at all,' speaking here of graces not given freely by
God, but acquired, by reason whereof some men are frequently
led into evil."   The celebrated Helinand of Froidmont, it may
be noted, speaks still more strongly of the dangers of music to
the Religious, " whether of instruments, or of the human
voice . . . . . as Orpheus with his lute followed his desire
even to hell. In further proof whereof, mark that thou shalt
scarce find a man of light voice and grave life . . . . . I have
seen numberless men and women whose life was so much the
more evil as their voice was more sweet."   Benvenuto, again,
while noting how Casella too belied Horace's sarcasm by singing
without delay at Dante's request, and while laying stress on the
sovereign virtues of good music, speaks of the danger of
elaborate church music, " wherefore Athanasius, to avoid vanity,
forbade the custom of singing in church, ... and a
certain good and prudent man who had the care of a great convent of nuns forbade them to celebrate their church services with
song."[3]   This Puritan estimate of song was far more common
before the Reformation than is generally realised ; and even
St. Francis was believed by many to have forbidden church
music.
     But to return to Brother Henry.   " In truth Brother Henry of

Pisa was my intimate friend, and such as he of whom the Wise Man saith 'A man amiable in society shall be more friendly than a brother'; for he himself also had a brother in the Order of my age, and I a brother of his age; yet he loved me far more, as he said, than his own blood-brother. And whereas Ecclesiasticus saith 'The token of a good heart and of a good countenance thou shalt hardly find, and with labour,' yet this could in no wise be said of him. He was made Minister of Greece, which is the Province of Romania, and gave me a letter of obedience, whereby, if it pleased me, I might go to him and be of his Province, with a companion of my own choice. Moreover, he promised that he would give me a Bible and many other books. But I went not, for he departed this life in the selfsame year wherein he went thither. He died at a certain Provincial Chapter, celebrated at Corinth, where also he was buried and hath found rest in peace. Moreover he foretold the future in the hearing of the Brethren who were in that Chapter, saying, 'Now are we dividing the books of departed Brethren; but it may be that within a brief while our own too shall be divided.' And so it came to pass : for in that same Chapter his books were divided."

Though Brother Henry worked no miracles himself, yet he had long been of the household of the miracle-working Patriarch of Antioch. The reader will not fail to notice how many of Salimbene's friends and acquaintances were distinguished in life or in death by these thaumaturgic powers. From the matter-of-fact frequency with which he notes the fact, one might almost fancy that he half expected the same of his own bones, when he should come in his turn to lie in the "good thick stupefying incense-smoke" of the choir at Montefalcone or at Reggio.* Miracles were in the air : the earlier volumes of Wadding teem with notices of obscure but wonder-working friars. In many cases, their very names had been forgotten within a century or two of their death ; only a vague memory was cherished among the Brethren that "a saint is buried in our convent."[4]

Another intimate friend was Brother Roland of Pavia, humble and eloquent, of whom Salimbene relates one miracle of the stereotyped pattern. There is, however, far more individuality in (556) "Brother Nicholas of Montefeltro . . . who was many years Minister of Hungary, and afterwards for many years, even to the day of his death, he dwelt in subjection in the convent of Bologna. He was humble beyond all men whom I have ever

---

* A miracle-working Brother Salimbene was in fact buried at Rodi ; but he can scarcely be our chronicler (Eubel. *Provinciale*, p. 53).

seen in this world. He neither thought nor would have others to think that he was anything at all : so that, when any man would do him reverence, forthwith he would fall to the ground and kiss his feet, if he might. When the refectory bell was rung for meals, it was he who came first to pour water into the lavatory for the Brethren's hands : and when strange Brethren came, he would hasten first of all the convent to wash their feet ; and though in appearance he was ill-fitted to perform such offices, for he was aged and corpulent, yet his charity and humility and holiness and courtesy and liberality and readiness made him skilful and pleasant and proper thereto. He lieth buried honourably in the church of the Friars Minor of Bologna. After his death God showed forth no miracle through him, for that he had prayed God that he might work none ; as also that most holy Brother Giles of Perugia had besought God to show forth no miracles on his behalf after his death. (This was the Brother Giles, whose life Brother Leo, one of the three special companions of St. Francis, wrote at some length.) But in his lifetime Brother Nicholas wrought three miracles—or God through him—which are worthy to be related. The first was that the Guardian of a certain convent had laid upon a certain young friar, who was also a clerk and sub-deacon, the duty of cooking the Brethren's soup or pottage for God's sake, until the cook, who was absent, should return. He then obeyed in all humility ; but by evil fortune his breviary fell into the pot and was utterly sodden with the pottage. Since therefore the book was thus foully destroyed, and the Brother wept and wailed,— for this was his greatest cause of grief, that the book was borrowed—Brother Nicholas hearing this, and willing to console him, said, ' See, son, weep no more, but lend me the book, which I need awhile for saying Hours.' And having taken the book, he went apart and poured forth his soul in prayer ; and behold, God restored it to its former beauty, so that no spot or blemish appeared thereon. And the Brother who had before wept so bitterly at the destruction of the book, seeing this, was comforted and filled with admiration, and gave praise to God." The next miracle of Brother Nicholas was of a more commonplace character ; but the third is truly original. " There was a certain youth in the convent of Bologna who was called Brother Guido. He was wont to snore so mightily in his sleep that no man could rest in the same house with him ; and, what is more, he made their waking-hours as hideous as their sleep-time : wherefore he was set to sleep in a shed among the wood and straw : yet even so the Brethren could not escape him, for the sound of that accursed rumbling echoed throughout the whole convent. So all the priests and discreet Brethren gathered together in the chamber of Brother John of Parma, the Minister-General, and told him of this boy, how he must be cast utterly forth from the Order by reason of this monstrous fault; and I myself was there present. And it was decreed by a formal sentence that he should be sent back to his mother, who had deceived the Order, since she knew all this of her son before he was received among us. Yet was he not sent back forthwith; which was the Lord's doing, Who purposed to work a miracle through Brother Nicholas. For this holy man, considering within himself that the boy must needs be cast out through a defect of nature, and without guilt on his own part, called the lad daily about the hour of dawn to come and serve him at his Mass: and at the end of the Mass, the boy would kneel at his bidding behind the altar, hoping to receive some grace of him. Then would Brother Nicholas touch the boy's face and nose with his hands, desiring, by God's gifts, to bestow on him the boon of health, and bidding him reveal this secret to no man. In brief, the boy was suddenly and wholly healed; and thenceforth he slept in peace and quiet, like any dormouse, without further discomfort to the Brethren. Afterwards he was transferred to the Province of Rome, where he became a priest and confessor and preacher, most serviceable and profitable to the Brethren, ever thankfully remembering the grace bestowed on him through the merits and prayers of the blessed Nicholas by God, Who is blessed for ever and ever. Amen."

Here again is one more Franciscan of the true type. (429) " Brother Thomas of Pavia was a holy and good man, and a great clerk. He had grown old in the Order; a man of wisdom and discretion, and of good and sober counsel. He was a friendly man, ready, humble, and kindly, and devoted to God, and a gracious and weighty preacher. He wrote a great chronicle, for he was very full and prolix; he made also a treatise of sermons and a great and most diffuse work of theology, which for its size he named 'The Ox.' He reformed the Province of Tuscany. He was a dear friend of mine, for I lived with him many years in the Convent of Ferrara; may his soul, of God's mercy, rest in peace! Amen." Many of Salimbene's other friends and acquaintances were distinguished authors of their time: Brother Benvenuto of Modena, a Greek scholar and a textual critic of the Bible, Master William of Auxerre, to whom the more famous Durandus was deeply indebted; Brother William of the Friars Preachers, " with whom I was familiar: for he was a humble and courteous man, though small of stature ";

and again, " Brother William Britto of the Friars Minor, whose Book is remembered of men ; and who in stature was like unto that other Brother William aforesaid, yet not in manners ; for he seemed rather wrathful and impatient, as is the nature of men who are small of stature : wherefore the poet saith :

' Seldom is the small man humble, seldom hath the long man reason ;
Seldom shalt thou find a red-head but his troth will smack of treason."*

Nearly all the portraits of good friars in this chronicle belong to the same general type :—learned men and busy workers of the first or second generation, who had grown grey in the Order, and whom our friend knew in the tranquil and honoured evening of their life. Here and there, however, we have glimpses of wilder natures in the ferment of their first overwhelming sense of sin, and in all the agonies of conversion. There is the Lord Bernardo Bafolo (1285—364), a knight of great wealth and renown, who entered the Order in its earliest days, and sought to share the reproach of Christ by causing his own servants to scourge him round the city at a horse's tail. As he passed thus by the portico of S. Pietro, " where the knights are wont to sit and make merry in their hours of ease, they were pricked to the heart, saying with groans ' In truth we have seen marvels this day ' ; and many were goaded by his example to leave the world." Two usurers, brethren by blood, restored their ill-gotten gains and joined the Franciscans ; and one of them caused himself to be scourged likewise all round the city, with a bag of money round his neck.   Bernardo Bafolo, whose father had distinguished himself at the storming of Constantinople in 1204, did not leave his own knightly courage behind him when he took the cowl : for " when he was a Friar Minor, and the men of Parma had marched with the Emperor's army against Milan, he ran to the fire which had been kindled in the Borgo di Santa Cristina ; and standing on the top of a burning house, he cut away with an axe and cast down on all sides the blazing timbers, that no other houses might take fire. And all men saw him and commended him that he had wrought prudently and valiantly ; and ' it was reputed him unto justice, to generation and generation for ever-more ' : for this doughty deed of his hath lived many years in men's memories. After this he crossed to the Holy Land, where he ended his days with all praise in the Order of St. Francis. May his soul by God's mercy rest in peace, for he began well and ended well."

* Vix humilis parvus ; vix longus cum ratione ;
Vix reperitur homo ruffus sine proditione (233).

But the greatest by far of Salimbene's friends was John of Parma, a man of very considerable intellectual force, and the Minister-General who trod most closely of all in the steps of St. Francis. For the life of this remarkable man Salimbene is by far our fullest authority : but he writes of him in so prolix and rambling a fashion (296 foll.), and John's life has so often been told elsewhere, that I will abridge it considerably here. His father was called Albert the Fowler ; for he loved fowling and made it his business. But John owed his education to an uncle, priest and Guardian of the Lazar-house at Parma, who sent him to the university. There he fell into an apparently fatal illness, "but one day he was comforted in the Lord and said in the bystanders' hearing, 'The Lord chastising hath chastised me, but He hath not delivered me over to death.'* After this he recovered suddenly of his sickness and began to study with fervour, and walked most manfully in the way of the Lord until he became a Friar Minor ; and then he began to go on most abundantly from virtue to virtue and was full of power and wisdom, and God's grace was with him. He was of middle stature or rather less ; he was shapely in all his limbs, and of a strong complexion and sound and stout to bear labours, both in walking and in study. His face was as an angel's face, gracious and ever bright of cheer : he was free and liberal and courtly and charitable, humble and mild and kindly and patient ; devoted to God and fervent in prayer, pious and gentle and compassionate. He sang Mass daily, and so devoutly that those who stood by felt some of his own grace : he would preach so fervently and well both to the clergy and to the Brethren that, as I have oft-times seen, he provoked many of his hearers to tears : he had a ready tongue that never stumbled, for he was most learned also, having been a good grammarian and a Master in Logic while yet in the world ; and in our Order he was a great theologian and disputator. He was a mirror and an example to all that beheld him ; for his whole life was full of honour and saintliness, and good and perfect manners : he was gracious both to God and man : learned in music and a good singer. Never saw I so swift a writer, in so fair and true a hand ; for his characters were exceeding easy to read. He was a most noble composer in the polished style ; and whensoever he would, he enriched his letters with many wise sentences. He was the first Minister-General who began to go round the whole Order

---

* Cf. Newman—"'All through (my fever in Sicily) I had a confident feeling I should recover . . . . and gave as a reason . . . . 'I thought God had some work for me.'"—*Letters.* vol i., p. 414.

and visit province by province, which had not been the custom
aforetime, except that Brother Aymo once went to England, which
was his native land.   But when Brother Bonagratia would have
thus visited the Order after the example of John of Parma,
the travail was more than he could bear, wherefore he fell
sick unto death within four years of his Generalship, and ended
his life at Avignon.   Moreover Brother John of Parma gave
licence to Brother Bonaventura of Bagnorrea* to lecture at Paris,
which he had never as yet done anywhere : for he was but a
Bachelor and not yet Master.   Moreover, at another time, during
the Chapter of Metz, the Provincials and Custodes said to Brother
John : ' Father, let us make some Constitutions.'   [*i.e.* bye-laws.]
But he answered and said, ' Let us not multiply our Constitutions,
but let us keep well such as we have.   For know that the Poor
Brethren† complain of you that ye make a multitude of Constitutions and lay them on the neck of your subjects, and ye who
make them will not keep them.'   For he looked more to a
Superior's hand than to his tongue : as we read of Julius Cæsar,
who never said to his soldiers ' Go ye and do that,' but ' Let us
go and do it,' ever associating himself with them."   He also
introduced uniformity into the Friars' services : for hitherto
they had made many changes each after his own fancy " either
contrary to the rubrics or altogether beside them, as I have seen
with mine own eyes."

   " Moreover, while he was Lector at Naples, and not yet
Minister-General, he passed through Bologna, and sat down
one day to meat in the guesten-hall with his companions and
with other strangers : then certain Brethren came and took
him by force from the table, that they might bring him to eat
in the infirmary.‡   But he, seeing that his companion was left
uninvited, turned back and said, ' I will eat nowhere without
my companion ' : which was thought great boorishness on the
part of the hosts, and the greatest courtesy and fidelity on Brother
John's part.   Another day, when he was General and would
fain find a moment's leisure, he came to the convent of Ferrara :
and, considering himself that the same Brethren were always
invited to eat with him—that is, the same who had dined with
him, were at supper also, and the same to-day, the same to-morrow
—he saw that our Guardian was a respecter of persons, which
displeased him.   So when Brother John was washing his hands

---

* Saint Bonaventura.

† *i.e.* the Spirituals, with whom he deeply sympathized.

‡ Where the food was always more delicate.

one day for supper, then the Brother on service asked of the Guardian, 'Whom shall I invite?'; and he answered, 'Take Brother Jacopo of Pavia and Brother Avanzio and such an one and such an one.' Now these four had already washed their hands in expectation, and stood ready, behind the General's back, as he had well seen from the first: wherefore he took up his parable, inspired perhaps by the Holy Ghost in the fervour of his spirit, and cried, 'Yea, yea! take Brother John of Pavia, take Brother Avanzio, take this one and that other!—take ten stripes for thyself, for that is a mere goose's song!' So they who had been invited to the meal were confounded and put to shame when they heard this: and the Guardian was no less ashamed, saying to the Minister, 'Father, it was for thine honour that I invited these to bear thee company, since I hold them the most worthy.' The Minister answered, 'Saith not the Scripture, "When thou makest a feast, call the poor, the maimed, the lame, and the blind: and thou shalt be blessed"? (and I heard all this, for I stood by his side). Then said the friar on service, 'Whom then shall I ask?' 'Invite,' said the Guardian, 'as the Minister shall bid thee.' Then said he, 'Go, call me the poor Brethren of the convent; for this office [of eating] is one wherein all know enough to bear their Minister company.' So that friar on service went to the refectory, and said to the feeblest and poorest Brethren, who seldom ate outside the refectory, 'The General inviteth you to supper: I bid you on his part to bear him company forthwith': and so it was. For Brother John, whenever he came to some fresh convent, would ever have the poor Brethren to eat with him, or else all together, or else these and those by turns, that they might have some refreshment by his coming. And thus he would ordain before his guest-table was full, that is, before he went into the refectory to eat, which he ever did forthwith after he was refreshed from his journey and his travail, when he stayed in any convent. So Brother John was no respecter of persons, nor bare he private love for any, but he was most courteous and free at table, so that, if divers sorts of good wine were set before him, he would cause equal portions to be poured out for all, or else he would pour it into a great cup, that every man might drink alike, which was esteemed by all to be an excellent courtesy and charity. Moreover, even when he was Minister-General, whensoever the bell was rung for cleaning the vegetables or herbs for the table, he would come to the convent-workers and labour with the other Brethren, as I have oft-times seen with mine own eyes: and, being familiarly known to him, I said to him, 'Father, ye do as the Lord taught: "He that is the leader among you, let him be as he that serveth." ' And he answered, ' " So it becometh us to fulfil all justice," that is, perfect humility.' Moreover he fulfilled his church services both nightly and daily, and especially Mattins and Vespers and the Conventual Mass, and whatsoever the Cantor laid upon him he obeyed at once, either beginning the antiphons or chanting lessons and responses or singing conventual masses. In short, he was full of all good deeds : he would fain write with his own hands even when he was a General, that he might by his labour earn wherewithal to be clothed : but the Brethren would not suffer this, for they saw him busied with the service of the Order, and therefore they gladly supplied him with all things necessary."

But John, as will be seen in Chapter XIII, was a Joachite ; he apparently did nothing to punish the rash author of the " Introduction to the Eternal Gospel " ; and the scandal of the book fell in a great measure upon him also. His restless energy had already worn out twelve secretaries one after the other : even his own iron frame and cheerful temper must have bent under the discouraging drudgery of visiting convent after convent that was drifting daily farther from the Founder's purpose :[5] and, if Salimbene is right, he met his sentence halfway, calling a special General Chapter to tender his resignation. For a whole day the Chapter refused to accept it, but at last, " seeing the anguish of his soul," they unwillingly consented, and besought him to name his successor : " and forthwith he chose Brother Bonaventura, saying that he knew none better in the whole Order. So Brother Bonaventura held the Generalate for 17 years, and did much good." According to Wadding, it was the Pope who had insisted on this resignation, partly on account of his Joachism, and partly because his efforts to enforce the strict observance of St. Francis's precepts had exasperated a section of the Order : and John gladly obeyed, alleging " his feebleness, his weariness, and his age."[6] Before his fall, John had won golden opinions on all sides : Salimbene tells us of the great respect with which he was treated by princes so different as the emperor Vatatzes ; Henry III of England ; and, " as I saw with mine own eyes," St. Louis and his brothers. Even Popes and Cardinals admired him, in spite of his Joachism. The worldly Innocent IV (304) " loved him as his own soul, and ever welcomed him with a kiss on the mouth when he came to see him, and thought to make him a Cardinal, but was himself overtaken by death." Alexander IV had loved him also ; and even now in his disgrace he found powerful defenders. St. Bonaventura did indeed permit the heresy-hunters to bait his old master, and would even have acquiesced in his imprisonment; the disgust of the Spirituals at this and other concessions to the "relaxed" party found utterance in the vision of blessed Jacopo dalla Massa (*Fioretti* chap. 48). It is true that the compiler of the *Fioretti* takes care, for scandal's sake, to suppress the great General's name: but the earlier versions of the vision in the *Actus* and the *Seven Tribulations* tell us plainly that the bitter adversary, with iron nails like razors, who would fain have torn John of Parma to pieces, was no other than Dante's guide through the twelfth Canto of the Paradiso. John was saved—not, as in the vision, by St. Francis stooping from heaven, but by the intervention of Cardinal Ottobono, afterwards Pope Adrian V. He was allowed to choose his own place of retreat, and selected the secluded hermitage of Greccio, where St. Francis had spent one Christmas and imitated the Manger of Bethlehem. Even in this his exile, he was still remembered at the Roman Court. (304) "When Master Pietro Ispano[7] was made first a Cardinal and then presently Pope John XXI, being a great dialectician and logician and disputer and theologian, he sent for Brother John of Parma, who also had the like qualities. For the Pope would fain have had him ever at his court, and thought to make him a Cardinal; but death overtook him before he could fulfil his purpose; for the vault of his chamber fell upon him and slew him." The next Pope, however, had no less respect for the saintly ex-General. (302) "A long time after [his retirement], Pope Nicholas III took him by the hand and led him familiarly through his palace, saying to him, ' Since thou art a man of much counsel, were it not better for thyself and for thine Order that thou shouldst be a Cardinal here with us at our Court, than that thou shouldst follow the words of fools who prophesy from their own heart?' So Brother John answered and said to the Pope, 'I care nought for your dignities, for it is sung in praise of every saint : "He sought no glory of earthly dignity, but came to the Kingdom of Heaven." As concerning counsel I say unto you that I could indeed give some counsel if there were any who would hear me. But in these days little else is treated in the Court of Rome but wars and buffooneries, instead of matters which concern the salvation of men's souls.' The Pope, hearing this, groaned and said, ' We are so accustomed to such things that we believe all that we say and do to be profitable.' Then answered Brother John, ' And the blessed [Pope] Gregory, as we read in his Dialogues, would have sighed at such things.' So Brother John was sent away and returned to the hermitage of Greccio where he was wont to dwell." Salimbene, in spite of his personal affection, agreed with the criticism passed by a fellow-friar on Brother John, that if he could have given up his Joachism he might have effected some real reform at the Court of Rome. He goes out of his way to account for John's clinging to the creed even after the shock dealt to it by Frederick's premature death in 1250; "Some men so cling to their opinions that they are ashamed afterwards to retract, lest they should seem liars : and therefore they cannot change their minds" (303). He himself once volunteered to go to Greccio and attempt to convert his old master : but he is unwontedly reticent as to the issue of this journey. Later on, however, he gives us two anecdotes of the holy man's life there : (310) a pair of wildfowl built their nest and hatched their brood under his study desk ; and again, an angel came and served for him at Mass when the poor little scholar, who should have served, had overslept himself. " Much more good," continues Salimbene, " have I seen and heard and known of Brother John of Parma, which would be worthy of record ; yet I must omit the rest for brevity's sake and because I am in haste to pass on to other things ; and because the Scripture saith, ' Praise not any man before death.' For he hath lived long and he liveth yet in this year 1284 wherein I write."[8]

Five years afterwards, in the year in which Salimbene himself probably died, John of Parma undertook a second journey to Constantinople for the conversion of the Greeks. He started with the blessing of his general, Acquasparta, and of Pope Nicholas IV, himself a Franciscan ; but at Camerino in the Apennines his strength failed him. As he entered the city he murmured the words of the Psalmist, " This is my rest for ever and ever ; here will I dwell, for I have chosen it." A few days later, he breathed his last among the Brethren, and in the presence of many citizens whom the renown of the stranger's sanctity had attracted to the convent. Dante's Ubertino da Casale, who in former days had made a special pilgrimage to Greccio for the sake of the old man's absolution and blessing, records the vivid and immediate renown of the miracles worked at his tomb. " Seldom do I remember to have read, for a long time past, so many miracles worked by any saint. . . . The less he hath been formally approved by that carnal Church which he most bitterly rebuked, the more richly he would seem to have been endowed in the heavenly Church with the manifold working of miracles." To Angelo Clareno he was one of the four great wonder-workers of the latter 13th century—witnesses of God's power in an age which had almost lost the power of miracles. A hundred and fifty years later, St. Bernardino of Siena calls him *Saint* John, and alludes to a record which attributes more miracles to him than to any other disciple of St. Francis. His tomb was still hung round with a multitude of votive offerings at the beginning of the XVIIIth century, when they were destroyed by "restorers." The original Gothic tomb, which is described as a work of great beauty, had perished at a still earlier restoration. His worship had long been officially recognised, if not by the Pope, at least by the city, so that it remained untouched by that Papal decree of 1675, which forbade the cult of unauthorised saints unless they could show a prescription of at least 100 years. John was formally beatified by Pius VI in 1777, so that Salimbene's friend has now his special Mass and Offices among the services of the Roman Church.[9]

Our chronicler claims also to have known intimately all the twelve " companions " or secretaries whom John wore out successively by his long journeys on foot from convent to convent ; and he paints most of them with vivid touches (550 foll.). First comes Brother Mark of the swift untiring pen ; " an honest and holy man who lived to a great age ; he was of Modena, and lies buried at Urbino where he coruscates with miracles. He was a good writer and swift and easily understood : and for the labour which he bore as companion to Ministers-general and in writing their letters, he earned for himself the decree in a general chapter that each priest in the Order should, after his decease, say a funeral mass for his soul. He was a special friend of mine, and he dearly loved Brother Bonaventura, the Minister-General, so that after his death, whensoever he recalled his great learning and all the graces that were his, he would burst into tears at the sweetness of that memory. Moreover, when Brother Bonaventura was to preach before the clergy, Brother Mark would go to him and say, ' Thou art but an hireling, and when thou preachedst last, thou knewest not what to say ; but I hope thou wilt not do so this time.' Thus said Brother Mark that he might provoke him to speak the better ; and yet he would write down all Brother Bonaventura's sermons for his own use ! But Brother Bonaventura rejoiced when Brother Mark reviled him, for five reasons ; first, because he was a kindly and patient man ; secondly, because therein he imitated St. Francis ; thirdly, because he was assured that the Brother loved him dearly ; fourthly, because he had an occasion of avoiding vainglory ; and fifthly, because it gave him an occasion of greater prudence." Next comes Brother Andrew of Bologna, Minister of the Holy Land and Penitentiary to the Pope. " The third was Brother Walter,

English by birth, and a truly angelic man.* He was a good singer, slender, and of seemly stature, a goodly man to see, of holy and honest life, well-mannered and learned. Moreover, Brother Walter was sent to stay at the Court of Rome, but he laboured all he could to be removed thence, rather choosing to be afflicted with the people of God than to have the pleasure of sin for a time, esteeming the reproaches of Christ greater riches than the treasure of the Egyptians. Yet I have heard of this Walter that afterwards against his will he was made a Bishop, I know not where. He was my friend. And note that all the comrades of Brother John of Parma were my intimate and familiar friends. The fourth was Brother Bonagiunta of Fabriano, a good Guardian and a learned man, a good singer, preacher and writer, bold, and of middling stature, and with a face like St. Paul. When I was a novice in the convent of Fano in the year 1238, he was a youth and lived there with me. He was first and last Bishop of Recanati. The fifth was Brother John of Ravenna, big and corpulent and black, a good man, and of honest life. Never saw I a man who so loved to eat macaroni with cheese"—yet, as a native of Parma, Salimbene must have had great opportunities in this line. " The sixth was Anselmo Rabuino of the city of Asti in Lombardy, big and black, with the figure and bearing of a prelate, and of honest and holy life ; he was a judge while in the world ; he was Minister of the Province of Terra di Lavoro." The Brethren looked upon him as a saint (315). " The seventh was Brother Bartolomeo Guiscolo of Parma, a great orator and a great Joachite, a courtly and liberal man, who in the world had been a Master in Grammar, of honest and holy life in the Order. He could write, illuminate, and preach. The eighth was Brother Guidolino Gennaro of Parma, a learned man and a good singer, who sang excellently both in harmony and in plainsong. His singing was better than his voice, for he had a very slender voice. He was a good writer, and his hand-writing also was good and fair. And he corrected texts well in the convent at Bologna, for he knew the text of the Bible excellently, and was of honest and holy life, so that the Brethren loved him. The ninth was Brother Giacomino da Berceto, Guardian of the convent at Rimini, a man of honest and holy life, and a good preacher, having a mighty voice. The tenth

---

* The text has "*Anglicus natione, et homo vere angelicus:* " there can be no doubt that the writer intended a pun here : (cf. *Sussex Arch. Coll.*, vol. vii, p. 219.) Salimbene seems always so interested in his English friends that it is a thousand pities he died a few years too soon to have known the Adam Goddam who (in spite of his truly medieval nickname) was a pillar of the English province in 1320 (Wadding, 1320, § 1).

was Brother Jacopo degli Assandri of Mantua, a man of honest and holy life, and excellently versed in the Decretals, and in giving counsel. The eleventh was Brother Drudo, Minister of Burgundy, lector in theology, who would daily preach to the Brethren concerning Divine influences, as I heard with mine own ears, when I was in Burgundy with him. He was a noble and comely man, and of incredibly honest and holy life, for he was marvellously devoted to God beyond all thought of man. The twelfth was Brother Bonaventura da Iseo, who was ancient both in the Order and in age, wise and industrious, and most sagacious, and a man of honest and holy life, and beloved of Ezzelino da Romano ; yet he played the lord ('*baronizabat*') above measure, seeing that his mother, as men said, was hostess of a tavern. He wrote a great volume of sermons for the Sundays and Feast-days of the year. His end was praiseworthy ; may his soul rest in peace ! And note that Brother John of Parma, when he was Minister-General, had not all the aforesaid comrades travelling with him at the same time, but successively ; for he would go round and visit the Order, and his comrades could not endure the labour— therefore he needed to have a multitude of comrades. These twelve aforesaid had in them much good which I have omitted for brevity's sake."

But Salimbene was not familiar with saints alone ; we get constant references to such personages as Buondio the Jew (394), or Asdente, the harmless cobbler-prophet of Parma, whom Dante thrust so rudely down to Hell.[10] He dwells, too, with pardonable pride on his noble friends. (467) "In the year 1261 died the Lord Simon de Manfredi. He was my friend, and a good and valiant fighter for the Church party at the time of the Great War." Again, (377) "The Lady Mabel, daughter of the Lord Markesopolo* Pallavicini, was married by her father before I entered the Order, and she came from Soragna to Parma, and lodged near the church of St. Paul. And her father gave her a dowry of £1,000 Imperial, and wedded her to the Lord Azzo, Marquis of Este,[11] who was a good man and courteous, humble and gentle and peaceful, and a friend of mine. For once I read to him the Exposition of the Abbot Joachim on the Burdens of Esaias, and he was alone with me and another Friar Minor under a fig-tree. The Lady Mabel likewise was devoted to me, and to all men of Religion, and especially to the Friars Minor, to whom she confessed, and whose Offices she always said, and in whose church at Ferrara she was buried

* ? Marchese Paolo.

by her husband's side, and rests in peace. She did much good in
her lifetime, and at her death scattered abroad and gave to the
poor many alms of her possessions. Seven years I dwelt at
Ferrara, where she likewise dwelt. She was a fair lady, wise,
clement, benign, courteous, honest, and pious, humble, and ever
devoted to God. She was not avaricious of her goods, but freely
she gave to the poor. She had a furnace in an inner chamber of
her palace, as I have seen with mine own eyes, and she herself
made rose-water and gave it to the sick ; wherefore the physicians
stationary* and apothecaries loved her the less. But she cared
for none of these things, if only she might succour the sick,
and please God. Many years she lived with her husband, and
was ever barren. But after the death of her husband she caused
a house to be built for her beside the convent of the Friars Minor,
and there she dwelt in her widowhood. May her soul, through
God's mercy, rest in peace, for she was a virtuous lady. After
the death of the Marquis she came to Parma, and I was there,
and heard from her that she was in marvellous comfort, for that
she was hard by the convent of the Friars Minor, and the church
of the glorious Virgin. Never saw I any lady who so brought to
my mind the Countess Matilda,[12] according to all that I have
found written of her." Her father, Markesopolo, had long since
found himself unable to keep up his old baronial dignity in the
new and prosperous Parma, "for he was noble and great-hearted,
and therefore took it ill that any man of the people soever,
whether of the city or of the country around, might send an
ambassador with a red fillet on his brow, and draw him to the
Palazzo Communale to go to law with him before the judges."
So he went off and fought in Greece, where he was treacherously
slain in his own house : ' for all things obey the power of money.'[13]
Moreover, the Lord Rubino, his brother, dwelt in Soragna, and
had to wife the Lady Ermengarda da Palude. She was a fair lady,
but wanton, of whom we might say with Solomon, ' A golden ring
in a swine's snout, a woman fair and foolish.' The Lord Rubino
was old and full of days, and sent for me in the year of the
great mortality (1259), and confessed to me and made his soul
right with God, and died in good old age, passing from this
world to the Father. But his wife took another husband, one
Egidio Scorza ; and afterwards she fell down from an upper
chamber, and died and was buried." For Salimbene is always
laudably anxious to bring his heroes to a good end, and to record
how his villains had their reward at last.

* *i.e.*, those who kept shops.

CHAPTER X.

The Siege of Parma.

IN spite of the distant thunder of the Brother Elias storm, Salimbene's first years in those Tuscan convents seem to have been among the most peaceful of his life. At Cremona, however, in the ninth year after his reception, he found himself a close spectator of one of the most savage and prolonged wars in civilized history. The conflicts of thirteenth century Italy between Pope and Emperor on the one hand, and jealous cities on the other, have seldom been surpassed in horror among Christian nations. The bitterest period of those conflicts began with the renewed excommunication and deposition of Frederick II by Innocent IV in 1245. Salimbene describes Frederick's spirit at this time as that of "a bear robbed of her whelps." The war speedily degenerated into a chaos of sickening atrocities and reprisals : I give a few of the entries as specimens.

In 1239 "The Emperor caused castles of wood to be made, to fight with the men of Brescia : and on those castles he placed the captives whom he had taken. But the men of Brescia smote the said castles with their mangonels, without any hurt to the captives who were therein ; and they for their part hanged up by the arms, without the palisade of their town, such of the Emperor's men as they had taken captive" (95). In 1246 "Tebaldo Francesco and many other barons of Apulia rebelled against the deposed Emperor Frederick; and after a long siege they were taken in the castle of Cappozio, and miserably tormented, both men, women, and little children." In the year following, "Ezzelino laid waste the whole diocese of Parma, on this side of the Lencia toward the castle of Bersello :—and the Mantuans for their part burnt the whole diocese of Cremona from Torricella downwards. For it was a fierce war, and tangled, and perilous" (178). In a war of this description, the first advantage would seem to lie with the more barbarous and unscrupulous of the two parties : and there can be little doubt that, on the whole, this bad pre-eminence was with the Ghibellines. With the help of his unspeakable lieutenant Ezzelino,

Frederick had devastated the north of Italy, and was already thinking of crossing the Alps to attack the Pope in his refuge at Lyons, when the sudden revolt of Salimbene's own native city struck the blow which was destined to ruin his hopes. It was the old story: the Imperialists of Parma had in the previous year expelled all the principal Guelfs from the city, and burnt their houses; so that these desperate men, having nothing further to lose, led a forlorn hope which turned the whole tide of the war. (188) "In the year of our Lord 1247 a few banished knights, dwelling at Piacenza, who were valiant, vigorous, and strong, and most skilled in war—these men were in bitterness of spirit, both because their houses in Parma had been torn to the ground, and because it is an evil life to wander as guest from house to house[1]—for they were exiles and banished men, having great households and but little money, for they had left Parma suddenly lest the Emperor should catch them in his toils—these men, I say, came from Piacenza and entered Parma, and expelled the Emperor's party on the 15th day of June, slaying the Podesta of Parma, who was my acquaintance and friend, and dearly beloved of the Brethren Minor.

Now there were many reasons why these banished men were easily able to take the city . . . The third reason is that on that day the Lord Bartolo Tavernario gave his daughter in marriage to a certain Lord of Brescia, who had come to Parma to fetch her; and those who met the exiles as they came to attack the city had eaten at that banquet, so that they were full of wine and over-much feasting; and they arose from table and fondly thought to overthrow all at the first onset. Seeing therefore that they were as men drunk with wine, their enemies slew and scattered them in flight. The fourth is that the city of Parma was wholly unfenced, and open in all directions. The fifth is that those who came to invade the city folded their hands on their breasts, thus making the sign of the Cross to all whom they met, saying, 'For the love of God and the Blessed Virgin His Mother, who is our Lady in this city, may it please you that we return to our own city, whence we were expelled and banished without fault of our own; and we come back with peace to all, nor are we minded to do harm to any man.' The men of Parma who had met them unarmed along the street, hearing this, were moved to pity by their humility, and said to them, 'Enter the city in peace, in the name of the Lord, for our hand also shall be with you in all these things.' The sixth is that they who dwelt in the city did not concern themselves with these matters, for they neither held with those who had come in, nor did they

fight for the Emperor; but bankers or money-changers sat at
their tables, and men of other arts worked still at their posts as
though nought were." Our author presently goes on to describe,
in the words which I have already quoted in full, that horrible
devastation of the country which he expressly dates from "the
time when Parma withdrew from Frederick's allegiance, and
clave to the Church."

To Salimbene, this revolt was but a natural consequence of
the Pope's ban, which had reduced the Emperor to the state of
"a bird whose wing feathers have been plucked away." But
the blow only roused Frederick to greater exertions. His son
Enzio, who was the nearest imperialist commander, might have
retrieved the disaster by a sudden counterstroke: but he lacked
the necessary nerve. (193) "When King Enzio heard that the
Guelf exiles had entered Parma by force, leaving the siege of
Quinzano, he came by a forced night march, not singing but
groaning inwardly, as is the wont of an army returning from a
rout. I lived in those days in the convent of the Friars Minor
at Cremona, wherefore I knew all these things well. For at
early dawn the men of Cremona were assembled forthwith with
the King to a Council, which lasted even to high tierce (*i.e.* past
9 o'clock); after which they ate hurriedly and went forth to the
very last man, with the Carroccio in their van. There remained
not in Cremona one man who was able to march and fight in
battle; and I am fully persuaded that if they had marched
without delay to Parma and quitted themselves like men, they
would have recovered the city. For if one enemy knew how
it fared in all things with his enemy, he might oft-times smite
him; but by the will of God King Enzio halted with the army
of Cremona by the Taro Morto, and came not to Parma, that
the Lord might bring evil upon them. For he wished to wait
there until his father should come from Turin. Meanwhile
succour came daily from all parts to the men of Parma who had
entered the city: and the citizens made themselves a ditch
and a palisade, that their city might be shut in against the
enemy. Then the Emperor, all inflamed with wrath and fury
at that which had befallen him, came to Parma; and in the
district called Grola, wherein is great plenty of vineyards and
good wine (for the wine of that land is most excellent), he built
a city, surrounded with great trenches, which also he called
Victoria, as an omen of that which should come to pass. And
the moneys which he minted there were called *Victorini*; and
the great church was called after St. Victor. So there Frederick
lodged with his army, and King Enzio with the army of Cremona;

and the Emperor summoned all his friends to come in haste to his succour. And the first who came was the Lord Ugo Boterio, a citizen of Parma, sister's son to Pope Innocent IV ; who, being Podesta of Pavia at that time, came with all the men of Pavia whom he deemed fit for war. Neither by prayers nor by promises could the Pope tear away this nephew of his from the love of Frederick ; and yet the Pope loved his mother best of all his three sisters—for the other two were likewise married in Parma.

After him came Ezzelino da Romano, who in those days was Lord of the Mark of Treviso, and he brought with him a vast army. This Ezzelino was feared worse than the devil : he held it of no account to slay men, women, and children, and he wrought such cruelty as men have scarce heard. On one day he caused 11,000 men of Padua to be burnt in the field of Saint George in the city of Verona ; and when fire had been set to the house in which they were being burnt, he jousted as if in sport around them with his knights. It would be too long to relate his cruelties, for they would fill a great book. I believe most certainly that as the Son of God wished to have one specially whom He might make like unto Himself, namely St. Francis, so the Devil chose Ezzelino. It was of the blessed Francis that it was written that to one servant He gave five talents; for never was there but one man in this world, namely the blessed Francis, on whom Christ impressed the five wounds in likeness of Himself.[2] For, as was told me by Brother Leo, his comrade, who was present when he was washed for burial, he seemed in all things like a man crucified and taken down from the cross.

Furthermore, after Ezzelino many nations came to Frederick's succour, as the men of Reggio and Modena, who were for the Emperor in their several cities, the men of Bergamo also, and other cities, as well of Tuscany as of Lombardy, and other parts of the world which held rather with the Emperor than with the Church. And they came from Burgundy and Calabria and Apulia and Sicily, and from Terra di Lavoro ; and Greeks, and Saracens from Nocera, and well-nigh from every nation under the sun. Wherefore that word of Esaias might have been said to him, ' Thou hast multiplied the nation, and hast not increased the joy ' : and this for many reasons. First, with the aid of his whole host he could but beset that one road from Parma to Borgo San Donnino ; while the rest of the city felt nothing of the siege. Again, whereas the Emperor thought in his heart utterly to destroy the city and to transfer it to the city of Victoria which he had founded, and to sow salt in token of barrenness over the destroyed

Parma ; then the women of Parma, learning this, (and especially the rich, the noble, and the powerful), betook themselves with one accord to pray for the aid of the Blessed Virgin Mary, that she might help to free their city ; for her name and title were held in the greatest reverence by the Parmese in their cathedral church. And, that they might the better gain her ear, they made a model of the city in solid silver, which I have seen, and which was offered as a gift to the Blessed Virgin ; and there were to be seen the greatest and chiefest buildings of the city, fashioned of solid silver, as the cathedral church, the Baptistery, the Bishop's palace, the Palazzo Communale, and many other buildings which showed forth the image of the city. The Mother prayed her Son : the Son heard the Mother, to whom of right He could deny nothing, according to the word which is figuratively contained in Holy Scripture, ' My mother, ask : for I must not turn away thy face.' These are the words of Solomon to his mother. And when the Mother of Mercy had prayed her Son to free her city of Parma from that multitude of nations which was gathered together against it, and when the night was now close at hand, the Son said to His Mother, ' Hast thou seen all this exceeding great multitude ? Behold, I will deliver them into thy hand this day, that thou mayest know that I am the Lord.' " In repeating this dialogue between the Virgin Mary and her Son, Salimbene is of course only a child of his time. It was a commonplace of thirteenth century theology, that " it was not right for the Son to deny His Mother aught" : and a far more blasphemous dialogue to the same effect, which is repeatedly recorded by the Franciscan and Dominican writers, may be found in the first chapter of " Lives of the Brethren." More popular ideas of the Virgin Mary's power over her Son are exemplified by Cæsarius's story of the simple-minded Cistercian lay-brother who was heard to pray, " In truth, Lord, if Thou free me not from this temptation, I will complain of Thee to Thy Mother." The convent was much edified by the lay-brother's simplicity, and by our Lord's humility in condescending to grant a prayer couched in such terms.[3] We have here only the grosser side of the rapidly-growing materialism : the great encyclopedist Vincent of Beauvais, who compiled his work with the help of St. Louis' library, writes of a Pope as saying that " Mary, the Mother of Jesus . . . is the only hope of reconciliation for [sinful] man, the main cause of eternal salvation " (*Spec. Hist.* vii. 95).

Meanwhile the Emperor pushed the siege with an energy proportionate to the bitterness of his disappointment. Salimbene had returned by this time to his native city—probably among those Guelf exiles from Cremona of whom he speaks so feelingly below : and here he found plenty of exciting incidents : for (196) " men went out daily from either side to fight : crossbowmen, archers, and slingers, as I saw with mine own eyes : and ruffians also daily scoured the whole diocese of Parma, plundering and burning on all sides : and likewise did the men of Parma to those of Cremona and Reggio. The Mantuans also came in those days and burnt Casalmaggiore to the ground, as I saw with mine own eyes. And every morning the Emperor came with his men, and beheaded three or four, or as many more as seemed good to him, of the men of Parma and Modena and Reggio who were of the Church party, and whom he kept in bonds : and all this he did on the shingles by the riverside within sight of the men of Parma who were in the city, that he might vex their souls. The Emperor put many innocent men to an evil death, as we see in the case of the Lord Andrea di Trego, who was a noble knight of Cremona, and of Conrad di Berceto, who was a clerk, and valiant in arms, whom he tortured in divers manners with fire and water and manifold torments. The Emperor was wont to slay of these captives at his will ; and especially when he made assault with outrageous words against the city, and when the battle went against him, then would he refresh his soul in the blood of these captives. At one time also certain knights of the Mark of Ancona deserted the Emperor, and fled to Parma ; because at the beginning of the rebellion the Emperor caused many knights of the Mark to be put in ward as hostages in the city of Cremona. And a messenger came from the Emperor bidding five of these knights, even as they washed their hands before supper, to mount their horses forthwith and ride with him to the Emperor. And when they were come to a certain field called Mosa, which is without the city of Cremona, he led them to the gallows, and they were hanged. And these butchers said, ' This is the Emperor's command, for ye are traitors ' ; yet they had come to his succour. On the day following the Brethren Minor came and took them down and buried them ; and scarce could they drive away the wolves from eating them while they yet hung on the gallows. All this I saw, for I lived at Cremona in those days, and in Parma likewise. It would be too long to recount all those of the Church party whom he slew and caused to be slain in those days. For he sent the Lord Gerardo di Canale of Parma into Apulia, and caused him to be drowned in the depths of the sea with a mill-stone at his neck ; and yet he had been at first one of his nearest friends, and had held many offices from him ; and ever he remained with him in the army without Parma. And the Emperor had but this one cause of suspicion against him, that the tower of his mansion in Parma was not destroyed.[4] Wherefore the Emperor would sometimes say to him, laughing in false and feigned jest, ' The men of Parma love us much, my Lord Gerard, for that whereas they tore down in their city the other Ghibelline buildings, they have as yet destroyed neither your tower, nor my palace on the Arena.' Wherein he spoke ironically, but the Lord Gerard understood him not. When therefore I left Parma to go into France, I passed through the village wherein the Lord Gerard then lived ; and he saw me gladly, saying that he was of much profit to the citizens of Parma. And I said to him ' Since the Emperor is besieging Parma, be ye wholly with him or wholly with the citizens, and halt not between two opinions, for it is not to your profit.' Yet he hearkened not unto me ; wherefore we may say of him with the Wise Man ' The way of a fool is right in his own eyes : but he that is wise hearkenth unto counsels.' And note that the Lord Bernard, son of Rolando Rossi of Parma, who was of kindred with the Lord Pope Innocent IV (for he had the Pope's sister to wife), better understood the Emperor's ironical speech than did the Lord Gerard di Canale. For when, as he rode one day with the Emperor, his horse stumbled, then the Emperor said to him, ' My Lord Bernard, ye have an evil horse, but I hope and promise you that within a few days I will give you a better, which shall not stumble.' And the Lord Bernard understood that he spake of hanging him on the gallows : wherefore he was inflamed with indignation against the Emperor, and fled from before his face.[5] Yet the Lord Bernard was the Emperor's gossip and most intimate friend, and well-beloved of him, and when he would enter into his chamber, no man ever denied him the door. But the Emperor could keep no man's friendship ; nay, rather, he boasted that he had never nourished a pig, but that at last he had its grease, which was as much as to say that he had never raised any to riches and honour but that in the end he had drained his purse or his treasure. Which was a most churlish saying, yet we see an example thereof in Pier delle Vigne, who was the greatest counsellor and writer of State papers in the Emperor's court, and was called by the Emperor his chancellor. And yet the Emperor had raised him from the dust ; and afterwards he returned him to the same dust, for he found an occasion of a word and a calumny against him, which was as follows. The Emperor had sent the judge Taddeo and

Pier delle Vigne, whom he loved above all, and who stood above
all others in his court, and certain others he had sent with them
to Lyons to Pope Innocent IV, to hinder the said Pope from
hastening to depose him ; for he had heard that to this end the
Council was being gathered together.   And he had straitly
charged them that none should speak with the Pope without
his fellow, or without the presence of others.   But after they
were returned, his comrades accused Pier delle Vigne that he
had often had familiar colloquy with the Pope without them.
The Emperor therefore sent and caused him to be taken and
slain by an evil death, saying in the words of Job ' They that
were sometime my counsellors have abhorred me : and he whom
I loved most is turned against me.'   For in those days the
Emperor was easily troubled in his mind, because he had been
deposed from the Empire, and Parma had fostered the spirit of
rebellion against him.

So Frederick's affliction and cursedness wherewith he was
inflamed against Parma, endured from the end of the month
of June 1247 to Tuesday the 18th of February 1248, on which
day his city of Victoria was taken.   For the men of Parma went
forth from their city, knights and commons side by side, fully
harnessed for war ; and their very women and girls went out
with them ; youths and maidens, old men and young together.
They drove the Emperor by force from Victoria with all his
horse and foot ; and many were slain there, and many taken
and led to Parma.   And they freed their own captives, whom
the Emperor kept in bonds in Victoria.   And the Carroccio of
Cremona, which was in Victoria, they brought to Parma, and
placed it in triumph in the Baptistery.   But those who loved
not the men of Cremona, (as the Milanese, and Mantuans, and
many others whom the men of Cremona had offended,) when
they came to see the Baptistery, and saw the Carroccio of their
enemies, carried off the ornaments of ' Berta ' (for so was that
Carroccio called) to keep them as relics.   So the wheels alone
and the framework of the carriage remained on the pavement
of the Baptistery : and the mast or pole for the standard stood
upright against the wall.   Moreover the men of Parma spoiled
the Emperor of all his treasure—for he had a mighty treasure
of gold and silver and precious stones, vessels and vestments.
And they took all his ornaments and his imperial crown, which
was of great weight and value, for it was all of gold, inlaid with
precious stones, with many images of goldsmith's work standing
out, and much graven work.   It was as great as a cauldron, for
it was rather for dignity and for great price than as an ornament

for his head ; for it would have hidden all his head, face and all, had it not been raised to stand higher by means of a cunningly disposed piece of cloth. This crown I have held in my hands, for it was kept in the sacristy of the Cathedral of the Blessed Virgin in the city of Parma. It was found by a little man of mean stature, who was called ironically Cortopasso (*Short-step*), and who bore it openly on his fist as men bear a falcon, showing it to all who could see it, in honour of the victory they had gained, and to the eternal disgrace of Frederick. For whatsoever each could seize became his own, nor did any dare to tear aught away from another : nor was a single contentious or injurious word heard there, which was a great marvel. So the aforesaid crown was bought by the men of Parma from this their fellow-citizen, and they gave him for it £200 Imperial, and a house near the Church of Santa Cristina, where of old days had been a pool to wash horses. And they made a statute that whosoever had aught of the treasure of Victoria should have the half for himself, and should give half to the community : wherefore poor men were marvellously enriched with the spoil of so rich a prince.

Now the Emperor's special effects which appertained to war, as his pavilions and things of that kind, were taken by the Legate, Gregorio da Montelungo ; but the images and the relics which he possessed were placed in the sacristy of the Cathedral Church of the Blessed Virgin, to be kept there. And note that of the treasures which were found in Victoria little remained in Parma ; for merchants came from divers parts to buy them, and had them good cheap, and carried them away—namely, gold and silver vessels, gems, unions, pearls and precious stones, garments of purple and silk, and of all things known that are for the use and ornament of men. Note also that many treasures in gold and silver and precious stones remained hidden in jars, chests, and sepulchres, in the spot where the city of Victoria was, and are there even unto these days, although their hiding-places are unknown. Note also that, after the destruction of Victoria, each man recognised so clearly the place in which aforetime he had had his vineyard, that no word of contention or quarrel arose among them. Moreover, at that time when Frederick was put to flight by the men of Parma, the Scripture was fulfilled which saith ' As a tempest that passeth, so the wicked shall be no more.' " Here Salimbene enters upon a lengthy exposition of the eleventh chapter of Daniel, the detailed fulfilment of which he sees in Frederick's career, and especially in the fact that his own illegitimate son Manfred poisoned him by means of a clyster, and was himself slain in battle by Charles of Anjou.

CHAPTER XI.

The Guelfs Victorious.

THOUGH Frederick never recovered from the blow that fell upon him at Victoria, he still hovered about Parma, ravaging the country and waiting for some unguarded moment. The Pope vainly attempted to stir up St. Louis against him. Meanwhile the war raged with varying success. Bernardo Rossi was slain in battle, to the disappointment of Frederick, who had hoped to take him alive and put out his eyes. Next year, however, the tide turned again and the Emperor's natural son Enzio was taken by the Bolognese. (329) " In the year 1249 the Podesta of Genoa came to our convent on the day of Pentecost to hear Mass. And I was there ; and the sacristan was Brother Pentecost, a holy, honest, and good man, who would have rung the bell for the Podesta's coming : but he said, ' Hear first my tidings, for the men of Bologna have taken King Enzio, with a great multitude of the men of Cremona and Modena, and German soldiers.' Now this King Enzio was a valiant man, and bold and stout-hearted ; and doughty in arms, and a man of solace when he would, and a maker of songs : and in war he was wont to expose himself most boldly to perils. He was a comely man, of middle height ; many years the men of Bologna kept him in prison, even to the end of his life. And when one day the gaolers would not give him to eat, Brother Albertino of Verona, who was a mighty Preacher in our Order, went and besought them to give him to eat for God's love and his. And when they gave no ear to his petition, he said to them, ' I will play at dice with you, and if I win, I may then bring him meat.' So they played, and he won, and gave the king meat, and remained in familiar converse with him : and all who heard this commended the friar's charity, courtesy, and liberality.[1] Moreover, the Lord Guido da Sesso, who was the chief of the Emperor's party in the city of Reggio, perished in the flight [of Enzio's army], for he was smothered with his war-horse in the cesspool of the leper-house of Modena. He was a most bitter enemy of the Church party, so that once when many had been taken by the King and doomed to the gallows, and would fain have confessed their sins, he would grant them no respite, saying, ' Ye have no need to confess ; for, being of the Church party, ye are saints, and will go forthwith to Paradise : ' so they were hanged unshriven. Moreover, in those days he would enter with other malefactors into the convent of the Friars Minor ; and calling together the Brethren in the Chapter-house he would demand of each in turn whence he came ; and he let write their names by his notary, saying to each, ' Go thou thy ways, and thou likewise go thy ways, and never dare to appear again in this convent or this city.' And so they expelled all but a few who kept the convent, and even these, as they went begging through the city for their daily needs, were reviled and slandered by him and his men, as though they carried false letters, and were traitors to the Emperor. Neither the Friars Minor nor the Preachers dared to enter the cities of Modena or Reggio or Cremona on their journeys, and if ever any had chanced to enter unwittingly, they were led to the Palazzo Communale and kept in ward ; and having been fed with the bread of affliction and the water of anguish for certain days, they were opprobriously driven out, cast forth and tormented, or even slain. For many were tortured in Cremona and in Borgo San Donnino. In Modena they took the Friars Preachers who had iron moulds for making holy wafers, and led them with many indignities to the Palazzo Communale, saying that they bore stamps to coin false and counterfeit money. Nor did they spare even the Brethren of their own party whose kin were said to be wholly on the Emperor's side, and who themselves also persevered therein ; for Brother Jacopo of Pavia was expelled and thrust forth with ignominy, and Brother John of Bibbiano and Brother Jacopo of Bersello among others ; and, in a word, all in the convent of Cremona who were of the Church party, were dismissed : and I was present in that year. Moreover, they kept Brother Ugolino da Cavazza long waiting in ward at the gate of the city of Reggio, and would not suffer him to enter in, though he had several blood-brethren of the Emperor's party in the city. To speak shortly, they were men of Satan, the chief of whom in malice was one Giuliano da Sesso, a man grown old in evil days, who caused some of the Fogliani family to be hanged, and many others to be slain because they were of the Church party ; and he gloried in these things, saying to his fellows, ' See how we treat these bandits.' This Giuliano was in truth a limb of the fiend ; wherefore God struck him with palsy, so that he was wholly withered up on one side, and his eye started from his head, yet without leaving its socket, but jutting forth outwardly like an arrow, which was loathsome to see. Moreover, he became so stinking that none dared come near him for his superfluity of nastiness, except a certain German damsel whom he kept as a leman, and whose beauty was so great that he who beheld her without pleasure was held most austere. This Giuiliano said in full assembly that it were better to eat quicklime than to have peace with the Church party, though he himself fed on good capons, while the poor were dying of hunger. Yet the prosperity of the wicked endureth not long in this world : for presently the Church party began to prosper ; and then this wretch was driven forth and carried secretly from the city, and died a mass of corruption, excommunicate and accursed ; unhouseled, disappointed, unanel'd. He was buried in a ditch in the town of Campagnola."

In 1250 Frederick gained his last victory against the rebellious city, on that very site of Victoria where his own army had been defeated. He drove them back in such headlong rout that his men would have entered the city pell-mell with the fugitives, had not the Blessed Virgin intervened by breaking the bridge and drowning Guelfs and Ghibellines together in the moat. As it was, the Ghibellines took the Parmese Carroccio with 3,000 prisoners. (335) " They bound their captives on the gravel of the River Taro, as the Lord Ghiaratto told me, who was bound there himself ; and they led them to Cremona and cast them chained into dungeons. There for vengeance sake, and to extort ransom, they practised many outrages on them, hanging them up in the dungeons by their hands and their feet, and drawing out their teeth in terrible and horrible wise, and laying toads in their mouths. For in those days were inventors of new torments, and the men of Cremona were most cruel to the captives of Parma. But the Parmese of the Emperor's party were still worse, for they slew many ; but in process of time the Church party in Parma avenged themselves wondrously."

An interesting side-light is thrown on this account of Salimbene's by the very impartial contemporary Chronicle of Parma published by Muratori (*Scriptores* vol. ix. p. 771 foll.) It tells us of savage reprisals on the part of the citizens : and how " many [imperialists] were caught coming in as spies hidden in hay or straw waggons, or in casks and chests : and such were tortured, confessed, and were burned on the river-beach of the city. And many women were thus caught, put to torment, and burned." The Emperor, adds the Chronicler, beheaded only some ten or twelve of his prisoners, and spared the rest, partly at the prayer

of the men of Pavia, partly because he recognised the uselessness
of such executions. But he kept in bonds about a thousand of
his Guelf prisoners : and "their kinsfolk rejoiced rather in their
death than in their life . . . for oftentimes these prisoners died
in the aforesaid prisons, slain with stench and terror." In the
year 1253 peace was made and all prisoners were released : but
of the thousand only 318 returned to their homes, "since all the
rest had died in the aforesaid prisons by reason of their grievous
and insupportable torments. For daily they were set to the rack,
and hanged upon the engines as upon a cross ; and oft-times
men denied them food ; and they suffered from the stench of
the corpses, for the dead were never drawn forth from prison
until the living had first paid the tax imposed upon them, and
[meanwhile] men gave them no bread : so that the living oft-
times hid their bread and other victuals among the bodies of the
dead, lest their cruel jailors should find them when they locked
up the prison. And the aforesaid prisons wherein the men of the
Church party lay bound were called ' The Hell ' ; and such
indeed they were. The dead had no sepulture, but were cast
into the Po."² The Chronicler expressly mentions that the death
of Bernardo Rossi in the battle of 1248 was avenged by the
cold-blooded execution of four of the chief Ghibelline captives
in Parma ; and that the Emperor retaliated by transporting
fourteen of his Guelf prisoners to his Apulian dungeons.

All this time the Parmese Ghibellines had taken up their
headquarters at Borgo San Donnino, a little town some fourteen
miles N.W. of Parma on the Emilian Way. They long counted
on some such sudden turn of fortune's wheel as that by which
they themselves had lost the city : for they had still partisans
among the citizens. (371) " But in process of time the Parmese
exiles at Borgo San Donnino besought their fellow-citizens of the
Church party that they would vouchsafe to take them into the
city again, for God's sake and the blessed and glorious Virgin's :
for they would have peace, since the Emperor was now dead. So
those made peace with them and brought them into their city,
as I saw with mine own eyes. But they, seeing their houses
destroyed (for this the Church party had done when they expelled
them) began to contend again and to attack the Church party ;
and seeing that Uberto Pallavicino was lord of Cremona and of
many other cities, they thought in their hearts to make him lord
of Parma also. At this the citizens quaked as a rush quakes in
the stream, and set themselves to hide many of their dearest
possessions. I also hid my books (for I lived at Parma then),
and many citizens of the Church party purposed to depart from

the city of their own free will, lest Pallavicino should come and
catch them and spoil their goods. Meanwhile, Parma was full
of rumours of his coming, and yet he came not so soon, since he
had other threads to weave. For he purposed first to take
Colurnio and Borgo San Donnino (as indeed he did), that he might
enter Parma more triumphantly afterwards : seeing that the
Guelfs, driven out from Parma, would have no place of refuge,
and would thus receive checkmate after cherishing the serpent
in their bosom. But suddenly in the meanwhile a man rose up
against him, who dwelt hard by the bridge-head of Parma. This
was a tailor, Giovanni Barisello by name, the son of a farmer
(such as the Parmese call *mezzadro*) on the estate of the Tebaldi.
For he took in his hands a cross and a book of the Gospels, and
went through Parma from house to house of the Ghibelline party,
and made each swear obedience to the Pope's bidding and to the
Church party ; for he had with him a full five hundred armed men
who followed him as their chief. Wherefore many swore obedience
to the Church and the Pope, partly of their free will, partly for
fear of the armed men whom they saw : and such as would not
swear went forth hastily from Parma to dwell at Borgo San
Donnino : for whensoever there was a division between the
citizens of Parma, the exiles had that city of refuge ever at hand ;
whose citizens rejoiced in the discords of Parma, and would have
rejoiced yet more to see her utterly destroyed. For they of Borgo
never loved Parma : nay rather, when Parma was at war, all the
ruffians of Lombardy would gather together there, and Borgo
would receive them gladly for the destruction and confusion of
Parma. Yet the Parmese had done well to Borgo, as I saw with
mine own eyes, for I lived there a whole year in 1259, when the
great plague was throughout Italy. The first benefit was, that
they gave them a Podesta yearly from Parma and paid the half of
his salary. The second, that the citizens might have at Borgo,
without contradiction of the Parmese, the market of all the land
on their side of the river Taro, which is five miles distant from
Parma : and thus they had ten miles of the Bishopric of Parma
for their market, and the Parmese five miles only. The third
was, that the Parmese defended them if they were at war with
the Cremonese or others. The fourth, that, though there were
but two noble houses in Borgo, the Pinkilini and the Verzoli,
and the rest were citizens and rich farmers, yet the Parmese
would marry their noble ladies among them, which was no small
matter. I think I have seen there a score of ladies from Parma,
clothed in fur of vair and in scarlet cloth. In spite of all these
benefits the men of Borgo were ungrateful, and well they deserved

their destruction by the men of Parma when a fit time was come. So this Giovanni Barisello, as he went through Parma and made all the suspects swear, came to the house of the lord Rolando di Guido Bovi, who dwelt at the bridge-head by the church of San Gervasio ; and, calling him forth from his house, he bade him swear fealty to the Church party without further delay, or else depart from Parma as he loved his life. This lord was of the Ghibelline party, and had been Podesta of many cities under the Emperor : yet when he saw so great a multitude gathered together and heard their demands and their threats, he did as the Wise Man saith ' The prudent man saw the evil and hid himself : the simple passed on, and suffered loss.' For he took the oath, saying ' I swear to stand by and obey the precepts of the Pontiff of Rome, and to cleave to the Church party all the days of my life, to the shame of that other most miserable and utterly filthy (*merdiferosae*) party of all that are beneath the sky.' This he said of his own, the Emperor's party, for that they had suffered themselves to be basely trodden under foot by such men. And the Parmese Guelfs loved him from thenceforth, for it was reckoned to his honour. Now this Giovanni Barisello who rose up in Parma was a man poor and wise, who delivered the city by his wisdom : wherefore the citizens were not ungrateful but repaid him with many kindnesses. First, they turned his poverty to riches ; secondly, they gave him a wife of the noble family of Cornazano ; thirdly, they ordained that he should ever be of the Council without further election, for he had mother-wit and was a gracious speaker ; fourthly, they permitted him to found and lead a gild called after his own name, on condition that it should ever be to the honour and profit of the Commune. This gild lasted many years ; but a certain Podesta of Parma, the Lord Manfredino di Rosa of Modena, would fain have destroyed it, for he would not that the men of Parma should be called after such a man's name : and he wished to rule the city with his own Council. Wherefore he bade Giovanni Barisello see to his own house and his own work, and leave this gild and this great show which he seemed to make : so Giovanni obeyed humbly, and that same day he went back to his board and took his needle and thread, and began to sew garments in the sight of his fellow-citizens. (The father of the aforesaid Podesta was of my acquaintance ; his mother and his wife were my spiritual daughters). Yet this Giovanni was ever beloved of the citizens, and had ever a place and a good repute in Parma. But in process of time King Charles of Anjou, hearing that the Parmese were a warlike folk, and friendly to him, and ever ready to succour the Church, sent word to them to found a gild in honour of God and the Holy Roman Church, which should be called the Gild of the Cross : of which gild he himself would be one ; and he would that all other gilds of Parma be incorporated in this, and that they should ever be ready to succour the Roman Church when she should need it. So the citizens formed this gild and called it the Gild of the Crusaders, and they inscribed King Charles in letters of gold at the beginning of the register, that this prince and duke and count and king and triumphant hero might be the captain and leader of this gild. And whosoever in Parma is not thereof, if he offend any of the gild, they defend each other like bees, and run forthwith and tear down his house to its very foundations, razing it so utterly to the ground that not one stone is left upon another : which strikes fear into the rest, for they must either live in peace or enter this gild. And so the gild hath increased marvellously, and the men of Parma are no longer named after Giovanni Barisello, but after King Charles and the Cross of our Lord Jesus Christ, to Whom is honour and glory for ever and ever, Amen."

Prof. Holder-Egger (p. 375. notes 4, 5,) points out inaccuracies of detail in this account : and Salimbene's narrative needs one important rectification which the author did not live to make : for in 1298 poor Barisello was taken prisoner and tortured to death. But the description of the gild's activity is fully borne out by the *Chronicon Parmense*, from which one extract may suffice. " In the year 1293 the Lord Podesta, with an armed force of 1,000 or more, made an assault after the customary fashion upon the houses of the Lord Giovanni de' Nizi (who was a *Frate Godente*), and of Poltrenerio de' Ricicoldi, by reason of certain injuries which they had done to some who were enrolled in the Gild Book." So valuable a privilege naturally led to abuses ; and we accordingly find that in 1286 the Gild Register had to be burnt "because many were found to be illegally enrolled therein. . . . Wherefore it was ordained that another new register should be compiled from that copy which was in the Sacristy of the Cathedral Church, and that it should be so rubricated with red ink as that no fresh names could be added thereto." But the political morality of a medieval Italian city rendered all such precautions useless. Only seven years later the Captain of the City and his notary, in collusion with another scrivener, falsified the register afresh, and fled the city on the discovery of their forgery.[3]

The Gild, however, had thoroughly done its work of ensuring Guelf supremacy in Parma. The first inquisition held by Bariselli with his 500 satellites had inaugurated a three days' reign of terror in the city, marked by robberies and ravages which the Podestas were powerless to prevent or to punish. Many Ghibelline houses were razed, or burned with such blind fury that even a raven's nest was consumed in the flames, in spite of the medieval superstition which reprobated so ominous an outrage. The palaces of the obnoxious Pallavicino were of course destroyed, and the site turned into a meat market, as in the case of the Uberti at Florence : Salimbene mentions a third case at Reggio under the year 1273. This destruction at Parma was probably in 1266. In 1268 the citizens already felt strong enough, with their allies, to attempt the complete reduction of Borgo San Donnino : "but after a long siege they retired, destroying the trees and corn and houses outside the walls, together with the vineyards. And that same year the men of Parma made peace" (475).

As the *Chronicon Parmense* tells us, this peace was received in the city with such wild rejoicing that many were crushed to death that evening in the crowd. The same year saw the defeat and death of Conradin, the last hope of the Ghibellines in Italy ; and it was evident that Borgo could no longer sustain the unequal struggle. The Parmese were planning the details of a great fortress to act as a perpetual check upon the rebel stronghold, when the Podesta and councillors came with the keys of their town to surrender at discretion. The Parmese might now spare themselves the expense of the new fortress : "they razed the walls of Borgo San Donnino to the ground, and filled up the moats, and commanded the citizens to quit the town and to rebuild their houses in a long street on either side of the high road towards Parma ; and thus they did, and thus it remains unto this day" (478). Eleven years afterwards, another great step was taken in the cause of peace. Parma had long since allied herself with her old enemy Cremona ; and now at last (505) "the Parmese restored to Cremona her Carroccio, which they had taken when they drove the Emperor from Victoria ; and so also did the Cremonese with the Carroccio of Parma which they had captured, restoring it now to the men of Parma ; and these restitutions were made with great honour and joy and gladness on either side."

So Parma now no longer fights for life and death, but is a definitely Guelf city at comparative peace. The stormcloud drifts away for a while, and we get only fitful glimpses of battle that flash and die out in the distance like summer lightning all round Salimbene's horizon ; but such flashes are still frequent and lurid enough. "In 1248 the town of Castellarano was taken by the Commune of Reggio and many were taken and slain ; and all men of Trignano and of the Bishopric of Reggio who were found in the said town were put to an evil death." In 1265 the Count of Flanders " destroyed the town of Capicolo, and all were slain therein, men and women and children, for that they had hanged one of the aforesaid count's knights." Salimbene records many other similar incidents under the years 1266-1280 : after which these monotonous notices of petty quarrels give way to fresh pictures of civil war on a larger scale. For the discords of Florence from which Dante suffered so cruelly were merely typical of the state of things throughout Italy. The Guelfs had hardly assured their supremacy over the Ghibellines, when they themselves split into new parties as savage and irreconcilable as the old. Salimbene complains (379) that " the Imperial party has been utterly destroyed in Imola, and the Church party from its envy and ambition is now divided into two factions. This same curse has now come to the men of Modena, and is to be found in Reggio also. God grant that it be not found in Parma, where the same matter is likewise to be feared." Again (370) " This city of Bologna was the last to drink of the cup of God's wrath, and she drank it even to the dregs, lest perchance she should be moved to boast of her righteousness and insult other cities which had already drunk of the cup of the wrath of God, and of His fury and indignation. For in that city were assassins, nor could she get the better of them." . . . . . here a page is cut out of the manuscript, which (as we learn from the ancient table of contents), treated " of the causes of the destruction of Bologna, and against the taking of usury and bribes, and concerning other sins."⁴ Italy, in short, remained for generation after generation in a state of anarchy and misery which among our own annals can be paralleled only in Stephen's reign ; when men said that God and His saints slept. Yet the sad facts must be faced : for it was from this violent ferment that noble minds like St. Francis and Dante took much of that special flavour which appeals so strongly to the modern literary mind. Here, as on many other points, Salimbene's evidence is all the more valuable that he himself was neither saint nor poet, but a clever, observant, sympathetic man with nothing heroic in his composition. All through his chronicle runs the feeling that, in this " hostelry of pain," the only fairly happy folk were fools at one end of the scale and friars at the other : that a man's only wise bargain was to destroy his house on earth that he might build himself a mansion in heaven.

Nor was his individual experience specially unfortunate for

that time : his long tale of slaughter and ravage includes scarcely
the most distant allusion to those wars in Tuscany which to
Dante and his commentator Benvenuto seemed worst of all.[5]
To Benvenuto, indeed, at the end of the 14th century, things
seemed if possible more intolerable than to Salimbene in the
middle of the 13th : he complains of even Sordello's bitter
Philippic as utterly inadequate. " In thy time, O Dante, certain
special evils did indeed oppress Italy, but those were small and
few [in comparison with to-day]. . . . I may say now of all Italy
what thy Virgil said of one city :—

> ' Look where you will, heart-rending agony
> And panic reign, and many a shape of death.'

Assuredly Italy suffered not so much from Hannibal or Pyrrhus
or even from the Goths and Lombards. . . .Thy lines, Dante,
were cast in happy days which may well be envied by all of us
who live in the wretched Italy of to-day."[6] Yet, a century later,
Savonarola might have looked back with regret even to the days
of despairing Benvenuto.[7] This decline, whether real or apparent,
was certainly not so rapid as each of those writers imagined ;
but it is plain that the good man was always uneasy in his own
age, and sighed fondly for a comparatively unknown past, or for
a future in which some sudden stroke of God's hand might create
a new heaven and a new earth. The saint's constant cry was
" Would God it were even ! " or else " Would God it were
morning ! " The conception of a world around us slowly yet
surely working out its own salvation by God's grace was almost
impossible to him. Nowadays, thanks to the work of saints in
all ages, and to this era of patient research and free discussion,
men are able to face the facts of human life with a serener eye.
We see how much richer the world has grown, from age to age,
by the lives of such men as St. Francis ; even though learned
and pious Italians of the 13th, the 14th, and the 15th, centuries
constantly yearned backwards to " the good old days " before
St. Francis was born. It is our privilege, in the broader light of
history, to see how the world is more truly Christian, on the
whole, than in our Lord's days : more truly Franciscan than in
the age of St. Francis : and how the loss of the past centuries is
not worthy to be compared with our present gain and our future
hopes.

CHAPTER XII

Wanderjahre.

SALIMBENE, as we have seen, had left Cremona—expelled, perhaps, by the Ghibelline authorities—and had come to Parma at the beginning of the siege. However, he did not see that siege to an end, but left the city after a few months with news for the Pope ; one of the thousand friars who swarmed on all the roads of Italy and did such yeoman service to the Guelf cause as despatch-bearers and spies. (53). " In that same year 1247, while my city was beleaguered by the deposed Emperor Frederick, I went to Lyons, and arrived there on the Feast of All Saints. And forthwith the Pope sent for me and spake familiarly with me in his chamber. For since my departure from Parma, even until that day, he had seen no messenger nor received no letters. And he was very gracious unto me ; that is, he heard the voice of my petition, being indeed a most courteous man, and a liberal." Elsewhere he specifies the favours here received from the Pope : permission for his mother to enter a convent of Clarisses (55), and for himself the coveted rank of a Preacher in his Order (178). This Pope had himself been a canon of Parma and on fairly intimate terms with Salimbene's father. Now, as the bearer of news from the front, our hero was fully conscious of his own importance ; and he dwelt fondly on the scene his whole life long. As he tells us later, he allowed himself in this interview to hint very plain doubts as to the good faith of the great Cardinal Ottaviano : (Dante *Inf.* x. 120,) and the scene as he describes it supplies a vivid commentary on the " *messagier che porta ulivo* " in Dante's meeting with Casella and his companions. (384) " The bystanders were there in such multitudes that they lay hard one on the other's shoulders in their eagerness to hear tidings of Parma[1] ; when therefore they who stood by heard me end my speech thus, they marvelled, and in my own hearing they said to each other, 'All the days of our life we have seen no friar so void of fear, and speaking so plainly.' This they said partly because they saw me sitting between the Patriarch of Constantinople and the Guardian, (for the Guardian had invited me to sit down, and I thought not fit to spurn and contemn such an honour;) and also because they saw and heard me speak so of so great a man, and in the presence of such an assembly. For in those days I was a deacon, and a young man of 25 years old."

But Lyons and the Pope were only the beginning of our friar's adventures on this journey. (206) "After the Feast of All Saints I set out for France.² And when I had come to the first convent beyond Lyons, on that same day arrived Brother John di Piano Carpine, returning from the Tartars, whither the Pope had sent him. This Brother John was friendly and spiritual and learned, and a great speaker, and skilled in many things. He showed us a wooden goblet which he bore as a gift to the Pope, in the bottom whereof was the likeness of a most fair queen, as I saw with mine own eyes; not wrought there by art or by a painter's cunning, but impressed thereon by the influence of the stars : and if it had been cut into a hundred parts, it would always have borne the impress of that image. Moreover, lest this seem incredible, I can prove it by another example. For the Emperor Frederick gave the Brethren a certain Church in Apulia, which was ancient and ruined and forsaken of all men. And, on the spot where of old the altar had stood, grew now a vast walnut-tree, which when cut open showed in every part the image of our Lord Jesus Christ on the Cross ; and if it had been cut a hundred times, so often would it have shown the image of the Crucifix. This was miraculously shown by God, since that tree had grown up on the very spot whereon the Passion of the spotless Lamb is represented in the Host of Salvation and the Adorable Sacrifice ; yet some assert that such impressions can be made by the influence of the stars."³ Brother John told the Brethren those stories which may still be read in his own book (Ed. C. R. Beazley, Hakluyt Soc. 1903) : remarkably true and sober accounts, on the whole, of China and the Far East. "And he caused that book to be read, as I have often heard and seen, when he was wearied with relating the deeds' of the Tartars. And when they who read wondered or understood not, he himself would expound and dissert on single points. When I first saw Brother John he was returning from the Tartars, and on the morrow he went his way to see Pope Innocent ; and I on mine to France. And I dwelt in Brie of Champagne ; first for fifteen days at Troyes, where were many Lombard and Tuscan merchants, for there is a fair which lasts two months. Then I went to Provins, from the 13th day of December until the 2nd

of February, on which day I went to Paris, and dwelt there a
week, and saw many pleasant sights. Then I returned and
dwelt in the convent of Sens, for the French Brethren gladly
kept me with them everywhere, because I was a peaceful and
ready youth, and because I praised their doings. And as I lay
sick in the infirmary by reason of the cold, there came hastily
certain French Brethren of the convent to me, with a letter,
saying, 'We have excellent news of Parma; for the citizens
have driven out Frederick, the late Emperor, from the city of
Victoria which he had built, and have taken the Emperor's
whole treasure, and also the chariot of the Cremonese; and here
is a copy of the letter from the men of Parma to the Pope.' And
they asked me to what purpose that chariot could be used. And
I answered them that the Lombards call this kind of chariot a
'Carroccio,' and if the Carroccio of any city be taken in war, the
citizens hold themselves sore shamed; even as, if the Oriflamme
were taken in war, the French and their King would hold it a
great disgrace. Hearing this, they marvelled, saying, 'Ha!
God! We have heard a marvellous thing.' After that I
recovered. And behold! Brother John di Piano Carpine was on
his way home from the king, to whom the Pope had sent him;
and he had his book which the Brethren read in his presence;
and he himself interpreted whatsoever seemed obscure and
difficult to understand or believe. And I ate with Brother John,
not only in the Convent of the Brethren Minor, but outside in
abbeys and places of dignity, and that not once or twice only,
for he was invited gladly both to dine and to sup, partly as the
Pope's Legate, partly as ambassador to the King of France,
partly because he had come from the Tartars, and partly also
for that he was of the Order of Friars Minor, and all believed
him a man of most holy life. For when I was at Cluny, the
monks said to me, 'Would that the Pope would ever send such
Legates as Brother John! for other Legates, so far as in them
lies, spoil the Church, and carry off all that they can lay their
hands upon. But Brother John, when he passed by our Abbey,
would accept nothing but cloth for a frock for his comrade.'[4]   And
know thou who readest my book, that the Abbey of Cluny is the
most noble monastery of Black Monks of St. Benedict in Burgundy;
and in that cloister are several priors; and in the aforesaid Abbey
the multitude of buildings is so great that the Pope with his
Cardinals and all his Court might lodge there, and likewise at
the same time the Emperor with all his; and this without hurt
to the monks: nor on that account would any monk need to
leave his cell or suffer any discomfort. Note also that the Order

of St. Benedict, so far as the Black Monks are concerned, is far better kept in lands beyond the mountains than among us in Italy.[5] Then from Sens I went to Auxerre, and dwelt there, for the Minister of France had assigned me specially to that convent." Auxerre interested him with its many tombs of Saints and martyrs, and as the dwelling-place of Master William, a great contemporary theologian and disputant, but one who "when he undertook to preach, knew not what to say : note the example of that cobbler in Brother Luke's sermon, who removed a mountain in the land of the Saracens and freed the Christians." But the city had another still more vivid interest for him : " I remember how, when I dwelt at Cremona, Brother Gabriel, who was a most learned and holy man, told me that Auxerre had more plenty of vineyards and wine than Cremona and Parma and Reggio and Modena together ; whereat I marvelled and thought it incredible. But when I dwelt myself at Auxerre, I saw how he had said the truth ; for not only are the hillsides covered with vineyards, but the level plain also, as I have seen with mine own eyes. For the men of that land sow not, nor do they reap, neither have they storehouse nor barn ; but they send wine to Paris by the river which flows hard by ; and there they sell it at a noble price. And I myself have encompassed the diocese of Auxerre three times on foot ; once with a certain Brother who preached and gave men the Cross for the Crusade of St. Louis ; another time with another Brother who, on the day of the Lord's Supper, preached to the Cistercians in a most fair Abbey ; and we kept the Feast of Easter with a certain Countess, who gave us for dinner (or rather, who gave to her whole court) twelve courses or diversities of food—and if the Count, her husband, had been there, then still greater plenty would have been served. The third time I journeyed with Brother Stephen, and saw and heard many noteworthy things, which I omit here for brevity's sake. And note that in the Province of France are eight custodies of our Order, whereof four drink beer, and four drink wine. Note also that there are three parts of France which give great plenty of wine,—namely, La Rochelle, Beaune, and Auxerre. Note that the red wines are held in but small esteem, for they are not equal to the red wines of Italy. Note likewise that the wines of Auxerre are white, and sometimes golden, and fragrant, and comforting, and of strong and excellent taste, and they turn all who drink them to cheerfulness and merriment ; wherefore of this wine we may rightly say with Solomon ' Give strong wine to them that are sad, and wine to them that are grieved in mind : Let them drink and forget their want, and remember their sorrow no more.' And know that the wines of Auxerre are so strong that, when they have stood awhile, tears gather on the outer surface of the jar. Note also that the French are wont to tell how the best wine should have three B's and seven F's. For they themselves say in sport

> ' Et bon et bel et blanc
> Fort et fier, fin et franc,
> Froid et frais et frétillant.' "

Here, as elsewhere where he is reminded of good cheer, Salimbene seizes the occasion for breaking out into a drinking song : it is of the usual type of clerkly medieval rhymes ; and I have tried to render it fairly literally, while softening down some of its inevitable crudities. It will no doubt be noted that the metre is one of those which hymn-writers very likely borrowed at first from secular songs, and which bacchanalian or erotic songsters undoubtedly borrowed back from the Church hymns, often with a very definite turn of parody.[6]

(219) " Now Master Morando, who taught grammar at Padua, commended wine according to his own taste in this fashion, singing

> ' Drink'st thou glorious, honey'd wine ?
> Stout thy frame, thy face shall shine,
>   Freely shalt thou spit :
>
> Old in cask, in savour full ?
> Cheerful then shall be thy soul,
>   Bright and keen thy wit.
>
> Is it strong and pure and clear ?
> Quickly shall it banish care,
>   Chills it shall extrude :
>
> But the sour will bite thy tongue,
> Rot thy liver, rot thy lung,
>   And corrupt thy blood.
>
> Is thy liquor greyish pale ?
> Hoarseness shall thy throat assail
>   Fluxes shall ensue :
>
> Others, swilling clammy wine,
> Wax as fat as any swine,
>   Muddy-red of hue.
>
> Scorn not red, though thin it be :
> Ruddy wine shall redden thee,
>   So thou do but soak :
>
> Juice of gold and citron dye
> Doth our vitals fortify,
>   Sicknesses doth choke :

But the cursed water white
Honest folk will interdict,
Lest it spleen provoke.'

" So the French delight in good wine, nor need we wonder, for wine 'cheereth God and men,' as it is written in the ninth chapter of Judges." The author here loses himself again in Biblical quotations—Noah, Lot, and the warnings of Proverbs—after which he goes on : " It may be said literally that French and English make it their business to drink full goblets ; wherefore the French have bloodshot eyes, for from their ever-free potations of wine their eyes become red-rimmed, and bleared, and bloodshot. And in the early morning, after they have slept off their wine, they go with such eyes to the priest who has celebrated Mass, and pray him to drop into their eyes the water wherein he has washed his hands. But Brother Bartolommeo Guiscolo of Parma was wont to say at Provins (as I have often heard with mine own ears) ' ale, ke malonta ve don Dé ; metti de l'aighe in le vins, non in lis ocli ; ' which is to say, ' Go ! God give you evil speed ! Put the water in your wine when ye drink it, and not in your eyes ! ' The English indeed delight in drink, and make it their business to drain full goblets ; for an Englishman will take a cup of wine, and drain it, saying, Ge bi, a vu,'[7] which is to say ' It behoveth you to drink as much as I shall drink,' and therein he thinketh to say and do great courtesy, and he taketh it exceeding ill if any do otherwise than he himself hath taught in word and shown by example. And yet he doth against the Scripture, which saith, ' . . . Wine also in abundance and of the best was presented, as was worthy of a king's magnificence. Neither was there any one to compel them to drink that were not willing.' (Esther i, 7). Yet we must forgive the English if they are glad to drink good wine when they can, for they have but little wine in their own country. In the French it is less excusable, for they have greater plenty ; unless indeed we plead that it is hard to leave our daily wont. Note that it is thus written in verse, 'Normandy for sea-fish, England for corn, Scotland [or Ireland ?] for milk, France for wine.'—Enough of this matter.—But note that in France, as I have seen with mine own eyes, the days are longer in the corresponding months than in Italy : namely, in May they are longer there than here, and in winter they are less. Let me return now to my own affairs, and speak of the French King.

" In the year 1248, about the Feast of Pentecost or somewhat later, I went down from Auxerre to the convent of Sens, for the

Provincial Chapter of our Order in France was to be held there ;
and the Lord Louis (IX), King of France, was to come thither.
And when the King was already hard by our convent, all the
Brethren went forth to meet him, that they might receive him
with all honour. And Brother Rigaud of our Order, Professor
of Theology at Paris, and Archbishop of Rouen, clad in his
pontifical robes, hastened forth from the convent, crying as he
went, ' Where is the King ?   Where is the King ? '   So I followed him, for he went by himself as a man distraught, with his
mitre on his head, and his pastoral staff in his hand.[8] For he
had fallen behindhand in robing himself, so that the other
Brethren had already gone forth, and stood on either side of the
street with their faces turned towards the King, in their eagerness
to see him coming. And I marvelled beyond measure within
myself, saying ' Certainly I have read oftentimes how the Sen-
onian Gauls were so mighty that under Brennus they took the
city of Rome ; but now their women seem for the most part like
handmaids : yet, if the King had passed through Pisa or
Bologna, the whole flower of the ladies of those cities would
have gone out to meet him.' Then I remembered that this is
indeed the custom of the French ; for in France it is the
burgesses only who dwell in the cities, whereas the knights and
noble ladies dwell in the villages and on their estates.

" Now the King was spare and slender, somewhat lean, and of
a proper height, having the face of an angel, and a mien full of
grace. And he came to our Church, not in regal pomp, but
in a pilgrim's habit, with the staff and the scrip of his pilgrimage
hanging at his neck, which was an excellent adornment for the
shoulders of a king. And he came not on horseback, but on
foot ; and his blood-brethren, who were three counts, (whereof
the eldest was named Robert, and the youngest Charles, who
did afterwards many great deeds most worthy of praise), followed
him in the same humble guise, so that they might have said in
truth that word of the prophet ' Woe to them that go down to
Egypt for help, trusting in horses, and putting their confidence
in chariots, because they are many, and in horsemen, because
they are very strong : and have not trusted in the holy One of
Israel, and have not sought after the Lord.'   Nor did the King
care for a train of nobles, but rather for the prayers and suffrages
of the poor ; and therefore he fulfilled that which Ecclesiasticus
teacheth ' Make thyself affable to the congregation of the poor.'
In truth he might rather be called a monk in devotion of heart,
than a knight in weapons of war.   When he had come into our
church, and had made a most devout genuflexion, he prayed

before the altar ; and as he departed from the church, and was yet standing on the threshold, I was by his side ; and behold, the treasurer of the cathedral of Sens sent him a great living pike in water, in a vessel of fir-wood, such as the Tuscans call ' *bigonza*,' wherein nursling children are washed and bathed : for in France the pike is esteemed a dear and precious fish. And the King thanked not only the sender, but him who brought the gift.

" Then cried the King in a loud and clear voice that none but knights should enter the Chapter-house, save only the Brethren, with whom he would fain speak. And when we were gathered together, the King began to speak of his own matters, commending himself and his brethren and the Queen his mother, and his whole fellowship ; and kneeling most devoutly he besought the prayers and suffrages of the Brethren. And certain Brethren of France who stood by my side wept so sore for devotion and pity that they could scarce be comforted. After the King, the Lord Oddo, Cardinal of the Roman Court, who had formerly been Chancellor of the University of Paris, and was now to go beyond the seas with him, began to speak, and concluded the matter before us in a few words, as Ecclesiasticus teacheth : ' Desire not to appear wise before the king.' After those two, Brother John of Parma, the Minister-General, (on whom in virtue of his office fell the task of replying), spake as follows : " ' Our King and lord and benefactor hath come to us humbly and profitably, courteously and kindly ; and he first spake to us, as was right ; nor doth he pray us for gold or silver, whereof by God's grace there is sufficient store in his treasury ; but only for the prayers and suffrages of the Brethren, and that for a most laudable purpose. For in truth he hath undertaken this pilgrimage and signed himself with the Cross, in honour of our Lord Jesus Christ, and to succour the Holy Land, and to conquer the enemies of the Faith and Cross of Christ, and for the honour of Holy Church and the Christain Faith, and for the salvation of his soul, with all theirs who are to pass the seas with him. Wherefore, seeing that he hath been a special benefactor and defender of our Order, not only at Paris, but throughout his kingdom ; and that he hath come humbly to us with so worthy a fellowship to pray for our intercession, it is fitting that we should render him some good. Now whereas the Brethren of France are already more willing to undertake this matter, and purpose to do more than I could impose upon them, therefore upon them I lay no precept. But, seeing that I have begun to visit the Order, I have purposed in my mind to enjoin on each priest of the whole Order to sing four Masses for the King and this holy fellowship. And if so be that the Son of God call him from this world to the Father, then shall the Brethren add yet more Masses. And if I have not answered according to his desire, let the King himself be our lord to command us, who lack not obedient hearts, but only a voice to prescribe.' The King, hearing this, thanked the Minister-General, and so wholly accepted his answer that he would fain have it confirmed under his hand and seal. Moreover, the King took upon himself all that day's cost, and ate together with us in the refectory ; and with us sat down to meat the King's three brethren, and the Cardinal, and the Minister-General, and Brother Rigaud, Archbishop of Rouen, and the Minister-Provincial of France, and the Custodes and Definitores, and the Discreti,[9] and all who were of the capitular body, and the Brethren our guests, whom we call ' foreigners.' The Minister-General therefore, seeing that the King had already a noble and worthy fellowship, was unwilling to thrust himself forward, according to the word of Ecclesiasticus, ' Be not exalted in the day of thy honour,' though indeed he was invited to sit by the King's side ; but he loved rather to practise that courtesy and humility which our Lord taught by word and example. Wherefore Brother John chose rather to sit at the table of the humble ; and it was honoured by his presence, and many were edified thereby : for consider that God hath not placed all the lights of heaven in one part alone, but hath distributed them in divers parts and in sundry manners for the greater beauty and utility of the heavens. This then was our fare that day : first, cherries, then most excellent white bread ; and choice wine, worthy of the King's royal state, was placed in abundance before us ; and, after the wont of the French, many invited even the unwilling and compelled them to drink. After that we had fresh beans boiled in milk, fishes and crabs, eel-pasties, rice cooked with milk of almonds and cinnamon powder, eels baked with most excellent sauce, tarts and junkets, [or curd-cheeses] and all the fruits of the season in abundance and comely array. And all these were laid on the table in courtly fashion, and busily ministered to us. On the morrow the King went on his way ; and I, when the Chapter was ended, followed him ; for I had a command from the Minister-General to go and dwell in Provence : and it was easy for me to overtake the King, for oft-times he turned aside from the high road to visit the hermitages of Brethren Minor or of other Religious, that he might commend himself to their prayers ; and so he did daily until he came to the sea, and set sail for the Holy Land. When therefore

I had visited the Brethren of Auxerre, which had been my convent, I went in one day to Urgeliac, a noble town in Burgundy, where the body of the Magdalene was then thought to lie. And the morrow was a Sunday; so at early dawn the King came to our church to pray for our suffrages, according to the word which is written in Proverbs ' Well doth he rise early who seeketh good things.' And he left all his fellowship in the town hard by, save only his three brethren, and a few grooms to hold their horses; and, when they had knelt and made obeisance before the altar, his brethren looked round for seats and benches. But the King sat on the ground in the dust, as I saw with mine own eyes, for that church was unpaved.[10] And he called us to him, saying, ' Come unto me, my most sweet Brethren, and hear my words '; and we sat round him in a ring on the ground, and his blood-brethren did likewise. And he commended himself to us, beseeching our suffrages: and after we had made answer, he departed from the church to go on his way; and it was told him that Charles still prayed fervently; so the King was glad, and waited patiently without mounting his horse while his brother prayed. And the other two counts, his brethren, stood likewise waiting without. Now Charles was his youngest brother, who had the Queen's sister to wife; and oft-times he bowed his knee before the altar which was in the church aisle hard by the door. So I saw how earnestly Charles prayed, and how patiently the King waited without; and I was much edified, knowing the truth of that Scripture ' A brother that is helped by his brother is like a strong city.' Then the King went on his way; and, having finished his business, he hastened to the vessel which had been prepared for him: but I went to Lyons, and found the Pope still there with his Cardinals. Thence I went down the Rhone, to the city of Arles, and it was the 29th of June."

We here take leave of the saintly King, of whose crusade Salimbene tells us briefly later on (320) that it failed " by reason of the sins of the French," and whom after this he only mentions cursorily here and there, without any first-hand touches. But the next stage of his journey brought him into contact with a man almost as celebrated in his own day as St. Louis himself: the holy Cordelier of Joinville's narrative (§§ 657 foll.), which is too vivid and characteristic to be omitted here. " King Louis," writes Joinville of the year 1254, " heard tell of a Grey Friar whose name was Brother Hugh: and for the great renown that he had the King sent for that Friar to see and hear him speak. The day he came to Hyères, we looked down the road whereby he came, and were aware of a great company of people,

both men and women, following him on foot. The King bade
him preach : and the first words of his sermon dealt with men
of Religion. 'My Lord,' said he, 'I see many more folk of
Religion in the King's court and in his company than should of
right be there'; and then 'First of all,' said he, 'I say that
such are not in the way of salvation, nor can they be, unless
Holy Scripture lie. For Holy Scripture saith that the monk
cannot live out of his cloister without mortal sin, even as the
fish cannot live without water.[11] And if the Religious who are
with the King say that his court is a cloister, then I tell them it
is the widest that ever I saw ; for it stretches from this side of
the great sea to the other. And if they plead that in this cloister
a man may lead a hard life to save his soul, therein I believe
them not ; for I tell you that I have eaten with them great plenty
of divers flesh-meats, and drunken of good wines, both strong
and clear ; wherefore I am assured that if they had been in
their cloister they would not have been so at their ease as they
now are at the King's court.' Then in his sermon he taught
the King how he should hold himself to please his people ; and
at the end of his sermon he said that he had read the Bible and
all the books that go against the Bible ; and never had he found,
whether in believers' books or in unbelievers', that any kingdom
or lordship was ever ruined or ever changed its lord, but by reason
of defect of justice : 'Wherefore' said he 'let the King look
well to it, since he is returning to his kingdom of France, that
he render his folk such justice as to keep God's love, that God
may never take the kingdom from him so long as he is alive !'
So I, Joinville, told the King that he should not let this man quit
his company, if by any means he might keep him : but he
answered 'I have already prayed him, and he will do nought
for me. 'Come,' said he, taking me by the hand, 'let us go and
pray him once more.' We came to him and I said to him,
'Sir, do as my Lord the King hath prayed you, to abide with
him while he is yet in Provence.' And he answered me in great
wrath, 'Be sure, Sir, that I will not do so : for I shall go to a
place where God will love me better than He would love me in
King's company.' One day he tarried with us, and on the
morrow he went his way. They have told me since that he lieth
buried in the city of Marseilles, where he worketh many fair
miracles." A fine, sturdy John-Baptist of a friar, this : but
how will he suit our chronicler, who is so far from sharing his
abhorrence of delicate fare and choice wines in Kings' houses ?
Excellently, according to Salimbene's own account ; nor is
there any reason to doubt his word. To begin with they had

common friends and strong common interests: for Joachism was a powerful freemasonry in the thirteenth century. Moreover, Salimbene was one of those who, without great pretensions to superior personal sanctity, are yet so sympathetic and sociable that the most intractable saints suffer their company as gladly as Johnson suffered Boswell's. Our friar, like so many others, constantly plumed himself on the theoretical strictness of that Rule which in practice he interpreted so liberally; and he took just the same æsthetic delight in the rugged sanctity of his friend. So from Arles he went to Marseilles (226) "and thence to see Brother Hugues de Barjols, or de Digne, whom the Lombards call Brother Hugh of Montpellier. He was one of the greatest and most learned clerks in the world, a most famous preacher, beloved of clergy and layfolk alike, and a most excellent disputant, ready for all questions. He would entangle and confound all men in argument; for he had a most eloquent tongue, and a voice as a ringing trumpet, or mighty thunder, or the sound of many waters falling from a cliff. He never tripped or stumbled, but was ever ready with an answer for all. He spake marvellously of the Court of Heaven, and the glories of Paradise, and most terribly of the pains of hell. He was of middling stature, and somewhat swarthy of hue—a man spiritual beyond measure, so that he seemed a second Paul or Elisha; for in his days he feared neither principalities nor powers; none ever conquered him or overcame him in word. For he spake in full consistory to the Pope and his Cardinals as he might have spoken to boys assembled in school; both at the Council of Lyons, and aforetime when the Court was at Rome: and all trembled as a reed trembles in the water. For once being asked by the Cardinals what sort of tidings he had, he rated them like asses, saying, 'I have no tidings, but I have full peace, both with my conscience and with God, which passeth all understanding, and keepeth my heart and mind in Christ Jesus. I know in truth that ye seek new tidings, and are busy about such things all day long, for ye are Athenians, and no disciples of Christ.'" This little incident forms a living commentary upon one of the precepts most frequently insisted upon in the Franciscan disciplinary writings. The friar of Shakespeare's plays—a sort of walking newspaper and ready *deus ex machina* for any innocent little plot that may be on foot—the indispensable confidant in all family matters, from the least to the greatest—was already fully developed in St. Bonaventura's time, and was the bugbear of the convent authorities, since he brought into the Order the oft-forbidden "familiarities with women," together with all sorts of other

purely worldly interests. To take only one quotation out of
many from the "Mirror of Novices" (p. 239); "Study thy
whole life long, so far as thou well mayest, to avoid familiarities
with secular persons ; for they are 'a perverse generation and
unfaithful children,' as the Scripture saith. And when thou
art brought among them by the compulsion of necessity or
[spiritual] profit, beware lest thou ever speak with them any
but profitable and honest words ; and if they themselves speak
of secular matters, or of the wars, or of other unprofitable
things, never follow them even though thou know of these
matters, but say with the Prophet 'That my mouth may not
speak the works of men.' . . . Moreover, flee from women, so
far as in thee lieth, as thou wouldst flee from serpents, never
speaking with them but under compulsion of urgent necessity ;
nor ever look in any woman's face ; and if a woman speak to
thee, circumcise thy words most straitly, for as the Prophet
saith ' Her words are smoother than oil, and the same are darts.' "
The rest of Hugh's long speech to the Cardinals, vivid as its
interest is for the student of medieval manners, belongs rather
to another place :[12] as indeed Salimbene himself must have
realized by the time he had come to the end of it : for he exclaims
again " Blessed be God that I am at last at the end of this
matter ! "

He goes on to enumerate Hugh's special friends : (232) the
first was John of Parma, "for whose love he became my familiar
friend also, and because I seemed to believe in the writings of
Abbot Joachim of Fiore." The second was the Archbishop
of Vienne ; the third, Grosseteste, Bishop of Lincoln ; the
fourth, Adam Marsh, the great Oxford scholar and adviser of
Simon de Montfort. While Salimbene was a youthful convert
at Siena he had already met Hugh, whose eloquence and
readiness in disputation had electrified him (233). Our
chronicler had again heard him preach on a solemn occasion
at Lucca : (234) for "it chanced that I came thither from
Pistoia at the very hour at which he must needs go to the
Cathedral Church, and the whole convent was gathered together
to go with him. But he, seeing the Brethren without the gate,
marvelled and said, 'Ha ! God ! Whither would these men go ? '
And it was answered him that the Brethren did thus for his
honour, and for that they would fain hear him preach. So he
said ' I need no such honour, for I am not the Pope ; but if they
will hear me, let them follow when I am entered into the church ;
for I will go on with a single comrade, and not with this multitude.'
Brother Hugh therefore preached with such edification and

comfort of his hearers that the clergy of the Bishopric of Lucca were wont to say many years after how they had never heard a man speak so well; for the others had recited their sermons even as a psalm which they might have learnt by heart. And they loved and revered the whole Order for his sake. Another time I heard him preach to the people in Provence, at Tarascon on the Rhone, at which sermon were men and women of Tarascon and Beaucaire, (which are two most noble towns lying side by side, with the river Rhone between; and in each town is a fair convent of the Brethren Minor). And he said to them (as I heard with mine own ears) words of edification, useful words, honeyed words, words of salvation. And they heard him gladly, as a John the Baptist, for they held him for a Prophet. These things find no credence with men who are themselves deprived of such grace; yet it is most ridiculous if I will not believe that there is any Bishop or any Pope because I myself am not a Bishop or a Pope! Moreover, at the court of the Count of Provence was a certain Riniero, a Pisan by birth, who called himself an universal philosopher, and who so confounded the judges and notaries and physicians of the Court that no man could live there in honour. Wherefore they expounded their tribulation to Brother Hugh, that he might vouchsafe to succour and defend them from this bitter enemy. So he made answer: ' Order ye with the Count a day for disputation in the palace, and let knights and nobles, judges and notaries and physicians be there present, and dispute ye with him; and then let the Count send for me, and I will prove to them by demonstration that this man is an ass, and that the sky is a frying-pan.' All this was so ordered, and Brother Hugh so involved and entangled him in his own words that he was ashamed to remain at the Count's court, and withdrew without taking leave of his host; nor did he ever dare thereafter to dwell there, or even to show his face. For he was a great sophist, and thought within himself to entangle all others in his sophistries. Brother Hugh therefore ' delivered the poor from the mighty, and the needy that had no helper;' and they kissed his hands and feet. Note that this aforesaid Count was called Raymond Berenger, (*Paradiso*, vi, 134), a comely man, and a friend of the Friars Minor, and father to the Queens of France and of England. Moreover, in Provence there is a certain most populous town named Hyères, where is a great multitude of men and women doing penitence even in worldly habit in their own houses. These are strictly devoted to the Friars Minor; for the Friars Preachers have no convent there, since they are pleased and comforted to dwell in

great convents rather than in small. In this town Brother Hugh
lived most gladly, and there were many notaries and judges and
physicians and other learned men, who on solemn days would
assemble in his chamber to hear him speak of the doctrine of
Abbot Joachim, or expound the mysteries of Holy Scripture, or
foretell the future. For he was a great Joachite, and had all the
works of Abbot Joachim written in great letters : and I myself
also was there to hear him teach."

These Franciscan Tertiaries of whom Salimbene speaks were
the nucleus of one of the earliest and most famous Béguinages,
under the direction of Hugh's sister St. Douceline, of whom
Salimbene gives a brief account lower down (554). " In another
stone chest by Brother Hugh's side is buried his sister in the
flesh, the Lady Douceline, whose fame God likewise showed
forth by miracles. She never entered any religious Order, but
ever lived chastely and righteously in the World. She chose
for her spouse the Son of God, and for the saint of her special
devotion the blessed Francis, whose cord she wore round her
body ; and almost all day long she prayed in the church of the
Friars Minor. There was none who spoke or thought evil of
her ; for men and women, religious and layfolk, honoured her
for her exceeding sanctity. She had of God a special grace of
ecstasies, as the Friars saw a thousand times in their church.
If they raised her arm, she would keep it thus raised from morning
to evening, for she was wholly absorbed in God : and this was
spread abroad through the whole city of Marseilles, and through
other cities also. She was followed by eighty noble ladies of
Marseilles, of middle and of higher rank, who would fain save
their souls after her example ; and she was lady and mistress of
them all." Of this saint, her asceticism and her trances, and the
wonderful power over others which she found in her single-
hearted devotion to God, the reader may find a full account in
Albanès' edition and translation of the thirteenth-century life
by one of her disciples, and in a recent essay by Miss Macdonell.

Here then dwelt Salimbene, for the second time in his life, in
an atmosphere of the most contagious religious enthusiasm,
thoroughly enjoying it all, and yet saved by his critical faculty
(as we shall presently see) from being swept off his legs altogether.
It is not difficult, I think, to trace in his history a very usual
type of religious development. The Alleluia of 1233 marked
his conversion, his first realization of a life to come ; an over-
powering appeal to his feelings while his intellect was as yet
utterly undeveloped. Now, as an impressionable and (for his
age) highly educated young man, he is brought into close contact

with a party leader of intense magnetic power, from whom, and from others of the same party, he imbibes a new and startling theory of Church statesmanship, and a philosophy of history which, even after experience had proved its partial falsehood, was so noble and true that it could not fail to influence all the rest of his life. Even in the ashes of Salimbene's old age lived the wonted fires of Joachism : after all his disillusions, and even through his period of antagonism to his old comrades, he was always a different man for having once accepted this 13th-century "Theory of Development." It is this which gives much of its charm to his book : one feels the mellow judgment of a man who, (to put it in terms of our own age), after having been "converted" as a boy in the Evangelical sense—after having been carried away at Oxford by Newman— has gradually settled down to views more consonant with the facts of human life than that earlier intense Tractarianism, and yet Tractarian in their sense of an eternal purpose for the Church amid the perlexing phenomena of daily life.

CHAPTER XIII.

Abbot Joachim's Theory of Development.

HOW is it that Dante assigned one of the most conspicuous places in his Paradise to a visionary, one of whose most important writings had been solemnly condemned by Innocent III at the great Lateran Council, and thought worthy of an elaborate refutation by St. Thomas Aquinas? It is not sufficient to say that Dante claimed in his poem an unusual liberty of private judgment; for three popes had patronized Joachim even in his lifetime ; and, strangest of all, his most dangerous speculations were never definitely condemned, even after they had been pushed to what seems their only legitimate conclusion, in a book which raised a storm throughout Latin Christendom. The real explanation of so strange a paradox is to be found in that comparative freedom of thought which makes the 13th century, especially in Italy, so living a period in the history of the pre-reformation Church. Dante, in fact, caused as little scandal by promoting Joachim to a high place in heaven as by degrading a canonized pope, Celestine V, to one of the most contemptible corners of the lower regions. The rigid framework and the inexorable discipline of the modern Roman Church are mainly the work of the Counter-Reformation; and the records of the 13th century show us, beneath much orthodox intolerance, an irrepressible diversity of religious life which in many essential respects reminds us rather of Anglicanism. The Church, as it embraced the whole population, embraced also every type of mind, from the most superstitious to the most agnostic : and many of these unorthodox elements worked far more freely, under the cloak of outward conformity, than is generally supposed. Almost all variations of opinion were tolerated, so long as their outward expression was fairly discreet : partly, no doubt, because the machinery of repression was as yet imperfect; but partly also because there was too much life and growth to be easily repressed. It was far less dangerous to hint that Rome was the Scarlet Woman, as Joachim did ; or again (with certain friars of whom Eccleston tells us), to debate in the Schools "whether God really existed,"[1] than to wear publicly and pertinaciously a frock and cowl of any but the orthodox cut.   Joachim's book against Peter Lombard was condemned as a public attack on a pillar of the Schools ; his evolutionary speculations were treated leniently because any other course would have enabled the secular clergy to triumph over the Friars, and no pope could afford to lose the support of the two Orders.

The story of the Abbot Joachim is admirably told by Renan, Gebhart, Tocco, Father Denifle, and Dr. Lea : a summary of these by Miss Troutbeck appeared in the *Nineteenth Century* for July 1902.   Born about 1132 in Calabria, where Roman religious ideas were leavened with Greek and even Saracen elements : by turns a courtier, a traveller, an active missionary, and a contemplative hermit, he has been claimed with some justice as a sort of St. John Baptist to the Franciscan movement : and he may be called with almost equal truth its St. John the Divine also.   The hateful and notorious corruption of the Church, which impelled Francis to found his Order, had previously driven Joachim into an attempt to interpret the world's history in the light of Scripture.   He found the solution of present evils in a theory of gradual decay and renewal, elaborated from St. Augustine's philosophy of history.   The visible Church, in Joachim's system, was no temple of stone, but a shifting tabernacle in this worldly wilderness ; pitched here to-night, but destined to be folded up with to-morrow's dawn, and carried one stage onward with an advancing world.   As Salimbene puts it (466) ; " he divides the world into a threefold state ; for in the first state the Father worked in mystery through the patriarchs and sons of the prophets, although the works of the Trinity are indivisible.   In the second state the Son worked through the Apostles and other apostolic men ; of which state He saith in John ' My Father worketh until now, and I work.'   In the third state the Holy Ghost shall work through the Religious."   In other words, the first state of the Church was taught by the Father through the Old Testament ; the second state by the Son through the New Testament ; the third state (which may be said in one sense to have begun with St. Benedict) shall be taught by the Holy Spirit.   Not that the Old and New Testaments are to be abrogated, or that a new Bible shall be revealed ; but that men's eyes shall be opened by the Spirit to see a new revelation in the time-honoured scriptures — an Eternal Gospel, proceeding from the Old and New Testaments as its Author the Holy Spirit proceeds from the Father and the Son.   And to these threefold

stages of inspiration correspond three orders of missionaries :
first, the patriarchs and prophets : secondly, the Apostles and
their successors the clergy : the third era of the Church shall be
an era of hermits, monks, and nuns, not superseding the present
hierarchy, but guiding it into new ways. Further, like nearly
all the prophets of this age, Joachim argued from the corruption
of the then world to the imminence of Antichrist, of the Battle
of Armageddon, and of all the convulsions foretold in the
Apocalypse as preceding the Reign of the Saints.

It is obvious how these prophecies would be caught at by all
who felt deeply the miseries caused by the wars between Pope
and Emperor ; and how to all good Guelfs Frederick would seem
a very sufficient Antichrist. The Friars, too, had every reason
to welcome prophecies of a millennium. to be heralded by new
Orders of surpassing holiness and authority : and the spiritual
Franciscans especially found in Joachism the promise of a reign
of glory after their bitter persecutions of the present time. Here
therefore was plenty of material for a great conflagration, to
which the match was set by one of Salimbene's friends, Gerard
of Borgo San Donnino. Appointed professor of theology at Paris
about 1250, he published four years later an *Introduction to the
Eternal Gospel*, containing one of Joachim's best-known works,
with a preface and notes of his own, The work created an
instant sensation, and was eagerly read by the laity. The saintly
John of Parma, General of the Franciscans and himself a strong
Joachite, certainly took no steps to punish the writer, and was
himself often credited with the authorship. But the University
of Paris, delighted to find a handle against the unpopular friars,
took the matter up. There seems no doubt that this book
pressed Joachim's theories to the antisacerdotal conclusions
which they would seem legitimately to bear, but which Joachim
himself had studiously avoided. Gerard regarded the sacraments
as transitory symbols, to be set aside under the reign of the Holy
Ghost ; and he predicted that the Abomination of Desolation
should be a simoniacal pope shortly to come —a prediction of
which many saw the fulfilment forty years later in Boniface VIII.
Gerard was further accused, we cannot tell now with what justice,
of seeing in St. Francis a new Christ who was to supersede the
Christ of the Second Age. Speculations like this, published in
the very Schools of Paris, could not be allowed to pass uncon-
demned : and the matter was brought in 1255 before a Papal
Commission : Gerard's work was condemned and suppressed, and
exists at present only in the extracts singled out by his accusers.
This event, as we have seen, brought about the fall of John of

Parma. Yet, all through this storm, Joachim's own prophecies
were never condemned ; the whole affair was hushed up as quietly
as possible, not only for the sake of the Franciscan Order, but
because there were so many others who had long held Joachim for
a prophet, feeling with him that traditional Christianity was a
failure, and that an altogether new world was needed for its renewal. The immense popularity of his prophecies--which were
quoted as authoritative by Roman Catholic divines even in the
17th century—goes far to explain many of the strangest religious
phenomena recorded by Salimbene. He himself believed to the
end in Joachim as a prophet, even after he had long given up
Joachism in the strictest sense.

He had received his first tinge of Joachism from Hugues de
Digne at Siena, and was confirmed in this creed at Pisa by an
Abbot of the Order of Fiore, and by his own Franciscan Lector
there. Again, at the very beginning of these his wander-years,
in December 1247, he had been brought under the immediate
influence of the future author of the notorious " Introduction."
(237) " When King Louis was on his first passage to succour the
Holy Land, and I dwelt at Provins, there were two brethren
wholly given to Joachism, who essayed all they could to draw
me to that doctrine. Whereof one was Brother Bartolommeo
Guiscolo, of my own city of Parma, a courteous and spiritual
man, but a great talker and a great Joachite, and devoted to the
Emperor's party. He was once Guardian in the Convent of
Capua : he was most active in all his works. In the world he
had taught grammar, but in our Order he knew to copy, to
illuminate, to compose writings, and to do many other things.
In his lifetime he did marvels, and in his death he worked still
more marvellously ; for he saw such things when his soul went
forth from his body, that all the Brethren present were in
admiration. The other was Brother Gerardino of Borgo San
Donnino, who had grown up in Sicily, and had taught grammar,
and was a well-mannered youth, honest and good, save for this one
thing, that he persevered too obstinately in Joachim's doctrine,
and clung so to his own opinion that none could move him.
These two lay hard upon me that I should believe the writings
of Abbot Joachim and study in them ; for they had Joachim's
exposition on Jeremias[1a] and many other books. And when
the King of France in those days was preparing to cross the seas
with other Crusaders, they mocked and derided, saying that he
would fare ill if he went, as the event showed afterwards. And
they showed me that it was thus written in Joachim's exposition
on Jeremias, and therefore that we must expect its fulfilment.

And whereas throughout the whole of France all that year men sang daily in their conventual Masses the psalm ' O God, the heathens are come into thy inheritance,' yet these two scoffed and said in the words of Jeremiah ' " Thou hast set a cloud before thee, that our prayer may not pass through " ; for the King of France shall be taken, and the French shall be conquered in war, and many shall be carried off by the plague.' Wherefore they were made hateful to the Brethren of France, who said that these evil prophecies had been fulfilled on the former Crusade. There was at that time in the convent of Provins a Lector named Brother Maurice, a comely man, and noble, and most learned, who had studied much, first in the World, at Paris, and then eight years in our Order. He had lately become my friend, and he said to me : ' Brother Salimbene, have no faith in these Joachites, for they trouble the Brethren with their doctrines ; but help me in writing, for I would fain make a good Book of Distinctions, which will be most useful for preachers.'

" Then the Joachites separated of their own free will; for I went to dwell at Auxerre, Brother Bartolommeo to dwell in the convent of Sens, Brother Gerardino was sent to Paris to study for the Province of Sicily, on behalf of which he had been received into the Order. And there he studied four years, and thought out his folly, composing a book, and publishing it abroad without the knowledge of the Brethren. And because for this book's sake the Order was evil-spoken of both at Paris and elsewhere, therefore the aforesaid Gerardino was deprived of his offices of Lector and Preacher, and of the power of hearing confessions, and of all priestly powers. And because he would not amend himself and humbly acknowledge his fault, but with wayward obstinacy persevered in his headstrong contumacy, therefore the Brethren cast him into prison and bonds, feeding him with bread of affliction and water of distress. Yet not even then would this wretch withdraw from his obstinate purpose ; but he suffered himself to die in prison, and was deprived of the burial of the Church and buried in a corner of the garden. Let all know, therefore, that due rigour of justice is kept among us against all that transgress : wherefore one man's fault is not to be imputed to the whole Order.[2]

" So when in the year of our Lord 1248 I was at Hyères with Brother Hugh (seeing that I was curious of the teaching of Abbot Joachim, and gladly heard him, applauding and rejoicing with him), he said to me, ' Art thou infatuated as those who follow this doctrine ? ' For they are indeed held infatuated by many, since although Abbot Joachim was a holy man, yet he had three hindrances to his doctrine. The first was the condemnation of that book which he wrote against Master Peter Lombard, whom he charged with heresy and madness. The second was that he foretold tribulations to come, which was the cause why the Jews slew the Prophets, for carnal men love not to hear of tribulations to come. The third hindrance came from men who believed in him, but who would fain forestall the times and seasons which he had prescribed : for he fixed no certain terms of years though some may think so. Rather, he named several terms, saying, ' God is able to show His mysteries yet more clearly, and they shall see who come after us.[3] '

" Now when I saw that judges and notaries and other learned men were gathered together in Brother Hugh's chamber to hear him teach the doctrine of Abbot Joachim, I remembered Eliseus, of whom it is written ' But Eliseus sat in his house, and the ancients sat with him.' In those days there came two other Joachites of the convent of Naples, whereof one was called Brother John the Frenchman, the other Brother Giovannino Pigolino of Parma. These had come to Hyères to see Brother Hugh and hear him speak on this Doctrine. Then also came two Friars Preachers returning from their General Chapter at Paris, whereof the one was called Brother Peter of Apulia, the Lector of their Order at Naples, and a learned man and a great talker ; and he was waiting a fit time to sail. To him one day after dinner said Brother Giovannino, who knew him very well, ' Brother Peter, what thinkest thou of the doctrine of Abbot Joachim ? ' To which he answered, ' I care as little for Joachim as for the fifth wheel of a waggon ; for even Pope Gregory in one of his homilies believed that the end of the world would come almost in his own time, since the Lombards had come in his days and were destroying all things.' Brother Giovannino therefore hastened to Brother Hugh's chamber, and in the presence of those aforesaid men said to him, ' Here is a certain Friar Preacher who will have nothing of this doctrine.' To whom Brother Hugh said, ' What is that to me ? To him shall it be imputed. Let him look to it when " vexation alone shall make him understand what he hears." Yet call him to disputation and I will hear his doubts.' So he came, but unwillingly, for he despised Joachim, and deemed that there were none in our convent to be compared with himself in learning or in knowledge of the Scriptures. Brother Hugh said to him, ' Art thou he who doubts of the doctrine of Joachim ? ' Brother Peter answered, ' I am he indeed.' ' Hast thou then read Joachim ? ' ' I have read him,' said he, ' with care.' ' Yea,' said Brother Hugh, ' I believe thou hast read him as a woman her Psalter, who when she is come to the end knows and remembers no word of that which she read at the beginning. So many read without understanding, either because they despise what they read, or because their foolish heart is darkened. Tell me now what thou wouldest hear of Joachim.' To whom Brother Peter answered, 'Prove me now by Esaias, as Joachim teacheth, that the life of the Emperor Frederick must be ended in seventy years (for he liveth yet): and that he cannot be slain but by God—that is, by no violent, but by a natural death.' To whom Brother Hugh said, 'Gladly ; but listen patiently, and with no declamations or cavils, for in the matter of this doctrine it behoveth to listen with faith.' " Here follows a discussion so long that I am compelled reluctantly to omit by far the greater part of it : though it contains one most interesting anecdote of the Saint (240). "As to the holiness of Joachim's life, beyond what is to be read in his Legend, I can cite one example wherein his admirable patience is shown. Before he was made Abbot, when he was a subordinate and private person, the refectorer was wroth against him, and for a whole year long always filled his jug with water to drink, wishing to keep him on the bread of affliction and water of distress; all which he bore patiently and without complaint. But when at the end of the year he was sitting beside the Abbot at table, the Abbot said to him, 'Wherefore drinkest thou white wine, and givest none to me ? Is that thy courtesy ?' To whom the holy Joachim answered, 'I was ashamed, Father, to invite you, for "my own secret to myself." ' Then the Abbot taking his cup, and wishing to prove him, tasted thereof, and saw that his merchandise was not good. So, when he had tasted this water *not* turned to wine, he said, 'And what is water but water ?' And he said to him, 'By whose leave drinkest thou such drink?' And Joachim answered, 'Father, water is a sober drink, which neither tieth the tongue, nor bringeth on drunkenness, nor maketh men to babble.' But when the Abbot had learnt in the Chapter-house that this injury and vengeance had been done of the malice and rancour of the refectorer, he would have driven him forth from the Order, but Joachim fell at the Abbot's feet, and prayed him until he spared to expel that lay-brother from the Order. Yet he reviled and rebuked him hard and bitterly, saying, 'I give thee for a penance that thou drink nought but water for a whole year long, as thou hast dealt unjustly with thy neighbour and brother.' " This story (of which Prof. Holder-Egger gives a different and less picturesque version from Joachim's biographer Luke of Cosenza) was well worth recording : but the rest of this long episode is chiefly interesting for the light it throws on medieval methods of theological discussion, which closely resemble those of the tavern disputants in *Janet's Repentance*. Brother Hugh is as mercilessly rhetorical as Lawyer Dempster ; and to Salimbene, as to Mr. Budd, the consideration that his hero had " studied very hard when he was a young man " and was always ready to answer any question on any subject without the least hesitation, entirely outweighs the fact that the event had proved him altogether wrong—for Frederick was now long since dead, at an age considerably short of the prophetical seventy years. Brother Hugh's methods, though every whit as reasonable as those of world-famed controversialists like St. Bernardino of Siena and St. James of the Mark, would carry but little conviction to-day. In vain did the sceptical Dominican ask for more real evidence, and protest against Merlin and the Sibyl being quoted as final authorities : in vain did he " turn to the original words of the Saints and to the sayings of the philosophers " : for " therein Brother Hugh entangled and involved him forthwith ; since he was a most learned man. Then Brother Peter's comrade who was a priest and an old and good man, began to help him, but Brother Peter cried to him ' Peace! Peace ' ! So when Brother Peter found himself conquered, he turned to commend Brother Hugh for his manifold wisdom. And when the aforesaid words had been ended, behold suddenly the shipman's messenger came for the Preachers, telling them to go hastily to the ship. So after their departure, Brother Hugh said to the remaining learned men who had heard the disputation, ' Take it not for an ill example if we have said some things which we should not have said ; for they who dispute of presumptuous boldness are wont to run hither and thither over the field of licence.' And Brother Hugh added ' These good men always boast of their knowledge, and say that in *their* Order is the foundation of wisdom. They say also that they have passed among unlearned men when they have passed through the convents of the Friars Minor, wherein they are charitably and diligently entertained. But by God's grace they shall not say this time that they have passed among men of no learning, for I have done as the Wise Man teacheth " Answer a fool according to his folly, lest he imagine himself to be wise." ' So the layfolk departed much edified and consoled, saying ' We have heard marvels to-day ; but on the Feast following we would hear somewhat of the teaching of our Lord Jesus Christ.' To whom Brother Hugh said, ' If I be still alive I will receive you gladly, and therefore come indeed.' Moreover, that same day the Friars Preachers returned and solaced themselves with us, for

they had no fit weather to sail. And after supper Brother Hugh
was familiar with them, and Brother Peter seated himself on the
ground at his feet, nor was there any who could make him rise
and sit on a level bench with him—no, not even Brother Hugh
himself, though he prayed him instantly. Moreover Brother
Peter, now no longer disputing or contradicting, but humbly
listening, heard the honeyed words which Brother Hugh spake,
(which indeed would be worthy to be related here, but I omit
them for brevity's sake, for I hasten to other things.) Then
Brother Peter's comrade said to me in private, ' For God's sake,
tell me who is that Brother, whether he be a prelate—a Guardian,
a Custos, or a Minister?' To whom I said, ' He has no prelacy,
for he will have none. Once he was a Minister-Provincial, but
now he is a private person, and he is one of the greatest clerks of
the world, and is so esteemed by all who know him.' Then said
he to me, ' In good truth I believe it, for never did I see a man
who speaketh so well, and is so ready in all knowledge. But I
wonder wherefore he dwelleth not in great convents.'[4] To whom
I said, ' By reason of his humility and sanctity, for he is more
comforted to dwell in little houses.' Then said he, ' God's blessing light on him, for he seemeth all heavenly.' And after many
commendations on both sides, the Friars Preachers departed,
consoled and much edified."[5]

This was in 1248: and Hugh's triumphant exposition of
Joachism was shattered in less than two years by the Emperor's
death—not after 1264, as it should have been, but as early as
1250. No doubt Hugh's robust faith survived the shock, for he
could still look forward to the Reign of the Holy Ghost, prophesied
to begin in the year 1260—a year which, by the bye, he never
lived to see. But when 1260 also passed without the expected
signs (though the Flagellants' mania of that year had given him
a brief gleam of hope) then Salimbene's faith in Joachism as an
-ism collapsed. (302) " After the death of the ex-Emperor
Frederick, and the passing of the year 1260, then I let that whole
doctrine go ; and I am purposed to believe no more than I can
see."

Yet he always kept up a lively outsider's interest, and gives
us a long account of a talk with the notorious Gerard of Borgo
San Donnino which took place, as Prof. Michael has shown, in
1256. The condemnation of the *Introduction to the Eternal
Gospel* naturally led to the punishment of its author, who
(456) "had been sent back [from Paris] to his own province
[of Sicily] ; and, because he would not draw back from his folly,
Bonaventura the Minister-General sent for him to join him in

France.   When therefore he passed through Modena, I dwelt there, and I said to him, since I knew him well : ' Shall we dispute of Joachim ? '   Then said he, ' Let us not dispute, but confer thereof : and let us go to some privy place.'   So I took him behind the dormitory, and we sat under a vine; and I said to him ' My question is of Antichrist, when and where he shall be born ? '   Then said he ' He is already born and full-grown ; and the Mystery of Iniquity shall soon be at work.'   So I said ' Dost thou know him ? '   ' I have not seen his face, but I know him well through the Scripture.'   ' Where then is that Scripture ? '   ' In the Bible,' said he.   ' Tell me then, for I know my Bible well.'   ' Nay, I will by no means tell it but if we have a Bible here.   So I brought him one, and he began to expound the whole 18th chapter of Isaiah, beginning ' Woe to the land the winged cymbal ' and so on to the end, as referring to a certain King [Alfonso] of Castile in Spain.[6]   So I said to him, ' Sayest thou then that this King of Castile now reigning is Antichrist ? '   ' Beyond all doubt he is that accursed Antichrist whereof all doctors and saints have spoken who have treated of this matter.'   Then I answered, mocking him, ' I hope in my God that thou shalt find thyself deceived.'   And as I thus spake, suddenly many brethren and secular folk appeared in the meadow behind the dormitory, speaking sadly one with another, : so he said, ' Go thou and hear what these say, since they seem to bring woful news.'   I went and returned and said to him, ' They say that the Lord Philip Archbishop of Ravenna [and Papal legate] hath been taken by Ezzelino.'   Then he answered ' Thou seest that the mysteries are even now begun.'   Then he enquired of me whether I knew a certain man of Verona dwelling in Parma, who had the spirit of prophecy and wrote of the future.   ' I know him well,' said I, ' and have seen his writings.'   ' I would fain have his writings : I beseech thee therefore to procure them for me if it be possible.'   ' Yea, for he is glad to publish them abroad, and rejoices greatly whensoever any will have them : for he has written many homilies which I have seen, and has left the trade of a weaver whereby he was wont to live in Parma, and betaken himself to the convent of the Cistercians at Fontanaviva.   There he dwells in worldly dress at the monks' expense, and writes all day long in a chamber which they have assigned to him : and thou mayest go to him, for the convent is no more than two miles below the high road.'   ' Nay,' said he, ' for my companions would not turn aside from the road ; but I beseech thee to go thither and procure me those books, and thou shalt earn my gratitude.'   So he went on his way, and I saw him no more : but when I had time I went to that convent.   There I found a friend of mine, Brother Alberto Cremonella, who entered the Order of Friars Minor the same day as I, ... but he quitted the Order during his novitiate, returning to the world and studying medicine, and after that he entered the Cistercian Order at Fontanaviva. where he was held in great esteem by all.   Seeing me therefore, he thought (as he said) to see an angel of God ; for he loved me familiarly.   Then said I that he would do me much favour if he would lend me all the writings of that man of Verona.   But he answered and said, ' Know, Brother Salimbene, that I am great and powerful in this house, and the brethren love me of their own lovingkindness and for my gift of physic ; and if thou wilt I can lend thee all the works of St. Bernard : but this man of whom thou speakest is dead, nor is there one letter of all his writings left in the world, for with mine own hands have I scraped all his books clean, and I will tell thee how and why.   We had a Brother in this convent who was excellently skilled in scraping parchment, and he said to our Abbot, " Father, the Blessed Job and Ecclesiastes warn us of our death : and it is written in Hebrews ' It is appointed unto men once to die : ' since therefore it is clearer to me than the light of day that I must some day depart this life, for I am no better than my fathers ; therefore, Father, I pray you vouchsafe to assign me certain disciples who would learn to scrape parchment : for they might be profitable to this convent after my death."   Since therefore there was none found but I who would learn this art, therefore after the death of my master and of this man of Verona, I scraped all his books so clean that not one letter is left of all his writings : not only that I might have material whereon to learn my art, but also for that we had been sorely scandalized by reason of those prophecies.'⁷   So I, hearing this, said in my heart, ' Yea, and the book of Jeremias the Prophet was once burned, and he who burned it escaped not due punishment ; and the law of Moses was burned by the Chaldees, yet Esdras restored it again by the aid of the Holy Ghost.'   So there arose in Parma a certain simple man whose intellect was enlightened to foretell the future, as it is written in Proverbs, ' God's communication is with the simple.'⁸   Moreover after many years, while I dwelt in the convent of Imola, Brother Arnolfo my Guardian came to my cell with a book written on paper sheets, saying, ' There is in this land a certain notary who is a friend of the brethren ; and he hath lent me this book to read, which he wrote at Rome when he was there with the Lord Brancaleone of Bologna, Senator of Rome ; and the book is exceedingly dear to him, for it is written and composed by Brother Gerard of Borgo San Donnino : wherefore do thou, who hast studied in the books of Abbot Joachim, read now this treatise and tell me whether there is any good therein.' So when I had read and understood it, I answered Brother Arnolfo saying : 'This book hath not the style of the ancient doctors ; but rather frivolous and ridiculous words ; wherefore the book is of evil fame and hath been condemned, so that I counsel you to cast it into the fire and burn it, and bid this friend of yours have patience with you for God's sake and the Order's.' So it was done, and the book burned. Yet note that this Brother Gerard who wrote the aforesaid book seemed to have much good in him. For he was friendly, courteous, liberal, religious, honest, modest, well-mannered, temperate in word and food and drink and raiment, helpful with all humility and gentleness. He was indeed such as the Wise Man writeth in Proverbs 'a man amiable in society, who shall be more friendly than a brother ' ; yet his wayward-ness in his own opinion brought all these good things to nought. It was ordained by reason of this Gerard that from henceforward no new writing should be published without the Order, save only such as had first been approved by the Ministers and the Definitors in a Chapter General ; and that if any did contrary to this rule, he should fast three days on bread and water, and his book should be taken from him." Gerard's book, according to our chronicler, "contained many falsehoods contrary to the doctrine of Abbot Joachim, and such as he had never written ; as for instance that Christ's Gospel and the teaching of the New Testament had led no man to perfection, and would be super-seded in the year 1260."

In judging the apparent coolness with which Salimbene speaks of his friend's disgrace and death, we must remember that he himself had given up the Millennarian side of Joachism, and was therefore compelled, like nine-tenths of the other Franciscans, to look upon Gerard as the man whose blundering obstinacy might easily have caused the defeat of the Orders in their great struggle with the secular doctors at Paris. Gerard was the intellectual black sheep of the Order ; Angelo Clareno, excluding him from the list of persecuted Spirituals, rejoices on the contrary to record that "he died as a heretic and excommunicate, and was denied Christian burial" after 18 years of imprisonment in Fran-ciscan dungeons (Arch. iv, 11, 283 ff.) ; and, considering the usual tone of medieval religious controversy, Salimbene's gener-ous tribute to Gerard's character is far more noticeable than his failure to sympathize with sufferings which a recantation would at any moment have ended. It is difficult for us in this age to realize even remotely the scorn which the most sympathetic men felt then for all poor fools who went to death as champions of unorthodox ideas. " This is the utmost folly " (writes Salimbene, p. 460), " when a man is rebuked by men of the greatest learning, and yet will not retreat from his false opinions against the Catholic faith . . . . no man, therefore, ought to be wanton and pertinacious in his own opinions." St. James of the Mark, again, was an able man and a real saint : but it is impossible to read without a shudder the reasons by which he overcame his natural reluctance to burn heretics.[9]

Frequent as are Salimbene's further allusions to Joachim, they mostly imply no more than that he still looked upon him as a man of great personal holiness, and endowed with the gift of foretelling certain particular events. He caught gladly, to the very end, at all Joachistic prophecies which fell in with his own views, but tacitly abandoned the rest.   He is especially fond of the spurious " Exposition of Jeremiah," with its prophecies of the greatness of the friars, and especially with the preference which it shows for the Franciscans over the Dominicans.   The Franciscans (it says) shall be the more popular and less exclusive Order : they alone shall last till the day of Judgment : for Salimbene, like most men of his time, was haunted by that vague, not always uncomfortable, foreboding of the near end of the world which contributed so much to the popularity of Joachism. He quotes how (579) " it was once revealed in a vision to a certain spiritual brother of the Friars Preachers that they would have as many Ministers-General as there are letters in the word *dirigimur* (" *we are governed* ") : which hath nine letters ; so that, if the vision be true, there are but two to come : namely, *u* and *r*. For the first letter signifieth *Dominic*, the second, *Iordan*, the third, *Raymund*, the fourth, *Iohn*, the fifth, *Gumbert* [*i.e.*, Humbert de Romans], the sixth, *Iohn the Second*, the seventh, *Munio*, who is now their General : whereof a like example is recorded by St. Gregory in the third book of his dialogues. And note that Abbot Joachim, to whom God revealed the future, said that the Order of Preachers should suffer with the rest of the clergy, but the Order of Friars Minor should endure to the end." The reference to St. Gregory is no doubt chap. 38, where the Pope, writing about 600 A.D., speaks of the probability— or, rather, the certainty—that the Last Judgment is close at hand. He therefore proceeds to relate a series of miracles designed to confute those " many folk within the bosom of Holy Church who doubt whether the soul survive the death of the flesh." Salimbene, as we may see from a sentence recorded above in his description of Hugh's argument, was critical enough to observe that these expectations of immediate judgment had been common at least from an early period of the Middle Ages. Later on he records another story showing how men's minds were haunted in his day by similar terrors of a coming Visitation of God. It may remind some readers of Chaucer's " Miller's Tale," the plot of which was probably taken from some 13th-century *fabliau.* (620) " In the year 1286 there died in the city of Reggio a certain man of Brescia, who had aforetime taught boys to read the Psalter, and feigned himself to be poor, and went about begging, singing also at times and playing the panpipe, that men might the more readily give. The devil put it into his heart that there would be a great famine ; wherefore he would roast crusts of bread and lay them in chests ; and he filled sacks with meal trodden down, which likewise he laid up in chests, against this famine which, as I have said, he hoped for at the devil's suggestion. But as it was said to the rich man in the Gospel ' Thou fool, etc.' so it befel this wretched miser. For one evening he fell into a grievous sickness beyond his wont, and, being alone in his house, he diligently bolted the door upon himself ; and that night he was foully choked by the devil, and shamefully mishandled. So on the morrow when he appeared not, his neighbours came together, men and women and children, and burst his door by force, and found him lying dead on the earth ; and they found the sacks of meal already rotten in one chest, and two other chests they found full of roasted bread-crusts. And it was found likewise that he had two houses in the city, in different quarters, which became forfeit to the Commune of Reggio ; that the common proverb might be fulfilled, ' *Quod non accipit Christus accipit Fiscus*—That which is not given to Christ goeth to the public treasury.' Moreover the children stripped that wretch naked, and bound shackles of wood to his feet, and dragged his naked corpse through all the streets and places of the city, for a laughing-stock and a mockery to all men. And, strange to relate ! no man had taught them to deal thus, nor did any reprove them or say that they had done ill. But when at last they came to St. Anthony's spital, and were weary with their labour, it chanced that a certain peasant came that way with an ox-waggon. The boys therefore would have bound this outcast corpse to the tail of his waggon, but he strove to hinder them ; then the boys rose up suddenly against that boor, and beat him sore, that he was fain at last to let them do as they would. They went out of the city therefore by the bridge of

S. Stefano, and cast the corpse from the bridge upon the gravel of the torrent called Crostolo, and then climbing down they heaped thereon a mighty pile of stones, crying ' Thy famine and thine avarice go down with thee to hell, and thy churlishness withal, for ever and a day.' Whence it became a proverb that men would say to miserly persons ' Take heed lest ye provoke the boys' fury by your churlishness.' "[10]

It is disappointing from many points of view that our chronicler so early lost sympathy with Joachism as a life-force : with that Joachism which was soon to inspire Dolcino, and after him Rienzi, and was so often the mainspring of those antisacerdotal sects which flourished all through the Middle Ages. For it can scarcely be out of place here to point out a more than superficial analogy between 13th century and 19th century religious life. Mysticism and Rationalism, little as they care to recognize each other, have strong secret affinities : enthusiasm may give a mighty impulse, but can never be sure what direction the forces thus liberated will finally take. Every fresh presentment of Christianity is double-edged in its truth as in its error. By means of his Theory of Development Newman reconciled himself to a Rome which, as he saw only too clearly, was very different from the Rome of the Apostles : he took the theory with him into his new church, and there it has borne unexpected fruit in the doctrines of Abbé Loisy and his school. To Newman, it was the high road from dreary Private Judgment to blessed Authority : to the modern intellectual Romanist, it is as easy a backward road from Authority to Private Judgment. Much of this same tendency may be traced in the history of Joachism. The Prophet of Calabria reconciled himself to the corruptions of the Church around him as to tokens which, after all, marked the imminent birth of a new era ; and his theory undoubtedly did much to create a favourable atmosphere for the coming friars, who were themselves deeply inspired by the conviction that old things were passed away, and all things were become new. When, however, after a generation or so, it became evident how little the Church in general was shaken from its old evil ways, then the restless energies of the new movement began in many cases to work backwards, rebounding with the very force of their own impact against so vast and inert a mass. The more men realized the living forces liberated by the Franciscan and Dominican reform, the more they were tempted to despair of a priesthood on which even such a shock could scarcely make an appreciable impression.[11] It was certain (so at least Joachim, truly interpreting the yearnings of his age, had taught), that the world was on the brink of a new and brighter era, with nothing now intervening save Antichrist and the Abomination of Desolation—the death-throes of a dying world from which the new world was to be born. Men whose every thought was coloured by this conviction—and thousands of the best and most pious, such as Adam Marsh, were more or less avowed Joachites—would find it difficult indeed to stifle antisacerdotal suggestions, as decade after decade passed without real reform within the Church.   So long as Frederick and his race were alive, so that the civil wars of Italy bore some real appearance of religious wars, so long good Church-men could always see Antichrist in the Empire.   But when, in the latter half of the 13th century, the Emperors became almost vassals of the Popes, and yet the world seemed rather worse than better—then at last men began to ask themselves whether the real enemy of the Church was not the Cleric himself : whether that Antichrist and that Abomination of Desolation, which by the Joachitic hypothesis were already let loose upon the world, could be any other than the Pope and his court, so powerful to fight with carnal weapons, and so powerless to reform the Church. And so among the Franciscans—who naturally counted a dis-proportionate number of enthusiasts and quick intellects, and with whom the liberties of the individual friar were often all the greater for his Order's well-earned reputation of subservience to the Pope—many among the Franciscans, first as zealous Spirituals and then as schismatical Fraticelli, became the chief exponents of the Antipapal element in Joachim's theories. Much is permitted to a man who is labelled with the label of a powerful party : and antipapalism often grew up unchecked among the Papal militia of the Middle Ages, just as Unitarianism grew up under the 18th century Presbyterianism, and as in our own generation a strict devotion to ritual will cover views on inspiration and on miracles which to the early Tractarians would have seemed unspeakably abominable. We can see this under our own eyes : we can trace much of the same tendency in the 13th century ; and it would have been welcome indeed if Salimbene had spoken as freely on this subject as he did on many others. But the old chronicler had already forgotten many of the interests of his youth ; and indeed this matter of Joachism is the one solitary case in which Salimbene seems ever to have cherished sectarian sympathies ; some of his most important and entertaining records, as will be seen later on, are directed against enthusiasts of his age whose religious zeal outran their discretion.   Nor is it easy to imagine that he ever fully sympathized—even under the daily influence of Brothers Hugh and John of Parma—with that passionate longing for a new world which was the soul of real Joachism. The world he saw and knew, with all its shortcomings, was a great deal too full of interest to be wished away. He was an Epicurean in the higher sense, recognizing that there are few pleasures in life so keen and abiding as that of learning; and that, so long as one is young and strong, there is no better way of learning than to travel among many men and many cities.

CHAPTER XIV.

Further Wanderings.

SALIMBENE, however happy in Brother Hugh's company, had no real business at Hyères, and could not stay there indefinitely. Accordingly (294) "I borrowed from him what he had of the Expositions of Abbot Joachim on the four Evangelists, and went to dwell in the convent of Aix, where I copied the book with the help of my comrade for Brother John of Parma, who was likewise a very mighty Joachite." Aix attracted him for those romantic but mythical traditions which may still be read in the Golden Legend, a book which was compiled by a contemporary of Salimbene's and probably an acquaintance: for he seems to have been in the Dominican convent of Genoa in this year 1248 when Salimbene spent some months at the Franciscan convent there. Martha and Lazarus and the Magdalene, with St. Maximin who had been one of the 72 disciples, and Martilla who had cried in the crowd "Blessed is the womb that bare thee," and Cedonius, the blind man of John ix. 2, had been put by the Jews on board a boat without sails or rudder; and "by God's will they came to Marseilles, where in process of time Lazarus was Bishop; and he wrote his book *On the Pains of Hell,* as he had seen them with his own eyes. But when I enquired after this book at Marseilles, I heard that it had been burnt by the negligence and carelessness of the guardian of the church."[1] (295) "When therefore I had written this book, the month of September was come, and Brother Raymond, Minister of Provence, wrote me word to come and meet the Minister-General. He wrote also to Brother Hugh to meet him, and we found him at Tarascon, where now is the body of St. Martha: so we went to visit her body—we twelve Brethren besides the General; and the Canons showed us her arm to kiss. So when we had said our Compline in the convent, and beds had been assigned to the guests to sleep in the same building with the General, he went out into the cloister to pray. But the strange Brethren feared to enter their beds until the General

came to his ; and I, seeing their distress,—for they murmured,
because they would fain have slept, and could not, for the bed-
places were lighted with bright tapers of wax—therefore I went
to the General, who was my very close and intimate friend, being
of my country, and akin to my kindred.   So I found him praying,
and said, ' Father, the strange Brethren, wearied with their
journey and their labour, would fain sleep ; but they fear to enter
their beds, until you be first come to yours.'   Then said he, ' Go,
tell them from me to sleep with God's blessing ' : and so it was.
But it seemed good to me to await the General, that I might
show him his bed.   When therefore he was come from prayer,
I showed him the bed prepared for him : but he said, ' Son, the
Pope's self might sleep in this bed:* never shall John of Parma
sleep therein.'   And he threw himself upon the empty bed which
I hoped to have.   And I said to him, ' Father, God forgive you,
for you have deprived me of my allotted bed, wherein I thought
to sleep.'   And he said, ' Son, sleep *thou* in that Papal bed ' ;
and when after his example I would have refused, he said to me,
' I am firmly resolved that thou shalt lie there, and that is my
command ' : wherefore I must needs do as he commanded."
Here at Tarascon Salimbene saw and admired two English friars,
of whom the principal, Brother Stephen, " had entered the Order
in his boyhood ; a comely, spiritual, and learned man, of most
excellent counsel, and ready to preach daily to the clergy ; and
he had most excellent writings of Brother Adam Marsh, whose
lectures on Genesis I heard from him."   Stephen, of whom
Salimbene has an interesting tale to tell presently, is possibly
the hero of one of the most charming anecdotes in Eccleston.
(R.S. p. 26.) " Brother Peter the Spaniard, who was afterwards
Guardian of Northampton and wore a shirt of mail to tame the
temptations of the flesh . . . had in his convent a novice who
was tempted to leave the Order : but he persuaded him with
much ado to go with him to the Minister.   On the road, Brother
Peter began to preach to him of the virtue of Holy Obedience ;
and lo ! a wild bird went before them as they walked on the way.
So the novice, whose name was Stephen, said to Brother Peter,
' Father, if it be as thou sayest, bid me in virtue of obedience to
catch this wild bird, and bid it wait for me.'   The Brother did
so : and the bird stood suddenly still, and the novice came up
and took it and handled it as he would.   Straightway his temptation was wholly assuaged, and God gave unto him another

---

* *Alla paperina* was a common Italian phrase to denote great comfort : cf.
Sacchetti Nov. 131 and 156.

heart, and he returned forthwith to Northampton and made his profession of perseverance; and afterwards he became a most excellent preacher, as I saw with mine own eyes."

Salimbene accompanied John of Parma down the Rhone again to Arles. (297) "And one day when the General was alone, I went to his chamber, and behold, after me came my comrade who was likewise of Parma, Brother Giovannino dalle Olle by name, and he said, 'Father, vouchsafe that I and Brother Salimbene may have the aureole.'* Then the General showed a jocund face, saying to my comrade, 'How then can I give you the aureole?' To whom Brother Giovannino answered, 'By giving us the office of Preachers.' Then said Brother John, 'In very truth, if ye were both my blood-brethren, ye should not have that office otherwise than by the sword of examination.' Then I answered and said to my comrade in the Minister's hearing, 'Hence, hence, with thine aureole! I received the office of Preacher last year from Pope Innocent IV at Lyons. Since therefore it hath once been granted to me by him who had all power, shall I receive it *now* from Brother Giovannino of San Lazzaro?' (For Brother John of Parma was called *Master Giovannino* when he taught logic in the world; and *di San Lazzaro* after the spital of San Lazzaro where his uncle brought him up.) Then answered my comrade, 'I would rather have the office from the Minister-General than from any Pope, and if we must needs pass by the sword of examination, then let Brother Hugh examine us.' 'Nay,' said Brother John, 'I will not that Brother Hugh examine you, for he is your friend and will spare you; but call me the Lector and Repetitor of this convent.' They came at his call, and he said, 'Lead these Brethren apart, and examine them on matters of preaching alone, and bring me word whether they are worthy to have that office.' It was done as he commanded: to me he gave the office, but not to my comrade, who was found wanting in knowledge. Yet the General said to him, 'Delay is no robbery. Study wisdom, my son, and make my heart joyful, that thou mayest give an answer to him that reproacheth.' Then came two young Brethren of Tuscany also, deacons and good scholars, who had studied many years with me in the convent of Pisa: and on the morrow, when they would have departed, they sent to the General through Brother

---

* It was commonly believed that a halo of special glory in heaven was reserved for virgins, or doctors, or martyrs, and that a preacher might rank for this purpose with a doctor. Salimbene, who certainly did not aspire to martyrdom, is glad to think that, through the Pope's grace, he is yet sure of his future crown of glory.[2]

Mark his companion, beseeching the office of Preacher and a
licence for the priesthood. The General was saying his Compline, and I with him : then came Brother Mark and interrupted
our Compline to give his message : to whom the General answered in fervour of spirit (as was his wont when he believed himself
to be stirred with zeal for God) saying 'These brethren do ill,
in that they beg shamelessly for such honours : for the Apostle
saith : "No man doth take the honour to himself." Lo these
men have come away from their own Minister, who knew them
and might have given them that which they seek from me :
let them therefore go now to Toulouse whither they are sent to
study, and continue to learn there ; for we need not their
preaching : yet at a fitting season they may obtain this.' Then,
seeing that he was wroth, Brother Mark withdrew from him
saying : 'Father, ye should rather believe that they ask not of
their own accord : for it might well have been that Brother
Salimbene had besought me to plead with you on their behalf.'
Then answered the General : 'Brother Salimbene hath been
all the while saying his Compline here with me : therefore know
I that it was not he who spake to thee of this matter.' So
Brother Mark withdrew saying, 'Father, be it as thou wilt.'
Knowing therefore that Brother Mark had not taken the
General's answer in good part, I went to comfort him when
our Compline was done. And he said unto me : 'Brother Salimbene, Brother John hath done evil in that he hath turned away
my face, and would not admit my prayers, even though the favour
were but small ; albeit that I pain myself for the Order, in following him and in writing his letters, though I be now advanced
in years.'" Brother Mark's distress gains additional pathos
from the character which Salimbene gives him elsewhere (see
Chap. ix) ; but the first fault was in his own indiscretion. John
of Parma was not among the many who, in St. Bonaventura's
words, "say the Hours sleepily and indevoutly and imperfectly,
with a wandering heart, and a tongue that sometimes omits
whole verses and syllables" : on the contrary, Angelo Clareno
assures us that he took his Breviary very seriously, always
standing and doffing his hood to recite, as St. Francis
had done : so that his old friend ought to have known better
than to interrupt him at Compline.[3] No doubt Brother
Mark's zeal had for a moment overrun his discretion : and
his disappointment was now all the more bitter. "If they
were priests," he complained, "then they might celebrate
Masses for both quick and dead, and be more profitable
to the Brethren to whom they go ; and God knoweth that I am

ashamed now to return to them with my prayer ungranted."
Salimbene, however sympathetic, could only remind him that
" patience hath a perfect work."

" That evening " (he continues) " the General sent for me and
my comrade, and said, ' My sons, I hope soon to leave you, for
I purpose to go to Spain; wherefore choose for yourselves any
convent soever, except Paris, in the whole Order, and take the
space of this night to ponder and make your choice, and tell me
to-morrow.' On the morrow he said, ' What have ye chosen ? '
So I answered, ' In this matter we have done nothing, lest it
should become an occasion of mourning to us ; but we leave it
in your choice to send us whithersoever it may seem good, and we
will obey.' Whereat he was edified, and said, ' Go therefore
to the convent of Genoa, where ye shall dwell with Brother
Stephen the Englishman. Moreover, I will write to the Minister
and Brethren there, commending you to their favour even as myself ; and that thou, Brother Salimbene, mayest be promoted to the
priesthood, and thy comrade to the diaconate. And when I come
thither, if I find you satisfied, I shall rejoice ; and if not, I will
console you again.' And so it was. Moreover, that same day
the General said to Brother Hugh his friend, ' What say ye, shall
we go to Spain, and fulfil the Apostle's desire ? ' And Brother
Hugh answered him, ' Go ye, Father ; for my part I would fain
die in the land of my fathers.' So we brought him forthwith to
his ship, which lay ready on the Rhone : and he went that day to
St.-Gilles, but we went by sea to Marseilles, whence we sailed
to Hyères to Brother Hugh's convent. There I dwelt with my
comrade from the Feast of St. Francis until All Saints ; rejoicing
to be with Brother Hugh, with whom I conversed all day long of
the doctrine of Abbot Joachim : for he had all his books. But
I lamented that my comrade grew grievously sick, almost to
death ; and he would not take care of himself, and the weather
grew daily worse for sailing as the winter drew on. And that
country was most unwholesome that year, by reason of the sea-
wind ; and by night I could scarce breathe, even as I lay in
the open air. And I heard wolves crying and howling in the
night in great multitudes, and this not once or twice only. So
I said to my comrade, who was a most wayward youth, ' Thou
wilt not guard thyself from things contrary to thy health, and art
ever relapsing into sickness. But I know that this country is
most unwholesome, and I would fain not die yet, for I would
fain live to see the things foretold by Brother Hugh. Wherefore
know thou, that if fitting fellowship of our Brethren shall come
hither, I will go with them.' And he said, ' What thou sayest

pleases me. I also will go with thee.' For he hoped that none
of the Brethren would come at that time. And behold, by the
will of the Lord forthwith there came one Brother Ponce, a holy
man, who had been with us in the Convent of Aix; and he was
going to Nice, of which Convent he had been made Guardian.
And he rejoiced to see us; and I said to him, ' We will go with
you, for we must needs come to Genoa to dwell there.' And he
answered and said, ' It is most pleasing to me. Go therefore
and procure us a ship.' So on the morrow after dinner we went
to the ship, which was a mile from our Convent, but my comrade
would not come, until, seeing that I was straitly purposed to
depart, he took leave of the Guardian, and came after us. And
when I gave him my hand to raise him up into the ship, he
abhorred it, and said, ' God forbid that thou shouldst touch me,
for thou hast not kept faith and good comradeship with me.'
To whom I said, ' Wretched man! know now God's goodness
towards thee. For the Lord hath revealed to me that if thou
hadst stayed here, thou wouldst doubtless have died.' Yet
he believed me not, until ' vexation did make him understand
what he heard '; for all that winter he could not shake off the
sickness which he had taken in Provence. And when on the
Feast of St. Matthew following I again visited Hyères, I found
six Brethren of that convent dead and buried, the first of whom
was the Guardian, who had accompanied my comrade to the
ship. So when I was come back to Genoa and had told my
comrade of these deaths, he thanked me that I had snatched
him from the jaws of death." It would have been a thousand
pities if he had died in his wayward youth : for he went afterwards as a missionary to the Christian captives in Egypt after
the disastrous failure of St. Louis' second crusade, "for the
merit of salutary obedience and for the remission of all his sins.
For he himself did much good to those Christians, and was the
cause of much more; and he saw an Unicorn and the Balsam
Vine,* and brought home Manna in a vessel of glass, and water
from St. Mary's Well (with which alone the Balsam Vine can be
watered so as to bear fruit) : and Balsam wood he brought home
with him, and many such things which we had never seen, which
he was wont to show to the Brethren : and he would tell also
how the Saracens keep Christians in bonds and make them to

* For this Balsam see Sir John Mandeville (chap. v), who gives an equally
miraculous, though quite different account of its methods of fructification. It
grows only near Cairo, and in "India the Greater, in that desert where the
trees of the sun and moon spake to Alexander. But I have not seen it, for I
have not been so far upward, because there are too many perilous passages."

dig the trenches of their fortifications and to carry off the earth in baskets, and how each Christian receives but three small loaves a day. So he was present at the General Chapter in Strasburg [A.D. 1282]; and on his way thence he ended his days at the first convent of the brethren this side of Strasburg [*i.e.* Colmar], and shone with the glory of miracles. So lived and died Brother Giovannino dalle Olle, who was my comrade in France, in Burgundy, in Provence, and in the convent at Genoa : a good writer and singer and preacher ; an honest and good and profitable man : may his soul rest in peace ! In the convent wherein he died was a brother incurably diseased, for all that the doctors could do, of a long-standing sickness ; yet when he set himself wholly to pray God that He would make him whole for love of Brother Giovannino, then was he forthwith freed from his sickness, as I heard from Brother Paganino of Ferrara, who was there present." In his company, then, Salimbene sailed to Nice, where they picked up a famous Spiritual, Brother Simon of Montesarchio. The three sailed on from Nice to Genoa ; and here our chronicler found himself again among good friends. (315) " The Brethren rejoiced to see us, and were much cheered ; more especially Brother Stephen the Englishman, whom afterwards the Minister-General sent to Rome as he had promised ; and he became Lector in the convent of Rome, where he died with his comrade, Brother Jocelin, after they had completed their desire of seeing Rome and her sanctuaries. Moreover, in the convent of Genoa when I arrived there was Brother Taddeo, who had been a Canon of St. Peter's Church in Rome. He was old and stricken in years, and was reputed a Saint by the Brethren. So likewise was Brother Marco of Milan, who had already been Minister : so likewise was Brother Anselmo Rabuino of Asti, who had been Minister of the Provinces of Terra di Lavoro, and Treviso, and had dwelt long at Naples with Brother John of Parma. There were also at Genoa Brother Bertolino the Custode, who was afterwards Minister, and Brother Pentecost, a holy man, and Brother Matthew of Cremona, a discreet and holy man : and all these bore themselves kindly and courtly and charitably towards us. For the Guardian gave me two new frocks, an outer and an inner, and the same to my comrade. And the Minister, Brother Nantelmo, promised to give me whatsoever consolation and grace I might require. He gave his own companion, Brother William of Piedmont, a worthy and learned and good man, to teach me to sing Mass. These have passed all from this world to the Father, and their names are in the Book of Life, for they ended their life well and laudably." Here in Genoa, therefore, Salimbene settled down for a while,

happy in his easily-won Preacher's aureole; but his companion
passed straight on to fight for a Martyr's crown.   (318) "In
this same year 1248, Pope Innocent IV sent Brother Simon of
Montesarchio into Apulia, to withdraw that kingdom and Sicily
from the dominion of the deposed Emperor.   And he drew
many to the Church party; but at last the Emperor took him
and had him tortured with eighteen divers torments, all of which
he bore patiently, nor could the tormentors wring aught from
him but praise of God; Who wrought many miracles through
him—may he be my Intercessor, Amen!   He was my friend at
the Court of Lyons when we travelled together to the Pope, and
when we travelled from Nice to Genoa we told each other many
tales.   He was a man of middle height, and dark, like St.
Boniface* ; always jocund and spiritual; of good life and proper
learning.   There was also another Brother Simon, called 'of the
Countess,' whom God glorified by miracles, and who was my
familiar friend at the convent of Marseilles this same year."
This Simon, also called Simon of Colazzone, was one of the
leaders of the Spirituals in their resistance to Brother Elias; but
the wily Minister, dreading his noble and royal connexions,
spared him when he scourged St. Anthony of Padua and
imprisoned Cæsarius of Spires.   A long list of his miracles, from
the Papal Bull of Beatification, may be found in Mark of Lisbon
(L. i. cap. x.)   The allusion to him here is important as a further
proof that, if Salimbene took for granted the "relaxed" view
of the Rule, it was not for want of zealous Spiritual friends.
John of Parma, Hugues de Digne, Bernard of Quintavalle, Giles
of Perugia, Illuminato, Simon of Colazzone, all six *Beati* and
miracle-workers, show that Salimbene kept the best of company
within his Order.   This lends all the more point to the story of
holy violence which he tells; a tale admirably illustrating those
encroachments by which the friars, to the detriment of their
own healthy influence in other directions, needlessly exasperated
the parish clergy.   (316) "There was in the city of Genoa a
certain Corsican Bishop, who had been a Black Monk of St.
Benedict, and whom King Enzio or Frederick, in their hatred
of the Church, had expelled from Corsica.   He now dwelt at
Genoa and copied books with his own hand for a livelihood; and
daily he came to the Mass of the Friars Minor, and afterwards
he heard Brother Stephen the Englishman teach in our Schools.
This Bishop consecrated me priest in the church of Sant' Onorato,

---

* Who is described in the *Golden Legend* as "a square-built and stout man,
with thick hair," and as " bearing pain readily."

which is now in the convent of the Friars Minor at Genoa. But
in those days it was not so—nay, rather, a certain priest had and
held it just over our convent, though he had no folk for his
parishioners. And when the Brethren came back from Matins
to rest in their cells, this good man troubled their rest with his
church-bells ; and thus he did every night. Wherefore the
Brethren grew weary, and so wrought with Pope Alexander IV
that they took that church from him. This Pope had canonized
St. Clare, and at the very hour whereat he celebrated the first
Mass of St. Clare, when he had said his prayer, the priest drew
near and said, ' I beseech you, Father, for love of the Blessed
Clare, not to take from me the church of Sant' Onorato.' But
the Pope took up his parable and began to say, in the vulgar
tongue, ' For the love of the Blessed Clare 1 will that the Brethren
Minor have it.' And thus he said many times over, so that he
seemed almost mad (*infatuatus*) to repeat it so often, and that
the priest groaned to hear it and departed from him."

CHAPTER XV

A Bishop's Conscience.

SALIMBENE had come to Genoa in November 1248 : in Feb. 1249 he was already on the move again : for (320) " It pleased Brother Nantelmo my Minister to send me to the Minister-General for the business of the Province. So I put to sea, and came in four days to Brother Hugh's convent at Hyères. And he rejoiced to see me; and, being Guardian for the time being, he ate familiarly with me and my comrade and none else but the Brethren who served us. He gave us a magnificent dinner of sea-fish and other meats, for we were at the beginning of Lent; and not only my comrade from Genoa, but even the Brethren of that convent marvelled at his great familiarity and complaisance with me : for in those days Brother Hugh was not wont to eat with any, perchance because Lent was at hand. And we spake much of God during that dinner, and of the doctrine of Abbot Joachim, and of what should come to pass in the world. When I left Genoa there was an almond-tree in blossom hard by our sacristy, and in Provence I found the fruit of this tree already big with green husk. I found also broad beans fresh grown in their pods. After dinner I went on my way to the Minister-General, whom I presently found at Avignon on his return from Spain ; for he had been recalled by the Pope to go among the Greeks, of whom there was hope that by the mediation of Vatatzes they might be reconciled to the Roman Church. Thence I went to Lyons with the Minister-General, and at Vienne we found the messenger of Vatatzes, who was of our Order, and was called Brother Salimbene, even as I. He was Greek of one parent, and Latin of another, and spoke Latin excellently, though he had no clerical tonsure. And when the General had come to the Pope, the Holy Father received him and vouchsafed to kiss him on the mouth, and said to him, ' God forgive thee, son, for thou hast delayed long. Why didst thou not come on horseback, to be with me the sooner ? ' To whom Brother John answered, ' Father, I came swiftly enough when I had seen thy letters ; but the Brethren by whom I have passed have kept me on the way.' To whom the Pope said, ' We have prosperous tidings, namely that the Greeks are willing to be reconciled with the Church of Rome ; wherefore I will that thou go to them with good fellowship of Brethren of thy Order, and it may be that by thy mediation God will deign to work some good. Receive therefore from me every favour which thou mayest desire.' So the Minister-General departed from Lyons when Easter week was passed.

" I found at Lyons Brother Ruffino, Minister of Bologna,* who said to me, ' I sent thee into France to study for my Province, and thou hast gone to dwell in the convent of Genoa. Know therefore that I take this very ill, since I bring students together for the honour of my Province.' And I said, ' Forgive me, Father, for I knew not that you would take it ill.' Then he answered, ' I forgive under this condition, that thou write forthwith an Obedience whereby thou mayest return to my Province whence thou hast come, with thy comrade who is now in Genoa.' So I did, and the Minister-General knew not of this Obedience when he was at Lyons. So I went on my way to Vienne, and thence through Grenoble and the valley of the Count of Savoy, where I heard of the fall and ruin of the mountain. For the year before, in the valley of Maurienne—between Grenoble and Chambéry--there is a plain called the valley of Savoy proper, a league distant from Chambéry, over which rose a great and lofty mountain, which fell one night and filled the whole valley ; the ruin whereof is a whole league and a half in breadth : under which ruin seven parishes were overwhelmed, and 4000 men were slain. I heard tell of this ruin at Genoa ; and in this year following I passed through that country, that is, through Grenoble, and understood it with more certainty ; and many years after, at the convent of Ravenna, I enquired of the fall of this mountain from Brother William, Minister of Burgundy, who was passing through that city on his way to a Chapter General : and I have written it faithfully and truly as I heard it from his mouth.[1] On this journey I entered a certain church dedicated to St. Gerard, which was all full of children's shirts.† Thence I passed on to Embrun, where was an Archbishop born of Piacenza, who daily gave dinner to two Friars Minor, and ever set places for them at his table, and portions of all his dishes before them. So if any came, they had this dinner ; but if not,

* Not the Ruffino of the Fioretti.

† No doubt as thanksgiving offerings for cures : perhaps the church was that of Gières by Grenoble.

he caused it to be given to other poor folk. Moreover, in that country dwell thirteen Brethren. Then came the Guardian and said to me, ' Brother, may it please thee to go and eat with the Archbishop, who will take it in excellent good part ; for it is long since the Brethren have eaten with him, because they are wearied to go thither so often.' But I said, 'Father, forgive me, and take it not ill : for I must depart without delay after meat ; but the Archbishop, hearing that I was from the Court, would hinder my journey by asking after tidings.' Then the Guardian held his peace, but I said softly to my comrade, ' I have bethought me that it is well to finish our journey while we have fair weather and good letters, that we may quickly answer those who sent us, and also lest the Minister-General come before us to the convent of Genoa ; for our own Minister would not take our journey in so good part : ' and that which I said and did pleased my comrade. So we departed therefore and passed through the lands of the Count Dauphin, and so came to Susa. And when we were come to Alessandria we found two Brethren of Genoa, to whom my comrade said, 'Know that ye are losing Brother Salimbene and his comrade at Genoa, for the Minister of Bologna is recalling them to his Province. But I, though I be of Genoa, will not go thither ; but I am purposed to return to my convent of Novara, whence the Minister took me when he sent me to the General. Now therefore take these letters and give them to the Minister Provincial of Genoa on the General's part.' Then he brought forth his letters, and gave them to my comrades [of Genoa]. So on the morrow we went from Alessandria to Tortona, which is ten miles' journey : and next day to Genoa, which is a far journey.* And the Brethren rejoiced to see me, for I was come from afar, and brought good tidings.

    " Now at Lyons I had found Brother Rinaldo, of Arezzo in Tuscany, who had come to the Pope to be absolved from his Bishopric. For he was Lector at Rieti, and when the Bishop of that city died, the folk found such grace in him that the canons of one accord elected him. And Pope Innocent, hearing of his learning and sanctity, would not absolve him, nay, rather, by the counsel of his brother Cardinals, he straitly commanded him to accept the Bishopric, and afterwards honoured him by consecrating him personally, while I was at Lyons. A few days therefore after [my return to Genoa] Brother Rinaldo returned as a Bishop from Lyons ; and on Ascension Day he preached to the people, and celebrated with his mitre on his head in the church of our

---

* It is between 35 and 40 English miles.

convent at Genoa. And by that time I was a priest, and served him at Mass, although a deacon was there, and a sub-deacon, and other ministers. And he gave the Brethren a most excellent dinner of sea-fish, and other meats, eating familiarly with us in the refectory. But the night following after Mattins, Brother Stephen the Englishman preached to the Brethren in the Bishop's hearing, and among other honied words (such as he was wont to speak), he told a story to the Bishop's confusion, saying : ' A certain Friar Minor in England, a layman, but a holy man, spake truly one day concerning the Easter candle. When it is kindled to burn in the church, it shines and sheds light around : but when the extinguisher is placed upon it, its light is darkened, and it stinks in our nostrils. So it is with a Friar Minor when he is fully kindled and burns with Divine love in the Order of St. Francis : then indeed doth he shine and shed light on others by his good example. Now I bethought me yesterday at dinner how our Bishop suffered his Brethren to bow their knees to him when dishes were placed before him on the table. To him, therefore may we well apply that word which the English Brother spake.'* The Bishop groaned to hear this ; and when the sermon was ended, he bent his knees and besought Brother Bertolino the Custode for leave to speak ; (for the Minister Provincial was not present) and, leave being given, he well excused himself, saying, ' I was indeed aforetime a candle, kindled, burning, shining, and shedding light in the Order of St. Francis, giving a good example to those that beheld me, as Brother Salimbene knows, who dwelt two years with me in the convent of Siena. And he knows well what conscience the Brethren of Tuscany have of my past life ; nay, even in this convent here the ancient Brethren know of my conversation : for it was on behalf of this convent that I was sent to study at Paris. If the Brethren have done me honour by bowing the knee before me at table, that hath not proceeded from my ambition ; for I have forbidden them often enough to do thus. But it was not in my power to beat them with my staff; neither could I nor dared I insist upon obedience. Wherefore I pray you for God's sake to hold me excused, seeing that there was neither ambition nor vainglory in me.' Having thus spoken, he bent his knees (as I myself saw and heard), confessing his fault, if by chance he had given evil example to any man, and promising to remove, as quickly as

---

* This anecdote gains point from the fact recorded by Eccleston and others, that the English Province was noted for its comparatively strict observance of St. Francis's rule.

might be, that extinguisher which by force had been set over him.
After this he commended himself to the brethren, and so we led
him honourably forth, and accompanied him to an Abbey of
White Monks without the city, where was an old man who had
resigned of his own free will the Bishopric of Turin that he might
live more freely in that cloister for himself and for God. Hearing
then that Brother Rinaldo was a mighty clerk and had lately been
made Bishop, he sighed and said : ' I marvel how thou, a wise
man, art fallen so low in folly as to undertake a Bishopric,
whereas thou wert in that most noble order of St. Francis, an
Order of most excellent perfection, wherein whosoever endureth to
the end shall without doubt be saved. Meseemeth therefore that
thou hast greatly erred, and art become as it were an apostate,
because thou hast returned to active life from that state of
contemplative perfection. For I also was a Bishop like unto
thee, but when I saw that I could not correct the follies of my
clergy who walked after vanity, then " my soul rather chose
hanging : " I resigned therefore my Bishopric and my clergy
and chose rather to save mine own soul. And this I did after
the example of St. Benedict, who left the company of certain
monks for that he had found them froward and wicked.'

" When therefore Brother Rinaldo had heard these words, he
made no answer, though he was a man of learning and of great wit ;
for the Bishop's words were to his mind, and he knew that he
had spoken truth. Then I answered and said to the Bishop of
Turin, lest he should seem wise in his own eyes, ' Father, lo thou
sayest that thou hast forsaken thy clergy, but consider whether
thou hast done well. For Pope Innocent III among many other
things said to a certain Bishop who would have refused his
Bishopric, " Think not that because Mary hath chosen the best
part, which shall not be taken away from her, therefore Martha
hath chosen an evil part in that she was busy about many things :
for, though the contemplative life be more free from care, yet is
the active life the more fruitful : though the former be sweeter,
yet is the latter more profitable : for Leah the blear-eyed surpassed in fertility of offspring the well-favoured Rachel." '

" When therefore I had spoken thus, the Bishops listened on
either side, but Brother Rinaldo answered me not a word, lest he
should seem to delight in his Bishopric. For he purposed in his
mind to lay down the load imposed upon him as soon as a fit
season should come. He went therefore to his Bishopric, and
when he was come thither the canons came to see him, and told
him of a certain wanton fellow-canon of theirs, who seemed
rather a layman than a clerk, for he had long hair even to his

shoulders, and would wear no tonsure. And the Bishop dragged him by the hair and smote him on the cheek, and called his parents and kinsfolk, who were noble, rich, and powerful, and said to them, ' Let this son of yours either choose the life of a layman, or wear such a habit as may show him to be a clerk ; for I can in no wise suffer that he go thus clad.' And his parents answered and said to the Bishop, ' It is our pleasure that he should be a clerk, and that ye should do to him whatsoever seems to you honest and good.' Then with his own hands the Bishop cut his hair and made him a tonsure, round and great, in the figure of a circle, that therein he might for the future be amended wherein he had aforetime sinned. And he to whom these things were done was grieved, but the canons rejoiced beyond measure.

" When therefore Brother Rinaldo could no longer dissemble with a whole conscience the works of his clergy, seeing that they would not return to the way of honesty and righteousness, he visited Pope Innocent IV, who was come to Genoa, and resigned the dignity which had been conferred on him at Lyons, saying that he was wholly purposed from thenceforward to be no Bishop. The Pope, seeing the anguish of his soul, promised to absolve him when he should be come to Tuscany ; for he hoped that perchance Brother Rinaldo would yet change his mind, which however was far from him. So Brother Rinaldo came and dwelt many days at Bologna, hoping that the Pope would pass that way into Tuscany ; and when the Holy Father had come to Perugia Brother Rinaldo came to him, and before the cardinals in Consistory resigned his office and benefice, laying his pontificals, that is, his staff, his mitre, and his ring, at the Supreme Pontiff's feet. And the Cardinals marvelled and were troubled, seeing how Brother Rinaldo seemed therein to derogate from their state, as though they were not in a state of salvation, being promoted to dignities and prelacies. The Pope likewise was troubled, for that he had consecrated him with his own hands, believing himself to have conferred a fit man upon the church of Rieti, as all held him to be, and as indeed he was. So the Cardinals and the Pope prayed him instantly for the love of God and for their honour and for the profit of the Church and the salvation of souls that he should not renounce his dignity. But he answered that they laboured thus in vain. And the Cardinals said, ' What if an angel hath spoken to him, or God hath revealed this to him ? ' Then the Pope, perceiving his steadfast purpose, said to him, ' Although thou wilt not have the thought and care of Episcopal rule, yet let the pontifical powers at least be left, and keep dignity and authority to ordain others, that thy Order may thus have some profit from thee.' And he answered, ' I will keep nothing whatsoever.' So, being absolved from his office, he came to the Friars that same day : and, taking his bag or wallet or basket, he besought leave to go with the almoner begging for bread. And as he went thus begging through the city of Perugia a certain Cardinal met him on his way back from the Consistory, perchance by the will of God, that he might see, teach, and hear. Who, knowing him well, said to him, ' Wert thou not better to be still a Bishop than to go begging from door to door ? ' But Brother Rinaldo answered him, ' The Wise Man saith in Proverbs, " It is better to be humbled with the meek than to divide spoils with the proud." As to my Bishopric, I grant indeed that it is more blessed to bestow spiritual gifts than to beg them from others : but the Friars Minor do indeed bestow such gifts ; whereof the Psalmist saith "Take a psalm and bring hither the timbrel," which is to say " Take spiritual gifts and bring hither temporal gifts."* Wherefore I will cleave to the end to this way which I have learnt in the Order, as the blessed Job saith, "Till I die I will not depart from my innocence : my justification, which I have begun to hold, I will not forsake." However, as the Apostle saith, "Everyone hath his proper gift from God, one after this manner, and another after that : " yet " Some trust in chariots and some in horses, but we will call upon the name of the Lord our God." ' The Cardinal, hearing this, and knowing that God had spoken through the mouth of his saint, departed from him, and reported all his words on the morrow to the Pope and Cardinals in Consistory : and they all marvelled. But Brother Rinaldo told the Minister-General, Brother John of Parma, to send him to dwell wheresoever he would ; and he sent him to the convent of Siena, where he was known to many ; and there he dwelt from All Saints until after Christmas, and so he died and went to God. Now as he lay sick of the sickness whereof he died, there was at Siena a certain canon of the cathedral church who had lain six years palsied in bed, and with all the devotion of his heart had recommended himself to Brother Rinaldo. He, about daybreak, heard in his dreams a voice that said unto him, ' Know thou that Brother Rinaldo hath passed from this world to the Father, and through his merits God hath made thee altogether whole.' And waking forthwith, and feeling himself wholly delivered from that sickness, he called his boy to bring his garments,

---

* This explanation is from the *Glossa Ordinaria*, and well exemplifies the confusion imported into medieval theology by this habit of arguing from farfetched traditional glosses as almost equal in authority to the Bible text.

and going to the chamber of a fellow-canon, told him of this new miracle, and both hastened forthwith to the Brethren to tell them this evident miracle which God had deigned to work that night by the merits of the blessed Rinaldo.   And when they were come out of the town gate they heard the Brethren chanting as they carried his body to church ; and so they were present at his funeral, and afterwards related the miracle with joy ; and the Brethren rejoiced, saying ' Blessed be God.'   Such was Brother Rinaldo of Arezzo, of the Order of the Friars Minor, Bishop of Rieti, who in his life wrought marvels, and in his death did yet greater wonders.   He was a man of most excellent learning, a great Lector in theology, a splendid and gracious preacher, both to clergy and to people, for he had a most eloquent tongue that never stumbled, and was a man of great heart.   Two years I dwelt with him in the convent of Siena, and saw him oft-times in those of Lyons and Genoa.   I could not have believed, if any man had told me, that Tuscany could have produced such a man, unless I had seen it with mine own eyes.*   He had a blood-brother in the Order of Vallombrosa, who was Abbot of the monastery of Bertinoro in Romagnola, (*Purg.* xiv. 112) a holy, learned, and good man, and a great friend of the Friars Minor ; may his soul rest in peace !

(332) " Moreover, in the year of our Lord 1249, after the Feast of St. Anthony of Padua I departed from the Convent of Genoa with my comrade, and we came to Bobbio, and saw one of the water-pots wherein the Lord turned water into wine at the wedding-feast, for it is said to be one of them.   Whether it be so indeed, God knoweth, to Whose eyes all things are naked and open.   Therein are many relics ; it stands on the altar of the monastery of Bobbio, and there are many relics of the blessed Columban, which we saw.   Afterwards we came to Parma, where we had been before, and there we did our business.   Now after our departure from Genoa, the Minister-General, Brother John of Parma, came thither ; to whom the Brethren said, ' Wherefore, Father, hast thou taken away from us our Brethren, whom thou hadst sent hither ?   We rejoiced in your love, for that they were here with us, and for that they are good Brethren, and full of consolation, and have behaved themselves well.'   Then the Minister answered and said, ' Where then are they ?   Are they not in this Convent ? '   And they said, ' No, Father,

---

* Compare the character which Salimbene has already given to the Tuscans in his account of the Great Alleluia, and Sacchetti's letter to Giacomo di Conte. The Saints of the Order came far more from mountain districts like Umbria and the Mark of Ancona than from the great towns.

for Brother Ruffino of Bologna hath recalled them to his Province.'
Then said the General, ' God knoweth I knew nothing of this
command ; nay, rather, I believed that they were in this house,
and marvelled much that they came not to me.' Afterwards he
found us at Parma, and said to us with a merry face, ' Ye are
much abroad, my children, now in France, now in Burgundy,
now in Provence, now in the Convent of Genoa, and now ye
purpose to dwell in that of Parma.   If I might rest as ye may
I would not wander so much abroad.'   And I said to him, ' On
you, Father, falls the labour of travelling by reason of your
ministry ; but know of us that true and pure obedience has
always been our part.'   Hearing this, he was satisfied, for he
loved us.   And when we were at Bologna, he said one day in his
chamber to the Minister, Brother Ruffino, ' I had placed those
Brethren in the Convent of Genoa to study, and thou hast
removed them thence.'   Brother Ruffino answered, ' Father,
this I did for their consolation, for I had sent them to France in
the days when the Emperor was besieging Parma, and thought
therefore to comfort them by recalling them.'   Then said I to
the Minister-General, ' Yea, Father, it was as he saith.'   Then
said the General to him, ' Thou wilt therefore place them well,
that they may be comforted, and attend to their studies, and
wander not so much abroad.'   To whom Brother Ruffino
answered, ' Gladly, Father, will I do them favour and comfort,
for your love and for theirs.'   Then he kept my comrade at
Bologna to correct his Bible for him ; but me he sent to Ferrara,
where I lived seven years continuously without changing my
abode."

CHAPTER XVI.

Settling Down.

SEVEN years on end! With what tell-tale emphasis Salimbene writes here, and repeats elsewhere, this significant phrase! Hitherto he had travelled about pretty much as he pleased; if only by getting different " obediences " from different authorities, and choosing whichever pleased him best : for we see clearly in his pages how impossible it was even for the untiring John of Parma to superintend more than a small fraction of so extensive an Order, with all its complicated details and overlappings of jurisdiction. One can realize too how easily the more wayward friars could manage to live in vagabondage for years ; and Wadding's records of constant complaints on this subject, in spite of vainly-repeated papal anathemas, are seen to be natural enough. From this arrival at Ferrara onwards, we find far fewer autobiographical records, until Salimbene's last few years brought him again into the mid vortex of civil war. It seems that for a period of about 32 years, from 1249 to 1281, our good friar lived a comparatively uneventful convent life, studying, preaching, writing, always observing no doubt, but with fewer experiences of the sort that would specially interest his niece in her convent. If only he had kept a business diary during those years, like his acquaintance the Archbishop of Rouen, and passed down to us a record of that daily convent life which was too trivial to be told to Sister Agnes !

Yet even this comparatively stationary and uniform life was not without many distractions. Prof. Holder-Egger points out that a chance observation of Salimbene's suggests the probability of brief wanderings even during the " seven continuous years " of Ferrara (p. 41, *note* 3). Prof. Michael had previously traced Salimbene's places of abode during the next few years, and they make a very varied list. After the Ferrara years came a long abode in Romagna—five years altogether at Ravenna, five at Imola, and five at Faenza, of which periods however the two last were certainly not unbroken and consecutive. One year he

spent at Bagnacavallo, and one at Montereggio : another year
he passed in his native Parma,—probably only off and on. In
1259 we find him in neighbouring Borgo san Donnino : twice
again in neighbouring Modena. He went on a pilgrimage to
Assisi, some time after 1270. He was at Forlì when it was besieged in 1273, and at Faenza during the siege of 1274. In
1281, at last, he came to end his days in his native province of
Emilia.

It is quite possible that, as Michael supposes, he worked hard
as preacher and confessor all these years, though the quotation
adduced scarcely goes so far as this : " I have now lived in the
Order many years as a priest and preacher, and have seen many
things and dwelt in many provinces and learnt much." (38)
He was no doubt always sociable, always busy, always popular,
but nothing in his chronicle seems to imply that he worked really
hard among the people : and certainly he always lent his heart
out with usury to just those worldly sights and sounds, just those
innumerable and thoroughly human trifles, which the disciplinarians of his Order tried so earnestly to exclude from a friar's life.

He read hard undoubtedly, or he would never have known his
Bible so well : though here and there his strings of quotations
seem to smack rather of the concordance, which was the invention of a 13th century Dominican, to whom our good Franciscan
pays a somewhat grudging tribute on p. 175. And he wrote
busily too,—witness the list of his writings, mostly compilations,
and now all unfortunately lost but one. First, in 1250, he wrote
his " Chronicle beginning : *Octavianus Cæsar Augustus.*" (217) :
in another place he tells us that he wrote three other chronicles
besides the one which has survived (293). One of these may be
the " Treatise of Pope Gregory X " to which he refers on page
245 (A.D. 1266) : and another the chronicle concerning Frederick
II (204, 344, 592). The " Treatise of Elisha " (293) and the
" Types and Examples, Signs and Figures and Mysteries of Both
Testaments " (238) were doubtless of a purely theological character. Another was apparently in verse, an imitation of Patecchio's satirical " Book of Pests." (464) Two other treatises
have been preserved by the happy impulse which prompted the
author to copy them bodily into the present chronicle : these are
the " Book of the Prelate," a violent pamphlet against Brother
Elias, from which I have already quoted and shall quote again
(96 foll.) and the " Treatise of the Lord's Body," mainly
liturgical (336 foll.)

But his life during these 32 years was by no means entirely
devoid of outward interest : as the rest of this chapter will show.

To begin chronologically with the seven years at Ferrara : here he found himself a close spectator of the cruelties of Ezzelino and his Brother Alberigo, and of the crusade which finally crushed the former. Here too he heard of Frederick's death, and saw the Pope come home in triumph from his long exile at Lyons. This was in 1251, while Europe was still shuddering at the failure of St. Louis' first crusade and mourning for thousands of Christians slain : but no news of public disaster to Christendom could spoil the Pope's private triumph. (445) "He came in the month of May to his own native city of Genoa, and there gave a wife to one of his nephews ; at whose wedding he himself was present with his cardinals and 80 bishops ; and at that feast were many dishes and courses and varieties of meats, with divers choice and jocund wines ; and each course of dishes cost many marks. No such great and pompous wedding as this was celebrated in my days in any country, whether we consider the guests who were present or the meats that were set before them : so that the Queen of Sheba herself would have marvelled to see it."

Meanwhile very different events were taking place in the land which the Pope had just left. The common people of France, indignant at the failure of their nobles in the Crusade, rose under a leader who boasted that he had no mere papal or episcopal authority, but a letter direct from the Virgin Mary, which he held night and day in his clenched hand. So writes Matthew Paris, whose very full account, from the lips of an English monk who had fallen into the hands of these Pastoureaux, confirms the briefer notice of Salimbene. (444) "In this year an innumerable host of shepherds was gathered together in France, saying that they must cross the sea to slay the Saracens and avenge the King of France : and many followed them from divers cities of France, nor dared any man withstand them, but all gave them food and whatsoever they desired ; wherefore the very shepherds left their flocks to join them. For their leader told how God had revealed to him that the sea should be parted before him, and he should lead that innumerable host to avenge the King of France. But I, when I heard this, said 'Woe to the shepherds that desert their sheep. Where the King of France could do so little with his armed host, what shall these fellows do ? ' Yet the common folk of France believed in them, and were terribly provoked against the Religious, more especially against the Friars Preachers and Minors, for that they had preached the Crusade and given men crosses to go beyond seas with the King, who had now been conquered by the Saracens.

So those French who were then left in France were wroth against Christ, to such a degree that they presumed to blaspheme His Name, which is blessed above all other names. For in those days when the Friars Minor and Preachers begged alms in France in Christ's name, men gnashed with their teeth on them ; then, before their very faces, they would call some other poor man and give him money and say, 'Take that in Mahomet's name ; for he is stronger than Christ.' So our Lord's word was fulfilled in them ' They believe for a while, and in time of temptation they fall away.' Wretched misery ! whereas the King of France was not provoked to wrath, but suffered patiently, these men were goaded to fury ! Moreover that host of shepherds destroyed a whole Dominican convent in one city so utterly that not one stone was left upon another, and this because the friars had dared to speak a word against them. But in this same year they were brought to nought, and their whole congregation was utterly destroyed." Matthew Paris tells us how the Pastoureaux owed much of their popularity to their attacks on the clergy, especially upon the friars : he looks upon these crusaders as precursors of Antichrist, but admits that many pious folk, including the severe queen Blanche herself, favoured their preaching at first, in spite of its entire lack of ecclesiastical authority. He speaks also in the strongest terms of the widespread infidelity in France at that time : " faith began to waver in the kingdom of France : " " the devil . . . . saw that the Christian faith was tottering to its fall even in the sweet realm of France." A few pages higher up, under the year 1250, after describing the outbreak of blasphemy among the French at the first news of St. Louis' failure, he adds : " Moreover the most noble city of Venice, and many cities of Italy whose inhabitants are but half-Christians, would have fallen into apostasy if they had not been comforted and strengthened by bishops and holy men of Religion."

After his nephew's wedding at Genoa, Innocent IV "came through Brescia and Mantua (445) to the great Abbey of San Benedetto di Polirone, where the Countess Matilda lieth buried in a tomb of marble : in whose honour the Pope with his cardinals recited the psalm *De Profundis* around her grave ; for they were mindful of the benefits which she had conferred in old time on the Roman Church and Pontiffs. Then he came on to Ferrara, where I dwelt. So when he should have entered the city, he sent word that the Friars Minor should come out to meet him, and abide ever by his side ; which we did all along the Via San Paolo. His messenger this time was a certain Brother of Parma

named Buiolo, who dwelt with the Pope and was of his family : and
the Pope's confessor was another Minorite, Brother Nicholas, [the
Englishman] my friend, whom the Pope made Bishop of Assisi :[1]
and there was likewise in the Holy Father's household my friend
and companion Brother Lorenzo, whom he afterwards made Bishop
of Antivari [in Greece], and there were yet two other Friars Minor
in the Pope's household. And the Pope stayed many days at
Ferrara, until the octave of St. Francis, and he preached a sermon
standing at the window of the Bishop's palace ; and certain
cardinals stood by him on either side, one of whom, the Lord
William his nephew, made the Confession in a loud voice after
the sermon. For there was a great multitude gathered together
as for judgment ; and the Pope took for his text ' Blessed is the
nation whose God is the Lord : the people whom He hath chosen
for His inheritance.' And after his sermon he said : ' The Lord
hath kept me on my journey from Italy, and while I dwelt at
Lyons, and on my way back hither ; blessed be He for ever and
ever ! ' And he added : ' This is mine own city ; I beseech you
to live in peace ; for the lord who was once your Emperor and
who persecuted the Church, is now dead.' Now I stood hard
by the Pope, so that I might have touched him when I would ;
for he was glad to have Friars Minor about him. Then Brother
Gerardino of Parma, who was the master of Brother Bonagrazia
[the Minister-General], touched me with his elbow and said :
' Hear now that the Emperor is dead : for until now thou hast been
unbelieving ; leave therefore thy Joachim.' Moreover in those
days when the Pope dwelt at Farrara, the cardinals sent us oft-
times swine ready slaughtered and scalded which men gave them
continually : and we in our turn gave thereof to our Sisters of
the Order of St. Clare. Moreover the Pope's seneschal sent word
to us saying : ' To-morrow the Holy Father will depart : send
me therefore your porters, and I will give you bread and wine
for yourselves, seeing that we have no further need thereof : '
and so we did. And when the Pope was come to Bologna, he
was received with great pomp by the citizens : but he tarried
little with them, departing in haste, and wroth for that they
besought him to give them Medicina, which is a Church estate
in the Bishopric of Bologna, and which they had long held by
force. He therefore would not listen to their petition, but said,
' Ye hold Church lands by force, and now ye beg the same as a
gift ? Get you hence in God's name, for I will not hear your
petition.' But at his departure he found many fair and noble
ladies of Bologna gathered together, who had come from the
villages to the road by which he must pass, for they were fain to

see him : so he blessed them in the Lord's name and went on his
way and dwelt at Perugia."

It will be seen that Salimbene was never slow to take the place
to which he felt himself entitled by his birth and his abilities :
and on one occasion at least, about the year 1256, he was
entrusted with the responsible office of peacemaker between
Bologna and Reggio. On another occasion (451) we find him a
guest at the villa of Ghiberto da Gente, Podesta of Parma, who
tried to make use of our friend to further his designs on Reggio :
but Salimbene did not like the job, and remembered opportunely
that "The Apostle saith in his second Epistle to Timothy : ' No
man being a soldier to God entangleth himself with secular
businesses.' " Later on, when Ghiberto had fallen from his high
estate in Parma, it was the friar's turn to plead, and equally in
vain. "Being in his villa of Campigine I said to him, ' What
now, my Lord Ghiberto? Why enter ye not into our Order ? '
Then he answered and said : ' And what would ye now do with
me, who am an old man of 60 years and more ? ' And I said :
' Ye would give a good example to others, and would save your
own soul.' He then answered and said : ' I know that ye give
me profitable counsel ; but I cannot hear you, for my heart is
wholly concerned with other matters.' And, in short, I besought
him long and instantly, but he would not listen to do well : for
he "devised iniquity on his bed," hoping to be avenged of the
men of Parma and Reggio who had deposed him from his lordship
there. He died at Ancona and was there buried : and he assigned
certain yearly rents of his meadows in the Bishopric of Parma
to the Friars Minor and Preachers, that they might enjoy them
during a certain term of years as conscience money for his ill-
gotten gains : and so they have indeed enjoyed them ; may his
soul of God's mercy rest in peace ! Amen." Salimbene's third
and last political mission will be told in its place under the year
1285.

1258 had been a year of famine ; and then (464) "Next
year a great pestilence fell upon men and women, so that at the
office of Vespers we had two dead together in our church. This
curse began in Passion-week, so that in the whole Province of
Bologna the Friars Minor could not hold their services on Palm-
Sunday, for they were hindered by a sort of numbness. And this
lasted many months : whereof three hundred and more died in
Borgo San Donnino, and in Milan and Florence many thousands ;
nor did men toll the bells, lest the sick should be afraid." Famine
and pestilence led to a great religious revival, beginning as usual
among the common people. (465) "The Flagellants came

through the whole world ; and all men, both small and great, noble knights and men of the people, scourged themselves naked in procession through the cities, with the Bishops and men of Religion at their head ; and peace was made in many places, and men restored what they had unlawfully taken away, and they confessed their sins so earnestly that the priests had scarce leisure to eat. And in their mouths sounded words of God and not of man, and their voice was as the voice of a multitude : and men walked in the way of salvation, and composed godly songs of praise in honour of the Lord and the Blessed Virgin : and these they sang as they went and scourged themselves. And on the Monday, which was the Feast of All Saints, all those men came from Modena to Reggio, both small and great ; and all of the district of Modena came, and the Podesta and the Bishop with the banners of all the Gilds ; and they scourged themselves through the whole city, and the greater part passed on to Parma on the Tuesday following. So on the morrow all the men of Reggio made banners for each quarter of the town, and held processions around the city, and the Podesta went likewise scourging himself. And the men of Sassuolo at the beginning of this blessed time took me away with the leave of the Guardian of the convent of the Friars Minor at Modena, where I dwelt at that time, and brought me to Sassuolo, for both men and women loved me well ; afterwards they brought me to Reggio and then to Parma. And when we were come to Parma this Devotion was already there, for it flew as ' an eagle flying to the prey,' and lasted many days in our city, nor was there any so austere and old but that he scourged himself gladly. Moreover, if any would not scourge himself, he was held worse than the Devil, and all pointed their finger at him as a notorious man and a limb of Satan : and what is more, within a short time he would fall into some mishap, either of death or of grievous sickness. Pallavicino only, who was then Lord of Cremona, avoided this blessing and this Devotion with his fellow-citizens of Cremona ; for he caused gallows to be set up by the bank of the River Po, in order that if any came to the city with this manner of scourging he might die on the gibbet : for he loved the good things of this life better than the salvation of souls, and the world's glory better than the glory of God. Nevertheless many brave youths of Parma were fully resolved to go thither, for they were glad to die for the Catholic Faith, and for God's honour and the remission of their sins. And I was then at Parma in the Podesta's presence, who said ' His heart is blinded, and he is a man of malice, who knoweth not the things of God. Let us

therefore give him no occasion of ill-doing, for he loved cursing, and it shall come unto him : and he would not have blessing, and it shall be far from him.' And he said, 'How seemeth it to you, my Brethren? Say I well?' Then I answered and said, 'You have spoken wisely and well, my Lord.' Then the Podesta sent heralds throughout the city of Parma, forbidding under the heaviest penalties lest any man of Parma should dare to cross the Po : so their purpose ceased. And this was the year wherein that age should have begun which was foretold by Abbot Joachim, who divideth the world into three states : and they say that this last state of the world began with these Flagellants of the year 1260, who cried with God's words and not with men's."
Manfred also kept the Flagellants out of his states by the threat of martyrdom, for he, like Pallavicino, was known to be as good as his word in these matters, and to wage perpetual war against religious enthusiasms which were only too likely to cause political complications in his dominions. This leads the Dominican chronicler Pipinus to lament the premature end of the movement in Italy : though it was to some extent kept up by formally constituted Gilds of Penitents in most of the cities. But elsewhere the revival degenerated into such superstitions and disorders as could be only too surely anticipated from such descriptions as Varagine and Pipinus himself give us in their chronicles. The Pope had never approved the movement, which was plainly an attempt of the common folk to come to God without human mediation ; and the clergy of Germany and Poland were compelled to suppress it as mercilessly as the Italian tyrants. The same superstition broke out with greater violence after the Great Plague of 1349, and again on several other occasions. Gerson wrote a treatise against it in 1417, recalling how often the movement had already been condemned by the authorities, and partly explaining its recrudescence by the favourite medieval quotation from Ecclesiastes (Vulg.) "The number of fools is infinite."[2]
The next important dates of which we are sure in Salimbene's biography find him at Ravenna : he was there in 1264 and 1268, and it is very likely that the five years' residence of which he speaks was continuous, except for short excursions to neighbouring towns. Our chronicler looked back very fondly to those five years at Ravenna. Everything in the old Imperial city appealed to him. The district was at peace, so far as there could be peace in 13th century Italy, and here were old families to associate with, and old books to read. He enjoyed, too, the antiquarian atmosphere of the city : it did his heart good to see the desecrated

tomb of the unorthodox Theodoric, and to think that (209) "the blessed Pope Gregory, when he came hither, caused his bones to be torn from the tomb of porphyry, (which is shown empty unto this day,) and thrown upon the dunghill and into the cesspool;" though it is almost certain that some other profane hand did what he ascribes here to the great Pope. Here also he could admire the tomb of his heroine the Empress Galla Placidia, with other similar monuments of the earliest Christian art: and he was naturally chosen as cicerone when a distinguished visitor came to see the churches of Ravenna (169), and earn the rich indulgences to be gained there. Last, but not least, Ravenna was a city of good living. As the Podesta boasted one day to Salimbene (482) "We have such plenty of victuals here that he would be a fool who should seek for more: for a good bowl of salt, full and heaped up, may be had here for a poor penny; and for the same price a man may buy twelve clean boiled eggs at a tavern; I can buy whensoever I will an excellent fat wild-duck for four pence in the proper season; and I have seen times when, if a man would pluck ten ducks, he might keep the half of them for himself." Here he lived out of reach of actual war, hearing only the distant echoes of those battles in the South which decided the fate of Frederick's last descendants. One Christmastide, on his way to preach at San Procolo near Faenza, he met the great French host passing southwards to conquer Manfred at Benevento. "And a great miracle then befel: for in that year wherein they came was neither cold nor frost nor ice nor snow nor mire nor rain; but the roads were most fair, easy, and smooth, as though it had been the month of May. Which was the Lord's doing, for that they came to succour the Church and to exterminate that accursed Manfred, whose iniquities well deserved such a fate: for they were many indeed.* For he had slain, as was said, his brother Conrad, who himself had slain his own brother Charles, born at Ravenna of the Emperor's English wife." (470)

Again, he remembers Conradin's defeat in 1268 by a strange natural phenomenon in which he doubtless saw an omen of that event. (480) "In that year and at that same season, there passed so great a number of those birds which destroy the grapes in the vineyards and are called in the vulgar tongue *turili*, [thrushes] that every evening between supper-time and twilight the open sky could scarce be seen. And at times there

---

* " Orribil furon li peccati miei." *Purg.* iii. 121

were two or three storeys of them one over another, and they stretched three or four miles, and after a brief space other birds of the same sort would take their place, flying and chattering and murmuring, and as it were, complaining. And so they did every evening for many days, coming down from the mountains to the valleys and filling the whole air. And I with the other Brethren was wont to go out and stand in the open air every evening to see and contemplate and marvel at them : and yet I was not in the open air, for they covered the whole sky. I say in truth that if I had not seen them, I could not have believed any who should have told me thereof." Salimbene's church at Ravenna was of course that in which Dante's bones were first laid, and outside which stands his present tomb : and the open air into which the Friars came out every evening to watch these portents in the sky would have been practically the garden of the present Hôtel Byron.

The one piece of fighting which took place even in the peaceful district of Ravenna was, according to our friar's account, simply owing to the greed of the Venetians, whom he accuses of methods not unknown to modern diplomacy. (481). They had "taken a fifty-years' lease " of a castle commanding the mouth of the Ravenna canal ; and now, at the very end of their 50 years, instead of preparing to quit, they were rebuilding the wooden bulwarks of their fortress in stone. Again, they entirely neglected the principle of the Open Door ; "so utterly closing this canal to the Lombards, that they can draw no supplies from Romagna or the Mark of Ancona : yet, but for this hindrance of the Venetians, they might draw therefrom corn and wine and oil, fish and flesh and salt and pigs, and all good things to sustain man's life." Moreover, their trade methods were so astute, and their *Visdomini* (consuls) were such active political agents, that the Bolognese found themselves outbought and outsold even in their own districts, and were compelled in self-defence to build a fortress at Primario, at the mouth of the Po, which might keep the Venetian fortress in check. (480) "And the Venetians came with a great fleet and all siege-engines and battered the tower with mangonels and catapults, and the men of Bologna defended their castle manfully, and the Venetians retired. And the men of Bologna remained there, as I think, some 2 or 3 years and 300 or 500 of them died by reason of the unwholesomeness of the sea-air, and of the multitude of fleas and gnats and flies and gad-flies. And Brother Peregrino di Polesmo of Bologna, of the Order of Friars Minor, went and made peace between the Bolognese and the Venetians, and the men of Bologna destroyed the castle which they had made and departed thence, and gave much wood of the said castle to the Friars Minor of Ravenna. The Venetians are greedy men and stubborn and outrageous, and they would gladly subdue the whole world to themselves if they could ; and they treat boorishly the merchants who go to them, both by selling dear, and by taking tolls in divers places of their district from the same persons at the same time. And if any merchant carries his goods thither for sale he may not bring them back with him : nay, but he must needs sell them there, will-he nill-he. And if by mishap of the sea any ship other than their own is driven to them with its merchandise, it may not depart thence except it have first sold all its cargo : for the Venetians say that this ship has been driven to them by God's will, which no man may gainsay." He had not only little sympathy with Venetian commercial methods, but he also disliked the city for its aloofness from the Guelf cause, and was ready to believe that the disastrous floods which ravaged Venice in 1284 were due to the Papal excommunication for its lukewarmness in the cause of Charles of Anjou. He even shows imperfect sympathy with that ancient pageant which we especially associate with the name of Venice,—the Espousal of the Adriatic—which he traces "partly to a certain idolatrous custom, whereby the Venetians sacrifice to Neptune."

It seems only fitting, however, that his memories of Ravenna should to us be redolent of the *Commedia*, though he left the city while Dante was still almost in the nursery. The Middle Ages were rich in pretenders, and Salimbene alludes briefly to many of these :—a false Count of Flanders, who was finally betrayed by his inability to remember at whose hands he had received knighthood : a false Frederick II : a whole crop of false Manfreds, whom Charles of Anjou destroyed one after another. (174 ; 472). But by far the most picturesque of these is a story of the famous " Casa Traversara," once so rich in noble lords and ladies, in courtesy and in love, of which Dante laments the extinction. (*Purg.* xiv. 107). Salimbene tells us of Paolo Traversario and his adversary Anastagio, who are prominent in that strange tale of unrequited passion and repentance which Dryden borrowed from Boccaccio[3] and entitled " Theodore and Honoria " : while the former is also commemorated as " the noblest man of all Romagna " in the 35th story of the still older " Novellino." He tells us how all the four noblest houses of Ravenna were now extinct ; of which the last and greatest was this of the Traversari. After Paolo's death, the house was represented by a single girl Traversaria, born out of wedlock, whom Innocent IV legitimated and married to his kinsman Tommaso Fogliani. Their only son, however, died in early youth, and the vast possessions of the house passed for a while to Lord Matteo Fogliani. (166) "But in process of time one Gulielmotto of Apulia came with a handmaid named Paschetta ; but he gave her the name of Ayca, saying that she was his wife, and daughter to the Lord Paolo Traversario : for in truth the Emperor Frederick had taken Paolo's daughter Ayca and sent her as a hostage to Apulia. Afterwards, however, when the Emperor waxed wroth against the girl's father, he caused her to be cast into a burning fiery furnace ; and so she gave up her soul to God. For a certain Friar Minor, Ubaldino by name, who dwelt in Apulia, and was a noble of Ravenna, and brother to the Lord Segnorelli, was present and heard her confession. And she was a most fair lady—and no wonder, for she had a most comely father. But this Paschetta, who gave herself out as Ayca, was foul and deformed, and beyond measure miserly and avaricious ; for I have spoken with her in the city of Ravenna, and seen her a hundred times. She had learnt from her mistress her father's manners, and the circumstances of the city of Ravenna : moreover, a certain man of Ravenna, whom I knew well, the Lord Ugo de' Barci, went oft-times to Apulia, and of his malice instructed her in these things, hoping for a reward if she were exalted. So Gulielmotto came with his wife to Ravenna, and the men of the city rejoiced to hear thereof and went out gladly to meet them. I also went out with a friar, my comrade, to without the gate of San Lorenzo, and stood waiting on the river-bridge to see what this might be. And as I waited, a certain youth came running, who said to me, ' And wherefore have not the other Brethren come ? In truth, if the Pope with his Cardinals were in Ravenna, he should hasten to behold this rejoicing.' Hearing this I beheld him, and smiled, saying, ' Blessed be thou, my son ; thou hast spoken well.' Now when they had entered Ravenna, they went forthwith to the church of San Vitale, to visit the grave of Paolo Traversario. When therefore Paschetta stood face to face with his sepulchre, she raised her voice and began to weep, as though she mourned for her father. And then she began to feign herself sick, for loathing that Traversaria [the illegitimate] should be buried in the sepulchre of her father : and after that they went to the lodgings ordained for them. All this was reported to me by one who saw with his own eyes, my friend Dom Giovanni, monk and sacristan of San Vitale. And on the morrow Gulielmotto spoke in the city Council, for he was a comely knight, and a great orator. And when he had ended his speech in open Council, the citizens promised and offered him more than he himself had asked ; for they rejoiced at this revival of the Lord Paolo's house. The Lord Philip likewise, Archbishop of Ravenna, was consenting thereto. So Gulielmotto had these possessions and lands, as well as ever the Lord Paolo himself had possessed them : and he abounded in money and goods, and built courts and mansions and walls and palaces, and prospered many years, as I saw with mine own eyes. Yet after this he rose up against the Church party, and was driven forth from Ravenna : and all his palaces and buildings were torn down. Moreover, that woman his wife, who feigned herself to be Ayca, had no son by him : yet she would send and fetch boys of five and seven years old from Apulia, whom she said to be her children. At length one of those children died : and she buried him in the sepulchre of the Lord Paolo, bursting forth into bitter lamentation and crying, ' O glories of Lord Paolo, where must I leave you ! O glories of Lord Paolo, where must I leave you ! O glories of Lord Paolo, where must I leave you !' At length, amid the multitude of wars, she ended her days at Forlì : and Gulielmotto returned to Apulia, naked and stripped of his possessions."

These years at and near Ravenna brought Salimbene into close contact with two more of the most striking figures in the Commedia—Guido da Montefeltro and Tebaldello. He was living both at Forlì and at Faenza when those cities were besieged by the Pope's Bolognese allies, and when the siege of Faenza was raised by Guido's brilliant victory at San Procolo, $2\frac{1}{2}$ miles from the city. He describes the terrible slaughter of the Bolognese knights : and how the four thousand common folk, huddled helplessly round their carroccio, presently surrendered in a body. Many of these prisoners, with their hands bound, were butchered in cold blood : the rest were brought in triumph to prison at Faenza. Ricobaldo, writing at Ferrara more than 20 years after the event, speaks with bated breath of this massacre, and breaks off with " But I must say no more, lest even now I awaken men's half-slumbering hate."[4] The battle took place on the Feast of St. Anthony of Padua, " and therefore " says Salimbene " the Bolognese cannot bear to hear the Saint's name mentioned in their city." (397) At Bologna and Reggio the dead knights lay at the church doors, each in his own coffin, while the men of Faenza swarmed out and carried to their houses the plunder of that vast camp which only a day before had threatened the very existence of their city. (490)

Six years later, Guido took Sinigaglia and put 1,500 Guelfs (it was said) to the sword (506); but next year saw the election of Martin IV, who soon showed himself desperately in earnest with the war, and who spent upon it the vast hoards which his predecessors had collected for the next Crusade in the East. So, although the men of Forlì held out bravely, yet (516) " every year Pope Martin IV sent against them a mighty army of French and of divers other nations, who destroyed their vines and corn and fruit-trees, with their olives and figs, almonds and fair pomegranates, houses and cattle, casks and vats, and all that pertaineth to country-folk. And the Pope spent in these years many thousands of florins, nay, many pack-loads of gold pieces. So when the city had come to the obedience of the Church, all the moats were filled in and the gates razed, and houses and palaces torn down, and the chief buildings shattered to pieces : and the chief men of that city went out and fled to divers hiding-places, that they might give way to wrath. But Count Guido da Montefeltro, who had been their captain and that of the Imperial party, made peace with the Church, and was banished for a while to Chioggia, after which he was sent to Asti in Lombardy, where he dwelt in great honour, since all loved him for his former probity, and frequent victories, and for his present wise and humble obedience to the Church. Moreover he was noble and full of sense and discreet and well-mannered, liberal and courteous and generous ; a doughty knight and of great courage and skill in war. He loved the Order of St. Francis, not only because he had kinsfolk therein, but also that the blessed Francis had delivered him from many perils, and from the dungeon and chains of the Lord Malatesta "—for, as Salimbene had pointed out before, his great victory was won on the Feast of St. Anthony of Padua, and the siege of Faenza was raised on St. Francis's day. " Yet for all that he was oft-times grievously offended by certain fools of the Order of Friars Minor. In the city of Asti he had a decent company and household, for many ceased not to lend him a helping hand." These remarks are all the more interesting for having been written before Guido had become a Franciscan and given his fatal counsel to Boniface VIII.

How difficult it was for him to refuse his services to the Pope, and how thoroughly men of Religion were expected to put even the least religious of their worldly talents at the service of their new Brethren, is shown not only by Salimbene's friar who was compelled to build siege engines (as will be seen later on,) but also by the two following anecdotes from Cardinal Jacques de Vitry's sermons.[5] " I have heard of a noble knight who left all his great possessions and became a monk, that he might serve God in peace and humility. But the Abbot, seeing that in the World he had been a man of many wiles, sent him to the fair to sell the aged asses of the convent and buy younger beasts. The nobleman loved not the task, but bent his will to obey. So when the buyers asked whether these asses were good and young, he deigned not to dissemble, but answered, ' Think ye that our convent is come to such poverty as to sell young asses that might be profitable to the house ?' When again men asked why they had so little hair on their tails, he replied, ' Because they fall oftentimes under their burdens ; wherefore, since we raise them again by their tails, these have lost their hair.'[6] So when he came home to the cloister without having sold a single beast, then a lay-brother who had gone with him accused him before the Chapter. So the abbot and monks, in white-hot wrath against him, set about beating him with stripes as for a grievous fault. He therefore said to them : ' I left behind in the World a multitude of asses and great possessions : therefore I was unwilling to lie for the sake of your asses, and to harm mine own soul by deceiving my neighbours.' So thenceforward they never sent him forth on worldly business." The other story is of a great advocate who for the same reason lost his causes when he had become a monk and was sent to plead for the convent. Both tales appear frequently in Preachers' manuals, and evidently appealed vividly to the medieval mind.

Salimbene twice mentions the double betrayal of Faenza by Tebaldello, whom Dante plunges for that reason into the hell of ice (*Inf.* xii, 123.), and of whom our friar says (505-6) " He was named Tebaldello de' Zambrasi, a great and powerful noble of the aforesaid city of Faenza ; he was base-born, but his brother Zambrasino, of the Order of Frati Godenti, had given him the half of his father's inheritance, for that those two brethren only were left of the family, and there was wealth enough for two : therefore his brother gave him an equal share of the inheritance and made him a nobleman. So this Tebaldello (whom I knew and have seen a hundred times, and who was a man of war, like a second Jephthah) betrayed his city of Faenza into the hands of the Bolognese. At that season the half of the citizens of Faenza were gone with the banished party of Bologna to lay siege to a certain town ; so that Tebaldello had watched for a fit time for his evil deed. [Then Pope Martin] sent his army oft-times against Forlì, and the Church party had the under hand, for they were conquered and taken and slain and put to flight : among whom fell Tebaldello also, who had twice betrayed his own city of Faenza; for he was drowned in the moat of the city of Forlì and smothered there together with his charger."

Such, then, were the events which Salimbene constantly saw and heard during the few remaining years which he spent in Romagna after that quiet life in Ravenna. In his terrible description of the devastation wrought by civil wars, his deepest pity is for this province of Romagna : and, in spite of all Martin IV's favours towards his own Order, the good friar never forgave this waste of crusade-money and this drenching of Italian soil with Christian blood.

His old age, as the Chronicle tells us plainly, was spent in his native province of Emilia—mainly at Reggio and Montefalcone, within easy reach of his early home at Parma. He may have settled in Reggio as early as the spring of 1281 : he was certainly there in August 1283 (526) : and the minuteness with which he chronicles the occurrences of 1282 in that district is a strong proof that he was then living there. The last event referred to is a Papal Bull of May 14, 1288, and the reference does not imply that this was very recent (625) : so that there is no reason to quarrel with Gebhart's guess that he died in 1289, or Clédat's that it was he himself whose trembling hand scratched out the unflattering notices of Obizzo when that tyrant became master of Reggio in 1290.

The events of these last years have a very special interest for us. Salimbene was of the same generation as Dante's father ; and all that he has told us hitherto is what the poet might have heard from his parents at his own fireside. But now we come to Dante's own age ; for Salimbene came to Reggio a little before the first salutation of Beatrice, and died about the time when Dante showed his real manhood at the battle of Campaldino. Life in the towns of Emilia was very like that in adjoining Tuscany : and what the friar tells us of his own experiences is practically what passed under the poet's eyes from his 17th to his 25th year.

CHAPTER XVII.

Taking in Sail.

SO our busy friend rested at last from his wanderings, and
came to end his days in the convents of his native province
—a land flowing with milk and honey, if only men could have
ceased for awhile from war. "This is the fairest spot in the
world," writes the Continuator of Ricobaldi's Chronicle: "conveniently hilly, yet with fruitful plains and lakes for fish; and
therein dwell men of kingly heart."[1] Parma and Reggio and
Modena are sleepy enough nowadays; very restful to the weary
traveller, with their Apennines hard by, and far off the Alps of
Trent and Verona looming in ghostly orange on the evening
horizon, high above that endless stretch of purple plain. But in
Salimbene's days this sleepy world was like a swarming bee-
hive, upon which the good old friar looked down as Lucretius'
philosopher contemplated the troubled sea of human error and
pain.

In those harder times a man was already aged at fifty: but
in 1282 Salimbene was in his 61st year, and had at least six more
to live. This year 1282 passed comparatively peacefully for the
cities in which he was most interested. His native Parma was
now reconciled again to the Church, after an interdict of three
years. For in 1279 the Dominicans had burned for heresy, first
a noble lady of the city, and then an innkeeper's wife, who had
once been her maidservant (501). On this, "certain fools"
attacked the Dominican convent and wounded some of the
Brethren (507); or, as the contemporary Chronicler of Parma
tells us with more detail "certain evil men, by suggestion of
the Devil, ran to the convent and entered it by force and
despoiled it, smiting and wounding many of the Brethren, and
killing one Brother Jacopo de' Ferrari, who was an aged man
and (as was reported) a virgin of his body; who was also blind
of his eyes, and had lived forty years and more in the Order."
Yet, in spite of her recent prosperity, Parma was not quite free
from war. Her citizens made a petty raid into neighbouring

territory, and destroyed some crops : again, they sent a force to garrison friendly Cremona while the Cremonese went to fight against the Ghibellines in Lombardy. Within the city itself, this was a gay year, in spite of the pulling down of certain rebels' houses and of a sudden scare in the summer, when " thunderclaps were heard at nightfall so horrible and so startling that they seemed almost visible and palpable, and many fearful folk fell to the ground " (511). There were many worldly pageants, which the good friar describes in the language of keen enjoyment, but with extreme brevity. This is all the more disappointing because even a few details, such as might so naturally have come from the pen of an observant man writing for his favourite niece, would have made us realize even more vividly Villani's description of the " noble and rich company, clad all in white, and with a Lord of Love at its head," which made Florence so gay for nearly two months of the next year 1283, and which it is so natural to connect with the occasion, in that same year, when Dante first exchanged speech with his Beatrice, " dressed all in pure white."[2] At Parma, two brothers of the great Rossi family were knighted, one of them resigning his canonry for the occasion, and the feastings lasted nearly a month. Again, there were other knightings at Reggio, and most noble festivities at Ferrara, where Azzo of Este was knighted and wedded to a niece of Pope Nicholas III. At Reggio, rival factions were reconciled by the mediation of the Friars Minor, and " many men and women, youths and maidens," were present at the solemn oath of reconciliation in the convent. Outside this narrow circle, however, the political horizon was dark enough. The Sicilians got rid of their French masters by the Sicilian Vespers : which Salimbene recounts with the brevity usual to him when he writes at second hand of distant events. " In the city of Palermo they slew all the French of both sexes, dashing their little ones against the stones, and ripping up the women that were with child : but the men of Messina treated them less cruelly, stripping them of their arms and their goods and sending them back to their master Charles " (508). The Vespers kindled a long and bloody war between Charles of Anjou and Peter of Aragon. Another war, equally long and bloody, was being fought out with redoubled energy by Martin IV, the French Pope whom Charles of Anjou had lately forced upon Christendom by kidnapping the dissentient Cardinals and intimidating the rest. Salimbene, staunch Churchman as he is, speaks very plainly about these papal wars, as will presently be seen. This greed for fresh territory was all the more blameworthy because even their earliest territorial possessions kept them constantly involved in political complications and their resultant wars. "The men of Perugia made ready to go and waste the lands of Foligno, and the Pope sent word that they should utterly desist, on pain of excommunication, since Foligno was of the garden of St. Peter. Yet the Perugians turned not aside from their purpose, but went and ravaged the whole Bishopric of Foligno even to the ditches of the city. So they were excommunicated; wherefore in their wrath they made a Pope and Cardinals of straw, and dragged them outrageously through the whole city: after which they dragged them to the summit of a hill, where they burned the Pope in robes of scarlet, and his Cardinals with him; saying, 'this is such a Cardinal, and this is such another.' And note that the Perugians thought to do a good deed in fighting against Foligno and ravaging the lands; for in former times there was much war between the two cities, and the men of Foligno raged so cruelly against the Perugians, on whom God sent at the same time such confusion, that one old woman of Foligno drove 10 Perugians to prison with a rod of reed: and other women did likewise; for the Perugians had no heart to resist them." (510).

1283 was a fairly quiet year too: there was a great cattle-plague, but the mortality did not spread among men until the year following. At Parma men built rapidly, almost feverishly, in those days of prosperity: the Friars Minor built a handsome refectory, the city walls and Baptistery rose rapidly: the Cathedral was adorned with its "porch-pillars on the lion resting:" a great stone bridge was built, and three fair new streets lined with houses and palaces; also a governor's palace and a canal—"but this canal was little worth: I myself could have planned a better canal for the service of Parma if I were lord of the city." Here a reader of the 14th or 15th century, provoked at Salimbene's self-sufficiency, has scribbled on the margin of the MS. "note the bestial folly of this fellow!" (519).

At Reggio, the little cloud of last year, no bigger than a man's hand, was coming up dark on the horizon. (515). "The Podesta was too remiss, and many manslaughters and crimes were done in the district, so that in one house in the city a man's enemies entered by a ladder and slew him in his bed. This Podesta was succeeded next year by the Lord Bernabo dei Palastrelli of Piacenza, who spared none, and destroyed many evildoers and robbers in his days. Many he slew and caused to be slain in his government; and therefore, because he kept justice well, the men of Reggio said that he was the destroyer of their city. But his predecessor was rather their destroyer, who was too remiss and negligent, so that many wars began in the city which last even to this day, and are a cause of destruction to the city, unless God shall ordain otherwise." God did not interfere to save them from the consequences of their quarrels : and next year saw the outbreak of savage civil wars at Reggio and Modena, though Parma was still in comparative peace. The last quarter of Salimbene's chronicle is largely taken up with the record of these sordid and barbarous wars, which I shall give only in the briefest summary, except for those personal touches which put Salimbene so high above most of his contemporaries. Again in 1284 Reggio dismissed its Podesta : not only because his acts were factious and partial, but also because he put them to shame with his uncouthness. " He had such an impediment in his speech as provoked his hearers to laugh ; for when in Council he would say ' Ye have heard what hath been proposed,' he said, ' Ye have heard what hath been propolt,' (*audivistis propoltam*), and so they mocked him as a tongueless man, for he was thick of speech. Yet the citizens were more worthy of scorn for electing to their lordship such men as are of no worth, for it is a sign that like loves like, and that they are ruled by private friendship, and care little for the common profit. . . . ." Indeed, the position of podesta was not so enviable in those days, and Sacchetti very naturally wondered how any man of sense could be tempted to take the office. Here is another instance from Salimbene : " The Lord Jacopo da Enzola, Podesta of Modena, had fallen ill and died in that city, and lay buried there in the Cathedral church : and on his tomb he was portrayed sitting with all honour on his horse, as became a knight ; and, for that in the days of his government all those manslaughters and misdeeds had been done, wherefrom sprang the divisions of parties and civil wars in Modena (for he had not done due justice and vengeance for them), therefore the men of Modena, provoked to wrath and troubled with indignation at the sight of these evils, put out the eyes of the Podesta's image, and defiled his tomb in so foul and swinish a fashion as may scarce be written here."[3] (608). Here again, as usual, outrage bred fresh outrage. " In process of time the citizens of Modena, sent to Parma two ambassadors, one of whom in full Council spake many opprobrious insults against this dead Podesta Jacopo da Enzola [who was a native of Parma]. Therefore his son Ghirardino, provoked to wrath by these words, wrought according to the saying of Scripture ' A patient man shall bear for a time, and afterwards joy shall be restored to him.' For when that ambassador who had reviled his father departed, Ghirardino followed after him along the road with certain wanton young men ; and after he was come into the Bishopric of Reggio he grievously wounded and maimed him, yet not so as to slay him : wherefore he was condemned by the men of Parma [to pay £1,000 Parmese :] which he paid to the last penny. All this I say to show that the men of Parma did well in keeping justice, and they did evil who kept it not at Modena."

With such rulers and such people, the story of Dante's Florence was repeated in every city. A jealous quarrel—a cry of " cosa fatta capo ha,"—a sudden murder in the streets—a consequent series of vendettas—and in a few weeks the city was cleft in twain by a gulf of implacable feuds. After some days of street fighting, the weaker party would be driven into exile, and its houses razed to the ground with every circumstance of indelible insult. Nothing tended so inevitably to perpetuate civil feuds in Italy as these wholesale expulsions of the beaten party and destructions of their houses. Many who first read how the houses of the Ghibellines at Florence were pulled down, and their stones used to build walls which should shut out all Ghibellines for ever from their native city—or how the great Piazza was made on the site of the houses of the exiled Uberti—are apt to look on these as isolated and exceptional instances ; but the chronicles of other cities show us that these barbarous reprisals were normal and incessant. The author of the *Chronicon Parmense* records twenty-four cases of house-wrecking in the forty years following 1265. These were all in consequence of quarrels between Guelf and Guelf, quite independently of the wholesale destruction of 1247, when " the Ghibellines' houses and towers were daily destroyed, and from the bricks and beams and planks men built walls and engines for the city." The provocation was usually a murder, but often merely a bloodless quarrel : as in 1285 when Marcherio da Montecchio " had had words with (*habuerant verba cum*) Gherardino Ansaldi by reason of the priory of St. Bartholo-mew," or in 1293 when " the Lord Podesta, with more than 1,000 armed men, ran as usual (*more solito*) to the house of the Lord Giovanni de' Nizi, who was a Frate Godente, and likewise to that of Poltrenerio de' Ricicoldi, by reason of certain injuries which they had committed against men of the Gild of the Cross," The result was that Italy swarmed from sea to sea with homeless and desperate men, degraded still more by that hand-to-mouth life and base companionship which Dante describes so bitterly (*Parad.* xvii. 58 foll.) The acts of the Provincial Synod of Milan, held in 1311, contain a long decree as to the means of raising an income for the many bishops who were wandering in

exile from their sees.[4]   Here is the light in which Salimbene saw
all this, anticipating Cacciaguida's prophecy by thirteen years
(1287—395). "Moreover, in this year all they who were of the
old party of the Emperor Frederick, who had long been cast forth
from their own cities and had wandered homeless in exile, thought
to take some city wherein they might thenceforth dwell without
reproach and without loathing, and wherefrom they might take
vengeance on their enemies unless they would live at peace with
them. They were driven to this by utter necessity : for indeed
they of the Church party utterly refused to show them bowels
of mercy or receive them to peace by opening their cities to
them." It speaks much for Salimbene's candour, that, good
Guelf as he is, he cannot help finding some sympathy and
justification for these Ghibellines at bay. Such exiles usually
seized a neighbouring town or castle from which they might
harass their former city and possibly some day, by a sudden
coup de main, enter again as victors and destroy their enemies'
houses in turn. Desperate themselves, they collected round
them all the desperate characters of the district. The Monk of
Canossa—probably one of those unfrocked clerics so often
conspicuous among the ruffian leaders of medieval wars—made
his den in Matilda's old castle, and was probably still there in
the year when Dante saw the transfigured Countess in his Earthly
Paradise. Here is another scene from Salimbene (592). When
the exiles stormed Magreba, "Nero da Leccaterra entered
into the church of the Blessed Virgin and set fire to it that it
might be utterly consumed, saying, 'Now, St. Mary, defend
thyself if thou canst!' Yet even as he spake these words of
malice and insult, a lance hurled by some other hand pierced
through his breastplate and entered even into his heart, and
suddenly he fell down dead. And, for it is certain that his own
men hurled no such lance, especially against their Captain,
therefore it is believed that the blow was dealt by St. Mercury,
both because he is the wonted avenger of wrongs done to the
Blessed Virgin, and also because he slew the apostate Julian with
his lance in the Persian war." This legend of Julian's death
by the lance of St. Mercury and at the command of the Virgin
Mary occurs first in the Life of St. Basil, whose prayers are
said to have brought about this vengeance ; it is told also by
Vincent of Beauvais ; and Caesarius quotes it as a proof that
Christian charity by no means forbids one saint to avenge injuries done to another : "St. Mercury the Martyr, though perchance in this life he prayed for his own murderers, yet stepped
down from the realms of glory to slay Julian."[5]

The brutalities committed on each side were awful. The destruction of houses and crops, orchards and vineyards, went on wholesale: our good friar spares a word of special regret for one particular vineyard "which made Vernaccia wine."[6] Prisoners were killed in cold blood or carried off like cattle : "the greater part of these 103 prisoners were bound with a single rope and led off to Reggio, where men threw them into chains and kept them bound in the common prison." On one attack, children were slaughtered in their cradles : at another time, the men vented their spite on the women (587). "In this year, when the women of Modena had come forth to gather grapes in the vineyards, the men of Sassuolo took 300 of them and led them to Sassuolo, and there cast them into prison . . . but they were quickly loosed, for the Modenese for their part took the women of Sassuolo." It is not surprising to find that these ruffians, losing heart in battle, "took to flight, casting away their arms and garments and all that they had, desiring only to save their souls ; " or that another, taken prisoner by the Monk of Canossa, "after but small persuasion of torture, became of his party and dwelt from thenceforth with him." Yet the men who did these things might be good churchmen, as churchmanship was often understood. Here is Salimbene's description of the Lord Burigardo, who cast the 300 women into prison. (589) "And note that he had certain virtues (*bonitates*) towards God : for he was so devout that he always had a chaplain of his own at his court, (as I saw with mine own eyes) who daily said Mass for him and celebrated divine service. When he was at Reggio he sent the Friars Minor a great branched candlestick to illuminate and honour the Lord's body, when it is elevated and shown to the people in the Mass." So far these people came up to the modern idea of the medieval robber-baron : but modern ideas of chivalry will find little satisfaction in the friar's chronicle. Only one trait of generosity is recorded in this whole dismal series of civil conflicts : and the very stress laid on this is eloquent as to the ordinary practice. (636) "The chief captain of the men of Gesso was the Lord Rolandino of Canossa, a fair and noble man, courtly and liberal, and who in his day had been Podesta of many divers cities. His mother was of the house of Piedemonte, a noble lady and most holy of life. Moreover the Lord Rolandino did one great act of courtesy which is worthy to be recounted and remembered. For when the men of Gesso had a truce with the men of Albinea, a certain man of Albinea came and complained to the Lord Rolandino that a man of Gesso had driven off his oxen. And he had the oxen forthwith restored to him, adding 'what wilt thou now?' Then the man answered 'I would have that man, whom I see standing there, restore me my garment which he hath.' So the Lord Rolandino prayed the man to restore the garment; and when he utterly refused, he himself took off his outer mantle and gave it to the man who had been robbed, saying 'Methinks thou hast now full satisfaction for thy garment: go now in peace.' When therefore the country fellow who had stolen the garment saw this, he was ashamed and fell at the Lord Rolandino's feet and confessed his fault."

Imagine the lot of the ordinary peasant in these times—the class of whom we often speak as the backbone of the country, fretting ourselves nowadays merely because they insist on flocking, like ourselves, to the towns! Castles and cities being generally too well fortified for attack, the whole story of the war is that of outrages and reprisals upon the peasants of either party. "The villagers dwelt apart almost after the fashion of the Sidonians, nor was there any that resisted their enemies or opened the mouth or made the least noise. And that night they burned fifty-three houses in the village, good and mean alike: and they would have burned all without distinction but that they desisted at the prayers of the Friars Minor who opposed themselves to the evildoers. So the men of Bibbiano seeing this gave £100 imperial to the men of Gesso, and made a truce with them for one year, that they might labour in safety and gather in the fruits of the earth." The majority of the peasants' possessions were thus at the mercy of their enemies: even their lives and portable goods were in comparative safety only when they neglected ecclesiastical prohibitions and turned the parish churches into fortresses. Short of this, there was no salvation but in bodily removal of their houses. (633) "The men of Castelli carried away their houses and rebuilt them round the mount of Bianello, on its very summit. Likewise did the men of Coresana and Farneto and Corniano and Piazzola round Monte Lucio, on its highest point; likewise also did the men of Oliveto; the men of Bibbiano also fortified themselves, fearing the war to come. But the men of San Polo d'Enza built their houses round the parish church, and digged moats and filled them with water, that they might be safe from the face of the spoiler." The ordinary farm-house was evidently slight enough in those days; for Salimbene thus describes the rejoicings after a battle: "that evening the citizens kindled a beacon of fire on the summit of the Tower of the Commune at Reggio in sign of joy and gladness, and to rejoice the hearts of their friends: and they for their part did likewise, showing lighted beacons, as the country folk do at

carnival times, when they burn down their cottages and hovels "
(639).

Nor was it only the peasants who suffered from what may be
called the contingent horrors of civil war. In those days of
exasperated party feeling, both sides were merciless to traitors,
real or suspected (1287—394). "The Monk of Canossa took
Bernardo Guglielmi, deacon of the church of S. Antonino at
Castelli, who confessed outright and of his own free will, without
torment (as they said who took him captive) that he would have
betrayed Bianello to the men of Gesso. So forthwith they slit
his windpipe, and dragged his dead body naked through the
town : afterwards they cast him forth like carrion without the
walls, and so he was buried in his bare shirt at the church of
S. Antonino. On St. John Baptist's day when I sang Mass at
Bianello, that same man sang the gospel to my Mass ; and that
same year, on the day following the feast of the beheading of St.
John Baptist, he also was beheaded. Moreover, they cut out
the tongue of his sister, Bertha by name, and cast her forth into
perpetual banishment. For they accused not only her but also
the dead man's leman or concubine of carrying evil news to and
fro between Gesso and certain abominable traitors at Castelli.
That deacon was an old man : he kept a concubine, and at his
last end he could not, or would not, make his confession. He was
slain by one Martinello, a murderer and notorious evildoer whom
the monk of Bianello kept in his castle. The year before, the
Monk's hired murderers had slain the parish priest of S. Polo,
on the same accusation that he was not truly of the Monk's party,
and for many other reasons which are not worthy to be told or
remembered. His four murderers supped familiarly with him
one evening ; and at night as he slept under his own roof and in
his own chamber, they slew him with their swords and deformed
his corpse with so foul a mockery that it was a horrible and
monstrous sight to see. But God brought swift vengeance on
them ; for before the year was past, Raimondello was slain by
the men of Gesso, into whose hands Giacomello likewise fell,
and they smote out two of his teeth and scarce left him his life ;
and God smote Accorto and Ferrarello in their own beds." On
another occasion Modena was nearly taken by a band of exiles
treacherously introduced by night : and next morning (1287—397)
" men began to enquire diligently who were the traitors who had
let them in. And they took the Lord Garso de' Garsoni and
hanged him at the Porta Bazoaria ; and in those days thirty-nine
men were hanged for the same cause, some of whom were said to
have been guiltless. The Podesta of Modena at that time was

the Lord Bernardino of Ravenna, son to the Lord Guido da Polenta," and therefore brother to Francesca da Rimini. . . "So the Lord Matteo Correggio went to Modena, and there in the Palazzo Communale, before the full council, he bitterly rebuked the Podesta, saying, 'Of a truth, my Lord Podesta, ye have brought a great burden upon us and upon this city, seeing that we must now dwell in fear our whole life long by reason of the headlong vengeance which ye have taken.'" Two similar instances of torture and random vengeance are recorded about the same time (1287—389).

One of the most hopeless features of these civil wars is the part played in them by Churchmen. Salimbene shows us bishops driven out of their sees for their share in these faction-fights : the archpriest of Fornovo murdered in one political quarrel : and the Bishop of Tortona in another, by the " Guglielmo Marchese " of *Purg.* vii. 134. The abbots of the great monasteries, again, were almost as rich and powerful as the bishops : and they too were generally chosen on political principles and expected to work for political ends.

San Prospero at Reggio was one of the great abbeys of Italy, though its princely revenues had within recent years been much diminished by lawsuits and wars. The Abbot's election in 1272 had been celebrated by a great feast " whereat all the clergy and men of Religion were present, and all the good men (*i.e.* the upper classes) of the city " (488). In 1284 we find the Abbot on the losing side in the civil strife at Reggio, and only enabled to retain his Abbey by making peace with his powerful enemies the Boiardi, ancestors of the famous poet. Now, however, in 1286, the Abbot fell under suspicion not only of giving help to the other party, but also of complicity in two recent murders— that of the brothers da Bianello and of the archpriest Gerardo Boiardi. The rest may be told in Salimbene's words (621) " The Abbot Guglielmo de' Lupicini was a good man indeed with regard to God and to man's honour ; but as regards worldly affairs he was simple, and churlish, and miserly ; for he treated his monks ill in the matter of their food, and therefore he found them traitors afterwards. For Bonifazio Boiardi, with the connivance of certain monks who stood ill with their Abbot for that he had dealt unkindly with them in the matter of victuals, took the monastery by assault on the feast of Pentecost, at the hour of dinner ; and, having despoiled it of all that he coveted, he departed. And the Abbot sought safety in flight and came to the convent of the Friars Minor, where he abode all that day and the night following ; then he went to the house of his brother by blood, named Sinibaldo, and dwelt there some days in doubt of mind and anguish of heart. Moreover, the said Bonifazio seized all the granges of the convent at the season of wheat-harvest, and afterwards he seized Fossola by force, and besieged and took and burnt Domomatta, where he slew a man who defended his oxen and would not yield them up; and another they beat and grievously wounded, leaving him half dead. And note that all these things had been foretold to the Abbot before the event; but in his simplicity and his miserliness he would not avoid them nor beware. But his friends, seeing that he was slow to guard himself, came of their own accord and uninvited, forty good men of Reggio in all, and kept the convent of San Prospero all night before Pentecost. But when the dinner hour came he thanked them not for the guard which they had held all night long, nor did he call them to dinner, but suffered each to go and dine at his own house while he himself went to dine at his palace with certain esquires and pages of his own. And lo, while he sat at meat and believed that all was at peace, suddenly he heard the bell which the traitor monks rang from the campanile. Then the secular enemies of the Abbot came forth swiftly from their hiding-places and rushed into the convent, wishing to make a fresh Abbot of their own; but by God's mercy the Abbot cast himself down from a certain small upper chamber which they call the ambulatory, and forthwith he waded through the city moat and came, as aforesaid, to the convent of the Friars Minor, trembling for fear as a rush trembles in the water. There all his friends who came to visit him cursed him, heaping reproaches and imprecations on his head; for they said that all this was befallen him by reason of his churlishness and avarice. Yet he bore all with much patience, knowing himself guilty in this matter. Moreover, the month before, that is in May, before these things had befallen the Abbot . . . ."

Here we have another lamentable gap of five sheets, torn out by some impatient reader who was no doubt offended by our friar's frank revelations. The Abbot's story, like most others of the kind, had a bloody sequel next year, when (625) "peace was made between the Lupicini and Boiardi, and two monks of San Prospero were slain. These were the monks who had betrayed both their Abbot and their convent. And in process of time within a brief space, another monk of the same convent was slain in revenge for those two, on his way to the court with another priest, for the Abbot had made him his proctor. He asked of his murderers 'Who are ye?' They answered and said 'We are the proctors of those two monks who were slain a few days

past ; and we have been sent to return blow for blow.' Thus
then they wounded him and left him half dead ; and he was
taken to the house of his parents, where he confessed himself
well, and fell asleep in the Lord. And within a few days the
mother of this monk, bowed down with grief, fell sick and gave
up the ghost." Dom Affarosi, the historian of S. Prospero.
gives us further details of these disorders. The Boiardi had
sacked not only the convent but the church. As the civil wars
went on, the affairs of the convent went from bad to worse, so
that the monks were obliged to desert it altogether and live in
their own hospice of S. Matteo. Not until some years after,
when the city had recovered a little quiet by throwing itself into
the arms of the despot Obizzo da Este, was Guglielmo's successor
able to begin restoring the ravages wrought on the Abbey by
these wars. The Parmese, dreading the effect of these quarrels
at Reggio and Modena on their own tranquillity, tried to make
peace but only earned the further enmity of the two jealous
cities. Shortly after our chronicler's death, Parma also " drank
of the cup of God's fury."

CHAPTER XVIII.

Fresh Storms.

THE reader will easily realize that politics were a vivid interest in those days; and it is natural that the friars' manuals should strictly forbid all listening to or repeating tales of worldly wars. This, however, if we may judge from Salimbene, did not render them less curious. Over and over again, he ends some fresh entry in his chronicle with a phrase like this : " Thus matters stand to-day, on the Octave of the Nativity of the Blessed Virgin : how they will end we know not ; yet, if life be spared us, we shall see." We need not wonder that divines and prophets were in great request throughout these uncertain times. " The Inner Party of Modena had a man of Brescia who called himself an astrologer and diviner, to whom they gave daily ten great pennies of silver, and nightly three great Genoese candles of the purest wax, and he promised them that if they fought a third time they should have the victory. And they answered him ' We will not fight on a Monday or a Tuesday, for that we have been conquered on those two days. Choose us therefore another day ; and know that if we gain not this time the promised victory, we will tear out thy remaining evil eye : ' for he was one-eyed. So, fearing to be found out in his falsehood, he carried off all that he had gained, and went his way without saluting his hosts. Then the men of Sassuolo began to mock them, ' as men who sacrifice to devils and not to God,' as it is written in Deuteronomy." Moreover, two of the soothsayers whom Dante has gibbeted were consulted in these civil wars. Asdente is first mentioned on p. 512, where he is described as " a poor working cobbler, pure and simple and fearing God and courteous and urbane : illiterate, but with great illumination of mind, so that he understood the writings of those who have foretold the future, as Abbot Joachim, Merlin, Methodius and the Sibyl, Isaiah, Jeremiah, Hosea, Daniel and the Apocalypse, and Michael Scot, who was astrologer to the deposed Emperor Frederick II. And many things have I heard from Asdente which in process of time came to pass, *viz.* that Pope Nicholas III should die in the month of August, and be succeeded by Pope Martin : and many other things which we hope to see if life be spared us. This man besides his own name, which is Master Benvenuto, is commonly called Asdente, that is toothless, by way of contrary, for he hath great and disordered teeth and an impediment in his speech, yet he understands and is understood well. He dwells at the bridge-head of Parma, hard by the city moat and the well, along the street which goes to Borgo San Donnino." He is mentioned again under 1284 (531) " When the ambassadors of Reggio were in their lodging in the suburb of Santa Cristina, hearing of Asdente the prophet of the men of Parma, they sent for him to consult him of their state, and laid it on his soul that he should withdraw no word of the future which the Lord purposed to bring about. So he answered that if they would keep themselves in peace to the Feast of Christ's Nativity they should escape the wrath of God : if not, they should drink of the cup of His wrath as the men of Modena had drunk. They answered him that they would keep well at peace, for they purposed to make intermarriages for peace and friendship. Yet he answered that they were doing all these things fraudulently, and under a cloak and veil of peace. Wherefore the ambassadors of Reggio returned, and ceased from their marriages, and are rather preparing themselves to make and gather together arms of war than to keep peace with each other, that the word of Michael Scot may be fulfilled in them, which he wrote in his verses wherein he predicted the future, ' And the factions at Reggio shall hold ill words together.' "

A little lower down we come for the third time to Asdente, and see again what injustice Dante has done him. (532) " In those days the Lord Obizzo, Bishop of Parma, invited to dinner the prophet of the men of Parma, who is called Asdente, and enquired of him diligently concerning the future. And he said that within a short while the men of Reggio and Parma would suffer many tribulations ; and he foretold likewise the death of Pope Martin IV, determining and specifying the times of all these things which I will not set down : and he foretold that three Supreme Pontiffs should succeed and be at discord with each other, one of whom should be lawful, and two unlawfully created : and he had foretold the ruin of Modena before it came to pass. This man is only so far a prophet, that he hath a mind illuminated to under-stand the sayings of Merlin and the Sibyl and the Abbot Joachim, and all who have foretold anything of the future. He is courteous and humble and familiar, and without pomp or vainglory. Nor doth he say anything positively, but rather, ' Thus it seemeth to me,' or ' Thus do I understand that scripture.' And when any man reading before him omits anything, immediately he perceives it, and says, ' Thou deceivest me, for thou hast omitted something.' And many come from divers parts of the world to inquire of him. A good three months beforehand he predicted the mishap of the Pisans ; for a man of Pisa came to Parma of set purpose to inquire of him, after Pisa had already fought twice with Genoa. For the men of Pisa and Genoa met three times in sea-fight, once in 1283, and twice in 1284. In the first two fights 6000 Pisans were reckoned among the dead and wounded, and while they still fought fiercely at sea, a man of Genoa boarded a Pisan vessel, and loaded himself with many plates of silver, and thus armed in steel and laden with silver, wishing to board his own ship again, he missed his mark, and plunged to the bottom like a stone, with his silver and his steel and perchance with many crimes on his head. All this I heard from our Lector at Ravenna, who was a Genoese, and newly come from Genoa. Note and consider the marvel that the Pisans were taken by the Genoese at the same season and month and day and place wherein they themselves had taken the prelates in the days of Pope Gregory IX of pious memory, that thou mayest see the truth of what the Lord saith ' He that toucheth you, toucheth the apple of my eye.' And note that the Parmese, of whom I am one, are wont to say that a vengeance of thirty years old is timely enough, and they say the truth.

So in this year 1284 the Pisans, seeing all the evil which the Genoese had inflicted upon them, and wishing to avenge themselves, built many ships and galleys and sea-vessels, in the river Arno, and when the fleet had been made ready, they ordained that none betwixt the ages of 20 and 60 years should stay at home, but all should go to the fight. And they scoured the whole of the Genoese shore, destroying and burning, killing and taking captives, and plundering. And this they did along all the shore from Genoa to Provence, desiring to find the Genoese and fight with them. But the Genoese had ordained that none of their citizens should remain at home between the ages of 18 years and 70, for all must go to fight. Thus they scoured the sea, desiring to find the Pisans. At last they found each other between the point of Corsica and Gorgona, and grappled their ships together after the fashion of sea-fights, and there they fought with such slaughter on either side that even the heavens seemed to weep in compassion, and many on either part were slain, and many ships sunken. But when the Pisans had already the upper hand, other Genoese came and fell upon them, wearied as they were.

Nevertheless, the battle still raged furiously on both sides. At last, the Pisans finding themselves worsted, yielded themselves to the Genoese, who slew the wounded, and kept the rest in prison : and even the victors had no cause for boasting, since fortune was cruel to either side; and there was such weeping and wailing in Genoa and Pisa as was never heard in those two cities from the day of their foundation to our times. For who without woe and bitter weeping can consider how those two noble cities, whereby all plenty of good things came to us in Italy, destroyed each other from mere ambition and pomp and vainglory, whereby each desired to overcome the other, as though the sea were not wide enough for the ships of both ! I care not to write here the number of captives and slain from either side, for they were diversely told. Yet the Archbishop of Parma, in his letter to his blood-brother the Bishop of Bologna, hath named a certain number, which also I care not to write ; for I expect Brethren Minor of Pisa, who will better tell me the exact number. And note that this murderous fight between Genoa and Pisa was foretold long before it happened. For in the town of San Ruffino in the Bishopric of Parma, women who were bleaching linen by night, saw two great oxen fighting and retreating, and again meeting to fight with each other. Moreover, after the fight of the Pisans and Genoese, many women of Pisa, fair ladies and noble and rich and mighty, gathered together in companies of thirty and forty at a time, and went on foot from Pisa to Genoa, to seek out and visit their captives. For one had a husband there, another a son or a brother or a cousin . . . And when the aforesaid women sought out their captives, the jailers would answer them, ' Yesterday thirty died, and to-day forty. We cast them into the sea, and thus we do daily with the Pisans.' So when those ladies heard such news of their dear ones and could not find them, they fell down amazed with excess of grief, and could scarce breathe for utter anguish and pain of heart. Then after a while, when their breath was come again, they rent their faces with their nails and tore their hair, and raising their voices wept with great wailing until their fountain of tears was dried. For the Pisans died in prison of hunger and famine, and poverty and misery, and anguish and sadness, for ' they that hated them had dominion over them, and their enemies afflicted them : and they were humbled under their hands.' Nor were they thought worthy of the sepulchres of their fathers, and they were deprived of burial rites. Moreover, when the aforesaid ladies of Pisa were come home, they found others dead whom they had left safe in their homes. For the Lord smote the Pisans with a plague in that year, and many died : nor was there any house without its dead. For the sword of the Lord's fury slew the Pisans, because they rebelled long time against the Church. Four years I dwelt in the convent of the Friars Minor at Pisa, a good forty years past ; and therefore I am sad for the Pisans, and have compassion on them, God knoweth! Note moreover that as there is a natural loathing between men and serpents, dogs and wolves, horses and gryphons, so is there between the Pisans and Genoese, Pisans and men of Lucca, Pisans and Florentines. So the Florentines and men of Lucca, who are bound with a chain of close friendship, hearing of this defeat of the Pisans, and seeing now their own favourable time, ordained an expedition against Pisa a little before Christmas in that same year ; with which expedition the men of Prato and Corneto also were to come and sweep the rest of the Pisans into their net, and raze the city if possible to the foundations, and blot it from the face of the earth. So the Pisans bethought them of a good counsel, and sent the keys of the gates of their city to Pope Martin, that he might defend them against their enemies. And he received them graciously and repressed the enemies that rose up against them."

We have seen how Asdente unmasked the treachery which underlay these pacific overtures : and Salimbene shows us more than once how the promised peace of those days might be worse than open war. He himself was one of the two friars selected as peacemakers between the cities of Modena and their exiled enemies. "They answered me most courteously and kindly, that they were most willing to make peace with their fellow-citizens." (590) But there was an evident want of good faith on both sides, and the war blazed up again. This leads our chronicler to remark "I have little trust of peace among Lombards : for their peacemakings are like the boys' game when they lay hand above hand upon their knees : and each, seeking to get the better of the other, withdraws his hand from below and strikes it upon the hand above, and thus each thinks to have the better : but oftentimes we see the conqueror conquered in his turn." And here, after giving instances of inextinguishable party hate at Parma and Bologna, Modena and Reggio, and Cremona, in which Imperialists and Churchmen had shown equal rancour and treachery, he goes on to quote Jeremiah ix, 4, 5 and Ecclesiasticus xii, 10-12 : "Take ye heed everyone of his neighbour, and trust ye not in any brother—distrust thine enemy for ever and ever." He quotes the old fable of the man and serpent who, for a while, lived on friendly terms until one day the latter

killed the child of the man, who cut off a great part of his tail
in revenge, and then felt generous enough to say " Shall we make
peace ? "   " No," said the serpent : " for thou wilt never forget
thy son's death, nor I my revenge when I see my mutilated tail.
Let each, therefore, work for his own hand as best he can, which
will be more profitable alike for thee and for me."

Moreover, Salimbene's descriptions show that these later wars
in Emilia were no less barbarous than those of Romagna which
he has already painted in such lurid colours. (1287-392) " Under
pretext of the peace above-mentioned the siege was raised and
the men escaped ; yet peace was never made, but the men of
Gesso did worse than before, plundering and spoiling the villages
of the Bishopric of Reggio, and taking prisoners, whom they
tortured with divers exquisite torments to extort money for
their ransom.   And they who did thus were hireling soldiers of
Bergamo and Milan and other ruffians from Liguria.   Once they
took a poor man who had never harmed them ; nay, who would
have served them if he had been able ; whom they led away
captive to Gesso and said to him ' Tax thyself,' which was as
much as to say ' Let us hear what thou canst give us.'   And
when he answered that he had nought to give, forthwith they
smote him in the mouth with a flint-stone, with which one blow
six of his teeth were smitten out, and the seventh was ready to
fall.   Likewise also they did to many others.   For some men's
heads they bound with a cord and lever, and strained it with such
force that their eyes started from their sockets and fell upon their
cheeks : others they bound by the right or left thumb only, and
thus lifted the whole weight of their body from the ground :
others again they racked with yet more foul and horrible torments
which I blush to relate : others they would hang by the little
toe of one foot, or seat them with their hands bound behind
their back and lay under their feet a pot of live coals, blowing
with the bellows to stir them yet more ; with others again they
would bind the great toe of their right foot with a bowstring to
one tooth, and then prick their backs with a goad that they
might tear out their own teeth ; or they bound their hands and
legs together round a spit (as a lamb is carried to the butcher)
and kept them thus hanging on that pole all day long, without
food or drink : or again with a hard and rough piece of wood they
would rub and grate their shins until the bare bone appeared,
which was a misery and sore pity even to behold.   And when the
chief men of Gesso rebuked them, saying that it was horrible to
see such things practised on Christian folk, then these ruffians
waxed wroth and threatened to depart from them if they suffered

not such things; wherefore the chief men must needs suffer them whether they would or not. Many other torments they invented and inflicted, which I have omitted for brevity's sake; but these I have written that it may be known how some men are more cruel than beasts: wherefore it is nought but just that they who do such things should be tormented with such devils in hell."

Meanwhile, whoever might have lost during these civil wars, the friars of Reggio had steadily grown. Already in 1256 they bought the Emperor's palace for their convent, and found occasion to enlarge it soon after. (463) Soon afterwards, when the Emperor of Constantinople passed through Reggio, it was the friars who lodged him, (no doubt by way of acknowledgment for their tenure of the palace): and the convent was the scene of brilliant festivities which brought rich gifts to the Brethren. (483) And now (582) they began to build a new church, laying the foundation stone on May 18th. But, as ill-luck would have it, "the whole May was a rainy month that year, so that it rained daily, and the country-folk were disquieted, for that they could do no work in the fields: and they laid the blame on the Friars Minor, who had dug up the graves of the dead for the foundations of their church." St. Francis would have shared the peasants' horror at this desecration, and still more at the present craving of his brethren for money and creature comforts. The men of Parma, complains Salimbene, "cared little for the friars, for they are ever indevout and hard-hearted towards men of religion." He comes back to this same subject later on (596) while speaking of the Bishop of Spoleto, known as "Master Roland of Parma, whose father was called Master Taberna, a comely and courteous man and an excellent tailor, who made the garments of the nobles. This Master Roland went to Paris in great poverty, and there he studied many years in divers sciences, and became a great clerk and full of knowledge: after which he became a very great advocate at the Pope's court, where he gained wealth and honour. And to the Religious of Parma he was ever hard and clownish, and never familiar or kindly: nor did he ever leave them anything at his death. And this cursed property is common to almost all the people of Parma—both clergy and laity, men and women, noble and commonalty—that they are always indevout and hard and cruel to Religious and other servants of God, whether of their own or of other cities, which would seem a most evil sign of the wrath of God upon them. For as Ezechiel saith ' Behold this was the iniquity of Sodom thy sister, pride, fulness of bread, and abundance, and the idleness of her and of her daughters, and they did not put forth their hand to the needy and to the poor,' so we may say of the city of Parma for its hardness and mercilessness towards the poor servants of God : and therefore I, Brother Salimbene of Parma, have been 48 years in the Order of Friars Minor, yet never would I dwell at Parma by reason of the indevotion which its citizens show and practise towards God's servants. For they care not to do them kindness, though at times they could easily help them if they would : for they are most liberal in largesse to play-actors and minstrels and buffoons. Certainly if a city so great as Parma were in France, then 100 Friars Minor would be settled to dwell there in all decency and comfort, and abundantly supplied with all things needful." Yet presently a Parmesan Cardinal did actually give £20 Imperial to the convent, and another £10 each to the two Brethren who went on an embassy to him at Rome (597)—which latter gift shows, even more clearly than Salimbene's commercial criterion of religion, how far the Order had already changed in the 60 years since St. Francis had written " I strictly forbid the Brethren, all and single, to accept coin or money in any way, whether directly or through a third person."   We see also how fast the friars were losing the unique popularity and influence which they had enjoyed so long as they were really poor. (627) " In this year, at the Carnival season, the men of Reggio disported themselves not after the fashion of other Christian people, who all and in every place revel and play the fool at that season (*stultizant et infatuantur*) ; but rather they kept silence as though they mourned their dead.   But in the season of Lent, when the time is sacred to God, then began they to play ; yet this is the acceptable time and the day of salvation, a time for giving alms and doing works of piety, moreover a time for confession and hearing of sermons, and visiting of churches, of praying, and fasting, and weeping, as the church lessons tell us. So in the solemn Lenten season the men of Reggio wrought not the aforesaid works of piety or devotion ; and although the Lord forbiddeth a man to use woman's apparel they heeded this not, but walked after their own inventions. For many of them borrowed garments from ladies, wherein they clothed themselves and began to play and wander through the city as in a tournament.   And, that they might the better resemble women, they painted white masks wherewith they covered their faces, caring nought for the penalty promised for such deeds. For the Scripture saith of sinners ' all faces shall be made like a kettle : ' and again ' the faces of them all are as the blackness of a kettle : ' and again ' their face is now made blacker than

coals.' (Joel ii, 6. Nahum ii, 10. Lam. iv, 8.) Woe to such
wretched Christians, who strive to turn the worship of the
Church into dissoluteness and vain talk! for certain wretched
Christians in the cities of Lombardy neither fast nor confess
their sins in the solemn season of Lent. And, since no flesh can
be found at that season in the market, therefore they eat in
secret the flesh of hens and capons; and after the hour of siesta
they sprawl all day long in the squares and under the porticoes,
playing with dice at games of hazard; and there they blaspheme
the Lord, and the Blessed Virgin His mother. Note that the
Apostle hath described certain signs of evil Christians who shall
live about the days of Antichrist; which signs seem to be fulfilled
in these men of our days who sin without shame. (1 Tim. iv, 1 :
2 Tim. iii, 1.) And note that for the many evils done by the
Jews, the Lord complained of them and removed them from
before his face (Jer. xxxii, 30.) See in the Bible. Yet not
even so will wretched sinners be warned; but they are as the
sluggard of whom it is written in Proverbs (xxii, 24-32) For in
the years before this date certain millers of the city, with cunning
and malice prepense, begged and obtained of the Friars Minor
certain old frocks, saying that they would cause them to be
cleansed in a fulling-mill : and afterwards, in the Carnival season
and at the hour of vespers, they clothed themselves in these
borrowed frocks as Friars Minor and danced in the public street.
Which folly they wrought at the instigation of the Devil, desiring
to lay a blot on the elect, that the passers-by might believe those
revellers to be Friars Minor, and the matter might thus redound
to the scandal and disgrace of the Order. But the Podesta of
the city, hearing of this, and being moved to bitter wrath by his
zeal both for the Friars and for the dignity of his office, fined
them heavily and issued a perpetual decree that no others should
ever dare to do likewise." Though two well-known preachers
publicly justified these lententide revels at Reggio, God showed
His displeasure by permitting the Monk of Canossa to make a
bloody incursion into the city shortly afterwards : (632) "and
that day I came down to Reggio from the convent of Montefalcone
and entered the city, and saw all these things with mine own
eyes : for all day I went round the streets while these things
were done. Moreover, on this day of tumult, after the hour of
noon, many ribalds and evildoers ran to the convent of the Friars
Minor and would have entered it and carried off the goods therein
deposited [by others]. But the Brethren seeing this rang the
great bell, and forthwith the Lord Guido da Tripoli came fully
armed on his charger, as I saw with mine own eyes, and smote

them with his mace and put them all to flight. And he looked on me and said 'Ha, Brethren, why have ye no stout staves wherewith to smite these ribalds, that they spoil not your goods?' Then I answered that it was not lawful to us to smite any man, as the Lord saith, 'If one strike thee on thy right cheek, turn to him also the other.' Yet He Himself showed that we should not do this to the letter, in that He answered to him who smote Him on the cheek, 'If I have spoken well, why strikest thou Me?' Yet a certain holy father fulfilled this to the letter : for when a demoniac had smitten him on the cheek, he turned the other ; and forthwith the demon, confounded at his humility, left the man's body and vexed him no more." Nor was this the only occasion on which rioters scented plunder in the friaries ; for "in this same year 18 ribalds of the men of Gesso purposed to come and despoil the Friars Minor in their convent of Montefalcone. But when this came to the ears of certain Lords, they frighted them by threats from their purpose ; so that the fools ceased from their folly." But, however the Friars had lost in real spiritual influence with the masses—however they might alarm even their patron the Pope by their encroachments on the duties and privileges of the parish clergy—they were still at the zenith of their popularity among the richer classes, to whom for many generations they were tactful and not too exacting confessors. Of this Salimbene gives us instructive glimpses on almost the last page of his chronicle. In spite of the peculiarly odious crimes with which he charges Obizzo of Este, one of the most conspicuous tyrants in Dante's *Inferno* ; in spite of the fact that Boccaccio put the Countess on very much the same moral plane as her husband, our chronicler is proud to relate how the former feasted the assembled Friars at the General Chapter of 1287, and how the latter was buried in their convent. This Chapter (it may be noted) was presided over by the Acquasparta of Par. xii. 124.

It is evident that the good old friar felt deeply both the public disasters around him and the decaying prestige of his Order ; for he more than once lets fall a word of discouragement. "These accursed parties and divisions in Italy cannot be healed or assuaged, by reason of men's wickedness and the Devil's malice" (591) : and again "the whole world is seated in wickedness." One symptom of the deep-rooted unrest was the appearance of an impostor claiming to be the Emperor Frederick, long since dead and damned. Another report, still more interesting to Salimbene, announced the impending conversion of the Tartars to Christianity : for "truthful travellers who have lately come from the Holy Land (to wit, Friars Minor and Preachers,) report that a very great and new marvel shall come to pass among the Tartars and Saracens. For they say that the son of the late king of the Tartars is purposed to be in Jerusalem for Easter Eve ; and if he shall see the fire coming down from heaven as the Christians assert, then he promises to slay all the heathen whom he can find." These reports of a wholesale and miraculous conversion of Tartars or other infidels were frequently circulated by " truthful travellers " in the thirteenth century. Roger Bacon shows us how they were begotten of men's belief in the approaching end of the world, to which this conversion would be a necessary preliminary (Matt. xxiv. 14).[1] The yearly miracle of fire at Jerusalem had been condemned by Gregory IX in 1238 as a barefaced forgery of the canons of the Holy Sepulchre : but it evidently flourished still, for Salimbene hints no suspicion whatever, though he was not uncritical for his age.

But amid all his records of war, and grave misgivings for the future, he never loses his interest in picturesque trifles. He has much to tell us of the obstinate ambition of the Parmese to get a bell which would be heard northward to rival Borgo San Donnino, and southward to Reggio—14 and 17 miles off. (584) They sent for a famous master who came from Pisa " like a great baron." The whole town marvelled at his elaborate preparations for the great mould. Vast sums were spent on three attempts, yet even the last and best of the three bells " could scarce be heard over the city of Parma," which was a providential blow to the citizens' pride. Two years later a fourth was made, which, before it had been hung in the tower, " fell down from its platform and hurt no man, save that it cut off the foot of a certain young man, wherewith he had once spurned his own father " (634). He is always much impressed by comets, eclipses, and earthquakes, and believes, of course, firmly in their occult influence on current events. Of plagues there are naturally frequent notices : *e.g.*, in 1285 (584) " in the village of Popilio in the Bishopric of Parma 80 men died within three months ; for this is a general rule or proved fact that, whensoever we have a cattle plague, the next year comes always a pestilence on men. The plague and sickness was so great that year in Rome, that bishops and mitred Abbots, between Easter and the Feast of the Assumption, died to the number of twenty-four (593). And, of strangers only, two thousand died in the city ; and the Friars Minor had oft-times four funerals in their church on one day. And there was an old bishop-elect from beyond the Alps, who had come to Rome for his consecration ; and he died with twenty-five of his attendants. Then I remembered the words of the prophet Amos ' Wailing

shall be in all streets, and they shall say in all the highways
Alas ! alas !' (v. 16, 17 : viii, 3)." Later on in the year (608)
"there was a terrible plague among the cats : for they fell sick,
and were covered with blotches like lepers, and in process of time
they died. Moreover, on the feast of St. Callistus (Oct. 14)
two stars appeared in conjunction at the hour of dawn ; and so
they appeared nightly for many days : but about the feast of
All Saints they began to separate again." Nothing seems to
escape him. He notices how rich one particular summer is in
butterflies, and augurs from it a rep^tition of past caterpillar
plagues. (547) Another year, there were "such a vast multitude
of gnats that their importunate bites made men aweary of their
lives . . . and the reapers ended not their harvest till the end of
July ; so that to Christian folk there seemed a punishment in
that which had been promised as a blessing to the Jews : 'the
threshing of your harvest shall reach unto the vintage, and the
vintage shall reach unto the sowing-time.' " Even his smallest
personal experiences are recorded to point a moral. (547) " In
this aforesaid year, on the Feast of St. Clara, I ate for the first
time *raviuoli* without any crust of pastry ; and this I say to show
how subtle is human gluttony in this appetite of bodily meats
in comparison of earlier men, who were content with the food
created by nature, whereof Ovid saith in the first book of his
Metamorphoses 'And, contented with the meats created of
nature's own free will, they picked arbutus berries and beechnuts
from the mountains, and cornels and blackberries clinging to
the rough brambles, and acorns fallen from the spreading tree
of Jove.' " *Raviuoli* are a sort of rissole : and it was evidently
looked upon as a *tour de force* to fry them without the usual
envelope of pastry.

Under the year 1285 he records an incident at Reggio which
illustrates admirably the medieval attitude towards inconvenient
trade combinations. (586) " In this year it was ordained in full
council of the citizens of Reggio, that fishmongers should sell no
fish from the beginning of Lent until after Easter, under penalty
of £25 Bolognese, and that none should buy of them under pain
of £10 Bolognese ; and this statute was most strictly kept. Now
the cause thereof was that, when knights or judges would enquire
of some fisherman 'At what price wilt thou sell this fish ? ' the
latter, though asked twice or thrice, would disdain to answer ;
nay, rather, he would turn away his face, and speak with his
partner, saying : ' Gossip, put the barrel or the chest in that
place !' according to the Proverb ' A servant will not be corrected by words : because he understandeth what thou sayest, and

will not answer.' Moreover, they demanded three or four *grossi* for a single small tench or eel. When therefore the fishermen and fishmongers saw how strictly and steadfastly men kept the statute made against them, and that they lost much thereby (for all their fish were numbered and placed in stewponds until after Easter) then they came to the Friars Minor and besought them to beg of the Podesta and the Captain and the Ancients and the whole council some relaxation of that statute : in which case they for their part would promise to sell reasonably and discreetly and courteously and good cheap to all who desired to buy of their fish. Yet not even so was the statute relaxed, as the Apostle saith of Esau, 'for he found no place of repentance, although with tears he had sought it.' Moreover, the citizens threatened to deal in like manner with the butchers at Eastertide, unless they sold their flesh in the shambles both courteously and reasonably. But the butchers hearing this did after the Wise Man's counsel 'The wicked man being scourged, the fool shall be wiser.' "

A similar quarrel between priests and people had already had much the same issue (504). "In the month of October 1280 a quarrel arose between the Lord Guglielmo, Bishop of Reggio, with the clergy of his city and bishopric on the one part, and the Lord Dego, Captain of the people, with the citizens of Reggio on the other part. This quarrel was by reason of the tithes, for the clergy seemed to wish to collect too much from the men of the people and all the citizens. Wherefore the Lord Captain, with the 24 Defenders of the People, made certain statutes against the lay-collectors of the said tithes, by reason of which statutes the Lord Bishop excommunicated the aforesaid Captain and 24 Defenders and the whole Council-General of the people, and therewithal he laid the whole city under an interdict. So the people were wroth at this, and chose other 25 from among themselves, among whom were 7 judges (among the aforesaid 24 there had been 4 judges), and made many other statutes against the clergy. First, that none should pay them any tithe, nor give them counsel, help, or favour, nor sit at meat with them, nor stay in their service, nor have any dealings of trade with them, nor dwell in their houses or at their farms, nor give them to eat or to drink—and many other such provisions there were, and a most grievous penalty was laid upon the breach of any one. Neither might any man grind their corn, nor bake their bread, nor shave them, nor do any service to them : and the aforesaid Wise Men claimed of their own authority to proclaim, resolve, and ordain in the aforesaid matters according to their own will and pleasure.

This claim was afterwards confirmed by the General Council of the People, and all the aforesaid laws were ratified and kept both by all the people and by the Knights and other chief men. So by reason of these laws many millers were condemned each to a fine of £50 of money of Reggio, for that they remained in the mills of the clergy against the aforesaid ordinances beyond the term fixed ; and many other persons were condemned also . . . In the month of November of the same year this matter of the tithes was peaceably concluded . . . to the effect that none should be compelled to pay tithes but according to his own conscience, and many other provisions which were written in the aforesaid treaty."[2]

CHAPTER XIX.

Last Days.

IT is natural enough that the tone of the old man's chronicle should grow sadder towards its end. The year 1285 was marked by many tragic occurrences. At Faenza, hard by, a noble was murdered, with his son, by some cousins in whose house they had sat down to dinner : at Cesena Malatesta of Rimini (the *Mastin Vecchio* of Dante, *Inf.* xxvii, 46) was nearly murdered by Taddeo da Buonconte, but just managed to slip away, though wounded, through the open door of the convent of the Austin Friars, where he took sanctuary. This same year saw the death of the four sovereigns who loomed largest on the horizon— Charles of Anjou, Peter of Aragon, Martin IV, and Philip the Bold of France : and our chronicler dismisses them with a characteristic epitaph (600) " Note that these four great men of whom I have made mention were all ' stout hunters before the Lord,' (*i.e.*, oppressors of mankind) . . . . . yet in one and the same year they went the way of all flesh. Whereof Primas hath written most excellently in his treatise ' Of this World's Life,' saying

> ' Out, alas ! dear life on earth,
> Why art thou so rich in mirth ?
> Since thou mayst not stay with me,
> Why must I so cling to thee ? ' "

Not only was there this public *memento mori*, but Salimbene had also to mourn a far nearer loss—that of two old friends (594). "About the Feast of St. Lucy died Bernabo di Regina, a native of Reggio, expiring suddenly in his bed without warning of illness. He was a dear friend of mine, and his words were the joy of canons, cardinals, and all prelates, with knights and barons and all who loved mirth ; for he spake most excellently in the French and Tuscan and Lombard tongues, and in divers other fashions. He could speak childishly, as children speak with each other ; or as women speak with women, discussing their own affairs in familiar speech with their gossips ; and he could imitate the fashion of address of the ancient preachers, as they held forth in the days of the Alleluia, when they took upon themselves to work miracles, as I saw with mine own eyes in those days."[1] The other friend was a lady, heroine of a domestic tragedy which recalls that of Pia de' Tolomei. We must go back a little, with Salimbene, to understand the circumstances of the family into which she married.

Ghiberto da Gente, Podesta of Parma for many years, became so unpopular that he was finally driven from the city, but kept a country villa not far off, at Campagine. In process of time, however, his sons became even more unpopular than the father : so that the whole race was driven forth utterly by the citizens in this year 1285, and their villa destroyed. (606—607). "For thou must know that Ghiberto had a son named Pino, whose wicked deeds provoked the men of Parma in many ways against Ghiberto's heirs : for first he attacked and took Guastalla, and would have held it in spite of Parma ; then he married a wife whom he afterwards caused to be murdered ; from which crime, by God's providence, much evil came afterwards upon him. Now his father Ghiberto was at first desirous to take this same lady to wife, when he dwelt in exile at Ancona after his expulsion from Parma : but Pinotto forestalled his father and secretly stole her away, for greed of her wealth and for the allurement of her comeliness. She was called the Lady Beatrice ; and she had much treasure and was a comely lady, alert and merry and liberal and courtly ; and she was exceeding well skilled in the games of chess and hazard,[2] and dwelt with Pino her husband at Bianello, which had once been a castle of the Countess Matilda. Oftentimes she would come to the convent of the Friars Minor at Montefalcone in the days when I dwelt there, for the sake of recreation and of speaking with the Brethren : and she related to me in familiar converse that men would have slain her ; and I knew of whom she spoke, and had compassion on her, and taught her that she should confess her sins and ever order her life well, that she might be ever ready to meet death. In those days her husband Pino departed in great wrath against the Lord Guido his cousin, as I saw with mine own eyes, and he took his wife with him to the village of Correggio, wherein he caused her to be smothered with a featherbed by a squire named Martinello, and in that same village she was buried ; and he had by her three daughters who are most comely damsels. And, seeing it is written that ' the soul of the wounded hath cried out, and God doth not suffer it to pass unrevenged,' therefore I must say somewhat of the misfortunes which befel her husband. First he became hateful, not only to the men of Parma, but even to his cousins and nephews : secondly he was taken by the ruffians of Sassuolo, who took from him for ransom his horses and £200 Imperial : thirdly, on a time when he would have avenged himself by plundering a wayfarer on the highway leading to Parma, the citizens sent to the village of Campagine, wherein he had his possessions, and ploughed up all his crops and green corn, and razed to the ground fourteen or twenty of his houses in the village : fourthly, the lady whom he took to wife after the murder of his first spouse could never be his lawful wife, since there were many hindrances on either side. She was named the Lady Beatrice even as his first wife, and was most comely, and daughter to the Lord Jacobino da Palude ; he espoused her in her widowhood of her first husband the Lord Atto da Sesso. Fifthly and lastly, once again he took certain men and cast them into chains in his dungeons, and would take no ransom for them, though they had never offended him nor owed him any obedience : wherefore the men of Parma, seeing that he was already outlawed and yet ceased not from evil, cast forth both Pino and all the heirs of Ghiberto da Gente from their village of Campagine. This Pinotto was named likewise the Lord Jacobino, and was a comely man and of great courage, bold and careless, and most haughty, as is the manner of the men of Parma."

The misfortunes which Salimbene so gladly records here may seem a light enough punishment for a cowardly murder ; but there was more to follow in later years. Next year the cousin Guido, whose conduct had occasioned Pino's jealousy, was himself murdered. (615) "For he was journeying from Reggio to Bianello with his kinswoman, the Lady Giovannina, wife to his brother Bonifazio, which brother followed without attendants at a distance of three miles ; and these three had only a few hackneys with them, and they were unarmed and without escort. The murderers of these two brethren were, first, one Scarabello da Canossa, who threw the Lord Guido from his horse and thrust him through with his lance as he lay on the ground so that there needed no second blow : and secondly, Azzolino, brother to the Abbot of Canossa, and son to the Lord Guido da Albareto, who smote off his head : and others there were, both on horse and on foot, who smote him with many strokes, 'and tore him with wound upon wound.' So likewise they did to his brother Bonifazio who followed hard on him. Then they laid the Lady Giovannina on her horse, wherefrom she had cast herself to fall upon her Lord Guido, believing and hoping that they would spare him for her sake, since she was their kinswoman ; and all day she journeyed alone and groaning in the bitterness of her heart, and came to Bianello ; and there she told her bitter tidings. And they that heard her lifted up their voices and wept most bitterly, until the fount of their tears was dried up. And all that night the bodies of the two brethren lay in that waste and solitary spot. Yet some say that the Lord Manfredino was moved to pity at these tidings, and took men and a waggon, and raised and joined together the bodies, and laid them in the church of the Templars midway on the road to Bianello. And next day came the men of Bianello, and carried off the bodies and buried them in their robes and armour in the sepulchre of their fathers, in the convent of the Friars Minor at Montefalcone ; and it was a Saturday, whereon men sang for the Epistle at Mass those words of Jeremiah, ' Let their wives be bereaved of children, and widows.' And, for that the Lord Rolandino of Canossa was cousin-german to this Scarabello, therefore he was accused before the Podesta : (for Scarabello himself had been already banished from Reggio, nor would he have appeared if he had been cited.) Wherefore the Lord Bonifacio, Podesta of Reggio, sent for the Lord Rolandino, who came before him with a very great multitude of armed men : so when the Podesta had learned his innocence in this matter he suffered him to go in peace and unhurt. Then the Lord Guido da Albareto was accused, and appeared and was kept ten days in prison, and gently tortured once only, and then sent away. And while he was being put to the torture, the men of Reggio thought they must needs have civil war for three reasons : first, by reason of these two brothers lately slain ; secondly, by reason of this great lord who was being tortured ; and thirdly, by reason of the parties at Reggio. (For there were two parties, each whereof called itself, and was indeed, of the Church party : for they of the Emperor's party had been cast forth from the city many years since, and still wandered homeless through the world.) But at the beginning, when the Lord Guido was to be put to torture, the Podesta besought him to suffer it in all patience for God's sake and his own ; more especially ' (he said) ' in that I am unwilling to inflict such pain, but I needs must do so, both by reason of my office, and by reason of the crime whereof you stand accused.' So the Lord Guido, knowing that the Podesta did this for the honour of both parties, suffered patiently that which afore would have been sour and bitter to him ; yet afterwards, when he knew the reason, he held it pleasant. And he said to the Podesta, ' If it be possible, let this chalice pass from me. Nevertheless, not as I will, but as thou wilt.' Yet there were some who said that the aforesaid Guido was spared all torment, with the help of money, which all things obey. For his son Roland, Abbot of Canossa, gave £100 Imperial to the Lord Guido da Correggio, and as much again to the Podesta of Reggio ; and by their favour he escaped this torment. So when it was noised abroad that he should be tortured, the Podesta would suffer none to be there with him but himself alone ; and then he caused him to sit awhile on a great balance for weighing flour, and spake familiarly with him of all these things which had befallen. So when he was come down from this instrument of torture[3] and lay in bed, he sent for his brother Jacopo da Palude and told him all that he had suffered in his torture : then he came down from the palace and went to the house of the Lord Rolandino of Canossa, which was hard by the piazza ; and there he dwelt at his ease, eating and drinking and merrymaking the whole day long. Yet before, when he came down from the Palazzo Communale, he had caused himself to be upheld by two men, one on either side, as desiring thereby to show that he had been grievously tortured by the Podesta. But the Lord saith ' There is nothing covered that shall not be revealed.' Moreover, concerning this Lord Guido da Albereto, it was told me by his son the Abbot of Canossa, speaking familiarly with me hard by the gate of the town of Gesso, that five years before his father suffered this mishap, he himself had enquired of a certain diviner of that which should befal his father ; whereupon the diviner showed him a book wherein was written ' He shall fall into the hands of a judge : ' as indeed came to pass. Whereby we see that not only prophets foretell the future, but even sometimes demons and sinful men ; yet the righteous foretell it better than they, as I may be able to show next year, if life be spared me. . . .

(617) "Now this Lord Guido da Bianello who was thus murdered was a comely man, and learned, and of great discernment and memory, and ready speech, and eloquence, sprightly and jocund and free and liberal, and of most familiar and pleasant company, and a lover and a great benefactor of the Friars Minor. For the Friars Minor had a convent on his lands, in the wood at the foot of Montefalcone, where he also was buried with his brother in the sepulchre of their fathers, as I have said above : God of His mercy grant that his soul may rest in peace, if so it may be. Amen. For while he lived he was an exceeding good friend to me and to Guido di Adamo, my brother in the flesh and in Religion, who likewise died and was buried at Montefalcone. Yet this Lord Guido was held to be a man of malice by them

that loved him not; and they accused him of many wicked-nesses; that is, that he was a slanderer and defamer of God's servants. And that is ever the wont of carnal men, gladly to defame God's servants, for they think themselves excused of their own sins if they may have holy men to bear them company. Moreover, men accused him that he was wont to say 'If I am predestined to eternal life, then shall I come thereto, whatsoever may be my sins; and if I am predestined to eternal damnation, so shall it be likewise, in spite of all good deeds.' In proof whereof he would bring forward that which is written ' Whosoever shall seek to save his life, shall lose it; and whosoever shall lose it, shall preserve it.' And such was his folly that, howsoever either I or other Brethren and friends of his might warn him to look to his ways, he scorned to hear us and would only answer, ' It is written, " He that is hasty to give credit, is light of heart, and shall be lessened." ' Yet I would answer against him (for he was most learned in the Bible) saying ' The Wise Man saith " Blessed is the man that is always fearful." ' And, as aforesaid, he would not hear me, but ever shook his head as though he scorned all that I spake to him. So I said to him, ' It is written in the Proverbs " The way of a fool is right in his own eyes : but he that is wise hearkeneth unto counsels." ' Yet when I had thus spoken, adding, ' I have said to thee all that in me lieth,' then answered he and said ' Ecclesiasticus saith " There are many words that have much vanity in disputing.' " . . . . Here five sheets have been torn out of the MS., no doubt as having scandalized some reader. This fatalistic infidelity, as will be seen below, was common among the upper classes in the Middle Ages.

The feud broke out again; and the Monk of Canossa made a murderous incursion into the city of Reggio, as above recorded, in revenge for the death of his kinsman. But the final vengeance only came in 1287 (638), when " on the 17th day of May was slain Pinotto, son of the Lord Ghiberto da Gente, in his villa of Campagine, by his nephews Ghibertino and Guglielmo. The cause of this murder was a certain mill, for the possession of which each party contended—nay, what is worse, he was slain for the sake of a *pinza* or small tongue of land behind the mill. But many days and years before this he had exchanged words of discord and contention with them and with their father; wherefore they came with certain evil doers and hired murderers and fell upon him with clubs and other weapons, and slew him. And note here three judgments of God. First, that all who were consenting and privy to the death of Pinotto's wife, the Lady

Beatrice of Apulia, were slain themselves also within a brief space : the first of whom was Pinotto himself; then the Lord Guido da Bianello. For the Lord Guido had given Pinotto cause for her death, since he would have lain with her, but she utterly spurned such a temptation, not only for the crime of adultery, but also for that Pinotto and Guido were cousins-german. The third was one Martinello, who smothered her one night with a featherbed in the villa of Correggio. The second judgment of God is that this same Martinello was not only present at the murder of Pinotto (whose wife he had already slain at his bidding) but also, being wounded at the siege of Montecalvolo, returned home, and there met his death by his own wife's treachery, whereof he was ignorant. The third marvellous judgment of God is that, if strangers had slain Pinotto, instead of his nephew, then those same nephews would have avenged his death for the honour of their house, and according to the vainglorious custom of worldly men."[4]

This, then, was a sad year for our sociable friar ; and his melancholy finds expression in the last words he wrote under this date. He has been speaking of certain noble families which he remembered in Parma, and of Friars who lived in the earlier heroic days of the Order ; and he goes on (1286—366) "I have written these matters aforesaid, for that I have seen and known wellnigh all these men whereof I have spoken ; and quickly, as in a brief space, they have passed from this life into another. If more noteworthy deeds were done in this year 1285 I remember them not. I have written the aforesaid in good faith, with truth for my guide, even as I saw each thing with mine own eyes. Here endeth the year 1285 : and here followeth the year which is to come."

Our chronicler's forebodings of evil were soon justified : for the year 1286 was not only destined to bring fightings and fears to Reggio, but was big from the first with those small troubles of life which are not always the most tolerable. "This year was a disordered wintertide, for all ancient saws were found false except one which men commonly say, 'February brief, yet most fulfilled of grief.' Which proverb was most plentifully fulfilled this year, above all that I have seen in all the days of my life : for seven times this February did God 'give snow like wool ; ' and there was a mighty cold and frost. And many blains and boils were engendered both in men and in hens, which afterwards broke out openly. For in Cremona and Piacenza and Parma and Reggio and many other cities and Bishoprics of Italy there were very many deaths both among men and among hens ; and in the city of Cremona a single woman lost, within a brief space, forty-eight hens; and a certain doctor of medicine caused some to be opened, and found on the tip of the heart of each hen a boil like unto a small bladder; he caused a dead man to be opened likewise, on whose heart he found the same. In those days, in the month of May, Master John the Leech, who dwelt at Venice and had a stipend from the city, sent a letter to his fellow citizens of Reggio, warning them to eat neither potherbs, nor eggs, nor hens' flesh throughout the month of May: wherefore a hen was sold in those days for five small pence. Yet certain wise women fed their hens with pounded rue mingled with bran or meal; by the virtue of which antidote they were liberated and escaped death." Then, when a bright spring sunshine had tempted the almonds and all the other fruit trees into their richest blossom, a sudden frost cut off all the hope of the orchards for that year, and men were but half consoled even by the plenty of corn and oil and wine which followed.

Moreover, it was a bad year for the Franciscan Order, and therefore for Salimbene, for whom the Order had no more convinced champion. Pope Honorius very nearly decided a quarrel between "certain prelates" and the Friars in favour of the former, and would certainly have done so but for his providential removal from this world in the very nick of time, in answer to the prayers of the Brethren (see chap. xxi below). Again, the Franciscans were boycotted by their old allies the Cistercians, whom the friars had at last alarmed by their enormous growth and (it must frankly be confessed) their continual pious encroachments (623). "A certain Friar Minor left our Order to enter that of the Cistercians, and he bore himself so well among them that they made him Abbot of a great monastery. Then the Friars, having a zeal of God, but not according to knowledge on this occasion, fearing moreover lest others might leave our Order after the example of this brother, took him and brought him back into his past Order and fed him with the bread of affliction and water of distress. The Cistercians hearing this were greatly troubled and incensed against the Friars, and this for five several reasons. First, for that they punished so sorely a man who deserved no punishment. Secondly, for that he had already been released from our Order. Thirdly, for that they took him clad in his own Cistercian habit. Fourthly, for that he had a great prelacy in their Order, being an Abbot. Fifthly, for that he had borne himself so excellently in their Order, as to his life and good manners, as to be acceptable and gracious to all men. Brother Bonagrazia, when he was Minister Provincial

of Bologna, had a like quarrel with the Abbey of Nonantola.
For a certain brother Guidolino of Ferrara left our Order and
entered among the Black Monks of St. Benedict, where he bore
himself so well and laudably in the Abbey of Nonantola that he
was beloved by all, and they chose him for Abbot.[5]   Wherefore
the Friars had a great altercation with those monks before the
Lord Giovanni Gaietano, who was then Protector of our Order
and who after was Pope Nicholas III ; and the Friars with much
violence obtained their desire that he should not be Abbot ; yet
the said monks spent £10,000 Imperial that they might have
him for their Abbot.   And finding that they laboured in vain to
procure his election, they chose no other in his room, but made
him lord of their Abbey as though he were their true Abbot.
See now how those monks loved him !   Yet he was like Joseph
of old, nor would he return evil for evil unto his brethren, though
he had it in his power and opportunity : nay, rather he studied
to do them good.   For he saw and welcomed our Brethren at
Nonantola as angels from Heaven, and prayed them to keep
two copyists always there at the expense of the Abbey, that they
might copy to their fill the original writings whereof it had great
plenty.   This Brother Guidolino was my close friend when we
dwelt together in the convent of Ravenna.   And note that the
Friars Minor obtained of Pope Nicholas IV (who was of their
own Order) the privilege that none who left their Order should
ever be promoted to any prelacy in another Order."   It is
obvious how often such a privilege must have roused the
indignation of the older foundations, already too often jealous of
the rapid growth of the Friars.   The Cistercian quarrel, however,
was settled by the personal intervention of the Emperor Rudolf
of Hapsburg, who loved both Orders alike.

The events of these last years were indeed a few degrees less
barbarous than what Salimbene had seen in his youth at the
siege of Parma, and later on during the civil wars of Romagna :
but his mind had lost something of its elasticity, and it now
seemed to him that the foundations of the earth were out of
course.   He was out of sympathy even with the democratic
movement of the century which the Friars, directly or indirectly,
had done so much to promote.   (1287—391) " In these days
the Commonalty of Bologna made heavy statutes against their
knights and all the nobles of their city, namely that whosoever
of the knights or nobles should wrong a man of the people's
guilds, that man should be so spoiled both in his villages and
in the city, in his houses and fields and trees, that of all his
possessions not one stone should be left on another.   And the

first to fall under this curse were the sons of the Lord Niccolo
de' Bazeleri, who were utterly despoiled by the people : wherefore
the knightly families of Bologna fear now to live in the city, for
the onslaughts of the furious Commonalty : and, like the French,
they dwell now on their country estates : wherefore the common
folk, who live in the city, may well be called henceforth the
bourgeois, as in France.   But let the Commonalty dread lest
God's wrath come upon them, for they do against the Scripture
(Levit. xix, 15).   Moreover the men of the people and country
folk are they through whom the world is ruined, but through
knights and nobles it is saved.   For Patecchio saith in his *Book of
Pests*

" Et quando de sola fit tomera, etc.,"

which is to say, that it is a pest when that is exalted which should
be lowly.   Remember the example of the butchers of Cremona,
one of whom had a great dog who bore patiently many insults
from another butcher's small dog ; but when the other would
not cease from his accustomed insolence, being at last provoked
beyond measure, he caught him by the throat and drowned him
in the Po.   And so are many in this world, who if they lived in
peace would be hurt by no man ; but because they go about
seeking quarrels of set purpose, therefore they find them.   That
same year the men of Bologna banished many of their fellow
citizens to dwell in exile in divers cities : and this was done by
the Commonalty, who had gained the mastery over the knights.
And note that the Holy Scriptures speak of the dominion of
certain persons as most mischievous ; that is, of women,
children, servants, and fools ; also of enemies and worthless
persons."
    He was evidently weary of politics : for, after a brief notice
of the faction fights at Parma between Guido Correggio and the
Bishop, he adds (398) : " And men spake of these things with
praise or reviling according to their love or their hate.   But the
blessed Augustine saith that we should care little for men's
judgment, giving for his reason that ' neither can injustice damn
a man, nor false praise crown him.' "
    But, looking at the wars beyond his own immediate neighbour-
hood, the good friar chronicles an event in which he evidently
took a personal interest of the liveliest sort.   In these, the last
words that he wrote, readers of Dante will recognize something
more than mere aversion to the foreigner as a foreigner : something of that filial compassion for Mother Italy which, even in
those minds in which party politics came foremost, necessarily

implied a hatred of the French. Salimbene had lived in France and made friends there; his own Guelfs owed their triumph in the peninsula mainly to a French prince, Charles of Anjou; but the foreigner could bring no lasting peace to Italy. On the contrary, his very presence implied, and tended to perpetuate, the discords which had made her a mere "hostelry of pain." The Frenchman in Italy, like our own Henry V and Bedford in France, was inevitably hated even by the party to whose political purposes he directly ministered: and Salimbene, who had so little sympathy with the political ambitions of the Popes, had naturally still less with the foreigners who had been imported to serve those ambitions. These concluding words of his chronicle form an admirable commentary on the striking fact that, to Dante, St. Louis himself is not the hero which even modern Protestants and freethinkers see in him, but simply the somewhat despicable brother of the hated Charles of Anjou.[6]

" Moreover, in this year 1287, many French ships were sunken in the sea beyond Naples by the fleet of Peter of Aragon. And many of King Charles' fleet who had survived the fight, common folk and knights, nobles and barons, were blinded by their captors. Which vengeance was just and merited, for they are most proud and foolish, an accursed folk who despise almost all other peoples of the world; and especially do they scorn the English and the Lombards (under which term they include all Italians and all on this side of the Alps): whereas in truth it is they who are despicable and scorned of all men. For to them we may apply that which is said in the trutannic verse of Trutannus

> The Vagrant with his pot of wine, warm in an ingle-nook,
> Will deem the wealthiest Eastern King scarce fit to be his cook.[7]

For when Frenchmen have well drunken, then they think to beat down and conquer the whole world at one blow. But they are deceived* . . . . therefore the French are proud beyond measure. And they afflicted the Kingdom of Naples, and Tuscany, and the Lombards dwelling in the kingdom of Apulia, and took from them their victuals without money and without price—corn and wine and milk, fish and flesh, capons and geese and hens and whatsoever they found fit for food. Nor was it enough that they gave no payment; but they beat men also and wounded them grievously. A man of Parma had a most fair wife; and when she asked of a certain Frenchman

* On this last page of the MS. a few words here and there are entirely illegible.

the price of the geese which she had sold him, not only did he refuse her all payment, but he wounded her grievously, with so sore a stroke that no second was needed; and yet he asked of her 'Wilt thou that I smite thee again?' Her husband hearing this quaked with indignation; and herein was no marvel: for whereas aforetime she had been most perfect in beauty, now all the rest of her life she halted in her gait by reason of that stroke. Wherefore I say that the rule of the French hath ever been most foul and cruel, and it is just that mishap should fall upon them and that they should be destroyed. Moreover in that same year the men of the ancient party of the Emperor Frederick, seeing that they could neither take by force nor hold Reggio nor Modena, went then and seized . . . . ." With these words the present manuscript breaks off, though, as we know from the author's own headline to fol. 356 (p. 590), there once existed more of it, in which he treated again of civil wars under the two texts "Mistrust thine enemy for ever and ever" and "Bring not every man into thine house" (Eccles. xii, 10 and xi, 31). The good friar, as we have seen, probably died either towards the end of 1288 or not long afterwards.

Chapter XX.

The Princes of the World.

WITH these last words of his chronicle Salimbene the man disappears suddenly and finally from our sight. But his outlook on the Italy of St. Francis and Dante is more interesting even than his personality : and many of his anecdotes, omitted hitherto as bearing only remotely on his life, are of extreme importance for the light they throw on contemporary society. I will therefore summarize these briefly here, with only such outside illustrations as are strictly necessary to give them their full significance.

I must begin by repeating that our author's love of small details and his familiar style have blinded some critics to his true authority as a chronicler. Miss Macdonell, for instance, complains that "the solemnity with which his judgments on men are received, is absurd : " but it is abundantly evident that, apart from her frequent failure to understand Salimbene's own words, she lacks the knowledge of other contemporary authorities which is necessary to form a sound opinion on this subject. It is natural enough that his lively style should at first sight suggest doubts of his accuracy. Yet, on comparing him closely with the most valuable of his contemporaries—distinguished Churchmen who wrote under a strong sense of responsibility—we find that his judgments on the principal figures and institutions of his time coincide in the main with theirs. St. Bonaventura, Roger Bacon, Adam Marsh, Bishop Thomas of Chantimpré, Cæsarius the novice-master of Heisterbach, have penned sadder words on the whole than Salimbene. The private Register of Archbishop Eudes Rigaud, like many other strictly official documents, bears the same testimony. Joinville, if we read him carefully from end to end, gives us an equally sad impression of the past, and equal hope, by comparison, for our own much-abused age. Salimbene is not less trustworthy as a historian for being instinct to his finger-tips with that life which most medieval chroniclers so sadly lack : and indeed his most startling pictures are corroborated by independent witnesses from his own and the next two centuries.

There is enough in Salimbene's more strictly autobiographical pages to show the general reader as much as he needs to realize nowadays of those barbarous and incessant wars which made Italy so miserable not only in Dante's day, but for generations before and after him. Moreover, Salimbene's judgments show us how little respect sober men often felt for the leaders on either side—for the Emperor and his princes or the Pope and his Legates. He could not help seeing some good both in Frederick and in Manfred, as he frankly confesses : but in his youthful days of Joachism he had looked upon Frederick as Antichrist (174), though in later life he thought this somewhat exaggerated. (362). Still, he always felt a mystery of evil about him, both in his birth and in his death : though his silence shows that Villani's and Dante's legends on both these subjects are of later growth than his day. To Salimbene, Costanza was simply a *femme incomprise* : and his version of her marriage is more consonant with known facts than Villani's. (358) " King William of Sicily on his deathbed bade his sons, I know not wherefore, never to marry their sister Costanza : wherefore they kept her by them until the 30th year of her age. But she was a froward woman, and troubled her brothers' wives and their whole household. So, considering that the Wise Man said truly, ' It is better to sit in a corner of the housetop, than with a brawling woman and in a common house,' they said among themselves, ' Let us marry our sister and put her far away from us.' " Although Costanza was 20 years younger at her marriage than Villani imagined, and only 40 when Frederick was born, yet already in Salimbene's day his enemies believed him a supposititious child. (43) " Now Frederick was born at Jesi ; and it was noised abroad concerning him that he was the son of a baker in that city, for the Empress Constance was aged and advanced in years [*multorum erat dierum et multum annosa*] when she espoused the Emperor Henry ; nor is she said to have had any son or daughter but this one ; wherefore it was said that she took him from his father (having first feigned herself great with child) and took him to herself that she might be thought to have brought him forth : which I am led to believe by three things. First, that women are indeed wont to do thus, as I remember oft-times to have found. Secondly, that Merlin wrote of him ' The second Frederick [shall be] of marvellous and unhoped-for birth ' ; thirdly, that King John [of Brienne], who was King of Jerusalem and father-in-law to the Emperor, one day with wrathful soul and

frowning brow called the Emperor in his own French speech the
son of a butcher, since he would fain have slain his kinsman
Gualterotto. And because the Emperor could not compass his
wish with poison, therefore it was to be done with the edge of
the sword, while they sat together at a game of chess : for the
Emperor feared lest by some chance the kingdom of Jerusalem
[or rather of Sicily] should fall to Gualterotto. But these things
were not hidden from King John, who went and caught his
nephew by the arm as he played with the Emperor, and withdrew
him from the game and reproached the Emperor bitterly in his
own French tongue, saying : ' Devil ! son of a butcher ! ' For
King John was tall and stout and of great stature, strong and
brave and skilled in war, so that he might seem a second Charlemagne : and when with his mace he smote on every side in battle,
then the Saracens fled from before his face as though they had
seen the devil, or a lion ready to devour them. Wherefore concerning him and Master Alexander [of Hales], who was the most
learned man in the world and was of our Order and taught at
Paris,—in their praise (I say) a song was made half in French
and half in Latin, which I have oft-times sung : and it began

> Avent tutt mantenent
> Nostris florent temporibus.

This King John, while he was being armed by his servants for
battle, would tremble as a rush quakes in the water. And when
they asked him wherefore he thus trembled, since he was a stout
and mighty fighter against his enemies in battle, then he would
answer that he cared not for his body, but feared lest his soul
were not well with God. This is as the Wise Man saith [Prov.
xxviii. 14, and Ecclus. xviii. 27] : moreover St. Jerome saith
" it is prudent to fear whatsoever may come to pass " . . . .
When this King John went into battle and was heated in fight,
none durst stand before his face, but they turned aside when they
saw him, for he was a brave and mighty warrior." The chronicler Pipinus, as I have already noted, gives another cause of
quarrel between John and Frederick : but there is no reason to
doubt that both are true.

     To Salimbene, as to Dante, Frederick was a man of heroic
proportions in his very sins. (348) " Of faith in God he had
none ; he was crafty, wily, avaricious, lustful, malicious, wrathful ; and yet a gallant man at times, when he would show his
kindness or courtesy ; full of solace, jocund, delightful, fertile
in devices. He knew to read, write, and sing, and to make songs

and music. He was a comely man, and well-formed, but of middle stature. I have seen him, and once I loved him, for on my behalf he wrote to Brother Elias, Minister-General of the Friars Minor, to send me back to my father. Moreover, he knew to speak with many and varied tongues, and, to be brief, if he had been rightly Catholic, and had loved God and His Church, he would have had few emperors his equals in the world." He goes on to enumerate several specimens of the Emperor's "curiosities" or "excesses," though for sheer weariness he will not tell them all. Frederick cut off a notary's thumb who had spelt his name *Fredericus* instead of *Fridericus*. Like Psammetichus in Herodotus, he made linguistic experiments on the vile bodies of hapless infants, "bidding foster-mothers and nurses to suckle and bathe and wash the children, but in no wise to prattle or speak with them ; for he would have learnt whether they would speak the Hebrew language (which had been the first), or Greek, or Latin, or Arabic, or perchance the tongue of their parents of whom they had been born. But he laboured in vain, for the children could not live without clappings of the hands, and gestures, and gladness of countenance, and blandishments." Again, "when he saw the Holy Land, (which God had so oft-times commended as a land flowing with milk and honey and most excellent above all lands,) it pleased him not, and he said that if the God of the Jews had seen *his* lands of Terra di Lavoro, Calabria, Sicily, and Apulia, then He would not so have commended the land which He promised to the Jews. But Ecclesiasticus saith : 'Speak nothing rashly, nor let thy heart be swift to utter thy speech before God : for God is in the heaven, and thou upon earth ; wherefore let thy words be few.' Take an example of that clerk who uttered against God such words as should not have been said : wherefore he was smitten forthwith by a thunderbolt from heaven, and fell dead. His fourth excess was that he oft-times sent one Nicholas against his will to the bottom of the Faro, and oft-times he returned thence ; and, wishing to know in sooth whether he had indeed gone down to the bottom and returned thence, he threw in his golden cup where he thought the depth was greatest. So Nicholas plunged and found it and brought it back, whereat the Emperor marvelled. But when he would have sent him again, he said : 'Send me not thither, I pray you ; for the sea is so troubled in the depth that, if ye send me, I shall never return.' Nevertheless the Emperor sent him ; so there he perished and never returned : for in those sea-depths are great fishes at times of tempests, and rocks and many wrecks of ships, as he himself reported. He might have said to Frederick in Jonah's words ' Thou hast cast me into the deep, in the heart of the sea, and the flood encompassed me about; all thy whirlpools and waves went over me.' This Nicholas was a Sicilian who once grievously offended his mother and provoked her to wrath ; wherefore she cursed him that he should ever live in the water and come seldom to land; and so it came about. Note that the Faro is an arm of the sea in Sicily hard by the city of Messana, where there is at times a mighty rush of waters, and great whirlpools which suck ships under and drown them; and therein are Syrtes and Charybdes and rocks of vast size, and many misfortunes. And on the other shore of this strait is the city of Reggio, whereof St. Luke writeth (Acts xxviii. 13). All that I have above written I have heard a hundred times from Brethren of Messana, who have been close friends of mine : for I had in our Order a cousin-german, Brother Giacomino da Cassio of Parma, who dwelt at Messana and told me those things which I have written above.[1] Moreover, Frederick had likewise other excesses and curiosities and cursed ways and incredulities, whereof I have written some in another chronicle : as of the man whom he shut up alive in a cask until he died therein, wishing thereby to show that the soul perished utterly, as if he might say the word of Isaiah ' Let us eat and drink, for to-morrow we die.' For he was an Epicurean ; wherefore, partly of himself and partly through his wise men, he sought out all that he could find in Holy Scripture which might make for the proof that there was no other life after death, as for instance ' Thou shalt destroy them, and not build them up ' : and again ' Their sepulchres shall be their houses for ever ' " [also Ps. xxxviii. 14, Ecclus. xlviii. 12, Ps. cvi. 5, Ecc. iii. 19-22, " and many such, which Solomon said in Ecclesiastes in the person of carnal folk : " after which Salimbene quotes several contrary texts, " all of which make for the destruction of the credulity of Frederick and his wise men, who believed that there was no life but this present, in order that they might the more freely employ themselves in their fleshly lusts and wretched ways."] " Sixthly, he fed two men most excellently at dinner, one of whom he sent forthwith to sleep, and the other to hunt ; and that same evening he caused them to be disembowelled in his presence, wishing to know which had digested the better : and it was judged by the physicians in favour of him who had slept. Seventhly and lastly, being one day in his palace, he asked of Michael Scot* the astrologer how

* Dante. *Inf.* xx. 116.   In spite of his later evil fame, he was honoured in his lifetime by two popes.

far he was from the sky, and Michael having answered as it seemed to him, the Emperor took him to other parts of his kingdom as if for a journey of pleasure, and kept him there several months, bidding meanwhile his architects and carpenters secretly to lower the whole of his palace hall. Many days afterwards, standing in that same palace with Michael, he asked of him, as if by the way, whether he were indeed so far from the sky as he had before said. Whereupon he made his calculations, and made answer that certainly either the sky had been raised or the earth lowered; and then the Emperor knew that he spake truth." (350 foll.) Yet Salimbene is careful to note that Frederick's cruelties might justly be excused by the multitude of his open and secret enemies, and that he had a saving sense of humour. (353) "He was wont at times to make mocking harangues before his court in his own palace, speaking for example after the fashion of the Cremonese ambassadors, who were sent to him by their fellow-citizens; one of whom would begin by praising the other with manifold words of commendation, saying 'This lord [my fellow] is noble, wise, rich, and powerful': and so after commending each other the ambassadors would at last come to their proper business. Moreover, he would suffer patiently the scoffings and mockings and revilings of jesters, and often feign that he heard not. For one day, after the destruction of Victoria by the men of Parma, he smote his hand on the hump of a certain jester, saying 'My Lord Dallio, when shall this box be opened?' To whom the other answered, ''Tis odds if it be ever opened now, for I lost the key in Victoria.' The Emperor, hearing how this jester recalled his own sorrow and shame, groaned and said, with the Psalmist, 'I was troubled, and I spoke not.' If any had spoken such a jest against Ezzelino da Romano, he would without doubt have let him be blinded or hanged. Again, another time he suffered patiently that Villano da Ferro mocked him at the siege of Berceto; for the Emperor asked him how men named the mangonels and catapults which were there, and Villano gave him for their names certain mocking words, namely 'sbegna' and 'sbegnoino.' But the Emperor did but smile and turn away." Moreover, he could himself play cruel practical jokes (591) "For one day, when he was excommunicated by Pope Gregory IX and had come to certain parts where was the Patriarch of Aquileia, the Lord Berthold, whom I have seen and known, a comely man and uncle to St. Elizabeth of Hungary,—then the Emperor sent word to him to come and hear Mass with him. But the Patriarch, knowing all this, called his barber and caused himself to be bled before he had seen the

Emperor's messenger ; then he sat down and began to dine, and sent word to the Emperor that he could not go and hear Mass with him, since he had been bled and was set down to meat. So the Emperor sent a second time, bidding him come forthwith, all impediments notwithstanding : whereupon, willing to redeem his vexation, he humbly obeyed, and came and heard Mass with him." To hear Mass with an excommunicate was of course a mortal sin, which the poor Patriarch had only aggravated by the trick of beginning his dinner beforehand : and the anecdote gains point from what Salimbene tells us on another page of the victim's grandeur. He has been speaking of superfluity in food and dress ; and he goes on (281) " It is reported, and truly reported (and this is altogether superfluous) that the Patriarch of Aquileia, on the first day of Lent, has at his table forty dishes, that is forty varieties and courses of food : and thus one less is set on every day until Holy Saturday : and he says that he does this for the honour and glory of his Patriarchate. Truly then Patriarchs of Aquileia took not this example from Christ, who fasted forty days and forty nights in the desert." The Patriarch was honourable and glorious, and uncle to St. Elizabeth ; and to hear Mass under these conditions was to crucify Christ afresh : but the Emperor was the Emperor, who (if he had been driven to it) was quite capable of having the great churchman ripped open to see whether the excuse of dinner was true.

That superabundant awe of the Emperor, which our Chronicler shared with so many others of his time, made him ready to attribute to Joachim's and Merlin's and the Sibyl's prophecies an authority scarcely second to that of Holy Writ. (174) " I could never have believed that he was indeed dead, had I not heard it with mine own ears from the mouth of Pope Innocent IV, preaching at Ferrara in full concourse of people ; for I was a Joachite, believing and expecting and hoping that Frederick would do yet more evil." So widespread was the reluctance to believe in the Emperor's final disappearance, that he was twice personated after his death : and ambassadors came from far countries to see the second of these pretenders. Even in his old age, Salimbene attributes the death of Pope Gregory X and Honorius IV, in part at least, to their flying in the face of Providence by attempting to set up new Emperors after Frederick's death, for it had been prophesied " by some Sibyl, as men say," that the Empire should end with him, (349 : 494 : 629).

Next to the Emperor and to St. Louis, the most striking kingly figure of the book is Charles of Anjou. Salimbene shows mingled admiration and repulsion for " him of the manly nose." He mentions neither the cynical greed with which Charles robbed unhappy Crusaders wrecked on his coasts,[2] nor his reputed guilt as the poisoner of St. Thomas Aquinas—but he repeatedly censures his ambition and violence and those of his French knights. At the same time, he bears the most emphatic testimony to his valour (599). A Campanian champion was reputed invincible in single combat : and all the knight-errant in Charles' soul was grieved to hear this man's praise. He therefore challenged the knight *incognito*, brushing aside impatiently his son's prudent quotation from Ecclesiasticus, " He that is high hath another higher, and there are others still higher than these." The champions fought like heroes of romance, until Charles was smitten senseless from his horse ; and the knight, horrified to find who it was that he had conquered, fled the country to avoid the vengeance which too often awaited a successful champion after medieval tournaments. Charles, on recovering his senses, was anxious to renew the fight : and his son had much ado to quiet him with a " Peace, father, for the leeches say that ye have two ribs of your body broken." Salimbene has much also to say of the abortive duel between Charles and Peter of Aragon : of Peter's pitiful evasions, and the accusations of treachery against Charles. (517 ff.) Yet Peter, for all his unknightly shifts on this occasion, was not unworthy to rest by his rival's side in that Valley of Flowers where Dante saw them on the brink of Purgatory. He was the hero of one of the earliest recorded Alpine ascents, climbing to the top of Canigou for mere adventurous curiosity. (598) A thunderstorm broke over the party half-way, and the other knights " fell to the ground and became as dead men for the fear and anguish that was come upon them." Peter had much ado to tempt them a little further upwards ; breath and courage alike deserted them, and he was obliged to finish the ascent alone. At the top he found a lake : " and when he had cast a stone into the waters, a monstrous dragon of loathly aspect issued therefrom, hovering round in the air until the face of heaven was darkened with the vapour of his breath : whereupon Peter went down again. Methinks that this achievement of his may be reckoned with those of Alexander."

Salimbene gives only the briefest glimpses of our own Edward I, first as a crusader, and then on his way back from the Holy Land to take possession of his crown : but he records two characteristic anecdotes of Henry III. (305) The pious king humbled himself to welcome John of Parma, and kiss him as an equal, silencing the murmurs of his knights with the reminder that this was for the honour of God and St. Francis. But then

Henry "was reputed a simple man." One day a jester cried aloud in his presence " Hear ye, hear ye, my masters ! Our king is like unto the Lord Jesus Christ." " How so ? " asked the King, hugely flattered. " Because our Lord was as wise at the moment of His conception as when he was 30 years old : so likewise our King is as wise now as when he was a little child." Henry, like other weak men, had his fits of sudden fury ; and he ordered the jester to be strung up out of hand. His servants, however, only went through an empty form of execution, and bade the unlucky fool keep carefully out of the way until the King should have forgotten. Of Manfred, again, he tells us disappointingly little, though he once implies a real sympathy at bottom for that bright and unfortunate figure, and his words go far to explain the feeling even among the Guelfs which dictated Dante's " per lor maladizion sì non se perde." (472) Of all the princes of his time, our good friar seems to have had the greatest admiration for the above-quoted John of Brienne. Not only was John the hero of almost as many martial legends as our own Cœur-de-Lion ; but he was persuaded to join the Franciscan Order on his death-bed ; and our chronicler is convinced that " he would have persevered in the Order all the days of his life, if God had prolonged his days." (44)

I will not attempt to follow Salimbene from point to point among the scores of petty princes who fought nominally for Pope or Emperor, but really for their own hand : yet much must be told of these men if we are to understand the age of Dante. Perhaps the most striking figures in the *Inferno* are the great Guelf and Ghibelline leaders. We find them in the Tombs of Fire or the River of Blood, or bound to their trees of anguish in the Forest of the Harpies ; and we long to know more of their life on earth. What brought these great soldiers and statesmen to this dolorous pass ? By what stealthy temptations, what mad passions, what fatal pressure of circumstances, did Satan gain such empire over these souls for whom Christ died ? Our footnotes give us a few dry sentences with a couple of dates ; and even Benvenuto da Imola, the great collector of Dante legends, too often fails us in our sorest need. The real commentator on Dante is Salimbene, not only directly by what he tells us of actual actors in the *Commedia*, but still more by his living portraits of their compeers. Yet his pictures of these men (like the words of all free-spoken medieval churchmen) are most unflattering to knightly society. From Ezzelino downwards—Ezzelino, who was the devil's chosen servant, as St. Francis was the chosen servant of Christ—there is scarcely one for whom we can feel real respect. Ezzelino once slaughtered in cold blood a crowd of prisoners variously reckoned, no doubt with medieval exaggeration, at eleven or twelve thousand. (367) "I believe in truth that no such wicked man has been from the beginning of the world unto our own days : for all men trembled at him as a rush quivers in the water, and not without cause : for he who lived to-day was not sure of the morrow. The father would seek out and slay his son, and the son his father, or any of his kinsfolk, to please this man : he would submit ladies to the foulest mutilations, and cast them into prison with their sons and daughters to perish of hunger." Scarcely less devilish was his brother Alberigo, on whom, when at last he fell, his infuriated enemies inflicted cruelties more bestial than those which he himself had exercised on them and theirs. Neither age nor sex was spared in these civil wars : to Papalist and Imperialist alike, death or bodily torture were not enough for an enemy, whose last moments must be still further embittered by the anguish and shame of his womenfolk ; and it was probably Alberigo's deathbed repentance and horrible fate which moved Dante to spare him the tortures of the River of Blood. "He was indeed a limb of Satan and a son of iniquity," writes Salimbene ; "but he died an evil death with his sons and daughters. For those who slew them tore the legs and arms of his little sons from their living bodies, in the sight of their parents, and therewith they smote the fathers' and mother's mouths. Afterwards they bound his wife and daughters to stakes and burned them, though they were noble maidens, and the fairest in the world, and guiltless : yet men so hated their parents that they would not spare their innocence. For the father and mother had brought terrible evil and horrible affliction on the Mark of Treviso : wherefore men came to Alberigo with pincers, and there in the market-place each tore a piece from his living flesh ; thus they destroyed his body in mockery and scorn and grievous torments. For he had slain this man's cousin, that man's brother, another's father or son ; moreover, he had laid so grievous taxes and fines on that land that they must needs tear down their own houses and lay the boards and beams and chests and casks and barrels on barges, and send them for sale to Ferrara, that they might have money to pay the taxes and redeem themselves. This I saw with my own eyes. And he feigned to be at war with his own brother Ezzelino, that he might the more securely do these evil deeds : nor did he spare to slay his own fellow-citizens and subjects. Moreover, in one day he hanged 25 of the greatest men of Treviso, who had in no wise offended or harmed him : but, because he feared they might harm him,

therefore he removed them from before his face by basely hanging them. And at the same time he caused 30 noble ladies, their
wives and daughters and sisters, to come and see them and to be
seen of them while they were hanged ; moreover, he would have
cut off the ladies' noses, but this was spared them by the grace
of one whom he called his bastard son, but who was not. Yet,
even so, their garments were cut away in the most foul and
shameful wise[3] ; and they were thus shown to the men who were
to be hanged. And these were hanged so near to the ground
that the ladies were driven among their feet : and they in the
bitterness of their soul smote the ladies' faces as they died with
their legs and feet : whose life was pain and anguish to them for
this foul mockery. After this, Alberigo caused them to be fer-
ried over the river Sila, that they might go whither they would ;
and with the shreds of garments which were left they bound
themselves about the middle like wild folk ; and all that day they
went 15 miles through an untilled land, among thorns and briars
and nettles and burrs and pricks and thistles, while the flies stung
their bare bodies ; and thus they went weeping, as indeed they
had cause ; and withal they had nought to eat. But God's help
must needs come where man's help fails, as we see in the story
of Susanna, and in the case of Esaias who, while he was being
sawn asunder with a wood-saw and was in vehement thirst, and
his tormentors would give him no water to drink at his request,
the Lord sent water from on high which flowed into his mouth.
So these ladies came that day, about nightfall, to the lagoons of
the Venetian Sea : and behold ! they were aware all at once of
a fisher alone in his little boat, to whom they cried for help : but
he was sore afraid, thinking to see some diabolical illusion, or a
crew of spirits, or monsters of the sea at least ; but at last by
God's grace, and for their instant prayers, he came to them. So
when they had told their whole story and all their woes, he said
' I pity you sore, nor will I leave you till God give you help :
yet, since my little boat may bear but one at a time, therefore
will I bring you one by one and set you down on dry land in
Saldino ; for if ye should stay here this night the wolves would
devour you. Then on the morrow, before daybreak, I will get
me a greater boat and bring you to St. Mark's church at Venice ;
where I hope God will give you help.' In brief, he brought all
over but one, the last, whom he led to his fisher's hut and fed to
her heart's content, and treated her with all kindness and courtesy and humanity and charity and honesty : and on the morrow
he exactly fulfilled all his promises. So when he had brought
them into St. Mark's church, he came to the Lord Ottaviano,

Cardinal of the Roman Court and Legate in Lombardy, who at that time was at Venice ; to whom he told the whole tale of these ladies and of their misfortunes, and where they now were. So the Cardinal came forthwith to them and gave them to eat ; and he sent word throughout the whole city that all should come to him swiftly and hastily without delay in the church of St. Mark : both men and women, small and great, young men and maidens, old men and young : for he would tell them (he said) such things as they had never heard, and show them such sights as they had never seen. What then ? swifter than the tale may be told, the whole city of Venice was gathered together to him on the Piazza of St. Mark, and from his lips they heard all the aforesaid story : and when he had finished speaking, he brought forward those ladies, in such foul array and such nakedness as that accursed Alberigo had devised to their dishonour ; and this he did to provoke the citizens unto the greater hatred against that tyrant, and pity towards these ladies. So when the Venetians heard the story, and saw the ladies as naked as I have said, then they raised a great shout and cried, ' Let him die ! let that accursed man die ! Let him and his wife be burnt alive, and his whole seed be rooted out from this world.' Then, by the common consent of the whole city, both men and women, he preached a crusade against that accursed Alberigo. So they went with one mind against Alberigo and wrought him much evil, yet they destroyed him not utterly : howbeit within a short time after that crusade he was utterly destroyed with all his seed, and suffered justly the aforesaid mockery and torments and woes. For one day, having lost his hawk, and being under the open sky, he made so foul and boorish a gesture at the heaven, in sign of mockery and contumely and derision, thinking thereby to take vengeance on God, as may scarcely be told : moreover, when he was come home, he went forthwith into the church and defiled God's altar in unspeakable wise, at that very spot where the Lord's Body is consecrated. Moreover his wife would call other noble ladies and matrons harlots and such like names, nor did her husband ever rebuke her and say, ' Wherefore sayest thou thus ? ' Nay rather, but he heeded it not, and she took heart from his heedlessness : so that it was a just vengeance which the men of Treviso wreaked upon them. But after the Cardinal had ended his sermon to the Venetians, then he commended those ladies to the citizens as he would have commended himself : and they succoured them most liberally both in food and in clothing : moreover the men of Treviso spared that man by whose grace the ladies had not lost their noses, and they suffered him to live and did him much kindness, whereof he was worthy ; for he oft-times restrained those tyrants from many iniquities which they would have done."

These two brothers are only the first in evil pre-eminence among a whole host of petty tyrants whom Salimbene enumerates under the year 1250, and to whom he frequently refers elsewhere. There, first, is Obizzo of Este—the flaxen head which emerges side by side with Ezzelino's shaggy black locks from Dante's River of Blood. In 1290 Obizzo became tyrant of Reggio ; and this explains why Salimbene's very unflattering description of him (167) has been so mutilated by some cautious hand that it is only legible here and there. To begin with, he was believed to have been a supposititious child, intruded by a trick into the noble inheritance of Este. Furthermore, " he caused his own mother to be drowned : for she had been a washerwoman, and the buffoons were wont to put him to shame for his base birth and his ignoble mother. Moreover it was reported of him that he violated the wives and daughters of both nobles and commons at Ferrara ; and he was ill-famed of many foul and incestuous connexions. Many other evils he did, and many shall he receive from God, unless he be converted to Him. He was so intimate a friend of the Cardinal Ottobono, who was afterwards Pope Adrian V, that he took his near kinswoman to wife : and his firstborn was the Lord Azzo [*Inf.* xviii, 56] who had a wife of the kin of Pope Nicholas III, a Roman by birth." We get brief glimpses of other figures familiar to us in the " Commedia "— Pietro Pagani (370), whose wife and sister were both Salimbene's spiritual daughters : Salinguerra, (165) " who was wont to say ' He hath given the heaven to the Lord of Heaven, but the earth to the children of men,' as who should boast of his own might here on earth. Yet he was drowned in the lagoons of Venice ; and, wise as he was, he had a foolish son, as Rehoboam was to Solomon." We get some glimpses of Buoso da Duera, who (363) " did much evil to others, and in the end himself also received much evil." Pinamonte, again, is mentioned at some length (436 ff) : " he was feared as the Devil : he was an old man and altogether bald-headed, and had a huge multitude of children ; among whom was a certain Friar Minor, Brother Philip by name, a good and honest man and Lector in theology, who was once Inquisitor, and took and scattered and destroyed many heretics of the district called Sermilione." To him, in 1283, the Cardinal-Legate Bernardo sent two friars as ambassadors for the sake of peace : " and the Lord Pinamonte received them courteously, both for their Order's sake and for the Cardinal's : notwithstanding it had been ordained that who-soever should bring a letter into Mantua should be beheaded. And he sent to the Friars Minor, for these messengers' sake, a waggon-load of good wine, and the half of a flitch of bacon ; and one of his sons sent to the Brethren a great and glorious pasty, with many other gifts. So the Brethren returned with the Lord Pinamonte's letters : what might be contained therein, God only knoweth. Moreover the Lord Pinamonte was wont to boast that he had never had any ill-fortune, but all things had succeeded as he had wished : which was a great folly, as the wise man saith in Proverbs [xxvii, 1]." Of Guido Vecchio da Polenta, father to the ill-fated Francesca da Rimini and grandfather to Dante's last patron Guido Novello, Salimbene gives us one of his few anecdotes worthy of the romantic conception of the Age of Chivalry. (606) After relating an instance of bitter and somewhat un-generous rivalry, he goes on : "The Lord Guido da Polenta of the city of Ravenna wrought far better than this, in that he avenged himself sufficiently, yet would not pass beyond measure. For when he was yet a boy, and the Emperor kept his father in chains, the Lord Guido Malabocca, brother of the Count Roger of Bagnacavallo, persuaded the Emperor to cut off the father's head ; wherefore the Lord Guido, when he was grown to man's estate, cut off in return the head of Guido Malabocca. Now, in process of time, as he was journeying to Bagnacavallo with a great following of armed men, and those who were his fellows on that journey would have persuaded him that he might now rid himself wholly of the Count Roger and never fear him more, yet he answered and said, ' We have done enough : suffice it then that we have done thus far : for evil may ever be done, but afterwards it may not be undone.' And so he suffered him to go free." The very emphasis with which the chronicler records this trait of ordinary generosity is significant ; and indeed all intimate records of the Middle Ages give very much the same unfavourable picture of the feudal nobility. Not that they were unworthy of the place they occupied in their own times and among their own circumstances :—but what circumstances, and what times ! No more damning judgment can be passed on medieval society than the continual cry of the apologist, perfectly true within its own limits, " You must not judge the man or the deed in that century as you would judge them in ours ! " Yet the best men of their own age made less allowance for them than we. Cardinal Jacques de Vitry, when he comes to speak of the sufferings of the common folk in the 13th century, exclaims outright " How mad are the men who rejoice when sons are born to their lords ! "[4] Page after page of Salimbene's book tells us of reckless bloodshed, cowardly murders, and treachery. Like the Knight of La Tour Landry, [p. 2 and *passim*] he shows us plainly and frequently the risks which a lady's honour ran in noble houses.[5] (pp. 27, 67, 427, 429) His average noble, like those of contemporary chronicles and even of many medieval romances, answers pretty well to the Byronic sarcasm—not quite a felon, yet but half a knight. We have the knightly forger of a will (1287—398), and the usual knightly Bluebeard. (483) "The Lord Jacobino di Palude on divers occasions slew many of his own house, namely, the father of his son-in-law, and his son-in-law, and the son of his own daughter, a little child still at the nurse's breast, whom he dashed against the earth, and his cousin-german, the Lord Arverio, with his two sons, and likewise another of his own house."

Salimbene is exceptional in giving us no hint of the frequency with which ladies were beaten in private life by their fathers and husbands ; but we have already had glimpses of their fate in time of war—and when was there not war ? The study of fresh documents makes it plainer every day that theory and practice were as widely divorced in medieval chivalry as in religion. Sacchetti, who was born about the time of Dante's death, complains repeatedly that money would buy knighthood for the vilest—mechanics, bakers, "usurers and cozening ribalds." His contemporary Fra Giordano da Rivalto implies the same : and Salimbene also shows us how great a part usury often played in family greatness (609). It was a mortal sin, of course ; and few figures are more pitiful in the *Inferno* than the usurers writhing and shifting under the rain of fire ; yet, as the good Benvenuto complains in his commentary, "He who taketh usury goeth to hell : and he who taketh none liveth on the verge of beggary." Moreover, there was always good hope of escaping the *doloroso foco :* it was only necessary to make a last confession to the friars and leave them some of the ill-gotten gains for conscience-money. We see this even in Salimbene : Ubertino and the Spirituals complain of it as one of the worst scandals in the Order ; and St. Bonaventura sadly admits something of the impeachment.[6] Though this process of buying nobility marks the beginning of a new world, yet the people in general were scarcely happier under this new aristocracy than they had been under the old. Canon Knox-Little, with even more neglect than usual of plain facts, asserts that the Franciscan Tertiary system broke the power of Feudalism before 1230, and had "emancipated the middle classes and the poor from feudal tyranny " before the death of Frederick in 1250. (pp. 217-220). No doubt the Tertiary system exercised a real democratic influence in the long run ; but it is almost incredible that anyone professing an acquaintance with Italian history could bring himself to write " What now ? Military service was swept away." To St. Bonaventura, the Tertiaries were mainly an ungrateful burden.[7] Often as Salimbene tells us of the Friars' services, either as peacemakers or as combatants against the pre-eminently feudal party, he has not a word to say for the Tertiaries : while for their aristocratic imitators, the *Frati Godenti*, he has as little sympathy as Dante had. (467) "In the year 1261 was composed and ordained the Rule of the knights of the Blessed Virgin Mary, by the mediation of Brother Ruffo Gurgone of Piacenza, who for many years had been minister Provincial of Bologna, and was then a Penitentiary at the Papal court. The Order was founded by Loderingo degli Andaloi of Bologna, who was its Prior and Prelate, and by other honourable and noble men. These knights are by the country-folk scoffingly called ' Godenti,' as who should say ' They are only become *Frati* that they may keep their goods for themselves alone, according to the word of that miser of whom Ecclesiasticus speaketh (xi. 18.)' Moreover I remember that this Order was founded in Parma at the time of the Alleluia, (that is in the days of the other great devotion), by the means of Brother Bartholomew of Vicenza of the Friars Preachers, who in those days had high rank in Parma, a good man who was afterward Bishop of Vicenza, his own native city. And the aforesaid Brethren had the same habit as these [Godenti], and a white saddle and a red cross : there was only this difference, that the Parmese Order were called Knights of Jesus Christ, and the Godenti, Knights of St. Mary. But the former lasted and endured many years, and at length failed : for I saw both their beginning and their end, and few entered into their Order. Likewise these Godenti are indeed multiplied like bread in the hand of a hungry man : and they think themselves to have done a great and noble deed in taking this habit : but they are little esteemed at the Court of Rome ; and this for four reasons. First, they have never used their wealth to build monasteries or hospitals, or bridges or churches, nor are they found to have done other works of piety. Secondly, that they have ravished much of others' goods, as great men are wont to do, nor have they restored their illgotten gains. Thirdly, after they have wasted their wealth in lavish expenses upon many vanities, and in banqueting with buffoons rather than with Christ's poor, they now beg of the Roman church and would fain get from the Pope and enter into the convents of better Religious than themselves, and expel these latter from their dwellings. Fourthly, for that they are most avaricious men. Fifthly and lastly," [for our chronicler finds an extra reason], "I see not whereunto they serve God's church or what profits they bring, unless perchance that they save their own souls, which St. Jerome calleth 'a holy boorishness, profitable to itself alone.' Enough of this matter : now must we rejoice with them that rejoice [*cum Gaudentibus*] and weep with those that weep, as the Apostle saith."

In spite of Salimbene's many aristocratic friends ; in spite of the consciousness of noble birth which never deserted him and coloured all his views, you may seek vainly from end to end of his long chronicle for more than one or two instances of real chivalry. Of mere vulgar barons of prey there are plenty : Ghiberto da Gente, for instance, whom the *Chronicon Parmense* accuses of abusing his judicial power to torture an innocent noble after failing to seduce his daughter ; and who after coming into power with the help of the butchers of Parma, showed himself as grasping and close-fisted as any *nouveau riche* of our own century (448) "He was greedy and avaricious beyond all measure ; so that, during his dominion, no man in Parma might sell any sort of victual except publicly ; and he made himself a partner with all who sold, that he might get his share of gain from all. Moreover he was so stingy that, when a knight of the court [*i.e.*, jongleur] had begged him for a gift, he said he would give him a shilling of Bologna to buy himself figs withal. I myself experienced and proved and saw and knew his boorish-ness and avarice and filthy stinginess [*merditatem*] in his villa of Campigine ; yet I had gone thither on his own service, with Brother Bernardino da Buzea." There is Uberto Pallavicino, again, (344) "a puny and weakly old man, and one-eyed (for, while he was yet in his cradle, a cock had picked out one of his eyes), whom in former days I have seen so poor that he was proud to have two squires riding abroad with him on sorry jades " : yet by his courage and audacity he won city after city, built palace upon palace, (one of which was "like a town in itself "), and exchanged his barren wife, like any Henry VIII, for another who might bear him a son. We see too the truth of Joinville's remark that many men of great pretensions belied their reputation in the hour of danger. Bartolino Tavernario, one of the greatest nobles in Parma, lived "many days and nights " in such anguish of his life for fear of Pallavicino and other enemies that "when he heard noises by night—as indeed he heard many such—he would flee forth on horseback from his villa into the field and tarry there sleepless all night long in the open air, ready at any moment for flight."[8]

(604) Another, it is true, commanded Salimbene's admiration by his coolness and courage under similar circumstances : for " one day when Pallavicino was to march with his 500 men-at-arms through one of the quarters of Parma, the Marchese Lupi bade a servant wash his feet in a tub under his portico in the very street ; for he wished to show how he cared no more for Pallavicino than for a goat's tail." (605) Rare indeed is such a picture as this following, of one who might pass for a living illustration of Chaucer's " verray parfit, gentil knyght." " The Count [Lodovico] di San Bonifazio, who should have been Lord of Verona, wandered through the world as an exile : yet he was wholly devoted to the Church party, a good man, and holy, and strong and doughty in arms, and skilled in war. In the year 1283 he lay dying, and by his testament he committed all his children into the hand of the lord Obizzo of Este, who received them courteously and treated them as his children, though formerly he loved not the count, for they had quarrelled concerning the city of Mantua. So in the night following the count died in the presence of the Friars Minor, to whom he had confessed : and he ordered excellently for the health of his soul. And the citizens of Reggio spent liberally on his funeral, as for a noble man who had been their Podesta and had been driven from his possessions for the sake of the Church party. And all the Religious of Reggio and many nuns were at his funeral, and all the citizens with many foreigners, and the noblest of the city bore him on his bier. His body was clothed in scarlet with fair fur of vair and a splendid pall ; and it was laid with the same magnificence on the Monday following in a fair tomb, exceeding fair, which the Commune had caused to be made at their own expense. His sword was by his side, and his gilded spurs on his feet, and a great purse at his belt of silk, and gloves on his hands, and on his head a most fair cap of vair and scarlet, and a mantle of scarlet trimmed with divers furs. And he left his charger and his armour to the Friars Minor. He was an honourable and holy man : so honourable that when he went through the city he never raised his eyes to look on any woman, whereat even the women and the fairest ladies marvelled. Moreover, on the anniversary of his death his wife sent a fair pall of purple samite for the altar of the Friars' convent at Reggio, where her husband was buried. May his soul, by God's mercy, rest in peace ! Amen." (368 ; 513).

CHAPTER XXI.

Neither Fish nor Flesh.

THE story of these worldly princes is taken mainly from a long digression in which Salimbene enumerates and characterises the rulers of his time. He then proceeds to give us the other side of the picture, and to estimate with his usual keen but sympathetic insight the Legates who had been commissioned by different Popes to champion the Church cause in Northern Italy : and who, in consequence of the worldly policy which was inseparable from the Temporal Power, were necessarily statesmen or warriors first of all, and churchmen only in the second place. These portraits are valuable as coming from a convinced and consistent Churchman who had yet independence enough to write of things and men exactly as he saw them, and as they were frankly discussed within the ranks of the Guelf party. It is very difficult for a modern reader to realize 13th century society. But here and there even a single episode, told frankly and in detail, gives the intelligent reader just that double evidence which we require—the conviction, not only that the thing is true in itself, but also that it is characteristic of the times—no mere artificial museum-specimen, but a real natural growth, drifted down the ages to us, with the soil of its home still clinging to its roots. Not all the crimes of Gilles de Retz are half so damning to 15th century society as the collateral evidence of the equanimity with which his misdeeds were so long suffered, of his own firm trust to meet his accomplice in Paradise, and of the tenderness with which his bones were brought by " damsels of high estate," to be buried honourably with the Carmelite friars of Nantes.[1] Similarly, even the sickening atrocities of Alberigo, and the no less sickening reprisals of his victims, carry in themselves less demonstrative force than the matter-of-course words in which Salimbene, a nobleman by birth and a man of Religion by profession, records how the victims were paraded before the crowd in their naked shame, until the Venetian citizens were sufficiently wrought up to the Holy War. So, again, many students to

whom the Inferno has given an inkling of the real life of the
tyrants, and who have a clear enough general recollection that
Dante saw grave faults in the Church of his time, may yet be surprised at these figures of Church champions drawn by Salimbene
from the life. He describes in chronological order the twelve
Papal Legates who, during his lifetime, had championed the
Church cause in Italy. The first was Ugolino, friend and protector of St. Francis, and later Pope Gregory IX. The next
was "The Cardinal" *par excellence*, Ottaviano, into whose mouth
later chroniclers put the despairing cry, "if there be such a
thing as a soul, then I have lost mine for the Ghibellines!"
(385) "He was a goodly man to see, and of noble birth ; for he
was of the sons of Ubaldino da Mugello in the Bishopric of
Florence ; he was of great repute among the Imperial party ; but
for his own honour's sake he sometimes wrought to the profit of
the Church, knowing that thereto he had been sent. When he
was Legate at Bologna, I oft-times ate with him, and he set me
ever at the head of his board, so that none sat betwixt me and
him but the friar my comrade ; and he himself took the third
place from the head of the table. Then I did as the Wise Man
saith in Proverbs : 'When thou sittest to eat with a ruler, consider diligently what is before thee and set a knife to thy throat' :
and this was right and proper, for the whole hall of this palace
was full of guests. Yet we had food in plenty and with all
decency, and choice wine was set before us, and all delicacies.
Then began I to love the Cardinal, as it is written in Proverbs
'Many will intreat the favour of the prince ; and every man is a
friend to him that giveth gifts.' But the Cardinal invited me and
my comrade to go and eat daily with him ; but I thought best to
do as Ecclesiasticus teacheth 'When thou art bidden of a more
powerful man than thou, depart, for thus will he bid thee all the
more.' Moreover, it was said of this same Cardinal that he was
the son of the Lord Pope Gregory IX ; perchance for that he
had loved him with special love. I have also seen the daughter
of this Cardinal, a nun in a certain convent[2] : and she invited
and prayed me instantly to be her spiritual father, (*devotus*) and
she my spiritual daughter (*devota*). She knew not whose daughter
she was, nor what a father she had. But I knew well, and
answering said to her, 'I will not have thee for a friend, for the
poet Patecchio saith, "It is a weariness when I cannot speak with
her," meaning to say, "It is a weariness to have a lady-friend to
whom her friend cannot speak," as thou art, being enclosed in a
convent.' And she said to me, 'Even if we may not converse
together, at least let us love each other in heart, and pray

mutually for each other's salvation, as St. James saith in his last chapter (v. 16).' And I thought within myself that she would have drawn me in little by little, and entangled me, that I might love her : so I told her the example of the blessed Arsenius." The reference is to St. Jerome's " Lives of the Fathers."[3] The aged Arsenius was visited in his desert cell by a noble Roman lady, who had dared the perils of the deep and of the wilderness to look once upon his face. She fell at his feet : but he rebuked her intrusion with such asperity that she dared not even look up, and could only falter, " I beseech thee, pray for me and deign to bear me in mind." " I pray to God," replied the Saint, " that He may blot all memory of thee from my soul." She was cut to the heart, went home, took to her bed and longed to die. Her own bishop, however, cured her by pointing out how subtle a flattery the Saint's rudeness implied to her charms ; and we may perhaps hope that the same reflection consoled Salimbene's fair friend. He pursues " Moreover the Lord Ottaviano was a most subtle man. For one day when there was a great procession, a certain jester raised his voice as the Cardinal went by and said in his hearing, ' Remove, all ye good folk, and give way and let the man pass who hath betrayed the Roman court and oft-times deceived the church !' Hearing this, the cardinal softly bade one of his men to shut the man's mouth with a gift of money, knowing that all things obey money. And thus he redeemed his own vexation ; for the jester took the gift, and went forthwith to another place where the Cardinal should pass by ; and then he spake in manifold commendation of him, saying that there was no better cardinal at the court, and that he was well worthy of the Papal tiara. Of such saith Micah : ' if one give not somewhat into their mouth they hallow war against him.' Moreover I have heard it said that if Pope Innocent IV had lived but a little while longer, he would have put down the Lord Ottaviano from his Cardinalate for that he was too much Imperial and wrought not faithfully for the Church. But he, knowing that he had not the Pope's favour, and that this had already been noised abroad by many at the Court and elsewhere, did thus to show that he had the Pope's favour. One day when all the Cardinals were hastening to go out from the Consistory and from the Pope's presence to their own homes, the Lord Ottaviano alone remained so long in talk with a clerk in the closet or chamber which was at the issue from the Pope's presence, until he knew that all the other Cardinals were gone forth, so that they who were in the palace hall might think him to have gone out last of all, wishing thus to show that the Pope had kept him to hold familiar converse and treat privily of great matters with him ; that they might thus think him the greatest cardinal of the court, and most powerful of all with the Pope, and in consequence might bring him gifts as to one who could help them in their business with the Pope."

The next Legate whom he describes is Gregorio da Montelungo, who lived in Ferrara shortly before Salimbene, and whose pet raven was already of legendary fame, like the raven of St. Francis.[4]   " Long ago, when he lived in Ferrara, he had a raven which he was wont to pledge for great sums of money, and afterwards to redeem faithfully by repaying the gold. For the raven spake like a man and was an excellent buffoon. For he would arise in the night and call forth from their inns the travellers who abode therein, crying ' Who will come to Bologna ?   Who will come to Dojolo ?   Who will come to Peola ?   Let him come, come, come !   Quick, quick !   Arise, arise !   Come, come ! Bring your baggage !   Off, off !   To the boat, to the boat ! Raise [the anchor], raise !   Yare, yare, yare !   Get off the boat ! Steer, steer !'   So the stranger guests, not knowing the wiles and deceits of this raven, would arise and carry their goods and baggage ; and well-nigh all night long they would wait by the Po bank for the ship to take them whither they would go : and they marvelled who could so have deceived them, for they heard no man by the river.   Moreover, this raven had such a feud with a certain blind man that, whenever he begged with bare legs and feet along the banks of the Po, the bird would come and peck his heels and calves, and draw back and cry injuriously to the blind man, ' now thou hast it, now thou hast it !'   But one day the blind man smote the raven with his staff and broke his wing, and said ' now *thou* hast it, now *thou* hast it !'   Whereunto the raven answered : ' now I have it, now I have it.'   And the blind man ' keep now that thou hast, take what is thine own and depart !   cozeners and deceivers provoke the wrath of God : I have smitten thee once and no second stroke will be needed.   Go to the physician, if by chance he may heal thee, for incurable is thy breaking, terrible is thy wound.'   So the lord Gregorio pawned his raven for a pledge and would never redeem him, but left him there, for that he was smitten.   So do very many, [*plures*] who leave their servants when they begin to fall sick." Salimbene pays a high tribute to the Legate's military genius and political orthodoxy : but his morals were no more irreproachable than those of Ottaviano.   (391) " He faithfully treated and wrought the affairs of the Church, and therefore he earned the Patriarchate of Aquileia and held it many years, even to his last end.   Yet it must be known of the Lord Gregorio da Montelungo that he was gouty and unchaste [*non bene castus*] : for I knew a leman of his. But many secular clerics who have lordships and prelacies and live in delights, seem to care little for chastity ; and they put into the Apostle's [Paul's] mouth that he said 'though not chastely, yet [live] cautiously.'⁵ But the Apostle wrote not thus : rather he wrote [1 Cor. xv, 33, 34 ; Gal. vi, 5-8 ; also Wisdom ix, 15, Eccles. xiv, 20, 21, and many other texts]. All this I have said, because certain worldly clerics, who desire to live after the flesh, lay upon the Apostle this crazy falsehood, saying that he said 'if not chastely, yet [live] cautiously.' Methinks I have heard them say it a hundred times : and certainly the Apostle taught no such doctrine : for he saith ' A bishop must be blameless, having his children in subjection with all gravity.'* After Gregorio da Montelungo the Lord Philip [Fontana], by the grace of God and of the Pope Archbishop of the holy church of Ravenna, was made Legate of the Apostolic See. This Legate was born in Tuscany in the district of Pistoia, and being yet a poor scholar he came to the city of Toledo, desiring to learn the art of necromancy. And as he sat one day in that city under a portico, a certain knight asked him what he sought. So when he said he was a Lombard, and why he was come thither, the knight led him to a certain great master of that art, an old man of hideous aspect with a hood over his head, to whom the knight recommended him, begging the necromancer for his sake to instruct this stranger in his art. The old man led him therefore into his chamber, and gave him a book, saying, ' When I am gone from thee thou must stay and study here.' Then departing from him, he diligently closed the door, and the whole chamber. So, as that youth read in the book, suddenly there appeared demons of manifold kinds and shapes ; for all seemed full of mice, cats, dogs, and pigs, which ran tumultuously hither and thither through the chamber. And forasmuch as he spake nothing to them, suddenly he found himself sitting outside the chamber in the street ; and the Master came and said to him, ' What dost thou here, son ? ' Then he told the Master what had befallen him, so that the old man brought him again into the chamber, and departed from him as before, and locked the door with care. And as he read, there appeared a multitude of boys and girls, running hither and thither through the chamber. For-

---

* Note that Salimbene omits ' the husband of one wife,' thus making the rest of the Latin text read as though *children* were used only metaphorically of the Bishop's flock.

asmuch as again he spoke nought to them, he again found himself sitting without in the street; wherefore his Master said : ' Ye Lombards are unfit for this art ; leave it to us Spaniards, who are fierce men, and like unto demons. But thou, son, go to Paris, and study in Holy Scripture ; for thou shalt yet be a mighty man in the church of God.' So he went and studied at Paris, and learned excellently, and returned to Lombardy and dwelt at Ferrara with the Bishop of Garsendino, who was one of the sons of Manfred of Modena, and brother of the Abbot of Pomposia. And the Bishop made him his chamberlain ; and after his death another Bishop was elected, after whom this Philip was elected Bishop of Ferrara, and remained many years Bishop Elect, until he was made Bishop of Ravenna. And when Pope Innocent IV came from Lyons to Ferrara, this Bishop there " . . . . . [Here some scandalised reader has torn a leaf out of the manuscript, which (as we learn from the ancient table of contents) related " how a certain nun disposed in her heart to forsake God unless He should come to her succour." The text then proceeds :] " It came to pass therefore at the time when kings go forth to war, that the Lord Philip, Archbishop of Ravenna, having been made Legate by the Lord Pope, came to Ferrara. (Now that which men call " the time when kings go forth to war " is the month of May, for then the weather is quiet and jocund and temperate, wherein the nightingale tunes her song, and grass is found abundantly for oxen and horses). The Legate then, being at Ferrara, gathered together all the citizens of that city and strangers from Padua, and preached from the great door of the Cathedral church of St. George, opposite to the church of San Romano. And all the monks and friars were there and all folk of the city, both great and small ; for they hoped to hear great marvels of God. Moreover, I also was by the Archbishop's side, and Buongiorno the Jew, who was my familiar friend, sat by my side, for he also would fain listen. The Legate therefore, standing in the gate of the Lord's house, began to preach in a loud voice, saying briefly that the time for words was now past, and we must keep silence, for the time is come to do those deeds which words do but represent. And he published how he had been made Legate by the Lord Pope against Ezzelino da Romano, and how he would fain raise an army of Crusaders to recover the city of Padua, and restore the expelled Paduans. And whosoever would be of his army in that expedition should have Indulgence and remission and absolution of all his sins. And let none say : ' It is impossible for us to fight against that man of the Devil whom even demons fear,' for it shall not be impossible with God, who will fight for us. And the Legate added, ' I say to you, to the honour and praise of God Almighty, and of the blessed Peter and Paul, his Apostles, and likewise of the blessed Anthony, whose body is held in veneration at Padua, that if I had in my army none but the orphans, the wards and the widows, and the rest who have been afflicted by this man Ezzelino, yet even with these I would hope to have the victory over that limb of Satan and son of iniquity. For now the cry of his wickedness is gone up to Heaven, and therefore they shall fight from Heaven against him.' So when he had finished his speech his hearers rejoiced : and he gathered together an army, and in due time marched forward to assault the city of Padua, which Ezzelino had most strongly fortified, garrisoning it with 1,500 knights, all stout men and skilled in war. Yet he himself dwelt elsewhere, for he feared as little for Padua as God fears lest the sky should fall, especially since the city had three rings of walls, and a moat both within and without, besides the knights and a multitude of people. For he held the Legate's army, with regard to their fitness to storm such a city, as a mere unarmed rabble without either courage or skill in war. Yet in that army there was a certain lay-brother of the Order of Friars Minor, a Paduan by birth, called Clarello, whom I have seen and known well, who was a man of great courage, and whose heart's desire was that the Paduans who had long been in exile should return now to their city. Seeing then that this occasion was favourable to him, and knowing how God hath chosen the weak things of the world to confound the things which are mighty, he undertook to be the standard-bearer of that army, if haply God would give them salvation through his hand. Wherefore he strode before the army and found a peasant there with three mares, whereof he took one by force and, mounting it, caught in one hand a pole to serve him for a lance, and began to gallop hither and thither, shouting valiantly, ' Ho ! ye soldiers of Christ ! Ho ! ye soldiers of the blessed Peter ! Ho ! ye soldiers of the blessed Anthony ! Cast away fear from you, be strong in the Lord.' In brief, the army was so cheered and comforted by these words of his that it was ready to follow him whithersoever he might go ; and thus cried Brother Clarello, ' On ! On ! At them ! At them ! Salvation is the Lord's. Let God arise, and let His enemies be scattered ! ' So the army followed him as its herald and standard-bearer, and set itself to storm the city. But the Lord struck fear into the hearts of those that were within, so that they dared not resist. For there was in the army another lay brother, also of the Friars Minor, a holy man and devout, who in the world had been the Lord Ezzelino's master-engineer, to build his machines and catapults and mangonels and battering rams, for the storming of cities and castles. Him the Legate commanded by holy obedience to strip off the habit of St. Francis (for the Legate loved that Order), and to put on a white habit, and build such an engine as might enable them to take the city by storm.[6] So the Friar humbly obeyed him, and forthwith built an engine which in front was all fire, and behind was full of armed men ; and the city was soon taken. Then the Church party, when they had entered the city, would neither hurt any in the city, nor did they slay nor take prisoners nor spoil goods, nor carry away anything ; but they spared all men and let them go free. And the others held themselves happy in their mere freedom from prison and other harm ; so the whole city exulted and rejoiced.[7] The Legate therefore, although his name had been renowned even before this time, yet was he far more renowned after the capture of the city of Padua. In old days he had been Legate in Germany, by reason of the Landgrave who had been made Emperor after Frederick's deposition, [i.e., Heinrich Raspe, d. 1247.] And at this time there were in Germany three Provinces, wherein were certain brethren of great dignity [solemnes,] who, despising the discipline of the Order, would not obey the Ministers ; and when they came to consult this Legate, he took them and handed them over to the power of the Ministers, that they might exercise judgment and justice on them according as the statutes of the Order demanded.[8] Now it came to pass that the Landgrave died ; and the Legate, being in another city, and hearing of the death of the Landgrave, feared Frederick's son, Conrad, who caused Germany to be most strictly guarded. He commanded, therefore, one of his household on no account to open his chamber to any man for several days ; for he purposed to flee, lest he should be utterly taken. Then, changing his garments, and taking with him a single comrade only, he came furtively and secretly to a convent of the Friars Minor, where he called the Guardian apart, and said to him, ' Knowest thou me ? ' And he answered, ' Truly, nay ! ' Then said the Legate, ' I know thee well : and I command thee by holy obedience to keep in thine own bosom all that I shall tell thee, and to disclose it to none until I shall give thee leave ; and to speak to no man but in my presence, and never in thy native German, but ever in the Latin tongue. The Landgrave is dead, and I am the Legate. Thou shalt therefore give me and my comrade a habit of the Order, and without delay thou shalt give me means to flee, and lead me to a safe place, that I be not taken

by Conrad.' To be brief, all this was done obediently and
gladly ; but when the Guardian would have led them forth from
the city, he found one gate shut, and likewise the second and the
third : yet through the third, by a space which was beneath the
gate, they saw a great dog creep out, and it seemed to them that
this was the only way whereby they also might pass. But when
they attempted it, it was found that the Legate was too fat to
pass through ; but the Guardian stood upon his body, and flat-
tened him by stamping it to the ground, and thus he crept forth.
When therefore all four were gone forth, they passed on and
came that day to dinner at a certain city, wherein was a Convent
of Friars Minor. And when these asked of the Guardian who
were these friends whom he brought with him, he answered,
' They are great Lombards. For God's sake show them charity
and courtesy and do them service.' So the guardian of that
house came with ten brethren of the convent, and ate with them
in the guest-house with the greatest familiarity and solace, being
much comforted to have such guests. When therefore the Legate saw that he was in a safe place, and had escaped all perils,
at the end of dinner he gave leave to the Guardian his guide
and fellow-traveller to make him known. Then that stranger-
guardian who had travelled with him, said to the brethren,
' Know, dearest friends, that this Brother with whom ye have
eaten is the Legate of the Lord Pope, and therefore have I
brought him to you, for that the Landgrave is dead, and here at
last we have no further fear of Conrad. But even the comrade
who travelled with me has known none of these things until
this very hour.' The brethren, hearing this, began to tremble as
a reed when it is shaken with the water. But the Legate said
to them, ' Fear not, brethren ! I know you, that ye have God's
love in you : ye have busily ministered to us, ye have shown us
courtesy and charity and familiarity ; the Lord repay you ! I
was even heretofore a friend to the Order of St. Francis : and
that friendship will I now hold fast all the days of my life.'
And so in truth it was. For he gave to the Friars Minor the
church of St. Peter the Great at Ravenna,[9] and granted us every
favour which we sought from him, of preaching, of hearing confessions, and of absolving from all cases of conscience which
were reserved for himself. He had a terrible and savage
household, yet they all revered the Friars Minor as apostles of
Christ, knowing that their Lord loved us dearly. For they
were full forty men-at-arms, whom he ever led with him, to be
guardians of his life and person ; and they feared him as they
feared the Devil. Nay, Ezzelino da Romano was scarcely less

feared ; for he gave his servants most grievous punishments. One day, as he went from Ravenna to Argenta (which is the Archiepiscopal palace), he caused one of his servants to be bound with a rope and plunged into the water, and thus they dragged him bound to the ship through the rolling waves, as though he were a sturgeon, because he had forgotten to bring salt. Another time he caused a certain other servant to be bound to a great pole and turned as on a spit, before the fire ; and when the men of his household wept for him with pity and compassion, the Legate, seeing the cruel sight, said to them, ' Poor wretches ! Do ye weep so soon ? ' and so bade that he should be taken away from the fire. Yet the man had already borne bitter anguish of soul and much roasting. Moreover, the Legate cast into chains a certain Amanato, his steward, a Tuscan ; and the rats devoured him in the prison, for he was accused of having wasted his master's goods. Many other cruelties he practised on those who were of his household, for his own vengeance and their punishment, and to strike fear into others. And therefore God suffered him to be taken, while he was yet Legate, by Ezzelino, who kept him carefully, and took him whithersoever he went, that he might the more carefully guard him. Yet he treated him with honour and reverence, although he had taken Padua from him. But He who liberated Manasses from his dungeon and restored him to his kingdom, liberated likewise this Legate in the manner following. A certain man of Reggio, named Gerardo de' Campsori, drew him forth from Ezzelino's dungeon and let him down by a rope from an upper chamber : and so he escaped in the Lord's name from Ezzelino's hands. But he was not unmindful of this loving kindness, but repaid the same man by making him a Cardinal[10] of Ravenna. Moreover, to Brother Enverardo of Brescia, a great Lector of the Order of Friars Minor, he gave the bishopric of Cesena, for that he was of his household, and had been taken prisoner with him ; which Brother Enverardo, after the death of Ezzelino, was freed from prison with all the other prisoners whom that accursed tyrant kept in ward. Moreover, this aforesaid Archbishop [of Ravenna] had two nephews, Francis and Philip ; but Philip was his own son, and was twenty-five or thirty years old, comely and fair as a second Absalom : and this Lord Philip, Archbishop of Ravenna, and Legate of the Roman court, loved him as his own soul. Whoever therefore was willing to fill the hands of these two men with gifts might have a prebend or whatsoever he demanded from the Archbishop ; and thus they became rich beyond measure. He had also a fair daughter, whom he would have given to wife to the Lord Jacopo di Bernardo : but he would not take her, both because she was not of lawful birth, and for that he would not take a dowry of Church goods, and also because he purposed to become a Friar Minor and die in that Order, as in truth he did. Moreover, the said Archbishop was sometimes so melancholy and gloomy and furious, and such a son of Belial, that none could speak with him. But to me he was always kind and familiar and courteous and liberal ; for he gave me the relics of the blessed Eliseus,[11] of whom we read in the Book of Kings, which were in a certain city called Cæsarea, hard by Ravenna, in the Monastery of St. Lawrence, in a stone coffin within the royal chapel ; and I carried off the principal and greatest bones of that body, and placed them within the high altar of the Friars Minor at Parma, where they are even unto this day, with the following epitaph, besides that which I had affixed first in leaden letters :—

> Hic virtute Dei—patris ossa manent Helysei,
> Quæ Salimbene—detulit ossa bene.

But I could not have the head of Eliseus, because the Austin friars had stolen it and carried it away unbidden. For the Archbishop cared more for war than for relics of Saints. Once when he was Legate he came to Faenza, where I then dwelt : and because he needed to enter a convent of the Order of St. Clara, and the Abbess wished to speak long with him, he sent for some brethren to be his comrades, both for honesty's sake and for his own honour. For he loved honour above all men in the world, as my judgment goes ; and above all men in the world he knew how to lord it and play the baron, as I have heard from others, and as it seemed to me likewise. We were therefore ten brethren that bare him company ; and after we had warmed ourselves by the fire (for it was a Saturday morning in the month of January, on the feast of St. Timothy), he robed himself in sacerdotal vestments, that he might enter the Convent decently and honestly. And when he would have put on his alb, and found it too close in the sleeves, he was troubled. And the Bishop of Faenza said to him, ' It is not close for me, for I put it on easily.' To whom the Archbishop said, ' How ! Is this alb thine ? ' ' It is mine,' said the Bishop. ' And where then is mine ? ' said the Archbishop ; and presently it was found that one of his servants had carried it to Ravenna. And the Archbishop said, ' In truth, I wonder much at mine own long-suffering, yet will I give him punishment ! I cannot inflict it here in his absence ; but delay is no robbery ! ' And I said to the Arch-bishop, ' Have patience, Father, for "patience hath her perfect work." And the Wise Man saith " By patience a prince shall be appeased, and a soft tongue shall break harness." ' Then the Archbishop said, ' The Wise man saith also in the xiii chapter of Proverbs " He that spareth the rod hateth his son ; but he that loveth him correcteth him betime." '* I, seeing that the Arch-bishop was wholly purposed in his own heart to punish the offender, said, ' Father, let us leave these words and speak of another matter. Do you celebrate ? ' And he said, ' No, I will that thou sing Mass.' And I said to him, ' I will obey you and sing Mass.' Then said the Archbishop, ' Will ye that I prophesy to you of the Pope to be ? ' (for the Papacy had been vacant since the death of Pope Urban IV of Troyes.) And we said, ' Yea, Father, tell us who shall be the Pope.' And he said : ' Pope Gregory IX loved much the Order of St. Francis. Now shall succeed Gregory X, who shall dearly love the Friars Minor.' (For he thought to speak thus of himself ; for he desired much to have the Papacy, and even hoped it ; both because he was a friend of the Friars Minor, and because the master of necromancy at Toledo had foretold that he would be great in the Church of God, and also because he saw himself already great, and that sometimes the Cardinals were at discord in the Papal election, and that at times men spake his name in this matter.) Then I answered and said, ' Father, if the Lord will, you will be that Gregory X : and you have loved us, and will love us yet more.' Yet it came not thus to pass ; for no Gregory X succeeded then, but Clement IV ; nor did this Arch-bishop of Ravenna ever come to the Papacy. So when this Archbishop and Legate had spoken the aforesaid words, he added, ' These are they who shall enter the Convent : firstly, all the Friars who are here ; then, of mine own company, let none enter but the Bishop of Faenza, the Archdeacon of Ravenna, and the Podesta of this city.' When therefore we were come to the door of the church, we found there a lay-brother with a smoking censer, and when he had censed the Legate the latter took the censer from his hands, and censed each friar as he entered the church, saying thrice, *de licenso ali frati me*, which being inter-preted is ' Incense to my Brethren.' Then we went to the stairs, and he leant on me, for honour's sake and for help, both in mounting and descending ; so that I held up his right arm, and

---

* This text was taken in the Middle Ages to apply equally to servants : See the *Moral Tales* of the Franciscan Nicole Bozon. (p. 25.)

the Archdeacon of Ravenna his left. And the church was on an upper floor, and the whole Convent of those ladies, to the number of 72, was there gathered together ; and after Mass had been solemnly celebrated, and all our council and business was ended, we went out from the Convent and found a plenteous fire kindled. And forthwith the bell ran to Nones, and the Legate took leave, and said, 'I invite ye all to dine with me.' I believe that he said full ten times over in the Tuscan tongue, *mo e' ve 'nvito, e si ve renvito*, which is, being translated, ' I invite you to dinner, and again I reinvite you.' Nevertheless those brethren were so fearful and shamefaced that I could not bring with me but two ; the rest went to eat in the Convent of the Brethren. When therefore I had come to the Bishop's palace, the Legate said to me, ' To-day is the Sabbath-day, and the Bishop and Podesta will eat flesh. Let us part from them, and go to the hall of the Palace, where we shall have abundantly to eat.' And he kept me and made me sit by his side at table ; and oft-times he said how he took it exceeding ill that I had not honoured him by bringing other Brethren with me ; for he had invited them all. And I dared not tell him that they would not come, for he would have taken it too ill ; but I told him that another time he should have the whole Convent. For he rejoiced much when men honoured him. Moreover the Archdeacon bare us company, and sat at a lower table by himself ; but he was my friend and acquaintance and sent me a present."

Here follows a long digression on the Council of Ravenna, in which Philip, despite his own lax morals, stoutly supported the Friars in their attempt to reform the morals of the parish clergy. Salimbene speaks again of his hopes of the Papacy, and their repeated disappointments ; and he gives a pathetic picture of the great man's last days. (429) " So the Lord Philip, Archbishop of Ravenna, after that he had fought many fights and gained many victories, became aged and weighed down with years and fell sick of the sickness whereof he died. And, wishing to die in his own land, he let himself be carried on a wooden litter by twenty men, ten and ten by relays ; and when he came to Imola, he would fain stay in the Convent of the Friars Minor, where at that time I dwelt ; and we gave him the whole Refectory to himself, and he stayed with us but one day. And when he was come to Pistoia, he sent for Brother Thomas of Pavia, who was his acquaintance and friend of old, and confessed to him and ordered well for the salvation of his soul ; and so he rested in peace, and was buried in the church of the Friars Minor at Pistoia. (430) Moreover, this Lord Philip, when he was in his villa called

Argenta on the banks of the Po, and when he went to and fro through his palace, was wont to go singing some responsory or antiphon in praise of the glorious Virgin, from one corner to another of that palace. And in summer time he would drink at each corner; for at each corner of the palace he had a pitcher of excellent and noble wine in the coldest water. For he was a mighty drinker, and loved not water with his wine, wherefore also he loved much the treatise which Primas wrote against mixing water with wine, which we will perhaps write in this book for the solace of some. Yet, you must know that water is most profitable in wine for many reasons: for watered wine doth not hurt the head or gnaw the stomach, or make the mouth to stink or impede the tongue, or inebriate or make a man wordy or provoke to lust: for (as St. Jerome saith) the belly that revelleth with wine is quick to foam into lust." With which excuse Salimbene quotes *in extenso* these most unedifying verses of Primas.

The next whom he names (433) was not strictly a Legate, (though Salimbene calls him so), but a Bishop of Mantua sent by the Pope to preach the crusade in Lombardy. He again was "a mighty drinker," and not unnaturally subject to fits of religious depression: yet he was "a courteous man, humble and kindly and open-handed and liberal." He had been a personal friend of Salimbene's eldest brother; and one day our autobiographer sat a long while with him in the palace where he lodged on his way through Ravenna. The Legate rose at last and went to the window: "Where, then, is your convent, Brother Salimbene?" "Then I pointed it out to him: a great church with a tall campanile like the donjon-tower of a fortress," in the shadow of which Dante's bones still lie. "Then said the Bishop, 'Do you believe, Brother Salimbene, that we bishops can come to heaven— we who are in so many labours and cares and anxieties by reason of the flocks committed to us—unless you Religious, who are in familiar converse with God, help us with your frocks and hoods?'" Salimbene comforted the Bishop with Prov. xv. 13, and xii. 25, and with a long quotation from St. Bernard's sermons on the Canticles, in which the saint argues that the monk, who from his safe castle of contemplation looks down upon the sin-spotted Bishop in the outer world, is like the woman at her spinning-wheel who should scold the man returning from battle; for (quotes St. Bernard from Ecclesiasticus) "better is the iniquity of a man than a woman who doth well." "These things" (pursues Salimbene) "are said [by St. Bernard] against the double temptation by which men of Religion are oft-times urged of the Devil either to run after the glory of Bishops or to judge rashly of their excesses. So when I had quoted all these sayings, the Bishop said : ' May the Lord reward thee, Brother Salimbene, for thou hast given me excellent comfort : thou art in truth, in the words of Ecclesiasticus, " a man of counsel who will not destroy understanding." ' After him another Legate was sent to Lombardy, a Cardinal who had been Archbishop of Embrun. (323) He was a man of worth in knowledge and song and letters and honest and holy life : and once when a minstrel had played his viol in the Legate's presence and begged for some gift, the Archbishop answered ' if thou wilt fain eat, I will give thee gladly for God's sake ; but for thy song and viol I would give thee nought, for I can sing and play as well as thou.' He always kept with him two Brethren Minor. (435) He transformed the Alleluia of St. Francis *O patriarcha pauperum*, into a hymn to the same air for the Blessed Virgin, *O consolatrix pauperum* : and he wrote the *Summa Copiosa**. After him a certain [Papal] chaplain was sent by the Lord Pope, who would have gathered knights from every city in help of King Charles against Manfred. When he came on this business to Faenza, he gathered together the Friars Minor and the Preachers in the Bishop's chamber, who was there with his canons ; and I likewise was present and heard his words. And he concluded our business in few words after the fashion of [his own] French, who speak briefly, and not like the men of Cremona, who delight in much speech : for he reviled Manfred and accused him to us of manifold crimes. Then he said that the French army would come quickly, and this was true, as I saw with mine own eyes at the Christmastide next following. Lastly he promised that the matter whereon they marched would quickly end well with victory ; and so it was : yet some of his hearers scoffed and derided him, saying : *Ver, ver, cum bon báton*, which was to say that the French should have the victory with good staves. After him another chaplain was sent as Legate, who contrived excellently to bring back the Church exiles of Cremona to their city ; for they had long been exiles and wanderers. Moreover he subtly expelled Buoso da Duera and Pallavicino from the lordship of Cremona, which they had long held and done much ill. So the Church exiles returned to Cremona and gave them tit for tat, destroying their towers and houses and palaces and seizing their lands and possessions, as is the custom in Lombardy. This Legate was followed by Cardinal Latino, a young man and lean of flesh, of the Order of Friars Preachers,

---

* A standard commentary on the Canon Law which goes by the name of his cardinalate, *Hostiensis*.

whom Pope Nicholas IV had made Cardinal and Legate for his kindred's sake. (169) He troubled all the ladies with a certain Constitution which he promulgated, wherein it was written that all women should have garments of length to reach to the ground, and only the measure of a single palm further ; for before this they trailed along the ground tails of garments a whole ell and a half long, whereof the Poet Patecchio writeth 'And trains of cloth, long-trailing in the dust.' And the Bishop caused this Constitution to be preached in all the churches, and imposed it strictly upon the women, and that no priest might absolve them of their sins but if they obeyed ; which to the women was bitterer than any death. For a certain lady told me in familiar talk that this tail was dearer to her than the whole of the rest of the garments wherewith she was clad. Moreover, the Cardinal enjoined that all women, both maidens and noble damsels, married and widows and matrons, should wear veils on their heads, which was horribly grievous to them. Yet for that tribulation they found a remedy, which for their tails they could not ; for they caused their veils to be made of fine muslin and silk inwoven with gold, wherein they showed ten times fairer than before, and drew beholders' eyes all the more to wantonness."[12] The twelfth and last Legate was that Cardinal Bernardo of whom we have already heard in connexion with Pinamonte. He had been created by Martin IV, and was his willing instrument in those wars of aggrandisement in which he wasted such incalculable blood and treasure. Salimbene constantly speaks with horror of this slaughter and waste ; he tells us that the Pope spent " 1,400,000 golden florins, which sum was from the tithes of all the churches which Pope Gregory X had gathered for the succour of the Holy Land, and which was thus diverted from its true purpose."

" These twelve abovenamed," adds our chronicler, "were the most noble Legates and Princes of the Church whom the Pope sent into Lombardy and Romagna, not only for the salvation of men's souls, but also against the wiles of that Dragon, the Emperor Frederick, who strove with his princes and followers to overthrow the liberty of the Church, and to corrupt the unity of the faithful." The remedy, however, was not so much more tolerable than the disease ; and we can well understand the complaint which Salimbene ascribes to the monks of Cluny : " The Pope's Legates rob the churches so far as in them lies, and carry off whatsoever they can." (213)

Chapter XXII.

The Princes of the Church.

BUT the Papal Legate was apt to be statesman first and churchman afterwards :—the nemesis of that Temporal Power in which so many besides Dante have seen one of the weakest points of the Roman Church. Let us turn now to other prelates who were in theory spiritual pastors first of all, and statesmen only accidentally.

Salimbene records the reign of sixteen Popes ; for most of these he has little to say, and they are far from bulking in his chronicle as they would in a similar book of modern memoirs. First, in time and in greatness, comes Innocent III. After quoting Sicardo's description of the great Pope's energy and successes, Salimbene goes on (31) " The Church flourished and throve in his days, holding the lordship over the Roman Empire and over all the kings and princes of the whole world. Yet this Pope sowed the seeds of the cursed dissensions between Church and Empire, with his chosen Emperors Otto IV and Frederick II, whom he exalted and entitled Son of the Church : but herein he may be excused, that he meant well. And note that this Pope was a bold man and stout of heart. For once he measured on his own person the Seamless Coat of our Lord, and he thought how the Lord must have been of small stature ; yet when he had put on the coat, it seemed too great for him ; so he feared and venerated the relic, as was seemly. Moreover he would sometimes keep a book before him when he preached to the people ; and when his chaplains asked why he did this, being so wise and learned a man, he would answer and say 'I do it for your sakes, to give you an example : for ye are ignorant and yet are ashamed to learn.' Moreover, he was a man who, as the poet saith, mingled his business at times with mirth, as this example may show. One day a minstrel of the Mark of Ancona saluted him, saying :

'Papa Innocentium,
Doctoris omnis gentium,
Salutat te Scatutius
Et habet te pro dominus.'

And when the Pope asked, 'Whence art thou then, Scatuzio?'
he answered:

'De castro Recanato,
Et ibi fui nato.'

To whom the Pope said:

'Si veneris Romam,
Habebis multam bonam,'

answering purposely in false grammar to the false grammar of
the Minstrel.   Moreover, one day as he preached to the people,
he saw how a certain scholar mocked at his words.   So when his
sermon was ended he called him apart into his chamber and
asked him why he had laughed at the Word of God which is
profitable for salvation of souls.   The scholar answered that the
Pope's were mere words, but that he himself could show deeds, as
for example raising of the dead and authority over demons.   So
the Pope learned from him that he was a necromancer who had
studied at Toledo: wherefore he besought him to raise a certain
dear friend of his own, with whom he would fain speak and hear
of his soul's health.   So they chose a desert and secret spot in
Rome, whereunto the Pope went as though he walked abroad for
air; and when he was come thither he bade his attendants pass
on and tarry until he came again to them.   They therefore did
as he had bidden, believing that he went down into this place at
the call of nature.   So the scholar raised up before his eyes the
Archbishop of Besmantova,[1] with the same pomp and vainglory
with which he was wont to come to Court.   First came his
servants to make ready his lodging, then a great multitude of
sumpter-mules with his treasures, then his squires to wait on
him, and then his knights, and himself last of all with many
chaplains round him.   The necromancer asked him whither he
went: and he made answer 'To the Court, to my friend Pope
Innocent, who would fain see me.'   Then said he 'Here is thy
friend Innocent, who would know from thine own mouth how it
standeth with thee.'   'Ill indeed,' said the Archbishop, 'for I
am damned by reason of my pomp and vainglory and my other
sins: and I did no penitence: wherefore I am doomed to dwell
with devils and with those who go down to hell.'   When there-

fore these speeches were ended on either side, the apparition vanished and the Pope went back to his attendants."

It is evident that Salimbene did not feel unmixed admiration even for the greatest Pope of the age. We have seen already (chap. vi) how little he valued Innocent's liturgical ordinances : and (as Prof. Michael points out) he dismisses in a few careless lines that great Lateran Council which made Transubstantiation a dogma of the Church and aimed at a sweeping reform of clerical learning and discipline (22). "Among other things, the Pope ordained that there should be henceforth no [new] Order of religious Mendicants : but this constitution was not kept, through the negligence of the prelates. Nay rather, whosoever will may clap on a hood and go begging and boast that he has founded a new Order. Hence comes confusion in the world ; for secular folk are burdened thereby, and their alms are not enough for those who labour in word and in teaching, and whom the Lord hath set to live by the gospel. For rude secular folk, who have no knowledge or discernment, leave as much by will to one wretched woman living in a hermitage as to a convent of thirty priests, who celebrate mass almost daily for the living and for the dead. May the Lord see to it, and change for the better all that is ill done ! The rest that was ordained at that Council I write not here, for weariness and for the avoidance of prolixity." Salimbene's contempt, apart from his obvious zeal for his own Order, is no doubt partly to be explained by the scanty practical result of that Council : but it is also true that Innocent in his own days often commanded a far less unreserved admiration than in ours. Many good Churchmen were quite as much scandalized by his political struggles as edified by his zeal for religion : e.g. St. Liutgardis spoke of him as only having just avoided damnation, and Caesarius thought little better of him. The conception of the Papacy in the 13th century was in many ways still far from its modern development. Nearly two centuries after Salimbene, even so orthodox a saint as James of the Mark, in controversy with the heretics of his time, could only claim that at least no two *consecutive* popes had taught heresy, for there had always been an orthodox successor to repudiate his forerunner's errors.[2] It must always be borne in mind that the " state of siege " (as Mr. Wilfrid Ward calls it) in which Romanism has lived since the Reformation has contributed very strongly to raise the characters of the Popes, and to teach them circumspection in their actions. Even in the 13th century (to say nothing of the far worse 200 years which followed) the average Pope generally cuts a poor figure in the pages of contemporary chroniclers : and it is a matter of common remark that Dante, who damns so many, mentions even the great Innocent only in a couple of words, as having ratified the Rule of St. Francis.

Of Honorius III Salimbene tells us that (33) "he deposed a Bishop who had not read Donatus : " *i.e.* who knew little or no Latin.

Gregory IX had been the Cardinal Ugolino of Franciscan history : Salimbene speaks of him as a man of strong feelings (88), but had little sympathy with his aggressive politics, which had for a moment well-nigh wrecked the Church (36). Later on, as we have already seen, he mentions the report that Cardinal Ottaviano was this Pope's son. Celestine IV and the inter-regnum of nearly two years are barely mentioned : but Innocent IV, who ruled eleven years and had been a friend of Salimbene's father, receives plenty of attention, though not always of a flatter-ing kind, in spite of his favour to the Friars. (61, 62). Indeed, nearly all the Popes of this period were staunch friends to the Franciscans, a fact which adds all the more weight to these criti-cisms, since Salimbene's strongest prejudices were those of his Order. He speaks repeatedly of Innocent's shameless nepotism (62, 176), and has no doubt that God smote him for a momentary weakness in siding with the parish clergy against the Friars. Certain German Friars, who had vainly waited long months for an audience, found their way in at last when all others had deserted the dying Pope, and promised to wash his body for burial : "for he remained on the straw, naked and abandoned of all men, as is the wont of the Pontiffs of Rome when they give up the ghost" (420). The sang-froid with which Salimbene speaks of God's judgment on this Pope will surprise only those who are unfamiliar with medieval chronicles. The learned and orthodox Wadding describes the affair at much greater length. He tells us how the friars in their trouble recited a daily Litany against the Pope's oppressive measure; and how the Virgin Mary was seen standing on the altar of their great church at Rome and saying "Son, hear them ! " Innocent fell ill at Naples, and died on December 7th, quoting with his last breath "Thou with rebukes dost chasten man for sin : " hence a proverb-ial saying at the Roman court "Beware of the Litanies of the Friars Preachers." Thomas of Chantimpré, himself a Domini-can and a suffragan Bishop at that time, asserts that the Pope was struck with palsy on the very day on which he signed the Bull. Thomas of Eccleston tells substantially the same story, and adds that " no beggar—not to say, no human being—dies a more miserable and viler death than all Popes die."[3]

Alexander IV (453) astounded the world by his freedom from nepotism : he neither made a Cardinal of his nephew nor an Abbess of his niece. Moreover he was a learned and zealous man and " a true and faithful friend, as we see in the case of Brother Rinaldo di Tocca of our Order, whom he loved more dearly than Jonathan his David, or Amis his Amiles.[4] For though the whole world had said aught of evil against him, the Pope would have believed no whit thereof, nor even lent ear thereto ; and he would go barefoot to open when Brother Rinaldo knocked at his chamber door, as was seen by one who was alone with the Pope in his chamber, namely, Brother Mansueto da Castiglione of Arezzo, my friend, from whose mouth I heard all this. This Pope would not meddle with wars, but passed his days in peace. He was big, that is, fat and corpulent, like another Eglon : he was kindly, merciful, just, Godfearing, and devout." " He died of a broken heart, considering daily the terrible and increasing strife among Christians,"says Wadding (an. 1261.)

Of his successor Urban IV, Salimbene had a poor opinion : and he attributes his death to the influence of the great comet of 1264. But the next Pope was again a man after his own heart. This was Clement IV, who had had a wife and children " in the World," and who as Pope "was so devoted to vigils, fastings, and prayers that God is thought to have remedied for his merits many disorders under which the Church then suffered." (476) After him came a disastrous interregnum of nearly four years, which men vainly attempted to prevent in future by passing ordinances to which nobody paid any attention. Then came Gregory X, the last of the good Popes in this chronicle. One case of nepotism is indeed reported of him ; he gave the Archbishopric of Ravenna, in favour of his kindred, to the Bonifacio Fieschi of *Purg*. xxiv, 29 ; " *che pasturò col rocco molte genti*" (83). All else that he tells us is very much to this Pope's credit. (488, 491) He hated simony : a rare virtue in that century : " he was a good man, just, and upright and God-fearing, and very zealous for religion ; and he purposed to do many things which were broken off by his death. In 1274 he celebrated a General Council at Lyons, wherein he appeared truly holy, for there he ordained many good constitutions." Moreover, he thought to cleave fast to Christ's commands, if he had lived : but he was carried off by death, even as Josiah, King of Judah, at that moment when he was most needed, for the sake of our wickedness who still survive him." But Salimbene finds two other characteristic reasons for the Pope's death—he had attempted to continue the imperial line after Frederick's decease, and had set his heart upon recovering the Holy Land : in each case, in flat neglect of Joachim's prophecies.

Nicholas III earned Salimbene's gratitude by making two Franciscan Cardinals : but the costly and scandalous wars of Martin IV had their real origin in Nicholas's acquisition of Romagna from the Emperor Rudolf : " for the Popes oft-times seek to extort gifts from the Empire by reason of a fresh accession, since the Emperor cannot fittingly refuse a demand at that moment " (509). Again, Nicholas was sadly given to nepotism, " for he ' built up Sion with blood,' as also certain other Roman Pontiffs have sometimes done.[5] I believe most surely in my conscience that there are a thousand Friars of the Order of the blessed Francis (whereof I am a poor and most humble Brother) who would be better fitted by their learning and holy life to receive the Cardinal's hat than many who are promoted by reason of their kindred by the Roman Pontiffs. We need not seek far for an example. Pope Urban IV promoted to the Cardinalate his nephew Anger, and exalted him in riches and honour above all the Cardinals of the Court : yet he was at first so miserable a scholar that he was wont to fetch back flesh from the market for his fellow scholars ; and in process of time it was found that he was the Pope's son—and so they promote and exalt their bastards, and say that they are their nephews, sons of their brethren.[6] Not so did the blessed Job, who saith of himself ' If as a man I have hid my sin, and have concealed my iniquity in my bosom,' etc. And certainly such men as these are thought most honourable when they are promoted to power and dignities, and have wealth and free access to the Pope ; but hearken now to a text which may comfort thee against any man who hath a fat prebend. ' If his sons be multiplied, they shall be for the sword, and his grandsons (*nepotes*) shall not be filled with bread.' Therefore . . . ." here follow six-and-a-half lines which have been scratched out, the only legible words being at the end " is loved, for that she is foul and deformed ; moreover, she is hunchbacked and of illegitimate birth." (170)

Of Martin IV he speaks frequently, showing little sympathy with his waste of blood and treasure in the Italian wars, and with his embezzlement of Crusade money : he is rather amused than otherwise that the Perugians should have burnt him and his Cardinals in effigy. (510) At the same time, he shows his leniency in omitting all mention of that gluttony and winebibbing which earned Martin a conspicuous place in Dante's Purgatory. Martin's successor, Honorius IV, passed among the Friars for an enemy of their Order ; and Salimbene probably wrote more about him than we shall ever know. For, under the year 1286, two passages of five sheets each have been torn from the MS., no doubt as containing more unedifying details than usual. The first evidently contained criticism of the Roman Court, since among the first words on the next page we read (618) " For the Cardinals are wont to care little for such things. Moreover, the Cardinals at that time had just such a Pope, a Roman named Jacopo Savelli, grasping and avaricious and of little worth and crippled with the gout.[7] He was called Pope Honorius IV : and not only was he no founder of new Orders of Religion, but, so far as in him lay, he was a great destroyer of those already founded and growing—being moved thereto by bribes from certain prelates of churches ; for all things are obedient unto gold." His death (thinks Salimbene) might partly be explained by his renewing Gregory X's attempt to continue the Roman Empire after Frederick's death, in the teeth of Joachim's prophecies : but the main cause was this aforesaid acceptance of £100,000 Tournois to curtail the privileges of the Friars. " And the Lord Matteo Rossi who was the cardinal, protector, governor, and corrector of the Franciscan Order, came weeping to the Brethren, and said to them with tears : ' My brethren, I have laboured all that in me lay to turn the Supreme Pontiff aside from his purpose ; yet could I not recall him from his evil disposition (*malignitate*) which he beareth in his heart towards you. Pray ye therefore to God who " bringeth to nought the designs of the malignant," that he may " deliver you from importunate and evil men." Pray ye also to the blessed Francis that he may deign to work his accustomed marvels against those who strive to trouble his Order, that all men living may know, and all who do evil, that it is not easy to fight against God and his servants.' Hearing this, the Brethren turned with one mind to beseech the Lord that He might deign to succour them in this peril ; and, for that ' the prayers of so many must needs be heard ' (as saith St. Augustine) therefore He who ' hath had regard to the prayer of the humble ; and hath not despised their petition ' that is, God—whereas Pope Honorius was about to promulgate the aforesaid decree on the morrow of Maundy Thursday—God (I say) smote him on the fourth day of Holy Week at even, and he died." (619, 629).

After all, Papal embezzlement, Papal immorality, Popes prayed to death by the faithful, are common phenomena enough in the 13th and 14th centuries. Matthew Paris speaks far more bitterly than Salimbene about the theft of Crusade money, though he never lived to see its grosser forms under Martin IV : and this was no doubt one of the main causes for that decay of crusading enthusiasm of which Etienne de Bourbon so bitterly complains (p. 174). If there is any medieval chronicler who wrote consistently of the Popes in terms that would satisfy a modern Roman Catholic, it may pretty safely be asserted that the majority did not. Salimbene's popes, it must be remembered, were after all far better than those of an earlier or a later age. His complaint as to the distribution of Church preferment, petulant as it sounds, is outdone by St. Dominic's successor, the blessed Jordan of Saxony. Here is the latter's reply to certain Bishops who complained that Friars, when raised to the episcopal rank, were less satisfactory than before. "Though I have passed many years in the [Dominican] Order, I do not recall a single instance in which his Holiness the Pope, or any Legate, or Cathedral Chapter, has ever asked me or any of our Superiors, or any General or Provincial Chapter, to find them a good bishop. On the contrary, they picked their own men at will, either for reason of nepotism, or from some other unspiritual motive, and so no blame can rest with us."

"Like Pope, like Cardinal," as all contemporaries assure us. The terrible accusations which Grosseteste brought against the Papal Court at the First Council of Lyons (1245) are if possible outdone by Hugh de Digne's diatribe against the Cardinals on that same occasion, as recorded by Salimbene. "I heard it" (he says) "from the mouth of Brother Hugh, and wrote it down even as I heard it, fully and faithfully." Fully indeed, for it would fill nearly twenty pages of this book, and I can give only the briefest summary here (226ff). Innocent IV had asked Hugh to attend and give an informal account of his Joachistic beliefs before the Cardinals in Consistory. They began by asking what news he brought—naturally enough, as the modern reader would think, seeing that the ordinary friar was a sort of professional go-between and newsbearer. But Hugh was of St. Bonaventura's opinion in the matter, and loathed the ready sociability of his ordinary brethren : in a moment his Provençal blood was up, and he felt himself "full of the fury of the Lord." Taking their worldly curiosity as the text of his sermon, he proceeded to "rate them like asses." First he compared them to St. Paul's Athenians, idly agape all day long for some new thing. Then he passed on to rebuke their notorious simony and nepotism, and the bribery that was rampant at the Roman Court. Both Pope and cardinals (he says) neglect to do as Jethro advised Moses ; i.e. choose fit men to govern in pastoral offices. At Rome, there is no relic half so efficacious as the bones of St. Gold and St. Silver : with money, a man may buy a judgment at his will. He quotes the University epigram :

> " On an *accusative* errand no suitor to Rome need wend,
> Unless he bring with him the *dative*, to make that Mammon his friend."

By this time his blood is well up, and he proceeds to hurl text after text at the princes of the Church. The bitterest invectives of Isaiah and Amos against rich men's luxury and wantonness, and of Christ against the Pharisees, had but prefigured the Cardinals—or, as pseudo-Joachim nicknamed them, the Grabbinals (*Carpinales*). Their very title and dignity is a mushroom growth : in Constantine's time no Cardinals were known : it was but yesterday in 1245 that Innocent IV gave them their red hats to distinguish them from the rest of the clergy[8] . . . "And ye travel not, except it be in pomp from your own lodging to the Pope's Consistory, and thence to your own table, where ye eat and drink sumptuously. Then ye journey to your bed and sleep softly ; after which ye are all day idle in your chambers, stagnating in sloth, and sporting with hounds and hawks, or with your nephews and your fat palfreys. Such is the business of your lives, nor do ye care what stranger lies in the street, who lacks bread, who needs clothing, who is to be visited or redeemed from captivity or buried. Surely ye might convert the whole world if ye followed what the Wise Man teacheth, ' Run about, make haste, stir up thy friend :' thus would men believe in you more than in their priests. Of the Lord it is said that He went about all Galilee, teaching in their synagogues. But the chief Pontiff, who is called Pope, and Bishop, and Servant of the Servants of God, remains shut in day and night, that they may gain money who keep him in prison. . . . St. Paul said ' There shall be a time when they will not endure sound doctrine : but according to their own desires they will heap to themselves teachers, having itching ears, and will indeed turn away their hearing from the truth, but will be turned unto fables.' Of whom in truth ye are, who inquire after fables and news. Tell me who of your whole College—I mean of you Cardinals—has yet been written on the roll of the Saints ? Certainly Pope Damasus was accused by you of adultery, St. Jerome was foully and shamefully driven away, but he did wisely in departing from you,[9] and was of more profit to the Church of God by withdrawing from you than if he had remained with you and had become Pope ; for if he had been Pope, perchance he might have made four Deacons and five Presbyters and fifteen Bishops in divers places, and would have

ordained patens of glass to be kept.[10]   But after his departure
from your midst he edited many books, and expounded many,
and translated the Bible. . . . I have spoken : it is enough."
    The Cardinals were cut to the heart and gnashed their teeth
at the bold friar : " It seemed long to them till he should depart
from them and go forth from the chamber, nor did they imitate
the Athenians in saying 'We will hear thee again concerning
this matter.' "   But the Pope, to his honour be it said, praised
Hugh for his fearless speech : it will be remembered that Innocent, with all his faults, had also a real regard for the incon-
veniently earnest John of Parma.   Moreover, Hugh had from
the first stipulated that he should have fair play, and be allowed
to finish his speech without interruption.   Salimbene, ever glad
to show his very great scripture knowledge, remarked that, if the
Cardinals had been less taken aback and more ready with their
Bibles, they might have answered Hugh with one or two contemptuous texts such as Prov. xvii. 28, or xxvi. 10 : or xix 25.
In this latter case they might have suited the action to the word
and caused him to be scourged.   To which Hugh answered that
he would have taken the stripes cheerfully, with the tranquil
conviction that he had had his money's worth of plain speech
beforehand : for he had thoroughly fulfilled his initial promise,
" I will touch the mountains, and they shall smoke."
    On this point, as on nearly all the others on which I touch in
these chapters, the significance of the evidence lies less even in
its intensity than in its universality.   That one or two men—
even specially distinguished men—should have "rated the
Cardinals like asses " is not so surprising : but the absence of
rebutting evidence is most remarkable.   Similar accusations of
corruption made by orthodox writers against the Court of Rome
during the last four centuries before the Reformation would fill
a volume.   Matthew Paris quotes the epigram :

> "The whole world for Rome's greed can not suffice
> Nor the world's harlots for its lecheries."

Wherever the Pope has made his abode—until quite recent times
—the morality of that city has alway enjoyed an evil reputation.
Hugh of St.-Cher, one of the few really learned and virtuous
Cardinals under Innocent IV, made a memorable farewell speech
to the citizens when the Papal Court was on the point of leaving
Lyons : " We found three or four houses of ill-fame when we
came hither [seven years ago], and now at our departure we
leave the whole city one continuous brothel."   Petrarch has still

harder words for Avignon during the years of the Pope's abode there : and its common nickname of "the sinful city" finds its way even into English parliamentary documents of the time. Exactly the same complaint was made against the city of Constance during the sitting of the Great Council in the next century. The iniquities of the city of Rome itself have always been proverbial : both Boccaccio and Benvenuto da Imola refer to them as notorious, and they are silently admitted even by Father Ryder in his reply to Littledale's *Plain Reasons*.[11]

Moreover, the Bishops as a class were if anything worse than the Cardinals. We have seen what Jordan of Saxony says about them : and Salimbene among others, makes the very same complaint: "Note that in my days many Friars Minor and Preachers have been raised to bishoprics, rather by favour of their family and their fleshly kindred, than by favour of their Order. For the canons of the cathedral church of any city care little to have men of religious orders set above them as prelates, however clearly they may see them to shine in life and doctrine. For they fear to be rebuked of them, while they would fain live in fleshly lusts and wantonness." At that Council of Lyons at which St. Bonaventura was the prominent figure, the good Gregory X had roundly asserted that "the prelates were the cause of the ruin of the whole world." This pope did what he could for reform during those brief years which were yet granted him "in a world too evil to retain him." By exerting the whole weight of his authority, he succeeded in enforcing the resignation of the great prince-bishop Henry of Liège, who for nearly thirty years had led a life almost incredible, but for the plain evidence of similar episcopal scandals even under Innocent III. Two abbesses and a nun were among his concubines ; and he boasted of having had fourteen children in twenty-two months. Though illiterate, and not made a priest till eleven years after, he had been elected for political reasons by the special exertions of Innocent IV, the Pope whose influence on the Church was perhaps strongest of all during Salimbene's lifetime. It has been pleaded that we must be lenient to the episcopal scandals of the Middle Ages, regarding the Church rather as an unwilling victim to rude and oppressive secular lords, who too often forced unworthy prelates upon her : but the plea will not bear a moment's serious examination.[12] The Papal Court had plenty of power to minimize or even stamp out such an abuse, if it had cared to throw into such a struggle those energies which it wasted in petty Italian civil wars, in the persecution of heretics, and in the collection of vast sums to be squandered on selfish and scandalous indulgences. What is more, contemporaries assure us that the Popes themselves were directly responsible for the unworthiness of the prelates. Salimbene, (as we have seen in Chapter VIII) quotes the saintly Cistercian Geoffroi de Péronne, whose spirit came back from the other world to announce that he would have been damned without hope if he had let himself be persuaded by St. Bernard and the Pope to accept the Bishopric of Tournai. Franciscan records tell us how a 13th-century scholar of Paris, being led down to hell in a vision, asked news of his lately deceased uncle the Bishop. " The demon replied, ' I know him not : so many Bishops come hither daily that I know not of whom thou speakest.' " We have small reason to look back fondly to an age when a Bishopric could be spoken of, even hyperbolically, as one of the high roads to damnation ; and when this aversion to the office was strongest among many of the very best men. Salimbene has told us already of poor Rinaldo and the ex-Bishop of Turin : and similar evidence meets us everywhere. Gregory X complained of the number of Bishops who besieged him for leave to resign their sees. Albert the Great, a man perhaps superior on the whole to his pupil Aquinas, accepted the Bishopric of Ratisbon for the sake of carrying out definite and sorely-needed reforms : the General of his Order treated this acceptance as a terrible fall. " Who would believe that you, in the very evening of life, would set such a blot on your own glory and on that of the Order which you have done so much to augment? Consider what has befallen such as have suffered themselves to be drawn into such offices : what their reputation now is, what fruits they have brought forth, how they have ended their lives ! " Later on, Albert resigned his see, and died as a simple monk at Cologne. Aquinas refused the see of Naples, Bonaventura that of York. Such refusals are specially plentiful in Franciscan chronicles : but they stare out from every page of the history of the times, down to the Gran Rifiuto of Celestine V, who, before taking the decisive step, used to weep alone in his cell ; " they say I have all power in this world over souls, and why cannot I ensure my own salvation ? " It is generally known that John of Salisbury debated more or less seriously the question " Can an Archdeacon ever be saved ? " but few know the earnest and far more significant discussion in Caesarius of Heisterbach. He begins : " A certain clerk at Paris pronounced a terrible judgment on Bishops a few years ago, saying, ' I can believe anything, but I cannot believe that any German Bishop can ever be saved : ' " and he goes on to quote Salimbene's Geoffroi de Péronne as saying, " The state of the Church is now come to such a pass that it is not worthy to be ruled but by Bishops doomed to damnation."[13]

Lurid as this picture is, it is quite in accord with other details we find in Salimbene, though he leaves the world-renowned sinners alone, and speaks merely of those who have come within his own ken. We have seen already how low one Bishop of his acquaintance estimated Episcopal chances of salvation (435, quoted in chap. xxi). He tells us of eight Bishops of Parma during his lifetime. The first, uncle to Innocent IV, was "honest of his person, as men report "—*i.e.*, chaste : a praise which of itself is significant. (69) His successor Grazia " was held by the Parmese to be a good Bishop : in truth he was no dissipator of the Episcopal revenues. After him came a certain Gregory, a Roman, who lived but a short time, and died at Mantua, a heretic and accursed. For when in his last illness they brought him the Body of the Lord, he would not take it, saying that he believed nothing of such a faith. When therefore he had been asked why he accepted the bishopric, he said, ' Because of its riches and honours ; ' and so he died, without the Holy Communion. After him Master Martin da Colurnio was Bishop, a man of no very distinguished birth ; after whom came Bernardo Vizi. From this Bernard, (who had founded the Order of Brethren of Martorano,,) although he had received the Bishopric from the Legate Gregorio da Monte-lungo, Pope Innocent IV nevertheless took it away and gave it to his brother Albert : for he dearly loved his kinsfolk." (69, 176, 1285—365) Albert, though useless as a Bishop, was however again " honest of his person." He never took priest's orders or obtained consecration, though he held the see for fourteen years. His death was the signal for an exact repetition of the previous jobbery : Master John was canonically and rightly elected, but " then came the Lord Obizzo Bishop of Tripoli, who was likewise a nephew of the aforesaid Pope, and took it from him." (69) Obizzo began less decently than his brother, but apparently lived to become quite a respectable specimen of an Italian Bishop. " He was rather like a knight, and may be described as we have above described the Lord Nicholas, Bishop of Reggio ; for he was a clerk with the clergy, a monk with monks, a layman with laymen, a knight with knights, a baron with barons : a great embezzler (*baratator*), a great waster, freehanded, liberal, and courtly. At first he wasted many lands and possessions of the Bishopric, and gave them to buffoons ; but as time went on, he recovered the lands which he had given away, and did much good in his Bishopric. He was a man of learning, especially in Canon Law, and most skilled in the office of a Churchman, and he knew the game of chess, and kept the secular clergy strictly under his rod, and he would give parishes and churches to those who did well by him." (62). About ten years after Salimbene's death, Obizzo was driven from Parma by a popular rising, and fled to Ravenna, where he succeeded Dante's Bonifazio as Archbishop.[14]

This is not a brilliant record for sixty years of Bishops, in a see which was as safe from undue secular influence as any in Europe. In truth, Papal appointments were generally quite as political as any others : and these illegal interferences with the freedom of election constantly resulted in bloody quarrels or at least in long vacancies, during which the people got on as best they could without a Bishop. So it was at Milan after the death of the pugnacious Leo : so at Modena (141): and Reggio, still nearer to Parma, was thus vacant for ten years, while two noble candidates of rival houses fought out their differences. (175) The Papal candidate entered at last into his see : but Salimbene's epitaph shows that he was of the type of Innocent's other creations. (518). "In this year died the Lord Guglielmo Fogliani, Bishop of Reggio, and he ordered ill for the health of his soul. For he was avaricious, illiterate, and almost as a layman. He was also as Zacharias saith 'a shepherd, and idol, that forsaketh the flock.' He loved to live splendidly or eat sumptuously every day for the pampering of his body. Oft-times he made great feasts to the rich and to his relatives, but from the poor he shut up the bowels of compassion. He dowered no girls ; he was a boorish man, that is, dull and rude : he had few who spoke well of him. It had been better for him had he been a swineherd or a leper than a Bishop. He left nothing to the Religious, nor to the Friars Minor or Preachers, nor to other poor : the poor Religious who were present that day at his funeral had naught to eat of his goods, or rather, of the goods of the Bishopric. I was present at his funeral and interment, and I know that a dog defiled his grave when he was laid therein.[15] He was buried below in the cathedral church, where the men of the people are laid (yet he was rather worthy to be buried on a dungheap ;) and he troubled many that were at peace. He held the Bishopric of Reggio for forty years save one month."

The avarice or wastefulness of the Bishops is a common medieval theme : many were the prelates of whom it might be said, as Innocent III said of the Archbishop of Narbonne, that he had a purse where his heart should have been. Cardinal Jacques de Vitry, with all his sense of responsibility, does not hesitate to tell us of a priest who suffered so terribly from an episcopal visit and from the insatiable demands of his Lordship's cook, that, in despair, he sawed several slices from the body of the great crucifix, and brought them roasted to the Bishop. " My larder is empty : I have nothing left for your table but these ribs of the Crucified."[16]   Salimbene bears out this picture : in three other places he describes covetous Bishops of his day. Of one (Genoa) he adds that " men even whisper a sinister report of him, to wit that he was not altogether a good Catholic," (317) but it is only fair to note that the author of the *Golden Legend* gives this bishop a good character : (Chron. Januense, col. 47), and Salimbene seems certainly mistaken in quoting a report that he was finally murdered. He goes on with another anecdote on which Prof. Holder-Egger throws doubt also : " The Bishop of Ferrara was no less miserly and covetous than he ; for when the Patriarch of Jerusalem had come from the Holy Land to Ferrara on a journey of business to the Roman Court, and besought the Bishop to lodge him for one night in his palace. he denied his brother that hospitality. So the Patriarch went to the Court of Rome ; and there after a short space he was made Pope by the title of Urban IV. So he wrote letters to the Bishop of Ferrara saying, ' Know now that I am Pope, and that I may render thee thy deserts for thy avarice and thy covetousness ; since the Apostle saith " a Bishop must be given to hospitality." ' Yet we read not that the Pope wrought the Bishop any evil : though, indeed, the latter feared it all the days of his life, which itself was a great vengeance. The aforesaid Bishop was a Brescian by birth, and a physician by his calling : then he was made Bishop of Piacenza ; and, going to the Court, he procured the Bishopric of Ferrara. At Piacenza he was wont to keep two Friars Minor in his palace ; but they had a miserable life in the matter of victuals, by reason of his avarice." Our chronicler describes the bestial debauchery of another (Faenza) in words which the Parmese editor felt bound to omit even from his Latin text. This satyr was succeeded by a mere party politician, who received a politician's reward, and was driven out by the other faction. " So this Bishop went to Bagnacavallo, where he tarried all night shut up in the campanile of the parish church, quaking with terror, since he feared for his own skin. He lived but a few days after this, and another Bishop was made in his room." (426). Indeed, good Bishops are rare in our chronicle : and the general level may be judged by Salimbene's enthusiasm over the Patriarch of Antioch, (179) " who was of the family of Roberti at Reggio. At the time of the great earthquake he was Bishop of Brescia ; and having left his chamber at the cry of a certain Friar Minor who dwelt with him whilst he was Bishop, immediately after he had quitted it the chamber fell in at the shock of the earthquake; and he so recognised this benefit from God, that he was wholly converted to Him. For immediately without delay he made a vow, and promised firmly to God that for all the days of his life he would keep his chastity, which he was not formerly wont to keep; and that all the days of his life he would eat no flesh, which vow he inviolably kept. Yet he gave abundantly to all of his household, according to the word of St. Chrysostom which saith, 'Wilt thou both appear and be holy, be austere with respect to thine own life, kindly with respect to the lives of others. Let men hear of thee as doing hard things, and commanding small things.' But there are some wretched men, who when they abstain and fast, would have all men do likewise, and when they are sad, would have all be sad, which, indeed, they do either from avarice or from churlishness. This Patriarch was wont to do as the Apostle saith to the Romans, 'Rejoice with them that rejoice, weep with them that weep,' which, indeed, he did excellently, for he could be sportive when he would. Wherefore, one day as he sat at meat with his whole court and many other guests, he saw how a certain jongleur hid by stealth a silver spoon. So the Patriarch called his servant and said to him, 'I will not return thee my spoon unless each one at this table shall first have returned thee his,' and so by this speech he made this seneschal careful, and recovered his spoon. Moreover, the said Patriarch was a man of small learning, but made amends for this defect by other good deeds which he wrought; for he was a bountiful almsgiver, and was wont daily to say the Office for the dead with nine lessons. Being, therefore, a man with small learning, who made up by good works for that to which he could not attain in books, he might have said 'Because I have not known learning, I will enter into the powers of the Lord,' and so forth (Ps. lxx. 15 Vulg.) : for, as St. Paul saith, 'The letter killeth but the spirit quickeneth.' Because therefore this Patriarch continued his good life from the time when he gave up his heart wholly to love of God, therefore God glorified him in death by miracles, thus showing that he had been His servant and friend. Which miracles I write not here for brevity's sake." Of another Archbishop (Embrun) Salimbene records "he was made a Cardinal of the Roman court, and was a man of worth in learning and in song and in letters and in honest and holy life. And one day when a jongleur had played his viol in the Archbishop's presence and begged for a gift, the prelate answered, 'if thou art in want of food, I will give gladly unto thee for God's sake : but I would give thee nought for thy song and viol-play, for I cau sing and play as well as thou.' " (323).

Another good Bishop's life shows that medieval belief in the mysterious significance of anniversaries and symmetrical periods of time, which comes out so strikingly in the " Vita Nuova." " At Marseilles a boy was born on the feast of St. Benedict, and named Benedict ; and after he had been weaned, he was set to learn letters on St. Benedict's day ; afterwards, well versed in literature and almost grown to manhood, he entered upon St. Benedict's day into the Order of Black Monks of St. Benedict : and in process of time he was made sacristan on that same day. Then, many years after, for his good life and manners, the monks choose him for their abbot on the Feast of St. Benedict ; and thus, step by step, on the Feast of St. Benedict the Canons of Marseilles chose him to be their Bishop, in which office he bore himself with all praise. At length on the same day he entered the Order of the Blessed Francis, wherein he lived humbly and with all praise for ten years, and breathed his last on the Feast of St. Benedict. He is buried in a marble tomb in the church of the Friars Minor of Marseilles, and God hath glorified him by miracles. He was, indeed, a man of venerable life, blessed both in grace and in name . . . Blessed be that Bishop, for he began well and ended well, and the Friars Minor of Marseilles had many good books through his favour ; for he would rather ' be humbled with the meek than to divide the spoils with the proud.' "

But there is one prelate in this book who needs no apology of any kind : a man little known compared with inspired madmen like Brother Juniper and Jacopone da Todi, yet a far truer son of the real Christlike Francis. Eudes Rigaud, Archbishop of Rouen, would scarcely have run stark naked through the streets with Ruffino and his master : but he plodded doggedly along the thorny path of office for 27 years, and men called him afterwards " The Model of Good Life."[17]   One of the greatest scholars of his time, he quitted his books to wrestle with the sordid ignorance of clergy and laity in a great province. Of noble birth, he was one of the few friars whom the princely state and income of a prelate never tempted away from their first simplicity : to the very last he valued his friendship of King Louis and his influence with the Popes mainly for the power they lent him in his daily warfare against the encompassing wickedness. Side by side with St. Bonaventura, he led the van of the reformers at the second council of Lyons ; and he has left to posterity the most valuable episcopal record of medieval Europe—an official diary so complete, that, except for two or three chance omissions, we may trace his movements and his labours from day to day for more than twenty years. It unfortunately does not begin until a month after Salimbene's meeting with him and St. Louis at Sens in 1248. But it does record the Archbishop's presence at Mantua, Ferrara, and Bologna early in 1253, when we know Salimbene to have been living at Ferrara ; and of this journey our chronicler tells us the following ancedote. (434) " The Legate dealt most generously at Mantua with Brother Rigaud and all his household, when he passed towards the Court of Rome : and he sent forward his seneschal to pay his expenses as far as Bologna : but Brother Rigaud would not suffer him, saying that he and his whole household could live with becoming splendour on the half of his revenue, wherefore the other half was superfluous to him. Yet he had on that journey eighty mounted attendants, and a proper household ; and when he sat at meat in the city of Ferrara he had with him four Friars Minor, who had gone to visit him. And he had before him on the table two great bowls of silver, wherein food was put for the poor, and his butler always brought two dishes of each kind of food, according to the diversities of meats, and laid them before Brother Rigaud : and he kept one dish for himself and ate therefrom, and the other he poured into the silver bowls, for the poor. And this he did with each course and each several sorts of meats. Now this Brother Rigaud was of our Order, and one of the most learned men in the world. He had been doctor of theology in the convent [at Paris] : being a most excellent disputator and a most gracious preacher. He wrote a work on the Sentences ; he was a friend of St. Louis, King of France, who indeed laboured that he might be made Archbishop of Rouen. He loved well the Order of the Friars Preachers, as also his own of the Friars Minor, and did them both much good : he was foul of face, but gracious in mind and works, for he was holy and devout, and ended his life well ; may his soul, by God's mercy, rest in peace ! He had a brother according to the flesh in the Order, a goodly man and learned, who was called Brother Adam le Rigaud. I saw both often and in divers places." Brother Adam appears prominently also in the diary, from which I shall quote later on to corroborate Salimbene's evidence as to the parish clergy. The bitterest epigrams of satirists and preachers, the most heartrending confessions of great administrators like St. Bonaventura, are less dismal on the whole than the daily prosaic tale of the struggles, and disappointments, and compromises of this other saint who faced the most thankless routine work under a system already rotten to the core. Eudes Rigaud was one of those true heroes who plod on through the discouragements which all men are apt to feel in their own generation, and from which most of us are tempted to escape in day-dreams of the past or of the future. We cannot help admiring poor Rinaldo for throwing off the Lord Bishop to beg round the town in his ragged frock, and presently to lay his weary bones in a grave which the poor folk honoured with their simple faith. But a closer acquaintance with the morals and manners of the 13th century would move most men to far deeper respect for his sturdy brother of Rouen, who laboured for nearly half a lifetime to make the crooked paths straight.

CHAPTER XXIII

Clergy and People.

IT is sometimes tacitly assumed that, however unworthy the clergy of the early 13th century might have been, the Franciscan and Dominican movements soon effected something like a radical reform. Such ideas as this are mainly fostered by a class of writers who read their Franciscan texts only in the light of carefully expurgated Church histories. Father Cuthbert, for instance, has prefaced his translation of Thomas of Eccleston with a long introduction which takes the most medieval licence with the facts of history. He describes (p. 4) the embarrassment caused to the clergy by the growth of urban populations in language almost strong enough to describe the present state of things. Yet the plain fact is that England in the 13th century had nearly 9000 parish churches to four million souls—or only about 450 per parish—and that the towns were, if anything, better off for priests than the country districts. There were of course great inequalities then as now : St. Peter's Mancroft at Norwich contained probably about 3000 souls : and Cæsarius speaks of a specially large parish in Germany which contained 10,000 : though here he probably takes the usual medieval licence with figures. But any attempt to represent the average medieval town parish as over-populated is contradicted by the most elementary facts of economic history : and such descriptions as Father Cuthbert's are simply random exaggerations of the already ultra-enthusiastic picture drawn by Prof. Brewer.[1] St. Bonaventura does indeed complain how great is the harvest and how few the labourers : but the context of this complaint, with its stress on the uselessness of the clergy and the perversity of their flocks, makes it perfectly consistent with the figures above quoted ; especially when it is borne in mind that Italian conditions were definitely worse than French or English in this respect. The saint, as one who both knew the facts and had reason to weigh his words, is our most unexceptionable Italian authority on this subject.[2] "The world," he complains, "seems far worse now than it was of old ": "many (*plures*) clergy weaken the laity both in morals and in faith by their evil example. . . . Very many of the clergy are notoriously unchaste, keeping concubines in their houses or elsewhere, or notoriously sinning here and there with many persons. . . . Simple folk might think that those sins among the clergy were not hateful to God, unless we preached against them; and silly women might think that it was no fault to sin with them; as it is well known that some have been so persuaded by the clergy. . . . Many (*plerique*) of them [cannot hear confessions, since] an honest woman fears to lose her reputation if she whisper secretly with them . . . Again, whereas the late Legate in Germany gave a general sentence of suspension from office and benefice against clergy who solicited nuns of any Order to sin, and of excommunication against all who actually sinned with them . . . it is to be feared that many have come under this sentence." Yet these go on in their parishes as if nothing had happened, and crucify Christ daily afresh: while their confession and absolution are void and their prayers ineffectual, and the parishioners have no right to attend their Masses. Even these, moreover, are only a small proportion of the parish priests who have lost almost all priestly powers, and are therefore worse than useless, deceiving their flocks with hollow ministrations, leaving them in their sins, and involving in their own excommunication those parishioners who ask them for Masses or offer them money.[3] For the unchaste, the illegitimately born, the simoniacal, the pluralists, those who have celebrated in defiance of their suspension—all these numerous clergy have become "irregular" and lost the power of binding and loosing from sin, unless (which is seldom the case) they amend and procure the removal of their disabilities. Moreover, even of those who have the strict right to bind or loose, few are able to use it properly. "There are in Italy so many inexperienced clergy that, even if they be well-taught in grammar and other knowledge, yet where a hundred or more rectors and vicars are gathered together, there are scarcely any (*vix pauci*) who have in fact enough knowledge of the Scriptures to manage either the souls committed to their care, or other things necessary for salvation . . . [The Prelates], given up to temporal cares, wink at these faults, so that there is scarce any hope of amendment: nay, even if at times they would fain correct such shortcomings and remove the unprofitable clergy, they have none better to put in their places." Therefore the Friars themselves are terribly hampered in their ministrations, since they dare not supersede the parish clergy too openly for fear of increasing what

is already the main cause of heresies—the contempt of the flocks
for their pastors. Almost incredibly dark as this picture seems,
it is borne out by the contemporary writers Eudes Rigaud in
France, Berthold of Ratisbon in Germany, and Salimbene in
Italy. Here, for instance, is the latter's report of the Council of
Ravenna in 1261. (403) It had been summoned at the Pope's
bidding to collect money against the invading Tartars: but
the parish clergy refused to contribute until they had discussed
the encroachments of the Friars upon their duties and privileges.
"So the Archbishop began hotly to defend the Friars, saying,
'Wretched madmen! to whom shall I commit the confessions
of layfolk, if the Friars are not to hear them? I cannot with
a safe conscience commit them to you : for if they come to you
seeking balm for their souls, and desiring to confess, ye give them
poison to drink. For ye lead women behind the altar under
pretence of confession, and there ye deal as the sons of Eli dealt
at the door of the tabernacle, which is horrible to relate and
more horrible to do. Therefore doth the Lord complain of you
through the mouth of the prophet Hosea " I have seen a horrible
thing in the house of Israel : these are the fornications of Eph-
raim " : for therefore are ye grieved that the Friars hear confessions since ye would not that they should hear your evil deeds.
Can I commit women's confessions to the priest Gerard here present, when I know well that he has a whole house full of sons and
daughters, and that he might not unfitly be spoken of in the
words of the Psalmist, "Thy children shall be like young
olive trees around thy table"? And would that Gerard were
singular in this matter, and had no partners like unto himself!'
So when the Archbishop had thus spoken his mind, all were
ashamed who were conscious of guilt in this matter." Salimbene
then goes on to record two incidents of which the first, though
told originally by the Bishop within whose experience it happened,
and repeated by Pope Alexander IV to St. Bonaventura, cannot
be reproduced here even in summary. (409) Its moral is the
same as that of this next here following. (411) "I knew
one Brother Umile of Milan, who was *Custode* of the Parma
Custody.[4] One Lententide, when he was dwelling in our convent
of Fano, he was busy in preaching and hearing confessions.
The mountaineers, men and women, hearing this, sent and
prayed him for God's sake and for the salvation of their souls,
to deign to come unto them ; for they would fain confess to him.
So he took a companion and went unto them preaching and
hearing confessions for many days, and working much good
there with his salutary counsels. So one day a certain woman

came to him for confession." It transpired that she had twice been not only invited, but forced to sin by the priests to whom she had come for confession. "He therefore said to her: '*I* have not invited thee to sin, nor will I so invite thee : but rather I invite thee to the joys of Paradise, which the Lord will grant thee if thou love Him and do penance.' So he gave her absolution, and said, 'What meaneth this knife which thou hast in thy hand, at such an hour as this?' She answered, 'Father, in truth I was purposed to stab myself and die in my despair, if ye had invited me to sin as the other priests had done.'" Any reader who cares to follow this subject up should refer to the story of the old canon of Lucca (426). Prof. Michael (p. 75) does Salimbene great injustice in complaining that our chronicler relates so many startling stories in such plain language. One of the worst of those stories (as we have seen) came to him through a Saint and a Pope. It is impossible to get away from such things in facing the real facts of the Middle Ages. So far from being exceptional in its plain speech, Salimbene's chronicle is at least as fit to be put into a girl's hands as many definitely "edifying" books of the Middle Ages. It will bear comparison in this respect with the collections of anecdotes for sermons made by Cardinal Jacques de Vitry, the Dominican Etienne de Bourbon, and the Franciscan Nicole Bozon ; with Bishop Thomas of Chantimpré's edifying treatise *De Apibus*, or with that standard book of religious instruction, the *Gesta Romanorum*. It is decidedly more decent than the manual which the Chevalier de la Tour-Landry wrote for his daughters, and which became at once the most popular educational treatise of the Middle Ages. If Salimbene, in speaking of the clergy of his time, uses language shocking to modern ears, it is because he has to describe a state of things entirely foreign to modern experience.* For indeed all thirteenth century writers who take their readers into their confidence speak practically with the same voice about the abuse of the Sacrament of Penitence. They show us the confessional treated as a farce on the one hand, or used for blackmail and seduction on the other : moreover, even the well-meaning "groper of consciences" would sometimes put into innocent

---

* The fullest evidence on this subject may be found in Dr. Lea's *Confession*, vol. i, p. 382, and *Celibacy*, pp. 350, 566, 632. Some who cannot deny the accuracy of Dr. Lea's quotations accuse him of playing the part of "the man with the muck-rake : " but readers who have gone over a good deal of the same ground in original authorities will only wonder at his moderation and self-restraint. He might have quoted indefinitely more to the same effect, but has rightly judged it useless to multiply evidence which is already absolutely conclusive to any open mind.

minds ideas hitherto undreamt of, yet henceforth never to be forgotten, as Cæsarius (for instance) complains. Nowadays, when confession is practised by only a fraction of the population, under the eye of unsympathetic critics and with hitherto unknown guarantees for publicity, the system is no doubt comparatively free from those worst scandals which were the despair of good Churchmen in the 13th century.[5] No apologist has ever dared to grapple at close quarters with the evidence brought forward thirty-eight years ago by Dr. Lea ; yet still the ordinary public has only a faint conception of the actual facts; and modern Englishmen have reason to be proud that their countrymen are so slow to realize abominations which haunted the saints of the Middle Ages like a nightmare. Moreover, it is necessary to protest against the mischievous modern plea that most of these clerical connexions were virtual, though not legal, marriages. Even if this were true, what religious denomination could hold up its head in any civilized country of to-day, if a large proportion of its clergy, (to suggest a very mild parallel,) habitually broke the law by marrying their deceased wives' sisters ? But the plea itself contains only a very small grain of truth, even if we consider 13th century England and Germany alone, where the clergy fought so hard for their ancient rights. On every side we have evidence that the tie was necessarily furtive, scandalous, and precarious. The Register of Salimbene's friend Eudes Rigaud, which gives us the very names of the worst clerical offenders in the diocese of Rouen between 1248 and 1261, shows us that scarcely any of these connexions can possibly have borne the character even of an informal marriage. Many of them were multiple : some even incestuous. None of the evidence packed into Dr. Lea's 650 learned pages—accurate as it is reluctantly allowed to be even by hostile critics—has the same quiet force as this diary in which the saintly Eudes wrote down sadly, from day to day, the results of his visitations. In very few dioceses in Europe can the conditions have been so favourable as in that of Rouen : yet here we find, at the first visitation, 18 per cent of the parishes possessing, *to the Archbishop's knowledge*, drunken or concubinary priests. Worse still, it was difficult to remove even these, and dangerous in many ways—for what security had the Archbishop for those who might take their places ? True, the offenders were *ipso facto* excommunicate : but they went on deluding their flocks with sacraments and services of which many were invalid in Canon Law : and even this very exceptionally strong prelate was almost powerless against the dead weight of their resistance. As his contemporary Bourbon put it, the clergy

cared more for a fine of a few shillings than for their bishop's
sentence of excommunication : and, later on, the University of
Oxford was driven to the same sad confession.[6]

Not half a century after St. Francis's death, it was already
impossible for the Friars to imitate him in kissing a priest's hand
as a rebuke to others who accused their pastor of immorality.
These few years had made it quite plain that, if the Friars were
ever to reform the Church, it must be in spite of the parish priests.
St. Bonaventura, as we have seen, was driven to speak of them
in terms which might well seem too violent in the mouth of a
modern Protestant : and I will here conclude with Salimbene's
racier, though not more damning, evidence. (425) "I have
found some priests lending out their money to usury and en-
riching themselves merely for the sake of their bastards : again,
I have found others keeping taverns, with the sign of the hoop,[7]
and selling wine, and their whole house full of bastard children,
and spending their nights in sin, and celebrating Mass next day.
And when the people communicate, they thrust the consecrated
hosts which remain over into clefts of the wall : though these
are the very body of our Lord. And many other foul things
they do and horrible to be told, which I pass over for brevity's
sake. They keep their missals, corporals, and church ornaments
in an indecent state—coarse, black, and stained : tiny chalices
of tarnished pewter ; rough country wine, or vinegar, for the
Mass. The hosts they consecrate are so little as scarce to be
seen betwixt their fingers—not circular, but square, and all
filthy with the excrements of flies.* Many women have better
shoe-bands than the cincture, stole, and maniple of many priests,
as I have seen with mine own eyes. One day when a Franciscan
friar had to celebrate Mass in a certain priest's church on a feast-
day, he had no stole but the girdle of the priest's concubine, with
the bunch of keys attached : and when the friar (whom I knew
well) turned round to say ' *Dominus vobiscum*,' the people heard
the jingling of the keys. (425). Am I then to preach for
tithes on these men's behalf ? or shall I for their sake abstain
from celebrating Mass in our convents, that they may the easier
get offerings to spend in this fashion ?   God forbid, God forbid ! "
And he quotes the evidence of the so-called *Devil's Letter*, which
was commonly believed in the Middle Ages. (419) " Certain it is
that, before the Friars Minor and Preachers had appeared in the
world, when the secular clergy and prelates were gathered to-

---

* Cf. *Mirror of Perfection*, chaps. 56 and 65, where Leo describes how St.
Francis used to carry a broom to sweep dirty churches, and tried to teach
priests to treat the consecrated host with more reverence.

gether at a synod, letters were thrown into their midst couched in
these terms : ' The Princes of darkness to the Prelates of the
churches, greeting. We give you abundant thanks, for that all the
souls committed to you are transmitted to us.' "8

Moreover, many of the parish clergy were as ignorant as they
were idle and immoral. Roger Bacon, casting about for an
illustration of parrot-learning which would at once be understood
by his hearers, wrote " just as boys gabble through the psalter
which they have learnt ; and as clerks and country priests recite
the Church services (of which they know little or nothing) like
brute beasts." St. Thomas Aquinas, St. Bonaventura, Cæsarius
of Heisterbach, St. Bernardino, St. Catharine of Siena, and
Sacchetti made similar complaints, which were echoed in many
great church councils during the times of St. Francis and Dante.
At two English synods, in 1222 and 1237, it was enacted, " Let
the Archdeacons see that the priests can rightly pronounce at least
the formula of consecration [in the Mass] and that of baptism,
and that they clearly understand the meaning of these two formulas."   The modern reader may well stagger at the abyss of ignorance revealed by these injunctions, and hesitate to press them to
their legitimate conclusion without further evidence. But we have
such evidence in abundance. For instance, the Salisbury Register
of St. Osmund, under the year 1222, contains a record of the examination to which a number of curates were submitted who had
long been serving livings in the gift of the Dean and Chapter.
Five of these men, who had been in priests' Orders for an average of nearly six years, were unable to construe or parse the very
first words of the Canon of the Mass—the most solemn portion
of the whole service, which could be learnt by heart almost in a
single day by a man to whom Latin is really familiar. What is
more, there is no hint of any measures taken to get rid of these
illiterate priests, though the Commissaries did superannuate
another worn-out curate whose toothless jaws mumbled so unin-
telligibly as to make it impossible, (according to Canon Law,)
that he should work the miracle of Transubstantiation. It may
be that curates were often hired for Dean and Chapter livings in
the cheapest market, as was notoriously the case with monastic
churches ; yet even so it is startling to find five such incapables
in seventeen parishes. But the contemporary Register of
Eudes Rigaud records six similar examinations of clergy,
with very similar results. One candidate could not even construe *annuus* : he dimly thought that it meant " often," and
when asked " How often ? " replied " Every day ! " Another,
whom the Archbishop found " unable to read competently or

to construe," promptly gave notice of appeal to the Pope. Johann Busch gives us similar evidence for Germany in the 15th century. Abbot Gasquet's attempts to whitewash English religious education in the later Middle Ages rest, like so many of his other theses, partly on disingenuous suppressions and partly on misquotation of his documents.[9] For, as the clergy were, so were their flocks. Bishop Haymo of Hythe, founding an almhouse in 1337 for the special benefit of men of good position who had come down in the world, made it a *sine qua non* that they should know the Lord's Prayer, the Ave, and the Creed: and we have plenty of evidence to show how necessary this stipulation was. What (for instance) must have been the ignorance of those lay populations to whom their clergy could quote St. Paul broadcast as having counselled Christians to " walk cautiously even if they did not live chastely " ? What was the education of those " many thousands " who, in consequence of the lying persuasions of indulgence-mongers, " falsely believe that they have done penance for all their sins with a penny or a halfpenny, and so go straight to hell? " These are the words of Brother Berthold of Ratisbon, perhaps the greatest popular preacher of the 13th century, of whom Roger Bacon speaks no less enthusiastically than Salimbene : and the testimony of Gascoigne two centuries later is more damning still. The plain proofs of popular ignorance and irreverence, though they have never yet been fairly faced, are bewildering in their multiplicity. The many-sided records of medieval life, public and private, show us the people going in and out as they pleased during Mass ; often coming in only for a moment at the Elevation, and forthwith " running off as if they had not seen Christ but the Devil." Among St. Louis's brief dying instructions to his sons we find " attend the service of Holy Church devoutly and without jesting talk." The knight of La Tour Landry impresses the same on his daughters : and his statement of the strictest theory on this point is eloquent as to the laxer practice of the majority : " sum clerkes susteineth that none shulde not speke no manere thing whiles they bene atte masse, and in especial atte the gospel, nor atte the ' per omnia.' " Silence during the Church services was among the nineteen points of self-denial to which Franciscan Tertiaries were pledged by their statutes. Visitations of great cathedral and collegiate churches record how the canons and vicars walked about during the service, chattered with women in the aisles, or across to each other in the choir, mocked aloud at the officiants, and played childish practical jests, dropping hot wax or snuffings from their candles upon the shaven pates of the

clergy in the stalls below them "to excite ridicule and perhaps
. . . open discord, or at least rancour and spite of heart." These
irreverences had become so ingrained that the Bishop of Angers
complained at the Ecumenical council of Vienne in 1311 "the
clergy of collegiate churches . . . impede and disturb divine
service, to the scandal of many " : and a formal statement to the
same effect was solemnly registered by the Pope in his collection
of Decretals. Moreover, church councils constantly complain
of the indevout way in which the service was gabbled. Benvenuto, in his note on Inf. vii, 125 ff, explains how Dante's
"this hymn they gurgle in their throats" contains a direct
satire upon the clergy : "since priests, whose duty it is to
sing hymns, labour most of all under the vice of *accedia* and
asinine sloth (*asinitatis*) ; wherefore such sluggards, when they
chant divine service, oft-times can scarce move their lips."
Etienne de Bourbon speaks even more strongly : a priest came
back from the dead to say that "an infinite multitude of clerks
and priests" suffered terribly in hell for the words they had
skipped or mumbled in their services. " I have heard " (he goes
on) " that a poor scholar came from Paris and helped a parish
priest to celebrate Mass. When the priest was saying his hours,
he so corrupted the verses that the scholar could not understand
a word, but only the sound : so he for his part began to cry
aloud in imitation of what he had heard in Paris of a workman
crying his wares (even as, for instance, botchers of old clothes cry,
or such as go about seeking old shoes, or muffin-men) ; and the
priest believed him to have said all his responses aright, for he
understood the clerk as little as the clerk understood him—that
is, he heard only the sound of his voice."[10]
    We need hardly wonder, then, that Berthold of Ratisbon
has to complain of ordinary lay folk habitually talking at
Mass "as if they were at market." " Nay, Brother Berthold,
we understand not the Mass," pleads a voice from the congregation. " The sermon indeed we can follow word by word, but
not the Mass : we know not what is being sung or read ; we
cannot comprehend it." The good friar finds the excuse so far
justified, that he spends the rest of his sermon in explaining
roughly the different stages of the ecclesiastical service. St.
Bernardino, again, interrupts one of his sermons with the same
complaint. " Fie on you, ladies ! for in the morning while I am
saying Mass ye make such a noise that I seem to hear a pile of
clattering bones, such a chatter do ye make. One says ' Giovanna ' ! another cries, ' Caterina ' ! and a third, ' Francesca ' !
Oh ! your fine devotion to hear Mass ! To my poor wits, it seems

to be mere confusion, without any devotion or reverence what-soever. Do ye not consider that here we celebrate the glorious body of Christ the Son of God, for your salvation? and that ye should stay so still that none should say a single *hush*! Yet here comes Madonna Pigara, and would fain sit in front of Madonna Sollecita. No more of this: 'first at the mill, first grind.'[11] Take your seats in order as ye come, and let none crowd in before you. And now to my sermon again." His contemporary, Gerson, complains in the same words as Berthold 200 years before: "they talk as if they were at market." Men and women scuffled and fought for precedence not only at the Communion but also at religious processions: such fights not infrequently ended fatally.[12] Apart from war and the name-less vices of the soldiery,[13] even in times of peace the churches were too often neglected by priests and people alike. Parish churches and cathedrals were used as barns; a Devonshire parson even brewed his beer within the sacred walls. If the Reformation had come in the middle of the 13th instead of the 16th century, there would have been comparatively little point in Dr. Jessopp's articles on "the Great Pillage." The separation of the sexes during service, often revived in our own day, was in those days a necessary measure of propriety. The vulgar proverb that "thunderbolts often fall on the church but never on the tavern," is justified by Bourbon on the ground of the profanities and indecencies which went on in God's house: and he is borne out by an anecdote which Wadding quotes.[14] Really devout people, of course, attended Mass daily: but St. Bernardino speaks as if the majority came only on Sundays, and with very scant reverence even then. To communicate every Sunday and holy day was very exceptional, and such superfluous devotion was sometimes strongly discouraged by the parish clergy.[15] Moreover, we get glimpses here and there of the most extraordinary irregularities even in the most ordinary ecclesiastical offices. Sacchetti mentions "a good many" who did not feel certain that they had been baptized, and whom he consoles by assuring them their faith in the fact would be taken by God as equivalent to the fact itself. The ignorant folk were withheld from accepting extreme unction by the grossest superstitions, and in Germany at least by the heavy fee which the clergy demanded for that sacrament. A Constitution of Archbishop Peckham (1281) complains that there were in England "numberless people grown old in evil days who had not yet received the grace of confirmation:" and there is similar evidence on this subject from Germany, Flanders, and

Austria. Yet it must be borne in mind how numerous and powerful the clergy were, what rights the law gave them over almost every part of their parishioners' lives, and how fully they insisted on those rights whenever they were pecuniarily profitable. Indeed, one of the main causes for the general irreverence was the fact that clergy and people were constantly quarrelling about tithes. It was a matter of common complaint that heretics found their strongest justification in the lives of the clergy : as Benvenuto comments on Purg. xvi. 102 : "we see, as a matter of fact, that the people catch vices more readily than virtues from the morals of the priests." Gower bears him out ; and the professor and the satirist are outdone in vehemence by the greatest saint of their time. "It is impossible," writes Mr. E. G. Gardner, "to reject the appalling picture of the corruption of the ministers of the Church that is given us by St. Catherine [of Siena] herself in certain amazing chapters of her *Dialogue*. The saint's own words make it abundantly clear that the lives of the great prelates of the curia and of the humblest parish priests alike were too often such that the fire from heaven, with which Dante and Petrarch had threatened the Cardinals, seemed as though it needs must fall."[16]

It need not surprise us therefore to find that, even in the 13th century, the heretics were often distinguished from the orthodox laity by their avoidance of profane oaths and by their wider religious knowledge. We know this on the testimony of their most determined adversaries. "They know the Apostle's Creed excellently in the vulgar tongue," says Etienne de Bourbon : "they learn by heart the Gospels of the New Testament in the vulgar tongue, and repeat them aloud to each other. . . . I have seen a young cowherd who had dwelt but one year in the house of a Waldensian heretic, yet had attended so diligently and repeated so carefully all that he heard, as to have learned by heart within that year forty Sunday gospels, not counting those for feast-days . . . . and other extracts from sermons and prayers. I have also seen some layfolk who were so steeped in their doctrine that they could even repeat by heart a great part of the Evangelists, as Matthew or Luke, and especially all that is said therein of our Lord's teaching and sayings ; so that they could repeat them continuously with scarce one wrong word here and there. This I say on account of their diligence in evil and the negligence of the Catholics in good ; for many (*plures*) of these latter are so negligent of their own and their families' salvation as scarce to know their Pater or their Creed, or to teach the same to their servants." Berthold of Ratisbon says the same of the Jews, that they knew their Bible better than Christian laymen, and were therefore dangerous adversaries. At the same time, the Church blindly attempted to right herself by suppressing these "heretical" scripture studies, instead of rivalling them by the thoroughness of her own instruction in orthodoxy : and even the enlightened Busch, who would allow the laity some religious books in their mother tongue, disapproved of "such lofty or divine books " as a translation of the Communion service : indeed, finding one in the hands of some nuns, he committed it to the flames. The modern apology that the authorities forbade only *unorthodox* translations of Bibles and religious books is demonstrably false.[17] The Friars had, it is true, brought a real change into religious education : yet even so the world of 1300 was far less in advance of 1200 than both were still behind our present age, with all its grievous shortcomings. The Friars did study the Bible, in the earlier generations at least ; and Salimbene himself is an admirable example. But they did little to spread the knowledge of the actual text among the people, who were fed on glosses and pious embroideries rather than on the plain facts of Bible history. One of the most popular books of this kind, St. Bonaventura's *Hundred Meditations on the Life of Christ*, contains a good twenty per cent. of glosses from the Fathers, or else of sheer romance, based upon the saint's own surmises of what might have happened, or on revelations vouchsafed to "a holy Brother of our Order." In spite of a general warning at the beginning of the book, and several others elsewhere, there is nothing in most cases to mark the transition from Bible fact to pious fancy. The Virgin Mary is constantly brought in as acting and speaking without the least Biblical authority. And the example thus set by one of the first men of the century was naturally followed by others : *e.g.* by the friar who wrote the very pretty but utterly unbiblical romance of the Magdelene, lately translated by Miss Hawtrey. Chaucer's keen eye noted this tendency on the Friars' part. (*Cant. Tales*, D. 1790, 1920). St. Bonaventura's book, apparently, was designed for the immediate use of the clergy, through whom it would filter to the people : but in this indirect process it would be just the extraneous features of these Biblical romances which would catch the hearers' fancy, and stick most surely. At the best, therefore, the great bulk of the people knew the Bible story only with a strong admixture of modern Franciscan notions.[18] Here again Chaucer helps us : his clerk Nicholas, reminding the carpenter of Noah's flood, has no doubt that he will remember the least Biblical feature in that event as conceived in the

later Middle Ages—the refusal of Noah's wife to embark
until she had drunk one more pot of ale with her jolly gossips
ashore. It is true that many of St. Bonaventura's fancies are
really beautiful : but it is difficult to realize nowadays how
inevitably even the most pious fancies ended in hateful falsehoods, among people who had no materials for criticism and
were not permitted free discussion. A single example may
suffice. The legends of the early martyrs had inspired many
generations of Christians ; and the pious enthusiasm with which
each martyrologist would outbid his predecessors in describing
their odour of sanctity and their joy under torments might well
seem harmless or even praiseworthy. Yet these legends, from
the 13th century onwards, served to steel the hearts of naturally
charitable men against the most devilish cruelties practised on
their fellow-Christians. St. James of the Mark, arguing with
those Fraticelli whose faith had originated in loyalty to the
Franciscan tradition, takes it as a plain note of uncatholicity
that their sect does not flourish, like the early Christians, under
the unrelenting persecutions to which it is subjected. Again,
(he argues) when a heretic is burnt the odour of sanctity is entirely wanting : "for instance, when the Pope Nicholas V was at
Fabriano, certain heretics were burned there, and the stench of
them filled the city three days long ; this I know, for I smelt
the evil savour all those three days even in our convent." Etienne
de Bourbon tells a similar story ; and St. Bernardino of Siena
was of the same mind.[19] When we consider in what blind
reliance on this and similar pious figments whole populations have
been exterminated at the bidding of men who thought to do God
service, we may well be thankful that the poorest in our own age
have at any rate some chance of checking mistaken glosses by
comparison with the text to which all Christians nominally appeal
in the last resort.

I am quite aware that much of what I have written in this
chapter will excite strong disapproval in many quarters, and
that in one sense the very strength of my evidence may render it
scarcely credible to modern readers. I would only repeat that
while I have often tried in vain to obtain any real evidence from
apologists of the Middle Ages, I am always ready to discuss this
and similar questions, at my own expense, with any competent
student of medieval history.

CHAPTER XXIV.

Faith.

IF we are to define faith as we define no other virtue, and measure it by its outward manifestation rather than by the inward working of the heart; if we esteem more highly the assent to certain dogmas imposed from without than the soul's own sincere effort to climb to the highest realities within its ken, then no doubt the 13th century was an age of faith compared with ours. But such a definition of faith, which would have made St. Paul's conversion impossible, and left him at best a staunch though tolerant Pharisee, is becoming daily more discredited. It seems strange that it should ever have grown up under the name of Christ, who valued the widow's mite not at its market price but at the rate of the inward effort which had prompted the gift. Measured by its living faith, the 13th century can claim no advantage, to say the least, over the 20th. Again, it is only a superficial view of history which would represent our ancestors as the merely passive recipients of a creed formulated by the Fathers of the church, and made binding on the consciences of the faithful by the decrees of Popes and Councils. On the contrary, many of the most distinctive tenets of Romanism grew up *from below*, and were only accepted later on by Priests and Bishops, Doctors of the Church and Popes. In many matters, of course, Dante's ideas are far in advance of the current religion of his age ; and in no matter more definitely than in his conception of purgatory as a place where the soul is conscious of its own happy growth in peace of mind as in fitness to appear before God. But many other elements of that religion which Dante learned first at his mother's knee, and could never seriously question in after life, had been born among the ignorant. Thence they had risen and spread slowly from generation to generation, until at last they had been brought into some sort of harmony with scripture and reason by Schoolmen who themselves also had sucked these doctrines in with their mother's milk. Since the times when Christianity first became a great world-creed, the mass of the faithful had never been really imbued with a knowledge of the New Testament : and they had retained, with or without sacerdotal permission, much of their old heathenism. Origen, writing about 230 A.D. to rebut the arguments of the philosopher Celsus, laughs at the learned pagan for contending that he can raise his mind to the Unseen by gazing at or praying to a statue ; he shames him by explaining how " a Christian, however unlearned, is persuaded that every corner of the world is a part of God's whole temple ; so that he prays everywhere with his bodily eyes closed, and, raising his spiritual eyes, soars in contemplation above the whole universe."[1] Little by little, however, the practice of image-worship crept in ; it was definitely legalized in 787, after a long struggle, by the 2nd Council of Nicaea ; and in the later Middle Ages Christians were burned for maintaining a doctrine which one of the greatest of the Fathers had described as notorious even among the most unlearned. We see the same process, to the very end of the 13th century, in the canonization of saints, in spite of a Bull of 1181 which claimed the right exclusively for Popes.[2] John of Parma is only one of hundreds who were worshipped without leave from the Pope—often without any leave at all. In each case it is the same story. The cult began among the people and lower clergy : the Bishops were gradually forced to take notice of it : by this time it was already an ineradicable part of popular religion, and the Pope had little choice but to sanction it. Or, as in many cases of very respectable cults which still survive, there was no papal sanction of any kind, until the Bull of 1675 granted a prescriptive right of existence to all worships, however little proof of authority they could show, which had enjoyed a continuous existence of 200 years. The feast of Corpus Christi, one of the most solemn and striking of all in the modern Roman Church, grew up entirely from below. It was first suggested by a visionary girl : the Office was composed by a young unlearned priest : but the worship caught like wild-fire among the people, and at last forced itself through all obstacles into recognition by Prelates and Popes.[3] The dogma of the Immaculate Conception was reprobated by St. Bernard, and formed no part of Dante's theology. It was consistently opposed throughout the Middle Ages by the Dominicans, the most learned Order in the Church : but the Franciscans, strong in the popular support, at last carried the day. Practically all the differences between Dante's creed and St. Paul's had originated thus in the popular imagination : and Salimbene better than most men shows us that imagination at work. He gives more than one admirable example of popular canonization : and his descriptions are corroborated by other con-

temporaries. (501) " In this same year 1279 appeared the cozening miracles of a certain Alberto who dwelt at Cremona. This
man was a wine-porter, loving the wine-pot, and living in sin ; *
after whose death, as men said, God wrought many miracles in
Cremona, Parma, and Reggio. In Reggio He wrought them in
the church of St. George and of the Blessed John the Baptist,
in Parma in the church of St. Peter, which is by the Piazza
Nuova, where all the wine-porters of the city were gathered
together ; and blessed was the man or woman who could touch
[his relics,] or give anything of his own. And they made
gilds in divers quarters of the town, and went out into the
streets and squares to gather together in pairs and walk in
procession to the church of St. Peter, where the relics of that
Alberto were kept. They bore crosses and banners, and
chanted as they went, and gave purple and samite and brocade
of Bagdad, and much money ; all which the wine-porters divided
among themselves, and kept to their own use. So the parish
priests, seeing this, caused this Alberto to be portrayed in their
own churches, that they might the easier obtain offerings from
the people. And not only in the churches was his likeness
painted in those days, but even on many walls and porticoes
of the cities and villages or country towns. Yet this is known
to be directly against the statutes of the Church, for no man's
relics may be held in reverence except they be first approved by
the Church of Rome, and written in the catalogue of the Saints.
Nor may any man be portrayed anywhere as a Saint except his
canonization be first published by the Church. Wherefore the
Bishops who suffered such abuses to be done in their dioceses or
under their rule would deserve to be removed from their bishoprics, and wholly deprived of their dignity. Yet he who was
absent from this solemnity was held for an heretic, and envious ;
and the seculars would say loudly and audibly to the Friars
Minor and Preachers ' Ye think that none can do miracles except
your own Saints : but ye are much deceived, as may be seen
now in this man.' But God swiftly purged this reproach
from His servants and friends by showing forth the lying men
who had espoused them, and punishing those who laid a blot
on the elect. For some came from Cremona claiming to have
brought relics of this Saint Alberto, namely, the little toe
of his right foot ; so that all the men of Parma were gathered
together, from the least even unto the greatest ; men and
women, young men and maidens, old men and youths, clerks
and laymen, and all the men of Religion : and in solemn pro-

---

* *Vini portator simul et potator nec non et peccator.*

cession, with many chants, they bore that toe to the cathedral church, which is dedicated to the glorious Virgin. When therefore the aforesaid toe had been laid on the high altar, there came the Lord Anselmo di Sanvitale, canon of the cathedral church and at one time vicar to the Bishop, and kissed the relic. Whereupon becoming aware of a savour (or rather, a stench) of garlic, he made it known to the other clergy, who themselves also saw that they were both deceived and confounded; for they found therein nought but a clove of garlic. And so the men of Parma were despised and mocked, for that they had walked 'after vanity, and become vain.' Wherefore the sinner or the sick man errs greatly who leaves famous Saints, and turns to call on one who cannot be heard. Note now and diligently consider that, as the men of Cremona and Parma and Reggio wrought folly of late with their *brentadore* Alberto, even so do the Paduans work folly with one Antonio a pilgrim, and the men of Ferrara with a certain Armanno Punzilovo: but the Lord came also truly in the blessed Francis and the blessed Anthony and St. Dominic and in their sons, in whom sinners should believe. Now this devotion to the false Saint had its origin in many reasons : among the sick, because they sought to be healed ; among the curious, because they desired to see new things ; among the clergy, on account of the envy which they have to modern men of Religion [*i.e.* the new Orders of Friars] ; among the Bishops and Canons on account of the gains thereby accruing to them, as is plain in the matter of the Bishop of Ferrara and his canons, who gained much by occasion of Armanno Punzilovo. Also [the devotion] grew among those who, having been driven from their cities for their adherence to the Emperor's party, hoped through these miracles of new saints to make peace with their fellow-citizens, whereby they might be brought back into possession of their earthly goods, and no longer wander homeless through the world." The contemporary author of the *Chronicon Parmense* gives Alberto a better character, and seems rather more inclined to believe in his miracles. He describes the Piazza outside the church of St. Peter as encumbered with booths, in which the sick lay ; and tells how a great part of the offerings to the new saint were devoted to the building of a hospital. Of Armanno Punzilovo we only know that, after he had been worshipped for thirty years, the inquisitors found him to have been a seducer and a heretic : whereupon his corpse was torn from its shrine and burned.[4] A still stranger case of the same sort happened in these days at Milan, though Salimbene does not mention it. A woman named Guglielma passed during her lifetime for an Incarnation of the Holy Ghost. She was worshipped for some years specially by people of the wealthy class, under the direct patronage of the Cistercian monks and without opposition from the Archbishop, until the matter was taken up by the Inquisition. The reader may have been struck by the serious failings which Salimbene attributes to these objects of popular worship in his time ; but moral excellence, though undoubtedly an advantage, was by no means a *sine qua non* in these cases. One of the scandalous cases quoted by Guibert of Nogent is that of an abbot whose claims to sanctity, under investigation, reduced themselves to this : that he had fallen down a well in a state of intoxication and so perished. Canonization, again, was one of the regular forms of popular protest in purely political quarrels : there was a constant stream of pilgrims to the tombs of Simon de Montfort, of King Henry VI, and even of the selfish and despicable Thomas of Lancaster, who worked far more miracles than many of his betters. While the soul of Martin IV was expiating in Dante's purgatory those surfeits of Bolsena eels and Vernaccia wine, his body was busily working miracles on earth. So also did the body of Gregory IX, a far more remarkable Pope, though he was believed by many to have had an illegitimate son, and certainly did more than any other Pope of the 13th century to degrade the first Franciscan ideal.

The wine-bibbing wine-porter at Parma, and the Incarnation of the Holy Ghost at Milan, were in the fresh bloom of their saintship on the day on which Dante first spoke to Beatrice : and Sacchetti shows us a similar picture after the poet's death. There was a strong popular movement to canonize Urban V, whose life contrasted favourably with that of most XIV Century Popes.[5] Sacchetti, writing to a friend in 1365, does not stick at calling it sheer idolatry. He complains that, in the great Baptistery of Florence—Dante's *bel San Giovanni*—the brand-new image of this unauthorized saintling " had before it a lighted wax torch of two pounds' weight, while the Crucifix hard by had but a mean penny taper. . . . If a man were new come into the world, without knowledge of divine things, and if we told him ' One of these two is the King of Everlasting Life ; ' then, considering the painting and the light, he must needs have believed that Pope Urban was He. . . . The cause of this is in the clergy, who consent to these things in their avarice, to make men draw to them. . . . You tell me how Marquis Ghino Cittadella once said that these new-fangled saints made him lose faith in the old. Are not this nobleman's words indeed true ?

and who is to assure us that there are not many (*assai*) who surmise that other saints began in this fashion, first with mere rays round their head and 'Beato' on the label under their feet; until in process of time the rays have become a halo, and the Beato a Saint? How can we believe in our priests, when they raise on high the bodies of these Beati, setting lights and waxen images round them, while our Lord and the Virgin Mother are portrayed in the gloom, almost on the level of the ground, and without a single light? . . . . The Friars Minor of Florence have the bodies of St. Bartolommeo Pucci and St. Gerard of Villamagna and Santa Umiliana de' Cerchi, who have passed from Beati to Saints; and are all honoured with many tapers, while our Lord and the Apostles, and even St. Francis, have none. And the Friars Preachers have the blessed Giovanna . . . . and the blessed Villana, a girl who dwelt in Florence, hard by mine own house, and who went about clothed like other folk; and now they make much of her, and St. Dominic stands aside." So also with the other friars: brand-new saints have almost driven St. Augustine and St. Benedict out of mind. As to the Santo Volto of Lucca, no man knows its history, and the most miraculous thing about it is its hideousness: two holy friars have preached openly against its worship.[6] Nor are the miracles less doubtful: a blind friend of Sacchetti's pressed into the crowd to touch one of these new saints, and came out as blind as he went, but with his nose cleft almost in half: a peasant returning from the same saint found that he had only lost his purse. "I have no space to tell how wide this error is spread in our days, solely because it brings grist to some men's mills. And the Pope pays no attention: he has greater things to do. . . . How many changes have there been, in my city of Florence alone, in the figure of our Lady! There was a time when all flocked to Santa Maria da Cigoli: then it was Santa Maria della Selva: then grew up the fame of Santa Maria in Pruneta: then Santa Maria Primeriana at Fiesole: then our Lady of Or San Michele: then all these were left in the lurch, all flock now after La Nunziata de' Serri, round whom so many images have been hung, one way or another, that if the walls had not been bound with chains of late, they bade fair to fall flat to the ground, roof and all. . . . And so our folk are clear of sin, God knows how, as though our Lady had more might to work graces in one place than in another!'"

This then was what men of learning and ability said to each other in 14th century Florence. But in Salimbene's Lombardy of a century earlier it was easier to keep some belief in these new saints—at any rate, in those of one's own Order or party. Salimbene seems as naïvely delighted as Charles of Anjou at the discovery of a fresh body of "the Magdalene, whole save for one leg" near Aix in Provence (520) "where I dwelt in the year when the King of France went on his Crusade, for I was of the convent there. When this body was found, her epitaph could scarce be read with a crystal glass, for the antiquity of the writing. And it pleased King Charles that the body should be displayed abroad and exalted and honoured, and that a solemn feast should be made in her honour. And so it was: wherefore the contentions and contradictions and cavils and abuses and falsehoods which were of old concerning her body are henceforth ended. For the men of Sinigaglia had formerly claimed to possess it, and the men of Vézelay had it likewise, as they said, and had even a legend thereof: but it is manifest that the body of the same woman cannot be in three places. (For this same cause there is a bitter quarrel at Ravenna concerning the body of St. Apollinare, for the men of Chiassi, which was once a city, say that they possess it: and the citizens of Ravenna claim to possess it too.) Now the Magdalene's cave, wherein she did penitence thirty years,[7] is five miles distant from Marseilles, and I slept there one night immediately after her feast. It is in a high rocky mountain, and great enough, if I remember well, to contain a thousand men. There are three altars and a dropping well of water like unto the well of Siloa, and a most fair road to it, and without is a church hard by the cave, where dwells a priest; and above the cave the mountain is as high again as the height of the Baptistery of Parma, and the cave itself is so far raised above the level ground that three towers like that of the Asinelli of Bologna could not reach it, if I remember aright: so that great trees which grow below show like nettles or bushes of sage; and since this region is utterly uninhabited and desolate, therefore the women and noble ladies of Marseilles when they come thither for devotion's sake bring with them asses laden with bread and wine, and pasties and fish, and such other meats as they desire. Here then is a miracle for the confirmation of the Invention of the Magdalene's body; which miracle the Lord showed through her to prove that it is hers indeed. In those days a young butcher was going upon the road, and an acquaintance asked him whence he came. He answered, 'From the town of St. Maximin, where the body of the blessed Mary Magdalene has been newly found; and I kissed her leg.' The other answered, 'Thou hast kissed no leg of hers, but rather the leg of an ass or a mare, which the clergy show to the simple for lucre's sake.' When therefore a great contention had arisen between these two concerning this matter, the undevout man who believed not in the Magdalene smote the devout man with many blows of his sword, yet he with the Magdalene's help took no hurt. Then he who was devoted to the Magdalene smote the undevout man but once, and there needed no more ; for he straightway lost his life and found his death. So the champion of the Magdalene, grieving that he had slain a man, even in self-defence, and fearing to be taken by the kinsfolk of the deceased, fled to the city of Arles and thence to St.-Gilles, that he might be safe there, and give place unto wrath. But the father of the slain man, by a bribe to a traitor, caused the slayer of his son to be cast into prison, for he was already condemned to be hanged. Yet in the night before his execution, as he lay awake in his cell, the Magdalene appeared to him and said, 'Fear not, my servant, defender and champion of mine honour, for thou shalt not die : I will help thee in due time, that all men who see may marvel and give thanks to God our Creator, Who worketh marvels, and to me, His servant. But when thou shalt be free, remember this kindness that I have done thee, and give the reward of this good fortune to God thy liberator, to the benefit of thine own soul.' With these words the Magdalene disappeared, and left the man comforted. Next day, when he was hanged on the gallows, yet his body felt neither harm nor pain ; and suddenly, in the sight of all who had come to see, there flew swiftly down from heaven a dove, dazzling white as snow, and alighted on the gallows, and loosed the knot round the neck of the hanged man, its own devotee, and laid him on the earth wholly unhurt. But when the officials and men of justice, at the instigation of the dead man's relatives, would have hanged him again, he escaped by the goodwill of the butchers, of whom a very great band was there, ready armed with swords and staves ; for he had been their comrade and friend, and they had also seen this stupendous miracle. Therefore when he had told all men how he had slain the man unwillingly to defend his own life and the Magdalene's honour, and how the Saint had promised him in his dungeon that she would free him when the time came, then they held themselves satisfied, and praised God and the blessed Magdalene who had freed him. And the Count of Provence, hearing these things, desired to see the man and to hear it from his own lips, and to keep him about his person at the court all the days of his life. Yet he answered that if any should offer him the lordship of the whole world he would not end his life anywhere but in the service of the Magdalene, in the town of St. Maximin, in the place wherein her body was newly found in this year 1283."

While entirely agreeing with Salimbene that the Magdalene's body could hardly be in three places at once, we may well decline to accept the butcher's evidence as conclusive. This saint is indeed one of the most ubiquitous and elusive of the whole calendar. Vincent of Beauvais describes her translation from Aix to Vézelay in A.D. 746 : though even then some men claimed that she was at Ephesus. In 898 her body was at Constantinople : in 1146 it was at Vézelay. In 1254 St. Louis went and worshipped it at Ste-Baume, which is the first hint we get of her ever having been in Provence. In 1267, again, the saintly king showed his impartiality by assisting in state at the solemn translation of the rival corpse of Vézelay, and dividing some fragments of the relics with the Papal Legate. In 1281, that Legate, now Pope Martin IV, gave to the Cathedral of Sens a rib from the Vézelay corpse, and declared in his accompanying Bull that this was the genuine body. Rome had spoken, and the dispute was for the moment nominally settled : yet here, only two years later, we find the Pope's particular friend Charles of Anjou ostentatiously patronizing the rival corpse ; and Salimbene, writing a year later again, imagines that the claims of Vézelay and Sinigaglia are dead for ever ! No doubt the perplexed faithful consoled themselves as Sir John Maundeville did for the similar multiplication of St. John's head : " I know not which is true, but God knows ; but however men worship it, the blessed John is satisfied."[8]

This is not the place to treat fully of 13th century infidelity : but its prevalence may be established by details as manifold and as startling as those which I have briefly summarized to indicate the prevailing ignorance and irreverence. Apart from noble ruffians like Alberigo and Nero da Leccaterra, who had apparently just enough belief in God's existence to lend point to their obscene blasphemies, four definite kinds of unbelief may be traced. There was the learned scepticism of the universities and of Frederick's court, well described in Renan's *Averroës* : and the scoffing scepticism of the rich and self-indulgent, conspicuous in *Piers Plowman* and in Sacchetti's *Sermons*. Again, a certain fatalism and semi-Mahomedanism was brought home from the Crusades : and the failure of these holy wars provoked, as we have seen, an explosion of popular infidelity throughout Europe. Lastly, there was the involuntary scepticism of the pious and faithful soul : a state of mind which is often ignorantly spoken of as purely modern. Joinville has recorded a stock instance of this : Franciscan and Dominican writers are full of similar indications, from St. Bonaventura downwards. Female saints were specially tortured with such doubts. Gerson wrote a long

treatise on the subject : but perhaps the most interesting confession comes from his younger contemporary, Johann Busch.[9]
" What temptations I suffered as a novice," (he writes) " and
especially concerning the Catholic faith, God alone knoweth,
from whom nothing is hid. . . . But God Almighty suffered
me to be thus tried, because in later years, taught by experience,
I liberated many who were buffeted with the same temptation."
Indeed the 13th century, which from our modern distance seems
at first sight to swim in one haze of Fra Angelico blue, shows to
the telescope its full share of barren sand and pestilent marsh.
Sensitive souls struggled then too for their faith, with an agony
that was often bitterest before the very altar and in the presence
of what should have been to them the bodily flesh and blood of
the Redeemer.   The duties to temporal and spiritual powers
were generally·in hopeless conflict : or, within the strictly religious
domain, a man had often no alternative but to disobey flatly
either his Bishop or his Pope.   His parish priest might well be
one with whom no honest woman dared be seen to whisper ; if
he wished to call in the friars instead, that right was frequently
denied him ; nor could he be certain that the friar himself was
such as we expect all clergy to be in the present century.   He
risked worshipping a villain as a saint, and saw the saints themselves often receiving less hearty recognition than in these days
of open unorthodoxy.

For an age must be judged not only by the few remarkable men
it produces, but still more by the attitude of the rest of the world
towards these men.   It is of course far easier to ticket a period
with just a dozen names—for even a great age produces no great
number of first-rate men—and to judge it accordingly.   But we
do not stop at the fact that St. Paul and the other apostles were
Jews of a certain generation : we ask further, " How did their
own generation accept their persons or their teaching ? "   Why
then should we be asked to stop at the fact that a certain century
produced Innocent III and St. Francis, Dante and Aquinas ?
Innocent was believed by some of his time to have barely escaped
damnation, and was often criticized with the greatest freedom
in his own Church.   St. Francis and his early missionaries were
treated by many who misunderstood them with a brutality from
which modern England impartially protects expelled monks from
France and Jews from Russia.   Florence was a true Nazareth to
Dante ; she would have burned him alive if she could have taken
him : and his *De Monarchia* was indeed burned as heretical by the
Papal Legate eight years after his death.   Aquinas's family tried
to prevent his becoming a Dominican and a Saint by foul and

barbarous means scarcely credible to us. He was finally poisoned (so at least Dante believed) by the King who had been the special creation and particular champion of the Church ; and within a few years of his death some of his doctrines were solemnly condemned at Paris and at Oxford. A greater intellect than Aquinas, Roger Bacon, was all but quenched in prison, and it is only by a miracle that we possess his writings. There was widespread disbelief in the Stigmata of St. Francis even towards the end of his own century. Bernard of Quintavalle, his first disciple, was hunted from forest to forest like a wild beast by the 'relaxed' Franciscans : Cæsarius of Spires, another of his truest disciples, was murdered by his conventual gaoler. St. Bonaventura is one of the most heartily abused men in the *Fioretti*. The greatest perhaps of the Franciscan Generals, John of Parma, narrowly escaped imprisonment for life ; while Raymond Gaufridi, his only successor who dared to take the side of the Spirituals, was poisoned.* So was Henry of Luxemburg, the one Emperor of the age whom Dante thought not unworthy of the throne ; so also was Kilwardby, one of the most efficient Archbishops of Canterbury. The great English prelates of the century were indeed peculiarly unfortunate. St. Edmund Rich died in exile, equally unable to tolerate or to reform that Henry III who, of all our English kings, was most after the Pope's own heart. St. Richard of Chichester, when first elected Bishop, was ignominiously rejected. St. Thomas Cantilupe was excommunicated by the no less saintly Peckham, who himself was on such bad terms with our great Edward I, that he retained his canonry at Lyons as a refuge in case of exile. Grosseteste's whole life was one long struggle with the powers of evil in high or low places ; and he died in bitterness of heart. Prominent in the lives of 13th and 14th century saints are the persecutions they endured at home, and the continued distrust even of their spiritual advisers. St. Louis, who was a great king as well as a real saint, could not escape even in his own chamber from the lords who cursed and called him nicknames in the antechamber.[10] It is far safer and more comfortable to be a good Roman Catholic in modern England than it was in Dante's Italy. Of most generations it may be said that they build the tombs of their prophets : but when we are inclined to doubt of our own age, let us remember that few centuries have been more ungrateful to their best men than the Thirteenth.

* Accusations of poison are so common in the Middle Ages that one can never in any particular case assert more than a probable suspicion : but the extreme frequency of these suspicions is in itself most significant.

CHAPTER XXV.

Believing and Trembling.

THERE is one side of Franciscan life which comes out less clearly in Salimbene's story than in other documents : for his was a naturally happy disposition. Many men and women of our own times whose backs are bowed under the burden of spiritual self-reliance, with its possible contingencies of doubt and mental agony—to whom God seems too distant and unapproachable without constant help from visible mediators—many such are attracted to a Church which promises an end of struggles and uncertainties. This promise may be more or less true in the case of modern Romanism, with its definite limitations, its mechanical completeness on the surface, and the ever-watchful discipline with which it represses attempts to pierce below the surface. Under the present free competition, a religion like this tends more and more to attract a certain type of mind in proportion as it repels other types : so that the Church which promises certainty without the pain of enquiry becomes more and more the Church of those who do not even wish to enquire. But in the 13th century the Church included *all* minds, except that small minority which was ready to risk the loss of friends, fortune, and life for the sake of an unpopular idea. It was therefore a living and growing Church in a sense very different to that of modern Romanism :—a Church in which Dante could write without misgiving " In religion, God cares for nought of us but the heart." And the individual soul, like the Church of which it was a part, had its own growing-pains, far more nearly resembling those of our own century than most men imagine. Even among laymen, sensitive minds were distracted by constant conflicts among their spiritual teachers. Dante had no doubt (though here he was probably wrong) that Pope Anastasius was a heretic. The heresy of Pope Honorius was openly proclaimed in the Breviary itself. St. James of the Mark, as we have seen, could only congratulate himself that at any rate no two *consecutive* Pontiffs have ever been heretical, and that God will never impute the guilt of such papal heresies to the flocks who follow them in ignorance. Men's faith was perplexed on all sides by visions and miracles often proved to be false; and the friar in his cell, so far from escaping these spiritual trials, was frequently tortured tenfold: the early legends show us glimpses of a veritable religious Inferno. The greatest saints had often the bitterest struggles: first with their own family and the World: then with religious doubts; then with unsympathetic superiors and companions even in religion; lastly with devils on their death-bed. For we need to realise that, if the 13th century looked far oftener than ours for the visible and tangible presence of God, yet it also realized with even disproportionate vividness the omnipresence of the Devil. Flashes of blinding spiritual light alternated with a horror of great darkness. Much of what is most harsh and repulsive in early Protestantism is a direct legacy of this medieval Satanology. Many of the best minds of the Middle Ages suffered Bunyan's own agonies of mind on the subject of Predestination. The *Fioretti* tells us how this despair tortured Ruffino, one of the Three Companions, in the very presence of St. Francis. Giles, a greater name still in the annals of the Order, was so buffeted of Satan that "he was wont to say with a sigh as he returned to his cell in the evening, 'Now I await my martyrdom.'" It was the penalty of the constant preponder-ance of sentiment over reason in the religion of the time, just as numb and weary doubts are the nemesis now of a reason which tyrannizes over sentiment. The early friars encouraged even the most hysterical manifestations. The gift of tears in prayer was especially coveted; and the blessed Umiliana, lacking these for a time, nearly blinded herself by trying to recall them artificially with quicklime. Visions and ecstasies were infectious; sensual enjoyments of taste, of smell, of touch were eagerly sought and highly prized in religion. Words of prayer would leave a literal taste of honey in the mouth or a smell of incense in the nostrils: again, the ecstasy of devotion would take more violent forms which seemed perilous even to the en-thusiastic David of Augsburg, and are altogether horrible to the modern mind, whether Catholic or Protestant.[1] Indeed, the crazy conceits and vain self-torturings recorded in the century from St. Francis to Dante have never been exceeded, and seldom equalled, in other Christian ages. So long as these inventions were not too antisacerdotal or too contrary to the then popular currents of religious thought, there was no extravagance that did not find its admirers and its imitators.

Devils, then, were everywhere plain to the eye of faith in the most ordinary and innocent operations of nature. To St. Edmund Rich, they rode on the thunderstorm and filled the winter twilight like rooks cawing their way home to roost. To St. Dominic, the fiend was incarnate in a wretched sparrow which interrupted his studies and which he therefore plucked alive, exulting in its shrieks. Thousands of devils would besiege one tiny Franciscan hermitage : friars would be seen brandishing their sticks in the air and driving them away like flies. But the fear of the visible devil was not the worst : there was always the horrible suspicion that he might be lurking under the disguise of an angel of light, of the Virgin Mary, of our Lord Himself. Long hours of tender spiritual talk, of rapturous visions, of graces begged and vouch-safed, of ecstasies faint with sweetness, would suddenly reveal themselves as a mere film of bright deceptions concealing the unspeakable abominations of Hell. Salimbene gives us a glimpse of this, though his stories are far less painful than others which might be quoted. He tells (569) of a friar to whom the Devil came habitually in the form of Saints Francis, Anthony, Clare, Agnes, the Virgin Mary, or Christ Himself. These visions promised that he should become Pope ; and he was delighted to think how much good he could then do. He refused, however, to follow certain " devilish and unhonest " suggestions of the Demon, who therefore told him that he had now lost the papacy by his disobedience. This leads Salimbene to tell a string of similar devilish deceptions, by way of warning readers how difficult it was to distinguish between false and true visions. To another Franciscan the Devil appeared in our Lord's shape ; a third was haunted on his deathbed by a demon assuring him that he was damned, and that his daily adoration of the Host at the Mass had been sheer idolatry.[2] Again, Brother Richard of England told Salimbene a strange incident which had happened in his own convent. " A simple and upright friar, fearing God and avoiding evil," dwelt in a hermitage near Naples : and the other Brethren esteemed him so highly that they made no scruple of leaving him at home alone when they went abroad on business. The Devil therefore, in the likeness of an angel, came and told him " thy life is most pleasing in God's sight : so that thou wouldst be altogether like unto His Son (in so far as human frailty permitteth) if thou hadst yet one thing, for lack whereof thou canst not be saved." The one thing lacking was, that he should literally crucify himself : and one day the Brethren found him half-dead, with one hand and both feet nailed to a cross. Salimbene does not tell us the last end of this friar : in the parallel incident, the visionary held impenitently to his own belief, till the discussion was ended by the Devil carrying him off. We might be tempted to dismiss such stories with a laugh, but for their significance as to the frequency of homicidal and suicidal delusions in the cloister ; for the monastic records teem with such stories. As Salimbene puts it, "some by the guile of these devils are persuaded to hang themselves ; others they drive to despair ; others they drown in the waters or dash to pieces from a precipice ; others they cast into the fire, whence they shall pass to where their worm shall not die, and their fire shall not be quenched."[3]

Sometimes indeed the tragedy turns to comedy : for instance, (571) " there was a certain Friar Minor of Provence who had eaten a partridge for his supper, and who then went to sleep. Wherefore that night in his sleep the Devil came and smote him with his fist, so that the Brother awoke in fear, and fell asleep again. Then came the Devil and smote him as before ; and again the Brother fell asleep. Lo then a third time the Devil came and smote him mercilessly with his fist, so that the Brother awaked and cried in fear, ' Ah God ! must I be slain for that I ate a partridge last night ? ' To whom the Devil replied, ' Ye murmur, ye are ungrateful and discontented ; I have taken from you the fruit of your prayers.' And with these words he departed from the friar, who now changed his life for the better : for perchance he had been faulty in those things whereof he was accused by the Devil. Hence we read that the blessed Francis said to his companion, one night when he was smitten of demons at the palace of a certain cardinal : " The demons are our Lord's bailiffs, whom He hath set apart to exercise men. For I believe that God hath suffered His bailiffs to fall upon us because our sojourn at the court of great folk is no good ensample to others.' " There is another charming story of a devil who entered into a peasant and made him talk Latin. " But he tripped in his Latin, whereat our Lector mocked him for his faults of grammar. To whom the demon said, ' I myself can speak Latin as well as thou, but the tongue of this boor is so gross and unhandy of speech, that for very uncouthness I can scarce wield it.' " Our chronicler presently goes on to relate another long and amusing, but very rambling, story about a demoniac peasant who also talked Latin : Miss Macdonell, who has evidently somehow misunderstood it, goes out of her way to found upon it a very unjust accusation of unfriendliness against Salimbene himself.[4]

But it was not always the Devil who got the best of these discussions. A friar of the Mark Tapley type, who was crying aloud the praises of God at a time when such utterances were discouraged as undignified by monastic moralists, "was rebuked by the Devil, who said that this place was neither fitting nor honest for the praise of God. To whom the friar answered and said, 'I am so wont to praise God that I cannot cease therefrom ; for I have learned in the Scriptures that He is everywhere, and should therefore everywhere be praised by His own, even as the Apostle saith "I will therefore that men pray in every place," wherefore even in this base place will I praise God with my mouth. For God abhorreth no uncleanness but the uncleanness of iniquity. But thou, wretch, who wert created to praise God in heaven, hast now lost it by thy pride. Prithee tell me now, wert thou of those who prayed the Lord to send them into the herd of swine ? ' To whom the demon said, 'Why askest thou this ? ' ' Because,' said the friar, 'like cleaveth to like. Thou art a swine, unclean by nature and by name ; thou lovest uncleanness and seekest uncleanness ; for thou wert created to dwell in heaven, and now thou goest from dunghill to dunghill, and spiest out the cesspools.' At which words the devil was ashamed, and departed from him in confusion. For all demons are utterly confounded and put to shame by whatsoever recalleth their lost glory and the present misery which they have brought upon themselves."

Another friar, a friend of Salimbene's, who "made 300 genuflections every night, and fasted daily his whole life long," put a devil to the blush by ridiculing the contrast between his former high place in heaven and his present lurking-place in the body of a miserable harlot. (570) Nor did this discomfited demon mend matters by attempting a diversion. "He paused and listened to a certain young friar who went singing through the convent : then said he to the Brethren who stood by, 'Hear ye that friar who sings as he goes through the house ? He is wholly mine.' So when that friar had come to the place where the demoniac was, the Brethren said unto him, 'This demon saith thou art wholly his.' Then was the Brother ashamed, being conscious within himself of certain faults : and, turning aside from him, he found a priest, to whom he confessed those sins whereof he had greatest remorse of conscience. Then he returned and said again to the demon, 'Tell me, wretch, what have I done that I should be wholly thine ? ' To whom the demon answered, 'A little while ago I knew well ; but now I have forgotten. Yet know thou beforehand, that I have bound such a chain to thy feet as, before forty days are past, shall draw thee out from this Order, and thou shalt go thy way and return to thy vomit.' And it came to pass as the Devil had said. See now the virtue of confession, whereby sins are hidden; for at first the Devil knew, yet after Confession he could know nothing." This anecdote is a very mild specimen of a type which even highly accredited medieval moralists frequently repeat with great gusto. The point is that confession not only annuls the guilt of sin before God, but also justifies the criminal in denying it altogether to his fellow-men: as we are told that, even in modern Ireland, a priest who has confessed and absolved a penitent of political murder will speak of him henceforth in public as "the innocent man."[5]

On the other hand, this casting out of demons had its dangerous side. (572) "A certain clerk named Guglielmo, who dwelt in Parma, was a comely man, strong and of great stature, evil-minded, and a conjuror of demons. So one day when the wife of one Ghidino, a blacksmith, was possessed by a demon, this aforesaid clerk came and began to conjure the demon to depart from her. To whom the demon said, 'I will indeed depart from her, but for thee I will weave such a web that thou shalt nevermore molest me nor drive me forth from my abodes; for know well that I will shortly cause thee to be slain, and thou shalt slay another.' And it came to pass even as he had said; for a few months afterwards, in that same city of Parma, the clerk fell out in a certain courtyard with Ardoino da Chiavari, and they so rushed upon each other that, the strong stumbling against the strong, both fell together. Our chronicler presently goes on to enumerate "the eight perils whereof the Apostle speaketh" (2 Cor. viii, 11, 26), and adds "as Brother Bonaventura the Minister-general said, in his sermons to the Brethren at Bologna whereat I was always present, 'to consent to the temptations and suggestions of demons is as though a man should throw himself from the summit of a most lofty tower, and, when he is fallen half-way, should seek to catch some pole or stake to arrest his fall.'"

These abbreviated quotations give but a faint idea of the place held by the Devil in even a well-balanced imagination of the Middle Ages. Difficulties and temptations change their forms as time goes on: yet then, as now, Christ brought to many souls not peace but a sword. In spite of the elaborate organization of the hierarchy and the theory of the sacraments, every man had still to work his own salvation with fear and trembling: and desperate pangs of conscience were a sign not of reprobation but of grace.

Moreover, as a vigorous soul is never without its struggles, so a vigorous Church has always its sects. Those who are curious to learn how Italy was distracted during this period should consult Dr. Lea's great History of the Inquisition. I have no room

here but for those religious aberrations which came under
Salimbene's own eyes. These all throw—unjust as it would be
to press the comparison too closely—very interesting side-lights
on the beginnings of the Franciscans themselves.

One sect originated indirectly with Salimbene's dear friend
and master, Hugues de Digne. (254) Two laymen, touched by
his preaching, came and begged admission to the Order : but he
refused and put them off with Joachitic parables which they
very naturally misunderstood. " Go into the woods," said Hugh,
" and learn to eat roots, for the Tribulations are at hand." They
took him literally, and formed an order of wild hermits whom the
Franciscans called derisively *Bushmen* (*Boscarioli*), but who
called themselves Friars of the Sack. " They made themselves
striped garments of black and white . . . . then in process of
time they made themselves a frock of sackcloth—not sackcloth
of hair [as in the Apocalypse] but almost of fine linen : and beneath this they had excellent tunics, and at their neck a mantle
of sackcloth, whence they are called Friars of the Sack. And
they caused sandals to be made for them, such as the Friars
Minor have : for all who wish to make some new Rule always
beg somewhat from our Order—either our sandals or our cord or
even our frock. But now we have a papal privilege that no man
shall wear such a habit as might cause him to be taken for a
Friar Minor : for the so-called Britti Friars of the Mark of
Ancona were wont to wear just such an habit : but Pope Alexander IV brought them into one congregation with the Austin
Friars." Meanwhile these friars waxed in numbers and became
indefatigable beggars, to the disgust of the older Mendicants.
" One day the Lady Giuletta degli Adhelardi, a devotee of ours,
seeing these Friars of the Sack begging their bread from door to
door in Modena, said to the Franciscans, ' I tell you truly,
Brethren, we had already so many bags and wallets to empty our
granaries, that this Order of the Sack was not needed.' " Salimbene, therefore, is convinced that Gregory X was divinely
inspired in abolishing the Order, as tending " to weary and
burden Christian folk with the multitude of beggars." He
goes on to explain how the Austin Friars were organized by
Alexander IV, who compelled half-a-dozen sects of begging
Hermits to coalesce into that single Order. Among these were
the Giambonitani, " founded by one Giovanni Bono, who lived
in the days of St. Francis ; his body was buried in my days at
Mantua, and his son I have seen and known, Brother Matthew
of Modena, a fat man." Yet he remarks complacently that
these Austin Friars existed even now only on sufferance, and in

daily peril of disruption. An Austin Friar might possibly have retorted the criticism on the Franciscan Third Order, which was already getting so seriously out of hand that St. Bonaventura seemed to look upon it as a hindrance rather than a help.[6]

The strangest story of all, however, is told on p. 255 ff., with even more than Salimbene's usual superfluity of repetitions and abusive epithets. In or about 1260—the year foretold for Joachim's Reign of the Holy Ghost, and actually marked by the rise of the Flagellants—a new Order arose. It grew up, as usual, among the common people. Salimbene was living in the convent of his native Parma, when one Gerardino Segarello applied for admission and was refused, being "of vile parentage, illiterate and a layman, unlearned and foolish."[7] Nothing daunted, he lingered in their churches, studying how to found a religion of his own. This was of course contrary to the definite decree of the Lateran Council (1215) : but we have seen already how little the decrees of that great Council were regarded. Segarello hit at last upon the idea of imitating our Lord's outward actions even more literally, and with even more scenic effect, than the Franciscans. His first suggestion came from a lamp-cover in their church, embossed with figures of the Apostles "wearing sandals on their feet, and mantles wrapped round their shoulders, according to the ancient traditions among painters." He conformed himself carefully to this model, letting his hair and beard grow, making a mantle of coarse woollen stuff which he threw over his shoulders, and "taking the Franciscan sandals and cord : for whosoever would make a new congregation must needs steal from our Order." Then, selling his house, he took the money and cast it "not to the poor, but to the rabble at play in the piazza, who departed to continue their dicing, and blasphemed the living God in the giver's very ears. He thought to fulfil Christ's counsel : yet Christ said not ' Give to the *rabble* ' but ' Give to the *poor* : ' give to those who praise God, and not to those who blaspheme Him and the virgin mother of Christ, who made the Son of God our brother. Again, wishing to make himself like to the Son of God, he caused himself to be circumcised, which is contrary to the words of the Apostle, (Gal. vi. 15). Moreover, he lay in a cradle wrapped in swaddling-clothes, and sucked milk from the breast of a certain ignorant woman. After that he went to a certain village called Collechio ; and standing in the midst of the road, in his simple folly he cried aloud to the passers-by ' Go ye into my Vineyard.' Such as knew him held him for a madman, knowing that he had there no vineyard : but the hill-folk, who knew him not, entered the vineyard that lay towards his outstretched hand, and ate other men's grapes, thinking themselves bidden thereto by the proper lord. Moreover he spake to none and saluted none, thinking thereby to fulfil that word of Christ's ' Salute no man by the way.' And often would he say the Lord's word ' *Penitenz-agite,*' (for he was too rude and unlearned to say ' *Pœnitentiam agite :* '*) and thus in process of time said his followers for many years, being rustics and unlearned men. If ever he were bidden to dine or to sup or to lodge, he ever answered in doubtful phrase, saying '1 will come or I will not come : ' which was against that word of the Lord ' Let your speech be Yea, yea, No, no.' So when he came to the house of the Brethren Minor, and asked whether this Brother or that were in the house, the porter would answer him scoffingly and derisively, saying ' Either he *is* in the house, or he is *not.*' This is as grammarians teach us, ' In whatever case the question is asked, in that same the answer should be made.' " Salimbene further accuses him of practising an ordeal not infrequent among ignorant enthusiasts in the earlier days of Christianity, but already repugnant to the moral sense of the 13th century.

Gerardino soon had about thirty followers. He called his Order the Apostles : Salimbene can never bring himself to write the name without some scornful addition ; often he parodies the Apocalypse : " They who say that they are Apostles and are not, but are the synagogue of Satan—a congregation of fools and lewd folk, and forerunners of the disciples of Antichrist." The first proselyte had been " a certain servant of the Friars Minor of Parma, Robert by name, who was a disobedient and wayward youth, of whom the Wise Man writeth in Prov. xxix, 19, 21 : whereof a certain tyrant said well ' the race of menials cannot be corrected but by torture.' Gerardino persuaded this servant to leave us and cleave to him : and this was to our great profit, for we got an excellent servant in his place, as it is written in Esaias ' instead of the shrub shall come up the fir-tree, and instead of the nettle shall come up the myrtle-tree.' " He was " like unto Judas Iscariot," not only because " he took away with him the Brethren's knife and cup and napkin, as though they had been his own," but also because he bare the bag of these false Apostles, to his own private profit. For, sad to say, " men and women gave to them more willingly than to us and the Dominicans." Yet this new Order could neither pray for men, nor preach, nor sing masses or other offices : they were merely " a congregation

---

* A.V. " Repent ! " Douay version " Do penance ! "

of rascals and swineherds and false and lewd folk ; of fools and of beastly ribalds,—ignorant as brute beasts—boorish and beastly men," who, like the Gibeonites, had crept in under false pretences among the Lord's chosen people, and deserved to be made mere hewers of wood and drawers of water—nay "*quibus magis incomberet purgare latrinos aut alia vilia opera exercere.*"

They were indeed mere religious tramps, spending their days in idle gossip, and coming back to their common doss-house only to eat and sleep. Salimbene complains bitterly that they actually carried money about with them :—for the Franciscan, though ready to accept any sum whatever through a third person, still carefully abstained from touching it with his own fingers, for Lady Poverty's sake.[8]   He is also shocked at their going about singly, unlike other Religious, who were bound to go about two and two for the avoidance of scandal.   Moreover, they talked and went about freely with women—as indeed St. Francis and the very earliest Brethren had done with St. Clare and her sisters. But "the malice of the times" had long rendered such ideal relations impossible to the Friars ; and Salimbene is all the more angry at the licence of the Apostles : "they run about the city all day beholding women."   Worse still, "they are not in a state of salvation, since some of them keep not the rule of chastity to which all religious Orders are bound : . . . . more-over, trusting to St. Paul's words (1 Cor. ix, 5), these, who believe themselves to be Apostles, led about with them the lady Tripia, sister to Brother Guido Putagio, who was many years their head : and likewise many other women also, who were an occasion of ruin to them.   So that, in literal truth, ribalds and seducers enter in among these Apostles ; and deceivers and robbers and fornicators, committing much folly with women and also with boys, and returning afterwards to their ribaldry." On another point also the Apostles pushed Franciscan ideas to a dangerous extreme.   "They would fain be content with one single tunic, believing this to be commanded them of God. Yet therein they err ; for when the Lord said, 'nor two coats,' He did not understand these words literally, to forbid more than one to such as might be in need, both for the washing away of dirt, and for avoiding harm from cold.   It is plain therefore that the Apostles of Gerardino Segarello are most foolish to be contented with a single tunic.   Moreover, they expose themselves to danger of cold and of grievous illness, or even of death : or again to much wretchedness, both of vermin, which they cannot shake off, and also of sweat and dust and filth.   For they can neither shake nor wash their tunic, unless they would be naked meanwhile. Whence one day a certain woman said scoffingly to two Friars Minor 'Know that an Apostle lieth in my bed at home, where he will remain until his tunic is dry, which I have washed.' The Brethren Minor, hearing this, began to laugh at the woman's folly, and that of the unwise Apostle." Nothing is apt to be more irritating than the exaggerated imitation of our own mannerisms : and though it was counted saintly in one Franciscan that he wore the same garment for thirty years, the same feat seemed merely sordid in an "Apostle." It is interesting, again, that our chronicler should apply to these Apostles the very text which was oftenest quoted against the Friars themselves by their adversaries : "they who creep into houses, and lead captive silly women loaden with sins, who are led away with divers desires : ever learning, and never attaining to the knowledge of the truth."

Salimbene is specially disgusted at these men's ignorance : "These fellows, who say that they are Apostles and are not, have neither book-learning nor mother-wit ; and when they would fain preach without scriptures they busy themselves with goat's wool and the fifth wheel of a waggon,[9] for they speak buffooneries and sow heresies abroad, 'understanding neither the things they say, nor whereof they affirm.' Of whom one may say with the prophet Micah : 'thou shalt sow, but shalt not reap; thou shalt tread the olives but not be anointed with the oil ; and the new wine, but shalt not drink the wine : ' which is to say that these ribalds of Brother Gerardino Segarello, who call themselves Apostles, shall have no reward of their preaching, for they know not what they say : nay, in the words of the Scripture 'they shall sow wind, and reap a whirlwind.'" The reference here to Salimbene's own aureole laid up for him in heaven is unmistakable : and he goes on to reckon up with pardonable complacency his own opportunities of learning, and the use he has made of them. "Forty and six years have I studied unceasingly : and even yet I have not attained to the wisdom of my forefathers. But these so-called Apostles are mere rustics, who ought rather to take the hoe and labour the earth, which crieth far and wide for tillage. In their congregation such men preached as, in our Order would scarce be suffered to wait at our tables, or wash our dishes, or go from door to door for bread." Of this he gives two very amusing instances. "A certain Friar Minor, who had a nephew not yet 15 years old, was causing him to be taught, that he might enter later on into the Order of Friars Minor. This nephew would write out sermons for the Friar his uncle, whereof he learnt four or five by heart : and since we received him not so quickly as he wished, he caused himself to be taken into the Congregation—nay, rather, into the Dispersion—of those who say they are Apostles and are not ; and these also let him preach in Cathedral churches those sermons which he had learnt. Many of these fellows would command silence ; and then would the boy speak to the assembled people. So one day when Brother Bonaventura da Iseo* was preaching at Ferrara in the church of the Friars Minor, he saw some of his hearers rise suddenly and run hastily forth. And he marvelled greatly ; for he was a famous and gracious preacher, whom men were wont to hear gladly, so that none would withdraw from his preaching until it was ended. So he asked why they had left the church in such haste, and the congregation told him ' A little boy of these Apostles is ready to preach in the Cathedral church, where the people is gathered together ; wherefore all are in haste to run and get themselves places.' To whom Brother Bonaventura answered ' I see that your heart is busied and troubled with other things ; wherefore I will dismiss you forthwith, for I should labour in vain if I preached longer. In truth we need not that Antichrist should come with his forerunners ; for he would find many followers among Christian folk. Go therefore to your child whom ye desire to hear, and let *him* confess you of your sins ; for to-day is that day wherein the Lord's words shall be fulfilled, saying " Behold, the hour cometh, and it is now come, that ye shall be scattered each one to his own, and shall leave Me alone : and yet I am not alone, because the Father is with Me." ' Therewith he dismissed them ; and all made such a haste to depart that none waited for the other. Another time, when I dwelt at Ravenna, those Apostles caused the aforesaid boy to preach in the archiepiscopal cathedral of the city of Ravenna ; and in so great haste did folk of both sexes run together that scarce would one await the other. Wherefore a certain great and noble lady of that land, who was a devotee of the Friars Minor,—the Lady Giullietta, wife of the Lord Guido, Son of Rizola da Polenta,—complained to the Brethren that she could scarce find a friend to go with her. And the Cathedral was already so full when she came thither that she was fain to stand without by the door ; yet that Cathedral church is so great that it has four aisles, beside the great nave, which contains half the space. Moreover, those fellows who call themselves Apostles were wont to lead round this boy of theirs from city to city, and made him preach in Cathedral churches ;

---

* Not the Saint, but a contemporary of some note in the Order.

and folk flocked thick together, and there was a vast congregation, and much gaping both of men and of women; for the men of our days delight in new things.[10] Wherefore it is strange that the Church should suffer boys to elect one of their fellows to sit in the Bishop's seat on the Feast of the Innocents."[11] Salimbene heads the whole of this paragraph "Of the folly of Christian folk." In short, he could see only two good points in these Apostles; first, the picturesqueness of their dress, which he admits not without a little natural envy; and secondly that they did really begin in or about the year 1260, the Great Year of Joachism. But this latter advantage was neutralized by the fact that there was no word of them in Joachim's prophecies, (or rather in the pseudo-Joachim,) which, as all the world knew, had foretold exactly the coming of the Franciscans and Dominicans.

All this, however, did not hinder the Apostles from growing rapidly. Among the ignorant folk Segarello's pious folly passed for a good imitation of the Friars' life. Nor was it popular among the ignorant only: for the Apostles had at least three powerful patrons in the Church—the Bishop Obizzo, the Notary Apostolic Albert of Parma, and the Abbot of the great Cistercian monastery of Fontanaviva. It was this latter who advised them not to build convents, but to tramp the country and live on alms. Segarello soon found himself an object of fervent worship, and his house a resort of pilgrims from all quarters. The devotees would "flock around him in a certain house, never opening their mouths but to cry with a loud voice a hundred times or more, ' Pater, Pater, Pater !' Then after a brief space they would begin again, and chant ' Pater, Pater, Pater !' after the wont of boys in grammar-schools, when they repeat in chorus at intervals the words which have been spoken by their master. But he honoured them in return by stripping himself and them so stark naked as to uncover their shame; and they stood round in array leaning against the wall; yet in no orderly or honest or good array. For he would fain strip them of all their worldly goods, that, naked, they might henceforth follow the naked Christ. For each of them at the master's bidding had bound up his garments and laid them in the midst of that building. Then, at the master's bidding, as they stood in this unhonest guise, was brought in (as Origen saith) ' woman, the fountain-head of sin, the devil's weapon, expulsion from paradise, mother of guilt, corruption of the old law.' To her Gerardino commanded that she should give back the clothes as she pleased to these poor folk thus stripped and denuded of their worldly goods : and they, when they were clothed again, cried out as before, ' *Pater, Pater, Pater !* ' Such then was the reward and guerdon they had for this honour done to their master, that he played the fool in their presence and made them to play the fool : therefore the Wise Man saith in Proverbs ' as he that casteth stone into the heap of mercury, so is he that giveth honour to a fool.' After this he sent them to show themselves to the world : so some went to the court of Rome, others to Compostella, others to St. Michael's mount,[12] and others even to the Holy Land." Salimbene saw such a troop in 1284, when " seventy-two of those who call themselves Apostles but are not, came by the high road through Modena and Reggio, old men and children together, on their way to Parma to see their founder Segarello, that they might give all their goods into his hand and receive his blessing, and wander by his leave through the world. So he brought them into a certain church in Parma ; and, stripping them all naked, he reclothed them and received them into his Order and blessed them, and then sent them to go whithersoever they would. Yet Pope Gregory X in full Council at Lyons [A.D. 1274] had forbidden their further multiplication ; but they cease not on that account to take the habit of that Religion, and to wander in their folly throughout the world, neither fearing God nor honouring man, (that is, the Supreme Vicar of Jesus Christ :) and yet they dream that they are in a state of salvation, though they obey not the Church of Rome ! Moreover, in that same year, a few days later, there came along the same highway twelve girls, with mantles wrapped round their shoulders, calling themselves the Sisters of the aforesaid Apostles, and seeking Brother Gerardino on the same errand. These men, who call themselves Apostles and are not—nay rather, they are ribalds, boorish and beastly men, leading with them women of this kind—yet they believed themselves to be doing what the Apostle saith ' Have we not power to carry about a woman, a sister, as well as the rest of the Apostles, and the brethren of the Lord, and Cephas ? ' " The indignation which plays such havoc with Salimbene's grammar was felt in other quarters also. In 1287, the Council of Würzburg stigmatized the Apostles as disorderly tramps, and forbade the faithful to support them. Meanwhile Segarello himself "remained at Parma, where he was born, and wrought much folly ; for he cast off his mantle wherein he had been wrapped, and made him a white over-mantle of coarse stuff without sleeves, wherein he seemed rather a buffoon than a man of Religion. Moreover, he wore pointed shoes, and gloves on his hands ; his words were ribald, foul, vain, and unhonest, and empty and ridiculous, rather from his folly and stupidity than from the malice of his heart." The decree of Pope and Council against the reception of new members was easily evaded, in the then state of ecclesiastical discipline. " Instead of obeying, they make the garments of their Order, and lay them apart in the sight of those who would fain join them, saying ' We dare not receive you, for that is forbidden us : but to *you* it is not forbidden : wherefore do ye as seemeth good in your eyes.' Thus have they grown and multiplied beyond all count ; nor will they rest or cease from their folly until some Pope, in his indignation, shall blot out the very memory of them from beneath the sky." Meanwhile "by the miserliness and sloth of the Bishops they are suffered to wander unprofitably about the world."

This multiplication had already brought its natural consequence —a schism in the Order. Gerard was no organizer, and had never cared to assume the formal headship. " They have no instruction, which is great folly : for, whereas beasts and birds and other creatures have all that they need from nature at their very birth, yet man's soul is created by God like a blank tablet, and they need a teacher. Therefore to these Apostles (not Christ's but Segarello's) who are teacherless, we may apply that saying in the Book of Judges ' in those days there was no king in Israel, but everyone did that which seemed right to himself ' (Now that clause is written four times in the Book of Judges, once in the 17th chapter, and twice in the next, that is in the first and last verse, and again at the end of the book.) Therefore in a certain town of Apulia, where the country-folk said ' we are all captains and good folk,' they were put to flight by a certain baron from France on his way to the Emperor : for they demanded toll of him, which also he would have paid if he had found a captain." From Robert, again, little was to be expected in the way of leadership : for " in process of time, while I dwelt at Faenza, he dwelt there also in the house of a certain Tertiary called brother Ghiotto [glutton] ; and " on Good Friday, at the hour at which the Son of God was crucified, he became apostate, and cut his hair, and shaved his beard, and took to wife a certain female Hermit. I had heard all this, but I was loth to believe it until I had asked him ; whereupon he confessed and denied not that he had in truth done all these things. Then I rebuked him sharply, but he made excuse, saying that he had never bound himself to obedience nor to chastity ; wherefore he might well take a wife. But I said to him that he had worn publicly for many years the habit of religion, and ought therefore in no wise to have taken to wife a

Hermitess dedicated to God ; and I added many authorities and examples to show him his folly and wickedness . . . sixthly and lastly, I showed him how all who fall away from God and become apostate come to an evil end, which I have proved not by experience only, (for I have seen it with mine own eyes and heard it from others) but also from holy Scripture. For either they are beheaded or burnt or slain with the sword or hanged on gallows, or surely they die by some other most evil and shameful and cruel death." Robert, however, only " began to scoff."

In default of Robert, Segarello found his Frate Elia in one Guido Putagio, a man of noble family and a personal friend of Salimbene's. Guido " manfully took the government to himself, and held it many years. But he went abroad too pompously with many horsemen, and made such lavish expenses and banquets as the Legates and Cardinals of the Roman Court are wont to make, wherefore his followers took it ill, and chose themselves another head, one Brother Matteo of the Mark of Ancona ; so that a division was made among them. They came to blows with one another—that is, the Apostles of Brother Matteo with the Apostles of Brother Guido Putagio—and gave an evil example to the laity at Faenza. For I dwelt there in those days, and can bear witness thereof. Brother Guido dwelt at Faenza in a little church which was in the orchard of the families of Alberghetti and Accherisi ; with whom were but few Brethren of his own party, and Brother Gerardino. It seemed therefore to the Apostles of the Mark that if they could have Brother Gerardino, who was their founder, they would obtain the victory ; so they would fain have carried him off by main force into the Mark : but this they might by no means do, so that either party fought against the other." The scandal of these conflicts was heightened by a worse incident. " In the year 1286, a certain rich young man, whose father and mother were still living, married a wife ; and on the day of his wedding he gave hospitality to three ribalds of the Order of those who call themselves Apostles and are not ; and these ribalds deceived him shamefully and horribly. So when the young man saw that he had been deceived, he caused them to be taken before the Podesta, and they were led to the gallows. When therefore this had come to the ears of the Lord Obizzo di Sanvitale, Bishop of Parma, (who had long protected this Order by reason of Gerardino their founder) he expelled them from Parma and from his whole Bishopric. This same Gerardino is now come to such a pitch of madness as to walk abroad clad like a buffoon ; and like a strolling actor or clown he trails his folly through the streets and squares of the city." Some years earlier, moreover,

Segarello had been in the Bishop's prison : for Salimbene wrote in 1284 that " on account of his follies, and his foul, carnal, and foolish words that he was wont to say, and the scandal that he gave with his unseemly ordeal of chastity, therefore the Lord Obizzo, Bishop of Parma, took and cast him bound into prison : but in process of time he brought him thence and kept him in his palace. So when the Bishop ate, he ate also in the hall of the palace, at a lower table with others. And he loved to drink choice wines and eat delicate meats; so when the Bishop drank some choice wine, then Segarello would cry in all men's hearing, desiring to drink of that same wine ; and forthwith the Bishop would send him thereof. So when he was fulfilled of delicate meats and choice wine, he would speak folly, and the Bishop, being a merry man, would laugh at the words and deeds of that fool, whom he took not for a man of Religion, but for a silly and senseless buffoon."

Segarello disappears here from Salimbene's pages, but not from the stage of history. Honorius IV had issued a special Bull against the Apostles about the year 1286 : but it was evidently not obeyed, for Nicholas IV reissued it five years later. The order was now proscribed : and in 1294 four Apostles were burned as heretics at Parma. Segarello abjured, and was condemned to imprisonment for life. He relapsed, however, and was burned in 1300, the year of Dante's vision.

We must, of course, allow for Salimbene's jealousy ; but his accounts tally with those from other sources. Almost incredible as it seems that these Apostles should have enjoyed distinguished ecclesiastical patronage, their story is less strange than that of their contemporaries the Guglielmites at Milan and the Neminians in France, of whom only one chance record has survived.[13] After all, why should not Segarello have passed so long for a saint, in an age which was accustomed to still more startling manifestations on the part of good Franciscans ? There is nothing in his outward conduct more eccentric than what we read of Fra Ginepro and Jacopone da Todi ; of Thomas the Irishman cutting off his right thumb to avoid the priesthood ; of St. Francis and Fra Ruffino climbing the pulpit " naked as they were born, save in their drawers only." Segarello, like these, had not only powerful protectors, but also distinguished disciples. The most eminent of these, Dante's Fra Dolcino, came forward publicly for the first time within a month or two of Segarello's death, and a dozen years of Salimbene's. A factitious importance was given to such enthusiasts by the widespread religious unrest of the age : an unrest which seemed as strong, after nearly a century of the

Friars' influence, as in those days when Francis first gained the world's ear by words of authority which contrasted strangely with those of the Scribes and Pharisees of his time. As in the year 1200, so also in 1300, thousands were sick at heart, doubting gravely of the official doctors, and therefore ready to follow any blatant quack who caught their fancy. A deep despair of the present world lay at the root of Dolcino's revolt. The Good Pope, to whom Roger Bacon and so many others had looked forward, seemed farther off than ever. Any man therefore could command a following by condemning the vices of the clergy and offering to lead others through blood and flame along the shortest path to heaven. On this idea, at least, Dolcino did stake his own life and happiness, and persuaded others to stake theirs. Few are recorded to have fought and suffered as those 1400 who followed him into the mountains ; fewer still have ever matched the constancy with which he himself bore the tortures of the Inquisition, and Margaret insisted on sharing them with him.

Chapter XXVI.

The Salt and its Savour.

THE reader has now seen how Salimbene and his contemporaries regarded the faith, the education, and the morals of a generation which is generally allowed to stand at the high-water mark of medieval life. Things were worse than this before St. Francis came; and again there was a falling-off in many ways when the Friars became as corrupt as the rest of the clergy. For the heroic days described in the Fioretti and Thomas of Eccleston and Jordan of Giano were brief indeed; and long before the first example of self-sacrifice had made its definite mark on the world, such self-sacrifice was already rare in the Order itself.[1] In brief, the Friars took the colour of the old world far more rapidly than their own better leaven worked among the people. In the divine inspiration of the earliest days Francis might almost have blessed his Order (if Order it could then be called) in Virgil's words to the purified Dante : " Free, upright, and whole is thy will, and 'twere a fault not to act according to its prompting; wherefore I do crown and mitre thee over thyself." But even before the Saint's death, Franciscanism could no longer be left safely to its own promptings. The stricter friars found themselves driven into a severity of discipline, a stern and sad view of human life such as became characteristic of later Puritanism.[2] Others at the opposite pole abused Franciscan liberty in vagabondage, gluttony, wine-bibbing and wantonness. The large majority, between these two extremes, tried more or less unconsciously to make the best of both worlds, and lived such a life as we see reflected in Salimbene's pages.

For Salimbene, in spite of all that may be said to the contrary by those who have formed their ideas from only one side of the early records, is quite the typical better-class Franciscan of the generation between St. Francis and Dante. He had many better friends, and many worse, but he himself was quite up to the average. That average may seem low indeed to those who know what St. Francis not only expected of all his Brethren, but obtained from many by the magnetism of his personal influence. Yet we must not judge of the Order from that first group of missionaries : for a serious rift appeared even in the saint's lifetime between Franciscan theory and practice, and widened rapidly into an almost impassable gulf.

Every friar on entry swore obedience to the Rule, which contained these words, written by St. Francis and solemnly ratified by the Pope : "I straitly command all my Brethren to receive in no wise either money or coin, whether directly or through any third person." The Brethren were further forbidden to possess houses of their own ; and on his deathbed the Saint solemnly laid it on their consciences never to explain away these plain words, nor to obtain Papal letters of interpretation, whether directly or indirectly. Each novice, as he was admitted, swore obedience to this Rule, and received in return a solemn and official assurance that by keeping it he would earn eternal life. Compare this theory with an incident which Salimbene relates without comment, and which is confirmed by official documents, exactly 30 years after St. Francis's death. (463) "This year . . . . in the month of May, the Lord Guglielmo Fogliani, Bishop of Reggio, sold to the Friars Minor of that city, that they might make their habitation there, the Imperial palace, which the Lord Nicholas his predecessor had had as a gift from the Emperor ; except that the Emperor kept the right of lodging there on his journeys. And the friars bought it, and paid for it with money which they had from the Sisters of the Order of St. Clare, to whom they sold their old convent. . . . . And because the friars had bought the aforesaid palace, (save for the Emperor's right of lodging there), therefore in process of time, they sent word to the Lord Rodolph, who had been elected Emperor by Pope Gregory X, that they possessed and dwelt in his palace in the city of Reggio, and they would gladly have his leave to dwell there. And he answered that he was exceeding glad to have such guests, and whatever rights he had therein he gave wholly and freely to the Friars Minor. And of this he gave them two indented letters, confirmed with his own seal, promising to confirm them yet more strongly if he were successful in getting possession of the Empire. And because the aforesaid dwelling was narrow, therefore the Friars Minor bought more ground and houses round about." Lower down he describes the buying of this new land and the building of the additions to the convent, "and the commune," he adds, "gave them valuers to value in good faith the price of the houses to be bought." Alberto Milioli, the contemporary chronicler of Reggio, adds the information (implied even in Salimbene's text), that the Friars evicted the unwilling sellers from their houses; and our friar's own words, "they made a new street," imply that these additions were of considerable value and extent. Yet the original palace must have been a very large building: for, even before the alterations, when the Emperor of Constantinople passed through the city, he solemnly knighted a noble "in the convent of the Friars Minor," on which occasion "all the knights and almost all the ladies of Reggio," were present. (483; 487) Only twelve years after St. Francis's death, in 1238, the Friars of Valencia were presented with a palace by a Moorish king, recently converted at the point of the sword; and dozens of cases might be quoted to show how rapidly and how completely the Order disobeyed their master's solemn precepts on this point. So also on the point of dress. The Rule bids them be content with two tunics, which they may patch with sackcloth. These patches were also used to thicken the tunics where the body was most sensible to cold.[3] But less than 15 years after St. Francis's death the friar who contented himself with two old frocks was already a *rara avis*. Salimbene (286) speaks with admiration of Brother Buoncompagno da Prato "a spiritual man: for when I dwelt with him in the convent of Pisa, whereas each Brother took two new woollen tunics yearly, yet he would never accept but one, and that an old one; and when I enquired the reason, he would answer me saying, 'Brother Salimbene, the Apostle saith, Every one of us shall render account to God for himself; and God shall also demand such an account, saying "Give an account of thy stewardship." Indeed, I shall scarce be able to satisfy God for this single tunic which I take.'"[4] Ubertino says that some friars in the Genoa province had two frocks and five under-tunics; and that all of the Milan province wore frocks of the finest cloth made in Italy. The appalling quibbles by which this kind of thing was justified may be read in the answer of the Community to these accusations. Indeed, here and elsewhere, the facts themselves are less significant than the jesuitry with which such flat disobedience was explained away even by men like St. Bonaventura. For the mere breach of their Rule the friars had indeed the precedent of centuries. The monk also was forbidden by his Rule to possess anything whatever of *private* property. Popes condemned the souls of "proprietary" monks to hell, and their bodies to the dunghill. Books of convent miracles swarm with tales of their damnation. On the very threshold of the Reformation, Cardinal Juan de Torquemada gravely decides that it is a mortal sin for any monk to say even of a book or any similar object (except by a mere slip of the tongue) " That is *mine*." On the other hand monks did in fact enjoy their private pocket-money, or even private incomes, for centuries, and would have enjoyed them for centuries more but for the violent interference of the State : yet even the crooked excuses offered for this breach of the Monastic rule seem straightforward compared with the jugglery of which Ubertino convicted his fellow-Franciscans. The degradation of the friars was unquestionably hastened by the habitual jesuitry with which their false position was defended.[5]

In this matter of buildings, especially, modern writers have painted even the earliest days in false colours which cannot but prove mischievous in the long run. Dr. Jessopp outbids Dr. Brewer, Canon Rawnsley outbids M. Sabatier, and Father Cuthbert outbids them all. But nothing can need a lie, and least of all the spirit of St. Francis, who loses far more than he gains by pious exaggerations. Professor Brewer, by a very natural slip, greatly exaggerated the meanness of the Cambridge Friars' chapel : but all the rest follow him without suspicion, in spite of the extreme inherent improbability of the story.[5a] Again, he exaggerated the meanness of the town or suburban districts in which the friars settled ; yet Dr. Jessopp outdoes these first exaggerations even in the case of the two Norfolk boroughs which lie close to his own home. He writes " The Friars settled outside the city walls at Lynn . . . . in a filthy swamp at Norwich through which the drainage of the city sluggishly trickled into the river, never a foot lower than its banks." These words are typical of the false perspective which dominates nearly all modern popular writings on the early Franciscans. Lynn had no town walls when the Friars settled there : and the later fortifications, never including a continuous wall, left the Greyfriars inside their enclosure by a good quarter of a mile ! Their site was then, as now, central and healthy. At Norwich, their site was separated from the river, first by one of the oldest streets in the town and then by a broad stretch of meadow. Of these meadows between the Friars and the river all were held by great folk : and in one of them, about 1300, Sir Thos. Roscelyn built himself a house which passed into the hands of other equally noted citizens.[6] Only a small fraction of the city could possibly have drained past the Friary : nearly all the streets lay on the other side of the slope, and drained into the other bend of the river. As the old antiquary Kirkpatrick puts it, the Friars had " a large parcel of land, and of a very pleasant situation." In London, where space was extremely scarce, they evidently did settle at first on an unpleasant site : but a beautiful Early English capital dug up on the site of Christ's Hospital shows that they very soon joined the many offenders against the constitution forbidding large or ornamental churches ; indeed, within a short space afterwards their church became one of the most magnificent in the city. If this was so even in England, where Franciscans prided themselves on their special strictness, we need not be surprised that in Italy, long before the century was out, they had given grave offence with their gardens and orchards and vineyards. The Spirituals attacked, and St. Bonaventura very lamely defended, their rapidly-growing habit of settling, "to the scandal of clergy and people," no longer in the country or the suburbs, but actually within the great towns ; where, in spite of the enormous cost of land, they yet managed to get their great burial-grounds and their orchards. This complaint is still further emphasized by Bernard of Besse's admission that the strict observance of St. Francis's ideal of poverty "is precluded in cities, by men's wickedness and by the multitude of the Brethren."[7] The Franciscan churches of Assisi, Florence, Padua, Todi, Bologna, Parma,—all built within a century of the Saint's death—are like so many cathedrals. The inference of poverty commonly drawn from the fact that the Friaries yielded little spoil at the Dissolution, and that they had sometimes sold their books even earlier, is extremely fallacious. It only shows that, whatever their income was, they spent it as fast as they got it ; or even, like other religious Orders, incurred heavy liabilities by living beyond it. The amount of plunder which could be squeezed at the present moment from the Salvation Army would be no true measure either of its actual income or of the comforts enjoyed by its officers : yet General Booth's financial arrangements are far more precise and business-like than those of the friars ; and a modern liquidator would have advantages which were altogether lacking in the 16th century. We have evidence that, long before Dante's death, the friars were collecting large sums of money which were not always spent on such worthy objects as buildings and church ornaments, illicit as even these were. Ubertino describes many of his brother Friars as begging all over the country, with servants at their heels bearing money boxes of which the masters alone kept the key : "and how they spend it, the tavern-keepers know, and the servants who bear the money. . . . . They have so corrupted the roads that such poor Friars as will not or cannot take bursars with them can now scarce find a living, since men believe they must possess money

like these others." Here we have already Chaucer's Friar, as
described by the Summoner, with his servant to carry the spoils.
Ubertino only stops short of the last and most intolerable
accusation—that, after writing down the benefactor's names to
be mentioned in his prayers—

> " Whan that he was out at dore anon,
> He planed away the names everichon : . . . .
> —Nay, there thou lixt, thou Somonour ! quod the Frere."

Yet for this also we have plain documentary evidence. The
still existing mortuary book of the Landshut Friary has had all
its earlier names carefully erased with pumice-stone to make
room for later entries ; so that even the special glory of the
convent's earlier days, "the Venerable Father Brother Conrad von
Weilheim," had no longer any share in the prayers of the later
Brethren. Similarly Ubertino tells us how the Friars would sell
the same wax taper ten times over to different devotees, each
of whom had paid for it in the hope of receiving its spiritual
benefit for himself alone.[8] The mere greed of money would
of itself have seriously impaired the Friars' authority over the
people : but the evil was increased by others which it drew in
its train. The earliest Brethren had braced themselves for their
missionary work by frequent retreats to solitary hermitages :
but in Salimbene's time they already crowded into the cities as
modern country-folk crowd into London. Of this he gives us,
quite incidentally, a remarkable example. After speaking of the
miracles of Brother Roland of Padua he goes on to speak of
the convent of La Vernia (556) "where the seraph marked
the Blessed Francis with the five wounds after the likeness of
our Lord Jesus Christ. So I saw all the places of devotion
which are there : and on the Lord's Day I celebrated the convent
Mass, and after the Gospel I preached to the assembled people,
both men and women. And note that, when I was at Alvernia,
Brother Lothario, who had formerly been my Custos at Pisa,
was still dwelling there, though old and infirm. I believe that
this convent would have been deserted by the Brethren (as he
said to me), unless it had been retained by his good offices." It
may seem almost incredible that a hermitage so sacred in
Franciscan tradition as La Vernia should have been almost
abandoned : but another sacred spot, Monte Casale, where
Brother Angelo joined the Order and St. Francis converted the
three robbers, was actually given up by the Brethren before
1450. Before that year of Jubilee in which Dante imagines
his poem, there were not many friars left who had enough

firmness of purpose to live the old simple life. Ubertino complains that the Order in general had already quite lost its faith in the promises of Christ and St. Francis, and relied instead on the money gained from burials of rich folk, absolutions of usurers, legacy-hunting, and fees for masses and spiritual services. And Salimbene shows us this process already actively at work. He bitterly regrets that the earlier loyalty to St. Francis's ideal should have lost to the Order the bodies of Count Raymund of Toulouse and St. Elizabeth of Hungary, and many other such rich prizes, including a whole convent, richly endowed, which Innocent IV had offered them at Lavagna. (61, 295.) He shows us usurers compounding for their sins by giving conscience-money to the friars (452 : 609). Moreover, even the grosser forms of usury received underhand encouragement from the very Church which damned them ; and none sinned more deeply in this respect than the ordinary friars, whom the Spirituals charged with habitually absolving the impenitent for the sake of a share in the plunder. Certain it is that the century of their first and strongest influence saw a rapid development of usurious practices, as the Franciscan Nicole Bozon himself complains, about the date of Dante's death. " Nowadays," he complains, "the old fashion is changed ; for those who once avoided to give such men the kiss of peace in church, are now ready to kiss their feet, . . . and they whose bodies were wont to be buried in the field or the garden are now entombed in churches before the High Altar."[9]

  Again, this growing thirst for money brought the Franciscans into collision with the other clergy and Religious—no longer now with the vicious and jealous only, but with the whole body outside their own Order. Already in Thomas of Celano's " Second Life" we find complaints of quarrels with their old friends and allies the Dominicans. Salimbene tells us plainly of the breach with their next nearest friends, the Cistercians. The Spirituals were justly scandalized by the Bulls which the laxer Brethren obtained to hinder other Orders from building convents within a certain radius of their own Friaries. The holy violence with which we have seen them evict a priest from his own church in Genoa was quite common, by Bonaventura's own confession. One by one, they obtained Papal privileges enabling them to encroach by force on parochial duties, and to compete for parochial fees. The consequences may be guessed. St. Francis had indeed protested on his deathbed " If I had the wisdom of a Solomon, and found paltry secular priests, I would not preach against their will in the churches wherein they reside." But, only 30 years afterwards, St. Bonaventura writes " If we were never to abide in parishes but by the priest's will, then we should scarce ever be able to stay long ; since, whether of their own motion or at others' instigation, they would eject us from their parishes sooner than heretics or Jews."[10]   Indeed, it was not long before the parish clergy began to retort the worst of the accusations brought against themselves by the Friars.   St. Francis himself, apparently, had not altogether escaped suspicion ; and he in turn sounded a plain note of warning to his Brethren in the eleventh chapter of his Rule.   Scandals, and sometimes more real difficulties, compelled the Franciscan authorities to renounce, over and over again, the official directtion of the Poor Clares.   Salimbene (421) tells us how one day at Faenza " as I was walking through the garden thinking of the Lord, I was called by a certain secular man of Ferrara named Matulino, a very great talker and composer of Canzoni and Serventesi, and one who noted us Religious and found fault with us : for he sat under a fig-tree with two Brethren of whom he asked questions ; and he cried to me ' Dan Friar, come hither and sit with us.' "   Matulino had lately been at dinner with the Bishop of Forlì, and there the clergy had made much the same complaints against the Friars with which St. Bonaventura deals in the *Quaestiones circa Regulam* and *Libellus Apologeticus* : for, (as Salimbene puts it) " it is plain that the priests and secular clergy always lie in wait for us and are glad to calumniate us . . . .   As to the sixth of these malicious accusations, that we are ladies' men ; that is, that we gladly see women and speak with ladies, and are in familiar talk with them, we say that these are the words of such as ' lay a blot on the elect '—that is, of buffoons and play-actors and such as are called Knights of the Court, who think to excuse themselves from their own vanity and wantonness in defaming others.'   Then answered Matulino and said ' I tell you in truth, Brother Salimbene, those were the words of the Bishop of Forlì, and not of a buffoon.   And, under my eyes, he arose from table and took a Bible and showed me how it was written " Sit not at all with another man's wife, nor repose upon the bed with her ; and strive not with her over wine, lest thy heart decline towards her, and by thy blood thou fall into destruction."   And he said that ye Friars Minor and Preachers do daily contrary to that Scripture ; and his clergy consented with him and confirmed his words.'   Then I answered and said ' The Bishop of Forlì is such as Ecclesiasticus saith " he lieth in wait and turned good into evil, and on the Elect he will lay a blot " ; and of his clergy I say that I care not for their praise, for Seneca saith " Care no more to be praised by base folk than if thou wert praised for base things."   We and the Friars Preachers are poor mendicants who must needs live on alms ; and among those who help us are women, as it is written in Ecclesiasticus " Where there is no wife, he mourneth that is in want " : for they are more merciful to help the poor and more pitiful to the afflicted than men, who are harder of heart.   Wherefore, when they send for us, we must needs go to them for their sick folk or for any other tribulation which they have, that we may make them some return of kindness and not be found ungrateful, since the Apostle saith "and be ye thankful."   We strive not with any women over wine ; for according to our constitution we dare not drink in cities, save with prelates and Religious and Lords of Manors.' "   This plea, which after all only rehearses the theory of Franciscan life and still leaves its practice to be proved, is reinforced by a digression in which our Friar brings against the clergy some of the accusations recorded in a previous chapter : and Matulino professed himself abundantly satisfied.   " But I said to him : ' five years I dwelt in the city of Ravenna, yet I never set foot in the house of the lord Marquis Michael, who is one of the greatest and most noble and richest of that city.'   ' And I,' said he, ' have been there an hundred times at meat with him.'   Then answered I ' Who therefore is the greater ladies' man, thou or I ? '   And he said ' I see that it is I : and you have hemmed me in and given me checkmate, nor have I more to answer.'   Then said I to Matulino "—and here follows the second little sermon against ladies' society and in praise of chastity from which I have already quoted in chapter viii : after which Salimbene ends in triumph, " Since, then, we are not ignorant of all these things, we are no ladies' men, as our friends assert against us, but (as it is written in the book of Tobias) ' we are the children of saints, and look for that life which God will give to those that never change their faith with him.'   What more shall I say ? "   What more, indeed ?   How could Matulino fail to become " such a friend of mine that I always found him ready to render me service ; but he lost nothing thereby, for I gave him to wife the daughter of a man of Ferrara who dwelt at Ravenna, by whom he had a great dowry . . . . for the girl's father confessed to me in that sickness whereof he died."

It is a long step from all this to the *Fioretti* or to Thomas of Eccleston : and indeed that intervening half century had wrought far-reaching changes among the Franciscans.   The fact is, that the very strictness of the Rule in theory hardened the average friar's heart against its literal observance in practice, just as the very Puritanism of the medieval theory of religion partly accounts for the absence of Puritanism in medieval practice. A limited number of men were precisians by profession, and the majority felt all the more dispensed from the necessity of imitating them ; as the crowds of our great towns claim a sort of vicarious merit in the achievements of their professional football-players. St. Francis's straightforward glance had already noted how many of his Brethren " were fain to receive praise and honour only by rehearsing and preaching the works that the saints did themselves achieve." So Ubertino asserts solemnly before God that, although there was no longer any real difference between friars and monks as to the reception of money, his brethren continued to glory in the unique strictness of their own Rule.[11]

Moreover, quite apart from their quarrels with the clergy, they rapidly lost popularity with the laity. Salimbene has told us how the country-folk attributed the barrenness of the earth to the malign influence of the Friars : and the same complaint meets us in a saying of Jordan of Saxony. St. Bonaventura and Ubertino, however else they differ, agree in frequently referring to the waning popularity of their Order.[12] Almost more significant are the disciplinary books of the early Franciscans, in their extreme and petty anxiety to avoid unsympathetic criticism. Mr. McCabe describes the painful efforts of the modern Franciscans to hide all their doings from even the most sympathetic outsiders : and there was just the same jealous secrecy in the 13th century.[13] Eccleston describes how Albert of Pisa, Minister General of the Order (d. 1280) " was wont to say to his companion, Ognibene by name, when they came to the house of spiritual friends, ' Eat now, eat : we may eat securely here ! ' For he was wont, so far as in him lay, to beware of all secular folk." He goes on to tell another story to point the same moral, that the less layfolk see of the inner life of the Religious, the more they are likely to honour them. St. Bonaventura's secretary shows the same jealous exclusiveness. " If novices are questioned about the doings of the Order, as of their fashion of fasting, their silence, or other points, let them plead that they are fresh to the Order, and pass the question on to a senior ; lest perchance, while they think themselves to answer wisely and well, they say something foolish and altogether unfit to be said. Let them reveal the secrets of the Order to none, however religious or familiar ; nor let them publish any statute, unless, perchance, it cannot conveniently be concealed." Again, " Let them never invite strangers, even their familiar friends, to visit the Offices of the Convent. Or if ever, at some man's urgent entreaty, they are permitted to show these, let them show only the more common buildings, not entering and going from place to place and from corner to corner, but standing at the door and, with all possible expedition short of discourtesy, furtively hiding all that can be concealed from the strangers' gaze. *There is no Religion where all things are open to all men.*" Moreover, even where the Friar thinks himself most secure, he must still be on his guard. " A certain Brother was wont to relate that he had discovered in certain lay folks' houses secret loopholes, whereby all that was unsuspiciously done in those houses could be clearly seen." " Let [friars] altogether avoid loud speech . . . . and especially when they are in woods or thickets: for, (as the vulgar proverb hath it) woods have ears, and the level plain hath eyes. Let them therefore abstain altogether, in thick and woody places, from all things which they would not say before secular folk ; unless perchance they wish to say anything under their breath, as it were, and in the Latin tongue. Miserable confusions from this cause are reported oftentimes to have befallen certain friars who have not used due caution." Even in the estimate of the gravity of an offence this consideration of scandal plays a great part. St. Bonaventura, commenting on the clause of the Rule which bids friars who have committed mortal sin to have recourse at once to their Provincial for absolution, adds—" This is to be understood of *notorious* sins only : for those which are secret should not be made public : since, other things being equal, a sin done publicly to the scandal of others is more grievous than a hidden sin, and therefore more grievously to be punished."[14]

Yet all this was a mere daubing with untempered mortar ; for, when it was known that so many scandals really existed, the very effort to conceal them did more harm than good. As the adversary objects to St. Bonaventura, " since the Religious are wont so studiously to conceal their doings, it is suspected that certain improprieties take place among them : for why else are things so studiously hidden, since there is no need to conceal that which is good ? " To which the Saint can only reply that this is partly in order to avoid vainglory, partly to conceal real shortcomings, but " mainly for the laity's sake . . . . for friars cannot look into all men's hearts and satisfy all with a reason why this or that is done [in their convents], since secular folk are rude, and prone generally to suspect evil of the Religious."[15] Yet there is nothing hid that shall not be revealed ; and from a thousand little scattered indications we can reconstitute pretty exactly the life of a Franciscan cloister. However, it is no part of my task here to present a full picture of the ordinary Friar's daily life: that would need a special volume to itself. I shall only attempt to bring out certain points which are necessary to the full appreciation of Salimbene's autobiography, yet on which the most accessible books tell us little or nothing.

Next to the matter of money and possessions, in which even the Papal Bulls mark clearly step by step the rapid lowering of the Franciscan ideal, perhaps the Friar's most natural and insidious temptation lay in the hospitality of the outside world towards his Order and himself. It is a matter of common observation that the customary inactivity of the modern Sunday generates, in all but the most earnest and ascetic minds, a positive craving for creature comforts; and the 13th century was no more able than our own age to supply enough really earnest and ascetic minds to form one tenth of the multitudes who crowded into the new Orders. "Why," asks St. Bonaventura's adversary, "do we see all Orders of Religious decay in religious life, even while they seem to advance in temporal prosperity and in certain ceremonial observances?" And the saint, admitting the fact, answers sadly that "one cause is the multitude of those that enter in." As Roger Bacon tells us, thousands of these converts were ignorant schoolboys: many others brought into the Order a mind and body broken by dissipation, like the typical husband of French Romance: and there can be no doubt that this collocation of those who knew nothing of real life with others who knew only too much of one side of it, reacted almost as injuriously on the discipline of the cloister as it notoriously did on that of the medieval universities. We find in these Franciscan manuals evident efforts to keep the old and the young apart to some extent, though nothing like the elaborate system of precautions which the Benedictines attempted. After all the goodwill of their first conversion, the majority found themselves still very human. The strictly ascetic minority, again, were too few, under the most favourable circumstances, to leaven the mass thoroughly; while in most places they were actually persecuted and imprisoned, or even done to death and buried with the burial of a dog, for their inconvenient puritan zeal. Hence we find very early indications of that recoil of oppressed nature which Mr. McCabe describes so graphically among the modern Franciscans. He relates how casuists permit a fast-dinner to be protracted for four hours, and how he himself has assisted at such which have lasted for three; statements which square well enough with the menu of the fast-dinner given by St. Louis, and with several other indications in our chronicle. Salimbene complains more than once of habitual self-indulgence on the part of the higher officials. Similarly, Ubertino writes " while Prelates guzzle daily, the sick are almost starved : " and again " so high has the flood of idleness and gluttony and continued familiarities with women risen, that I rather wonder at those who stand than at those who fall."[16]

The early Franciscan documents show us at every turn how the ultra-ascetic ideal defeated its own object. The whole tragedy of the Friars' decay during the lifetime of those who had known the founder himself, may be found written in St. Bonaventura's *Quæstiones circa Regulam* and his two *Epistles* to the Provincials of the Order. As the early heroes of Franciscanism dropped out of the ranks—some by premature death, others eking out a crippled existence in the convent infirmaries after the ascetic excesses of their earlier days—a new generation grew up which, while it knew the old rigours mainly by hearsay, had the plainest ocular testimony of the irregular luxuries with which the discrepit Religious were daily pampered. The enormous popularity of the Order, and the indiscriminate reception of candidates, contributed still more to relax the earlier discipline. St. Bonaventura bewails the growing extravagance of their buildings and private expenses, and their wearisome demands, direct or indirect, upon the charity of the laity, so that the wayfarer already fears a friar as he would fear a robber. The Saint himself " would willingly be ground to powder," if so he could bring the Order back to its purity of only half-a-century ago : but (as Father Ehrle points out) the downward impetus was too strong, and the " relaxed " party made rapid strides even during the Saint's long generalate.[17] Moreover these relaxations among the large majority necessarily entailed sufferings upon the strict minority, who, as even moderates like St. Bonaventura and David of Augsburg complain, were already not only despised but actually persecuted.[18] It only remained that the too strict observance of St. Francis's Rule and Testament should be publicly condemned as heresy ; and this was done by John XXII in 1317. From that time forward, friars were burned by their fellow-friars for loyalty to the first traditions of the Order ; since, helplessly subject as they were to the Roman hierarchy, they were not even allowed for many years to form separate congregations of their own for the strict observance of the Rule. This must alway be borne in mind when we are tempted to draw invidious parallels between the Franciscans and, for instance, the Wesleyans. The price which St. Francis had paid for the official recognition of his Order by

Innocent III was in fact the degradation of the whole ideal. From the moment that the Friars became a sort of papal militia, they must needs conform to the general policy of the Roman Court, and come to terms with the greed, the ambition, and the corruption for which that Court long had been, and was long to be, notorious. The Wesleyans, as an independent body, have thus been able to work more powerfully for good on the Church which they left, than the Friars could act on the Church to which they clung. In the face of powerful spiritual rivals, Anglicanism has had no chance of holding her ground but by her learning and her good works. On the other hand, when once the Roman Court had succeeded in assimilating the Friars, she had little further to fear from their inconvenient reforming energy. Under its garb of poverty, the Order soon became notorious for its flattery of the rich. The friars of the 13th century had indeed protested almost with Luther's violence against the abuses of the indulgence system : but the friars of the 15th and 16th centuries were the chief pardon-mongers.[19] When we speak of schism as a great evil, let us also admit that even greater evils may conceivably spring from conformity to a system deeply corrupted in practice. The failure of the Franciscans is in fact a direct justification of the policy of our Reformers : for certainly one of the most potent causes of Franciscan corruption lay in a false notion of Authority. It was that notion which enabled the less spiritual majority among the Friars, while swearing obedience to the Rule and boasting the strictness of that Rule, to torture or put to death those few who really followed the Rule.

Of this, however, Salimbene gives us little direct evidence, though his chronicle supplies us with the most valuable indirect corroboration of bitter and repeated complaints from contemporaries. It is natural, after all, that he should accept papally approved relaxations as a matter of course, and spend little ink on the dissentient Brethren who clung in spite of persecution to a doomed cause. Of horrors outside the convent he has plenty to tell us : but, so far as the inner life is concerned, the greater part of his Chronicle reflects his own cheerful and slightly cynical humour. In it we see plainly the average Friar, deep in admiration for the Saints of his Order, yet without any strong personal desire for martyrdom : full of fellow-feeling for the sinners, yet keeping himself pure on the whole from all grosser transgressions. If at times his manners and his morals seem strange to us, the fault lies not in the man but in his age. The more intimate study of medieval life, while it deepens our interest and affection for the separate figures which flit over that strange stage, is apt to increase our horror of the gloomy background behind even the gayest and brightest groups of actors.   Then, as now, most men struggled with more or less success against disorder and crime : but our hearty recognition of their honest efforts ought not to blind us to the rottenness of many institutions which they sought to uphold, or to the barbarous conditions which too often rendered their labours fruitless.

CHAPTER XXVII.

Conclusion.

I HAVE tried to show, through a faithful summary of Salimbene's autobiography with contemporary illustrations, how life would have looked to us if we had been born in the age of St. Francis and Dante. If I seem to have laid undue stress on the darker side, I would plead two considerations. First, if I had contented myself with a bare translation of Salimbene offhand—or, for the matter of that, of any among half-a-dozen others of that century whom I could name—the picture thus presented would still have seemed almost incredibly dark to the modern English reader. Imagination staggers at the moral gulf that yawns between that age and ours. Secondly, plain speaking on this subject is rendered imperative by the persistent misrepresentations of those who champion dying theories in our own day. Reactionaries build themselves an imaginary past, just as the *femme incomprise* takes refuge, in the imaginary homage of distant friends, from the unsympathetic common-sense of those among whom she has to live. The whole Middle Ages cry out to us from Dante's great poem " Who shall deliver us from the body of this death ? " and I have chosen Salimbene's chronicle for my main theme because he shows us more clearly than any other what was the Body of that Death. I am aware that many will refuse to accept this picture as true : but, as I have already said, I gladly challenge comparison with other contemporary evidence.

Meanwhile it is essential to a comprehension of our own life that we should face honestly and answer as truly as possible the question whether the morality of the " Ages of Faith " stood higher or lower than that of our own time. If the things that are more excellent have been steadily fading from the world during these 600 years, then it should clearly be the aim of civilization to hark back to the ideal of one central and absolute religious authority. If, on the other hand, the struggle among different creeds has tended towards a steady elimination of evil and growth of good—if many theories of the past, however massive and imposing, have shown themselves as little fitted to survive, as little worthy of regret, as the Mammoth or the Mastodon—then we may continue without misgiving to shape our creed by the Pauline maxim " Prove all things, hold fast that which is good." I have tried, in the spirit of that maxim, to appreciate those real virtues of Romanism which make it still a living creed, and have changed it gradually for the better in spite of its professed immutability. But I have not attempted to conceal my conviction that its exclusive pretensions are flatly contradicted by the history of the very time at which they seemed most nearly justified : and that the world is far purer and better for the decay of sacerdotalism. One tenth of the abuses that reigned in the 13th century would have sufficed to wreck any Church in a less barbarous age. If Romanism dominated the Western world for three whole centuries longer, it was mainly because it maintained a Saturnine supremacy by devouring its own children. The Inquisition ruthlessly murdered every non-Roman organization in its cradle : and all the while, within the Church itself, men hoped for better things till hope grew sick. Dante, with the Franciscan reform not yet dead around him, could still look for the regeneration of Romanism from within. But Langland, a couple of generations later, though he hated heretics as heartily as Dante did, had already lost Dante's hope in the Church. For him, the last stronghold of Christianity had already succumbed to the assaults of Antichrist and the treachery of the Friars. Henceforth his pattern of simple faith, his Piers Plowman, must shake the dust of the past from his feet, and wander forth alone to the world's end in search of the Christ that is to be.[1] Wiclif himself scarcely condemns the prelate and the parish priest more outspokenly than St. Bonaventura : it was only that the Englishman's bolder logic and his century of later experience drove him to a conclusion which the Saint had studiously avoided. Wiclif was the first great philosopher and theologian to confess frankly that the Medieval Church would never be reformed except by a revolution from within and by violent pressure from the laity without.

Much, however, of the generous modern over-estimate of medieval society is due to the admiration for medieval art. Men have jumped to the hasty but mistaken conclusion that the artists whom we now admire so much had greater honour in their own country than their modern successors have.[2] Again, the men who built and adorned our churches (it is argued), must have been better men than we. Yet this indirect argument from art to morals is utterly fallacious. Perugino was a rank materialist, who could never be persuaded of the immortality of the soul :[3] Raphael painted his Madonnas in the midst of a society rotten to the core : and the peculiarly modern art of landscape may teach us the same lesson. Six hundred years hence, the enthusiastic student of Turner will be tempted to imagine that Englishmen of the 19th century loved their country scenery better than any race in any age. Yet never has man done more to ruin the landscape ; never has he crowded more blindly from the fresh fields into the smoky town. Now that we are falling in love with the country again, preserving ruins and lakes by Act of Parliament, and planning our new Garden Cities, who dares on that account to promise us another Turner, or even another David Cox ? The art of the Middle Ages stood at that exquisite moment when the first rays of sunrise glisten on the dews of night, and colour its parting clouds. In those wild days, building was the one possible investment, and the church the one building which offered the artist some real hope of protection for himself and his work. The true artistic greatness of the Middle Ages begins with the 11th century, when art and learning began to leave the cloister which had sheltered them in the germ, and to spread freely through the world. The greatest works of those days were carried out not *by* celibate monks or clerics, but only *for* monks and clerics. The real artists were the most Bohemian of craftsmen — wandering masons, who loved wine, women, and song, but whose too riotous fancies were chastened by the spirit of asceticism among the clerical patrons that directed the general lines of their work. Even so, the glories of medieval art often seemed superfluous, wasteful, and actually semi-pagan, to the noblest minds of the time. So long as the spirit of St. Bernard lived in the Order, there was no Cistercian school of architecture ; and before ecclesiastical art had grown to maturity in the 13th century, the monasteries were already verging on moral decay. St. Francis, again, gave a powerful impulse to art : but only indirectly, and against his own will. The splendid basilica at Assisi, Sta. Croce at Florence, and all the great Franciscan churches which we admire now, were as definitely false to the Saint's spirit as was the Golden Calf to the Mosaic Law.[4] Art was not the product of medieval religion, but of worldliness under some restraint of religion. Many details of church carving are too licentious to be photographed or modelled ; and some at least of our most beautiful English cathedrals were built in part from the fines collected from unchaste priests, in part from more questionable sources still.[5]

The last and most potent cause of modern ignorance of the past lies in the dissatisfaction which many feel with the present world. In all ages, there are many minds of the type so familiar to us in everyday life ; unsympathetic to the family or the servants with whom their lot is immediately cast, and spending all their tenderness on cats or dogs or foreign missions. In its milder forms, most men feel this temptation more or less strongly : and many who can see no good in the flesh and blood of the 20th century can see no harm in the ghosts of the 13th. Yet it is idle to seek God in a corner of the past, while we reject the facts of the present. To find only poetry in distant history, only prose in our own age, is not imagination but dulness of imagination : not love of a purer ideal, but bat-like blindness to the broader light. Every spring-time reminds us afresh that the world is eternally young, and that any generation's weary complaints of old age are merely ridiculous to posterity. There is more hope in the world now, and more of the buoyancy of youth, than 600 years ago when Bernard of Morlaix sang dolefully "The times are waxing late . . . The judge is at the gate." That ideal of a fast-approaching external judgment was natural enough in days when men feared that Christ and His Saints slept. With us, the truer ideal is that of a present and perpetual judgment : a world in which God asks us daily : " Can you trace My finger everywhere here, or can you only find the Devil's ?—Are you seeking among your living fellow-men for My kingdom, or are you quarrelling with your own age, and whimpering for institutions which had not enough of My spirit to preserve them from decay ? " It is easy—at a safe distance of 600 years—to wax sentimental over a dead world which is often all the more picturesque to us because we never dream of living there. It needs a truer effort of faith and charity to see real good in a vulgar fellow at the meeting-house over the way, who daily vexes our righteous soul by preaching our own God in formulas which are not our own. But which is the more truly Franciscan—to chant with wearisome iteration the glories of those past Rolands and Olivers of the faith, or to accept modern facts and make the best of them ? How, again, shall we plead Dante's authority for a policy of idle regret ? Thoroughly as he mastered the religious ideas of his time, he has anticipated enough of ours to assure us that he would have been no mere reactionary if his lot had been cast with us. It is quite inconclusive to plead his passionate attachment to the Church as he knew it then : just so may the noblest of women, and the most clear-sighted, cling to some incurably drunken husband. If, again, the ideal Church of his vision bore a close resemblance to the real Church whose decay he lamented, so also a good woman's ideal always resembles some unworthier object in the flesh. Assuredly, if Dante had lived in the age of modern discoveries, he would no more have neglected science than theology, but would have struggled to possess the future, leaving the dead to bury their dead.

For Dante and St. Francis are great only as they anticipate the world that is to be. While sharing the inevitable belief in the decay of their own age—inevitable then, because true History was impossible—they rose by faith high above the pessimism of their contemporaries. Such too is the real greatness of their century, beneath the purely imaginary virtues with which it is often credited. That age is truly great, not in the false appearance of monumental completeness which it presents to a distant eye, but in the ferment and struggle which are only apparent to a closer scrutiny. We are often told to admire in the Middle Ages a pastoral of the 18th-century pattern : clean-washed sheep with pink ribbons round their necks lying in the tranquil shade, while a shepherd, in pink ribbons, pipes to them through the livelong day. But in fact they felt themselves as shepherdless as we :

> " A thousand of men tho thrungen togyderes,
> Criede upward to Cryst and to His clene Moder
> To have grace to go with hem, treuthe to seke,
> Ac there was wyghte non so wys, the way thider couthe,
> But blustreden forth as bestes, over bankes and hilles,
> Til late was and longe."
>
> (P. Plowman. B. v., 517).

In short, they struggled and suffered manfully, as generation after generation has done after them : and with the stripes of these our ancestors we ourselves are healed, if we will only accept their experience. Our later time has inherited a world for which the Middle Ages groaned and travailed in pain : yet half our teachers seem to spend their best energies in trying to put us out of patience with it. In our fight against the evil of our own times, often discouraging enough, we may brace ourselves by pausing for a moment to measure the world's past progress. There is no fear of present evils and defects being ignored : poverty and crime, luxury and levity, force themselves only too plainly on our notice. The encompassing hosts of wickedness are as visible to the honest Agnostic on one side as to the honest Romanist on the other. But the progress of the past is an earnest of far greater progress in the future. It is melancholy to see good men of every generation spending their whole energies in daubing the bulging bulwarks of the old world, which the next generation abandons as useless. Meanwhile, if we would only look steadily upwards instead of downwards, we should see how many more are with us than with them ;—how truly the whole mountain is full of horses and chariots of fire round about us.

APPENDIX A.

———

NOTES ON THE CHAPTERS.

———

CHAPTER I.

1. These lacunæ existed already in the 16th century, when a transcript of the Chronicle was made.

2. For growth of luxury see Murat. ix, pp. 128 ff and 669 : Ben. Im. vol. v, p. 150 : for slaves see Biagi, p. 333, and Wadding, 1274, p. 423.

3. Ps. xliv, 3. I have thought it best to give nearly all the Bible quotations from the Douai version, as more exactly representing the Vulgate, which Salimbene of course always quotes. The page references are to the text of Salimbene in *Mon. Germ. Hist. Scriptt.*, t. xxxii. In some cases, however, I have not been able to secure in time the paged sheets of this standard edition ; in such cases I give the year under which Salimbene records the matter, together with the page of the Parma edition. Thus the reference (1250-237) will enable the reader to verify my quotation on p. 237 in the Parma edition, or under the year 1250 in either edition. Whether the whole of the *Chronicle* was written for Sister Agnes has been questioned by Father Michael, who however gives no very cogent reasons for his doubt. Certainly Salimbene's freedom of speech supplies no proof that it was not written for a nun : see chap. iii, note 7.

4. Michael, p. 2.

5. *e.g.* The early history of the city and diocese of Tournai, in the *Corpus Chronicorum Flandriæ*, 1841, t. ii, pp. 480 following. Similarly, Abbot Guibert of Nogent tells how he has been pestered to deliver imaginary panegyrics on unknown saints : and his words imply that such requests were frequent and difficult to refuse. (Migne. *Pat. Lat.*, vol. clvi, p. 624). When, in 1282, a general chapter of the Franciscans was held at Strassburg, "the Minister-General . . . . . . enjoined Brother Philip,

minister of Tuscany, to enquire diligently, if perchance he could find the day and hour on which the stigmata of Jesus Christ were imprinted on St. Francis' body. So he found a lay-brother, perfect in all virtues, to whom had been vouchsafed many revelations directly from St. Francis, to the effect that on the day of the Exaltation of the Holy Cross . . . . the Lord Jesus . . . . imprinted on him those marvellous wounds." (24 *Gen.*, p. 374).

6. *Occasional Papers.* Vol. i, p. 87 (Macmillan, 1897).

7. She speaks of Cantarelli's as "an Italian version, for which it is difficult to say one good word" (p. 60) : yet, where Salimbene has *Rex Hyrtacus*, and Cantarelli's Italian has naturally *il Rege Irtaco*, Miss Macdonell mistranslates this as "King of Ithaca " (p. 259) ; and by a similar misunderstanding of Italian she converts Salimbene's *swineherds* into *swine*. There are very many other such mistakes, often small in themselves, but going far to explain Miss Macdonell's under-estimate of Salimbene's value as a serious historian.

For a conspectus of all that is at present known about Salimbene we must await Prof. Holder-Egger's introduction : but meanwhile a very good bibliography may be gathered from Prof. Michael's *Salimbene und seine Chronik*" (Innsbruck, 1889), pp. 1-5 and 87-94. The author, though his theological bias is obvious and natural, subordinates it generally to the interests of historical truth. His book shows a truly German industry and mastery of detail, though it is interesting to an Englishman to mark the natural limits of a Jesuit professor's familiarity with the Bible text. On page 123 he quotes the similes of the she-bear robbed of her whelps, and the eagle that hasteneth to the prey, as specimens of Salimbene's picturesque phrases : the context shows that he has no suspicion of their Biblical origin.

CHAPTER II.

1. Cæs. Heist. dist. x, cap. 99. Bert. Rat. *Pred.* I, 402.

2. Vinc. Bell. Spec. Doct. x, 12. Northumberland Assize Rolls (Surtees Soc., vol. 88), p. 341. L. Gautier, La Chevalerie, pp. 342-9 ; A. Schulz, Höfisches Leben, vol. ii, p. 163 ; La Tour, chaps. 17-19 ; Bern. Sen. *Pred.* II, 103, 115 ; Pipinus in Murat, ix, 647 ; Bourbon, p. 241 (where the editor misses much of the point of the story by referring *Imperator quondam* to Barbarossa, not realizing that this was the stereotyped phrase applied to Frederick II by good churchmen after the sentence of deposition pronounced on him by Innocent IV in 1245) ; Ben. Im., vol. v,

p. 150 ; Arte, p. 74. The statutes of medieval towns often yield very interesting evidence. Those of Castellarquato, near Piacenza (about 1350 A.D., pub. 1876, p. 179 ff), give a tariff of fines for defamatory language or assaults. The former list varies from 20 pence for calling another *Tapeworm!* through a rising gradation of *Cagasangue!* and similar picturesque epithets, to £10 imperial for *Forger!* or *Traitor!* Pulling the hair or scratching, if without effusion of blood, cost £1 ; with blood, £2, unless the assault were committed "by way of correction," in which case it was condoned altogether. Biting was assessed at £2 10s. without blood, and £5 with blood. An assault without arms, if it drew blood from the victim's body, cost £10 ; if from his face, £15. With arms and blood, the tariff was £20 per wound inflicted, *plus* the doctor's bill. To throw a stone and miss cost £1 ; the too successful marksman must, however, pay £10, or, if the missile struck his victim's face, £20. This elaborate tariff (of which I have given only brief specimens) was, however, inapplicable to "ribalds, prostitutes, or vile and abject persons," who were to be fined or punished at the judge's discretion. Other equally interesting tariffs at medieval universities may be found in Rashdall, vol. ii, pp. 415, 614. As the example of Cianghella may suggest, the idea of self-control even in church was foreign to the mass of the people. Bishop Quivil of Exeter complains, in his Synod of 1287, that the services were often scandalously interrupted by two or three parishioners scuffling for the same seat ; Chaucer twice alludes to similar quarrels of women for precedence or salutes in church ; and I shall have occasion to quote St. Bernardino to the same effect (Wilkins Concil, vol. ii, p. 139, Cant. Tales, Prol. 450 and B. 3091). The scuffle of the two Archbishops for precedence in Westminster Abbey, York finally sitting on Canterbury's lap, and getting his clothes torn almost off his back, is only one of a dozen similar instances which might be quoted (Gervase of Canterbury, R.S., vol. i, p. 258). The Bishops' registers are full of solemn "reconciliations" of churches and churchyards polluted by bloodshed in brawls.

3. The 14th-century commentator, Benvenuto da Imola, speaks as if this boyish vandalism were quite common—quite apart from the pleasure which older ruffians found in destroying churches or palaces in war-time (vol. i, pp. 115, 461).

4. For this, "the earliest of all the poets of Northern Italy known to us," see Gaspary's Hist. of Early Italian Literature. Salimbene frequently quotes him, and paid him the compliment of an imitation, as he tells us (464).

5. Bert. Rat. *Pred.*, vol. i, p. 89, and ii, 205.

CHAPTER III.

1. For Leo see Fleury, an. 1240, xxxiv, and 1267, liii.

2. For Gerard of Modena, see Wadding, 1244, p. 109, and 1251, p. 277. Bartholomew of Vicenza seems, like his fellow-townsman John, to have had two sides to his character. Prof. Holder-Egger points out (p. 74, note 1) that he is almost certainly the friar who was chosen in 1231 to arbitrate between Genoa and Alessandria, but who disgraced his office by falsifications and interpolations of documents.

3.
> " Et Johannes johannizat
> Et saltando choreizat.
> Modo salta, modo salta,
> Qui celorum petis alta !
> Saltat iste, saltat ille,
> Resaltant cohortes mille,
> Saltat chorus dominarum,
> Saltat dux Venetiarum, &c."

4. For this satire, and Guido Bonatti's testimony, see Prof. Holder-Egger's notes, pp. 77, 78.

5. For a more orthodox explanation of the delay in St. Dominic's canonization, see p. 30 of the works of his successor, Jordan of Saxony (Ed. Berthier, Fribourg, 1891).

6. The story of the philosopher Secundus may be found in Vincent of Beauvais, *Spec. Hist.* x, 70. Though designed to point a moral in its time, it again is scarcely suitable for modern print.

7. *Cf.* Archiv, iii, 458, for a decree of the general chapter of Terni forbidding friars to have obscene books in their possession. A similar prohibition of *cantilenæ lascivæ* may be found in the Franciscan Constitutions of 1290, edited by Prof. Little. (Eng. Hist. Review, July, 1903, p. 493.) Similarly, in his instructions to preachers, Cardinal Jacques de Vitry finds it necessary to record the warning, " scurrilia tamen aut obscena verba vel turpis sermo ex ore predicatoris non procedant" (Vit. Serm. p. xliii, note). To realize how much need there was for this admonition, the reader should refer to A. Méray, " La Vie aux Temps des Libres Prêcheurs," vol. ii, pp. 143 ff, 243. It is a book which must often be used with caution for historical purposes : but the quotations on those pages tell their own tale. Gerson complained of the obscene talk of university professors, by which their pupils were corrupted (ii, 763). The manners of ordinary society

in this respect are clearly shown by Chaucer : but, in view of
attempts often made to avoid the natural inferences from the
Canterbury Tales, it may be worth while to add further references
here.   The licence allowed in society games may be inferred from
a "Ragman Roll," printed in Wright and Halliwell's *Reliquiæ
Antiquæ*, and from the fact that medieval moralists and preachers
condemn dancing with practical or literal unanimity, and frequently even attendance at weddings.   The book of the Knight of
La Tour Landry shows how a particularly careful nobleman talked
to his daughters : next to this book, there is perhaps no document
so significant of medieval manners in this respect as the sermons
which St. Bernardino delivered in the great square of Siena, and to
which he expressly asked the mothers to bring their daughters.
(*Prediche*, vol. ii, nos. xix-xxii : especially pp. 98, 108, 110, 132,
135, 137, 138, 140, 142, 143, 149, 150, 167-172.)   Yet that
even this licence of speech was insignificant compared with that
which the manners of the time often permitted, may be gathered
plainly from the horror with which he describes the common
sins of 14th century society in this respect.   (*Opera*, vol. iii,
p. 367*b*.)   We get similar evidence from Sir Thomas More, as I
have pointed out in *Med. Studies*, no. 6 ; and from one of the
early chapters in Raimondo da Vigna's "Life of St. Catherine
of Siena."

8.   Compare this reference to Guido with what Salimbene says of him
later on, in the chapter which I have entitled "Settling Down."

9.   Guibert is specially concerned to combat the error of the monks of
St. Médard at Soissons, who boasted the possession of one of our
Lord's milk-teeth, fallen out in the course of nature when He
was nine years old.   Incidentally he refers to those who prided
themselves on still stranger relics—*umbilicum et praeputium
Domini*.   Even Innocent III treated these relics seriously (*De
Sacro Altaris Mysterio*, Lib. iv, c. 30), discussed the claims of two
rival præputia, and summed up (very nearly in the words of Sir
John Maundeville), "yet it is better to commit all to God than
to define rashly either way."*   The encyclopædic learning of the
late Father Denifle, sub-librarian of the Vatican, has unearthed
no less than seven churches which claimed this strange relic
(*Désolation des Eglises*), vol. i, p. 167 : (*cf*. J. B. Thiers, *Traité
des Superstitions*, Avignon, 1777, p. 365, from whom it appears

* The plea that all these duplicate relics were really fragments of one genuine
relic is, I believe, quite modern, beginning with Wadding and other 17th century
scholars whose bias was definitely apologetic.   In many cases the plea is demonstrably false, for different churches claimed the relic *in its entirety*.   Mr. J. C.
Wall ("Shrines of British Saints," p. 9) writes in a very misleading fashion on
this subject.

that it had a Mass of its own). Guibert, bolder and more logical
than the great Pope, decides that, if we are to believe in the
resurrection of the body, we cannot suppose the risen Christ to
have left a tooth or any other such relic on earth (col. 631). The
monks of Soissons, he concludes, can therefore only be absolved
from heresy on the charitable supposition that they are liars:
nor can he admit that the alleged miracles afford any valid proof
of the relic's authenticity.   As a somewhat earlier chronicler
puts it "miracles are sometimes wrought by evil spirits, by God's
permission and as a punishment for men's sins." (Rodulfi Glabri
Monachi Cluniacensis Hist. lib. iv, c. 3.)   Guibert's treatise
should be read in its entirety : but the following extracts will
give some idea of the attitude of a very distinguished scholar
and churchman in St. Bernard's generation towards popular
beliefs (col. 621).   "A certain most famous church (he is probably speaking of Laon Cathedral) was sending round wandering
collectors of this kind, and had employed a preacher to beg
money for its restoration.   This man, swelling beyond all
measure in his sermon over the relics which he bore, brought
forth a casket in my presence.   'Know ye,' said he [to the con-
gregation], 'that this casket contains some of the bread which
our Lord pressed with His own teeth : and, if ye are slow to believe, behold this illustrious man' (for thus he spake of me) 'of
whose great learning ye yourselves are witnesses, and who will
rise up, if need be, as a witness to the truth of my words.'   I
confess that I blushed to hear this : and (but that I feared in
the presence of those at whose prompting he spake, lest I should
offend them even more than the speaker himself),* I should have
exposed the fraud.   What shall I say ? not even monks—let
alone the secular clergy—abstain from such filthy lucre, or shrink
from speaking heresies on matters of our faith even in my
presence.   [And I must be silent] for, as Boethius said 'I should
be rightly condemned as a madman if I were to dispute with
madmen.' "   As Guibert says in another place (624) "There are
things written about some saints which are much worse than old
wives' fables, and unfit even for the ears of cowherds."   While
the clergy hold their tongues, old women and ignorant hussies
sing these legendary saints' lives, and will attack the rash
sceptic not only with abuse but with their distaffs (622).   Men
are put as saints under the altars who, living, were scarcely fit
to come into the sanctuary (615) : villages and little towns
"daily" invent saints of their own to rival the St. Martins and
St. Rémis of the great churches : and Guibert quotes in this context, I Sam., xvii, 29, "Each nation made its own God" (622).

---

* The text of this parenthesis seems corrupt in parts, but its general sense is
obvious.

He illustrates this manufacture of relics from his own experience (625). "Those who worship they know not what, even though it be in fact a holy relic, are yet never free from great danger. If on the contrary it be no relic at all, then they live in most terrible sacrilege : for what could be more sacrilegious than to worship as divine that which is not divine ? . . . . . Hear a tale which may explain my complaints and show the truth of what I have advanced. Odo, bishop of Bayeux, natural son to Robert count of Normandy, and blood-brother to William the First of England, eagerly sought the body of St. Exuperius his predecessor, who is worshipped with the utmost reverence in the town of Corbeil. He paid, therefore, the sum of one hundred pounds to the sacristan of the church which possessed these relics, that he might take them for himself. But the sacristan cunningly dug up the bones of a peasant named Exuperius, and brought them to the bishop. The bishop, not content with his mere assertion, exacted from him an oath that these bones which he brought were those of Saint Exuperius. 'I swear,' replied the man, 'that these are the bones of Exuperius: as to his sanctity I cannot swear, since many earn the title of saints who are far indeed from holiness.' Thus the thief assuaged the bishop's suspicions and set his mind at rest. . . . . . See now what disgrace this bishop's bargain brought upon religion, when the bones of this profane peasant Exuperius were thrust into God's holy altar, which perchance will never more be purged of them. I can recall so many like deeds in all parts that I lack time and strength to tell them here ; for fraudulent bargains are made, not so much in whole bodies as in limbs, common bones being sold as relics of the saints. . . . ."

Compare this with a parallel passage from Cardinal Jacques de Vitry about 1220 (*Hist. Occ.*, c. 10). After a vivid description of the traffic in false relics and indulgences, the blackmail exacted by preachers for ill-gotten gains, and the drunkenness and debauchery in which much of the money thus extorted from the laity was spent, the Cardinal goes on : "Those who send these aforesaid filthy and blasphemous fellows to preach for the building of their churches, and the bishops who grant them their letters of authorization, shall give account to the strict judge for all their perverse deeds." While the minds of the faithful were thus poisoned by the habit of revering false relics and false miracles, the belief was commonly exploited to their own sinister purposes by rascals even in the highest ecclesiastical circles. There is a typical instance from the Winchester annals (*Annales Monastici*, R.S. ii, 100, A.D. 1262). The prior of St. Swithun's was imprisoned for his sins, and, escaping by fraud, said that St. Thomas of Canterbury had set him free by a miracle : in token whereof he hung his chains at the Canterbury shrine " pro ludibrio, ne dicam pro miraculo," remarks the indignant chronicler of the monastery.

The Papal Letter referred to in the text may be found in Raynaldus, Ann. Ecc., an. 1238, § 33 : cf. Caes. Heist., dist. ii, c. 24 : Thos. Cant. II, xxvi, 7, 8.   The latter writes : " I remember what I once heard from a very simple-minded layman at Cambrai.   Certain monks had made him a solemn promise which they had not kept : so, not seeing how else he could excuse them, he said, ' Those men break their promise to me by a daily lie ; but I believe that they lie by leave of their Abbot.'   This is still remembered as a proverb in those parts where some monk fails to tell the truth : ' Let him alone,' ' men say, ' for he lies by his Abbot's leave.' "   Thomas blames their habit of excusing such falsehoods by the example of Abraham, Sarah, Isaac, and other patriarchs.   The fraud which he relates with approval may be found in II, xxv, 13.

With regard to the case of St. Francis, see Sabatier, *Vie de St. F.*, pp. 64, 65 : Knox-Little, *St. Francis*, p. 94.   The Three Companions say (chap. vi), " restore [to thy father] the money which thou hast ; for, *since it is perchance ill-gotten*, God willeth not that thou pay it to Church uses."   Thomas of Celano, *Leg. Antiq.* (Ed. Rosedale, p. 14) : " He restored the money to his father . . . at the persuasion of the Bishop, a most pious man, for the reason that it was unlawful to expend *anything ill-gotten* on pious uses (eo quod non liceret de male acquisitis aliquid in sacros usus expendere)."   Nowhere do the early authorities, I believe, claim that the horse and cloth sold at Foligno were the saint's own : they simply say, venditis . . . quæ portaverat (or portabat).   For admitted "pious thefts," see Wadding, 1242, p. 80 ; 1252, p. 281 ; 1297, p. 359 ; and Ana. Fra. iii, 164, 425, 551.

10.   Dav. Aug., p. 357.

11.   This book is now lost.

12.   These two sermons on Antichrist have been edited by Schönbach, " Studien zur Geschichte der altdeutschen Predigt," IV.   For information as to the preacher see E. Bernhardt " Bruder Berthold v. Regensburg." (Erfurt, 1905).

13.   The vivid impression made by Berthold's sermons may be realized, even through legendary exaggerations, from an anecdote quoted from an anonymous chronicler in Pfeiffer's edition of Sermons (vol. i, p. xxi), and recorded in the Chronicle of the 24 Generals, p. 238.   " Once when he was preaching against the vice of lechery, a certain prostitute who heard him was smitten with such pain by the arrow of his word, shot from so

valiant and direct a bow, that she gave up the ghost." Berthold
prayed her back to life : " And among other things she revealed
how in that same hour wherein she died 60,000 men were called
from life in divers parts of the world; of whom three only
entered purgatory. The rest were plunged into hell, all but one
Friar Minor, who passed through Purgatory and, suddenly
taking with him two souls which had confessed to him, went up
with them to Paradise."

14. The version of this story given by Wadding explains that
Berthold had Papal authority to grant several days' Indulgence
to his listeners at every sermon, and that on this occasion he
had granted one of ten days.

15. Berthold was exceeding his powers in admitting a new member
into the Order; but he hoped that the General would ratify his
decision.

16. This address to a single definite reader, who knew Bologna, adds
to the probability that our chronicler is here thinking of his
niece.

CHAPTER IV.

1. Michael, p. 70 : but cf. Carmina Burana (Ed. Schmeller, Breslau,
1883), p. 71. For Primas see Cæs. Heist. Dist. ii, c. 15 ; Boccaccio's Decameron, G. i, n. 7, and the references given by Prof.
Holder-Egger, p. 83, note. For Feast of Fools, Gerson, vol. ii,
pp. 555A, 636D, 641c ; Od. Rig., pp. 44, 384, 472. Sacchetti.
Serm. p. 22. For the transitory nature of these Revivals, see
Murat., vol. ix, p. 55, and xxiii, 839.

2. Ecc. i, 15, Vulg. This text was a great favourite with medieval
moralists, whose pale ghosts must have rejoiced far more to welcome Carlyle's disembodied spirit than Wordsworth's.

3. Obizzo ii : see Dante, *Inf.* xiii, 110.

4. Bacon, ed. Brewer, R. S., p. 426—Rashdall, vol. ii, p. 385—Jac.
de Varagine in Murat, vol. ix, p. 45.

5. Miss Macdonell (p. 263) is misled by Cantarelli's translation into
imagining that the friars only *promised* him an excellent meal
this evening, and actually *gave* him cabbages : thus missing the
whole point of the story. This supper in the infirmary before
his admission was in fact excellent ; only, when once he was ad-

mitted, he must needs eat cabbages at his daily meals in the refectory, like the rest of the Brethren.

6. "Milvus ait pullo, dum portaretur ab illo, cum *pi pi* faris, non te tenet ungula talis."

7.   "Homini avari, e pien d'ogni empietate,
               Che lor par proprio ire in paradiso
               Quando hanno il figlio dal padre diviso!"

(Drama of 14th or 15th century, quoted in D'Ancona, *Origini del Teatro*, etc., vol. i, p. 189). Bern. Bess., pp. 297, 399. Salimbene, as his own artless revelations often show, would have learnt more easily than most otherwise amiable boys that renunciation of home ties which has always been preached as one of the first duties of a Religious. As the Mirror of Monks puts it (a treatise often printed among St. Bernard's works), "the Religious should be like Melchizedek, without father, without mother, without genealogy." Again, Brother Giles, paraphrasing Luke xiv, 26 after his own hyperbolical fashion, advised the intending postulant to "go forthwith and slay his parents, his brothers, his sisters, and his cousins" (24 *Gen.*, p. 92 : cf. 98). Though we may scarcely need Prof. Holder-Egger's warning that the man's account of the boy's ever-ready Biblical quotations are not to be taken too literally, it transpires plainly enough from this and other episodes that Salimbene, if he did not slay his father and mother, at least did not strive officiously to keep them alive.

8. This is the Illuminato of Dante, Par. xii, 130.

9. The actual word here used by Guido, though unfamiliar to polite English ears, is said to be still commonly used in Italy as a term of abuse for monks and friars.

CHAPTER V.

1. There was, nevertheless, another Br. Ognibene in the Order at the same time as our chronicler. He is mentioned by Eccleston (p. 59) as the Companion of Albert of Pisa in England.

2. This description is strikingly like the fresco of the vocation of S. Ranieri in the Campo Santo of Pisa. Salimbene could not of course have seen that actual painting ; but his imagination might well have been struck by the story, which may be read in the *Acta Sanctorum*, or in the old Italian translation of Benincasa's Life of S. Ranieri, published at Pisa in 1842.

3. *E.g.*, the story (recorded in Vincent of Beauvais and the Golden Legend) how St. John the Evangelist turned pebbles into gems and sticks into gold (p. 46): again, stories from St. Gregory's Dialogues and (nominally at least) from the *Vitae Patrum.* The Bible misquotation is p. 51, line 43 : God in the third person, p. 52, ll. 39, 40. Prof. Holder-Egger assumes that Christ's speech must have ended somewhere before this, but there is no such indication in the text; and the simplest explanation seems to be that our good friar had become thoroughly muddled with his own arguments.

4. *Hist. Occ.*, p. 349 : the *s'étaient crus* of Sabatier, *Vie de St. F.*, p. cxxiii, is distinctly misleading.

5. Matt. Paris an. 1244 (p. 558), and 1250 (695), 1252 (731).—Mon. Franc., pp. 86, 90, 96, 101, 105, 213 and *passim* —Browne Fasc. ii, 251. *Cf.* Grosseteste. Epistolæ. R.S., pp. 434, 440— AA. SS. Oct. iv, 712—Bonaventura Quæstio ii, circa Regulam —Vinc. Bell. Spec. Doct., lib. ii, dist. ii, pars 2 : Spec. Hist. lib. xxx, c. 107—Quétif-Echard. Scriptt O. P. i, 25, notes A2 and B.—Vit. Frat. cap. I, § ii, iii,—Thos. Cant., pp. 253 (lib. ii, c. 37). AA. SS. Ap. III, prologus primus in vitam S. Cath. Senensis, sect. iii and iv.

6. Archiv., vol. iii, p. 453.

7. Bacon ed. Brewer, R.S., pp. 24, 30, 33, 38, 398—404, 426, 475.

8. See an article by the present writer in the *Independent Review* for June, 1905, reprinted as No. 5 of *Medieval Studies.* (Simpkin, Marshall & Co., 6d.)

9. Gerson, vol. i, p. 201A, vol. ii, pp. 555F, 649B, 712A. The Church, he says, is as though smitten with an incurable disease, and remedies do but make her worse. Compare the striking anecdote told by Salimbene's contemporary, Etienne de Bourbon (p. 217). Etienne had been informed by Petrus Hispanus—apparently not Dante's pope of that name, but a fellow-friar—how a holy man watching in prayer saw a vision of a fair lady who announced herself to be that Holy Church on whose behalf the devotee uttered so many groans and prayers. "And then she took off the resplendent crown which she wore and bowed her head towards him. And he saw the crown of the head cleft crosswise in four parts, and vermin bubbling forth from her brain, and her wounds reeking with corrupted blood in all four quarters. 'Behold !' said she : 'from what thou canst see of my head thou mayst now understand my corruption and pain in the rest of my limbs." A strikingly similar vision of the Franciscan Order smitten with leprosy is recorded in Angelo Clareno's *Seven Tribu-*

lations—but, indeed, it would be easy to fill a whole book of this size with similar complaints from orthodox medieval churchmen.

10. We may gather from frequent allusions in inquest and assize rolls that many houses in the towns of the 13th century were built of wattle and clay. The burglar's line of least resistance was often not a door or a window, but a more or less decayed portion of the house wall.

Chapter VI.

1. *Independent Review*, Feb., 1905. *Contemporary Review*, Aug., 1905 (reprinted as *Medieval Studies*, nos. 3 and 4).

2. Newman's Letters, Ed. Mozley (1891), vol. ii, p. 481 : cf. Ana. Fra. vol. iii, pp. 118, 269, 360 and *passim*. Wadding, an. 1246, p. 158 : 1261, p. 178 : 1277, p. 22 : Eubel. Prov. *passim*.

3. For puritanism in architecture see Eccleston, col. vii ; Archiv. vi, pp. 34-36, 70 ; Ana. Fra. ii, 123 ; Wadding, an. 1242, p. 17 ; Actus S. Francisci ed. Sabatier, p. 203 ; D. Bernardi Ep. ad Guil. Abbatem, cap. xii.—For music Dav. Aug., p. 28 : R. Bacon ed. Brewer, R.S., p. 297 ; Archiv. vi, p. 70 ; Wadding, an. 1250, p. 241.—For vandalism Od. Rig., pp. 426, 572 : Sacchetti Serm. vii : Frati, p. 82 : Bern. Sen., vol. i, p. 208 ; Wadding, an. 1236, p. 429 ; 1279, 462 ; 1280, 467 ; 1291 ; Actus S. Francisci, cap. xl. For Calvinistic ideas of hell Bonav. Quæst. Circ. Reg. xix and Soliloq., c. iv : Aquinas sup. quæst. XCIV (XCV) art. iii. Gerson, vol. ii, p. 676E. In fact (as Dr. Brown has pointed out in his recent able essay on *Pearl*) this Calvinistic idea is not the exception, but the almost universal rule among medieval schoolmen. (For Angela, see Wadding, an. 1309, § xi).

   St. Bernard's bitter condemnation of elaborate architecture or ornament for monastic churches, though perhaps the most instructive document of its kind, is too long to quote here ; but I subjoin a shorter passage from the *De Claustro Animæ*, printed among the works of Hugh of St. Victor, but probably written by his contemporary, Hugh Foliot (Migne Pat. Lat., clxxvi, col. 1053). "Let the Brethren's buildings be not superfluous, but humble ; not delightful, but decent. Stone is useful in building, but of what use is carving in the stone?" Such show might indeed be permitted in the Temple under the Old Testament dispensation, and nowadays "let it be permitted (if it be permitted in any case) to those who dwell in towns or villages frequented by layfolk, that such simple minds as are not delighted by the subtleties of Holy Scripture may be held fast by the delight of of painting [or sculpture] : but, for us [monks] who delight in solitude, a horse or ox is better in the field than carved on the wall." Gerson is not at all sure that the multiplicity of images does not lead the common folk into idolatry : and Chaucer's contemporary, Eustache Deschamps, composed a poem which he entitled " Balade, que on ne doit mettre es eglises nulz ymaiges entaillez, fors le crucifix et la vierge, pour doubte d'ydolatrier." (Works, vol. viii, p. 201). There is one stanza of the poem, which (if we had no other evidence) would show the futility of Abbot Gasquet's contention that even the common people worshipped images without any risk of idolatry :

> " Car l'ouvraige est forme plaisant ;
> La painture dont je me plain,
> La beauté de l'or reluisant,
> Font croire à maint peuple incertain
> Que ce soient Dieu pour certain,
> Et servent par pensées foles
> Telz ymages qui font caroles (*i.e.*, stand in a ring)
> Es moustiers ou trop en mettons ;
> C'est tres mal fait : a briefs paroles
> Telz simulacres n'aourons."

4. Bern. Bess., pp. 303-309, 405.—St. Bonaventura in the same volume, pp. 234, 249, 262-265.—Dav. Aug., pp. 32 ff, 188, 325 ff, 286 ff.—Bern. Bess., 364, 347.—Mirror, chap. 96.— Dav. Aug., pp. 46, 48. I will quote a few of these warnings in full. St. Bonaventura (262) : " Avoid in all places all women and beardless youths, except for reasons of necessity or manifest profit." Again (239) : " Flee from women as far as in thee lieth, as from serpents ; nor even speak with any except under compulsion of urgent necessity ; nor even look in the face of any woman. . . . . . For Augustine saith 'with women we must speak roughly, briefly and stiffly : nor are they less perilous for being holy women : for, the holier they are, the more they entice us, and under the cloke of smooth speech creeps in the slime of most impious lust. Believe me, who am a bishop : I speak the truth in God, I lie not. I have known cedars of Lebanon and bell-wethers of the flock to fall by this pretext :—men whose ruin I should no more have suspected than that of St. Jerome or St. Ambrose.' " St. Bonaventura's secretary (381), after warning the friar never to kiss even his mother, if he can well avoid it, or " his sister or niece, of however tender age," adds, " how can it be lawful to touch that which is not lawful to gaze upon ?" David of Augsburg (188) : " How many have frequented spiritual women under the excuse of spiritual friendship and of obtaining their prayers ! See, what purity in their first intention, viz.,

charity and devotion ! Then follow long talks, now of God, now of their own mutual love and faith, and loving looks and little presents exchanged for memorials of friendship. . . . At last follow false goods, but true evils, namely, embraces, kisses, touching of hands and breasts, and the like ; all of which are suspicious signs of carnal affection and preludes of foul works. Last of all, as the guilt of what hath gone before, follows im- modesty, that is, open works of iniquity." There, again, is an anecdote of St. Dominic's successor, Jordan of Saxony, a saint, and a man of sound common sense (*Vit. Frat.*, p. 146): "A certain friar accused a brother friar in Chapter of having touched a woman's hand. He replied, ' She was a good woman.' Then answered the president (Jordan of Saxony), ' Rain is good and earth is good, yet from their mingling mud is formed : so also is it even with the good hand of a man and of a woman ; for when they join together evil thoughts and affections sometimes arise.'" S. Bernardino of Siena, enumerating the cases in which a friar may lawfully appeal to the higher authorities against the deci- sion of his immediate superiors, specifies "also if he were to be compelled by the superiors of any monastery to hear confessions, and through such confessions should frequently fall into frailty on account of the foul things which he hears in the confessional . . . . also if any woman were to solicit him to sin with her by signs or words or presents" (*Opp.*, vol. iii, p. 442). Many friars tried to live up to this ascetic creed : admiring chroniclers record how St. Louis of Toulouse was asked by his mother, after a long absence, " ' Am I not your mother, who may lawfully kiss you ?' To whom her virginal son replied, ' I know, my Lady, that you are my mother and a woman, whom it is not expedient for a servant of God to kiss ' " (24 Gen., p. 434). Also, "Brother Jacopo di Benedetto da Todi, a man of great perfection, was so firmly rooted in purity of mind and body that (as he said) he cared to see the head and face of the fairest woman no more, or perchance even less than an ass's head " (*Ibid*, p. 460). Yet we may see clearly, even from Salimbene, how little the majority were inclined to avoid all social intercourse with women, and how easy it might be to fall into spiritual familiarity with a nun. A little later, Alvarez Pelayo, a learned Spanish Franciscan, who became a Papal Penitentiary, complained of the frequency with which familiarity between nuns and their *devoti*, or spiritual directors, led to sin. "Scarce any nun is without her carnal *devotus* . . . . and she holds herself neglected who has no such devotee, or rather corrupter. Secular folk and nuns' relations know this, and murmur and are scandalized and complain to the Superiors, but to small purpose ; for the flame of the flesh is a consuming fire." (*De Planctu Ecclesiæ*, fol. 243A ; lib. ii, art. 73). These words, from a churchman in such high position, lend double significance to Salimbene's tales of the Abbess of Gatharola, and the poor nun who had Cardinal Ottaviano for her father; and they make us understand the frequent attempts of some of the best Franciscan Generals to cut the male part of the Order altogether apart from the female (cf. Wadding, 1245, p. 140; 1250, p. 223; 1255, p. 537; 1263, p. 218). In this last passage St. Bonaventura asserts most earnestly "the secret evil and hidden danger" of such relations. Moreover, there was the further chance of scandal even where there was no guilt, as St. Bonaventura says again in repudiating the care of the béguinages: "if any of these [béguines] were of evil repute for any crime of fornication or adultery, forthwith men who perchance love us not would publish this abroad to our infamy, saying, 'Lo! these barefooted Sisters bring forth little barefooted children for them! but of whom should they conceive such if not of those who are busy about them all day long? And wanton clergy or laymen, in their hatred of us, would be more unfriendly to those Sisters, either to corrupt them or to bring them into evil fame, since their disgrace would fall upon us rather than upon others.'" (*Libell. Apol.*, Quæst. xvi). These passages, out of ten times as many which might be quoted, may suffice to show the reader how much greater were the perils of monastic life in days when the Religious swarmed everywhere, and public opinion was comparatively lenient, than in our days of few monasteries, efficient police, and strong public opinion.

5. Friars and food, see McCabe, "Twelve Years in a Monastery," p. 263, and "Life in a Modern Monastery," chap. iv : Eccleston R. S., p. 19 : Bonav. Quæst. circ. Reg. ix : Bert. Rat. Sermones, p. 30 : Archiv. vol. iv, pp. 77, 80. cf. 187 : Bern. Bess., chaps. xxi, xxii, xxxii : Hugo de S. Victore de Inst. Novitiorum. (Migne. Pat. Lat., vol. 176), col. 949c : Humb. de Romanis Speculum Religiosorum (Cologne, 1616), p. 136. "Indecenter agitur" (says B. Bess., p. 352) . . . "si quis tussit aut sternutat non aversa facie a mensa; raro enim hoc fit sine qualicunque emissione reliquiarum oris ; si nudam manum in mensa naribus emungendis vel carni nudæ scalpendæ apponit, vel manum ipsum ad vestimenta detergit." The handkerchief or napkin, though not absolutely unknown even in the 13th century, was seldom or never used for its chief modern purpose. The 14th century " Boke of Curtasye " warns :—

> " If thou spitt ouer the borde, or elles opon,
> Thou shalle be holden an uncurtase mon . . .
> If thy nose thou clense, as may be-falle,
> Loke thy honde thou clense, as wythe-alle,
> Priuely with skyrt do hit away,
> Other ellis thurgh thi tepet that is so gay."

(*Manners and Meals.* E.E.T.S., p. 301, cf 25). A quotation from Hugh of St. Victor's rules for the table behaviour of Austin Canons, will enable the reader to see how nearly monks and friars approached each other in this respect. (Migne *Pat. Lat.* clxxvi, 949). "Let nothing be done with noise or tumult . . . do not as some do, who on sitting down to table show their intemperance of mind by a certain uneasy agitation and confusion of their limbs. They wag their heads, stretch out their arms, spread out their hands on high, and not without great boorishess (as though they would swallow down the whole meal at one gulp), they strain and stretch with unseemly gestures. They pant, they gasp for anguish : you might fancy that they were seeking some easier inlet to their clamorous maw, as though the straitness of their gullet could not minister in proper abundance to their hungry stomach. . . . Some at their meals, in their anxiety to empty the dishes, wrap in the cloth, or throw upon it, the sops reeking with fat or gravy that have been poured over them ; until at last (having meanwhile gutted the inward parts of the dish) they put back the sops as they were. Others, as they drink, plunge their fingers half-way into the cup. Others wipe their greasy hands on the frocks, and turn again to handle the food. Others again fish out their vegetables with bare fingers instead of a spoon ; so that they seem to seek to wash their hands and refresh their belly with one and the same broth. Others thrust again into the dish their half-gnawed crusts or sops, and dip into the cups the leavings of their own teeth in the guise of sippets. These things (as I have said above) would be shameful for me to describe, but that I have been forestalled by such as do them in deed."

6. *Cf.* a Reviewer in the *Church Times* for Aug. 26th, 1904, who complains that the average Englishman judges monks by "the consciousness of what he himself should (*sic.*) be and do if he were placed in a cloister," and who goes on to betray complete ignorance of monastic life as described by monks themselves.

7. Friars in church, see esp. Bern. Bess., pp. 301-341. Bonav., pp. 56, 218 of same vol.: Dav. Aug. pp. 7, 107 : Cæs. Heist., vol. i, pp. 202-206, 222, 250 (2), 283, 284, 333 : vol. ii, p. 104 : Vit. Frat., p. 206. Nic. Clar. Serm. iii in Nativ. Domini. (in Mabillon's St. Bernard, 1719, vol. ii, p. 584). Thos. Cant. pp. 334, 335, 405. Italie Mystique, p. 71.

8. The law might indeed forbid : but the reader will see later on that the secular clergy were often almost incredibly irreverent in medieval churches.

9. Talking, laughing, etc., Eccleston R.S., p. 20. Vit. Frat., p. 144. Bonav. l. c. 207. Bern. Bess. 328, 357, 377, 395, 396. Archiv., vol. iii, p. 168. Bern. Bess. 340, 302. This same habit of public criticism during service is noted by Bishop Grandisson among his clergy in Exeter Cathedral. Too often one officiant would trip in his reading ; when the rest, who should rather have mourned his fault, would cry aloud in the vulgar tongue, "Cursed be he who spake that last lie" (*Reg.*, p. 586).

10. For sanitary rules in church, etc., see Bern. Bess. 327, 328, 338, 339, 364, 368, 370, 406. Flamenca (ed. P. Meyer), line 3, 131 ; cf. T. Wright, Domestic Manners, pp. 162, 277, 366.

11. *Mantellos curtos usque ad nates.* For this, and other wilful singu-larities, the General Crescenzio da Jesi "valiantly exterminated them." (xxiv Gen., p. 263. Cf. 469, and Ubertino's description of the Brethren's dresses in *Archiv.*, iii, 56).

12. *Archiv.*, iii, 65.

13. Cæs. Heist. dist. iv, c. 48 : cf. iii 8, iv 6, xii 5. For monastic and general ideas of personal cleanliness in the Middle Ages see Busch. introd., p. xxiv, and p. 584 : Consuetudines S. Aug. Cant. (H. Bradshaw Soc. 1902), p. 195 : Winchester Obe-dientiary Rolls (Hampshire Record Soc.), p. 71 : cf. 36, 87 : R. Steele, Medieval Lore, p. 51 : Vinc. Bell. Spec. Hist. xxviii 128, and xxix 116 : Register of Peckham, R.S., vol. i, p. 1. : Maitland, Dark Ages, 1890, p. 85. David of Augsburg mentions vermin among the petty trials which no religious can escape : "oportet nos pati morsiones pulicum et similium bestio-larum" (259) ; cf. the Dominican *Vitae Fratrum*, p. 39, where Father Conway renders a plain word of the original by the euphemistic phrase "and other discomforts." Etienne de Bourbon is even more plain-spoken about the inconvenience of the elaborately dressed wigs which were in vogue among 13th century ladies, and which had to be built up with such toil and kept so carefully undisturbed. Such fashionable ladies, he says, are "the devil's martyrs" : just consider "the pain and labour which they suffer in getting and dressing [the hair], washing and combing, dyeing and anointing, suffering vermin and nits and lice therein, etc., etc." (pp. 233, 240). Michelet was too hasty in asserting that Europe forgot to bathe for 1,000 years ; but it is none the less true that the daily tub draws a hard and fast line between polite society in the 20th century and in the 13th. This is clearly shown by many detailed descriptions of the knight's morning toilette : *e.g.* Petit Jean de Saintré pt. i, c. ix :

Manners and Meals E.E.T.S., p. 179: Flamenca, l. 224 ff.
cf. 1556 ff. See again the words of St. Vincent Ferrer (in
a sermon quoted by Thureau-Dangin *St. Benardin de Sienne.*
Chap. iv, § ii. (Paris, 1897.) "What does a man do on
awakening in the morning? He does ten things: opens his
eyes, sits up in bed, half dresses, gets out of bed, spits, puts on
his drawers, washes his hands, etc., etc." L. Gautier, in his
La Chevalerie, shows clearly enough that the bath was not unknown, but entirely fails to see that this was the *warm bath*,
taken as a luxury or by doctor's orders. Siméon Luce points
out that public bathing establishments of this kind were to be
found sometimes even in villages in 13th century France: but
his assertions on this and similar points are summed up very in-
accurately and apologetically by Abbot Gasquet (*Gt. Pestilence*,
pp. 54-56: cf. Luce, chap. iii).

14. Cf. Ubertino's contention (Archiv. iii, p. 176), that "the Rule
     alloweth no change of garments, for outer or for inner wear . . .
     yet, since the Brethren need now and then (*interdum*) to wash
     their frocks [which the Rule compelled them to wear day and
     night], St. Francis ordained that some should be kept in com-
     mon, more or less according to the numbers of the brethren;
     which common frocks might be used by the sick." Thomas of
     Eccleston (R.S. p. 33), mentions how "Brother Elias sent word
     round that the Brethren should wash their own drawers: so the
     Brethren of the English Administration washed theirs, according
     to his bidding; but they of the Scottish Administration waited
     for further orders." This probably involved the problem of the
     lavandaria, or washerwoman, which had long been a serious
     difficulty in the older orders, and became acute later on among
     the Friars also, as Ninguarda's 16th century Visitations show.

15. For friars' morality see Ana. Fra. iii, p. 268. Piers Plowman, B.
     xx, 345. Ben. Im. vol. v. p. 85. Busch, p. 45. Gerson, vol.
     i. p. 194E., ii, 641C. Gower., Vox Clamantis, lib. iii, l. 837;
     and the parallel passages in his *Mirour de l'Omme.*

16. *Contemporary*, Dec., 1905, and April, 1906: cf. reply by Father
     R. H. Benson in the June number, and my rejoinder in July.
     I cannot help regretting that Father Benson, from a dislike of
     controversy which I know to be genuine in his case, has de-
     clined to allow me to reprint his essay under the same covers
     as my two (*Medieval Studies*, No. 6, "The Truth about the
     Monasteries"). I had already dealt with Abbot Gasquet's
     falsifications of the real evidence in my first *Medieval Study*,
     "The Monastic Legend." The matter was also discussed at
     some length in the *Tablet* (Dec. 6, 1905, to the following Feb-

ruary) : but my antagonist in that paper, Father Gerard, whom I had convicted of gross and palpable mis-statements, altogether declined to let me reprint the whole correspondence. I have since permitted the Protestant Reformation Society to reprint my letters, with summaries of Father Gerard's, in a pamphlet entitled, " Catholic Truth and Historical Truth."

17. *Monumenta Franciscana*, p. 55. Father Cuthbert's translation (" The Friars, and how they came to England ") destroys the real sense of this passage, by omitting the crucial word *ordinis*, thus making it appear as if the friars' difficulties were incurred in reforming other institutions than their own.

18. Cf. Eccleston's description of the General Aymon of Faversham, who through his early asceticism " became at last so feeble and delicate that he could scarce live without roast meats and warm food " (R.S., p. 22). Similarly Bourbon (p. 422) describes the extent to which St. Bernard, after ruining his own health, was forced to set a dangerous example to his brother monks.

19. Bert. Rat. Serm., p. 11 : cf. 8, 9, 13, 14, and *passim.*—Bonav. Quæst. circ. Reg. xix : cf. the even stronger language of his contemporary, David of Augsburg, as to the scorn and persecution to which strict friars were already subjected by the laxer majority (pp. 110, 285, 331).—Bert. Rat. Serm., pp. 29, 41, 71, 90.

Chapter VII.

1. In theory, divorce in the modern sense is not permitted by the Roman Church ; but it was generally easy for influential persons to obtain a decree of nullity on different pretexts, or (as apparently in this case) to take the law into their own hands and practically change wives at pleasure. For the absurd and immoral anomalies of the Canon Law on the question of marriage, see the chapter on this subject in Pollock and Maitland's " History of English Law."

2. Cf. Brother Thomas Hibernicus, who imitated a certain St. Mark in cutting off his thumb to escape the priesthood (Eubel. Prov., p. 51), and Conrad of Offida, one of the greatest of the early friars. " Brother Andrew asked Brother Conrad of Offida why he never celebrated, since he was priest and was [formerly] wont to celebrate frequently : whereunto he answered, ' Know, Brother Andrew, that before I was made priest, I was for full seven years continuously in such a mood that in all created things— stocks and stones and whatsoever else they might be—in all, I

say, I was wont to behold God wrapped in sweet celestial light:
and then I was so comforted that I thought to possess a Paradise
everywhere. And at that time it was burdensome to me to
serve at mass, for that it distracted me from this consolation,
when I must needs serve the priest in his mass. How then
could I now celebrate mass, though I receive the Lord's body on
Sundays and feast days for the reverence and efficacy of the
Sacrament? And meseems that, before I was a priest, St.
Francis appeared more often to me than now: and at times he
would lean his head on my breast, and would speak to me at
greater length than now.'" (Ana. Fra., iii, 427.)

3. For St. Francis see H. Böhmer, Analekten z. Gesch. des. F. v.
Assisi. (Tübingen, 1904), pp. 28, 39. The former reference is
translated at length, though not very correctly, by Miss Macdonell, p. 152. The hermitage system went on at least till 1220,
six years before the saint's death: Sabatier, p. 199.

4. Salimbene, pp. 100 foll. Lempp. (p. 116) thinks that his opinions
can scarcely be taken as altogether typical on this point; that the
Order can scarcely have drifted so far in so short a time. But it
had undoubtedly drifted at least as far from the Saint's purpose
in the direction of extravagant buildings and reception of money:
and even the love of money is not a more natural instinct than
that the learned members of a religious Order should resent such
an equality, or even preponderance, of the unlearned, as was the
rule under St. Francis.

5. Cf. Dante, Inf., xxiii, 3. After the example of the earlier
monastic Orders, friars were commanded always to go about two
by two, to avoid scandal: and the same regulation was enforced
on the inmates of colleges at medieval universities.

6. Salimbene here exaggerates: Haymo of Faversham (1240-1244)
did indeed forbid their promotion to offices, but they were still
admitted to the Order, as Prof. Holder-Egger points out (p. 103,
note 6).

CHAPTER VIII.

1. For Guido Bonatti see Dante Inf., xx, 118, and Prof. Holder-
Egger's note on this page 163.

2. It is noteworthy that St. Bonaventura was here of an opposite
opinion to his contemporary Salimbene. He specifies this
"frequent re-election of officials as one of the chief causes of the
decay of a religious Order," and gives his reasons at length.
(Quæst circ. Reg., xix.)

3. Cf. his Life by Bonaventura, viii, 9, 10. I have already noted (*Medieval Studies*, no. 3) how little the Order in general seems to have shared Francis's love of animals. From the time of the General Chapter of Narbonne, at least (1260), it was a strict rule " that no animal be kept, for any Brother or any convent, whether by the Order or by some person in the Order's name, except cats and certain birds for the removal of unclean things."

4. Such assertions as that in Mr. F. S. Stevenson's *Grosseteste* (p. 148), that the early part of the 13th century was the " golden age of English monasticism " cannot be taken without very considerable qualification. There is a strong tendency among modern writers to ignore the large body of irreproachable evidence as to widespread and serious abuses in all, or nearly all, the Orders long before 1250. Guibert of Nogent, early in the 12th century, describes the monasteries of his time as dumping grounds for young men of good family who could not otherwise be provided for, and who therefore spent their monastic life in idleness and dissipation of the common revenues. (Migne. Pat. Lat. clvi, col. 850) : Jacques de Vitry, early in the 13th, and Roger Bacon, towards the end of the same century, bear testimony at least as unflattering. See note 5 to chap. 12, and appendix D, in which I have put a small selection from the vast mass of available evidence.

5. Among the witty and improper pieces of prose and verse contained in the Franciscan MS. Harl. 913, is one on the Abbot of Gloucester's Feast, in which the Brethren make this complaint. See *Reliquiae Antiquæ*, i, 140.

6. For Pietro Peccatore see Dante, Par., xxi, 122, and Toynbee's *Dante Dictionary* s.v. *Damiano* and *Pietro degli Onesti*. It is very possible that Dante confused the two men ; but these words of Salimbene's seem to show conclusively that the second was the real Pietro Peccatore.

7. Cf. Father Cuthbert's *The Friars, and how they came to England*, pp. 105, 106, in which a doubtful sentence of Prof. Brewer's is exaggerated out of all moderation and reason. Apart from such passages as this of Salimbene's, and hundreds of other briefer testimonies to the same spirit among the records of the early friars, (e.g. *Bonaventura's Life of St. Francis*, v. 5), Father Cuthbert's theory is flatly contradicted by two passages of the very chronicle which he has undertaken to edit (pp. 207, 233). His only medieval reference in its support is to Chaucer (Prol. 212, 213), where the poet obviously intends slyly to convey that same accusation against the Friars' morality which is outspokenly

pronounced in *Piers Plowman*, B. xx. 344. Father Cuthbert's work, though the *Church Times* commends it warmly "to all who are vexed with Dissenters," abounds in such purely imaginary presentations of history ; and his translation of Thomas of Eccleston, apart from a few obvious blunders, is disfigured by one or two very unfortunate misrepresentations.

CHAPTER IX.

1. Cf. *Purg.*, xi, 81.

2. For the extent to which Latin hymnology was indebted to popular songs, see Du Méril, pp. 26 ff.

3. Helinand in Vinc. Bell. *Spec. Hist.*, l. xxix, c. 144—Ben. Im., vol. iii, p. 75.

4. Some instances of the rapid oblivion which overtook even miracle-workers may be found in Wadding 1212, § 42 : 1233, p. 369 : 1235, p. 401 : 1282, p. 114 : 1291, p. 281 : 1305, § 4. The seven bulls said to have been addressed in 1216 to seven bishops about the Portiuncula Indulgence were all lost by 1281, or at latest by 1330 (Sabatier, p. 415 : cf. 24 *Gen.*, p. 372 note). Bartholomew of Pisa, when he wrote his book of the *Conformities*, was unable to ascertain where Simon of Assisi was buried. Already in 1360 the important book of the Minister-General Crescenzio da Jesi, on the lives of early Friars, was half destroyed : "some of it is left, the rest has perished through neglect." St. Adhémar de Filsin died in 1309 : half a century later the Chronicler of the *Twenty-four Generals* writes "although much had been written of his life and miracles, all have been lost by carelessness" (Ana. Fra., pp. 160, 263, 464: cf. 216 and 372 *note*). I shall have occasion to return to this subject of medieval negligence of books. (Chap. xiii, note 6).

5. See the confessions of W. de Notyngham in *Mon. Franc.* R.S., p. 71, and compare those of Adam Marsh, on p. 336.

6. Wadding, 1256, pp. 2 ff.

7. Dante. Par. xii, 134.

8. Miss Macdonell (pp. 246 foll.) brings out well the unselfish humility of John's last thirty years, though here again she twice misreads Salimbene, and misapplies to John some words of Ubertino which were really written of St. Francis.

9. These testimonials to John of Parma are quoted in full by Affò, Vita di Gioanni di Parma (Parma, 1777), pp. 181, 182. Miss Macdonell puts the date of his beatification wrongly in 1770.

10. " Ugolino the shearer," whom Miss Macdonell quotes to prove Salimbene's want of snobbishness, even towards humble friends, would in fact be a man of wealth and position in the city. The *"tonsores"* (not *shearers*, but *shearmen*) were clothdressers, possessing a quarter of their own in 13th century Oxford, Norwich, and elsewhere ; and a master-shearman, such as the context implies Ugolino to have been, would be a wealthy man.

11. Not the Azzo VIII of Inf. xviii, 56 and Purg. v, 77 ; but his great-grandfather, Azzo VII, who died in 1264.

12. The great heroine of the Church party, and probably the Matelda of Purg. xxviii, 40 foll.

13. Ecc. x, 19 (Vulg.) Those who groan over the power of " the almighty dollar " in the modern world, may be consoled to learn that this text was repeated in the Middle Ages with wearisome iteration by writers of all classes, and certainly with at least as much justice as at present.

CHAPTER X.

1. These and half-a-dozen similar sentences in Salimbene form an admirable commentary on Par. xvii, 58.

2. With regard to Salimbene's remark about the five talents Prof. Holder-Egger falls into a curious error. Not recognizing the allusion to the Parable of the Talents, he notes, " I have never read this incident in the lives of St. Francis : nor do I see how it can be bold of a man who would not touch money." Salimbene, with the usual Franciscan ingenuity in finding types of St. Francis throughout Holy Scripture, has no doubt that St. Matthew's words " to one he gave five talents " prefigured the one Saint to whom Christ had given his five wounds. For it must be borne in mind that this miracle of the Stigmata, not uncommon since, was still unique when Salimbene wrote.

3. Cæs. Heist. Dist. vi, c. 30.

4. The Parmese had torn down all the exiles' houses and built their city walls with the materials (Murat. ix, p. 773D).

5. This is the Bernardo Rossi whom Salimbene compares with Charlemagne : a flattering description which Miss Macdonell, blindly following Cantarelli's translation, transfers to the Emperor Frederick.

CHAPTER XI.

1. Cf. Ben. Im., iii, 320 (commentary on Purg., xi, 134 ff). Prof. Holder-Egger throws doubt on this story : very unnecessarily, as I cannot help thinking. The fact that Enzio was at one time treated well in prison affords only a very slight presumption in favour of his continued good treatment, especially in the Middle Ages.

2. For the horrors of prison life even under ordinary circumstances see Gross, *Office of Coroner* (Selden Soc.), pp. 79 ff. Six prisoners died in Northampton Gaol, within little more than a year (1322-3), of "hunger and thirst and cold."

3. Chron. Parm. in Murat., ix, pp. 810, 823, 825.

4. One of the most crying sins of Bologna is branded by Benvenuto da Imola, vol. i, pp. 522 ff. (Commentary on *Inf.* xv, 106 ff.)

5. *Ben.* i, 128 : cf. 222—though in iii, 397 he seems to say that all provinces of Italy were alike desolate.

6. III, 181, on *Purg.*, vi, 76 foll.

7. Sermon iv, p. 93.

CHAPTER XII.

1. Miss Macdonell, again misled by the Italian translation, represents the courtiers as *standing* on each other's shoulders !

2. Lyons was then nominally in the Empire.

3. This latter tree is described also, in much the same language, in the *Chronicle of the Twenty-four Generals*, p. 354.

4. This unflattering account of Papal Legates is borne out by the distinguished John of Salisbury, who writes : " Not even do the Papal legates keep their hands altogether free from bribes ; for sometimes they rage with such fury in their provinces as though

Satan had come out from before the Lord's face to scourge His church . . . . I do not say this of all legates, however." (Migne. Pat. Lat. cxcix, col. 580.)

5. This remark about the Benedictines is all the more significant, because the journal of his contemporary, Odo Rigaldi, shows that even these stricter French monasteries were already in such a state of decay as would not be tolerated in modern England.

6. For these parodies see Du Méril, pp. 204 *note*, 222 *note*.

7. *i.e.*, in modern French "J'ai bu: à vous!"—"I have drunk, now it's your turn!"

8. For Eudes Rigaud, one of the most remarkable prelates of the Middle Ages, see the chapter below on "The Princes of the Church."

9. See *Archiv.*, vol. vi, p. 129.

10. It was not only in churches that the scantiness of medieval furniture frequently necessitated sitting on the ground, e.g., Joinville, vi, § 37 "li roys . . . mist la main à terre, et dist: 'Seez-vous ci, bien près de moy, pour ce que on ne nous oie.'" Cf. *ibid* iv, § 27; Eccleston R.S., p. 60; Rashdall i, pp. 438, 561. This explains, though it can scarcely justify, the frequency of scuffles for seats during the service.

11. Cf. Chaucer, *Prologue* i, 179. The ascription of these words to "Holy Scripture" will surprise none of those who know what quasi-Biblical authority was usurped in the Middle Ages by some most unbiblical books: this quotation is in fact from Gratian's *Decretum*.

12. See below: "Princes of the Church."

CHAPTER XIII.

1. One of the spurious writings called forth by the popularity of Joachim's prophecies.

2. The same "rigour of justice" was also inflicted on friars whose only crime was that of interpreting the Rule too literally. Perhaps the worst case was that of Bro. Pontius Potugati, who had refused to give up for the burning certain writings which he possessed of the Spiritual Jean de Pierre d'Olive. "Nam vin-

culis ferreis compeditum et catena ferrea, infra carcerem fetidum
artum et cæcum ligatum includunt, et affigentes trunco cathenam
in tantum eum coarctant et stringunt ut non alibi, nisi ubi sedere
ferro gravatus cogebatur, posset secedere vel modicum ad requisita
nature, super nudam humum urina pedum suorum et stercore
stratam, fetentem et lutosam, infixus sordido limo jacebat. . . . .
Infirmatus tandem jacebat vel potius reclinatus sedebat sub
pondere ferri in fetoribus stercoris et urine animo letus et cari-
tatis igne succensus, infinitas Deo gratias refferens spiritum Deo
reddidit. . . . Custos . . . duobus fratribus laycis robustis corpore
mandat, in fossis orti foveam aliquam facere et in ea corpus hora
secreta projectum humo operire.   Accedunt fratres hii injuncta
perficere, et dum laborant corpus semisepultum in vermibus et
stercore a cathena et ferreis vinculis solvere, a lumbis deorsum
inveniunt [per] multitudinem vermium ex magna parte corrosum.
Intuentes vero vultum ipsius obstupuerunt, eo quod quedam
claritas refulgebat in facie ejus, que videbatur naturam hominis
excedere, et esse potius angelica quam humana."—Angelo Clareno
in *Archiv.* ii, p. 300.   Other similar cases may be found described in Dr. Lea's *Inquisition*, vol. iii, pp. 1-89.

3. Joachim was generally understood to have fixed the year 1260 for
    the beginning of the New Era: and indeed Salimbene himself
    says as much on p. 466.   It is significant of the widespread un-
    rest and expectation of change that, in the great dispute between
    the Mendicants and the University of Paris, both parties were
    agreed as to the mysterious significance of the year 1260.
    (Rashdall i, 383, note 1.)

4. Further allusions to the love of the Dominicans for great convents,
    and to the relations between them and the Franciscans, may be
    found on pp. 88 ff of the *Mon. Germ.*, and 337 of the Parma
    edition (an. 1285).

5. For further information about Gerard and his book, see Rashdall i,
    345 ff.

6. This was of course a *pis-aller*; Frederick, the original Antichrist,
    being now dead.

7. This systematic destruction of older MSS. for the sake of fresh
    writings was especially common in Italy, *e.g.* the library of
    Bobbio, not far from Parma, contained a very large proportion
    of palimpsests.   There is a strong tendency among modern
    writers to exaggerate the responsibility of the Reformation for
    the destruction of books as well as for that of ancient buildings.
    Visitations and similar documents supply us with abundant evi-

dence of books lost or decayed through the fault of clerical custodians; it is by no means rare to hear of books completely lost to posterity, as that attributed to Lazarus, of which Salimbene tells us a few pages lower down, and those of which I have already spoken in note 4 to chap. ix. The number of books written in monasteries has also been grossly exaggerated. Eudes Rigaud's register shows us that the Norman monks in Salimbene's day seldom did any writing at all. It may be doubted whether, if there had been no Reformation, we should possess many more medieval books and buildings than we do at present. For instance, there is more ancient stained glass left in English than in Italian churches; and no country can compare with ours in the completeness of its medieval episcopal records. It is characteristic of the amount of detailed research which still needs to be done, that so good a scholar as Prof. Medley can write (*Social England*, illustrated edition, vol. ii, p. 762) "large numbers of copyists were at work in every monastery and nunnery throughout the land." This is simply to accept uncritically the exaggerated ideas set afloat by S. R. Maitland in his *Dark Ages*— ideas which sprang out of a natural reaction from the still more uncritical acceptance, a generation earlier, of Robertson's misstatements as to the booklessness of the Middle Ages. For the small amount of writing done in the monasteries of Normandy, even in the 13th century, and the frequent neglect of their books, see the Register of Abp. Eudes Rigaud, pp. 76, 145, 339, 361, 407 (2), 496, 555, 556, 572, 577, 578 (2), 585, 593, 596, 597, 601, 609, 612, 619, 622 (2), 628, 630, 632, 633, 639. Even great monasteries like Eu and Tréport had nobody on the premises who could re-write the dilapidated service-books. Compare the evidence of Nicke's Norwich Visitations (Camden Soc., 1888, pp. 178, 295), and of Gascoigne (pp. 73, 112), who tells us plainly that the 15th century monks were rather destroyers than producers of books.—At the Augustinian Priory of Taunton, in 1339, five of the twenty-three Brethren were unable even to sign their names to a document, and therefore commissioned Brother John Coker to sign for them. (Reg. Rad. de Salopia. Somerset Record Soc., p. 351). Cf. Gerson, *de Laude Script.*, Consid. x, and especially xii.

8. The seer thus raised up in Parma is no doubt Dante's Asdente, of whom Salimbene will speak at length later on.

9. See his treatise in Baluze-Mansi, Misc. ii, p. 595 ff: especially 600, 604, 609, 610: cf. Bourbon, p. 25.

10. It is possible that the *pueri* of this passage were simply the city loafers, "undesirables," and lower classes generally. The

Chronicon Parmense describes a similar scene of mob-rule in 1294 (Murat. ix, 827a), where *pueri* is evidently used in this sense.

11. Here, for instance, are the words of S. Giovanni Capistrano in the life of his contemporary S. Bernardino : " All Italy then (about 1420) lay wholly sunken in vices and crime. . . . . There was no devotion to be found amongst Religious and Clerics, no faith among their flocks, no mercy, modesty, or morality (*disciplina morum*)." Savonarola, of course, spoke equally strongly.

CHAPTER XIV.

1. The steps by which the Magdalene became one of the greatest saints of the Middle Ages are interesting to trace. Many of the romantic tales which had grown up round her and her family may be found in the *Golden Legend* : but the high-water mark is reached by the pseudo-Cavalca, whose legend of the saint has recently been translated by Miss Hawtrey (Lane, 1904).

2. For the *aureola* see Ducange (who quotes Josephus Angles in 4 Sent., dist. xlix, art. 6), and Bonav. Compend. Theol. Verit., lib. vii, cap. 29. This is a work of doubtful authorship : it is also ascribed to Albertus Magnus and Thomas Aquinas. The virgins' crown will be white, the martyrs' red, and the doctors' green : each will proceed from a certain redundancy of spiritual joy shining forth in outward shape : cf. Dante, Par. v, 131-137 ; xi, 18 ; xvii, 121-123 ; xviii, 55-63, etc., etc.

3. For John of Parma's extreme reverence see Angelo Clareno in Archiv. ii, 267.

CHAPTER XV.

1. Miss Macdonell (p. 278) adduces it as a special proof of Salimbene's curiosity that he should have *turned aside to see* this landslip : but he nowhere speaks of having actually seen it, and only implies that he learnt what he tells us on his natural road from Lyons to Genoa. This fall of Mont Grenier, more terrible even than the Goldau catastrophe, is mentioned by Matthew Paris (an. 1248), who attributes it to the divine wrath at the greed and lust and brigandage of the inhabitants of that valley. On the other hand, Étienne de Bourbon (p. 182) explains that God's object was to punish an unscrupulous clerical politician named Jacques Bonivard, who had wrongfully seized a priory near

Chambéry, and had no sooner taken possession than the landslip overwhelmed him.

CHAPTER XVI.

1. Nicolaus Anglicus or Brito, bishop of Assisi in 1247. He is described as a man of great learning and high moral character.

2. For the Flagellants see Murat. ix, 704 ; Affò, vol. iii, p. 259. Fleury an. 1259, § 62. Gerson, vol. i, pp. 636-643.

3. Boccaccio, Decameron, G. v, n. 8.

4. Ricobaldo an. 1275, in Murat. ix : Chron. Parm. an. 1275.

5. Vit. Ex., pp. 20, 21.

6. I have already pointed out in the *Independent Review* of Feb., 1905 (*Medieval Studies*, no. 3), how little the contention of the Marquis de Rambures in his *L'Eglise et la Pitié envers les Animaux* is borne out by actual medieval facts.

CHAPTER XVII.

1. Ricobaldi Ferrarensis Additamentum (Murat. ix, 190c).—Murat. ix, p. 792.

2. Dante, Vita Nuova. cap. iii.—Murat. ix, p. 801.

3. I point out lower down (chap. xxiii) how mistaken is the common idea that this sort of vandalism originated with the Reformation : and I have dealt more fully with the same subject in *Medieval Studies*, nos. 3 and 4.

4. This decree of the Synod of Milan is in Murat. ix, p. 570.

5. Cæs. Heist. Dist. viii, c. 52.

6. *Purg.* xxiv, 24.—Salimbene smacks his lips on another page (572) over the recollection of this choice vintage, àpropos of which he quotes " the verses of a certain buffoon, who wrote :

'O precious juice of the vine, what gift hath life like thine ?
If two sorts come to the feast, then fill me a cup of the best !
Small is the profit to me if I suck down less than three ;
Sweet is the fourth full bowl, and deep is the calm of my soul ;
But the fifth cup sets me adaze, and my memory all in a maze ;
With the sixth I desire no more, but sprawl full length on the floor.' "

CHAPTER XVIII.

1. R. Bacon, ed. Brewer. R.S., p. 402.

2. The transactions of Church Synods in the Middle Ages are full of
    notices of such tithe quarrels. One of the most interesting of
    these is recorded in the diocese of Exeter at this same time. It
    was naturally the pettiest tithes which often caused the deepest
    irritation, and especially that on milk. The parson preferred to
    receive this in the more convenient form of cheese : but recal-
    citrant parishioners, as Bishop Quivil complained, hit upon an
    exquisite artifice to rid themselves of the vexatious tribute.
    They "maliciously brought their tithe of milk to church in its
    raw state ; and then, more iniquitous still, if they found no man
    there to receive it, they poured it out before the altar to the dis-
    honour of God and of the Church." (Wilkins, Concilia. ii, 160.)

CHAPTER XIX.

1. Miss Macdonell, by some strange misunderstanding, seems to
    attribute this gift of mimicry to Salimbene himself (p. 383).

2. "*De ludo schacchorum et alearum optime noverat.*" Salimbene had
    no business to know this, for by Canon Law not only were all
    men forbidden to play at games of hazard, but it was sinful even
    to abet or watch the players, especially for an ecclesiastic ; and
    this prohibition had been recently renewed by the great Lateran
    Council of 1215. Even chess enjoyed a very bad reputation :
    and St. Peter Damian speaks of it as a positively criminal game
    for a bishop. St. Benardino triumphs in the success of a mission-
    preacher who "burned . . . . . many chessboards, and converted
    more souls than I could tell" (Prediche i, p. 73). This was no
    doubt because the game was usually played for money and led to
    much quarrelling : a murder at chess is among the stock in-
    cidents of medieval romance, and Salimbene himself give us an
    instance later on (chap. xx). See B. Petri Damiani, lib. i,
    ep. x (Ed. Paris, 1743, t. iii, p. 227). Cf. Rashdall, vol. ii,
    p. 671, and T. Wright, *Homes of Other Days*, pp. 214 ff ;
    Domestic Manners, pp. 198 ff. An admirable essay on Dante
    and the games of his time, in which much use is made of Salim-
    bene's evidence, has been contributed by Mr. E. Armstrong to
    the *Modern Language Review* (April and June, 1906).

3. The Latin word *aculeus* used here by Salimbene marks his sarcasm
    even more plainly. The *aculeus* or *equuleus* was a bar of wood

with a sharp upper edge, which the victim was forced to bestride as on horseback, with weights hung to his ankles. The *Chronicon Parmense* speaks of these mock-trials as frequent during the long period of Ghiberto da Gente's rule at Parma. (Murat. ix, 778).

4. Cf. Inf. xxix, 20, where the shade of Geri del Bello scorns his cousin Dante for not having continued the family vendetta.

5. Prof. Holder-Egger points out (p. 624, note 3) that Guidolino was elected in place of a murdered abbot, Landolfo.

6. *Purg.* vii, 127-129. How thoroughly Italian Dante's feeling was on this point, is shown by Benvenuto da Imola's comments on *Inferno* xxix, 122 (vol. ii, p. 409). "To understand this matter, thou must know that the French have been from ancient times the vainest of all nations, as may often be read in Julius Celsus (*sic*), and may be seen to-day in deed : for we see them daily invent new habits and new shapes of garments. Whence there is not a limb of the Frenchman which hath not its own fashion : for they wear chains on their necks, bracelets on their arms, points at their hose ; and garments so short as to show their nakedness and the dishonourable parts of their body which should rightly be hid : while the honourable part, the head, which should be shown free, is covered by a hood over their face ; and so may it be said of many of their vanities. Wherefore I marvel much, not without indignation of mind, when I see Italians, and especially our nobles, seeking to follow in these men's footsteps and learning the French tongue, and asserting that no tongue is fairer than the French : which I cannot see : for the French is a bastard of the Latin tongue, as plain experience showeth. For, since they cannot rightly pronounce *cavaliero*, they corrupt the word and say *chevalier* : and in like manner they cannot say *signor* but *sir*, and so with the rest. Whereof we have a testimony herein, that even now when they would fain say 'speak in the vulgar tongue,' they say 'speak *Romance*,' and their vulgar tongue is called the *Romance*. Wherefore it is not meet that Italians should willingly submit their own nobility to less noble folk."

7. Dum Trutannus in *m* pateram tenet, et sedet ad *pir*,
    Regem Cappadocum credit habere cocum.

i.e. "While Trutannus sits at the fire with a wine-pot in his hand, he dreams he has the king of the Cappadocians for his cook." The reference is evidently to Horace, Ep. i, 6, 39. *Trutannus* is the typical drunken vagabond of medieval satire, the *Roi des Truands* of Victor Hugo's *Notre-Dame*.

CHAPTER XX.

1. For a long description of this Nicholas see Murat. ix, p. 248.

2. In 1270 a fleet of Sicilian and Genoese crusaders was wrecked off Trapani : Charles of Anjou appropriated everything of value that could be recovered from the wrecks, " alleging an injurious law of King William and a longstanding but infamous custom." Muratori *Annali d'Italia*, an. 1270, and *Scriptt.* vi, 551a. The poisoning is, of course, referred to by Dante, Purg. xx, 69 : cf. the authorities quoted for and against in Toynbee's *Dante Dictionary*, p. 532.

3. It is impossible to translate Salimbene's description fully, either here or lower down : but I subjoin a few references to enable the student to realize how characteristic such scenes are of the Middle Ages. The De Antiquis Legibus Liber (Camden Soc., p. 75) describes the obscene mutilations practised on Simon de Montfort's corpse for the gloating vengeance of a noble lady his enemy : cf. Ben. Im. i, 416, iii, 111, and A. Schulz. Höfisches Leben. i, p. 453. Such mutilations are spoken of as perfectly natural in Murat. Scriptt. ix, p. 130.

4. Vit. Ex., p. 64.

5. La Tour, p. 2 and *passim* : Salimbene, pp. 27, 67, 427, 429. In the first of these passages, Salimbene is speaking of Nicholas, bishop of Reggio, who " loved the friars minor so well, that he would fain have given them the cathedral church to occupy : and the canons who then held it consented thereto, and for love of the Brethren they would have gone to occupy chapels in divers parts of the city : but the friars in their humility would not suffer this ; nay, they utterly refused it. This bishop received an accusation against his steward, that this man was wont to withdraw from the friars the dole of bread which the bishop had commanded : wherefore he called him to his presence and rebuked him sore (Ecclus. iv). Moreover, knowing, as Solomon saith, that ' a servant cannot be taught with words, for he understandeth what thou sayest and scorneth to answer,' he laid him in strictest keeping within a dark dungeon, and fed him with the bread of tribulation and the water of anguish : after which he drave him forth from his service : God's benison be upon him ! for he knew that the race of servants cannot be corrected but by torments,' as a certain tyrant said to them that nourished St. Hippolytus [in the Golden Legend]. As Patecchio saith ' blessed be the Marquis of Montferrat, who was gentle to all men but to

serving-men.' [*Scutiferis*: literally *squires*]. Wretched fellows!
for when they are exalted and honoured in the courts of great
folk, then they become miserly, to show themselves good husbands and guardians of their lords' goods : robbing from the poor
and the righteous that which they waste afterwards on their
harlots ; and meanwhile in some parts the wives and daughters
of their lords become lemans of servants and stewards and
bailiffs, for they can have nothing whatsoever of the goods of the
house but by the hands of such menials. Most avaricious are
such lords, who love their worldly goods better than their own
honour, or the bodies of their wives and daughters! Mine own
eyes have seen and proved all these things." Marriage itself,
though in theory a sacrament of the church, was generally a more
or less definitely commercial bargain ; and nobody needed to
visit Gretna Green in an age when the mere promise by word of
mouth exchanged between two children in the presence of witnesses constituted a perfectly binding marriage without any
ecclesiastical formalities, though the priest's blessing was useful
to guard from contingent difficulties. Here is a scene from
Siméon Luce's *Du Guesclin*, p. 139 ff. " Cette frénésie de luxe,
où se laisse emporter la noblesse, n'a d'égale que la corruption
des mœurs. Froissart, cet historien, on pourrait presque dire ce
chantre de la chevalerie, a raconté longuement un brillant fait
d'armes de Galehaut de Ribemont contre les Anglais . . . Ce que
le chroniqueur de Valenciennes se garde bien de dire, et pourtant
il était trop rapproché du théâtre des événements pour l'ignorer,
c'est que ce même Galehaut avait commis l'année précédente
l'attentat le plus audacieux dont les annales judiciaires de cette
époque, si riche pourtant en scandales, aient gardé le souvenir.
En 1356, Marie de Mortagne, fille unique de Guillaume de Mortagne, sire d'Oudenarde, est restée orpheline à l'âge de huit ou
neuf ans, avec six mille livres de revenu annuel : c'est alors la
plus riche héritière de Flandre et de Hainaut. Aussi, obtenir la
main de cette fillette est le rêve que caressent tous les gentils-
hommes de cette région. En attendant qu'elle soit en âge de se
marier, Marie vit au château de Tupigny sous la garde de la dame
de Tupigny, d'Eustache et de Galehaut de Ribemont, ses cousins
germains, impatients de voir mûrir cet épi blond dont ils se
promettent bien les grains les plus dorés. Malheureusement pour
eux, un chevalier de leurs amis, Jean de Fay, a déjà jeté, lui
aussi, un regard de convoitise sur cette riche proie. Pendant
qu'Eustache et Galehaut sont allés servir le roi Jean dans cette
néfaste expédition qui se termine par la défaite de Poitiers, Jean
profite de leur absence pour enlever à l'église pendant la messe,
avec l'aide d'une de ses sœurs nommée Clémence, la richissime
héritière. Il l'emmène en son château du Fay, trouve un prêtre
pour bénir leur mariage, et le tour est joué. Quelle n'est pas la

déconvenue des deux Ribemont lorsqu'à leur retour en Picardie, ils s'apercoivent qu'on les a prévenus Un avide oiseleur a mis la main sur la petite colombe, alors que les premières plumes lui poussaient à peine. Galehaut, surtout, moins riche que son frère en sa qualité de cadet, est inconsolable, et il guette dès lors l'occasion de reprendre celle qu'il considère comme son bien. Jean de Fay et Marie de Mortagne sont mariés depuis plus de deux ans ; ils habitent le château du Fay, en Vermandois. Un matin qu'ils reposent tranquillement ensemble, Galehaut, qui s'est introduit par surprise dans le château, envahit avec l'aide de Baudas de Hennin, sire de Cuvilliers, chevalier, de Colard de la Cauchie, de Bernequin de Bailleul et de Bridoulet d'Atiches, écuyers, la chambre nuptiale, arrache Marie de Mortagne, toute nue et tremblante de frayeur, des bras de son mari, puis la conduit dans son manoir de Sorel, situé à quatre lieues du Fay où il la tient enfermée dans une tour pendant plusieurs semaines. Enfin, comme la jeune femme, révoltée sans doute de passer ainsi de main en main comme une marchandise qu'on s'arrache, refuse de faire les volontés de ce nouveau ravisseur, Galehaut, qui veut que son équipée lui rapporte au moins quelque chose, prend le parti de transporter sa cousine germaine an château de Dossemer, dans le souverain bailliage de Lille, où il la vend en mariage à un chevalier de Gand, nommé Pierre Pascharis, " au prix de deux mille quatre cents florins d'or, plus deux draps d'écarlate." Voilà le vilain revers de cette chevalerie, affolée de luxe, de tournois, de parade, dont Froissart n'a voulu voir que les prouesses et les élégances.

In war, the lot of women was of course infinitely less enviable. To quote Luce again (p. 67) "Il n'est pas de crime que l'on ne puisse se faire pardonner quand on sert fidèlement le roi à la guerre. Un chevalier, nommé Guillaume d'Agneaux, a commis en basse Normandie quatre viols bien avérés, un sur la personne d'une jeune fille, trois sur la personne de femmes mariées, mais il sert le roi sur mer sous les ordres de Jean de Vienne, amiral de France ; et le sage, le pieux Charles V accorde purement et simplement à ce monstre le pardon de ses atrocités." Even this is out-done by the case of Sir John Arundel towards the end of the century. This ruffian and his crew first carried off nuns wholesale from a convent near Southampton and then threw them overboard to lighten the ship during a storm. (Walsingham, R.S., vol. i, p. 420, quoted in "Social England," vol. ii).

6. Sacchetti, Nov. 153.—Giordano da Rivalto Prediche, p. 250 (Bologna, 1867).—Ben. Im. i, p. 579.—Archiv. iii, 107.— Bonaventura Quæst. xxvi, circa Regulam. In the Middle Ages all taking of interest, directly or indirectly, was held a mortal sin, and Pope Clement V expressly declared in the Council of

Vienne (1311) that it was heresy to deny the wickedness of usury : the offender was to be excommunicated and deprived of Christian burial unless he repented, confessed, and made all restitution in his power. This law however was as freely broken as most others : we constantly find monasteries in debt to money-lenders : even the best of English bishops were compelled to borrow at usury the enormous sums which had to be paid to the Papal court for their appointment : and Matthew Paris (an. 1250, 1253), complains bitterly of the protection afforded by the Popes to these bloodsuckers, adding, "In England at this time there were scarce any who were not taken in their toils." Usury was perhaps most regularly practised in the South of France (see Toynbee, Dante Dict., art. *Caorsini*) : but the Lombard merchants were also very frequently bankers : and indeed as trade began to grow in Europe it was found impossible to carry it on without the forbidden usury. In spite of these hard facts, usury re-mained a mortal sin until long after the Reformation, in theory at least : nor am I aware that the solemn decision of Pope Clement V has ever been reversed.

7. Libellus Apologeticus Quæst. xvi, in which the saint deals with the question ' why do you not give more encouragement to the Third Order ?'

8. Prof. Holder-Egger seems hypercritical in pointing out that, as Salimbene's other data prove Bartolino to have stayed at Noceto only from Oct. 27th to Dec. 7th at most, thus "many days and nights" cannot be true (p. 604, note 1). Six weeks—or even the half of six weeks—would indeed be an uncomfortably long time to spend under these nightly excursions and alarms.

CHAPTER XXI.

1. Michelet. Hist. de France, liv. xi, c.l. M. Reinach (Revue de l'Université de Bruxelles, Dec. 1904) has shown that Michelet was too hasty in taking literally the probably exaggerated testi-mony of contemporary witnesses ; but the arguments by which he attempts altogether to explode that testimony show a strange estimate of what is reasonably to be expected from a 15th century law report.

2. The convents were too often dumping-grounds for natural children of great men : even in the 17th century, Wadding boasts that a Poor Clare of the 13th century was " the *legitimate* daughter of the king " (1259, p. 117 : and he vaunts shortly afterwards two " legitimate daughters of marquises.")

3.   Vitæ Patrum ii, c. 61 : cf. Golden Legend (Temple Classics), vol. vii, p. 79.

4.   Ana. Fra., vol. iii, p. 196. " A certain raven was offered to St. Francis during his lifetime, and the bird became so domesticated among the Brethren by the merits of the holy father, and so learned, that he seemed endowed with human reason. For he would go into Choir with the Brethren at all their Hours ; and while the Brethren washed their hands before meat, the raven also washed his beak, and, coming into the refectory, took his food with the Brethren, and after a while, by the mere grace of God, the bird began to speak intelligibly. So St. Francis, seeing this with amazement and joy, once in the refectory bade him go to the infirmary to care for the sick and minister to their necessities. Wondrous to relate ! Immediately the raven, like a reasonable creature, obeyed the servant of God implicitly. He would go through the city of Assisi at the man of God's bidding, with a servant following him, and entering rich men's houses he would beg alms after his own fashion for the sick. So men naturally marvelled, and gave alms to the servant, who brought them to the sick Brethren. One day when the bishop was celebrating and collecting alms, the raven begged of him according to his wont. The bishop would give nothing at the moment, but promised to give some other time ; wherefore the raven, as if in indignation, took the bishop's mitre and carried it to a butcher ; and then taking meat for two sick Brethren, left him the mitre as a pledge. The bishop wondered to hear this, and paid the price to recover his mitre. Another day a knight was walking unshod through the streets in summer-time, and refused the raven's prayer for alms ; whereupon the bird ran after him and pecked him with his beak on the shin, and the knight forthwith struck him again with his staff. So another day the raven found the aforesaid knight riding between Assisi and the Portuincula with a fair helmet or cap upon his head ; and, remembering how the knight had once struck him, he snatched the cap from his head, and left it hanging high on a tree. So the knight dismounted and climbed to the top of the tree for his cap. But the raven forthwith swooped upon the horse, and smiting him sore with his beak, urged him to a gallop, and so was revenged of the knight. When St. Francis died, the raven fell grievously sick, and would eat nothing. But when the Brethren told him to go to the saint's tomb, he obeyed forthwith, and would not leave it, or eat, or drink, but died there of grief."

5.   The phrase was doubtless commonly current in the Middle Ages : Gower alludes to it in speaking of the number of evil clergy in his day (Vox Clamantis, bk. iii, l. 1327).

" Tales nec caste curant neque vivere caute,
De quibus exempla sunt modo saepe mala."

Cf. Fuller, Church History, bk. vi, sect. iii, c. x, § 7, "The *Charta Magna*, as I may call it, of monastical practice, 'si non caste, tamen caute.'"

6. Miss Macdonnell (p. 287) has misread this passage, evidently not fully realizing the sacredness of the Franciscan habit. Her account of the two Germans and of Rinaldo of Arezzo on the same page is equally inaccurate.

7. This too favourable description, which Salimbene no doubt heard as a tradition in the Order, is in direct variance with the accounts of eye witnesses, themselves of the Church party. (Murat. Scriptt. tom. viii, 299 and 694). Only five men were murdered, but "the violent plunder of the houses was more than can be described or imagined."

8. These were the friars who clung to the original Franciscanism of the *Fioretti* and the *Mirror of Perfection*, and who resisted the relaxations introduced by Brother Elias. It is from Salimbene alone that we learn the character of the Legate who compelled the German province to conform to these relaxations.

9. This is the church by which Dante's tomb now stands.

10. *i.e.* a canon of the cathedral. For the steps by which this title came to be applied exclusively to members of the sacred college, see Ducange, s.v.

11. Prof. Holder-Egger points out (p. 400, note 3) that the chronicler Thomas of Pavia records the finding of this body in 1231, and tells how the great Bonaventura was glad to get a single tooth. Parma is too near Ravenna for Salimbene to have successfully imposed on his brother-friars with a totally different body; we must therefore infer that the relic had cheapened very much between 1231 and 1270, when the archbishop died. This however is a common medieval phenomenon : we may see from inventories that relics were constantly disappearing from churches : the charm of novelty seems rapidly to have evaporated, and they were either stolen or allowed to disappear by mere neglect : for popular worship was apt to tire as quickly and as unaccountably as it had sprung up.

12. Much curious information about contemporary ladies' costume may be found in Bourbon, esp. pp. 228, 231, 233, which cast inter-

esting sidelights also on contemporary manners. Bourbon is specially indignant at their cosmetics and false hair : "they paint themselves like idols" : "they are like images of Janus, old in front and young behind."

Chapter XXII.

1. Probably Gerard, Archbishop-elect of Albano, who died in 1211.

2. Liutgardis quoted in Hurter's *Innocent III.*, l. xxi.—Cæs. Heist. dist. ii., cap. 30.—Jac. de Marchia in Baluze-Mansi Misc., vol. ii., p. 599.

3. Wadding III, 325 : Thos. Cant. II, x, 21 Eccleston R.S. p. 66 : his words are "quam Papa *quicunque.*" Here, as in other places, Father Cuthbert's translation is not true to the too plain-spoken original. Compare Pipinus's account of another papal deathbed (Murat ix, 750). "Pope Clement V possessed in his lifetime a flood of riches ; yet on his deathbed he was stripped even of his clothes by the servants, so that only one wretched cloak could be found to cover his corpse withal, as was reported afterwards by the Religious who were then present. Moreover, it is said that on the night whereon he died he was so deserted by all, that his body was partly burnt by the fire of some tapers which fell upon him."

4. A well-known medieval romance of two knights who had sworn blood-brotherhood.

5. This was a common scriptural quotation against nepotism : of Grosseteste's letters. R.S. p. 437.

6. See the satire quoted by Benvenuto da Imola (ii, 408) upon the sons of the clergy masquerading as their nephews.—"Sæpe sacerdotes filios dixere nepotes."

7. Prof. Holder-Egger quotes similar unflattering descriptions of Honorius from other writers, including the verdict of Brunetto Latini, "fu avarissimo come cane." (618, note 4).

8. The author of the *Golden Legend* speaks almost equally strongly of the Cardinalate as an upstart dignity. Murat. Scriptt. ix, p. 22.

9. Cf. Golden Legend (Temple Classics) vol. v, p. 201. St. Jerome "blamed the jollity and lavish life" of some of the clergy, who

revenged themselves by falsely accusing him of unchastity :
whereupon he retired from Rome to Constantinople.

10. Salimbene, as Prof. Holder-Egger points out, is here parodying the
records of the early Popes which he found in the *Liber Pontificalis* of Ravenna. The Professor appears to think that nearly
all this speech is Salimbene's own invention : but the main contents are in perfect harmony not only with what we know of
Hugh from other sources (*e.g.* Joinville § 657, Angelo Clareno in
Archiv. II, 282, and Ana. Fra. III, 405), but also with Grosseteste's speech at Lyons (Browne, Fascic II, 250).

11. Matt. Paris an. 1251, and Petrarch in Lea's *Celibacy*, p. 342. In
1311 Bp. Guillaume Durand presented a petition to the Pope in
full ecumenical council, one clause of which ran " moreover [we
pray] that public brothels be not held hard by the Churches of
the Roman Court and hard by the palace of the Lord Pope, nor
near the houses of prelates elsewhere [in Avignon]. And we
pray that the Lord Pope's Marshal and other similar officers may
receive nothing from the prostitutes and pimps of the same
brothels." (Baluze. Vit. Pap. Aven. col. 810). Benvenuto
comments on Inf. xix, 106 (II, 59) " Wherefore the modern
poet Petrarch will have it that this great Babylon is Avignon,
the new Babylon in France, which may truly be called Babylon
the Great, not for the circuit of its walls but for its greed of
souls (*non ambitu murorum sed ambitu animarum*). She is in
truth the mother of fornication, lechery, and drunkenness, full
of all abomination and uncleanness, and she sitteth indeed between the devouring waters of the Rhone, the Durance and
the Sorga ; and the woman's adornment fits well with the prelates themselves, who are wrapped in with purple, gold, silver,
and precious stones ; and that band of prelates is indeed drunken
with the blood of the holy martyrs of Jesus Christ." With
regard to Rome, Benvenuto (vol. i, p. 95) also repeats Boccaccio's
story about the Jew who was converted by the extreme wickedness of that city, arguing within himself that only a true religion
could have escaped suffocation in such a hot-bed of vice. He
speaks almost equally strongly below, p. 118, and ii, 186. For
Constance see Lea, p. 390.

12. Such, at least, is the apparent drift of Dr. Barry's plea on pp. 630,
652, of the Cambridge Modern History, vol. I. For Gregory
X, and Henry of Liège see Fleury, an. 1273, 1274.—For other
bishops worthy to be placed by Henry's side see Fleury an. 1245,
1248, 1251, 1257, and Innocent III, Epp. xiv, 125, xvi, 158 :
and for their general unpopularity see Ana. Fra. iii, 648.

13.   For Geoffroi de Péronne see also Peter of Blois, Ep. 102, Cæs, Heist. ii, 28, Etienne de Bourbon, pp. 249, 421.—The scholar's vision, Ana. Fra. iii, 297.—Gregory's complaint, Fleury, an. 1274 : for the other names : ibid. 1260, 1280, 1285, 1294.—Jo. Sarisb. Ep. 166. (Migne. Pat. Lat. cxcix, 156.)—Cæs. Heist. II, 27, 28 : cf. 39, 40. In connection with these and the abundant similar quotations which might be made from medieval documents, it may interest some readers to see a passage from the Roman Catholic *Monitor* (March 22nd, 1901). "In reference to the recent appointment of Dr. Ingram it [the *Church Times*] declares that 'he takes up a burden that is almost frightful,' and again, 'the burden is terrible. The strongest may bow and break beneath it.' We believe the *Church Times* says that which is strictly true. The burden imposed on Dr. Ingram is very grievous. The language of the *Church Times* confirms the truth that the new line of Bishops have not the grace of Orders to support them. Language of this kind could not be used of true Catholic Bishops. They have a load, but they have grace to bear it. The task is proportioned to the strength. They may die under it but they fall unconquered and glorious. The words above quoted are neither Primitive nor Catholic." An equally astounding historical mis-statement about the seal of confession was made publicly for similar polemical purposes by Cardinal Gibbons : see Lea, *Confession*, I, 414.

14.   For Obizzo see Chron. Parm. an. 1295 : for Reggio, Affarosi I, pp. 227, 252,

15.   Clement V protested in a bull against this introduction of hounds and hawks into the sanctuary : and Gerson, a century later, complained of the same practice, adding that such animals showed no more respect for the sacred places than mere protestant beasts. Yet, at the very time when Gerson was complaining, the *Ménagier de Paris* was advising good folk to bring their hawks to church, that they might thus grow used to crowds of men and lose their native shyness : and the Editor points out in a footnote how certain canonries carried with them the express right of bringing hawks into church. This evidence is specially significant, since the *Ménagier* is singled out by M. Léon Gautier, in his apology for the Middle Ages, as one of the four books that give the purest idea of medieval manners—the other three being Ville-hardouin, Joinville, and the Knight of La Tour-Landry. The *Chronicon Parmense* tells an amusing story of a dog which for twenty years always followed funerals into the church.—Decret. Clement, lib. iii, tit. xiv, c. ; Gerson ii, 630D. *Ménagier* ii, p. 296. Léon Gautier, *La Chevalerie* (Paris, 1891), p. 448. Murat. ix, 779.

16. Vit. Exemp., p. 2.

17. For Odo Rigaldi see his Register (Ed. Bonnin, Rouen, 1852): P.
Feret, *La Faculté de Théologie de Paris au M.-A.* (Paris, 1894,
etc.); Hist. Litt. de la France, vol. xxi, pp. 616 f, and a few
fresh and valuable details in Ana. Fra. vol. iii, (see index).

CHAPTER XXIII.

1. The Yorkshire Chantry Surveys published by the Surtees Society
(vols. 91 and 92) frequently plead the number of " housling
people,"—*i.e.*, those over 14, who were bound to attend the yearly
Easter communion—in different parishes, as a reason for not
suppressing particular chantries. Though the parishes for which
these figures are given are therefore naturally larger than the
average, yet the 107 specified for the county of York yield an
average of only 821 housling people—or from 1,300 to 1,500
souls—per parish. In the city of York itself, the seventeen
parishes specified had only an average of from 400 to 450 souls.
Merston, with only 320 housling folk, is spoken of as a "wide
and great " parish. The only instances, I believe, in which the
parish priests had to deal with more than 1,000 housling people
apiece were at Kyldewike and Halifax (pp. 407, 421). Thorold
Rogers calculated that England had one priest to every fifty souls
in the later Middle Ages : Abbot Gasquet is probably nearer the
truth in putting the proportion at one to 100. (*Great Pestilence*,
pp. 166, 205). Sir Thomas More felt very strongly that the
Church would have done better with a far smaller and more select
body of ministers (English works, pp. 224, 227). The proportion
of ministers of every denomination to the present population of
England seems to be about one in 900. Sacchetti (Nov. 28)
shows us how small was the average Italian parish, for he
distinctly implies that, as a rule, the parson knew all his flock by
sight. Cæsarius speaks of a Lombard Bishop who knew all the
folk in his diocese : this is probably a picturesque exaggeration
(ii. 29). I owe the Norwich calculation, with other valuable
information about town life, to the Rev. W. Hudson, F.S.A.,
editor of the Medieval volume of the Records of the city of
Norwich. A quotation from Hoeniger in Gasquet's *Great
Pestilence* (p. 66) goes some way in support of Cæsarius's assertion as to the size of some German parishes : but it must be
remembered that these would be endowed to maintain more than
one priest.

2. His most important writings from this point of view are the two
treatises in which he defends the Friars against charges of en-

croachment on the duties of the parish clergy (*Libellus Apologeticus* and *Quare Fratres Minores Praedicent*).

3. Bourbon, p. 259, quotes a Cardinal Legate as asserting that the devil gained more souls thus than in any other way—whole parishes swept to hell by communicating with an excommunicate ! Similarly, the Bishop of Angers asserted at the council of Vienne that it was common to find a parish with three or four hundred excommunicate, " and I have known one with as many as 700." (Lib. Guil. Major. p. 477 : cf. Fleury an. 1311. § 51).

4. He was a man of some note in the Order : see chap. x. above : but he must be distinguished from the Bro. Umile of the *Fioretti*.

5. I give here only supplementary evidence to that contained in Dr. Lea's *Confession*. The allusion in my text is to Cæsarius, Dist. iii., cap. 47. Chapters 40-47 of this book are sufficient by themselves to show that Salimbene's descriptions are not exaggerated. Cæsarius there tells us of the priest who, at the Easter confession, would cast his stole over six or eight penitents in a batch, and make them repeat a general confession after him : so that his successor found his flock willing to own vicariously to all the sins of the decalogue, but utterly recalcitrant to personal and first-hand confession. Another would say off-hand, "Do the same penance as my predecessor gave you," or "the same penance I gave you last year." Some are willing to absolve a heavy tale of sins for the gift of a hen and a pint of wine ; another is accustomed to use the confessional for blackmailing purposes : such are ready "to kill souls for a handful of barley," as Ezekiel says. The 47th chapter, referred to in my text, should be carefully studied by those who believe that such manuals as St. Alfonso Liguori's are without danger in practice, and unclean only to the unclean Protestant mind. Cæsarius tells us also of the female penitent who tempts her confessor ; and again a converse illustration which might serve as a worthy pendant to the tale which St. Bonaventura told to Salimbene. Nor does he thus exhaust his stock of instances : "I might show thee by very many examples how great evils are brewed in confession by wicked priests who fear not God , but I must spare the Order, spare the sex, spare Religion." Later on, however, he so far forgets this resolve as to record an incident if possible still more damning, though the point which interests him is less the opportunity of seduction in the confessional than the abuse of the consecrated Host as a love-philtre. (Dist. ix., cap 6.). Bourbon relates (p. 257) a story of a lady soliciting a Bishop to sin in the confessional, and bringing counter-accusations against him when he resisted her : such anecdotes are by no means infrequent in collections of moral tales. But far more damning are the frequent warnings of sober coun-

sellors to ladies that they should avoid the company of the clergy as much as possible. St. Catherine of Siena, writing to her niece in her convent of Montepulciano, says : " go to confession, and tell your need, and when you have received your penance, flee ! Take care, too, that [your confessors] be not of those with whom you have been on friendly terms : and marvel not that I speak thus, for thou mayst oft-times have heard me say (and this is truth) that conversation under the perverse title of ' spiritual fathers' and ' spiritual daughters' *(col perverse vocabolo de' divoti e delle divote)*, spoils souls and the customs and observances of religious Orders." (Lettere. Ed. Tommaseo vol. I p. 100.) The reader will perhaps here remember what I have already quoted from Alvarez Pelayo about these *divoti* and *divote*,* and will be prepared to find the same idea repeated in St. Bernardino's very explicit warning to widows (Prediche, vol. II, p. 185) " O widow, if thou be not wise, thou wilt take harm : beware with whom thou hast to converse. Wilt thou do well ? then have no conversation with good or with bad : oh ! thou wouldst have good friars, oh ! thou would'st have holy priests : I tell thee no ! with nobody. Believe me, thou wilt do better to stay at home.—What ? may I not associate *(usare)* with good and holy men, that they may teach me ?—Yes, but with a wall between you—Oh, but my devotion which I have taken upon myself ?—I tell thee no ! let it be. . . . . Take care to remove peril for thine own part, and thou wilt keep thyself from ill fame, and other men from scandals and sins. . . . Go not too often to places where thou may'st easily take harm. Stay not too long in church : take away every occasion [of evil] ; give all good example of thyself and thy life.† . . . Why, if it is seen that one woman talks with a friar, seven others will murmur against her. And even though their converse be only in church, and the friar be there by the side, not speaking to her, they still murmur ; nay, if one glance alone can be caught, there is no need of more !" And the saint goes on to relate a story which matches those of Salimbene on this subject. Again, in the very popular rhymed precepts for girls reprinted by Montaiglon (Recueil de Poésies. Franç. des xve and xvieSS, vol. II, p. 22), the moralist writes :

> Fille, hormis confession
> Seulette ne parlez à prebstre
> Laissez-les en leur eglise estre,
> Sans ce qu 'ilz hantent vos maisons.

* Chapter VI, note 5.

† The church was a common trysting-place for lovers : cf. the Prologue to Boccaccio's Decameron and Sacchetti, Serm. VII, "men were wont to go to church for prayer : but now they go to drive bargains in all sorts of sins, and specially in lechery, with all evils that tongue can tell." Almost stronger are the words of St. Bernardino (Opera. vol. I, p. 208).

A similar warning by the mission-preacher Geiler von Kaisersberg is quoted by A. Méray (Libres Prêcheurs, vol. II, p. 149 : cf vol. I, 142, 144). Moreover, when the confessor was honest, he was too often a mere bungler : and the blessed Raimondo da Vigna records of his heroine St. Catherine " if this holy virgin had had no other afflictions . . . than those brought upon her by her most indiscreet [spiritual] preceptors, she might yet have been called a martyr for all that she suffered." (AA. SS. Ap. vol. iii, p. 882 : cf. ibid. lib. i, c. v, § 84.)

6. Bourbon p. 268 : Munim. Acad. R.S. p. 305 : cf. Rashdall, ii, 689, note 3.

7. A hoop, a branch of a tree, or a wisp of straw were ordinary tavern-signs. The first seems to have been the most usual on the continent in the 13th century : David of Augsburg speaks of it as the ordinary inn-sign (p. 218) ; and Prof. Holder-Egger seems to be mistaken in tracing a connexion between the circle and the clerk's circular tonsure. After all, the hoop is still a common enough English sign : it probably was at first simply a barrel-hoop.

8. The earliest form of this Devil's Letter seems to be in Odo of Cheriton's sermons : see Prof. Holder-Egger's note. The fullest account of these documents may be found in Wattenbach's article "über erfundene Briefe u.s.w." in Sitzungsberichte der Berliner Acad. 1892, p. 91 ff. A reviewer who ought to have known better having questioned the pertinence of Salimbene's evidence here, I may refer doubting readers to the criticisms of three distinguished bishops, and of Humbert de Romans, general of the Dominicans, before the two great reforming councils of Lyons and Vienne. (Raynaldus an. 1273 § 6 ff : Labbe-Mansi. Concilia, xxiv, 109 ff : the latter is summarized in Fleury, an. 1311, § 51). It is noteworthy that the documents of 1311 show if anything a worse state of things than those of 1274.

9. Compare his versions of the Colyton and Culmstock reports with the originals in Stapeldon's Register, pp. 111, 130. I have exposed his manipulation of the other evidence in the *Contemporary Review* for Oct. 1906 and the *Churchman* for Apl. 1907 (reprinted as *Medieval Studies*, nos. 7 and 8). Guibert of Nogent, speaking of a gathering of important churchmen in the presence of Pope Paschal II, (d. 1118) mentions casually that "some [of the priests] scarce knew the rudiments [of Latin]" (Migne. Pat. Lat. 156, col. 913). St. Bernardino (Prediche. II, 127) tells a tale of four priests, who had a heated dispute as to the correct Latin for the four words of consecration in the Mass—" This is my Body." One only could repeat the words correctly : another

was wont to say *Hoc est corpusso meusso*, and the last confessed
" I don't bother myself about it : I just say an *Ave Maria* over
the wafer,"—thus, as the Saint remarks, living from day to day
in mortal sin, and teaching his whole parish to commit idolatry
by worshipping an unconsecrated wafer. The Bishop of Mende,
in his memoir for the Council of Vienne " se plaint que même
entre les hommes lettrés, il' s'en trouve très peu qui soient bien
instruits de ce qui regarde les articles de foi et le salut des âmes,
ce qui les expose (ajoute-t-il) à la risée des infidèles quand il faut
conférer avec eux " (Fleury, an. 1311 § 52). His colleague, the
scarcely less distinguished Bishop of Angers, asserted on the same
occasion " the law of God, the articles of faith, and other things
pertaining to the religion of the Christian faith and to the
salvation of souls, are almost utterly unknown to the faithful."
(Lib. Guil. Major. p. 477). The other authorities referred to in
the text are R. Bacon, Ed. Brewer, R.S., p. 413.—Aquinas
Contra Impug. Religion, cap iv, § 10.—Bonaventura Libell.
Apologet. Q.I.—Cæs. Heist. vii, 4 and 5.—Dialogo di Santa
Caterina, cap. 129.—Sacchetti serm. 27, cf. Nov. 35.—Labbe
Concil. xxii, col. 1159, and xxiii, col. 458.—Reg. of. S. Osmund
R.S., i, p. 304.—Od. Rig., pp. 159, 174, 217, 332, 395, 787.—
Busch., p. 441.

10. Bp. Haymo in Thorpe's Registrum Roffense, p. 413—Bert. Rad.
Pred. I. 393.—Gascoigne, pp. 118, 123—Bern. Sen. I, 495, cf.
112—Joinville §§ 297, 742 : cf. St. Louis's life by his Queen's
Confessor in AA. SS. Aug. V, c. iii, § 38.—La Tour pp. 40-42.
—Müller Anfänge p. 147.—For the visitations see Od. Rig., Reg.
Grand, the Southwell visitations (Camden Soc.)—Bp. of Mende
in Labbe-Mansi, vol. xi, p. 536.—Decret. Clem. lib. III, tit. xiv,
1.—Ben. Im. I, 271.—Bourbon, p. 185.

11. This proverb is quoted by the Wife of Bath : Cant. Tales, D. 389.

12. Bert. Rad. Pred. I, p. 493.—Bern. Pred. II, 109.—Gerson, vol.
II, pp. 630 and 641.—Chaucer, Cant. Tales Prol. 376, 449.—
Grosseteste (R.S. p. 162) enjoined throughout his diocese " let
not rectors and parish priests permit their parishioners to strive
for precedence in their procession with banners at the yearly
visitation of the Cathedral Church ; for thence not only fights
but death are wont to come about." Fifty years later, Bp.
Giffard of Worcester proclaimed " in consequence of the recent
disturbance and drawing of blood in the Cathedral Church of
Worcester, that all incumbents of churches and chapels shall
give out for four Sundays before the feast of Pentecost, that no
one shall join in the Pentecostal processions with a sword or
other kinds of arms " (Reg. Giffard, p. 422). In 1364, Bp.

Langham of Ely repeated Grosseteste's complaint of occasional deaths on these occasions (Wilkins III, 61) : and a milder complaint of the same nature from a fifteenth century Bp. of Chichester is quoted by Cutts (Parish Priests and their People, p. 122).

13. See Denifle's La Désolation des Eglises *passim*. Sacchetti writes (serm. VII, on Matt. xxi, 13). " Per queste parole si puo comprendere come li viventi uomeni e donne son divoti al tempo d'oggi nelli templi di Dio. Io per me mi vergognero quasi di scriverlo, che cosa è a dire, che ogni brottura e ogni crimine e peccatto in quelli li mondani sono discorsi a usare. In molti tempi dell' anno vanno li gioveni e le giovene donne vane alli monasterii a fare le delicate merende con balli e canti e con stormenti, ladove ciascuno da simile cose si doveria guardare, e l'onesta si rimane dall' uno de' lati. Cominciasi per li difetti de' Cristiani una guerra. Conducesi gente a piede e a cavallo : non si possono negli alberghi delle terre questi tali acconciare. È dato loro, che si chiama alloggiamento nelle chiese di Dio ; e qui con tutti li vizi che dire si possono, dimorano giocando, dove continuo si biastemma Dio e' Santi, adoperando la lussuria in tutti e modi dissoluti, insino la sodomia a piè degli altari : e però si puote bene dire apertamente oggi : *Vos fecistis illam speluncam latronum.*" Similar testimony is borne by Frati, p. 82, and Bern. Sen. I, 208.

14. For corn and brewing in churches see Reg. Stapeldon, p. 337, and Statuta Communitatis Parmæ, p. 320. It was Salimbene's friend, Gerard of Modena, who obtained the removal of this corn from the cathedral. Markets were held at the same time in the Cathedral of Ravenna, and barrels stored there (Labbe-Mansi. xi, 1583). The synod of Durham in 1220 complains of the dirty state of churches and their use as warehouses (Wilkins I, 580) : one of the most frequent subjects dealt with by church synods in all counties was that of markets, games, and dances in churches and churchyards. For the dilapidation of the churches see Reg. Grand, pp. 570 ff and 604 ff ; Reg. Stapeldon *passim ;* Visitations of St. Paul's Churches (Camden Soc., N.S.), Reg. St. Osmund (R.S.), p. 275 ff. For the separation of the sexes, Bern. Sen. Vita Cap. xlix, and Savonarola Serm. xxvi. For churches and lightning, Bourbon, p. 269, cf. Wadding, 1236, 420.

The best way of explaining medieval conditions to the general reader is to quote at some length a single visitation out of many which might be adduced : it is one of those recorded in the York Fabric Rolls, (Surtees Soc. pp. 242 ff), and shows a state of things fairly common even in the most stately cathedrals.

The date is 1409. "The chantry-priests do not celebrate masses as they are bound by the terms of their chantries : very many (*quam plures*) masses are left unsung by the defect of the clergy. The dignitaries do not come to the choir at double feasts and feasts of nine lessons, as they should. The deacons and incense-bearers do not come into the choir as they ought : and at the time when they are in the choir they chatter and do not behave themselves as they ought. The choirboys are not taught as they should be in singing, nor do they walk sedately and decently, as they should, in the processions. Both dignitaries, vicars, and other ministers wander about excessively and habitually (*nimis et communiter*) in the Cathedral, even while divine service is being celebrated in the choir. The books in the choir, viz., two called 'standards,' and the processional books, by reason of their age, their discordance, and their excessive fewness, are too defective, causing divers and numerous defects and discordances among those who sing in choir. Part of the Bible, and the books of sermons from which the Legend is read in choir, are worn-out and defective in those parts where the lessons are read. Within the vestry, the proper sedate silence is not observed as it should be by the Cathedral ministers ; but noisy disorders commonly take place there while service is being said in the choir, and especially while the minister on duty for the week is preparing for the celebration of High Mass ; which disorders frequently impede and disturb the devotion of the celebrant. The prebendaries pay irregularly the salaries for the vicars' common hall. . . . Very many (*plura*) vestments and ornaments and jewels belonging to divers chantries are in an exceedingly defective state, and perhaps some have been made away with, by the default of the custodian and of due inquisition in this matter . . . ." After other complaints of pecuniary mismanagement and defective service-books, the report goes on : "Within the Cathedral and its gates, and especially during the greatest and most solemn festivals of the year, public markets (*mercimonia*) are held, not without public, notorious and enormous degradation to the House of God, contrary to the teaching of the Gospel. The vicars wander too much in the Cathedral, with their robes on, at time of Divine Service. Divers vicars are too much given to chattering and talking together in the choir during service."

15. Bern. Sen. i, 490. For communion see Aquinas Summa Pars iii, Q. lxxx, art x. (Migne vol. iv, col. 806). Pope Anacletus (he says) had prescribed daily communion ; then, as faith gradually failed, Pope Fabianus thrice a year at least : ''at last, since the charity of many began to grow cold by reason of the abundance of iniquity, Innocent III enjoined . . . that the faithful should communicate at least once a year, at Easter." He goes on to speak of weekly

communion as a counsel of perfection.   For exceptional devotees
who kept this see Ana. Fra., 106, 392, 427, Bourbon p. 149, and
compare Salimbene's Guglielmo di Sanvitale " a most conscientious
youth, who would be confessed at least once a week " (62).   For
clergy who grudged to let their parishioners communicate, see
Cæs. Heist. dist. ix, c. 25, 26, 46 : in the last case the priest
" waxed wroth, and answered with indignation ' ye women always
wish to communicate at your own will.' "   The great Bishop
of Mende, in his memoir for the Council of Vienne in 1311,
suggested that the Church should return to the ancient custom
of three communions a year : but among the sixteen articles
of complaint drawn up by the Devon rebels of 1549 was one
requiring that the laity should go back to the system of yearly
communions, the Reformers having increased the frequency of
celebration, (Raynaldus. an. 1311, § 54 note : Gairdner, English
Ch. in the 16th century, p. 268.)

16.   For baptism, Sacchetti. Serm. xiv. : cf. Gascoigne, p. 197.   For
extreme unction, Bert. Rat. Pred. i., 304, ii., 89, and Wilkins
Concilia i, 583, 595, 599, 600, 616, 670, 690 : ii, 135, 295.
These cover the years from 1220 to 1308, and cast an interesting
sidelight on religious education also.   The reasons why parishioners feared extreme unction are given most fully in Bp. Quivil's
Constitutions (ii. 135) : " they foolishly imagine that if perchance
they recover after the reception of extreme unction, it is altogether
forbidden them to eat flesh, go barefoot, or know their own lawful
spouses again."   For confirmation, see Wilkins Concilia ii., 53 :
Fleury an. 1287 : Corpus Chronicorum Flandriæ ed. De Smet,
vol. ii, p. 507 : Quellen und Forschungen hrsg. vom. K. Pr.
Historischen Institut in Rom. (Loescher), vol. v, p. 180.   For
the irreverence bred of tithe-quarrels, see Wilkins ii, p. 160, and
passim.—Ben. Im. iii, 442 (on Purg. xvi, 102) : Gower, Mirour
de l'omme. 20, 593 ff.   E. G. Gardner in Hibbert Journal.   Apl.
1906, p. 571.

17.   Bourbon pp. 299, 307, 308.   Bert. Rat. Pred. ii, 531 : cf. Gerson,
vol. i, p. 204, 268, 349 ; vol. ii, pp. 552, 761, 762, and De Laud.
Script., Consid. xi., xii. : Busch., p. 731.   Gerson expressly
specifies this want of religious education as a main cause of the
notorious decay of the Church in his days (early 15th century).
For the question of Bible reading, cf. Trevelyan's Wycliffe pp.
130, 361, and the Church Quarterly Review for Oct., 1900, and
Jan., 1901, where Abbot Gasquet's misstatements on this subject
are exposed.   The Church Quarterly points out (p. 285) how,
after Mr. F. D. Matthew had exposed in the English Historical
Review a definite and fundamental misstatement of fact by the
Abbot, the latter yet reprinted this part of his essay without

correction, although he attempted to meet other criticisms of Mr. Matthew's. I have further shown that even Sir Thomas More, from whose apologetic writings the Abbot had quoted to show that the Church went on the principle of "the open Bible," very definitely repudiates that principle. Not only does More admit that no orthodox writer had made any translation which any printer would dare to publish in the face of ecclesiastical censure, but he further asserts his own conviction that the most orthodox translations ought to be lent by the Bishop only with great precautions " to such as he perceiveth honest," and that even to such well-meaning students the Bishop might well forbid the reading of St. John's Gospel or the Epistle to the Romans, as liable to misinterpretation. (*Contemporary Review*, Oct., 1906, reprinted in *Medieval Studies*, No. 7).

18. One of the best instances of this is to be found in the Book of the Knight of La Tour-Landry, written (as he assures us) with the help of four clerics, of whom two were priests. His distortions of Bible narrative are almost incredible : the story of Ruth, for instance, contains scarcely more than the heroine's name in common with the scripture narrative. (p. 3 : of chap. xci.)

19. Baluze-Mansi, Misc. ii., 600, 610. Bourbon, p. 286. Bern. Sen. vol. i, p. 431.

Chapter XXIV.

1. *Cont. Cels* vii. 44 (Ed. Spencer. p. 362.) A part of this is quoted in Dr. Littledale's " Plain Reasons," and is prudently ignored by the Roman Catholic Father Ryder in his reply. There are in Father Ryder's book several similar instances of convenient blindness to facts which it would be difficult either to deny or to explain away.

2. But see Lea, *Inquisition*, iii. 91, for the extent to which bishops still exercised the right.

3. Fleury. an. 1264 § 26.

4. Further references to Alberto and to Punzilovo may be found in Lea's History of the Inquisition. Compare Guib. Nov., p. 614 : but the whole of this treatise should be studied. For the gain accruing to the clergy from these new saints see ibid. : also Sacchetti's Letter to Giacomo di Conte. (Serm. p. 214 ff.), quoted below in my text. The Church councils of Rouen (1445) and Angers (1448) make the same complaint : the former even forbids

giving names to different images (our Lady of Redemption, our Lady of Pity, of Consolation, of Grace, etc.) as an invention probably due to the desire of squeezing more money from men's pockets. Abbot Gasquet, in his *Eve of the Reformation*, speaks of the alleged connection between saint-worship and clerical greed with a bland ridicule which carries weight only with readers accustomed to modern enlightenment and modern ideals of clerical honesty. If he had taken the trouble to look into the actual evidence, he would have found himself compelled, in common prudence, to leave the question alone.

5. For this canonization see Father Denifle's short article in Archiv. iv, 349 : also Baluze. Vit. Pap. Aven. i, 413.

6. For the *Santo Volto*, or miraculous portrait of Christ, see the demon's scoff in Inf. xxi, 48. Benvenuto (ii, 106) tells the legend that Nicodemus painted it, with other marvellous details ; but he adds : " Believe thou as much of this as thou wilt, for it is not one of the Articles of Faith."

7. The Magdalene's abstinence from food was (as we are assured) rivalled by St. Catherine of Siena alone, who became in consequence so emaciated " ut in obitu repertum sit, umbilicum ejus renibus adhaerere." So at least reports one of her confessors, Fra Tommaso Caffarini (AA. SS. Ap. vol. iii, p. 877 *note*).

8. Even Innocent III, as I have pointed out above, was obliged to acknowledge the same embarrassment in dealing with these duplicate relics : " it is better to commit all to God than to define rashly either way," (see note 9 to chap. III).

9. Joinville § 46 " [St. Louis] told me how William Bishop of Paris [1228-1248] had spoken to him of a great Doctor of Divinity who had come to him saying that he would fain speak with him. Then said the Bishop : ' Doctor, tell me your will.' And when he would fain have spoken to the Bishop, he fell to weeping most bitterly. So the Bishop said to him 'Doctor, say on, be not disconsolate : for no man can sin so sore as that God can no more pardon him.' ' And I say unto you, my Lord,' said the Doctor, ' that I cannot keep back my tears, for I hold myself an infidel, since I cannot bring my heart to believe in the Sacrament of the Altar, as Holy Church teaches it : and I know well that this is one of the Devil's temptations.' " The Bishop, with admirable sense, comforted him by pointing out how such trials only gave him the opportunity of showing his essential faith. cf. Gerson, Tractatus de Fœda Tentatione in the 4th vol. of his works : Busch. Lib. Ref., cap. ii., (p. 395).

10. For St. Louis see the remarkable anecdote in Ana. Fra., vol. i, p. 413 ff. " One day a certain God-fearing knight, very familiar and intimate with St. Louis, said to him : ' my lord, I will depart from your court, for I can bear it no longer.' ' Why so ?' asked the King. ' By reason,' said the knight, ' of that which I hear and see.' For he heard pestilent folk reviling the King, who (they said) bore himself rather like a monk than a king. So St. Louis said, ' have patience ; I will by no means suffer thee to leave me : as often as thou wilt let us go apart from these worldly folk, and comfort each other by talking of God and heavenly things. Care not for the words of fools : I will tell thee that which befalls me sometimes as I sit in my bed-chamber. I hear some crying " Brother Louis ! " [as to a friar,] and cursing me, not thinking to be heard of me. Then I think within myself that I might cause them to be slain ; but I see that this befalls me for my great good, if I bear it patiently for God's sake : and in truth I say unto thee, that I am not displeased at this injury which they do to me.' "

Chapter XXV.

1. Dante. Convivio. Trat. iv, c. 28. Giles in Ana. Fra. iii, 112, 296. For Umiliana, Wadding an. 1246, p. 157, cf. Bern. Bess. p. 321, Cæs. Heist., ii, 19. St. Louis' Life, by Q. Margaret's Confessor (in AA. SS.), cap. v, § 56. Dav. Aug. De. Ext. et. Int. Hominis Compositione Lib. III, c. 66.

2. St. Edmund Rich in Golden Legend (Temple Classics), vol. vi, p. 234. St. Dominic in Lives of the Brethren, tr. J. P. Conway (Newcastle, 1896), p. 290. For these devilish suggestions see Dav. Aug. p. 360, Bonaventura Sermo vi. de Decem Præceptis, and Bourbon, p. 199. Many similar pseudo-divine appearances, counselling suicide or homicide or other deadly sins as special degrees of religious perfection, may be found in Wadding, an. 1253, pp. 317 foll. ; 1261, 141, 1293, 317 (cf. 1291, 253, and the quotation from Alvarez Pelayo, 1318, § 43): St. Bernard Sermo vi, de x. Præceptis : Vitry Ex. p. 34 : 24 Gen. pp. 308 foll. (cf. 315) : Renan's " Christine de Stommeln," in Nouvelles Etudes, p. 353 ff. Cæs. Heist. iii. 127 : Thos. Cant. Lib. ii. c. i. § 14. An instance given by Wadding (1322, 45) specifies the *fœdos tactus* which are probably referred to here by Salimbene, and certainly by David of Augsburg. For the devils like flies see Wadding *loc. cit.*

3. An exactly similar occurrence in Spain is told in *Analecta Francis-cana*, iii, 309 : cf. Vitry, *Exempla* p. 34. Sir Thomas More tells

a similar story of a woman who hoped to attain canonization by suicide (*English Works*, p. 1188); and another of a carver who wanted his wife to crucify him on Good Friday (p. 1193).

4. (p. 257) There is in the original no trace of the almost treacherous change of tone of which she complains.

5. Cæsarius alone gives many instances of this immoral teaching about confession (ii. 23 ; iii. 2, 3, 6, 18 : x. 35), and many more may be found in the note to Bourbon, p. 448 : cf. *Athenæum*, No. 4025, p. 834.

6. Eccleston (R.S., p. 72) gives an equally uncomplimentary account of the origin of these Friars of the Sack. For the Third Order see Bonav. Libell. Apol. xvi.

7. For Segarello and Dolcino see Lea's *Inquisition*, vol. iii, p. 103 ff.

8. Even St. Bonaventura seems to attach real importance to this jesuitical distinction : see his Epistle of 1257 . . . . "pecunia, nostri Ordinis paupertati super omnia inimica, avide petitur, incaute recipitur *et incautius contrectatur*." Ubertino da Casale, a few years later, describes how the Friars who collected large sums of money salved their consciences by keeping a servant to touch it, though they kept the key of the bag to themselves. (Archiv. III, 67).

9. '*Lana caprina*:' see Horace Epist. I, xviii, 15.   The fifth wheel of a waggon, '*quinta rota plaustri*,' is a favourite phrase of Salimbene's for an insignificant trifle : it is used also by Matthew Paris.

10. '*Gaudent novitate moderni*,' a tag of a verse which is quoted in another thirteenth century chronicle, as Prof. Holder-Egger points out, and (in a slightly different form) by Bp. Guillaume le Maire of Angers.

11. This, of course, is the "Boy Bishop," an institution closely connected with the Feast of Fools. Abbot Gasquet describes it with characteristic inaccuracy on pp. 165 ff. of his Parish Life in Medieval England, suppressing in his quotation from the Sarum Statutes Bishop Mortival's complaint of the "manifold disorders" which formerly had caused "some damage both to persons and to the Cathedral," (see Rock. Church of our Fathers, ed. Frere, vol. iv, p. 255, note).   The Boy Bishop was in fact long tolerated even by the pious prelates who (like Grosseteste) looked upon the Feast of Fools as downright devilish : but

already in 1260 the provincial Council of Cognac forbade it ; and it was formally abolished by a decree of the ecumenical council of Bâle in 1431. It lingered long, however, and was only killed at last by the Reformation and the Counter-Reformation.

12. Prof. Holder-Egger refers this to the sanctuary of St. Michael on Monte Gargano : but, as Salimbene lays evident stress on the distances covered by these pilgrims, it is possible that he may refer to the French sanctuary.

13. See Father Denifle's essay in Archiv. IV, 330 ff. A certain Radulfus, about 1290, got it into his head that whenever the word *nemo* (*no man*) occurred in Latin writings, it was no mere negation, but referred to a person of that name, whom he proved to be identical with the Son in the Holy Trinity. His own reading (as may well be believed) was small : but he paid monks and clerks to make a collection of such passages, mainly from the Bible, from which he composed a "Sermon upon Nemo" which he dedicated to Cardinal Benedict Caietan, afterwards Boniface VIII. The sermon still exists in different versions, and an adversary assures us that Radulfus founded a sect of Neminians, among whom he names Peter of Limoges. This adversary, Stephanus de S. Georgio, "must have been as great a fool as Radulfus to think of refuting him," as Denifle truly remarks. Here is the beginning of Radulfus's sermon :—
"Beloved, God at sundry times and in divers manners spoke in times past to the fathers by the prophets, who preached darkly and with uncertain voice that the Only Begotten Son of God would come to redeem those who sit in darkness and in the shadow of death ; but in these last days He speaketh openly by His Holy Scripture, preaching, setting forth, and testifying the most blessed Noman as His own compeer, born before all ages, (as it is written in the 138th Psalm [v. 16], 'days shall be formed, and Noman in them :' that is, He was before the Prophet David himself), yet hitherto unknown to mankind by reason of their sins. But our Lord and Saviour Himself, whose nature it ever is to spare and show pity, and Who never leaves His own unheard, hath taken pity on the people redeemed by His precious blood ; and, having removed the old darkness altogether from our eyes, hath vouchsafed to discover to us the precious treasure of this most glorious Noman ; that whereas, to our great loss, he hath hitherto been hidden, we may be able henceforth to behold him with the eye of faith. The blessed Noman, therefore, is found in Holy Scripture to be co-eval with God the Father, and in essence most like unto the Son, as not created nor proceeding, but born : wherein this is plainly said by the Psalmist, 'Days shall be formed, and Noman in them.'

Afterwards his authority grew deservedly so great that, as though scorning earthly things, he soared with marvellous flight to the highest heaven, as it is written ' Noman hath ascended into heaven.' " And so on, through, " Noman hath seen God," " Noman knoweth the Father," " Noman knoweth the Son," " Noman can do these signs which thou dost," and a long catalogue of similar quotations. Stephanus, in his treatise addressed to the same Cardinal Caietan, takes these quotations one by one, and explains each painfully away : after which he proceeds to confute Radulfus by a string of counter-quotations from the Decretals : *e.g.*, " Noman sunk in sin," " to Noman did God give easy occasion of sin," " to Noman doth the Church shut her breast when he would fain return :" and he clenches the matter with the triumphant argument that God, Who would have all men saved, would therefore have Noman damned ever-lastingly : after which he concludes by calling on the secular and religious authorities present at the Provincial Council of Paris to burn these Neminians and their writings. One might be tempted to take it all for an elaborate hoax but for the abundant medieval evidence of the same sort, and for the fact that Stephen's memoir is solemnly filed among the Vatican archives.

CHAPTER XXVI.

1. Part of this chapter appeared in a rather fuller form in the *Hibbert Journal* for Jan., 1907. It was attacked in April by the Franciscan Fathers Cuthbert and Stanislaus, with great vehemence but little pretence of documentary proof. A little of this will appear in my rejoinder (July) : but consideration for the Editor's space obliged me to postpone the full exposure of their ignorance on elementary points of Franciscan history to a separate reissue of the article (*Medieval Studies*, No. 9).

2. Father Cuthbert's attempt to contrast the " gloomy, laughter-lack-ing spirit " of the " sectary " with the holy joy of the Friars is not only inconsistent with the tenour of Franciscan disciplinary writings, but is contradicted by so well-known an authority as Brother Leo, who assures us that St. Francis himself " did specially abhor laughter " (*Mirror* § 96). The strict Franciscan was as a rule cheerful only in comparison with the lachrymose piety of the other Religious of the Middle Ages : many of his tenets were such as are emphasized now only by gloomy fanatics. I have pointed this out at length in *Medieval Studies*, Nos. iii and iv.

3. " *Usque ad umbilicum ante et usque ad renes retro, buscum tunicæ sacco operientes.*" This, and the habit of wearing the second frock over the first, gave the early Friars' figures that extraordinarily unwieldy shape which we see in Giotto's pictures. See Ubertino in *Archiv.* iii, 173 ff., which is full of curious details about the Friars' dress.

4. Miss Macdonell, not recognizing the reference to the Rule, has again been misled by the Italian translation and missed the point of this passage.

5. For the quibbles about money, etc., see for instance Archiv. iii., p. 150, and Bonaventura Lib. Apol. Q. 6, 13, 18. For monks' pocket-money, Kitchin's Obedientiary Rolls (Hampshire Record Soc.), pp. 94, 95 : Jessopp's Norwich Visitations (Camden Soc., p. 77, and *passim.*) : for the vain attempts to check this abuse see the various General Chapter Acts of the Benedictines given by Wilkins and Reynerus.

5a. Eccleston's words are (R.S. p. 18) " Et sic aedificabant fratres capellam ita pauperrimam, ut unus carpentarius in una die faceret, et erigeret una die xiv coplas tignorum "—" and so the Brethren built a chapel so miserably poor that a single carpenter made in one day, and set up in one day, 14 pairs of rafters " (see Ducange s. v. *Cupla*). I am informed by an intelligent carpenter that this would point to a building some 20 or 25 feet long by 10 or 12 broad : the rafters would in this case be from 7 to 9 feet long each, and it would be a man's work to cut them one day out of the rough spars, and set them up in another day. Indeed, it would scarcely be possible for a single man to set up unaided any larger rafters than these. We have here a miserably small chapel indeed, but far from Prof. Brewer's " their chapel was erected by a single carpenter in one day," or Father Cuthbert's " one carpenter built it in one day."

6. See Mr. Hudson's excellent little *History of the Parish of St. Peter Permountergate* " (Norwich 1889).

7. Bernard of Besse in Ana. Fra. iii, p. 674. For friaries *inside* towns see Archiv. ii. 258, and iii. 84, 116 : Bonav. Libell. Apol. Q., vi., xix.

8. The friar's money-box is very conspicuous in the 23rd cut of Holbein's Dance of Death. (Lyon, 1538.) For Ubertino's complaints see Archiv. iii. 70, 104 : for Landshut, see Eubel. Oberdeutsche Minoritenprovinz (Würzburg, 1886), p. 239, cf. Archiv. iii. 105. For the unpopularity which this begging bred see Archiv. iii., 105, and St. Bonaventura's two Circular Letters.

9. Monte Casale in Fioretti i. c. 26 : its abandonment is recorded in Eubel. Provinciale, § 143. Bozon. Ed. Toulmin Smith (Soc. des Anciens Textes Français, 1889), p. 35. Cf. Bonav. Quaest. circ. Reg. xxvi, and Archiv. iii. 107, 165.

10. For evictions of clergy, cf. Bonav. Lib. Apol. Q. xi. : for friar unpopularity with parish priests, ib. Quæst. X.

11. Ubertino in Archiv. iii, 67.

12. Jordan in Vit. Frat. p. 138. Eccleston, R.S., p. 59 : Bern. Bess. p. 371, 384.

13. *Life in a Modern Monastery*, pp. 53 foll. This book, and the equally interesting *Twelve years in a Monastery*, describe a state of things extraordinarily similar in most respects to what may be gathered from medieval documents. The similarity is all the more striking because the author had evidently not studied the inner history of his Order in the past.

14. Here, for instance, is an extract from the diary of one of the strictest prelates of the Middle Ages, Archbishop Eudes Rigaud of Rouen (p. 42). He is visiting a Chapter at Pontoise. " Richard de Triguel is accused of sin with a certain prostitute ; yet there was no great scandal : we warned him to desist. Again Master Robert is accused with the gardener's daughter, and has but lately had a child by her, but the scandal is not great : we warned him to desist. Moreover, he behaves improperly in going barefooted outside his door to a certain workshop where women of ill fame are often congregated : we warned him to desist from such behaviour." (p. 42.) This hushing-up spirit is constantly traceable in medieval visitation records ; cf. Gower Mirour de l'Omme. 1. 20,137, and Mr. A. F. Leach's preface to the Southwell visitations. (Camden Soc., pp. lxxv, lxxxv, lxxxix). Ubertino da Casale and Angelo Clareno accuse their fellow-friars of great duplicity in hiding the misdeeds of the Order (Archiv. ii, 300, 301, 353 : cf. Piers Plowman's Creed Ed. Skeat. 1. 625 ff).

15. Quæst. circ. Reg. Q. 21.

16. Bonav. Quæst. circ. Reg. xix. : cf. his first circular letter "modis omnibus volo quod restringatis receptionem multitudinis": Bacon, ed. Brewer, R.S., p. 426. Martene De Antiquis Ritibus, lib. v., c. v., and *passim*. Ubertino in Archiv. iv., 77, 80, 187.

17. See Bonaventura's first Circular Letter, and his words in Archiv. iii., 517, with Ehrle's comment, ib. p. 591.

18. Bonav. Quæst. xix. circa Regulam. " Already the early brethren are becoming a laughing-stock, instead of being taken as examples." Dav. Aug. p. 110, "now of spiritual delights and the taste of inward sweetness, which surpass beyond compare all delights of this world as honey surpasses dung,—of this there is now scarce any mention or effectual desire or zeal, even among those who seem to themselves to have climbed high in Religion : nay rather, it (sic) is despised, derided, and held as a folly and abomination in these days; and men of this kind suffer perse-cution from other Religious and are thought possessed of demons, and are called heretics." cf. ibid. 285, 331. The *locus classicus* for the persecution of the Spirituals is of course Angelo Clareno's *Seven Tribulations*, published almost entirely in Archiv., vols. i— iv : but, a century later, we find St. Catharine of Siena speaking if possible still more strongly : the Order to which she specially refers is probably the Dominican. "They [the evil Religious] fall like famished wolves on the lambs who would fain keep their Rule, scoffing at them and mocking them. And these wretches with their persecution, their misdoings and their scoffs, which they inflict on good Religious and keepers of the Rule, think to cover their own defects : but they discover them far more." (Dialogo. Cap. 124). In the same chapter and again more emphatically in c. 162, she speaks of the multitude of evil Religious compared with the really good. The contemporary Gower bears the same testimony in his Mirour de l'Omme and Vox Clamantis.

19. Berthold of Ratisbon constantly harps on the soul-slaying abuses of Indulgences (Pred. i. 132, 148, 154, 208, 394 : ii. 12, 219). For the later Friars see Wycliffe's works *passim*, and Bishop Gardiner as quoted in Abbot Gasquet's Eve of the Reformation, p. 438. It is strange, however, that Abbot Gasquet can have made such a statement as that on which Bishop Hedley relies in his article in the *Nineteenth Century* (Jan., 1901, p. 170), con-sidering the appalling revelations of the Oxford Chancellor Gascoigne as to Indulgence abuses in 1450 (Lib. Ver., pp. 118, 119, 123, and *passim*). Men go about, says Gascoigne, selling indulgences "sometimes for twopence, sometimes for a good drink of wine or beer, sometimes for the stake of a game of ball, sometimes for a prostitute's hire, sometimes for fleshly love," with the result that "sinners say nowadays 'I care not what and how many sins I commit before God, for I can get with the greatest ease and expedition a plenary remission of all guilt and penalty by absolution and the indulgence granted me by the Pope, which I have bought for four pence, or six pence, or a game of ball." Bishop Hedley's whole article is vitiated by similar historical misstatements, none the less serious because

they are evidently made in pure ignorance. He knows nothing even of Berthold's words, though they are quoted in so orthodox a Romanist history as that of Prof. Michael (Gesch. d. d. Volkes im xiii, Jhtd. Vol. ii, p. 166).

Chapter XXVII.

1. P. Plowman, B. xxi, 241 ff.

2. Benvenuto's commentary on Dante's mention of the great miniature-painter Oderisi shows clearly enough how far the thirteenth century artist was from commanding such social consideration as their most successful brethren command in our own day (III, 310: on Purg. XI). "Note here that some men wonder ignorantly here, and say 'wherefore hath Dante here named humble and obscure craftsmen' (homines ignoti nominis et *bassae artis*), when he might more worthily have named most excellent men who thirsted sore for glory and wrought fair and noble works. But certainly the poet did thus with great art and with excellent justice ; for thus he gives us tacitly to understand that the great craving for glory seizes on all men with so little distinction, that even lowly craftsmen (*parvi artifices*) are anxious to gain it, even as we see that painters put their names on their works, as Valerius writeth of a famous painting." The tone of this comment is all the more remarkable because of the allusions to Grotto and Cimabue in the context. It is very doubtful whether the great artists of the past received more consideration in official quarters than now-a-days : certainly it would be difficult to find a modern author of Benvenuto's calibre writing of great artists as he does.

3. "He was a person of scant religion, and never could get himself to believe in the immortality of the soul; wherefore with words suited to his own flinty brain he most obstinately rejected all good doctrine. He had all his hope in the gifts of fortune ; and for money he would have undertaken to do any ill deed·" (Vasari. Life of Pietro Perugino *ad. fin.*)

4. About 1230 A.D., a friar of Gloucester was very severely punished by the Visitor for having painted a pulpit ; and Eccleston was convinced that many others bitterly expiated in purgatory their share in building those beautiful churches which we admire. Wadding quotes an early visionary who went further : according to him, an otherwise excellent friar was sent to hell for this sole cause (Eccleston R.S. col. v: cf. Actus s. Francisci cap. lxx, Wadding an. 1242 § 17.)

5. Those who (like Dr. Gasquet) argue so confidently from art to morals, should consider the following facts quoted by Mr. A. F. Leach from the Visitations of the Wells Cathedral clergy. " In 1511 . . . a Vicar Choral convicted of several adulteries was ordered [as a punishment] 'to paint one king before the choir door which is not yet painted ; and, if he escaped prosecution in the king's court, to paint another king not yet painted.' This experiment seems to have been so successful that, another chantry priest having been ordered ' candle penance ' for a similar offence, it is commuted to ' painting the image of St. Michael and its canopy.' " (*Visitations of Southwell.* Introd. p. 87). Browning's *Lippo Lippi* exactly typifies one phase of medieval life.

For the custom of devoting the fines of unchaste priests to cathedral fabrics see p. 42 of C. A. Swainson's, " A Cathedral of the old Foundation " (i.e., Chichester, A.D. 1287) : two Norwich visitations of 1498 and 1499 (Reg. Morton in Lambeth Library, ff 77a, 77b, and M. S. Tanner, 100 in Bodleian, ff 56a, 65a.) : also the constitutions of Chichester in Wilkins, i. 692 : and Ripon Chapter Acts (Surtees Soc.) pp. 292, 294. Similarly in the diocese of Wells, the Archdeacon of Bath, for incontinence and other offences (including the unpardonable guilt of contumacy), was not deprived, but fined 100 marks for the fabric fund (Reg. R. de Salopia, Somerset Record Soc., p. 429, A.D. 1340). Gascoigne (pp. 121, 123) speaks very strongly of the scandalous extortions for the York Cathedral fabric, and the immoralities by which the indulgence-mongers sometimes raised contributions.

APPENDIX B.

FULL TITLES OF THE BOOKS

(Which are quoted only by their short titles in the notes.)

AA. SS.—Acta Sauctorum : (references here are to the *London Library* copy.)

Affò.—I Affò : Storia di Parma. (Parma, 1792.)

Ana. Fra.—Analecta Franciscana. (Quaracchi, 1885, etc.)

Archiv.—Archiv für Litt-und ·Kirchengeschichte d. Mittelalters. Ed. Denifle und Ehrle.

Arte.—Arte, Scienza, e Fede ai Giorni di Dante. (Milan, 1901.)

Ben. Im. Benvenutus de Imola. Comentum super Dantis Comœdiam. (Florence, 1887.)

Bern. Bess.—Bernard of Besse in " Selecta pro instruendis fratribus scripta S. Bonaventuræ." (Quaracchi, 1898.)

Bern. Sen.—B. Bernardini Senensis Opera. Ed. de la Haye (1636).

Bern. Sen. Pred.—Le Prediche Volgari di S. Bernardino. (Siena, 1880.)

Bert. Rat. Pred.—Berthold. v Regensburg. Predigten, ed. Pfeiffer. (Vienna, 1862.)

Bert. Rat. Serm.—Bertholdi a Ratisbona Sermones ad Religiosos. Ed. Hoetzl. (Munich, 1882.)

Biagi.—Guido Biagi. The Private Life of the Renaissance Florentines. (Blackwood's Maga., vol. cliii, pp. 328 ff.)

Browne Fasc.—Fasciculus rerum expetendarum et fugiendarum. Ed. Browne. (London, 1690.)

Busch.—Joh. Busch. Chron. Windeshemense et Liber de Reformatione. Ed. Grube. (Halle, 1887.)

Cæs. Heist.—Cæsarii Heisterbachensis Dialogus Miraculorum. (Ed. Strange. Cologne, 1851.)

Dav. Aug.—David de Augusta. De exterioris et interioris hominis compositione. (Quaracchi, 1899.)

Du Méril.—Poésies Populaires Latines du M-A. par. Edélestand du Méril. (Paris, 1847.)

Eccleston.—Thomas of Eccleston's Chronicle in *Monumenta Franciscana* R.S., 1858.

Eubel. Prov.—Provinciale O. F. M. vetustissimum. Ed. C. Eubel. (Quaracchi, 1892.)

Frati.—La Vita Privata di Bologna, da L. Frati. (Bologna, 1900.)

Gascoigne.—Loci e Libro Veritatum. Ed. Rogers. (Oxford, 1881.)

Gautier.—Léon Gautier. La Chevalerie (nouvelle édition, 1883).

Gerson.—Joannis Gersonii Opera. (Paris, 1606.)

Guib. Nov.—Guiberti de Novigento Opera. (Migne *Pat. Lat.*, vol. 156.)

La Tour.—The Book of the Knight of La Tour Landry. E.E.T.S., 1868.

Lib. Guil. Major.—Mélanges Historiques. Choix de Documents. Tom. 2, Paris, 1877.—Liber Guillelmi Majoris Episcopi Andegavensis.

Matt. Paris.—Chronicle of M. P. Ed. Wat. (London, 1684.)

Michael.—E. Michael, S. J. Salimbene und Seine Chronik. (Innsbruck, 1889.)

Mon. Franc.—Monumenta Franciscana. Ed. Brewer, R.S., 1858.

Müller Anfänge.—Karl Müller. Die Anfänge des Minoritenordens u. s.w. (Freiburg i/B, 1885.)

Murat.—Muratori Scriptores Rerum Italicarum.

Od. Rig.—Regestrum Visitationum Odonis Rigaldi. Ed. Bonnin. (Rouen, 1852.)

Rashdall.—H. Rashdall. The Universities of Europe in the Middle Ages. (Oxford, 1895.)

Reg. Grand.—Episcopal Registers of Exeter. Ed. Hingeston-Randolph. Grandisson (1327-1369).

Reg. Stapeldon.—Stapeldon's Register in same series (1307-1326).

R. S.—Chronicles and Memorials published under the direction of the Master of the Rolls.

Sacchetti Nov.—Le Novelle di Sacchetti. (Milan. Sonzogno, 1876.)

Sacchetti. Serm.—I sermoni, le lettere, ed altri scritti di Sacchetti. Ed. Gigli (Florence, 1857).

Thos. Cant.—Thomæ Cantimpratani Bonum Universale de Apibus. (Douai, 1597.)

Vinc. Bell.—Vincentii Bellovacensis Speculum Quadruplex. (Douai, 1624.)

Vit. Exemp.—The Exempla of Jacques de Vitry. Ed. Crane. (Folk-Lore Society, 1890.)

Vit. Frat.—Vitæ Fratrum O. P. Ed. Reichert. (Louvain, 1896.)

Wad.—Wadding. Annales Minorum. (References are to the *London Library* copy.)

Wilkins.—Wilkins. Concilia Magnæ Britanniæ et Hiberniæ.

Appendix C.

Quæ hic sequuntur quamvis non omnibus legenda sint, illis tamen haudquaquam prætereunda, qui scire studeant qualis illis temporibus hominum vita vere fuerit. Hoc unum lector benevolus in mente retineat, omnia pæne quæ hic ponuntur a fratre Salimbene pro amicis suis, et præcipue, ut videtur, pro fratris sui filia, moniali Ordinis Sanctæ Claræ, scripta esse. Paucissima ipse ex aliis fontibus adjeci, quæ ad intellectum rerum in hoc libro scriptarum utilia videbantur. Numeri ad paginas meas referunt, ubi tales materias jam brevissime perstrinxi, sicco pede transiens. Signum *"Mon. Germ."* cum numero indicat paginam editionis novæ quam etiam nunc curat vir doctissimus O. Holder-Egger : *"Ed. Parm."* significat paginam editionis Parmensis anni MDCCCLVII, ubi verba in hac Appendice relata aut stant aub stare debent.

11. Vix credibile est, quantum inter homines medii ævi, præsertim inter scholares et clericos, vitium pæderastiæ vulgatum fuerit. Testimonia hujus rei vix enumeranda sunt ; perpauca tamen e tot indiciis hic pono. Scribit Benvenutus de Imola (vol. i, pp. 522 sq.) clericos et litteratos sui temporis maximam copiam peccandi contra naturum habere ; adjicit etiam se primo molestissime tulise Dantem tales viros hujus sceleris tam aperte arguisse (*Inf.* xv, 106 sq.) ; postea tamen, cum Bononiæ in scholis legeret, "experientia teste" didicisse " quod hic sapientissimus poeta optime fecit." Testatur Cancellarius Parisiensis Joannes Gerson, theologus ævi sui præstantissimus, in scholis præsertim atque inter monachos aut moniales hujusmodi vitium vigere : " exercent parentes utrique cum utraque progenie et affines affinibus in adolescentia, senesque cum junioribus tam in religione quam in scholis et alibi. Dubitaverim prosus si non deteriores mores trahunt aliquando pueri et puellae hac occasione in parentum domiciliis et religionum ac scholarum contuberniis quam facturi erant in prostibulis lenonum vel meretricum" (*Opp.* ed. Paris, ii, 629 : cf. 380, 637, 680, 762). Horrenda ac vix alias credibilia monet Beatus Bernardinus Senensis inter prædicationem publicam (*Pred. Pop.*, Siena, 1884, pred. xx, vol. ii, p. 142 : cf. pp. 98, 108, 140, 150, necnon vol. iii, p. 136 et *Opera Latina*, vol. iii, pp. 188 sq.) Arguit Bernardinus " infinitatem hujus peccati . . . nam Christiani erant per Christum a pagania purificati ab isto vitio, sed reversi in eodem (*sic.*) sunt pejores quam prius. His tamen etiam pejora in Universitate Romana seculo sedecimo publice ac quasi solemniter agebantur, testantibus coram magistratu duobus professoribus : (vide scriptum A. Bertolotti apud

Giornale Storico della Lett. It., *vol. ii, pp.* 144 *sq.*) Notandum est, inter folia illa quæ a lectore quodam irato ex Salimbenis Chronica excissa sunt, fuisse quæ (ut index antiquus testatur), de peccatis urbis Bononiæ tractabant (*Mon. Germ.*, p. 371 : ubi in nota sic legitur : " Hæc de exciso f. 363, leguntur : De causa destructionis Bon[onie] et de usuris non accipiendis et munera e de aliis peccatis ac. 363, 364 "). Nota item, Salimbenem ejusdem vitii pseudapostolos Segalelli accusare (vide p. 304 hujus libri : *Mon. Germ.*, pp. 269 sq.)

18. Vita Prima S. Francisci auctore Thoma de Celano c. i. (Ed. Rosedale, p. 6.)

"Quoniam hec pessima consuetudo una [*sic* : fortasse legendum *in*] doctrina puerorum apud eos, qui christiano censentur nomine, sic undique inolevit ; et perniciosa doctrina hec velut lege publica ita ubique firmata est et prescripta, ut ab ipsis cunabulis remisse nimis et dissolute filios suos studeant educare. Primo namque cum fari vel balbutire incipiunt, turpia quedam et execrabilia valde signis et vocibus edocentur pueruli nondum [lege, vixdum] nati : et, cum tempus ablactationis advenerit, quedam luxu et lascivia plena non solum fari sed et operari coguntur. Non audet aliquis eorum, etatis timore coactus, honeste se gerere, quoniam ex hoc duris subjacet disciplinis. Ideo bene ait secularis poeta : Quia inter exercitationes parentum crevimis, ideo a pueritia nos omnia mala sequuntur. . . . . . sed et cum paulo plusculum etate profecerint, se ipsis impellentibus, semper ad deteriora opera dilabuntur . . . . Cum vero adolescentie portas cœperint introire, quales eos fieri arbitraris ? Tunc profecto omni dissolutionis genere fluitantes, eo quod liceat eis explere omne quod libet, omni studio se tradunt flagitiis deservire. Sic enim voluntaria servitute servi effecti peccati, arma iniquitati exponunt omnia membra sua ; et nichil in se christiane religionis in vita seu in moribus preferentes solo christianitatis nomine se tuentur. Simulant miseri plerumque se nequiora fecisse quam fecerint, ne videantur abjectiores, quo innocentiores existant. Hec sunt misera rudimenta in quibus homo iste [sc. S. Franciscus], quem sanctum hodie veneramur, quoniam vere sanctus est, a pueritia versabatur." Cf. Gerson, ii, 310.

27. *Mon. Germ.*, p. 79. "Nam cum quadam die [fratur Deustesalvet] ad domum Predicatorum ivisset, et illi invitassent eum ad prandium, dixit quod nullo modi ibi staret, nisi ei darent de tunica fratris Johannis, qui in domo illo erat, ut pro reliquiis reservaret. Promiserunt et magnam petiam de tunica sibi dederunt, cum qua post prandium purgato ventre posteriora terxit, et petiam dejecit in stercora. Postmodum accipiens perticam stercora revolvebat, clamens et dicens : ' Heu, heu ! succurrite, fratres, quia reliquias

sancti requiro, quas perdidi in latrina!' Cumque vultus suos
inclinassent ad orificia camerarum, cum pertica stercora revolvebat
valenter, ut stercorum fetorem sentirent. Infecti itaque tali
odoramento erubuerunt cognoscentes se a tali trufatore delusos.
. . . . . Cum autem quadam die tempore yemali per civitatem
Florentie ambularet, contigit ut ex lapsu glatiei totaliter caderet.
Videntes hoc Florentini, qui trufatores maximi sunt, ridere
ceperunt. Quorum unus quesivit a fratre qui ceciderat, utrum
plus vellet habere sub se. Cui frater respondit, quod sic,
scilicet interrogantis uxorem. Audientes hoc Florentini non
habuerunt malum exemplum, sed commendaverunt fratrem
dicentes : ' Benedicatur ipse, quia de nostris est.'"

46. *Mon. Germ.*, p. 40. "Dixit igitur michi pater meus : 'Fili dilecte,
      non credas istis pissintunicis'—id est, qui in tunicis mingunt—
      'qui te deceperunt, sed veni mecum, et omnia mea tibi dabo.'"

69. Bern. Bess. Speculum Disciplinæ pars. i, cap. xv, 3 (ed. Quaracchi,
      p. 327). "Indignum quoque in divino officio venandis vermi-
      culis et mactandis intendere, quibus palam in oratorio digitos aut
      ligna fœdare frons inverecunda non metuit." Ibid. cap. xxiv, 2
      (p. 364). "Nares non in aliorum aspectu, sed ad partem cum
      duorum tantum aut trium appositione digitorum emungant;
      seorsum etiam spuendum est, maxime in conventu fratrum, ne
      loca publica, sive in choro sive alibi, sputo fœdentur, et astantium
      oculi offendantur. Pudet quidem in ipso chori deambulatorio ad
      pedes suos palam fratribus spuere nec pudere."

204. *Mon. Germ*, p. 608. "Dominus Jacobus de Henzola mutinensis
      fuit Potestas, et ibi infirmatus et mortuus et sepultus ad
      majorem ecclesiam, et in tumulo in equo, ad modum militis,
      honorifice fuit depictus ; et, quia tempore suæ potestariæ facta
      fuerunt illa homicidia et maleficia, quæ fuerunt initia futuræ
      guerræ in Mutina, . . . provocati Mutinenses, irati, turbati, et
      indignati, et videntes mala quæ ille occasione venerant super eos,
      eruerunt oculos Potestatis depicti et cacaverunt super tumulum
      ejus." Confer ea quæ de Alberico de Romano narrat Salimbene
      (*Mon. Germ.*, p. 367). "Nam quadam die, quia perdiderat
      accipitrem suum, cum esset sub divo, extraxit sibi bracas et culum
      ostendit Deo in signum opprobrii et convitii atque derisionis,
      credens se ex hoc de Deo ulcisci. Cum autem fuit domi, ivit et
      cacavit super altare in eo loco proprie, ubi consecratur Dominicum
      corpus."

218. Ed. Parm., 393. "Aliquos vero ligabant solum modo per pollicem
      manus dextræ sive sinistræ et totaliter totum corpus hominis
      suspendebant a terra ; et aliquos etiam, ligando testiculos, sus-

pendebant, etc., etc." Cf. Guib. Novig., p. 933, ubi de Thoma de Codiaco (*Coucy*) sic legitur : " cum enim captos ad redemptionem quoslibet cogeret, hos testiculis appendebat propria aliquoties manu, quibus saepe corporea mole abruptis, eruptio pariter vitalium non tardabat. Alteri suspenso per pollices aut per ipsa pudenda, saxo etiam superposito, humeros comprimebat, et ipse subter obambulans, cum quod habere non poterat ab eis extorquere non posset, fustibus super eorum corpora tandiu bacchabatur, donec ei placentia sponderent, aut in poenis morerentur."

248. *Mon. Germ.*, 367. " Omnes maiores et meliores et potentiores et ditiores et nobiliores delevit [Icilinus] de marchia Trivisina, et mulieres castrabat et cum filiis et filiabus in carceribus includebat, et ibi fame et miseria peribant."

248. *Mon. Germ.*, 364. Albericus . . . XXV de maioribus Trivisii fecit una die suspendi . . . et XXX nobiles mulieres, matres istorum, uxores, filias, et sorores, fecit venire ut viderent suspendendos, et ipsi eas ; quibus voluit nasum precidere, sed benefitio cuiusdam quem appellabat filium suum spurium, sed non erat, fuit dimissum. Verumtamen usque ad mammillas fuerunt vestes earum precise, ita quod totum corpus cuiuslibet earum nudum erat, et viderunt eas qui suspendendi erant.* Et ita iuxta terram fuerunt suspensi, quod iste mulieres cogebantur per tibias eorum transire, et cum tibiis et pedibus vultum earum percutiebant, dum moriebantur in amaritudine animarum suarum. . . . Post hec fecit eas poni ultra fluvium qui dicitur Silva vel Siler, ut irent quo vellent. Et fecerunt sibi coopertoria de modico indumento quod habebant circa mammillas, et operuerunt sibi membra genitalia, id est pudenda, et ambulaverunt tota die illa, etc., etc." Postridie, auxilio piscatoris cujusdam, Venetias in ecclesiam sancti Marci vectæ sunt. " Audiens hec Cardinalis [Octavianus, Legatus in Lombardia], sine mora venit ad eas et dedit eis comedere. Et misit per totam civitatem dicendo, quod celeriter atque festine et sine aliqua mora omnes venirent ad ipsum ad ecclesiam Sancti Marci, tam viri quam mulieres, tam parvi quam magni . . . quoniam talia diceret eis que nunquam audiverant, et talia ostenderet eis que nunquam viderant. Quid plura ? Dicto cicius congregata est tota civitas Venetorum ad eum in platea ecclesie sancti Marci, et audiverunt ab eo totam historiam suprascriptam. Quam cum recitasset, fecit venire dominas illas ita dehonestatas et nudas sicut ille maledictus Albricus dehonestari fecerat. Hoc ideo fecit cardinalis, ut magis provocaret Venetos contra illum et magis induceret ad miserendum istis. Cum autem audivissent

* " Idem facinus referunt Ann. S. Iustinæ Patav. SS. XIX, p. 178," *Editoris nota.*

Veneti omnem historiam supradictam et dominas ita nudatas con-
spexissent, elevata voce clamaverunt : etc., etc."
  Quam usitatæ fuerint tales turpitudines, ex duobus exemplis
colligi potest. Narrat *De Antiquis Legibus Liber* (C. S., 1846,
p. 75) mortam Simonis de Monteforti A.D. 1266 ; ubi sequuntur
hæc verba : "Capud vero dicti comitis Leicestrie, ut dicitur,
abcisum fuit a corpore, et testiculi sui abcisi fuerunt et appensi
ex utraque parte nasi sui, et ita missum fuit capud suum uxori
Domini Rogeri de Mortuo Mari apud castrum de Wiggemora :
Pedes vero et manus sue abcisi fuerunt, et missi per diversa loca
inimicis suis ad magnum dedecus ipsius defuncti ; truncus autem
corporis sui tantummodo datus est sepulture in ecclesia de Eves-
ham."   Cum his confer quae citat A. Schulz de sacerdote in
civitate Basileensi (A.D. 1297) "cujus testiculi, ob raptum ab eo
perpetratum, abscissi et in platea publica suspensi sunt." (Höfisches Leben. i, 453 : cf. Ben. Im. i, 416.)

251. *Mon. Germ.*, p. 168. "Item dictum fuit de [Opizone] quod filias
et uxores tam nobilium quam ignobilium de Feraria constuprabat.
Item diffamatus fuit quod proprias sorores cognoverit necnon et
et sororem uxoris."

253. *Mon. Germ.*, p. 27. "Benedicatur [episcopus Reginus, qui
villicum suum dure puniverat] ; sciebat enim quod genus servorum nisi cum supplicio non emendatur, sicut dixit quidam
tyrannus nutritoribus sancti Ypoliti. 'Benedicatur,' dicit Patte-
clus, 'marchio Montisferrati, qui omnibus pepercit nisi scutiferis !'
Miserrimi homines, qui postquam exaltati et honorati sunt in
curiis magnorum, efficiuntur avari, ut ostendant se bonos conser-
vatores et custodes rerum dominorum suorum, et subtrahunt
pauperibus et viris iustis quod postea suis dant meretricibus ; et
interdum in aliquibus partibus dominorum uxores et filie servorum
et canavariorum et gastaldorum efficiuntur amasie, eo quod de
rebus domus nichil nisi per manus talium habere possint omnino.
Miserrimi tales domini, qui plus diligunt res temporales quam
honorem proprium et corpus uxorum et filiarum. Hec omnia
vidit oculus meus et probavit singula."
  Ibid., p. 428. "Usque adeo Matulinus [poeta quidam] factus
est meus amicus, ut semper invenirem eum paratum ad servitia
impendenda. Sed nec ipse aliquid perdidit inde, quia dedi sibi
uxorem filiam cuiusdam Ferrariensis qui habitabat Ravenne, ex
qua habuit magnam dotem, adjuvantibus apud marchionem
[Estensem] domno Guidone de Polenta et domno Adhegerio de
Fontana. Confitebatur enim mecum pater puelle in illa infirmitate
de qua mortuus est, et ipso volente et consentiente feci hoc totum.
Et dixit michi pater puelle : 'Frater Salimbene, retribuat vobis
Dominus, quia filia mea remansisset in taberna post mortem meam

et forte facta fuisset meretrix, nisi vos fuissetis qui maritastis eam. Iam letus moriar, ex quo constat michi quod filia mea bene est maritata.'"

265. *Mon. Germ.*, p. 398. "Cumque vellet eos extra civitatem perducere, invenerunt portam unam clausam, similiter secundam et tertiam. Sed per tertiam, per vadum, quod erat subtus portam, viderunt quendam magnum canem exterius exeuntem, et visum est eis eodem modo posse eos exire. Quod cum attemptassent, propter grositiem legatus exire non poterat. At guardianus posuit pedem super nates ipsius et calcavit comprimendo ad terram, et ita exivit."

286. *Mon. Germ.*, p. 608. "Funeri ejus interfui et sepulturæ: et scio quod canis cacavit super eum postquam sepultus fuit. In majori ecclesia fuit sepultus inferius, " etc., etc.

287. *Mon. Germ.*, p. 426. Ego autem cognovi talem episcopum, qui de die in lecto suo denudabat iuvenculam mulierem, ut eam diu videret et tangeret, et ponebat florinos aureos super corpus illius et coxas, quos postea donabat eidem, et dicebat quod non erat plus mundus. Et erat senex et inveteratus dierum malorum. Et post paucos dies quadam nocte fuit suffocatus a quodam qui attinebat eidem, et totum thesaurum suum, quem repperit, asportavit. Et istius episcopi interfui sepulture. Iste fuit Faventinus episcopus . . . Cognovi etiam quendam canonicum quem diabolus strangulavit, et fuit sepultus in sterquilinio juxta porcos. Hunc pluries invenerunt in lecto suo cum quadam nobili muliere, quem amasiam retinebat, fratres Minores, quando summo diluculo ibant ad eum ad aliquid inquirendum; erat enim iuris peritus. Iste fuit Iohannes de Bondeno Ferrariensi, qui X annis stetit in ordine fratrum Predicatorum et postea apostatavit et intravit ordinem canonicorum sancti Frigdiani de Luca et cum eis fuit aliquibus annis; postea inde egressus factus est canonicus Ferrariensis in matrice ecclesia [sc. cathedrali]. Cum autem habitaret in ecclesia sancti Alexii et ibi quandam dominam nobilem, pauperem Paduanam, ab Icilino expulsam, retineret amasiam, inventus fuit in lecto a diabolo sine confessione et viatico suffocatus."

294. *Mon. Germ.*, p. 403. Ducitis enim mulieres post altare causa confitendi et ibi eas cognoscitis. quod nefas est dicere et peius operari."

294. *Mon. Germ.*, p. 409. "Narratio trufatoria, sed vera, quam retulit papa Alexander IV fratri Bonaventure, generali ministro O.F.M. . . .

Frater Bonaventura generalis minister interrogavit papam Alexandrum IV utrum placeret ei quod fratres Minores confessiones audirent, et ipse dixit ei: 'Immo volo penitus, quod ipsi audiant. Et dicam tibi orribilem exemplum et truffatorium. Quedam mulier confitebatur sacerdoti suo in ecclesia sua. Ille vero volens eam cognoscere et carnaliter cum ea dormire cepit eam de opere venereo multum sollicitare. Cumque in ecclesia post altare juxta locum dominici corporis violenter vellet eam opprimere, dixit ei domina illa, 'Nec locus requirit nec tempus, ut hic nepharia et venerea opera perpetrentur. Alio loco et tempore poterunt congruentius ista fieri.' Hec autem dicebat volens evadere manus eius. Sacerdos vero sperans habere propositum acquievit et habuit secum quedam familiaria verba : tamen, quando domina illa recedebat ab eo ut domum rediret, dixit ei sacerdos : 'Domina, recordemini illius uegotii, quod scitis, scilicet depostetiarum.'* Cui illa dixit : 'Optime recordabor.' Cum autem esset domi, quantum aforis apparebat, fecit pulcherrimam turtam, que intrinsecus humano stercore plena erat, et pro exenio misit eam sacerdoti cum enghestaria optimi vini et albi. In hoc solum fuit ex parte mulieris defectus ; quia debebat urinam propriam sacerdoti transmittere, sicut merdam propriam transmisit in turta. Videns vero sacerdos tam pulcherrimam turtam cogitavit quod tali exenio episcopus dignus esset, et misit episcopo. Cum autem episcopus cum suis discumberet, precepit servienti ut divideret turtam et apponeret discumbentibus. Quod cum seorsum faceret, invenit merdam intrinsecus et aborruit, et reservavit turtam, ut episcopo posset ostendere. Cum autem episcopus instaret, ut turtam portaret minister, dixit ei : 'Satis habetis modo ; alia vice Domino concedente habebitis melius.' Quid plura ? Postquam episcopus vidit talem turtam, contra sacerdotem indignatus est valde et misit pro eo et dixit ei : ' Dicatis michi, domne sacerdos ; Quis docuit vos mittere tales turtas et maxime episcopo vestro ? Quid promerui aut in quo unquam offendi vos, ut mihi talem injuriam faceretis mittendo turtam humano stercore plenam ? ' Quod cum audisset sacerdos, obstupuit et dixit episcopo : ' Pater, in veritate ego non feci fieri illam turtam, immo talis domina misit, et ego credidi quod vos essetis tali exenio dignus, et ideo misi vobis causa utilitatis atque honoris, credens turtam optimam esse.' Quod cum audisset episcopus, accepit satisfactionem. Et licenciato sacerdote accersivit dominam illam, volens huius rei cognoscere veritatem. Ipsa vero confessa est et non negavit quod ideo fecit hoc ut sacerdotem truffaret qui eam, cum confiteretur, de opere venereo invitabat, volens in ecclesia et post altare cum

* **Nota** viri doctissimi O. Holder-Egger : "hoc verbum non invenitur in Glossario mediæ et infimæ Latinitatis. Formatum videtur ad instar vocis *in-præsentiarum* a *depost.*"

ea peccare. Episcopus vero dominam illam ex eo quod fecerat multipliciter commendavit et sacerdotem punivit egregie. Et iste idem episcopus, qui tale exenium habuit, dixit pape Alexandro IV hec omnia, referendo ei totam historiam supradictam, et papa Alexander retulit fratri Bonaventure . . . Et adjecit papa dicendo ' Quapropter volo penitus quod fratres Minores de mea conscientia et licentia confessiones audiant secularium personarum.' "

" Alia narratio dolorosa. . . .

Cognovi quemdam fratrem Humilem de Mediolano, qui fuit custos Parmensis custodie. Hic dum habitaret in loco fratrum Minorum de Fanano, tempore quadragesimali instabat predicationibus et confessionibus audiendis. Quod audientes illi de Alpibus, homines et mulieres, miserunt rogando ut amore Dei pro salute animarum suarum dignaretur ad eos accedere, quia volebant confiteri cum eo. Et assumpto socio ivit ad eos et multos dies predicavit et confessiones audivit, et multa bona fecit consilia salubria eis dando. Quadam autem die venit ad eum quedam mulier volens confiteri, et dixit ei : ' Heu me ! pater, mulier infelix nimis ego sum.' Cui frater : ' Dic tu prius iniquitates tuas, et narra, si quid habes, ut iustificeris. De omnibus ergo peccatis tuis culpabilem te proclama, et sic absolutione recepta postea eris felix.' Et dixit : ' Quadam die, dum irem sola per viam, invenit me quidam homo et violenter oppressit atque cognovit. Accessi ergo ad unum de sacerdotibus volens confiteri. Qui duxit me post altare, et revelato sibi peccato meo violenter oppressit me ibidem atque cognovit, non veritus locum sacrum nec honorem Dei neque me plurimum deplorantem. Idem accidit michi cum secundo et tertio sacerdote, quia quilibet me cognovit et post altare juxta dominicum corpus mecum peccavit, dum eis crederem confiteri.' Postquam igitur de omnibus peccatis suis fideliter est confessa, absolvit eam frater et dixit ei : ' Quid sibi vult cultellus iste quem habes in manu, et ad quid tempore isto et hora deservit ?' Et dixit ei : ' Pater, in veritate cogitabam me gladio occidere et in desperatione mea mori, si invitavissetis me de peccato sicut fecerunt alii sacerdotes.' Cui frater dixit : ' Nec invitavi nec invitabo, sed potius invito te ad gaudia paradisi, que dabit tibi Dominus, si dilexeris eum penitentiam faciendo. Vade in pace, dilecta filia, et amplius noli peccare.' "

297. *Mon. Germ.*, p. 425. " Item inveni aliquos . . . totam domum filiis spuriis plenam habentes et cum focaria sua tota nocte in eodem lecto jacentes et in crastinum celebrantes."

317. David de Augusta. *De ext et Int. Hom. Compositione.* Lib. III., cap. 66 (Ed. Quaracchi, p. 359). Cum de visionibus revelationibus et consolationibus religiosis auctor locutus sit, hæc verba

adjicit : " Non videtur autem prætereundum, quod quidam, de-
cepti a seductoriis spiritibus, vel propriis falsis opinionibus, putant
sibi apparere in visione vel ipsum Christum vel ejus gloriosissi-
mam Genitricem et non solum amplexibus et osculis, sed etiam
alis indecentioribus gestibus et actibus ab eis demulceri ; ut, sicut
spiritus ipsorum interius ab ipsis consolatur spiritualiter, ita et
caro exterius sibi congruo oblectationis sensu sensibiliter demul-
ceatur et carnaliter consoletur. Quod non tantum esse falsum
et seductorium, sed etiam blasphemia gravis esse liquido
comprobatur. Spiritus sancti visitatio, sicut contra omnia vitia
reprimenda et detestanda infunditur, ita etiam singulariter contra
carnales illecebras opponitur ; et ubi spiritus munditiæ suo jubare
resplenduerit, continuo omnes pravæ voluptatis motus evanescere
et velut tenebras, superveniente lumine, disparere necesse est. De
his vero qui cum aliquando dulcedinem spiritualem sentiunt continuo etiam corporalis delectationis pruritu illecti fœdantur, nescio
quid judicem, nisi quod potius eligo illis carere floribus quos de
luti sordibus legere deberem. Et sicut illos damnare non audeo
qui inviti quandoque in hujusmodi spiritualibus affectionibus
carnalis fluxus liquore maculantur, ita etiam excusare nescio qui
tali fluxui ex consensu condelectantur, qualiscumque eorum in-
tentio videatur." Cf. Wadding, 1322, p. 45, " Multis [B.
Johannem de Alvernia dæmones] illusionibus perturbare tentarunt
. . . . fœdos et obscœnos ei tactus representabant."

320. *Consuet S. Augustini Cantuarensis*, p. 186. " Nec [fratres] pro-
nuncient aliquas orationes vocales dummodo secreta naturæ faciunt,
ne verba Dei sancta vilescant."
    Mon. Germ., p. 570.   " Quidam religiosus, dum in loco
privato ad requisita nature sederet et Deum laudaret, fuit repre-
hensus a demone, quod locus ille non erat ydoneus, sed inhonestus
ad Deum laudandum. Cui respondit frater et dixit : ' Ita sum
divinis laudibus assuetus, quod a laude Dei cessare non possum,
nam scriptura teste didici quod Deus est ubique, ergo ubique est
laudandus [a suis], quod etiam apostolus docuit I. ad Timo. II :
*Volo viros orare in omni loco, levantes puras manus sine ira et
disceptatione.* Igitur qui omnem locum dicit, nullum excludit.
Quapropter et ventrem meum purgabo et Deum meum luadabo.
Deus enim non nisi sordes vitiorum abhorret. Sed tu miser, qui
factus eras, ut Deum laudares in celo, propter superbiam tuam
celum perdidisti, ... et nunc vadis per sterquilinia visitando
latrinas."

324. *Mon. Germ.*, p. 257. " Post hec, cum hospitaretur [Segalellus]
apud aliquam mulierculam viduam, filiam nubilem et speciosam
habentem, dicebat sibi a Domino revelatum quod cum illa puella
debebat illa nocte nudus cum nuda in eodem lecto dormire, ut

probaret si castitatem servare possit necne. Consentiebat mater reputans se beatam, et puella minime hoc negabat." Vide etiam editoris notam, ubi Segalellus docuisse probatur (teste Bernardo Guidonis) "quod jacere cum muliere et non commisceri ex carnalitate maius est quam resuscitare mortuum." Cum his confer Sacchetti *Nov. CI.*

325. *Mon. Germ.*, p. 268 sq. "Quod autem isti Apostoli non sint in statu salutis, pluribus rationibus possumus demonstrare . . . . . Secunda ratio, est, quod aliqui eorum non servant castitatem, ad quam omnes religiosi tenentur . . . Apostoli autem, non Christi sed Ghirardini Segalelli, male servant castitatem. Nam, ut michi dixerunt, quando vadunt per mundum, ad meretrices declinant et in domibus in quibns hospitantur, si a lascivis mulieribus sollicitantur ad peccatum sive ad peccandum, consentiunt eis, et parva est pugna [hic citantur Ecclus. xxiii. 24, xix. 25 ; Osee iv. 14, 15, etc., etc.] . . . Cogitat enim virgo vel iuvencula, quando aspicitur a spadone, dicens; 'Si isti religiosi, qui spadones debent esse iuxta verbum Domini, [Matt. xix. 12] non reputant peccatum lasciviam carnis, ego quare reputabo?' Et ita dant ei maleficiendi occasionem, necnon et sibi ipsis . . . Item Apostoli Ghirardini Segalelli masculi in masculos turpitudinem operantur, maxime senes cum iunioribus qui ingrediuntur ad eos, ut dixerunt michi. Et ideo aut combustione aut carcere essent digni," etc., etc.

328. *Mon. Germ.*, p. 264. "Ipse vero pro hoc honore tale beneficium rependit eisdem, quod se et omnes alios denudavit usque adeo, quod etiam membra genitalia sine bracis et aliquo velamine nuda essent, et stabant appodiati ad murum in acie circum circa, sed non in acie ordinata nec honesta nec bona."

331. *Mon. Germ.*, p. 620. "Tres ribaldos recepit hospitio ex eis qui se dicunt Apostolos esse et non sunt, qui suaserunt juveni ne uxorem cognosceret nec cum ea in eodem lecto prima nocte dormiret nisi quando dicerent ei. Hoc autem dicebant, quia volebant juvenem praevenire atque decipere et prius cum uxore dormire, sicut factum est, quia omnes tres illa nocte iverunt ad lectum ejus unus post alium facto modico intervallo et cognoverunt eam," etc., etc.

CLERICAL CELIBACY.

THERE is probably nothing which draws so sharp a line between medieval and modern Society as the status of the clergy—their immense numbers, their privileges, and the celibacy which made it possible to treat them so entirely as a separate caste. Since even reviewers who ought to have known better have thrown doubt on the trustworthiness of Salimbene's evidence on this point, I subjoin here a few documents supplementary to the mass of evidence which is to be found in the six hundred closely-printed octavo pages of Dr. Lea's "Sacerdotal Celibacy in the Christian Church." Many readers may not care to pursue the subject ; but those who do can scarcely fail to realize how strictly Salimbene has kept within the facts.

A. *Popes.* The *Chronicle of Meaux* was written at the Cistercian Abbey of that name in Yorkshire, by Abbot Thomas of Burton, at the end of the fourteenth century. On p. 89 of vol. iii he speaks of Pope Clement VI, who instituted the fifty-years' Jubilee,* and against whom the Cistercians as a body had certainly no grudge. The Chronicler goes on : "Now this same Pope Clement VI had been lecherous beyond measure his whole life long. For every night at vespertide he was wont, after the cardinals' audience, to hold a public audience of all matrons and honourable women who wished to come. At last some men, speaking ill of him on this account, began to stand by the palace doors and secretly to number the women who went in and who came out. And when they had done thus for many days, there was ever one lacking at their egress from the number of those who had entered in. When therefore many scandals and obloquies arose on this account, the confessor of the Lord Pope warned him frequently to desist from such conduct, and to live chastely and more cautiously.† But he ever made the same answer, 'Thus have we been wont to do when we were young,

---

* The great Jubilee Indulgence was first instituted by Dante's Boniface VIII in 1300, and was intended to recur only once in a hundred years : Clement VI short-ened this period by half, and held the second Jubilee in 1350.

† Cf. Salimbene's " Si non caste, tamen caute."

and what we now do we do by counsel of our physicians.' But when the Pope was aware that his brethren the Cardinals and his auditors and the rest of the Court murmured and spake ill of him on this account, one day he brought in his bosom a little black book wherein he had the names written of his divers predecessors in the Papal chair who were lecherous and incontinent; and he showed by the facts therein recorded that these had better ruled the Church, and done much more good, than the other continent Popes. Moreover on the same day he raised to the Cardinalate one of his sons, a boy of sixteen, who was afterwards Pope Gregory XI. This Clement VI was succeeded by Innocent VI, who, like his predecessor Clement, promoted his own sons and brethren and nephews to Cardinals and Bishops, so that scarce any were left in the Sacred College who were not of his kin or of the aforesaid Clement's." The chronicler's account is no doubt exaggerated, in parts at least: but the significance of the story lies in the fact that it was believed and recorded for posterity by a man in Abbot Burton's position. Hardly less significant is the praise occasionally bestowed by chroniclers on popes of exceptional virtue. Peter of Herentals thinks it worth while to note that Gregory XI "died a virgin in mind and body, as some have asserted" (Baluze, Vit. Pap. Aven. i, 483): and similarly Wadding is proud to record of Salimbene's Nicholas III, "he kept perpetual virginity" (An. 1280, § 93). Indeed, the scandals sometimes forced even the laity to interfere. In 1340, the King of France felt bound to complain publicly to the Pope, who had legitimized "three brothers, born of a detestable union, that is to say of a Bishop in pontifical dignity, degree, or order, and an unmarried woman." The word in the original being *Pontifex*, it is possible that the father may have been one of the Pope's predecessors, several of whom were notoriously unchaste. (Baluze, Vit. Pap. Aven., p. 600).

B. *Bishops.* Here is Cardinal Jacques de Vitry's account of the state of things about the time of St. Francis's birth. "The cause of all these evils [monastic decay, etc.] was the indiscipline and insufficiency and ignorance of the prelates; for it was not only while the shepherds were asleep, but with their help, that the enemy sowed tares in the midst of the wheat . . . . In those days scarce any could be found who sorrowed for Christ's sufferings, even though He had an infinite number of ministers; scarce any setting themselves up as a wall for the Lord's house, or eaten up with zeal for the house of God, or catching the little foxes that destroy the Lord's vines. For, crucifying again to themselves the Son of God, and making Him a mockery, they not only made His limbs bare of all substance by the greed of their avarice, but also stripped them of virtues by the example of their iniquity. At night among harlots, next morning at the altar; caressing the daughter of Venus by night, and on the morrow handling the Son of the Virgin Mary, they trod under foot the Son of God, and esteemed the blood of the Testament unclean." (Hist. Occ. cap. v).

C. *Secular* (*i.e. non-monastic*) *Clergy.* I have already referred to the fact that St. Bonaventura condemns them in language almost as strong as Wiclif's: here again is what is said of them by St. Anthony of Padua when Salimbene was a boy. He speaks of clergy who "flay the faithful by forced offerings, whereon they fatten their horses, their foals, and the sons of their concubines." (Opera. ed. de la Haye, p. 334). How little the Friars succeeded in reforming this, may be judged from the words of another celebrated Franciscan, Alvarez Pelayo, a Papal Penitentiary who wrote about a generation after Salimbene (1320). He says: "The Parish Priests . . . . live very incontinently (and would that they had never vowed continence)! especially in Spain and South Italy, in which provinces the children of the laity are scarcely more numerous than those of the clergy . . . . They often sin most abominably with women of their parish whose confessions they hear." He goes on to describe, in language strikingly like Salimbene's, their irreverent treatment of the consecrated Host and carelessness of proper ceremonies at mass, their keeping of taverns, their greed for offerings and negligence of their duties. (De Planctu Ecclesiæ, lib. ii, artic. xxvii). Gower speaks equally strongly and fully (Mirour de l'Omme 20, 593 ff, and Vox Clamantis, bk. iii, l. 193 ff.) But more eloquent still are the fragmentary statistics of visitations which have survived. Here are the words in which Salimbene's acquaintance, Eudes Rigaud, Archbishop of Rouen, sums up his first ruridecanal visitation. (A.D. 1249. Reg. p. 17):
"We caused to be called together and visited, at St. Aubin, the priests of the deanery of Longueville [which contained 42 parishes and 3 chapelries]. We found that Richard, priest of Roumesnil, has long kept a certain woman and had a child by her, yet he has been corrected by the archdeacon and the ill report has ceased. Item, the priest of Appeville is ill-famed for drunkenness. Item, we found that the priest of Martigny, ill-famed for incontinence, is non-resident and absents himself from rural chapters. Item, the priest of Ste-Foy is ill-famed of a woman by whom he has two children, as several witnesses have deposed; and he sells his corn at the end of the year. Item, the priest of St. Germain of a woman by whom he has a child. Item, the priest of Torcy le Petit, of the wife of Gautier de Laistre. Item, the priests of Chapelle and Boisrobert are ill-famed for incontinence. Item, the priest of Mesnilobert is ill-famed of a certain woman. Item, the priest of Appeville, of Reialle's wife. Item, the priests of Arques and Arceaux are said to be incontinent. Item, the priests of St.-Honoré, of Appeville, of Arques, of Fresnoy and of Autels are ill-famed for drunkenness. We warned and rebuked them, and threatened them that, if they are found again ill-famed of such transgressions, we would punish them heavily." The rest mainly concerns the unclerical attire of the priests and other smaller faults.

Eleven incontinents and four drunkards out of forty-five parishes is nearly double of the general average of these visitations: though, again, there were in other deaneries a good many worse individual offenders than any on this list. But even more significant is the comparative impunity of the offenders, though for generations church councils had attempted to stamp out the evil by enacting the severest punishments not only on the clergy but on their partners. Any one of these Norman black sheep would at once have been deprived under the modern Anglican régime; and it is significant of the difference between our century and theirs to trace their actual careers. In 1259, Eudes began a second ruridecanal visitation which even his untiring energy failed to complete (p. 329 ff.) Here, after this ten years' interval, we find the priest of Appeville still "a drunkard and a sot": Roumesnil is as "ill-famed of witchcraft, and kept his daughter in his house": and there were two fresh incontinents who had not appeared on the earlier list, one of whom "had sometimes taken harlot into his house." The Archbishop adds "all these things we corrected and bade them amend: moreover we warned the priests generally, all and singular, to abstain from foul, mocking, and jesting words, especially before layfolk: and that they who had not close cassocks should buy them by mid-Lent." A later notice in the diary discloses that the priest of Boisrobert is "ill-famed of the wife of a certain clerk named Bigre, and of a certain Englishwoman: we enjoined him to expel altogether the said Bigre and his wife." (516). The priest of Mesnilobert, too, is heard of again. (139, 192, 655). In 1252 he was found to be helping his uncle, prior of the hospital at Neuchâtel, to consume in riotous living the revenues of that pious foundation. In 1254 he was cited to answer for certain misdeeds which were recorded in another register, now unfortunately lost. The result was that he gave an undertaking in legal form to resign when called upon; whether he amended his ways, or whether this written promise was later enforced against him, there is nothing to show. The rector of Fresnoy (669) was solemnly warned in 1264 for non-residence and neglect of Church services, and for beating a parishioner's wife with his fists. The priest of Autels (786 and 402) proved unsatisfactory, and it was ordered in 1252 that he should be pensioned off or exchange his living: in 1261 he, or his successor, resigned. The rector of Torcy le Petit (146) was in 1252 kicked in his own churchyard by the Lord Jean de Peletot, Kt., who was forced to put himself at the Archbishop's mercy for a fine. But the strangest career from among these misdemeanants of 1248 was that of the priest of Martigny, near Dieppe. On Aug. 5th, 1257, "Gerard, priest of Martigny, appeared before us and confessed that he had kept for three years one of his parishioners named Matilda, and had frequently (*pluries*) known another girl: and we assigned him a day, viz., Aug. 16th, to proceed legally upon his confessions legally made in our presence: but at length he gave a formal undertaking that, if it should befall him to relapse, his living might be taken as resigned." By canon law, of course, his living ought long ago to have been vacated. This formal undertaking, signed before witnesses, is duly filed in the Appendix of the Register. On December 25th, 1261, the same Gerard was summoned to answer for having wounded a vassal of the Lord Thomas of Beaumont with a sword; he pleaded self-defence, and an enquiry was instituted, we are not told with what result.   On the 20th July, 1265, "he was cited by his archdeacon on a fresh accusation of incontinency but denied it on oath; and we fixed the 16th August to hear the result of such inquisition as the Archdeacon should make in the mean time."   This inquisition was unfavourable: for on August 17th he was cited to appear on January 8th next for compurgation by the oaths of six other priests (at his own choice within certain obvious limitations) who would swear with him that they believed him innocent.   This was the usual lenient procedure for clerical offenders; and the great Oxford Chancellor Gascoigne describes in very strong language the iniquities to which it gave rise at the University. (Mun. Acad., R.S., p. 536).   Apparently Gerard found the requisite number of obliging colleagues; for there is no more of him, nor any record of a vacancy at Martigny, in the Register, which lasts to the end of 1269.   (See pp. 17, 283, 417, 523, 525, 658).

It is not at all uncommon to find such a paragraph as " we *warned* the priest of St. Peter's to abstain from tavern-haunting, immoderate wine-bibbing, gadding about and unhonest consorting with women: for he was exceedingly ill-famed of such offences."   Here, again, is another case in detail, illustrating the leniency with which offenders were treated.   On November 9th, 1261, "we fixed December 15th for [John] priest of Civières, who is of manifold evil report for divers vices, to purge himself with the oaths of eight other priests from the accusations of incontinence, adultery, manifold assaults, and tavern-haunting."   On December 16th John appeared without his compurgators: he was allowed a respite until the Wednesday before Christmas: on which day he failed to appear at all.   Meanwhile the Archbishop instituted an inquisition into his case: from which it appeared that he was also under ill report of buffoonery, and that the witnesses who deposed to his offences were " good and grave men ": he was therefore cited again and appeared on April 1st, 1262.   Here a day was again fixed for his purgation (April 17th): meanwhile, if he had any real proof of innocence to bring, he might bring it next day (April 2nd): however, "neither he appeared, nor any on his behalf."   He evidently failed to find compurgators, for on June 7th he was forced to sign a deed admitting that he "lay under grievous ill report . . . . . of incontinence with my own parishioners and with other women, of tavern-haunting, of assault; and seeing that my father the Archbishop might deal hardly with me on that account, if he were so minded," he therefore swears in due legal form to resign his benefice when called upon by the Archbishop.   Two years later, September 21st, 1264, he is again "under manifold ill report of incontinence" and is given the 17th October on which to appear with six compurgators.   He did not appear: but on November 5th "he appeared with seven priests, in readiness to purge himself of many vices whereof he was accused, and whereof he lay also under manifold ill-report. But we, fearing his fury and that of the priests that were with him,* and recalling that undertaking which he had formerly given us concerning the aforesaid matters, thought best to remit him this purgation, assigning to him the Tuesday before Christmas to fulfil what is contained in the said letter, as he promised under his own oath." On the 3rd May, 1265, he was at last brought to bay and compelled to beg for mercy : upon which the Archbishop made him swear that he would consider his living as vacant on July 29th and allow another to be put in his place. On the 8th of August it is at last recorded that he has actually resigned in due form. (pp. 415, 417, 423, 434, 497, 502, 516, 524, 666).

There are many other cases worse in certain respects than either of these—priests who had formed incestuous connexions, or with married women, or with two or three different women, or who regularly haunted the neighbouring convents. There are many others also showing almost as strongly as those I have quoted the difficulty of enforcing the law, even when the prelate happened to be one of the most energetic in Christendom, and the diocese one of the most civilized. In many cases Eudes simply bound down the priests to heavy fines in case of relapse ; in others (and these among the worse), he compelled them to exchange into other provinces, where no doubt they had an easier time.

I am publishing similar visitation records for England in *Medieval Studies*, No. 8, " Priests and People," which will probably be ready in August, 1907. In these English records, the clergy and their flocks are presented side by side : and the former supply, in proportion to their numbers, from five to ten times as many incontinents as the laity. I say from five to ten times, because it depends whether we accept Thorold Rogers's calculation that the clergy formed fifty per cent. of the total population, or Abbot Gasquet's more probable contention that they formed only one hundred per cent. It is worth while to consider for one moment what this means in modern figures. There would be, under medieval conditions, about 350,000 priests in the United Kingdom at the present day ; and, if we may take as a standard Bishop Morton's *Norfolk Visitations* of 1499 (Bodleian MS., Tanner, 100, f. 56), there would be about 2,500 notorious black sheep among them ! The Ripon and Beverley Chapter Acts show a state of things even worse.

D. *Religious* (i.e. monastic clergy). I have already pointed out in *Medieval Studies*, Nos. 1 and 6, how strong and unimpeachable is the evidence of monastic decay from A.D. 1200 onwards ; and the list of authorities might be much extended. Cardinal Jacques de Vitry speaks

---

* *Timentes ne ipse cum eisdem presbyteris deliraret*, a phrase which is sufficiently explained by Gascoigne (l. c.) ' no townsman of Oxford dare object . . . for, if he were to object against these false purgations, then the accused and his compurgators would secretly maim or slay him.' It is possible that Eudes remembered how nearly one of his predecessors in the see of Rouen was stoned to death for his zeal in enforcing the laws against concubinary priests.—Pommeraye, p. 98.

of the monks before the Franciscan movement as "keeping an outward show of piety but denying its inward virtue . . . disobedient, murmurers, backbiters, bearing Christ's cross unwillingly, unclean and incontinent, walking after the flesh and not after the spirit." Turning to the nuns, he asserts that a girl's virtue was safe among none but those of the Cistercian Rule (Hist. Occ., caps 4 and 5). Fifty years afterwards St. Bonaventura writes, "Seeing that . . . the late Legate in Germany pronounced a general sentence of suspension from office and from benefice against clergy soliciting nuns of any order whatsoever, and of excommunication against those who seduced them; and whereas Pope Gregory IX confirmed this, and granted to few confessors the power of absolving such offenders, it is to be feared that many are bound by these sentences, who think not in their hearts that they need the grace of absolution or dispensation; yet they minister in this state, and keep their cures of souls, and receive church benefices while under this anathema." Gower, who had no personal enmity against the monks, speaks even more strongly a century later. In some monasteries, he says, chastity is dead, and lechery has taken her place: very many (*plures*) monks go to hell for women, and nuns are sometimes seduced by the very visitors whose office it is to guard them (Vox Clamantis iv, 327 ff, 461, 495: much of this is repeated in his Mirour de L'Omme). His contemporary St. Catherine of Siena asserts that unnatural vices reigned among religious and parish clergy as much as among other classes: the stench of these sins tortured her so that she longed for death as a relief. There was little discipline in the monasteries, because the superiors were often as bad as the rank and file: monks and nuns sin together "and oft-times (*spesse volte*) they go so far that both abandon Holy Religion, whereby he is become a ruffian, and she a public harlot" (Dialogo, ch. 125: cf. 162). Scarcely a generation later, the great Gerson made the same accusation of unnatural vices, and wrote, "I actually doubt whether boys and girls do not sometimes learn worse morals . . . at the schools and among monks and nuns (*in religionum et scholarum contuberniis*) than they would in brothels." (Ed. Paris, 1606, ii, 628).

In 1414, almost at the same time as Gerson wrote these words, the University of Oxford addressed to Henry V a series of articles for the reform of the Church, probably in view of the Council of Constance. Although several of these articles are strongly anti-Lollard, yet those in which the University touches different failings of the clergy could scarcely have been more strongly expressed by Wiclif himself. The "Religious" exempt from episcopal jurisdiction were very numerous: probably nearer a half than a third of the whole number in England: and the University complains: "Whereas exempt Religious, at the Devil's persuasion, are frequently defiled with fleshly vices, and are not punished by their own superiors, but their sins remain unpunished, therefore it seems expedient to appoint that the ordinaries may have full power to punish and reform all Religious, and especially for the crime of fornication committed outside their cloister." (Wilkins, iii,

363). The next generation brings us to another distinguished name, Tritheim, an abbot of that Congregation of Bursfeld which owed its reform to Thomas à Kempis's Congregation of Windesheim : and this leads me to point out an extraordinarily ineffectual criticism by a writer in the *Contemporary Review* for September, 1906, who professes considerable familiarity with medieval history. He is offended at my speaking of the plain evidence for monastic decay, and writes : " on the whole the standard was much higher than one might expect. It is noticeable that Thomas à Kempis barely hints at the possibility of moral laxity." This criticism betrays a very strange ignorance of monastic history. Thomas à Kempis belonged to a particularly small and select Congregation at the period of its earliest and purest activity, and was not at all likely to write of gross sins. Yet, on the other hand, a scarcely less distinguished contemporary, himself a member of the same Congregation, has left enough and to spare of that evidence which it did not come within the province of Thomas à Kempis to give—I allude to the *Liber de Reformatione* of Johann Busch, which my reviewer would have done well to read side by side with à Kempis. Johann Busch, a Provost in his own Order, spent himself in the effort to reform other monasteries and bring them under the strict Bursfeld rule : he records the most startling details, and tells how his life was more than once in danger from those whose immoralities he attempted to check. Tritheim, who wrote some thirty years after Busch, and who was an Abbot of this same reformed Congregation of Bursfeld, shows how short-lived that reform had been. For seventy years, he says, scarcely one Abbot of his own house of Spanheim had died in harness : nearly all had given up the apparently hopeless task of bringing their monks to order. Again and again Tritheim enumerates the great monastic reforms of the past—including this of Bursfeld which owed so much to the friends of Thomas à Kempis—but only to lay stress on their evanescence. Addressing his fellow-Abbots at the Chapter General of 1493 he asks " where are those terrible oaths of all the Abbots of our province, whereby they swore to Cardinal Cusanus before the altar of St. Stephen at Würzburg that they would observe the Rule ? . . . . . Behold Fathers, ye have 127 abbeys under the authority of your Chapter, whereof . . . . . scarce 70 have remained under the Reform. . . . . See the manner of life both of abbots and monks, whose smoke goes up round about, which, though it be known, I blush to tell, and ye (most reverend Fathers) shudder to hear ! For the three vows of Religion [poverty, obedience and chastity], which by reason of their excellence are called ' the substantial vows,' these men care no more than if they had never promised to keep them . . . . . The whole day is spent in filthy talk . . . they despise the vow of poverty, and know not that of chastity." Again, nobody (he says) builds new churches or endows monasteries nowadays ; " for the laity say ' Lo ! sinful priests and monks have gotten to themselves riches : lo ! they despise the worship of God and waste their substance with harlots.' " (Preface to

Homilies—De Statu et Ruina, c. xi—Oratio III : cf. De Viris Illust. lib. i : Declamatio ad Abbates, c. ii, iii, and v).

In the case of the cloistered clergy, as in that of the parish priests, these unfavourable judgments of distinguished and orthodox churchmen are borne out by official records. The *Liber de Reformatione* of Johann Busch is, in itself, sufficient to explain the depth of that moral impulse which undoubtedly underlay those wild passions and frequent injustices of the Reformation. Abbot Gasquet's *Henry VIII and the English Monasteries*, with all its show of full documentary evidence on less important points, ignores most unaccountably the mass of obvious and unimpeachable evidence against the monasteries during the four centuries preceding the Reformation. When we take this ignorance in conjunction with his constant professions of familiarity with the subject, his flat refusal either to give chapter and verse for some of his most important statements or to discuss them publicly, and the fact that his strongest support has for some time come from anonymous articles and anonymous books, it is difficult not to conclude that the defenders of the monastic legend are at last driven to the last ditch in which the defenders of the Loretto legend are now fighting abroad—that of more or less wilful ignorance and of misrepresentations hurled from the dark corners of periodical literature. Any reader who cares to realize the shifts to which Abbot Gasquet's supporters have by this time been reduced, even in their own journals, may refer to the *Tablet* for Dec. 9, 1906, and following numbers, and *Demain* for May 3, 1907, ff.

INDEX.